American Casino Guide

2018 Edition

<u>Written and Edited By</u>

Steve Bourie

<u>Assistant Editors</u>

Matt Bourie

<u>Contributing Writers</u>

Linda Boyd
John Grochowski
H. Scot Krause
Henry Tamburin
Jean Scott

This book is dedicated to the memory of Walter Thomason. A truly great guy who will forever be missed by his friends and family.

American Casino Guide - 2018 edition

Published By:
Casino Vacations Press, Inc.
P.O. Box 703
Dania, Florida 33004
(954) 989-2766

e-mail: info@americancasinoguide.com
website: americancasinoguide.com

ISBN-13: 978-1-883768-27-0
ISSN: 1086-9018

Table of Contents

About Your Guide 5
Your Best Casino Bets - Part I 7
Your Best Casino Bets - Part II 11
Casino Comps 15
Players Clubs and Comps 17
Taking Advantage of Players Clubs 19
A Look at Gambling Systems 23
Meet Stanford Wong - The "Guru" of Blackjack 27
Slot Machines 35
Slot Machine Trends - 2018 41
Video Poker 47
"Not So Ugly Deuces" Optimum Strategy 58
Video Poker: Another Brick in The Wall 61
Blackjack 67
Blackjack FAQs 85
Roulette 89
Baccarat 95
Craps 102
A Few Last Words 117
ALABAMA 119
ARIZONA 121
ARKANSAS 127
CALIFORNIA 129
COLORADO 142
CONNECTICUT 148
DELAWARE 151
FLORIDA 153
GEORGIA 159
IDAHO 161
ILLINOIS 163
INDIANA 170
IOWA 175
KANSAS 181

LOUISIANA.......... 183
MAINE.......... 190
MARYLAND.......... 191
MASSACHUSETTS.......... 193
MICHIGAN.......... 194
MINNESOTA.......... 200
MISSISSIPPI.......... 206
Biloxi Map.......... 209
Tunica Map.......... 215
MISSOURI.......... 219
MONTANA.......... 225
NEVADA.......... 227
Las Vegas Map.......... 252-253
Reno Map.......... 271
NEW JERSEY.......... 278
Atlantic City Map.......... 279
NEW MEXICO.......... 283
NEW YORK.......... 289
NORTH CAROLINA.......... 295
NORTH DAKOTA.......... 296
OHIO.......... 298
OKLAHOMA.......... 301
OREGON.......... 317
PENNSYLVANIA.......... 320
RHODE ISLAND.......... 323
SOUTH CAROLINA.......... 324
SOUTH DAKOTA.......... 325
TEXAS.......... 333
WASHINGTON.......... 335
WEST VIRGINIA.......... 342
WISCONSIN.......... 344
WYOMING.......... 349
Casino Index.......... 351
Reference Map of U.S.......... 359
Coupon Directory.......... 361
Casino Coupons.......... 363

About Your Guide

This guide has been written to help you plan your visit to casino gambling areas and also to help you save money once you are there. The first edition of this guide began 27 years ago as an eight-page newsletter and it has continued to grow each year as casino gambling has spread throughout the country. We have listed information on all of the states that offer any type of traditional casino table games or slot machines (including video lottery terminals). We have also included stories to help you understand how casinos operate; how video poker and slot machines work; how to make the best plays in blackjack, craps, roulette and baccarat; and how to take advantage of casino promotional programs. Additionally, we have included a casino coupon section that should save you many times the cost of this book.

Virtually every casino has a "comp" program whereby you can get free rooms, food, shows or gifts based upon your level of play. If you plan on gambling during your trip to the casino, you may want to call ahead and ask their marketing department for details on their programs. There are also stories in this book to help you understand how "comp" programs work and how to best take advantage of them.

One more suggestion to save you money when visiting a casino is to join their players club. It doesn't cost anything and you would be surprised at how quickly those points can add up to earn you gifts, cash, food or other complimentaries. Also, as a club member you will usually receive periodic mailings from the casino with money-saving offers that are generally not available to the public.

When using this guide please remember that all of the listed room rates reflect the lowest and highest prices charged during the year. During holidays and peak periods, however, higher rates may apply. Also, since the gambling games offered at casinos vary from state to state, a listing of available games is found at the start of each state heading. We hope you enjoy your guide and we wish you good luck on your casino vacation!

Your Best Casino Bets - Part I

by Henry Tamburin

The majority of casino players leave too much to chance when playing in a casino. To put it bluntly, they don't have a clue as to how to play. They are literally throwing their money away with little chance of winning. Luck most certainly has a lot to do with your success in a casino but what really separates the winners from the losers is the skill of the players. Granted, there is no guarantee that you will win, but on the other hand, there is no guarantee that you must lose. My objective in this article is to educate you on the casino games so that at the very least, you'll be able to enjoy yourself in the casino with maximum play time and minimum risk to your bankroll.

Let's begin our understanding of casino gambling by learning how casinos win as much as they do. They don't charge admission, and they certainly don't depend on the luck of their dealers to generate the income they need to pay their overhead. In fact, they guarantee themselves a steady income by having a built in advantage, or house edge, on every bet. Think of it as a very efficient hidden tax that generates them a guaranteed daily profit.

Here's an example of how this works. Suppose we take a coin and play heads or tails. Every time you lose a flip of the coin you pay me $1. Every time you win a flip, I pay you 90¢. Would you play? I hope you said no. Here's why. In this simple game I would have an advantage over you and I created that advantage by not paying you at the true odds of one-to-one (or $1).

Casinos do this very same thing to create their advantage. They simply pay off winning bets at less than the true odds. For example, the true odds of winning a bet on number 7 on roulette are 37-to-1 (the latter means you have 37 chances to lose vs. one chance to win). If you get lucky and the roulette ball lands in the number seven slot, you'd expect the casino to pay you 37 chips as winnings for the one chip you bet on number 7 (37- to-1 payoff). If they did that, the casino's advantage would be zero. However, as I mentioned above, the casinos create their advantage by paying off winning bets at less than true odds. In the case of our bet on number 7, the winning payoff is 35 chips (instead of 37 chips). The two chips the casino quietly kept is what pays their bills. Mathematically, the casino advantage is 5.26% on this bet which simply means day in and day out, the casino expects to win (or keep) 5.26% of all money wagered in roulette.

The casino games with the lowest casino advantage (less than 1.25%), and your best bets, are blackjack, craps, baccarat, and video poker. Now don't sell the ranch and run over to your nearest casino just yet. These games, plus table poker, are your best bets but you must learn how to play these games properly to enhance your chances of winning. Here are some tips to get you started:

BLACKJACK - This is your best casino game, but you must learn how to play your hands (when to hit, stand, double-down, split, etc.). This is known as the basic strategy. Learn it and you can reduce the casino's advantage to virtually zero. And if you learn how to keep track of the cards as they are played (i.e. card counting) you can actually turn the tables on the casino and have the edge over them! Do not try to play blackjack if you haven't learned the correct basic strategy. If you do, your chances of winning are slim. Also, it's wise not to make any side bets that may be offered on your table and please stay away from any game which only pays 6-to-5 for an untied blackjack. Blackjack tournaments are also popular and here players compete against other players with the player with the most chips at the end of the round advancing. Tournament prizes can be substantial. Playing and betting strategy for blackjack tournaments, however, is different than playing blackjack in a casino so bone up on your tournament skills before considering playing in a tournament.

CRAPS - The game of craps intimidates most casino players because of the complicated playing layout and the multitude of bets. In fact craps is an easy game to play. And it also has some of the best bets in the casino (and also some of the worst). Your best bet is the pass line with odds and come with odds. Next best is a place bet on six or eight. Stay away from all other bets on the layout because the casino's advantage is too high. If you really enjoy the game of craps you might consider learning dice control – it's not an easy skill to learn and it requires a lot of practice but if you get good at it, you can have the edge over the casino.

ROULETTE - Every bet on the American roulette layout (with 0 and 00 on the wheel) has a high casino advantage. That goes for bets straight up on numbers that pay 35-to-1, as well as even money wagers on red or black. Atlantic City players get a break. If you bet on an even money payoff bet and 0 or 00 hits, you lose only half your wager. This cuts the casino's advantage in half. Also, some casinos offer a European layout with only one zero. This is a better bet than wheels with 0 and 00.

BACCARAT - Many casinos offer a low stakes version called mini-baccarat. Not a bad game to play. If you bet on the bank hand, the casino's edge is only 1.17%. And when you play baccarat, there are no playing decisions to make which makes the game very easy to play. However, this game is fast with many decisions per hour. It's best to play slowly. One way is to only bet on the bank hand after it wins (meaning you won't be betting on every hand which will slow down your play).

BIG SIX WHEEL - Stay away from spending a lot of time (and money) at this game. The casino's advantage is astronomical (11% to 26%). Its drawing card for the novice player is the low minimum bet ($1). Save your money for the better games.

PAI GOW POKER - Strange name for a casino game. The game is a cross between Pai Gow, a Chinese game of dominoes, and the American game of seven-card poker. Players are dealt seven cards and they must arrange (or set) their cards into a five-card poker hand and a two-card poker hand. Skill is involved in setting the two hands which can help reduce the casino's advantage.

SLOT MACHINES - Casinos earn more money from slot machines than all the table games combined. The casino's advantage varies from one machine to another. Typically the higher denomination machines ($1 and up) pay back more than the nickel, quarter and fifty-cent machines. Slots are not your best bet in the casino, but here are a few tips: It's wise to play one coin only in machines where all the payouts increase proportionally to the number of coins played (i.e. there is no jackpot for playing maximum coins). However, if the machine has a substantial jackpot when you play maximum coins, then you should always play the maximum number of coins the machine will accept or you won't be eligible for a bonus payoff for the jackpot. Don't waste hours looking for a machine that's "ready to hit." Join the players clubs, always use your players club card when you play, and try to schedule your play time when the casino offers multiple points. Joining is free and you'll be rewarded with discounts and other freebies. Machines that have lower jackpots pay smaller amounts more frequently which means you normally get more playing time for your money. Playing machines that have bonus rounds and fancy graphics may be fun, but the house edge on these machines is usually higher than traditional reel spinning machines. Likewise, the house edge is higher for linked machines that have those life-changing mega jackpots. Some casinos now certify their machines to return 98% or more and these machines are your best bets. Also, consider playing in slot tournaments where you are competing against other players, rather than the house, and the prizes can be substantial.

VIDEO POKER - Your best bet if you enjoy playing slot machines. Skill is involved as well as learning to spot the better payoff machines. For example, on the classic jacks-or-better game, always check the full house and flush payoff schedule. The best machines on jacks or better pay nine coins for a full house and six coins for a flush for each coin played. These machines are known as 9/6 machines. They are readily available; seek them out. The same analogy holds for bonus poker, double bonus, deuces wild, jokers wild, etc. video poker games. There are good pay schedules and bad ones, and it's up to you to know the difference and play only the higher paying schedules with the correct playing strategy (readily available on the Internet, in books, and on strategy cards).

KENO - This casino game has a very high casino advantage (usually 20% and up). Stay away if you are serious about winning.

ULTIMATE TEXAS HOLD 'EM - A relatively new game that has exploded in popularity in recent years. This game is based on Texas Hold 'em and just like Let It Ride, players play against the house rather than against each other. Each player at the table must make two bets of the same amount on the ante and blind to play with an option to make a "trips" side bet that pays with a three-of-a-kind or better. The player has to make the best five-card poker hand using their two cards and the five community cards, and has the option to bet or check at three different times throughout the hand. This game has a house edge of 2.19% with proper playing strategy. There are several pay tables for the trips bet, with the two most popular having house edges of 3.50% and 6.18%. So it is usually a good idea to avoid that bet.

MISSISSIPPI STUD - Another relatively new game to casinos, Mississippi Stud is different from other poker-based games because the player is paid based on the poker value of their hand made from two cards dealt to them, plus three community cards. They are not playing against another player or the dealer. The player makes an ante bet and receives two cards face down then makes a bet that must be one to three times their initial ante bet to see the first community card. They must then make another bet of one to three times their ante bet to see the second community card and then do it again a third time to see the final community card. The strategy for the first decision with two cards is rather simple. Make the big, 3x bet with any pair, and make the small 1x wager with either any face card, any two medium cards (6 through 10), or with a 5/6 suited or better. The other decisions are much more complex and can be found online.

LET IT RIDE - This casino table game is based on the all-American game of poker. Like Caribbean Stud Poker, players compete against the house rather than against each other. What makes this game so unique is that the players can remove up to two of their initial mandatory three bets if they don't think they can win. The objective is to end up with a five-card poker hand of at least 10's or higher. The higher the rank, the greater the payoff; up to 1,000-to-1 for the royal flush. The casino edge is about 3% and about 70% of the hands will be losing hands. If you are lucky enough to catch a high payoff hand, be smart, push your chair back, and take the money and run!

THREE CARD POKER - One of the more successful table games in recent years, you can wager on either the Ante/Play or Pair Plus. You win your Ante/Play bet if your three card poker hand beats the dealer's hand. If you wager Pair Plus, you win money if your three card hand contains at least a pair or higher (the higher the ranking hand, the greater the payout). There are different paytables – the best pays 4-1 for a flush rather than 3-1. The optimum playing strategy is to raise on Q-6-4 or higher and avoid playing the Pair Plus if the flush pays only 3-1.

Henry Tamburin, Ph.D., has over 50 years experience as a blackjack player, writer, author, and instructor. His latest book is the Ultimate Blackjack Strategy Guide, which is FREE to read on https://www.888casino.com/blog/blackjack-strategy-guide/. See his ad on page 88.

Your Best Casino Bets - Part II

by Steve Bourie

In the previous story Henry gave you his choices for your best casino bets based on which ones offer you the best mathematical odds. Now, Henry is a great mathematician who is truly an expert at crunching numbers to figure out what the theoretical odds are, but what about real life? By this I mean - at the end of the week, or the month, or the year, how much does a casino really make from blackjack, or craps, or roulette? Sure, you can do the math to calculate the casino advantage on a bank hand in mini-baccarat as 1.17%, but at the end of the day what percent of those bets on mini-baccarat actually wind up in the hands of the casino? Is it precisely 1.17%? Or is it less? Or is it more? And, if you knew how much the casino truly averaged on all of the games it offered, which one would turn out to be your best bet based on that information?

To find the answer to this question I began my search by looking at the annual gaming revenue report issued by Nevada's State Gaming Control Board. It lists the win percentages, based on the *drop* (an explanation of this term is provided later), for all of the games offered by the casinos and, as Henry stated in his story, blackjack, baccarat and craps were among the best casino bets. The first column below lists the actual win percentages based on the "drop" (an explanation of "drop" follows shortly) for Nevada's various games for the fiscal year from July 1, 2016 through June 30, 2017:

Game	Win %	Adjusted Win %
Keno	26.21	26.21
Race Book	15.22	15.22
Slot Machines	6.72	6.72
3-Card Poker	31.75	6.35
Sports Pool	5.04	5.04
Let It Ride	24.53	4.91
Pai Gow Poker	20.74	4.15
Bingo	3.93	3.93
Pai Gow	17.56	3.51
Roulette	17.37	3.47
Craps	14.88	2.98
Twenty-One	14.48	2.90
Baccarat	13.71	2.74
Mini-Baccarat	11.74	2.35

Before we go on to the other games though you'll need a brief explanation of how the win percentages are calculated and we'll start off with a basic lesson in how casinos do their accounting.

Casinos measure their take in table games by the drop and the win. The drop is the count of all of the receipts (cash and credit markers) that go into the drop box located at the table. Later, an accounting is made to see how much more (or less) they have than they started with. This amount is known as the win (or loss).

What the first column in the table shows you is how much the casinos won as a percentage of the drop. For example, on the roulette table for every $100 that went into the drop box the casino won $17.37 or 17.37%. What it doesn't tell you, however, is how much the casinos won as a percentage of all the bets that were made. In other words, the drop tells you how many chips were bought at that table, but it doesn't tell you how many bets were made with those chips. For example, if you buy $100 worth of chips at a blackjack table and play $10 a hand you don't bet for exactly 10 hands and then leave the table, do you? Of course not. You win some hands and you lose some hands and if you counted all of the times you made a $10 bet before you left the table you would see that your original $100 in chips generated many times that amount in bets. In other words, there is a multiplier effect for the money that goes into the drop box. We know that for every dollar that goes into the drop box there is a corresponding number of bets made. To find out exactly what that number is I asked Henry for some help. He replied that there is no exact answer, but during a 1982 study of the roulette tables in Atlantic City it was discovered that the total amount bet was approximately five times the amount of the buy-in. This means that for every $100 worth of chips bought at the table it resulted in $500 worth of bets being made.

The multiplier effect for the money that goes into the drop box is also dependent on the skill of the player. A blackjack player that loses his money quickly because he doesn't know good playing strategy will have a much lower multiplier than a player who uses a correct playing strategy. For purposes of this story, however, we'll assume that they balance each other out and we'll also assume that all games have the same multiplier of five. We can now return to our win percentage tables and divide by five the percentages for those games that have a multiplier effect. These new adjusted numbers let us know approximately how much the casinos actually won as a percentage of the amount bet on each of those games. Keep in mind, however, that besides bingo there are three other game categories that do not need to be adjusted: keno, race book and sports pool. They need no adjustment because there is no multiplier factor involved. On these particular games the casinos know the exact total of the bets they take in and the exact total of the bets they pay out.

After calculating our adjusted win numbers we can now go back and take another look at which games are your best casino bets. The worst game, by far, is keno with its 26.21% edge. Next comes the race book with 15.22%, followed by slot machines at 6.72% and then three-card poker at 6.35%

Sports betting has a casino win rate of 5.04% but that number actually deserves a closer look because there are really five different types of bets that make up that figure: football - 4.15%; basketball - 5.72%; baseball - 4.66%; sports parlay cards - 16.48%; and other sports (golf, car racing, etc.) - 5.67%. As you can see, all sports bets carry a relatively low house edge, except for sports parlay cards which you may want to avoid.

Next on our list is let it ride at 4.91%. That's followed by pai gow poker at 4.15%; and bingo at 3.93%.

Usually bingo would rank as one of the games with the worst odds, but not in Nevada where it's sometimes used as a "loss leader." Just like your local Kmart runs especially low prices on a couple of items to bring you into the store where they believe you'll buy some other items, Nevada casinos use bingo to bring people into their casinos, believing that while they're there they'll play other games and also develop a loyalty to that casino. So, if you're a bingo player Nevada casinos are the best places you'll ever find to play your game.

Next is pai gow at 3.51% and then roulette at 3.47%.

Finally, we come to the four best casino bets that all have roughly the same edge of less than three percent: craps at 2.98%; twenty-one (blackjack) at 2.90%; baccarat at 2.74%; and mini-baccarat at 2.35%.

So there you have it. Mini-baccarat is your best casino bet! Henry said it was a good game to play and he was right. But didn't he also say that blackjack was your best casino bet? Was he wrong about that? Not really, because he prefaced it by saying "you must learn how to play your hands."

You have to remember that of all the table games offered in a casino (other than poker) only blackjack is a game of skill. This means that the better you are at playing your cards, the better you will be able to beat the house average. The 2.90% figure shown is just an average and if you learn proper basic strategy you can cut it down even more which would then make it your best bet. Good luck!

Casino Comps

by Steve Bourie

In the world of casino gambling a "comp" is short for complimentary and it refers to anything that the casino will give you for free in return for your play in their casino.

Naturally, the more you bet, the more the casino will be willing to give you back. For the truly "high roller" (those willing to bet thousands, tens of thousands or even hundreds of thousands on the turn of a card) there is no expense spared to cater to their every whim, including: private jet transportation, chauffeur-driven limousines, gourmet chef-prepared foods, the finest wines and champagnes, plus pampered butler and maid service in a $10 million penthouse suite. But what about the lower-limit bettor?

Well, it turns out that pretty much any gambler can qualify for comps no matter what their level of play and if you know you're going to be gambling anyway, you might as well ask to get rated to see what you can get on a comp basis.

When you sit down to play be sure to tell the dealer that you want to be rated and they'll call over the appropriate floorperson who will take down your name and put it on a card along with information on how long you play and how much you bet. The floorperson won't stand there and constantly watch you, instead they'll just glance over every once in awhile to see how much you're betting and note it on the card. If you change tables be sure to tell the floorperson so that they can continue to track your play at the new table.

Usually a casino will want you to play for at least three hours and virtually all casinos use the same formula to calculate your comp value. They simply take the size of your average bet and multiply it by: the casino's advantage on the game you're playing; the decisions per hour in your game; and the length of your play in hours. The end result is what the casino expects to win from you during your play and most casinos will return anywhere from 10% to 40% of that amount to you in the form of comps.

So, let's say you're a roulette player that averages $20 a spin and you play for four hours. What's that worth in comps? Well, just multiply your average bet ($20), by the casino's advantage in roulette (5.3%) to get $1.06, which is the average amount the casino expects to make on you on each spin of the wheel. You then multiply that by the number of decisions (or spins) per hour (40) to get $42.40, which is the average amount the casino expects to make on you after one hour. Then, multiply that by the total hours of play (4) to get $169.60, which is the average amount the casino expects to make on you during your four hours of play. Since the casinos will return 10% to 40% of that amount in comps, you should qualify for a minimum of $16.96 to a maximum of $67.84 in casino comps.

One thing to keep in mind about comps is that you don't have to lose in order to qualify. The casino only asks that you put in the time to play. So, in our example if, after four hours of gambling, our roulette player ended up winning $100, they would still be eligible for the same amount of comps.

The last thing to mention about comps is that some casino games require skill (blackjack and pai gow poker), or offer various bets that have different casino advantages (craps) so those factors are sometimes adjusted in the equation when determining the casino advantage in those games. Just take a look at the chart below to see how the average casino will adjust for skill in blackjack and pai gow poker as well as for the types of bets that are made in craps.

Game	Game Advantage	Decisions Per Hour
Blackjack	.0025 (Card Counter) .01 (Good Basic Strategy) .015 (Soft Player)	70
Roulette	.053	40
Craps	.005 (Pass Line/Full Odds) .01 (Knowledgeable) .04 (Soft)	144
Baccarat	.012	70
Mini-Baccarat	.012	110
Pai Gow Poker	.01 (Knowledgeable) .02 (Average)	25

Players Clubs And Comps

by Steve Bourie

Before you start playing any kind of electronic gaming machine in a casino, you should first join the casino's players club to reap the rewards that your play will entitle you to. What is a players club you ask? Well, it's similar to a frequent flyer club, except that in these clubs you will earn cash or comps (free food, rooms, shows, etc.) based on how much money you put through the machines.

Virtually all casinos in the U.S. have a players club and joining is simple. Just go to the club's registration desk, present an ID, and you'll be issued a plastic card, similar to a credit card. When you walk up to a machine you'll see a small slot (usually at the top, or side) where you should insert your card before you start to play. The card will then record how much money you've played in that particular machine. Then, based on the amount you put through, you will be eligible to receive cash (sometimes) and comps (always) back from the casino. Naturally, the more you gamble, the more they will give back to you.

Some casinos will give you a free gift, or some other kind of bonus (extra slot club points, free buffet, etc.) just for joining and since there's no cost involved, it certainly makes sense to join even if you don't plan on playing that much. As a club member you'll also be on the casino's mailing list and you'll probably be receiving some good money-saving offers in the mail. Additionally, some casinos offer discounts to their club members on hotel rooms, meals and gift shop purchases.

While almost no casino will give you cashback for playing their table games, virtually all casinos will give you cashback for playing their machines. The amount returned is calculated as a percentage of the money you put through the machines and it basically varies from as low as .05% to as high as 1%. This means that for every $100 you put into a machine you will earn a cash rebate of anywhere from five cents to $1. This may not seem like a great deal of money but it can add up very quickly. Additionally, some casinos (usually the casinos with the lower rates) will periodically offer double, triple or quadruple point days when your points will accumulate much more rapidly.

One other point to make about cashback is that the vast majority of casinos (about 90%) offer a lower cash rebate on their video poker machines than they do on their slot machines. Generally, the rate is about one-half of what the casino normally pays on its slot machines. The reason for the reduced rate is that video poker is a game of skill and knowledgeable players can achieve a greater return on video poker games than they could on slots. Since the casino will make less money on video poker games they simply reduce their cash rebates accordingly. This is very important to keep in mind, especially if you're a bad video poker player, because you'll probably only be earning half the cash rebate you could be getting by just playing the slots.

Of course, the best situation is to be a smart video poker player in a casino that offers the same cash rebate to all of its player regardless of what kind of machine they play. This way you could be playing a good VP game, combined with a good rebate, and this will allow you to be playing at a near 100% level!

Not all casinos will give you cashback. Many casinos will send a freeplay offer to you and you must return to the casino on a specific date to use it. This is called a bounce back offer and it is the preferred method for most casinos. Keep in mind, if you won't be going back to that casino, a bounce back offer won't be of much use to you.

While not every casino's club will give you back cash it is standard for every club to allow you to earn "comps" for your machine play. "Comps" is short for complimentaries and it means various things that you can get for free from the casino: rooms, meals, shows, gifts, etc.

Once again, the comp you will earn is based on the amount of money you put through the machines but it is usually at a higher level than you would earn for cashback. After all, the real cost to a casino for a $15 meal is much less than giving you back $15 in cash so the casinos can afford to be more generous.

When it comes to players club comp policies they basically fall into one of three categories. Some casinos have clubs that allow you to redeem your points for either cash at one rate, or comps at a reduced rate that will cost you fewer points. In these clubs, for example, you might have a choice of redeeming your 1,000 points for either $10 in cash or $20 in comps.

Another option (one that is commonly used by many "locals" casinos in Las Vegas) is for the casino to set a redemption schedule for each particular restaurant, or meal. For example: breakfast is 800 points, lunch is 1,200 points and dinner is 1,600 points. These are popular programs because players know exactly what is required to earn their comp.

At the other extreme, many casinos base their comps on your total machine play but won't tell you exactly what's required to achieve it. At the MGM Resorts properties in Las Vegas, for example, you will earn cashback at a set schedule but you'll never quite know what you need to earn a food comp. You just have to go to the players club booth, present your card, and ask if you can get a buffet or restaurant comp. The staff will then either give it to you or say you need some more play on your card before they can issue you a food comp.

And which casinos have the best players clubs? Well, that would really be dependant on what's most important to you. If you're visiting from out of town you would probably want a club that's more generous with room comps so you could save money on your accomodations. However, if you're going to be playing at a casino near your home you would be more interested in which casino offers the best cashback rate and food comps. Whatever the situation, be sure to give most of your play to the casino that offers the best benefits for you and you'll soon be reaping the rewards of players club membership!

Taking Advantage of Players Clubs

by H. Scot Krause

Players clubs originated in Atlantic City over 30 years ago as a way to begin recognizing and rewarding the casino's good players. Today, players clubs are the casino's most powerful marketing tool and the player's best benefit the casino has to offer. It's the best of both worlds for both the player and the casino.

To begin, perhaps the word "club" is a little misleading, since there are no dues to pay, meetings to attend or any of the usual aspects associated with joining a club. You do get a players club membership card (also called a players card) which is your key to unlocking the benefits and rewards of the casino you're playing in.

Typically, your players club membership card is a plastic card, with your identifying number on it, that you will use while playing at any of the casino's slot or video poker machines or while playing table games. It resembles a credit card, but only in its appearance, and is in no way an actual credit card. I mention that because there are some people who actually, mistakenly believe they will be inserting a credit card into their slot machine and play on credit, and therefore they refuse to get their players card and are basically denied any and all benefits they are entitled to!

So let's start at the beginning and walk through the players card program, when and why to do it and discuss some benefits, rewards and perks. When you enter any casino for the first time, ask someone immediately where you can find the players club or players club booth before you put any money into a machine. At the booth, you should find a rather friendly group of employees who will get you started, signed up and get your card for you pronto.

You'll probably need to fill out a short application form or at least give your identification card to the clerk. It's simply a way to register the card in your name. You usually don't need to give your social security number if you don't want to, but always give your birthday and anniversary dates when asked. They help identify you with the casino in case others have your same name and many times the birthday benefits are nothing short of fantastic. Adding your e-mail address and signing up for text messages will also get additional offers sent to you.

Always ask the players club personnel about how to use the card and any other current promotions or benefits in addition to using your card. There will usually be a brochure or literature available that you can take explaining all the club benefits. There may also be a sign-up bonus such as a free gift, free slot play or free points when you register. Be sure to ask. Sometimes an easily obtainable coupon may be required and the clerks can tell you where or how to get one. Finally, I like to request two cards when I join, and you might like to do the same. You'll find that you may lose one, or want to play two machines at one time. That's it! You're on your way.

When you're out on the casino floor, you'll notice a slot on the machines that your card fits into. When you decide which machine you want to play, put your card in the slot and leave it in the entire time you play that machine. (Note: Take a moment to look for the card reader slot and not the bill acceptor. If you accidentally put your card in the bill acceptor you'll probably strip the magnetic reader off your card and it won't work).

Most machines will have some type of reader that will display your name, points earned or at least let you know your card has been accepted. It's not a swipe card, and you must leave it in the machine while you play. It's simply counting the coins, or credits, that go through the machine while you're playing and giving you credit in the form of points for the amount of money that cycles through the machine. (Some casinos consider time on the machine as well as money being cycled, but that is a little more rare than in years past). Now, while you're playing, you'll be earning valuable points that become redeemable for anything from cashback to restaurant complimentaries (referred to as "comps") show tickets, gifts, reduced room rates or free rooms, to almost any amenity you may want or require.

Check your card while you're playing to make sure it's working properly. If you sit idle for a period of time while you're ordering a cocktail or what have you, the card reader may stop working and you'll need to reinsert it. Be sure to keep your card in the machine until you have completed your play and cashed all coins or tickets out of the machine. Some clubs base their points on a coin-out system, rather than coin-in and some slot machines actually may pay a bonus when you cash out on certain games!

Your players club rewards are based on total play and your rewards may vary according to point formulas created exclusively for the casino at which you're playing. I do caution you not to continue to play beyond your comfortable gambling range and budget just to earn a point level or comp. Let the comps fall in place as you play or when you return again in the future. Which brings me to another interesting thought. I've heard players refuse to get a card because they believe they won't return to the casino again. First of all, you never know what your future plans may hold. Second, you may earn enough points while you're on this trip to at least earn a small comp or some cash back before you leave.You'll at least get on the casino's mailing list for future specials and events. You may win a jackpot that will allow you to return sooner than you originally thought was possible. And finally, with as many consolidations and buy-outs as there are in the casino industry today, the casino you're playing at today may be owned by someone else tomorrow, who may in turn, be closer to your home, and you'll be able to use your points with them. There's just no good excuse not to get a players card at any casino you visit.

Here are a couple other tips when you plan to visit a casino and need to get a players club card. Sometimes you can apply or sign-up in advance by mail registration or visiting the casino's website on the Internet. They will often mail you the card in advance or have it already prepared for you when you get to the casino. Call and ask ahead of time for this service and you'll save time and won't have to stand in long lines when you hit the casino floor. Sometimes, when you receive your card by mail or Internet sign-up, you'll get additional offers, coupons, gifts and funbook offers along with it. On the other hand you may find a coupon or a rebate offer that offers a bonus if you sign up in person with the coupon in hand. Try to investigate a little before signing up as to which way may be the best way for you to enroll in the club.

Many casinos now also employ players club ambassadors, cash hosts, or enrollment representatives who will sign you up on the casino floor, making it even easier for you to enroll in the club. They often have additional incentives or perks they can give you when you sign up with them. You might also check to see if a card you have from another casino might work where you're playing now. Many casino corporations are beginning to combine their clubs to offer you benefits at any of their respective properties. We're sure to see more of this as consolidations and mergers continue to take place.

Now, let's take a little closer look at the benefits and reasons why you want to belong to these players clubs. Obviously, the casinos want your business and will go to great lengths to have you return. In addition to the points you're earning while playing, which will entitle you to various comps as mentioned previously, your most valuable asset from joining the players club will be your mailing list advantage. Offers to players club members are mailed often and repeatedly for room specials, many times even free room offers, meal discounts (two for ones), and often other free offers. We've been mailed match play offers, double and triple point coupons (and higher), show and movie theater tickets, spa specials, gifts and gift certificates, drawing tickets, and a myriad of other offers.

The casino offers are based on levels of play, and better offers including lavish parties, Superbowl and New Year's Eve invitations, free participation to invited guest slot tournaments, limousine services, and even free round-trip airfare are offered to the casino's best players. Don't rule yourself out just because you don't think you'll reach those levels of play to be awarded those opportunities. Everyone is rewarded in some way for even the most nominal play. Just wait until your birthday rolls around and I can almost guarantee you'll get some fabulous offers from the casinos to spend your celebration with them!

Finally, we'll now take a look at some of the myths regarding players clubs and players cards and dispose of them accordingly. Here are some of the arguments I've heard against players club cards, or excuses as to why players don't use them...

"I never win when I play with my card." The truth is your results would be the same regardless if you had a card in or not. There is no relation between the card counting coins through the machine and what comes up on the screen when you push the button. The card just records how much money is wagered. It has no memory of whether you have won or lost and it doesn't care.

"I don't want to be tracked," or "I don't want the casino to know how much I'm playing," or "I don't want the IRS to have my records." In fact, you do want the casino to track you so you can be rewarded for your play. They have no way of knowing you or how they can help and reward you unless they know who you are, what you're playing and how much you're spending. The IRS does not have access to your gambling activities, but you, in fact, do. The players club can provide you with a year end win-loss record of your play that may help you offset wins with losses for tax purposes.

"I don't need a card, I'm a local," or "I'm a tourist." Basically, you're one or the other, but either way you still should have a card. The casino's computers usually separate locals from tourists and tailor their offers accordingly. If you're going to play anyway, get a card!

"I always lose those cards." You can always have another card made. Get extras made. Why play without it? It's like losing your wallet. The card has so much value for you, yet you leave it in the machine. You don't forget your airline frequent flier card at the airport, or your grocery savings card when you go shopping, do you?

"I don't need a card, I'm leaving in an hour." It doesn't matter how long you will be staying or how soon you will be leaving. Remember that all-important mailing list, and that you just might return some time in the future or play at a sister property somewhere else. (Don't worry. Most casinos do not sell their mailing list names. They want you for themselves and are very selfish!)

All-in-all, I've never heard of one good reason not to join a players club. In fact, I hope I've given you enough good reasons to always join every players club at every casino you ever visit. Good luck and happy Players clubbing!

H. Scot Krause is a freelance writer, gaming industry analyst and researcher. Scot reports, researches, and specializes in writing about casino games, events, attractions and promotions. His work is regularly featured in several gaming publications and he writes the popular "Vegas Values" weekly column for the American Casino Guide website.

A Look at Gambling Systems

by Jean Scott

Jean Scott is a retired teacher who never stopped teaching, just switching her subject from high school English to smart casino gambling. She and her husband Brad have been extremely successful gamblers for 33 years. She has continuously shared their secrets on TV, in countless articles, and presently in the blog "Frugal Vegas" you can access at http://jscott.lvablog.com/. She has written five books in the Frugal Gambler series and the following excerpt is from the "Show Me the Money" chapter of Jean's newest book: THE FRUGAL GAMBLER CASINO GUIDE, which updates the information in her previous books to help gamblers adjust to the changing casino environment.

Question: Can any system help me win?

Answer: The word "system" connected with gambling has a negative connotation and is often paired (incorrectly) with the words "loser" or "scam." However, you can't dismiss all systems. Blackjack card-counting and video poker correct-strategy play could be called systems—and they work. Even a system that tells you how to make the best bets in craps and which ones you should avoid helps you lose less. So some systems can be valuable to gamblers.

So how can you spot the bad systems? This isn't always a simple task, but here are some of the characteristics of charlatan systems.

• It's easy! There's no easy way to beat casinos—never has been, never will be. If someone did happen to stumble on one that anyone could do, the casinos would change the games, the rules, or the policies to plug up the hole so fast your head would spin.

• It's secret! "Only 200 people in the whole world are being offered this surefire way to win at XXX." We get these letters in the mail frequently. Why us? As gambling-product buyers, our address is obviously on a lot of direct-mail lists. But I seriously doubt that only 200 people in the whole world are offered these "surefire" winning systems.

• You'll win every time you play! One ad on the Internet said its system was "like going to the bank for a withdrawal." Why is the seller sharing this information? Shouldn't he be out there madly making his own withdrawals before the casinos catch on?

• It costs more than $50. A number of years ago, before home computers were common and not much was written about gambling based on sound mathematics, some good blackjack systems for counting cards were worth the $100 or $200 being charged for them. However, today, a wealth of published information is available on every aspect of gambling and almost all of the really trustworthy materials (books, software, strategy aids) can be bought for less than $50, most of it much lower.

• It's a money-management system that promises you can beat a negative-expectation game. Most of these come-ons offer up complicated betting systems that don't (and can't) change the math over the long term. A few might change the win/loss pattern, so you'll have lots of small wins. But if you continue to use these systems, you'll lose; the fewer, but large, losing bets will wipe out all of those prior small wins.

• It's a progressive betting system based on raising your bets after a loss. In a popular version of this, called the Martingale, you double your bet after every losing hand. The dealer can't beat you every hand forever, goes the thinking. That's true, but there's a good chance he can beat you long enough for your system to crash, either by reaching casino bet limits or by your bankroll hitting zero. This is one of the surest systems to use if your goal is to go broke.

• It's a progressive betting system based on raising your bets after a win. Many progressive systems that require you to increase your wager modestly after a win can safely be used to break the monotony of flat betting. But again, they can't move a negative-expectation game into positive territory in the long term. You may have winning streaks, but over time, most assuredly, you'll lose an amount close to what the casino edge says you should, just as you would have if you'd been flat betting.

• It has quit-and-start-again requirements that ignore proven mathematical theories about the long term. Short-term goals can be a way of managing your bankroll and your state of mind. However, short-term sessions, all taken together, do add up to the long term, whether you want to believe it or not. The machines, cards, and dice don't know whether this is your first hand in a new session or your thousandth hand in an ongoing one. Thus, the odds of the game don't change.

• It advocates changing your machine or sizing or placing your bets only at specific times, again ignoring math principles. Some valid techniques are associated with this "choice" feature—blackjack card-counting, for example—but they're based on sound computer-validated principles of mathematics. The arbitrarily chosen systems have no math basis. Wait for a crapshooter to make three passes, then jump in? The odds against you aren't changed. Switch machines after you've won $150? In four hours of play on a slot machine, whether done all at one machine in one session or over a whole day of jumping from machine to machine, the casino edge remains the same.

I've seen scores, maybe hundreds, of systems over my 30 years of casino gambling. A few are useful. Some are harmless, but a waste of money to buy. But most of them are cruel, giving false hope that will be disastrous to your wallet. Don't be taken in; most of these system promoters are selling dreams and fantasies. Nothing takes the place of study, practice, and discipline.

With all that said, I'll now state that as long as you aren't fooled into believing that these "wait" or "jump-around" or "start-and-stop" techniques will make you a long-term winner at negative-expectation games, many of these snake-oil systems do have redeeming factor.

I hear you: "I can't believe you said that, Ms. Stick-to-the-Math!" It's true. I'm in favor of any system that slows down your rate of play on negative-expectation games. The more downtime you can schedule, the less you'll lose. When you're doing something other than putting money at risk, you're saving money. But you don't have to spend your hard-earned money for some complicated system advertised in a magazine to do this. Make up your own system! You'd be surprised how interesting that can be. Here are some examples.

Crapshooters bet only when an attractive person of the opposite sex has the dice; if an ugly shooter comes up, just stand by.

If you lose three spins straight on a slot machine, punish the machine by cashing out and looking for a friendlier one.

If you're playing video poker and lose your first bill in, put the machine in "time out" and play the next one for 15 minutes before you go back to the naughty one.

Play roulette only if there's a blonde dealer.

Sit down at a blackjack table only if the dealer looks older than you. Depending on your age, you might have to shop around a long time.

The point is, whenever you aren't actually in action at a negative-expectation game, you're "winning."

Look for an ad for Jean's newest book,
THE FRUGAL GAMBLER CASINO GUIDE, on the next page.

Frugal Gambling with the Queen of Comps

The Frugal Gambler Casino Guide

Jean Scott • 304 pages • $12.71 ($16.95 Retail)

When *The Frugal Gambler* was published in 1998, Jean Scott became a household name to casino players across the country. Since then, Jean's frequent national publicity, her long-term success in casinos around the world, and the solid low-rolling advantage-play techniques she's divulged in *More Frugal Gambling* and *Frugal Video Poker* have catapulted the Frugal series into the ranks of all-time best-selling gambling books.

Bigger and better than anything she's done previously and based on 30 years in the frugal trenches, *The Frugal Gambler Casino Guide* is Jean Scott's ultimate statement on low-roller gambling and goals: how to lose less and play longer.

To order visit ShopLVA.com OR CALL **1-800-244-2224**

Don't miss the 2019 edition of
the American Casino Guide

Completely Updated
More Casinos! • More Coupons!

On Sale - November 1, 2017

Ask for ISBN #978-1-883768-28-7 at
your favorite bookstore or call (954) 989-2766
or order online at: americancasinoguide.com

Meet Stanford Wong - The "Guru" of Blackjack

by Steve Bourie

If you've ever read any stories about the game of blackjack you've probably heard of Stanford Wong. He's the author of numerous books on the subject, as well as the brains behind some computer software programs that can analyze the game inside and out. His most popular book, Professional Blackjack, is used as a bible by many professional players and is one of the best books for anyone who wants to learn how to counts cards.

I often refer to Wong's books during the course of my work and although we have talked on the phone I must admit that I really didn't know much about his background. In the 30 years that I've been reading about gambling I don't ever remember seeing any stories about how he came to be a blackjack expert. I thought it might be interesting to explore this subject and Wong Graciously agreed to let me interview him by telephone from his home in La Jolla, California.

Wong was born in Georgia during World War II and his family briefly moved to a few other states before settling in Beaverton, Oregon. He began his schooling there and always had an affection for playing games. "Any new game that I would hear about I would learn the rules and I would figure out how to play it," he says. "But what always turned me on about any new game was figuring out the optimal strategy.

When I first learned tic-tac-toe for example, I really didn't want to play the game with other people, I wanted to figure out where, if I moved first, should I make my mark? Or, if I moved second, and given where you made your mark, where should I make my mark? I was probably five or six years old when I figured that out. But that was what always interested me about games: learning the strategy."

As he grew up Wong also says he spent a lot of time playing card games. "It was the sort of thing that our family and relatives did whenever they got together. There were probably a dozen different card games that my folks and I played, depending on what set of relatives, neighbors or friends we were playing with and I essentially grew up with a deck of cards in my hand. It was just a way of life and it wasn't anything we did for money, it was just a competitive sort of thing"

Wong believes he led a rather normal lifestyle and never considered playing cards to be anything other than a minor diversion until he read Ed Thorp's book *Beat The Dealer* in 1963 which suddenly gave him other ideas. "I thought 'hey this is neat!' This guy's really got something here and maybe I can make some money in the casinos," he says. "Actually, before that book came out I was doing my own work on analyzing blackjack but I really didn't do it with the idea of taking on the casinos. I just did it as a hobby because I thought it was an interesting game and I thought I could figure out what the strategy should be."

And how old was he when he developed those blackjack strategies? Just 14! "It was fun," he says. "You got to look at some of the interesting problems that were involved in calculating 'should you hit or stand on 16 against a dealer's 10?' I thought it was interesting to figure out the formulas for doing that."

Wong was 20 at the time he read Thorp's book and, not surprisingly, he turned to the book's appendix first. "Thorp had calculated all the probabilities for hitting and standing for every situation and I compared his data with the calculations I had done. I noticed that his numbers matched my numbers exactly so I thought 'hey, this guy's giving us the true information.' Actually, I had only done the calculations for deuces through 10's and I hadn't done the aces yet because they took a lot of time. At that point I abandoned the rest of my calculations because I would have been doing what he had already done and I knew his numbers were correct."

Then an udergraduate student at Oregon State University, Wong was still too young to enter a casino but he enjoyed learning how to count cards using Thorp's 10-count system. "I practiced on evenings and weekends," he says. "Since I was a student I didn't have that much time for it and I just did it as a challenge. I had to wait a few months until I was 21 before I could go to Nevada and visit the casinos."

One week past his 21st birthday Wong traveled to Reno at the start of the summer with a classmate who had also taken the time to learn card-counting. "It was interesting because we won money right off the bat," he professes proudly. "We thought 'gee, what an easy way to make money.' We just had one of those fabulous win streaks. We started with a $300 bankroll and made something like $250. Our minimum bet was $1 and our maximum was $4."

During that first weekday afternoon in Reno he strolled into the Horseshoe Casino and found he was the only customer in the place. "There wasn't even anybody playing slots," he says. "All of the dealers and the pit boss were watching me because they had nothing else to do and I didn't know how to behave because I had never watched other players. So here I am just sitting back in my chair winning hand after hand and all of these silver dollars were piling up in front of me. I had about 250 of them and finally it dawned on me that I wouldn't be able to carry them all." At that point he stopped playing and when the dealer asked him why, he said "This is all the money I can carry. If I win any more I won't have any way to carry it." Then the dealer asked if she could "give him a check for those silver dollars?" and he replied "I don't want your check. I want this money." The dealer then explained to the novice player that she would exchange his silver dollars for chips out of her rack which he could then take to the cashier's cage to be redeemed for cash. Still unsure about what she was proposing to him, Wong wondered "are they trying to cheat me or is this the normal procedure? There were no other players there that I could ask but I finally agreed to it. Then, I must have ran over to the cashier's cage because it was like I was afraid that the chips were going to lose their value by the time I got there. I was so relieved when the cashier finally gave me $20 bills for those little pieces of plastic which I wasn't sure had any real value. That's how naive I was."

Of course, the blackjack games were a little different back in that summer of 1964. "They were all single-deck games and they dealt out 50 of the 52 cards," says Wong. "They only burned one card and they wouldn't deal the last card. If you got a dealer to yourself it was a fabulous game. The rules were you could double any two cards and the dealer would hit soft 17."

Following his successful first trip Wong continued to make visits to Reno or Lake Tahoe whenever he had a break from his academic studies and the following summer he felt ready to take on Las Vegas. However, after three days in Vegas he gave up because he was discouraged by the widespread cheating which he saw. "It seemed like every place in Vegas was cheating," he says. "I couldn't find an honest game. I remember one place where I saw the dealer cheating. It was an obvious move and he noticed that I saw him do it. Suddenly, he got this big smile on his face as if I were admiring his handiwork and he was proud of what he had done. There was no shame on his part and it was just like well, that's the way we deal the game in this town." Following his experience in Vegas Wong returned to Reno to practice his skills. "There were a couple of places in Reno that cheated but we stayed away from them. The rest were all honest."

In 1965 Wong completed his undergraduate studies and the following year he received his MBA from Oregon State. He stayed there as a teacher for two more years and during that period he met and married his wife (they're still married). Naturally, he was still playing in Reno and Lake Tahoe as often as he could and in 1968 he was drafted into the Army. Following his two-year tour of duty Wong enrolled at Stanford University (located about 30 miles south of San Francisco) to pursue a PhD in finance. Being closer to Las Vegas he decided to visit the city again and he says he "was pleasantly surprised to see that Las Vegas was dealing honest blackjack games. Somehow Las Vegas got 'cleaned up' between the years of 1965 and 1970."

For the next five years Wong visited Nevada casinos once or twice a month while pursuing his PhD and also while helping to raise his son (born in 1971) and his daughter (born in 1974). In 1974 he began teaching finance courses full-time at San Francisco State and it was during his last term at S.F. State in 1976 that Wong found himself in a bit of a dilemma. "I was making more money playing blackjack than teaching classes and I didn't want to have to go to all of the faculty meetings. I thought they were a waste of time and instead of sticking around for meetings I would rather pop over to Las Vegas," he says. Since he had signed a contract he felt obligated to continue to teach his classes but he really didn't need the money so he made a deal with the school to teach for free in return for not having to go to the meetings. The University agreed and paid him a salary of $1 for his last term of teaching at the school. That, according to Wong, was his "last real job."

In 1975 Wong published *Professional Blackjack* which, he says, he really didn't intend to write and the book sort of evolved. It seems that lots of people were always asking him to teach them how to count cards but he didn't have time for that. Instead, he wrote an explanation of how to count cards which he handed out to anyone who asked him for help. When those people came back with questions, he would write out the answers and then add that information to his original explanation to make it even more comprehensive. "The original write-up of how to count cards kept getting bigger and bigger," he says. "The other thing I did was that I worked out strategies on the computer that Thorp didn't have in his book. Thorp didn't cover surrender, for example, so I worked out my own surrender indexes. I also worked out strategies for games where the dealer stood on soft 17. Eventually, I looked at all of that material and thought if I put it all together, along with an explanation of how to play the game, it could be a book but it was all sort of accidental."

Once he was ready to publish his book Wong decided that he needed a pen name. After all, he had been playing under his real name in the casinos and he didn't want them to know that he was an expert in card counting. "I really liked Nevada Smith, but somebody else already had that name," he says. "I had a preference for complicated first names and simple last names so I went to my friends in the PhD program at Stanford and asked for suggestions. Denny Draper, who's now a professor at U.S.C., suggested Stanford Wong and I said 'that's it!' It's got the mystique of the Orient and it's got an academic ring. So, I have to give him credit for coming up with my name."

In 1976 Wong moved to La Jolla (near San Diego) and the following year decided he wanted to try to make a living "for a year or two" from his publishing business and playing blackjack. He finally got his Ph.D. in 1978 and initially thought he would become a college professor but, he says, "it turned out that I really enjoyed what I was doing and I was making enough money that I never got back to teaching."

Wong soon got the urge to broaden his horizons by traveling in search of good blackjack games. "I made a lot of trips to Asia," he says. "Korea had wonderful blackjack. So did Macau, Indonesia and the Philippines. They all had great games back then." When asked if his trips were successful, he responds with an enthusiastic, "oh yeah." And was he successful enough that he started getting barred? "Only at a few little Korean casinos," he says. "The problem at that time was that they just didn't have enough customers. If there were only four customers they could keep track of each customer and know exactly how they were doing. I just won too much money too fast and they said 'sorry sir, we don't want you here anymore.' I would assume that they were sophisticated enough to know that I was counting cards but their attitude was 'you're winning from us, you're too good for us, please don't play here anymore' and I could understand that."

Weary from his long trips to Asia, and eager to spend more time at home with his family, Wong resumed his visits to Las Vegas where he found that he could continue to play as long as he didn't spend too much time in any one place. He developed an index card system where he kept track of his play. He had a card for every casino with details on: the date of his visits, how many hours he played, which shift he played on, and the results of his play (dollars won or lost). Then, when he was planning his next visit he would pull out his cards and select a group of casinos where he hadn't played in a while and visit them. This way he wouldn't become too well known to any particular casino's personnel.

Wong continued to visit Vegas once or twice a month and says he continued to make money even though the casinos "did things to make the games more difficult to beat, with multiple decks being one example." "However," he says "at the same time, players developed skills too. There are skills that I have now that I didn't have in 1978. For a while there was a really good way to make money by looking for warped hole cards, especially on insurance. You just looked at the shape of the dealer's hole card and if it was bent one way it was either an ace or a 10 and if it was bent the other way it was a small card. Plus, I had no idea about 'tells' when I first started playing blackjack. That's when you use the dealer's body language to learn something about their hole card."

And did he always win? "Oh there's no such thing as always making money," he says. "Sometimes I would win and sometimes I would lose but at the end of the year I would be ahead."

Wong's comment here brought up a widespread misconception that many people have about card counters. Most people think that counters always win whenever they play but that just isn't true. "The edge that a card counter has over a casino is much, much smaller than the edge that a casino has over their players, " he explains. "The average blackjack player thinks 'every time I play I lose but as a card counter you've got an edge so every time you play you must win.' However, it doesn't work that way because the counter's edge is much smaller. Just as there are gamblers who occasionally come back as winners because they got lucky there are also card counters who get unlucky and the casino beats them. It just happens."

Wong believes that some of the best opportunities for blackjack players today may be in the special promotions that the casinos are continuously offering. "One of the best things now is all of the 'freebies' that the casinos are giving out," he proclaims. Anybody that plays a lot of blackjack has got more than they need in the way of room and food comps, plus many casinos are sending out coupons that are valid for cash at the cage or they're sending out matchplay offers that can be played at the tables just like cash. There's a lot of free money being given out to entice people to play. So part of the income for a professional player now, or even a regular player, is in these free cash offers. That wasn't the case 20 or 30 years ago."

When asked if there is any way a basic strategy player can come out ahead in the long run, Wong replies: "Well, it depends what you mean by come out ahead. You have to look at each individual and ask what is it that they want? There are a lot of people on our website bj21.com, for example, that don't really need the money they make playing blackjack. They're just looking for some fun. These are people who are successful as medical doctors, or lawyers, or something else outside of the world of blackjack but they're very competitive. They love Las Vegas and they really like the idea that when they go there they can stay at luxurious accommodations and eat meals in fabulous restaurants and somebody else will pay for them. So for them, as long as they're playing a game that's breakeven or better, they're happy because they get to live like kings but they don't have to pay for it."

And does Wong himself play for comps? "I don't do that," he says. His preferred method is to count cards and make sure he is only playing in positive decks (where the count favors the player, unlike negative decks where the count favors the casino). This means that he is constantly changing tables in search of positive situations and it's a system that is popular with card counters. The method is known as "Wonging" and, of course, it's named after him.

"I like the idea of walking around and finding positive counts," he says. "I'll sometimes play neutral counts or go to a table where a dealer is shuffling but if I get a count of -2 after the first hand, I'm gone. If it's -1 I might stick around for a second hand but I basically just stick around for positive counts. If I were to sit at one table making minimum bets in negative counts it wouldn't be worthwhile. In the first place I don't want to waste my time making minimum bets and in the second place that's going to look bad to anyone who's watching me when I hit a good count and start raising my bet. I'd rather have them see me only betting $200 a hand. I don't want them to see me sometimes betting $25 and sometimes betting $200."

But don't the casinos know him as Stanford Wong when he plays there? "Quite a few people in the casinos know me but they tend to be the higher-ups, they're not the people down on the floor" he says. "As long as I keep my bets low enough, basically the people who are watching me don't know me at all. At a lot of these places in Nevada the point where the attention starts is $100 and as long as you keep you bets under $100 you're flying under their radar. There are also some places where you can bet up to $300 or $500 before they start paying attention, so I like to bet as much as I can but the really important thing is to stay under their radar. If they'll let me bet $500 and nobody's going to care I'll stick $500 out there."

When asked if he has any words of wisdom for the average blackjack player Wong makes the point that players should be sure that they're getting the freebies that their action warrants. "If you're betting enough to earn free meals then you should make sure that the casino is paying for your meals," he says. "Also, you've got to know if you're playing with an edge and if you're not counting cards then you're not playing with an edge. If you like to play and you're not a card counter then my advice is to play as slowly as possible in order to get your comps."

By urging non-counters to play slowly Wong is referring to the fact that casinos always base their comp formulas on the amount of time you spend at the tables plus the average amount of your bets. "Typically they'll want four hours but they're going to say four hours whether it's a busy table and you're playing 40 hands an hour or it's an empty table where you're playing by yourself and putting in 200 hands an hour," he says. "If you're not counting cards make sure that you're playing at a table where there are lots of other players. It helps if they're all laughing and having a good time and the dealer's joking along with everyone and the game is moving as slowly as possible. But if you're a card counter I would advise you to do just the opposite because you want to get in as many hands per hour as possible. You would want to play at the times of day when the casino is empty and you're the only player at the table and the dealer is really fast."

Of course there are some blackjack players who believe that you don't have to be a card counter in order to have an edge over the casino. Many of these players believe that you can use money management, or progressive betting systems to overcome the casino edge but Wong doesn't believe that's possible. "That's hogwash," he says. "Money management does not give you an edge over the casino. The first thing you've got to do is count cards so you play well enough to get an edge over the casino. Once you've got that edge that's where money management comes in. But if you're not playing with an edge then proper money management says to keep your money in your pocket and don't risk it at all."

Looking back on the start of his career in blackjack Wong says he was surprised at how things worked out. "I just thought it would be interesting to do for a while and I didn't see it as a lifetime thing. I thought I would just be doing it for a short time but it kept stretching out and stretching out."

Although he's had great success playing blackjack Wong is quick to admit that he would be "bored stiff" if that was all he did. "I just wouldn't be doing that anymore," he says. "When I first started playing the money I made was important to me because I needed it to pay bills but then I got to the point where I had plenty of money and I really didn't have to play blackjack for big money anymore. So I started asking myself what do I really want to do with my time? Do I want to sit in a smoky casino and make these boring decisions over and over again and have these huge ups and huge downs in my bankroll if I really don't need the money that badly? So I started to think of different things to do and what happened is that I got into more things that I could write about. I got into tournaments and wrote a book on that, plus books on horse racing, video poker, sports betting and now I have my own website at bj21.com. There's always something new to come along that keeps my interest up."

And is he happy with way things turned out? "Of course," he says. "I consider myself as being very fortunate in being able to do basically whatever I wanted to do for my whole adult life and what I really enjoy doing is figuring things out." There are an awful lot of gamblers out there who are glad he did!

Slot Machines

by Steve Bourie

Virtually anyone who visits a casino, even for the first time, is familiar with a slot machine and how it operates: just put in your money, pull the handle and wait a few seconds to see if you win. It isn't intimidating like table games where you really need some knowledge of the rules before you play and it's this basic simplicity that accounts for much of the success of slot machines in the modern American casino.

As a matter of fact, the biggest money-maker for casinos is the slot machine with approximately 65 percent of the average casino's profits being generated by slot machine play. As an example, in Nevada's fiscal year ending June 30, 2017 the total win by all of the state's casinos was a little more than $11.4 billion. Of that amount, $7.28 billion, or slightly less than 64 percent, was from electronic machine winnings.

With this in mind, you must ask yourself, "can I really win money by playing slot machines?" The answer is a resounding yes...and no. First the "no" part: in simplest terms a slot machine makes money for the casino by paying out less money than it takes in. In some states, such as Nevada and New Jersey, the minimum amount to be returned is regulated. In Nevada the minimum is 75 percent and in New Jersey it's 83 percent. However, if you look at the slot payback percentages for those particular states in this book you will see that the actual average payback percentages are much higher. In New Jersey it's close to 91 percent and in Nevada it's slightly more than 93 percent. Even though the actual paybacks are higher than the law requires, you can still see that on average for every $1 you play in an Atlantic City slot machine you will lose 9¢ and in a Las Vegas slot machine you will lose 7¢. Therefore, it doesn't take a rocket scientist to see that if you stand in front of a slot machine and continue to pump in your money, eventually, you will lose it all. On average, it will take you longer to lose it in Las Vegas rather than Atlantic City, but the result is still the same: you will go broke.

Gee, sounds kind of depressing, doesn't it? Well, cheer up because now we go on to the "yes" part. But, before we talk about that, let's first try to understand how slot machines work. All modern slot machines contain a random number generator (RNG) which is used to control the payback percentage for each machine. When a casino orders a slot machine the manufacturer will have a list of percentage paybacks for each machine and the casino must choose one from that list. For example, a manufacturer may have 10 chips available for one machine that range from a high of 98% to as low as 85%. All of these chips have been inspected and approved by a gaming commission and the casino is free to choose whichever chip it wants for that particular brand of machine.

In almost all instances, the casino will place a higher denomination chip in a higher denomination machine. In other words, the penny machines will get the chips programmed to pay back around 87% and the $25 machines will get the chips programmed to pay back around 98%. A casino can always change the payback percentage, but in order to do that it usually must go back to the manufacturer to get a new RNG that is programmed with the new percentage. For this reason, most casinos rarely change their payback percentages unless there is a major revision in their marketing philosophy.

And what exactly is a random number generator? Well, it's a little computer chip that is constantly working (as its name implies) to generate number combinations on a random basis. It does this extremely fast and is capable of producing hundreds of combinations each second. When you pull the handle, or push the spin button, the RNG stops and the combination it stops at is used to determine where the reels will stop in the pay window. Unlike video poker machines, you have no way of knowing what a slot machine is programmed to pay back just by looking at it. The only way to tell is by knowing what is programmed into the RNG.

As an example of the differences in RNG payout percentages I have listed below some statistics concerning various slot manufacturers' payback percentages in their slot machines. Normally, this information isn't available to the public, but it is sometimes printed in various gaming industry publications and that is where I found it. The list shows the entire range of percentages that can be programmed into each machine:

AGS	
River Dragons	86.00% - 94.00%
Fu Nan Fu Nu	86.00% - 95.00%
Ainsworth Game Technology	
El Toro Wild	85.00% - 96.00%
PAC MAN	86.00% - 94.00%
Aristocrat	
African Storm	87.86% - 94.84%
Britney Spears	86.00% - 96.00%
The Walking Dead	88.50% - 93.50%
Midnight Stampede	88.11% - 96.51%
Wild Panda	88.00% - 95.00%
Sharknado	87.82% - 90.01%
Aruze Gaming	
Money Rush	87.02% - 97.94%
Ultra Stack Lion	87.20% - 96.00%

Scientific Games

Black & White 5 Times Pay	84.49% - 96.72%
Black & White Sevens	87.00% - 95.00%
Blazing 7's Double (reel)	88.00% - 95.98%
Cash Spin	85.72% - 88.38%
Dancing Drums	84.14% - 92.19%
Heidi's Bier Haus	86.07% - 95.44%
Hot Shot Progressive	85.41% - 96.01%
Hot Spin	87.59% - 89.99%
Money Wheel	85.38% - 96.08%
Triple Cash Wheel with Quick Hit	85.49% - 93.95%
Spin & Win (3-Reel)	83.24% - 94.00%
Reel 'em in/Compete to Win	86.92% - 96.15%
Cash Crop	86.36% - 94.92%
Monty Oython and the Holy Grail	90.31% - 90.32%
Monopoly Real Estate Tycoon	86.00% - 94.00%
Price is Right - Plinko Jackpots	87.00% - 96.00%
Quick Hit Ultra Pays	85.49% - 95.97%

IGT

Dangerous Beauty 2	87.50% - 98.00%
Diamond Jackpots	87.90% - 96.50%
Elephant King	85.03% - 98.04%
Enchanted Unicorn	85.00% - 98.00%
Dark & Stormy	92.50% - 98.00%
Gong Xi Fa Cai	85.09% - 96.01%
Ocean Magic	86.00% - 96.00%
Red White and Blue	85.03% - 97.45%
Texas Tea	87.00% - 97.00%
Wolf Run 2: Into The Wild	85.00% - 98.00%
Bejeweled	86.55% - 89.18%
Top Dollar Premium	80.00% - 96.00%
IC Money	85.20% - 97.02%
Zuma	84.15% - 94.16%
Sphinx 3D	86.00% - 92.00%

Konami Gaming

African Diamond	82.13% - 96.03%
Big Africa	85.50% - 98.10%
Dungeons & Dragons	87.20% - 96.10%
Frogger: Great City Wild	82.20% - 96.10%

Incredible Technologies

Crazy Money Deluxe	85.20% - 94.00%
Money Roll	85.15% - 94.00%
Money Rain Deluxe	85.10% - 94.06%

Once again, keep in mind that casinos generally set their slot paybacks based on each machine's denomination. Therefore, penny machines will probably be set towards the lower number and $5-$25 machines will be set towards the higher number.

Okay, now let's get back to the "yes" part. Yes, you can win money on slot machines by using a little knowledge, practicing some money management and, mostly, having lots of luck. First, the knowledge part. You need to know what kind of player you are and how much risk you are willing to take. Do you want to go for the giant progressive jackpot that could make you a millionaire in an instant or would you be content walking away just a few dollars ahead?

An example of a wide-area progressive machine is Nevada's Megabucks where the jackpot starts at $10 million. These $1 machines are located at more than 125 Nevada casinos around the state and are linked together by a computer. It's fine if that's the kind of machine you want to play, but keep in mind that the odds are fairly astronomical of you hitting that big jackpot. Also, the payback percentage is lower on these machines than the average $1 machine. During Nevada's fiscal year ending June 30, 2017 Megabucks averaged a little less than 87% payback while the typical $1 machine averaged a little less than 94%. So, be aware that if you play these machines you'll win fewer small payouts and it will be very difficult to leave as a winner. Unless, of course, you hit that big one! If you really like to play the wide-area progressive machines your best bet is probably to set aside a small percentage of your bankroll (maybe 10 to 15 percent) for chasing that big jackpot and saving the rest for the regular machines.

One other thing you should know about playing these wide-area progressives is that on most of them, including Megabucks, you will receive your jackpot in equal payments over a period of years (usually 25). You can avoid this, however, by playing at one of the casinos that link slot machines at their own properties and will pay you in one lump sum. Be sure to look on the machine before playing to see how it says you will be paid for the jackpot.

Knowledge also comes into play when deciding how many coins to bet. You should always look at the payback schedule posted on the machine to see if a bonus is payed for playing the maximum number of coins that the machine will accept. For example, if it's a two-coin machine and the jackpot payout is 500 coins when you bet one coin, but it pays you 1,200 coins when you bet two coins, then that machine is paying you a 200-coin bonus for playing the maximum number of coins and you may want to bet the maximum two coins to take advantage of that bonus. However, if it's a two-coin machine that will pay you 500 coins for a one-coin bet and 1,000 coins for a two-coin bet, then there is no advantage to making the maximum bet on that machine and you should only bet the minimum amount. To see more on this subject, watch my video titled "The Slot Machine - When to bet Maximum Coins" on our YouTube channel at www.youtube.com/americancasinoguide.

Knowledge of which casinos offer the best payback percentages is also helpful. When available, we print that information in this book to help you decide where to go for the best return on your slot machine dollar. You may want to go to the Las Vegas Strip to see some of the sites, but take a look at the slot machine payback percentages for the Strip-area casinos in the Las Vegas section and you'll see that you can get better returns for your slot machine dollar by playing at the off-Strip area casinos.

The final bit of knowledge you need concerns players clubs. Every major casino has a players club and you should make it a point to join it before you insert your first coin. It doesn't cost anything to join and as a member you will be able to earn complimentaries from the casinos in the form of cash, food, shows, drinks, rooms or other "freebies." Just make sure you don't get carried away and bet more than you're comfortable with just to earn some extra "comps." Ideally, you want to get "comps" for gambling that you were going to do anyway and not be pressured into betting more than you had planned.

Now let's talk about money management. The first thing you have to remember when playing slot machines is that there is no skill involved. Unlike blackjack or video poker, there are no decisions you can make that will affect whether you win or lose. It is strictly luck, or the lack of it, that will determine whether or not you win. However, when you are lucky enough to get ahead (even if it's just a little) that's where the money management factor comes in. As stated earlier, the longer you stand in front of a machine and put in your money, the more likely you are to go broke. Therefore, there is only one way you can walk away a winner and that's to make sure that when you do win, you don't put it all back in. You really need to set a "win goal" for yourself and to stop when you reach it. A realistic example would be a "win goal" of roughly 25 percent of your bankroll. If you started with $400, then you should stop if you win about $100. The "win goal" you decide on is up to you, but keep in mind that the higher your goal, the harder it will be to reach it, so be practical.

And what if you should happen to reach your goal? Take a break! Go have a meal, see a show, visit the lounge for a drink or even just take a walk around the casino. You may have the urge to keep playing, but if you can just take a break from the machines, even it's just for a short time, you'll have the satisfaction of leaving as a winner. If, later on, you get really bored and find that you just have to go back to the machines you can avoid a total loss by not risking more than half of your winnings and by playing on smaller denomination machines. If you made your winnings on $1 machines, move down to quarters. If you won on quarters, move down to nickels. The idea now is basically to kill some time and have a little fun knowing that no matter what happens you'll still leave as a winner.

And now, let's move on to luck. As stated previously, the ultimate decider in whether or not you win is how lucky you are. But, is there anything you can do to help you choose a "winning" machine? Not really, because there is no such thing. Remember, in the long run, no machine will pay out more than it takes in. There are, however, some things you could try to help you find the more generous machines and avoid the stingy ones. Keep in mind that all slot machine payback percentages shown in this book are averages.

Like everything else in life, slot machines have good cycles where they pay out more than average and bad cycles where they pay out less than average. Ultimately, what you want to find is a machine in a good cycle. Of course if I knew how to find that machine I wouldn't be writing this story, instead I'd be standing in front of it with a $100 bill in my hand getting ready to play it. So, I guess you'll have to settle for my two recommendations as to how you might be able to make your slot bankroll last longer.

First, is the "accounting" method. With this method you start with a pre-determined number of credits and after playing them though one time, you take an accounting of your results. If you have more than you started with you stay at that machine and start another cycle. Just keep doing this until the machine returns less than you started with. As an example, let's say you start with a $10 credit voucher. After making 10 $1 bets you see how many credits you have left on the machine. If it's more than $10 you start over again with another 10 $1 bets and then do another accounting. If, after any accounting, you get back less than the $10 bankroll you started with, stop playing and move on to a different machine. This is an especially good method because you have to slow down your play to take periodic accountings and you will always have an accurate idea of how well you are doing.

The other method is even simpler and requires no math. It's called the "baseball" method and is based on the principle of three strikes and you're out. Just play a machine until it loses three times in a row, then move on to another machine. Both of these methods will prevent you from losing a lot in a machine that is going through a bad cycle. To see more on this subject, watch my video titled "10 Tips To Stretch Your Slot Machine Bankroll" on our YouTube channel at www.youtube.com/americancasinoguide

Slot Machine Trends - 2018

by John Grochowski

Ever since the dawning of the video slot age, casinos have been flooded with hundreds of new games every year.

Three-reel slots such as Double Diamond and Blazing 7s held their popularity for decades. Video slots reach peak popularity and enter a decline phase in a matter of months.

In part, the games are designed to do exactly that. Within a few months, players have thoroughly explore games, played all the bonus events, seen the special features and are ready to see the next crop of latest and greatest games.

Some popular favorites remain on casino floors for longer periods, of course, and even inspire successor games, but slot design is an eternal game of "can you top this?"

Among the continuing trends are more multi-tiered progressive jackpots, new games in popular game families, eye-catching ways to deliver wild symbols to create frequent winners, use of pop-culture themes and, in video poker, multiplier features that require extra wagers.

One area that casinos and manufacturers alike hope will gather enough following to become a trend is a move into fully skill-based video gaming. Let's take a look at a few recent examples with games that either made their way into casinos in 2017 or were awaiting regulatory approval before making their debuts. In nearly all cases, the games make their initial impact on Nevada and players in some markets will be experiencing these slots for the first time in 2018.

PROGRESSIVE JACKPOTS

DRAGON LINK, Aristocrat Technologies: You can win multiple progressives on a single spin in a game that builds on Aristocrat's popular Lightning Link progressives, and that's a great base. For 2016, Lightning Link was named the leading slot in North America in the annual Eilers Fantini survey, ending a five-year run at the top for IGT's Wheel of Fortune.

As in Lightning Link, you're looking for pearls onscreen for bonus credits and possible progressive jackpots, and it's possible to win multiple progressives in a single bonus spin.

When you get six or more pearls, you collect credits from each, with a shot at one or more jackpots.

The multilevel progressive Dragon Link is on Aristocrat's premium Arc Single cabinet. It's Asian-themed with base games that include Autumn Moon, Panda Magic and Golden Century. It's available as a multidenominational game, so you can choose 1, 2, 5 or 10 cents, as well as $1 and $2 for the big players.

RIVERBOAT QUEEN, Everi: You're at the helm for fun and credits with an on-screen bonus wheel, and you'll enjoy cruising toward a multitier progressive jackpot.

Riverboat Queen has an unusual nine-reel, 32-payline configuration on Everi's Core HDX cabinet. The Core HDX features dual widescreen touchscreens on 23-inch monitors and a premium three-way sound system.

When bonus symbols land on the first, fifth and ninth reels, you earn a spin of the bonus wheel onscreen to the right of the main reels. Spins of the wheel can bring bonus credits and additional spins, and the credits mount up fast if you're lucky enough to get the maximum nine spins.

Max bets put you in contention for the progressive jackpots. Landing four through nine Riverboat Queen symbols on the reels puts you in jackpot land, with your jackpot tier corresponding to the number of Riverboat Queen symbols.

NEW VERSIONS OF OLD FAVORITES

SPHINX 4D, International Game Technology: ll How could IGT top Sphinx 3D? With Sphinx 4D, which adds a dimension of touch to the experience.

Recognizing that Sphinx 3D were reaching out to catch the virtual coins that appeared to pop out of the screen in big wins, IGT designed a game that can track hand movement. When launching a free-spin bonus, try moving your hand close to the screen. Lightning-like lines will appear around your hand, and you'll feel a small tingling.

Push your hand in and draw it out, and the energy discharge follows your hand. A quick flick, and the electrical effect disappears and the bonus launches.

It's a very cool effect, enhancing what's already an amazing experience.

MONEY RAIN SUPER SKY WHEEL, Incredible Technologies: Incredible Technologies has come a long way in a few short years creating slot games. Creative and different from the beginning, IT has upped its presence with experience in market needs and game math.

IT had its first megahit in Money Rain, and now is using the game to introduce its Infinity Super Skybox cabinet, you can't miss it. The recommended configuration is four machines side-by-side, each topped by a 55-inch monitor. The four monitors are linked and make an imposing 123-inch display when the Sky Wheel bonus is in play.

One feature is the money catch bonus – you touch the screen to collect currency as it flies by.

Some of that currency awards spins on a Super Sky Wheel that stretches across the four overhead monitors. There, you can win progressives or credits. The wheel has a ring within a ring, and on the inner ring you can win respins, with up to 20 Sky Wheel spins possible.

You'll be thrilled that sometimes when it rains, it pours.

POP CULTURE FAVORITES

SEINFELD, Scientific Games: Jerry and the gang are all here with classic moments from the TV legend.

Seinfeld is on Scientific Games' Gamescape cabinet with five video screens. At eye level, there's a triptych, with a main screen straight ahead and smaller panels angling out on either side. And there's big bonus and video clip fun in the top box screens.

The main screen has four set of video reels. You can play one if you like and still be eligible for all the character bonuses. Or you can bet bigger and play all four.

There are bonuses featuring Jerry, Elaine, George and Kramer, of course. But secondary characters also are featured, such in the Festivus Bonus. You use a motion sensor to grab the Festivus pole while Jerry Stiller as Frank Costanza announces, "A new holiday is born: Festivus for the rest of us." When you have the pole, it launches the Festivus free spins.

Then there's the Soup Nazi, a fun bonus event featuring custom content actor Larry Thomas recorded in a green-screen shoot at Scientific Games' Chicago facilities.

In the Soup Nazi bonus, cartons of soup roll by on a conveyor. Some reveal bonus credits, others contain a character's face. If you get a character, it's worth a trip to a bonus wheel that's superimposed on the Soup Nazi. Some wheel segments are open so you can see Thomas beneath. Other spaces award credits, but if the wheel lands on an open space and the Soup Nazi's face shows, it's "No soup for you!" and the round ends.

THE SIMPSONS, Scientific Games: Animators lent a hand in a revamped game that has TV-level fun. Highly anticipated as one of the hottest slots of 2016, The Simpsons was held back a year to become one of the hottest of 2017. Why?

"The Simpsons" license holders saw and like the game, but thought they could improve on animation and scripts to make it stand out more.

They then worked with Scientific Games to create custom content with animators from the series, with one of their writers doing scripts and voiceover sessions with "The Simpsons" voice actors Hank Azaria and Dan Castellaneta.

The result is gorgeous. You're going to want to stop by the game just to see the animated introductory dream sequence with a tuxedoed Homer wafting from craps table to roulette to the doughnut buffet.

WILD DISPLAYS

PHOENIX PRINCESS, Konami: Extra wilds in the top box and drop to the main screen and make for some regal payoffs.

A five-reel video slot, Phoenix Princess is available to casinos in 20-, 30- and 40-line versions. Each have Action Stacked Symbols on all reels, and when the stacks match, you're credit meter will soar.

During regular play, wild symbols can appear on the second through fifth reels, while in free-spin mode the wilds appear on the second, third or fourth reels. However, it's during the free spins that extra wild can appear up top and drop into random positions on the man screen. With up to 20 free spins possible, that can mean a wild ride.

DREAMSCAPE, Everi: Mystery Wilds and up to 97 free spins possible, the dream here is of big wins on the freebies. Dreamscape is on Everi's new Platinum MXP cabinet with a 40-inch integrated touchscreen, an interactive sound chair with Earthquake Shakers and 6.2 surround sound.

The game features five video reels with 80 paylines. Scattering five-to-10 bonus symbols across the reels triggers free spins. You can relaunch the bonus during free spins, adding a trigger payoff on each relaunch and making possible up to 97 freebies.

Mystery Symbol Upgrades and Mystery Symbol Bursts occur randomly to up your winnings. For those who bet the max, there are progressive jackpots triggered when six or more jackpot symbols land on the reels. With 13 or more symbols, you win the top progressive tier.

VIDEO POKER WITH EXTRA BETS

ULTIMATE X BONUS STREAK, International Game Technology: Bonus Streak builds on the success of Ultimate X, the most popular of video poker bonusing games. It's available in Triple Play, Five Play and Ten Play formats, each with a 10 credit per hand maximum bet.

As in Ultimate X, winning hands bring multiplier for subsequent hands. There are exceptions: The smallest-paying hands, Jacks or Better and two pairs, do not bring multipliers on Bonus Streak.

Here's the new wrinkle players will love. You don't just get a multiplier for the next hand. You get a streak of multipliers. On non-wild card games, three of a kind, flushes and straights bring multipliers on the next three hands. If it's a full house or better, you get a five-hand streak.

Not only that, the multiplier increases for each hand on the streak. When you have the maximum streak, multipliers are 2x, 3x, 4x, 8x and 12x – that is, payoffs on a winning hand are doubled on the next play, tripled on the one after and so on.

If you have a winner during the streak, it increases payoffs for the remainder of the streak to 12x. That's a bonus video poker players will want to see again and again.

SKILL-BASED GAMES

FROGGER, Konami: One of the most popular arcade games of all time makes its casino debut in retro style. A favorite in arcades and home gaming systems for more than 30 years, Frogger has come to slot formats in two themes: Great City Wilds and Woodland Wilds. Both have four-level progressive jackpots, but the bonus gamers will look forward to is the Frogger Bonus.

With a strong tie to the arcade game, the Frogger bonus will be instant nostalgia for longtime players and fun for everyone. It launches randomly with a mystery trigger, and it takes you to the classic Frogger course, crossing roads and rivers – watch out for cars! You get three lives at the start of the bonus as you collect credits and get a chance at the progressive jackpots.

There's much more to the skill-based story. Some gamemakers are confining skill to bonus events such as in Frogger and Scientific Games' Space Invaders. Other companies, notably GameCo, are pushing ahead with games that are entirely skill-based, such as Nothin' But Net, where players must time a button push to maximize chances of putting a ball through a hoop.

Baby Boomers and many Generation X players, long comfortable with spinning video reels and bonus events, might prefer the Frogger approach. But casinos are hoping full-skill games, which look and feel more akin to recreational games such as those you find online, will be an entry into wagering as Millennials come of casino age.

This is all new enough that neither approach can be called a trend, but both are on the watch list for those who want to see the future of gaming.

John Grochowski is the best-selling author of The Craps Answer Book, The Slot Machine Answer Book and The Video Poker Answer Book. His weekly column is syndicated to newspapers and Web sites, and he contributes to many of the major magazines and newspapers in the gaming field

Video Poker

by Steve Bourie

Okay, who knows the main difference between video poker and slot machines? C'mon now, raise your hands if you think you know it. If you said "a slot machine is a game of luck and video poker is a game of skill" then you are correct! When you play a slot machine there is no decision you can make which will affect the outcome of the game. You put in your money; pull the handle; and hope for the best. In video poker, however, it is your skill in playing the cards which definitely affects the outcome of the game.

Okay, who knows the other major difference between video poker and slot machines? Well, you're right again if you said "you never know what percentage a slot machine is set to pay back, but you can tell a video poker machine's payback percentage just by looking at it." Of course if you knew that answer then you also knew that video poker machines almost always offer you better returns than slot machines (provided you make the right playing decisions).

Now for those of you who didn't know the answers to those two questions, please read on. You others can skip the rest of this story as I am sure you're eager to get back to your favorite video poker machine.

First, let's cover the basics. Video poker has virtually the same rules as a game of five card draw poker. The only difference is that you have no opponent to beat and you can't lose more than your initial bet. First, you deposit from one to five coins in the machine to make your bet. You are then shown five cards on the video screen and your goal is to try to make the best poker hand possible from those cards. Since it is a draw game, you are given one opportunity to improve your hand. This is done by allowing you to discard from one, up to all five cards from your original hand. Of course, you don't have to discard any if you don't want to. After choosing which cards you want to keep (by pushing the button below each card), you then push the deal button and the machine will replace all of the other cards with new cards. Based on the resulting final hand the machine will then pay you according to the pay schedule posted on the machine. Naturally, the better your hand, the higher the amount the machine will pay you back.

That's pretty much how a video poker machine works from the outside, but what about the inside? Well, I had a few questions about that so I visited International Game Technology, which is the world's largest manufacturer of video poker machines (as well as slot machines), in January 2001 and spoke to their chief software engineer, James Vasquez. Here's what Jim had to say in answer to some questions about how his company's machines work:

Let's talk about the difference between video poker and slot machines. It's my understanding that with video poker you can't control the number of winning and losing combinations programmed into the computer chip, instead its based on a 52-card deck with a fixed number of combinations. Is that correct?

Vasquez: Yes, assuming there are no wild cards.

When the cards are dealt is it done on a serial basis where it's similar to cards coming off the top of a deck? Or, parallel where there are five cards dealt face up and one card is unseen underneath each of the initial five cards?

Vasquez: It's serial and the five later cards aren't determined until there is more player interaction at the time of the draw.

They aren't determined at the time of the deal?

Vasquez: No. They're determined at the time of the draw. That varies with the jurisdictional regulation actually. Some lottery jurisdictions tell you that you have to draw all 10 at once. Different jurisdictions write into their rules how they want it done, specifically on poker, because it's a simpler game and they understand it. They say they either want all 10 done at once, or however they want.

How is it done in Nevada? All ten at once, or five and five?

IGT: In Nevada it's five and five.

The talk with Jim Vasquez confirmed that in most regulated jurisdictions video poker machines use a Random Number Generator to shuffle a 52-card deck and then choose five cards to display to the player. (By the way, when played without wild cards, there are exactly 2,598,960 unique five-card poker hands that can be dealt to a player.) Then, when the deal button is pushed, the next group of cards is chosen and dealt to the player.

One point must be made here regarding random outcomes in video poker machines. Please note that gaming regulations always require video poker machines to have random outcomes. You should be aware that there are casinos operating in places that do not have gaming regulations. Examples are cruise ships which operate in international waters, some Indian reservations that are not subject to state regulations, and virtually all Internet casinos. You should also be aware that the technology exists for machines to be set so they do not act randomly. These machines can be actually programmed to avoid giving the players better hands and they wind up giving the house a much bigger advantage. These machines are illegal in Nevada, New Jersey, Colorado and all other states that pattern their gaming regulations after those states. You may, however, come across them in unregulated casinos.

One final point you should keep in mind - IGT is not the only manufacturer of video poker machines. There are quite a few others and they may engineer their machines to work in a different manner. Their RNG may not stop in the same way and their draw cards may be dealt differently. IGT, however, is by far the largest and it is the type of machine you will most often encounter in a casino.

Now that you understand how a video poker machine works let's learn how to pick out the best paying ones. In the beginning of this story it was mentioned that "you can tell a video poker machine's payback percentage just by looking at it." That's true, but it takes a little bit of knowledge to know the difference among all the different types of machines. An example of some of the different machines available are: Jacks or Better, Bonus, Double Bonus, Double Double Bonus, Joker Poker and Deuces Wild. To make it even more confusing, not only are there different machines, but each of those machines can have a different pay schedule for the same hand.

Fortunately, every video poker machine's payback percentage can be mathematically calculated. Not only does this let you know which machines offer you the best return, but it also tells you the best playing decisions to make on that particular machine based on the odds of that combination occurring. The bad news, however, is that it's fairly impossible to do on your own so you'll have to either buy a book that lists all of the percentages and strategies or buy a computer program that does the work for you. Take a look at the tables on the next few pages and you'll see some different types of video poker games and their payback percentages (when played with maximum coin and perfect strategy). For those of you with a computer there are several software programs on the market that can determine the exact payback percentage for any video poker machine. They retail for prices from $29.95 to $59.95, but can be purchased at discounted prices at www.americancasinoguide.com/video-poker-software. Besides calculating percentages, they also allow you to play different types of machines and analyze hands to show you the expected return for each play. You can set these games to automatically show you the best decision, or to just warn you if you make a wrong decision.

If you have no desire to get quite that serious about learning video poker then I'll try to provide some general tips to help you out. First, you'll need to find the machines that offer you the highest returns. One of the best is the 9/6 Jacks or Better machine. Of course, you're probably wondering "what is a 9/6 Jacks or Better machine?" Well, the Jacks or Better part refers to the fact that you won't win anything from the machine unless you have at least a pair of Jacks. The 9/6 part refers to the payback schedule on this kind of machine.

As stated earlier, each machine can have a different payback schedule and there are at least 20 different kinds of payback schedules available on Jacks or Better machines. In Las Vegas the two most common Jacks or Better machines you will find are 8/5 and 9/6. Here's a comparison of their pay schedules (per coin, for five-coin play):

Hand	9/6	8/5
Royal Flush	800	800
Straight Flush	50	50
4-of-a-Kind	25	25
Full House	**9**	**8**
Flush	**6**	**5**
Straight	4	4
3-of-a-Kind	3	3
Two Pair	2	2
Jacks or Better	1	1

As you can see, the schedules are identical except for the better payoffs on the 9/6 machines for Flushes and Full Houses. The payback on a 9/6 machine is 99.5% with perfect play, while the 8/5 machines return 97.3% with perfect play. Of course, it doesn't make any sense to play an 8/5 machine if a 9/6 machine is available. Yet, you'll often see lots of people playing an 8/5 when a 9/6 can often be found in the same casino. The reason they do that is because they don't know any better; you do. Always look for the 9/6 machines. They can be usually found in most downtown Las Vegas casinos at the quarter level and in many Strip casinos at denominations of $1 and higher. In other states they won't be found as easily, and sometimes, not at all.

One other common machine you will come across is an 8/5 Jacks or Better progressive. These feature the same 8/5 pay table as above except for the royal flush which pays a jackpot amount that is displayed on a meter above the machine. The jackpot will continue to build until someone hits a royal flush; then it will reset and start to build again. When the progressive jackpot (for five coins) on a 25¢ machine first starts out at $1,000 the payback is only 97.30%, but when it reaches $2,166.50, the payback is 100%.

Another good tip is to restrict your play to the same kind of machine all the time. Each video poker machine has its own particular strategy and what works best on a Jacks or Better machine is definitely much different from what works best on a Deuces Wild machine. I usually only play 9/6 Jacks or Better machines because that is what I practice on and I automatically know the best decision to make all the time. Keep in mind that when you calculate the payback percentage for a video poker machine the number you arrive at is based on perfect play. As an example, a 9/6 Jacks or Better video poker machine has a 99.5% payback with perfect play. This means that, theoretically, it will return $99.50 for every $100 played in the machine, but only if the player makes the correct decision every time. If you make mistakes, and most players do, the return to the casino will be higher. If you play several different kinds of machines it becomes increasingly harder to remember the correct play and you will make mistakes. Therefore, it only makes sense to memorize the correct decisions for one kind of machine and to always play on that same kind of machine (of course, in order to learn those proper strategies, you may want to buy that book or software).

Jacks or Better Pay Table Variations

(Per coin with maximum coin played and perfect strategy)

9/6		9/5	
Royal Flush	800	Royal Flush	800
Straight Flush	50	Straight Flush	50
4-of-a-kind	25	4-of-a-kind	25
Full House	***9***	***Full House***	***9***
Flush	***6***	***Flush***	***5***
Straight	4	Straight	4
3-of-a-kind	3	3-of-a-kind	3
2 Pair	2	2 Pair	2
Jacks or Better	1	Jacks or Better	1
Payback	**99.54%**	**Payback**	**98.45%**

8/6		8/5	
Royal Flush	800	Royal Flush	800
Straight Flush	50	Straight Flush	50
4-of-a-kind	25	4-of-a-kind	25
Full House	***8***	***Full House***	***8***
Flush	***6***	***Flush***	***5***
Straight	4	Straight	4
3-of-a-kind	3	3-of-a-kind	3
2 Pair	2	2 Pair	2
Jacks or Better	1	Jacks or Better	1
Payback	**98.39%**	**Payback**	**97.28%**

7/5		6/5	
Royal Flush	800	Royal Flush	800
Straight Flush	50	Straight Flush	50
4-of-a-kind	25	4-of-a-kind	25
Full House	***7***	***Full House***	***6***
Flush	***5***	***Flush***	***5***
Straight	4	Straight	4
3-of-a-kind	3	3-of-a-kind	3
2 Pair	2	2 Pair	2
Jacks or Better	1	Jacks or Better	1
Payback	**96.15%**	**Payback**	**95.00%**

Bonus Poker Pay Table Variations

(Per coin with maximum coin played and perfect strategy)

8/5 Bonus	
Royal Flush	800
Straight Flush	50
Four Aces	80
Four 2s 3s 4s	40
Four 5s-Ks	25
Full House	***8***
Flush	***5***
Straight	4
3-of-a-kind	3
2 Pair	2
Jacks or Better	1
Payback	**99.17%**

7/5 Bonus	
Royal Flush	800
Straight Flush	50
Four Aces	80
Four 2s 3s 4s	40
Four 5s-Ks	25
Full House	***7***
Flush	***5***
Straight	4
3-of-a-kind	3
2 Pair	2
Jacks or Better	1
Payback	**98.02%**

10/7 Double Bonus	
Royal Flush	800
Straight Flush	50
Four Aces	160
Four 2s 3s 4s	80
Four 5s-Ks	50
Full House	***10***
Flush	***7***
Straight	5
3-of-a-kind	3
2 Pair	1
Jacks or Better	1
Payback	**100.17%**

9/7 Double Bonus	
Royal Flush	800
Straight Flush	50
Four Aces	160
Four 2s 3s 4s	80
Four 5s-Ks	50
Full House	***9***
Flush	***7***
Straight	5
3-of-a-kind	3
2 Pair	1
Jacks or Better	1
Payback	**99.11%**

10/6 Double Double Bonus	
Royal Flush	800
Straight Flush	50
Four Aces w/ 2, 3 or 4	400
Four 2, 3 or 4 w/A-4	160
Four Aces	160
Four 2,3 or 4	80
Four 5-K	50
Full House	***10***
Flush	***6***
Straight	4
3-of-a-kind	3
2 Pair	1
Jacks or Better	1
Payback	**100.07%**

9/6 Double Double Bonus	
Royal Flush	800
Straight Flush	50
Four Aces w/ 2, 3 or 4	400
Four 2, 3 or 4 w/A-4	160
Four Aces	160
Four 2,3 or 4	80
Four 5-K	50
Full House	***9***
Flush	***6***
Straight	4
3-of-a-kind	3
2 Pair	1
Jacks or Better	1
Payback	**98.98%**

Deuces Wild Pay Table Variations

(Per coin with maximum coin played and perfect strategy)

Full Pay	
Natural Royal Flush	800
Four Deuces	200
Wild Royal Flush	25
5-of-a-kind	15
Straight Flush	9
4-of-a-kind	***5***
Full House	3
Flush	2
Straight	2
3-of-a-kind	1
Payback	**100.76%**

Short Pay	
Natural Royal Flush	800
Four Deuces	200
Wild Royal Flush	25
5-of-a-kind	15
Straight Flush	9
4-of-a-kind	***4***
Full House	3
Flush	2
Straight	2
3-of-a-kind	1
Payback	**94.34%**

Deuces Deluxe	
Natural Royal Flush	800
Four Deuces	200
Natural Straight Flush	50
Wild Royal Flush	25
5-of-a-kind	15
Natural 4-of-a-kind	10
Wild Straight Flush	9
Wild 4-of-a-kind	4
Full House	4
Flush	3
Straight	2
3-of-a-kind	1
Payback	**100.34%**

Not So Ugly (NSU) Deuces	
Natural Royal Flush	800
Four Deuces	200
Wild Royal Flush	25
5-of-a-kind	***16***
Straight Flush	***10***
4-of-a-kind	***4***
Full House	***4***
Flush	***3***
Straight	2
3-of-a-kind	1
Payback	**99.73%**

Now that you've decided which machines to play, you'll need some help with strategy. On the next page is a chart that will give you an excellent simple strategy to use for both 9/6 and 8/5 video poker machines. For each dealt hand, start at the top of the chart, and hold the cards for the first available hand type.

The chart was derived from calculations using the video poker software program called Optimum Video Poker by Dan Paymar. The chart does not take into account any penalty card situations (where the holding of some cards can lessen your chance of getting a straight or a flush), but it will still give you an expected return of 99.5429%, which is within 0.001% off of perfect play. Most players would lose more through inadvertent deviations from a chart with several penalty considerations. Although the chart was created specifically for 9/6 paytables, it can also be used for 8/5 games for a return of 99.29% (within 0.002% of perfect play).

Optimum Strategy Chart For 9/6 Jacks or Better

1. Royal Flush
2. Straight Flush
3. 4 of a kind
4. Any 4 card Royal Flush
5. Full House
6. Flush
7. 3 of a kind
8. Straight
9. 4 card Open-ended Straight Flush
10. Two Pairs
11. 4 card Inside Straight Flush
12. High Pair (Jacks or higher)
13. 3 card Royal Flush
14. 4 card Flush
15. 4 card Open-ended Straight with 3 high cards
16. Low Pair (2's through 10's)
17. 4 card Open-ended Straight with 1 or 2 high cards
18. 3 card Inside Straight Flush with 2 high cards
19. 3 card Open-ended Straight Flush with 1 high card
20. 4 card Open-ended Straight with no high cards
21. 3 card Double Inside Straight Flush with 2 high cards
22. 3 card Inside Straight Flush with 1 high card
23. 3 card Open-ended Straight Flush with no high cards
24. 2 card Royal Flush (Q-J)
25. 4 high cards (A-K-Q-J)
26. 2 card Royal Flush with no 10
27. 4 card Inside Straight with 3 high cards
28. 3 card Double Inside Straight Flush with 1 high card
29. 3 card Inside Straight Flush with no high card
30. 3 high cards with no Ace (K-Q-J)
31. 2 high cards (Q-J)
32. 2 card Royal Flush (J-10)
33. 2 high cards (K-Q or K-J)
34. 2 card Royal Flush (Q-10)
35. 2 high cards (A-K, A-Q or A-J)
36. 1 high card (J or Q)
37. 2 card Royal Flush (K-10)
38. 1 high card (A or K)
39. 3 card Double Inside Straight Flush with no high card
40. Redraw (All New Cards)

To use the chart just look up your hand and play it in the manner that is closest to the top of the chart. For example: you are dealt (6♣,6♦,7♥,8♠,9♣). You keep (6♣,6♦) rather than (6♦,7♥,8♠,9♣) because a low pair (#16) is higher on the chart than a four-card straight with no high cards (#20). Remember to always look for the highest possible choice on the chart when there are multiple ways to play your hand. As another example: you are dealt (8♣,8♦, J♥,Q♥,K♥). You keep (J♥,Q♥,K♥) rather than (8♣,8♦) because a three-card royal flush (#13) is higher on the chart than a low pair (#16). As a final, but radical, example of how to play your hand by the chart what would you do if you're dealt (6♥,10♥,J♥,Q♥,K♥)? Yes, you have to break up your flush by discarding the 6♥ and go for the royal flush because the four-card royal flush (#4) is higher on the chart than the pat flush (#6). When looking at the 9/6 chart there are a few things that should seem rather obvious:

1) A low pair is relatively good. Of the 40 possible hands, a low pair is #16 which means there are 24 hands worse than a low pair. If you look at the 15 hands that are better than a low pair nine of them are pat hands that require no draw. Of the other six hands, five of them are four card hands and the remaining hand is a three-card royal flush.

2) Don't hold three cards trying to get a straight or flush. Nowhere on the chart do you see that you should hold three cards to try for a straight or flush. In some instances you should hold three cards to try for a straight flush, but never a straight or flush.

3) Rarely draw to an inside straight. Inside straights (6,7,_,9,10) appear only twice on the chart and only in rather bad positions: #27 (with three high cards) and #25 (with four high cards). It is much easier to draw to an outside straight (_7,8,9,10_) where you can complete your straight by getting the card you need on either end. Open end straights appear three times on the chart and in much higher positions than inside straights: #20 (with no high cards), #17 (with one or two high cards) and #15 (with three high cards).

4) Don't hold a kicker. A kicker is an unpaired card held with a pair. For example (8,8,K) or (K,K,9) are examples of hands where an extra card (the kicker) is held. Never hold a kicker because they add no value to your hand!

If you want to make your own video poker strategy charts there are some special video poker programs that can do this for you. For information on buying these programs, go to www.americancasinoguide.com/video-poker-software.html With these specialized video poker software programs you can then print out the strategy charts and bring them with you into the casino.

For your information there are exactly 2,598,960 unique poker hands that can be dealt on a video poker machine (when played without a joker). Depending on the strategy that is used, on a 9/6 Jacks or Better machine a royal flush will occur about once every 40,000 hands; a straight flush about every 9,000 hands; four-of-a-kind about every 425 hands; a full house about every 87 hands; a

Other Video Poker Game Pay Tables

(Per coin with maximum coin played and perfect strategy)

Pick'Em Poker (five coin payout)	
Royal Flush	6,000
Straight Flush	1,199
4-of-a-kind	600
Full House	90
Flush	75
Straight	55
3-of-a-kind	25
Two Pair	15
Pair 9's or Better	10
Payback	**99.95%**

All American Poker	
Royal Flush	800
Straight Flush	200
4-of-a-kind	40
Full House	8
Flush	8
Straight	8
3-of-a-kind	3
Two Pair	1
Pair Jacks or Better	1
Payback	**100.72%**

Double Joker Full-Pay	
Natural Royal Flush	800
Wild Royal Flush	100
5-of-a-kind	50
Straight Flush	25
4-of-a-kind	***9***
Full House	5
Flush	4
Straight	3
3-of-a-kind	2
2 Pair	1
Payback	**99.97%**

Double Joker Short-Pay	
Natural Royal Flush	800
Wild Royal Flush	100
5-of-a-kind	50
Straight Flush	25
4-of-a-kind	***8***
Full House	5
Flush	4
Straight	3
3-of-a-kind	2
2 Pair	1
Payback	**98.10%**

flush about every 91 hands; a straight about every 89 hands; three-of-a-kind about every 14 hands; two pairs about every 8 hands; and a pair of Jacks or better about every 5 hands. The interesting thing to note here is that both a flush and a straight are harder to get than a full house, yet a full house always has a higher payback. The majority of the time, about 55% to be exact, you will wind up with a losing hand on a 9/6 machine.

The next bit of advice concerns how many coins you should bet. You should always bet the maximum amount (on machines returning 100% or more) because it will allow you to earn bonus coins when you hit the royal flush. Example: for a royal flush on a 9/6 machine with one coin played you receive 250 coins; for two coins you get 500; for three coins you get 750; for four coins you get 1,000 and for five (maximum) coins you get 4,000 coins. This translates into a bonus of 2,750 coins! A royal flush can be expected once every 40,400 hands on a 9/6 Jacks or Better machine and once every 40,200 hands on an 8/5 Bonus Poker machine. The odds are high, but the added bonus makes it worthwhile. If you can't afford to play the maximum coins on a positive machine then move down to a lower denomination machine. And, if you absolutely insist on playing less than the maximum, be sure to play only one at a time. It doesn't make any sense to play two, three or four coins, because you still won't be eligible for the bonus.

One important thing to keep in mind when you look at the total payback on these video poker machines is that those numbers always include a royal flush and the royal flush plays a very big factor in the total return. As a matter of fact, the royal flush is such a big factor on video poker machines that you are actually expected to lose until you get that royal flush. Yes, even by restricting your play to video poker machines with a more than 100% payback you are still expected to lose money until you hit a royal flush. Once you hit that royal flush it will bring your cash back up to that 100% level but until it happens you should be fully aware that you are statistically expected to lose money.

According to video poker expert Bob Dancer, "on a 25¢ Jacks or Better 9/6 machine you will lose at a rate of 2.5% while you are waiting for the royal to happen. Another way to look at this is quarter players who play 600 hands per hour can expect to lose about $18.75 per hour, on average, on any hour they do not hit a royal." You really have to keep in mind that there are no guarantees when you play video poker. Yes, you are expected to get a royal flush about once every 40,000 hands but there are no guarantees that it will happen and if you don't get that royal flush it could cost you dearly.

A final tip about playing video poker concerns players clubs. Every major casino has a club and you should make it a point to join the players club before you insert your first coin. It doesn't cost anything to join and as a member you will have the opportunity to earn complimentaries from the casinos in the form of cash, food, shows, drinks, rooms or other "freebies." When you join the club you'll be issued a card (similar to a credit card) that you insert in the machine before you start to play and it will track how much you bet, as well as how long you play. Naturally, the more money you gamble, the more freebies you'll earn. Just make sure you don't get carried away and bet more than you're comfortable with just to earn some extra comps. Ideally, you want to get comps for gambling that you were going to do anyway and not be pressured into betting more than you had planned. Many clubs will also give you cash back for your play and that amount should be added into the payback percentage on the kind of machine you'll be playing. For example, let's say a slot club rebates .25% in cash for your video poker play. By only playing 9/6 Jacks or Better machines with a return of 99.54% you can add the .25% rebate to get an adjusted figure of 99.79%. This means that you are, theoretically, playing an almost even game, plus you're still eligible for other room and food discounts on top of your cash rebate.

"Not So Ugly Deuces" Optimum Strategy

by Steve Bourie

The following strategy chart was created with a software program called Optimum Video Poker by Dan Paymar. The program can be used to practice video poker just like a regular game. However, it can also show you how to use the best strategies, analyze any video poker game, plus it can create customized strategy charts for any video poker game.

To buy this program at a discounted price, or to learn more about it, plus other similar programs, go to: www.americancasinoguide.com/video-poker-software.html

There are numerous pay tables for Deuces Wild games, but keep in mind that this chart only applies to the "NSUD" pay table found in the previous story.

If followed accurately, the expected return (when playing maximum coin) is 99.71%, which is less than 0.012% off of perfect play.

To use the chart, count the number of deuces in the hand that you are originally dealt. Then, hold the first hand-type available in that group.

Four Deuces

1. Just the Deuces

Three Deuces

1. Wild Royal
2. 5 of a Kind
3. Just the Deuces

Two Deuces

1. Wild Royal
2. 5 of a Kind
3. Straight Flush (SF)
4. 4 of a Kind
5. 4 card Royal Flush
6. 4 card SF
7. 4 card Inside SF
8. 4 card SF (2-2-5-6)
9. 4 card SF (2-2-4-5)
10. Just the Deuces

One Deuce

1. Wild Royal
2. 5 of a Kind
3. Straight Flush (SF)
4. 4 of a Kind
5. Full House
6. 4 card Royal Flush
7. Flush
8. 4 card SF
9. 4 card Inside SF
10. Straight
11. 4 card Double-Inside SF
12. 3 of a Kind
13. 4 card SF (Ace low)
14. 3 card Royal Flush
15. 3 card SF
16. 3 card Inside SF
17. Just the Deuce

No Deuces

1. Royal Flush
2. 4 card Royal Flush
3. Straight Flush (SF)
4. 4 of a Kind
5. Full House
6. Flush
7. Straight
8. 4 card SF
9. 3 of a Kind
10. 4 card Inside SF
11. 3 card Royal Flush
12. 3 card Inside SF (Ace low)
13. 4 card Flush
14. 2 Pairs
15. 3 card SF
16. 1 Pair
17. 4 card Straight
18. 3 card Inside SF
19. 3 card Double-Inside SF
20. 2 card Royal Flush (no Ace)
21. 3 card Inside SF (Ace low)
22. 4 card Inside Straight
23. Redraw

Dan Paymar, the creator of Optimum Video Poker, also offers the following advice for using this strategy chart.

Note that any deuces in the dealt hand are included in the hand type description. For example, "4 card Straight Flush" in the "1 Deuce" group could be 2-5♥-6♥-7♥ or 2-9♥-10♥-J♥ (where the non-deuces are all the same suit), but not 2-10♥-J♥-Q♥ since that would be a 4 card Royal Flush which is higher in the chart. A hand such as 2-6♥-8♥-9♥ would not qualify since that would be a 4 card Inside Straight Flush which is lower in the chart.

This strategy is optimized. That is, there are no penalty considerations, and it's simplified in situations that occur infrequently and have very small EV difference. The total net "cost" of this optimization is less than 0.012% off of perfect play and less than 0.005% off of the best published professional strategy for this game. Most players will actually achieve better payback with this strategy than they would with a professional strategy due to many fewer inadvertent deviations from the chart.

Why is this game called "Not So Ugly Deuces"? The original full pay Deuces Wild has the per-coin payoff schedule 1-2-2-3-5-9-15-25-200-800. A game analysis shows that the 5-for-1 payoff for four of a kind contributes over 32% of the game's payback. Many casinos offer this game, but with the quads payoff reduced to 4-for-1. With no strategy change, this reduces the payback by 1/5 of that 32% or more than 6%. This game has the 4-for-1 quads payoff, but increases the payoffs for four other hands. The result, assuming perfect strategy, is 99.726% payback, so many players clubs benefits put it to just about 100%. Multiple points days and/or off-point comps can also make it attractive to advantage players.

Visit our website:
americancasinoguide.com

- Casino News
- Casino Travel Info
- Casino Promotions
- U.S. Casino Directory
- Casino Discussion Forum
- Money-saving Casino Offers
- FREE Educational Gambling Videos

Video Poker: Another Brick in the Wall

by Linda Boyd

Line 1: "We don't need no education,
Line 2: We don't need no thought control,
Line 3: No dark sarcasm in the classroom,
Line 4: Teacher leave them kids alone!
Line 5: Hey! Teacher! Leave them kids alone!
Line 6: All in all it's just another brick in the wall
Line 7: All in all you're just another brick in the wall"

Pink Floyd, Lyrics by bassist Roger Waters

Some still debate the meaning of this iconic song, but it's definitely not an ode to traditional education. Ironically, they did need an education because beyond the grammatical errors (deliberate) is the fact that if you listen carefully you'll notice the chorus, sung by a group of kids, makes mistakes in lines 4, 5, and 6 from the song writer's words. (Chorus deviations, line 4 "those", line 5 "those" line 6 "you're" instead of Waters's written words.) The errors aren't a big deal except to point out that a little education wouldn't have hurt since I saw no recognition of this mistake when checking Roger Water's lyrics against what was sung.

In truth, I'm a Pink Floyd fan and like their brick in the wall analogy; it applies to lots of things in life. However, and contrary to this song, if you're placing bets involving odds you really do need an education. I'm referring to any game with a skill component. I don't think many would argue that a lack of understanding of all the nuances in poker, blackjack and most table games gives the player a big disadvantage against both the house and other players.

This is also true of video poker games. Sure, some people will win with the odds stacked against them, but if you play long enough you won't outrun the numbers. Gamblers don't need more bricks in the wall unless their goal is to construct glitzier pleasure domes for the house.

Bricks in the Wall: If you base your video poker plays on oddball anecdotal stories then you're more likely to go for long shot plays too often. The reason I describe these moves as "too often" is sometimes it is correct to draw for an unlikely result because the stakes are high enough to offset the risks. In other words, if your game is 9/6 Jacks or Better and you're dealt a straight, but four of the five straight cards are to a royal, then your best bet is to hold four to the royal. This, however, is a simple hold and very intuitive. How about correct video poker plays that are closer calls? In other words, should you hold three cards to the royal flush or a paying pair? The answer to that question depends on the game you are playing and the payout for the royal flush. Nowadays many video poker games have progressive royals. In my book, The Video

Poker Edge, I have broken down the correct play to the number of coins paid for the royal flush in a specific game.

The biggest bricks in the wall, however, are to assume all games are played the same or that you can guess the correct hold based on a small sampling of past events or your intuition. Your holds should be based solely on the best long-term results as indicated by tutorial software.

Table 1.1: 9/6 Jacks or Better Pay Table

Hand: 5-Coin Return	9/6 JOB
Royal Flush	4000
Straight Flush	250
4 of a Kind	125
Full House	45
Flush	30
Straight	20
3 of a Kind	15
Two Pair	10
Jacks or Better	5

Table 1.2: 9/6 JOB Hand Frequency (Assuming Correct Play)

Hand	Frequency: 1 in
Royal Flush	40,390.55
Straight Flush	9,148.370
4 of a Kind	423.2722
Full House	86.86431
Flush	90.78932
Straight	89.05221
3 of a Kind	13.43207
2 Pair	7.735214
Jacks or Better (Pair)	4.660157
Nothing	1.833400
Expected Return	**99.5439%**

Note: If you deviate from correct play then the frequency for the listed hands will differ; however, you will never improve your theoretical results from the ER listed in Table 1.1.

Hand Frequency: There are 2,598,960 possible dealt hands; far too many to know the statistically correct holds off the top of your head. Also, keep in mind that every single time changes are made in the pay schedule (found by pushing the "see pays" button on a video poker machine), it can alter the way hands should be played. That's why, for the purpose of having an accurate hand frequency table, I had to select a specific game and assume computer-correct play. If you choose to play 8/5 JOB (Jacks or Better), for example, some of the holds would be slightly different, especially on a progressive game. In this case you would only have a few minor differences so you could use the 9/6 JOB strategy with little change to the ER (expected return) for your chosen game. If, however, you chose an entirely different game, say 9/6 DDB (Double Double Bonus) you would have more strategy deviations. Of course, the frequency of dealt hands remains the same for every poker game using a deck of 52 cards.

Understanding the Data: You may think there is so much data that practicing a game is futile. After all, over two and a half million possibilities on the deal seems staggering at first glance. If you've tried to use video poker strategy masters there will be around 120 lines to check out after each dealt hand. That's why you'll rarely see them used inside a casino. Pros are slowed down too much on a positive game (ER over 100% with correct play) and the average Joe can't use them. Why? There's so much data that small print with many abbreviations and color coding was needed. Using small font and color-coded information inside a noisy poorly lit casino just doesn't work. These are not strategy cards but hand hierarchies. I have actual strategy cards, free in the back of my book, which can easily be used inside a casino.

The most important thing to understand by looking at the data in Table 1.2 is that the odds of achieving a given hand in conjunction with the payout when the hand is achieved are the sole factors in determining the correct holds. There are no psychological factors, like in table poker ("play the players, not the cards") so there is no debating over correct computer-perfect play. In fact, the absolute certainty of the statistically accurate holds in video poker are the main reason that table poker snobs claim it's not as difficult a game. Not at all true, by the way. It's just that the felt game requires a different set of skills then the video poker version.

Downgraded Games: I'm sure you've seen people just plop down at the first open seat at a bank of video poker devices. That's due to a lack of education fostering the belief that the pay schedule doesn't matter. In fact, when I've pointed to a 9/6 JOB game at the same bank as an 8/5 JOB game players have said "it doesn't matter, they're set to pay the same". Completely false information if the device has an RNG (random number generator). All devices in Nevada, Arizona and most other jurisdictions are required by law to have an RNG making the probabilities of being dealt any of the 52 virtual cards equal. With that in mind you have to ask yourself whether you'd rather be paid 45 coins for a 5-coin wager or 40 coins. The odds of achieving the full house are the same whether you're playing 9/6 JOB, 8/5 JOB or any other JOB game. (There are some 7/5 and even 6/5 JOB games out there.)

The fact that so many perpetuate the incorrect information that all machines are "programmed" to pay the same allows casinos to get away with downgrading pay schedules. They figure why offer a better ER if players don't know the difference?

Talking to Wrong People: Many gamblers believe that the best video poker players can be found in Nevada's "locals" casinos and I concur. After all, if nothing else, they know they're going to do better with video poker games that have a higher ER.

Beyond looking for the best pay schedules there are still many misconceptions about the credentials of the chatty stranger beside you knowing the best cards to hold. Often I've heard people say, "that guy is from Nevada, so he knows the right way to play" or claim a mechanic gave them the best game plan. If an individual hasn't practiced on the software or with mathematically correct strategy cards then they will not know the correct holds with any degree of certainty. The bottom line is that it's your money and therefore you should take the time to learn accurate holds for yourself instead of depending on a player seated next to you in your favorite casino.

Gullibility: If a statement sounds like it's off the wall and far-fetched, then it probably is. For example, I've heard people make comments like "I play in this casino all the time and the machine you're on deals lots of sevens". No need to argue, but that sort of comment makes no sense at all if you truly believe there's a RNG inside the device. In fact, if you believe these kinds of statements then you are accusing the casino of having a non-random device, or cheating, and therefore are foolish to be playing there. (There is an exception for states that are in jurisdictions that allow video lottery terminals, VLT's, which may not have RNG's. Be aware that some VLT's have RNG's while others do not, depending on legislative requirements.) Use your common sense to make decisions involving your bankroll and don't rely on quirky statements that fly in the face of logical thinking.

Removing the Bricks: It's good to know that games involving skill give a big advantage to those with the best education on the topic. Now it remains to figure out how to learn the basics for your game of choice. In fact, you're just as well off playing slots if you ignore correct plays and just guess at which cards to hold based on hunches. Nowadays there are plenty of materials out there to teach you the mathematically correct holds and remove the bricks in the wall that prevent you from getting the best odds at video poker.

Books: There are many good books for video poker players. Make sure the book you purchase has a recent publishing date. (My 2006 Edition of The Video Poker Edge sold out so the book you'll get from Amazon or Square One Publishers is the 2010 Second Edition.)

Software: There's a lot to choose from but you should make sure there is a teaching function to the software you use for practice. Often you get fancy graphics, but the software doesn't tell you the correct holds when you make a mistake. What good is practice if you to repeat the same errors over and over again? Also, make sure you have downloaded the free American Casino Guide

App, for both Apple and Android users. I consider the best video poker tutorial software on the market by far to be Dean Zamzow's WinPoker. The graphics mirror those you'll find in the casino, he uses 100% computer-perfect play and there are several different learning modes. You can adjust the pay schedules for your favorite game, say Jacks or Better, to exactly match the ones on the games you play in your favorite casino. Zamzow's software is easy to use and it's also lots of fun due to all the whistles and bells. It can be ordered at a discount price at www.americancasinoguide.com/video-poker-software.html

Checking Pay Tables: If you only play a few times per year and just don't want to spend much time practicing you can simply check the pay schedules for each version of your game and choose the one with the biggest payouts for the same hand. This is very easy to do. For example, if you're playing DDB (Double Double Bonus Poker) you may find a 10/7, 10/6, 9/6 DDB and an 8/5 DDB in the same casino. The numbers refer to the per coin payout for the full-house and flush respectively; the rest of the pay schedule will be the same. Of course, choose the 10/7 version (You can still find a few of these at locals casino in Las Vegas). If people shun the games with really poor pay schedules, then management will eventually remove the device or upgrade the pay table.

Communicating with Management: Most management teams want to keep their player base happy. If you find a bank of 8/5 JOB machines the ER is a paltry 97.2984% with perfect play. Most people make mistakes so the actual ER is several percentage points less than the theoretical return. In the case of 8/5 JOB that would be around 95% or less. The casino knows the exact ER for each device since the results are regularly checked. This translates to wiggle room for the casino to keep their frequent players from going elsewhere and still make a big profit. You may, therefore, suggest having a progressive bank of 8/5 JOBs and have a chance of getting a bank of them.

Correct Information: Regardless of whether you're relying on word-of-mouth tips, facts from a book, or tutorial software you're better off with no information than incorrect statements. There are several ways you can make sure you have reliable data.

Locals: Mostly the skinny from locals on current promotions, location of good video poker progressives (paying the same for all winning hands but a bonus for the royal and sometimes four of a kind outcomes), and best food deals is absolutely accurate. If you're traveling through the Midwest it's always a good idea to ask questions of local players. Otherwise go to the slot club counter get a free player's card and pick up flyers on the desk. Once you have a card make sure you slide it through a kiosk located on the casino floor.

Strategy Cards: Be aware that there is a huge difference between hierarchy charts and strategy cards. For all the reasons discussed earlier in this article you'll find hierarchy charts useless in a casino setting. That's why casinos "generously" allow you to bring them with you. In fact, I've watched many people trying to use them and invariably, after much study, they choose incorrect holds. On the other hand, good video poker strategy cards have a short list of possible dealt hands, say 12 to 14 vertical lines, and are extremely easy to use as well as accurate. Good ones take many years to write and test several prototypes before selecting the best format for players. You will know whether they work for you by practicing with them on tutorial software before heading for a casino. If you can't use them during practice they won't do you any good during casino play either.

Final Thoughts: Pink Floyd's classic rock song, "Another Brick in the Wall" has lyrics that are meaningful for both poker and video poker players, especially the first two lines.

"We don't need no education, We don't need no thought control" is the antithesis of what you actually do need if you're playing table poker or any felt game with a skill component.

Just check Amazon.com under poker books and you'll find hundreds of brilliant works worth their weight in gold if you're an online or casino player. Those who want to be long term winners absolutely need an education. How about "thought control"? The world's top and most successful competitors know that "thought control" or at least "thought reading" is an attribute for them. Just watch a genius like Phil Ivey stare down others during play as he seems to be reading their mind while they unconsciously reveal their hidden cards. Phil Hellmuth, Daniel Negreanu, Daniel Coleman, Eric Seidel, Antonio Esfandiari, Jamie Gold and many others are no slouches at this either. Why do you think Phil Laak, poker player and commentator (aka "the Unabomber"), wears a hood during play?

How about video poker? It's very different from table poker. For one thing "tells" (mannerisms that give away your hand) are worthless. The cards speak for themselves so you can blabber away during play with immunity from paying an outcome price. Thought control isn't even a factor and would be totally worthless to a player. However, you do in fact need an education so you can learn the computer perfect holds for any dealt hand. Pink Floyd should absolutely salute this honest form of poker giving the best odds to the best educated players with incontrovertible rights and wrongs; purely objective all the way.

Video poker players will want to tear down all the bricks in the wall that block them from using the most statistically accurate and objective strategy for a maximum theoretical return. If players fail to make use of all the educational resources designed to help them then they are simply giving the casino a bigger edge. I can't imagine any player wanting the house to have more bricks in their walls due to their own lack of a basic education.

Linda Boyd, a long-time table game player before turning to video poker, writes for numerous gaming magazines. Her book, "The Video Poker Edge," includes free removable pay schedules and her free strategy cards for the eight most popular games. The second edition is available at amazon.com, Square One Publishers and major bookstores. www.squareonepublishers.com, or see page 60 in this book.

Blackjack

by Steve Bourie

Blackjack is the most popular casino game in America and one of the biggest reasons for that is its relatively simple rules that are familiar to most casino visitors. Blackjack also has a reputation as being "beatable" and although that is true in some cases, the vast majority of players will always be playing the game with the house having a slight edge over them.

At most blackjack tables there are seven boxes, or betting areas, on the table. This means that up to seven people can play at that table and each player has their own box in front of them in which they'll place their bet. Now, before you take a seat at any blackjack table the first thing you should do is to take a look at the sign that's sitting on each table because it will tell you the minimum amount that you must bet on each hand. If you're a $5 player you certainly wouldn't want to sit at a table that has a $25 minimum so, once again, be sure to look before you sit down.

Once you're at the table you'll need chips to play with and you get them by giving your cash to the dealer who will exchange it for an equal amount of chips. Be careful, however, that you don't put your cash down into one of the betting boxes because the dealer might think you're playing it all on the next hand!

After everyone has placed their bets in their respective boxes the dealer will deal out two cards to each player. He will also deal two cards to himself; one of those cards will be face up and the other face down. Now, if you've ever read any brochures in a casino they'll tell you that the object of the game of blackjack is to get a total of cards as close to 21 as possible, without going over 21. However, that really isn't the object of the game. The true object is to beat the dealer and you do that by getting a total closer to 21 than the dealer, or by having the dealer bust by drawing cards that total more than 21.

The one thing that's strange about blackjack is that the rules can be slightly different at each casino and this is the only game where this happens. If you play baccarat, roulette or craps you'll find that the rules are virtually the same at every casino in the U.S. but that isn't the case with blackjack. For example, in most jurisdictions all of the casinos use six or eight decks that are always dealt from a rectangular box called a *shoe* and the cards are always dealt face up. In Las Vegas, some casinos will offer that same kind of game while others will offer games that use only one or two decks that are dealt directly from the dealer's hand and all of the cards will be dealt face down. To make it even stranger, some casinos in Las Vegas will offer both kinds of games in their casinos and the rules will probably change when you move from one table to

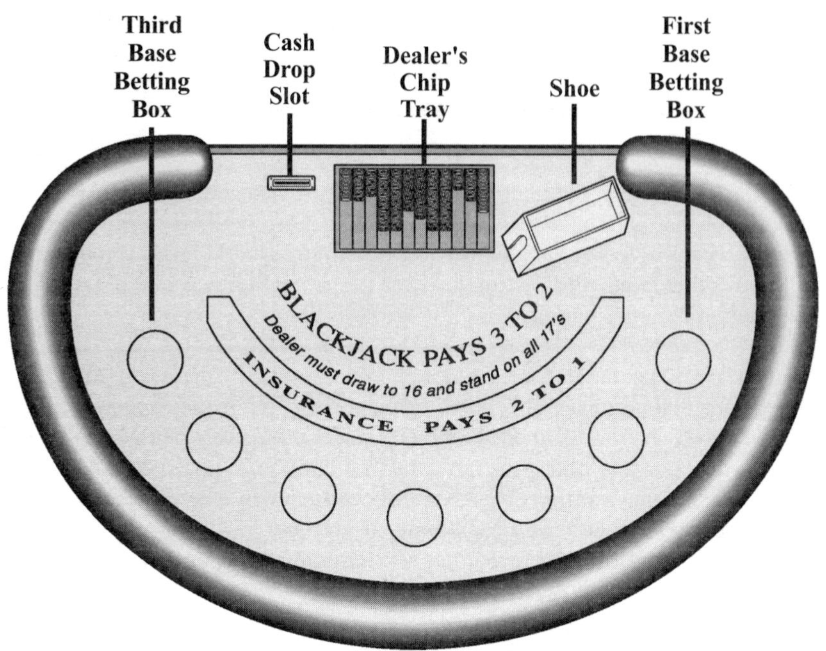

Typical Blackjack Table Layout

another. There can also be other rule variations concerning doubling down and splitting of pairs but we'll talk about those later. For now, just be aware that different casinos can have different blackjack rules and some of those rules will be good for you while others will be bad for you. Hopefully, after reading this story you'll know the good rules from the bad ones and which tables are the best ones to play at.

For our purposes, we'll assume we're playing in a casino that uses six decks of cards that are dealt out of a shoe and all of the player's cards are dealt face up. By the way, whenever you play blackjack in a casino where the cards are dealt face up don't touch the cards. In that kind of game the dealer is the only who is allowed to touch the cards and if you do happen to touch them they'll give you a warning not to do it again - so, don't touch the cards!

After the cards are dealt the players must determine the total of their hand by adding the value of their two cards together. All of the cards are counted at their face value except for the picture cards - jack, queen and king which all have a value of 10 - and the aces which can be counted as either 1 or 11. If you have an ace and any 10-value card you have a blackjack which is also called a natural and your hand is an automatic winner, unless the dealer also has a blackjack in which case the hands are tied. A tie is also called a ***push*** and when that happens it's a standoff and you neither win nor lose. All winning blackjacks should be paid at 3-to-2, so if you bet $5, you would be paid $7.50. You should avoid playing at any game that pays 6-to-5 (or even money) for blackjacks.

If the dealer has an ace as his up card the first thing he'll do is ask if anyone wants to buy ***insurance***. When you buy insurance you're betting that the dealer has a blackjack by having a 10 as his face down card. To make an insurance bet you would place your bet in the area just above your betting box that says "insurance pays 2-to-1" and you're only allowed to make an insurance bet of up to one-half the amount of your original bet. So, if you originally bet $10 you could only bet a maximum of $5 as your insurance bet. After all the insurance bets are made the dealer will check his face down card and if it's a 10 he'll turn it over and all of the insurance bets will be paid off at 2-to-1. If he doesn't have a 10 underneath, the dealer will then take away all of the losing insurance bets and the game will continue. By the way, according to basic strategy, insurance is a bad bet and you should never make an insurance bet.

If the dealer has a 10 as his up card the first thing he'll do is check to see if he has an ace underneath which would give him a blackjack. If he does have an ace he'll turn it face up and start collecting the losing bets that are out on the table. If he doesn't have an ace underneath the game will continue. In some casinos, however, the dealer won't check his hole card until after all of the hands are played out.

If the dealer doesn't have an ace or a 10 as his up card the game continues and the dealer will start with the player to his immediate left to see if they want another card. If a player wants another card they indicate that with a hand signal by tapping or scratching the table with their finger to show they want another card. Taking a card is also known as ***hitting*** or taking a hit. If a player doesn't want another card they would just wave their hand palm down over their cards. Not taking another card is known as ***standing***. The reason hand signals are used is because it eliminates any confusion on the part of the dealer as to exactly what the player wants and it also allows the security people to follow the game on the closed-circuit cameras that are hung from the ceiling throughout the casino.

Keep in mind that the hand signals will be slightly different if you're playing in a casino where the cards are dealt face down and you're allowed to pick them up. In that situation a player would signal that they wanted another card by scratching the table with the edges of the two cards they're holding. If they didn't want another card, they would simply place their two cards under the bet in their box.

In either case, if a player draws another card the value of that card is added to the total of the other cards and the player can continue to draw cards unless he gets a total of more than 21 in which case he busts and loses his bet.

When a player doesn't want any more cards, or stands, the dealer then moves on to the next player and after all of the players are finished then it's the dealer's turn to play. While each player can decide whether or not they want another card the dealer doesn't have that option and he must play by a fixed set of rules that require him to draw a card whenever his total is 16 or less and to stop when his total is 17 or more. If the dealer goes over 21 then he has busted and all of the players remaining in the game will be paid 1-to-1, or even money, on their bet.

If the dealer doesn't bust then each player's hand is compared to the dealer's. If the player's total is higher than the dealer's then they win and are paid even money. If the player's hand has a total that is lower than the dealer's hand then the player loses his bet. If the player and the dealer have the same total then it's a tie, or a push and neither hand wins. After all of the bets have been paid off, or taken by the dealer, a new round begins and new hands are dealt to all of the players.

When deciding how to play your hand there are also three other options available to you besides standing or hitting. The first is called ***doubling down*** and most casinos will allow a player to double their bet on their first two cards and draw only one more card. To do this you would place an amount equal to your original bet right next to it and then the dealer would give you one more card, sideways, to indicate that your bet was a double down. To double down in a game where the cards are dealt face down you would turn up your original two cards and tell the dealer you wanted to double down. Then, after you double your bet, the dealer would give you one more card face down. Some casinos may have restrictions on this bet and may only allow you to double down if the total of your two cards is 10 or 11, but it's always to your advantage if they allow you to double down on any two cards.

Another thing you can do is ***split*** your cards if you have a pair and then play each card as a separate hand. For example, if you had a pair of 8's you would place a bet equal to your original bet right next to it and tell the dealer you wanted to split your pair. The dealer would then separate your two 8's and give you one card on your first 8. Unlike doubling down, however, you are not limited to only getting one card and you can play your hand out normally. When you were finished with your first hand the dealer would then give you a card on your other 8 and you would play that hand out. Although you aren't usually limited to just one card on your splits, there is one instance where that will happen and that happens when you split aces. Almost all casinos will give you just one card on each ace when you split them. Also, if you get a 10-value card with your ace it will only count as 21 and not as a blackjack so you'll only get even money on that bet if you win. Besides splitting pairs you can also split all 10-value cards such as jack-king or 10-queen but it would be a very bad idea to do that because you would be breaking up a 20 which is a very strong hand and you should never split 10's. By the way, if you wanted to split a pair in a casino where the cards are dealt face down you would simply turn your original two cards face-up and tell the dealer that you wanted to split them.

The last option you have is not available in most casinos but you may come across it in some casinos and it's called ***surrender***. With the surrender option you're allowed to lose half of your bet if you decide you don't want to play out your hand after looking at your first two cards. Let's say you're dealt a 10-6 for a total of 16 and the dealer has a 10 as his face-up card. A 16 is not a very strong hand, especially against a dealer's 10, so in this case it would be a good idea to surrender your hand and when the dealer came to your cards you would say "surrender." The dealer would then take half of your bet and remove your cards. Surrender is good for the player because in the long run you will lose less on the bad hands you're dealt and you should always try to play in a casino that offers the surrender option.

All right, we've covered the basics of how to play the game of blackjack and all of the possible options a player has, so the next question is how do you win? Well, the best way to win is to become a card counter, but for the average person that isn't always possible so let's start off by taking a look at basic blackjack strategy.

Computer studies have been done on the game of blackjack and millions of hands have been analyzed to come up with a basic formula for how to play your hand in any given situation. The main principle that these decisions are based on is the dealer's up card because, remember that the dealer has no say in whether or not he takes a card - he must play by the rules that require him to draw a card until he has a total of 17 or more. Now, according to these computer calculations the dealer will bust more often when his up card is a 2,3,4,5 or 6 and he will complete more hands when his up card is a 7,8,9,10-value card or an ace. Take a look at the following chart that shows how each up-card affects the dealer's chance of busting:

Chance The Dealer's Up Card Will Bust

2	35%
3	38%
4	40%
5	43%
6	42%
7	26%
8	24%
9	23%
10	21%
Ace	11%

As you can see, the dealer will bust most often when he has a 5 or 6 as his upcard and he will bust the least amount, approximately 11% of the time, when his upcard is an ace. This means it's to your advantage to stand more often when the dealer's upcard is a 2 through 6 and hope that the dealer will draw cards that make him bust. It also means that when the dealer's upcard is a 7 through ace he will complete more of his hands and in that situation you should draw cards until you have a total of 17 or more.

Now let's show you how to play your hands by using the basic strategy and we'll start off with the ***hard hand*** strategy and hard hand means a two-card total without an ace. A hand with an ace is known as a **soft hand** because the ace can be counted as either a 1 or an 11. So, if you had an ace-6 you would have a soft 17 hand and if you had a 10-6 you would have a hard 16 hand. Later on we'll take a look at how to play soft hands, but for now we'll concentrate on the hard hand totals. Oh yes, one more thing, the following basic strategy applies to casinos where they deal more than one deck at a time and the dealer stands on soft 17, which is the situation you'll find in the majority of casinos today. So, keep in mind that the strategy would be slightly different if you were playing against a single deck and it would also be slightly different if the dealer hit a soft 17.

Whenever your first two cards total 17 through 21, you should stand, no matter what the dealer's up card is.

If your cards total 16, you should stand if the dealer has a 2 through 6 as his upcard otherwise, draw a card. By the way, 16 is the worst hand you can have because you will bust more often with 16 than with any other hand. So, if that's the case then why would you want to ever hit a 16? Well, once again, those computer studies have shown that you should hit a 16 when the dealer has 7 through ace as his upcard because in the long run you will lose less often. This means that yes, 16 is a terrible hand, but you should hit it because if you don't you will lose even more often than when you do take a card.

If your cards total 15, you should also stand if the dealer has a 2 through 6 as his upcard otherwise, draw cards until your total is 17 or more.

The same rules from 15 and 16 also apply if your cards total 14. Stand if the dealer has a 2 through 6, otherwise draw cards until your total is 17 or more. The same rules also apply if your cards total 13. Stand if the dealer has a 2 through 6, otherwise draw cards until your total is 17 or more.

When your cards total 12 you should only stand when the dealer has a 4,5 or 6 as his upcard, remember - those are his three weakest cards and he will bust more often with those cards, so you don't want to take a chance on busting yourself. If the dealer's upcard is a 2 or a 3, then you should take just one card and stop on your total of 13 or more. Finally, if the dealer has a 7 through ace as his upcard then you should draw cards until your total is 17 or more.

Basic Strategy - Single Deck

Dealer stands on soft 17 · Double on any 2 cards · Double allowed after split

Your Hand	Dealer's Upcard									
	2	**3**	**4**	**5**	**6**	**7**	**8**	**9**	**10**	**A**
17	ALWAYS STAND ON HARD 17 (OR MORE)									
16	-	-	-	-	-	H	H	H	H*	H
15	-	-	-	-	-	H	H	H	H*	H
14	-	-	-	-	-	H	H	H	H	H
13	-	-	-	-	-	H	H	H	H	H
12	H	H	-	-	-	H	H	H	H	H
11	ALWAYS DOUBLE									
10	D	D	D	D	D	D	D	D	H	H
9	D	D	D	D	D	H	H	H	H	H
8	H	H	H	D	D	H	H	H	H	H
A,8	-	-	-	-	D	-	-	-	-	-
A,7	-	D	D	D	D	-	-	H	H	-
A,6	D	D	D	D	D	H	H	H	H	H
A,5	H	H	D	D	D	H	H	H	H	H
A,4	H	H	D	D	D	H	H	H	H	H
A,3	H	H	D	D	D	H	H	H	H	H
A,2	H	H	D	D	D	H	H	H	H	H
A,A	ALWAYS SPLIT									
10,10	ALWAYS STAND (NEVER SPLIT)									
9,9	Sp	Sp	Sp	Sp	Sp	-	Sp	Sp	-	-
8,8	ALWAYS SPLIT									
7,7	Sp	Sp	Sp	Sp	Sp	Sp	**Sp**	H	-*	H
6,6	Sp	Sp	Sp	Sp	Sp	**Sp**	H	H	H	H
5,5	NEVER SPLIT (PLAY AS 10 HAND)									
4,4	H	H	**Sp**	**Sp**	**Sp**	H	H	H	H	H
3,3	**Sp**	**Sp**	Sp	Sp	Sp	Sp	Sp	H	H	H
2,2	**Sp**	H	Sp	Sp	Sp	Sp	H	H	H	H

- =Stand H=Hit D=Double Sp=Split *= Surrender if allowed

shaded boxes show strategy changes from chart on next page

Basic Strategy - Single Deck

Dealer stands on soft 17 · Double on any 2 cards · Double NOT allowed after split

Your Hand	Dealer's Upcard									
	2	3	4	5	6	7	8	9	10	A
17	ALWAYS STAND ON HARD 17 (OR MORE)									
16	-	-	-	-	-	H	H	H	H*	H*
15	-	-	-	-	-	H	H	H	H*	H
14	-	-	-	-	-	H	H	H	H	H
13	-	-	-	-	-	H	H	H	H	H
12	H	H	-	-	-	H	H	H	H	H
11	ALWAYS DOUBLE									
10	D	D	D	D	D	D	D	D	H	H
9	D	D	D	D	D	H	H	H	H	H
8	H	H	H	D	D	H	H	H	H	H
A,8	-	-	-	-	D	-	-	-	-	-
A,7	-	D	D	D	D	-	-	H	H	-
A,6	D	D	D	D	D	H	H	H	H	H
A,5	H	H	D	D	D	H	H	H	H	H
A,4	H	H	D	D	D	H	H	H	H	H
A,3	H	H	D	D	D	H	H	H	H	H
A,2	H	H	D	D	D	H	H	H	H	H
A,A	ALWAYS SPLIT									
10,10	NEVER SPLIT (ALWAYS STAND)									
9,9	Sp	Sp	Sp	Sp	Sp	-	Sp	Sp	-	-
8,8	ALWAYS SPLIT									
7,7	Sp	Sp	Sp	Sp	Sp	Sp	H	H	-*	H
6,6	Sp	Sp	Sp	Sp	Sp	H	H	H	H	H
5,5	NEVER SPLIT (PLAY AS 10 HAND)									
4,4	NEVER SPLIT (PLAY AS 8 HAND)									
3,3	H	H	Sp	Sp	Sp	Sp	H	H	H	H
2,2	H	Sp	Sp	Sp	Sp	Sp	H	H	H	H

- =Stand H=Hit D=Double Sp=Split *= Surrender if allowed

Basic Strategy - Multiple Decks

Dealer stands on soft 17 • Double on any 2 cards • Double allowed after split

Your Hand	Dealer's Upcard									
	2	**3**	**4**	**5**	**6**	**7**	**8**	**9**	**10**	**A**
17	ALWAYS STAND ON 17 (OR MORE)									
16	-	-	-	-	-	H	H	H*	H*	H*
15	-	-	-	-	-	H	H	H	H*	H
14	-	-	-	-	-	H	H	H	H	H
13	-	-	-	-	-	H	H	H	H	H
12	H	H	-	-	-	H	H	H	H	H
11	D	D	D	D	D	D	D	D	D	H
10	D	D	D	D	D	D	D	D	H	H
9	H	D	D	D	D	H	H	H	H	H
8	ALWAYS HIT 8 (OR LESS)									
A,8	ALWAYS STAND ON SOFT 19 (OR MORE)									
A,7	-	D	D	D	D	-	-	H	H	H
A,6	H	D	D	D	D	H	H	H	H	H
A,5	H	H	D	D	D	H	H	H	H	H
A,4	H	H	D	D	D	H	H	H	H	H
A,3	H	H	H	D	D	H	H	H	H	H
A,2	H	H	H	D	D	H	H	H	H	H
A,A	ALWAYS SPLIT									
10,10	ALWAYS STAND (NEVER SPLIT)									
9,9	Sp	Sp	Sp	Sp	Sp	-	Sp	Sp	-	-
8,8	ALWAYS SPLIT									
7,7	Sp	Sp	Sp	Sp	Sp	Sp	H	H	H	H
6,6	Sp	Sp	Sp	Sp	Sp	H	H	H	H	H
5,5	D	D	D	D	D	D	D	D	H	H
4,4	H	H	H	Sp	Sp	H	H	H	H	H
3,3	Sp	Sp	Sp	Sp	Sp	Sp	H	H	H	H
2,2	Sp	Sp	Sp	Sp	Sp	Sp	H	H	H	H

- =Stand **H=Hit** **D=Double** **Sp=Split** ***= Surrender if allowed**

Basic Strategy - Multiple Decks

Dealer stands on soft 17 • Double on any 2 cards • Double NOT allowed after split

Your Hand	Dealer's Upcard									
	2	**3**	**4**	**5**	**6**	**7**	**8**	**9**	**10**	**A**
17	ALWAYS STAND ON HARD 17 (OR MORE)									
16	-	-	-	-	-	H	H	H*	H*	H*
15	-	-	-	-	-	H	H	H	H*	H
14	-	-	-	-	-	H	H	H	H	H
13	-	-	-	-	-	H	H	H	H	H
12	H	H	-	-	-	H	H	H	H	H
11	D	D	D	D	D	D	D	D	D	H
10	D	D	D	D	D	D	D	D	H	H
9	H	D	D	D	D	H	H	H	H	H
8	ALWAYS HIT 8 (OR LESS)									
A,8	ALWAYS STAND ON SOFT 19 (OR MORE)									
A,7	-	D	D	D	D	-	-	H	H	H
A,6	H	D	D	D	D	H	H	H	H	H
A,5	H	H	D	D	D	H	H	H	H	H
A,4	H	H	D	D	D	H	H	H	H	H
A,3	H	H	H	D	D	H	H	H	H	H
A,2	H	H	H	D	D	H	H	H	H	H
A,A	ALWAYS SPLIT									
10,10	ALWAYS STAND (NEVER SPLIT)									
9,9	Sp	Sp	Sp	Sp	Sp	-	Sp	Sp	-	-
8,8	ALWAYS SPLIT									
7,7	Sp	Sp	Sp	Sp	Sp	Sp	H	H	H	H
6,6	**H**	Sp	Sp	Sp	Sp	H	H	H	H	H
5,5	NEVER SPLIT (PLAY AS 10 HAND)									
4,4	H	H	H	**H**	**H**	H	H	H	H	H
3,3	**H**	**H**	Sp	Sp	Sp	Sp	H	H	H	H
2,2	**H**	**H**	Sp	Sp	Sp	Sp	H	H	H	H

- =Stand H=Hit D=Double Sp=Split *= Surrender if allowed

shaded boxes show strategy changes from chart on previous page

Basic Strategy - Multiple Decks

Dealer hits soft 17 • Double on any 2 cards • Double allowed after split

Your Hand	Dealer's Upcard									
	2	**3**	**4**	**5**	**6**	**7**	**8**	**9**	**10**	**A**
17	STAND ON ALL - EXCEPT SURRENDER* AGAINST DEALER'S ACE									
16	-	-	-	-	-	H	H	H*	H*	H*
15	-	-	-	-	-	H	H	H	H*	H*
14	-	-	-	-	-	H	H	H	H	H
13	-	-	-	-	-	H	H	H	H	H
12	H	H	-	-	-	H	H	H	H	H
11	D	D	D	D	D	D	D	D	D	D
10	D	D	D	D	D	D	D	D	H	H
9	H	D	D	D	D	H	H	H	H	H
8	ALWAYS HIT 8 (OR LESS)									
A,8	STAND ON ALL - EXCEPT DOUBLE AGAINST DEALER'S 6									
A,7	D	D	D	D	D	-	-	H	H	H
A,6	H	D	D	D	D	H	H	H	H	H
A,5	H	H	D	D	D	H	H	H	H	H
A,4	H	H	D	D	D	H	H	H	H	H
A,3	H	H	H	D	D	H	H	H	H	H
A,2	H	H	H	D	D	H	H	H	H	H
A,A	ALWAYS SPLIT									
10,10	ALWAYS STAND (NEVER SPLIT)									
9,9	Sp	Sp	Sp	Sp	Sp	-	Sp	Sp	-	-
8,8	ALWAYS SPLIT - EXCEPT SURRENDER* AGAINST ACE IF ALLOWED									
7,7	Sp	Sp	Sp	Sp	Sp	Sp	H	H	H	H
6,6	Sp	Sp	Sp	Sp	Sp	H	H	H	H	H
5,5	D	D	D	D	D	D	D	D	H	H
4,4	H	H	H	Sp	Sp	H	H	H	H	H
3,3	Sp	Sp	Sp	Sp	Sp	Sp	H	H	H	H
2,2	Sp	Sp	Sp	Sp	Sp	Sp	H	H	H	H

- =Stand **H=Hit** **D=Double** **Sp=Split** ***= Surrender if allowed**

Basic Strategy - Multiple Decks

Dealer hits soft 17 • Double on any 2 cards • Double NOT allowed after split

Your Hand	Dealer's Upcard									
	2	3	4	5	6	7	8	9	10	A
17	STAND ON ALL - EXCEPT SURRENDER* AGAINST DEALER'S ACE									
16	-	-	-	-	-	H	H	H*	H*	H*
15	-	-	-	-	-	H	H	H	H*	H*
14	-	-	-	-	-	H	H	H	H	H
13	-	-	-	-	-	H	H	H	H	H
12	H	H	-	-	-	H	H	H	H	H
11	D/H	D/H	D/H	D/H	D/H	D/H	D/H	D/H	D/H	D/H
10	D/H	D/H	D/H	D/H	D/H	D/H	D/H	D/H	H	H
9	H	D/H	D/H	D/H	D/H	H	H	H	H	H
8	ALWAYS HIT 8 (OR LESS)									
A,8	ALWAYS STAND - EXCEPT D/S AGAINST A DEALER 6									
A,7	D/S	D/S	D/S	D/S	D/S	-	-	H	H	H
A,6	H	D/H	D/H	D/H	D/H	H	H	H	H	H
A,5	H	H	D/H	D/H	D/H	H	H	H	H	H
A,4	H	H	D/H	D/H	D/H	H	H	H	H	H
A,3	H	H	H	D/H	D/H	H	H	H	H	H
A,2	H	H	H	D/H	D/H	H	H	H	H	H
A,A	ALWAYS SPLIT									
10,10	ALWAYS STAND (NEVER SPLIT)									
9,9	Sp	Sp	Sp	Sp	Sp	-	Sp	Sp	-	-
8,8	ALWAYS SPLIT - EXCEPT SURRENDER* AGAINST ACE IF ALLOWED									
7,7	Sp	Sp	Sp	Sp	Sp	Sp	H	H	H	H
6,6	H	Sp	Sp	Sp	Sp	H	H	H	H	H
5,5	D/H	D/H	D/H	D/H	D/H	D/H	D/H	D/H	H	H
4,4	H	H	H	H	H	H	H	H	H	H
3,3	H	H	Sp	Sp	Sp	Sp	H	H	H	H
2,2	H	H	Sp	Sp	Sp	Sp	H	H	H	H

- =Stand H=Hit D=Double Sp=Split *= Surrender if allowed

D/H=Double if allowed, otherwise hit D/S=Double if allowed, otherwise stand

When your cards total 11 you would always want to hit it because you can't bust, but before you ask for a card you should consider making a double down bet. If the casino allows you to double down then you should do that if the dealer has anything but an ace as his upcard. After you double down the dealer would give you just one additional card on that hand. If the dealer's upcard is an ace then you shouldn't double down. Instead, you should hit the hand and continue to draw until your total is 17 or more. If the casino doesn't allow you to double down then you should just hit your hand and then, depending on your total, play it by the rules you were given for the hands that totaled 12 through 21. Meaning, if you had an 11 and the dealer had a 5 as his upcard, you should take a card. Then let's say you draw an ace which gives you a total of 12. Well, as noted before, if you have a 12 against a dealer's 5 you should stand and that's how you should play that hand.

If your total is 10 you would, once again, want to double down unless the dealer showed an ace or a 10. If the dealer had an ace or a 10 as his upcard you should hit your hand and then use the standard rules for a hand valued at 12 through 21. Therefore, if you had a 10 and the dealer had an 8 as his up card you would want to double down and take one more card. If you weren't allowed to double, then you would take a hit and let's say you got a 4 for a total of 14. You should then continue to hit your hand until your total is 17 or more.

If your total is 9 you would want to double down whenever the dealer was showing a 3,4,5 or 6 as his upcard. If the dealer had a 2 as his upcard, or if he had a 7 through ace as his upcard, you should hit your hand and then use the standard playing rules as discussed before. So, let's say you had a 9 and the dealer had a 4 as his upcard you would want to double down and take one more card. If you weren't allowed to double then you should take a hit and let's say you got a 2 for a total of 11, you would then take another hit and let's say you got an ace. That would give you a total of 12 and, as mentioned previously, you should stand on 12 against a dealer's 4.

Finally, if your total is 8 or less you should always take a card and then use the standard playing rules that were already discussed.

Now, let's take a look at splitting pairs, but keep in mind that the rules for splitting will change slightly depending on whether or not the casino will allow you to double down after you split your cards. Most multiple-deck games allow you to double down after splitting so that's the situation we'll cover first and then we'll talk about the changes you need to make if you're not allowed to double down after splitting.

As noted earlier, when your first two cards are the same most casinos will allow you to split them and play them as two separate hands so let's go over the basic strategy rules on when you should do this.

The first thing you should remember is that you always split aces and 8's. The reason you split aces is obvious because if you get a 10 on either hand you'll have a perfect 21, but remember that you won't get paid for a blackjack at 3-to-2, instead it'll be counted as a regular 21 and you'll be paid at even money. If you have a pair of 8's you have 16 which is a terrible hand and you can always improve it by splitting your 8's and playing them as separate hands.

The next thing to remember about splitting pairs is that you never split 5's or 10's. Once again, the reasons should be rather obvious, you don't want to split 10's because 20 is a great hand and you don't want to split 5's because 10 is a great hand to draw to. Instead, you would want to double down on that 10, unless the dealer was showing a 10 or an ace as his upcard.

2's, 3's and 7's should only be split when the dealer is showing a 2 through 7 as his upcard. Split 4's only when the dealer has a 5 or 6 as his upcard (remember 5 and 6 are his weakest cards!), 6's should be split whenever the dealer is showing a 2 through 6 and finally, you should always split 9's unless the dealer is showing a 7, 10 or ace. The reason you don't want to split 9's against a 10 or an ace should be rather obvious, but the reason you don't want to split them against a 7 is in case the dealer has a 10 as his hole card because in that case your 18 would beat out his 17.

If the casino will not allow you to double down after splitting then you should make the following three changes: For 2's and 3's only split them against a 4,5,6 or 7; never split 4's; and for a pair of 6's only split them against a 3,4,5 or 6. Everything else should be played the same.

Now, let's take a look at how to play ***soft hands*** and, remember, a soft hand is any hand that contains an ace that can be counted as 1 or 11. For a soft hand of 19 or more you should always stand.

For soft 18 against a 2,7 or 8 you should always stand. If the dealer shows a 9, 10 or an ace you should always take a hit and for a soft 18 against a 3,4,5 or 6 you should double down, but if the casino won't allow you to double then you should just hit.

For soft 17 you should always take a hit, but if the casino allows you to double down, then you should double against a dealer's 3,4,5 or 6.

For soft 16 or a soft 15 you should always take a hit, but if the casino allows you to double down then you should double against a dealer's 4, 5 or 6.

For soft 14 you should always take a hit, but if the casino allows you to double down then you should double against a dealer's 5 or 6.

Finally, for a soft 13 you should always take a hit, but if the casino allows you to double down then you should double against a dealer's 5 or 6.

The last thing we need to cover is surrender which, as noted before, isn't offered in many casinos but it is an option that does work in your favor and if available, you should play in a casino that offers it. The surrender rules are very simple to remember and only apply to hard totals of 15 or 16. If you have a hard 16 you should surrender it whenever the dealer has a 9, 10 or ace as his upcard and if you have a hard 15 you should surrender it whenever the dealer has a 10 as his upcard. That's all there is to surrender.

Now that you know how to play the game and you have an understanding of the basic strategy let's take a quick look at how the rule variations can affect the game of blackjack. As noted before, various computer studies have been made on blackjack and these studies have shown that each rule change can either hurt or help the player by a certain amount. For example, a single-deck game where you can double on any first 2 cards (but not after splitting pairs), the dealer stands on soft 17 and no surrender is allowed has no advantage for the casino when using the basic strategy. That's right, in a game with those rules in effect the game is dead even and neither the casino nor the player has an edge!

Take a look at the following chart and you'll see how some rules changes can hurt you or help you as a player. Minus signs in front mean that the casino gains the edge by that particular amount while plus signs mean that you gain the edge by that amount.

RULES THAT HURT YOU	
Two decks	-0.32%
Four decks	-0.49%
Six decks	-0.54%
Eight decks	-0.57%
Dealer hits soft 17	-0.20%
No soft doubling	-0.14%
BJ pays 6-to-5	-1.40%
BJ pays 1-to-1	-2.30%

RULES THAT HELP YOU	
Double after split	+0.13%
Late surrender	+0.06%
Resplit Aces	+0.14%
Double anytime	+0.20%

As you can see, it's always to your advantage to play against as few decks as possible. The house edge goes up substantially as you go from 1 deck to 2, but the change is less dramatic when you go from 2 to 4, or from 4 to 6, and it's barely noticeable when you go from 6 to 8. You can also see that you would prefer not to play in a casino where the dealer hits a soft 17 because that gives the dealer a slight edge. You would also want to play in a casino where you're allowed to double down on your soft hands or else you would be giving another added edge to the casino.

You can also see from these charts that you would want to play in a casino where you were allowed to double down after splitting cards and you would also want to play in a casino that offered surrender. The other two rule variations that help the player are somewhat rare but they were put in to show you how these rules changes can affect your odds in the game. Some casinos will allow you to resplit aces again if you draw an ace to one of your original aces and this works to your advantage. Also, some casinos will allow you to double down on any number of cards rather than just the first two. In other words, if you got 2-4-3-2 as your first four cards you would then be allowed to double down on your total of 11 before receiving your 5th card. If they allow you to do this then, once again, you have a rule that works in your favor.

The point of showing you these charts is to help you understand that when you have a choice of places to play you should always choose the casino that offers the best rules. So, if you find a single-deck game with good rules you could be playing an even game by using the basic strategy, or at worst be giving the casino an edge of less than one-half of 1%.

Now, there is one way that you can actually have the edge working in your favor when you play blackjack and that's by becoming a card counter. As mentioned before, card counting is not for the average person but it really is important that you understand the concept of card counting and if you think you'd like to learn more about counting cards then it's something you can follow up on later.

Many people think that to be a card counter you have to have a photographic memory and remember every single card that's been played. Fortunately, it's not quite that difficult. Actually, the main concept behind card counting is the assumption that the dealer will bust more often when there are a lot of 10's in the deck and that he will complete more hands when there are a lot of smaller cards in the deck. Now, if you stop to think about it, it makes sense doesn't it? After all, the dealer has to play by set rules that make him take a card until he has a total of 17 or more. If there are a lot of 2's, 3's and 4's in the deck the dealer won't bust very often when he draws cards, but if there are a lot of 10's in the deck then chances are he will bust more often when he is forced to draw cards.

The card counter tries to take advantage of this fact by keeping a running total of the cards that have been played to give him an idea of what kind of cards remain in the deck. If there are a lot of 10 cards remaining in the deck then the counter will bet more money because the odds are slightly in his favor. Of course, if there are a lot of small cards remaining then the counter would only make a small bet because the odds would be slightly in favor of the dealer. Another thing that the card counter can do is to change his basic strategy to take advantage of the differences in the deck.

There are at least a dozen different card counting systems but let's take a quick look at a relatively simple one (it's also the most popular) and it's called the ***high-low*** count. With this system you assign a value of +1 to all 2's, 3's, 4's, 5's and 6's, while all 10's, Jacks, Queens, Kings and Aces are assigned a value of -1. The remaining cards: 7, 8 and 9 have no value and are not counted.

+1 = 2, 3, 4, 5, 6
-1 = 10, J, Q, K, A

When you look at these numbers you'll see that there are an equal number of cards in each group: there are five cards valued at +1 and five cards valued at -1. This means that they balance each other out and if you go through the deck and add them all together the end result will always be a total of exactly zero.

What a card counter does is to keep a running total of all the cards as they're played out and whenever the total has a plus value he knows that a lot of small cards have appeared and the remaining deck is rich in 10's which is good for the player. But, if the total is a minus value then the counter knows that a lot of 10-value cards have appeared and the remaining deck must be rich in low cards which is bad for the player. To give you an example of how to count let's say the following cards have been dealt on the first hand from a single deck:

2, 3, 3, 4, 5, 5, 5, 6, = +8
J, K, Q, A, = -4
Total = +4

As you can see, there were eight plus-value cards and four minus-value cards which resulted in a total count of +4. This means that there are now four more 10-value cards than low cards remaining in the deck and the advantage is with the player. Naturally, the higher the plus count, the more advantageous it is for the player and counters would be proportionally increasing their bets as the count got higher. The card counter would also be using the same basic strategy we spoke about previously, except for certain instances where a slight change would be called for.

On the other hand, if the count is negative, a card counter will always bet the minimum amount. Of course, they would prefer not to bet at all, but the casinos don't like you to sit at their tables and not bet so the counter has to bet something and the minimum is the least they can get by with.

There is one more important thing to explain about card counting and it's called the ***true count***. The true count is a measure of the count per deck rather than a ***running count*** of all the cards that have been played and to get the true count you simply divide the running count by the number of decks remaining to be played. As an illustration, let's say you're playing in a six-deck game and the count is +9. You look at the shoe and estimate three decks remain to be played. You then divide the count of +9 by three to get +3 which is the true count. As another example, let's say you're in an eight-deck game with a count of +12 and there are six decks left to be played. You divide +12 by six to get +2 which is the true count. To put it another way, a +2 count in a double-deck game with one deck left to be played is the same as a +4 count in a four-deck game with two decks left to be played, which is the same as a +6 count is a six-deck game with three decks left to be played, which is the same as a +12 count in an eight-deck game with six decks left to be played.

For the card counter, it is crucial to always take the running count and then divide it by the number of decks remaining in order to get the true count because all betting and playing decisions are based on the true count rather than the running count.

Of course, if you're playing in a single-deck game the running count and the true count are initially the same. The more you get into the deck, however, the more weight is given to the running count because there is less than one deck remaining. So, if the running count was +3 and only a 1/2-deck remained you would calculate the true count by dividing +3 by 1/2 (which is the same as multiplying by 2/1, or 2) to get a true count of +6. As another example, if the running count was +2 and about 2/3 of the deck remained you would divide +2 by 2/3 (the same as multi-plying by 3/2 or, 1 and 1/2) to get +3.

As you can see, the count becomes much more meaningful as you get closer to the last cards in the deck and that's why casinos never deal down to the end. Instead, the dealer will insert a plastic card about 2/3 or 3/4 of the way in the deck and when that card is reached the dealer will finish that particular round and then shuffle the cards. How far into the deck(s) that plastic card is inserted is known as the ***penetration point*** and card counters always look for a dealer that offers good penetration. The card counter knows that the further into the deck(s) the plastic card is placed the more meaningful the true count will be and the more advantageous it will be for the card counter.

So, now that you know how those card counters keep track of the cards, what kind of advantage do you think they have over the casino? Well, not too much. Depending on the number of decks used, the rules in force, and the skill of the counter, it could be as much as 2% but that would be at the high end. Probably 1% would be closer to the actual truth. This means that for every $1,000 in bets that are made the card counter will win $10. Not exactly a huge amount but there are people out there who do make a living playing the game.

Blackjack FAQs

by Henry Tamburin

Blackjack continues to be the most popular table game in casinos. The reason is that it is an easy game to learn how to play, it's a beatable game, and it's possible to win often by learning the correct playing strategies (i.e., the house edge can be very low). What follows are the most frequently asked questions about the game and my responses.

Does it make a difference where I sit at a blackjack table?
Where you sit has no effect on the odds against you. My advice, if you are a beginner, is to sit in the middle because this will give you a little more time to decide how to play your hand. (The first base player, or player to the far right, is the first to act; the third base player, far left, is the last to act.) Now, if you are a card counter using a traditional counting system (e.g., Hi-Lo), it's best to sit at third base so you can see and count as many cards as possible before acting on your hand.

Do unskilled players affect your chances of winning?
I know many players believe the answer to this is "yes" because of the times they've lost a hand when another player misplayed his or her hand. But in the long run, the skill of other players on your table has no effect on your odds of winning. Yes, you'll remember the times you lose a hand when someone misplays his. But how many times have you congratulated a player who misplayed his hand that resulted in everyone on the table winning? Blackjack players have selective memory. Bottom line: Ignore how other players act on their hands and focus instead on how to play your hands as accurately as possible.

Why does the house edge against a player increase when the rules specify the dealer must hit soft 17 rather than stand?
A dealer will bust more often when she must hit soft 17 instead of standing, which is good for the player; however, this is more than offset by the fact that when she doesn't bust, what would have been a 17 often ends up to be a higher total that may now beat the player's hand. (A soft 17 is a lousy hand not only for the dealer but also for the player, which is why it's better for players to hit or double down on soft 17.)

Which is the best blackjack game to play?
You want to play blackjack games that offer the best rules. For example, some of the better rules are: blackjack pays 3-2, dealer stands on soft 17, player may double down on any first two cards, double down after pair splitting, resplit aces, and surrender. The games you want to definitely avoid

are those that pay only 6-5 (or worse, even money) for a blackjack. As a general rule, a single-deck game that pays 3-2 for a blackjack often has better odds than a multi-deck game that pays 3-2 (but not always; you need to carefully compare the rules). (Note: You will find a list of common rule variations and their effect on the player's expected return on the blackjack page at wizardofodds.com)

Why should you split 8s against a dealer's 10 and turn one losing hand into two?
Oftentimes we are dealt terrible hands and we have to make the best of them. Such is the case with a pair of 8s against a dealer's 10. Your choice is to either surrender the hand (when the rules allow it); stand on your 16; hit your 16; or split the 8s and play two hands, each starting with an 8. No matter which option you choose, you will lose more money than you will win in the long run. However, the math gives the edge to splitting the 8s because in the long run you'll less money than the other playing options. (Trust the math!)

Do progressive betting systems work?
No they don't. Whether you won or lost the previous hand has no effect on your chances of winning the next hand.

Is bringing a strategy card to the table legal?
Yes. Just don't lay the strategy card on the table; simply hold it in your hand. (For security reasons, casinos don't allow anything on the table except drink holders and ash trays.)

Is it better to play heads up against a dealer or on a table full of players?
If you are a basic strategy player, you are better off playing on a full table because you will get fewer hands to act on per hour and, therefore, have less exposure of your bankroll to the house edge. If you are a card counter, your hourly win rate will increase when you play heads up because you will be playing more hands when you have the edge.

Can blackjack really be beaten?
Yes, but you must learn the strategies on how to do it.

If blackjack can be beaten, why do casinos offer the game?
Simply because the majority of the public won't take the time or effort to learn the well-documented strategies that could give them the mathematical edge when they play. Instead they rely on hunches and guessing when they play, which results in a ton of profit for casinos.

Is card counting legal?
Using your brain when you play blackjack is not illegal; therefore, card counting is not illegal.

I tried card counting and found it too difficult. Is there anything else I can try?

I assume you tried to learn a traditional card counting system like Hi-Lo. There are simpler (albeit less powerful) counting systems that are much easier to master that can give the recreational player either a break-even game or a slight edge over the casino. Three that I recommend are Speed Count, the Ace-Five count, and the Ace-Ten Front count.

How do casinos get away with excluding card counters from playing blackjack? Isn't this discrimination?

The Nevada courts have allowed casinos to exclude card counters because technically they are private property, and under the ancient common law right (the so-called "Innkeeper's Right to Exclude or Eject Guests") a property owner could exclude anyone from his property for any reason, or even without a reason. Many players and lawyers believe that barring skillful players from playing blackjack is an unconstitutional form of discrimination. However, the Supreme Court prohibits discrimination only against persons who are members of "protected classes" based on (among others) race, creed, sex, national origin, age, or physical disability (i.e., card counters are not, unfortunately, a "protected class"). Therefore, until a law is passed or blackjack players bring a challenge, casinos will continue the practice of barring card counters (or for that matter, any player for any reason, which casinos don't always reveal to a barred player). (Note: In some gaming jurisdictions, such as in Atlantic City and Missouri, regulations don't allow casinos to bar card counters.)

Why should I go through the trouble of learning card counting when the casinos can throw me out?

If you are a skillful card counter, there is always the risk that a casino could ask you to stop playing. The question then becomes: Do the benefits of having the edge over the casino outweigh the risk of getting barred? In my opinion, the answer is "yes," but only after you learn how to disguise your skills to minimize this risk. (You'll find plenty of information in blackjack books or the Internet on how to camouflage your play.)

Henry Tamburin, Ph.D., has over 50 years experience as a blackjack player, writer, author, and instructor. His latest book is the Ultimate Blackjack Strategy Guide, which is FREE to read on https://www.888casino.com/blog/blackjack-strategy-guide/. See his ad on page 88.

THE ULTIMATE BLACKJACK STRATEGY GUIDE

The *Ultimate Blackjack Strategy Guide*, written by blackjack expert Henry Tamburin, Ph.D., is the most extensive and comprehensive introduction to the casino game of blackjack that you will find anywhere. Best of all, the book is FREE to read. Just go to

https://www.888casino.com/blog/blackjack-strategy-guide/

Roulette

by Steve Bourie

Virtually all American casinos use a double-zero roulette wheel which has pockets numbered from 1 to 36, plus 0 and 00 for a total of 38 pockets. This is in contrast to Europe where a single-zero wheel is used and the game has always been the most popular in the casino.

There are usually six seats at the roulette table and to help the dealer differentiate what each player is betting every player is assigned a different color chip which they purchase right at the table. Each table has its own minimum chip values and that information is usually posted on a sign at the table. As an example let's say a table has a $1 minimum chip value. This means that when you give the dealer your money the colored chips he gives you in return must have a minimum value of $1 each. So, if you gave the dealer $50 he would ask what value you wanted on the chips and if you said $1 he would give you 50 colored chips.

If you prefer, you could say you wanted the chips valued at $2 each and he would just give you 25 chips rather than 50. You can make the value of your colored chips anything you want and you'll notice that when the dealer gives you your chips he'll put one of your chips on the railing near the wheel with a marker on top to let him know the value of your chips. Later on when you're done playing at that table you must exchange your colored chips for regular chips before leaving. The colored chips have no value anywhere else in the casino so don't leave the table with them.

Besides the minimum chip value, there is also a minimum amount that must be bet on each spin of the wheel. Once again, the minimums are probably posted on a sign at the table. If it says $2 minimum inside/$5 minimum outside this means that when betting on any of the 38 numbers that pay 35-to-1 the total of all your bets must be $2. You could make two different $1 bets or one $2 bet, it doesn't matter except that the total of all your bets on the numbers must be at least $2. The $5 minimum outside means that any of the outside bets that pay 2-to-1, or even money, require that you bet $5 each time. On the outside bets you can't make a $3 bet and a $2 bet to meet the minimums - you have to bet at least $5 every time. After you've exchanged your cash for colored chips you're ready to place your first bet so, let's see what your options are:

You can make a ***straight*** bet where you only bet on one number and if it comes in you'll be paid 35-to-1. The casino advantage on this bet is 5.26% and by the time you're done with this roulette section I'm sure you'll be very familiar with that number.

Another choice you have is to do a ***split***. This is where you put a chip on the line that separates two numbers. If either number comes up you'll be paid at 17-to-1. The casino advantage on this bet is 5.26%.

If you put a chip in an area that splits 4 numbers this is called a ***corner*** bet and if any one of those 4 numbers comes in you will be paid off at 8-to-1. The casino advantage on this bet is 5.26%.

If you put a chip at the beginning of a row of 3 numbers, this is called a ***street*** bet and if any one of those 3 numbers shows up you will be paid off at 11-to-1. The casino advantage on this bet is 5.26%.

You can also put a chip on the line between two streets so that you have a ***double street*** covered and if any one of those 6 numbers come in you'll be paid off at 5-to-1. The casino advantage on this bet is?... you guessed it...5.26%.

The only other bet you can make on the inside numbers is the ***5- number*** bet where you place one chip in the upper left corner of the number 1 box. If any one of those 5 numbers comes in you'll be paid off at 6-to-1 and what do you think the casino advantage is on this bet? 5.26%? Nope, I gotcha... it's 7.89%. Actually, this is the worst possible bet on the roulette table and the only bet you'll come across that doesn't have a 5.26% house edge on the double-zero roulette wheel. You should never make this bet.

One quick word here about "to" and "for" when discussing odds. Whenever the odds are stated as "to" this means that in addition to the stated payoff you also receive your original bet back. In other words, if you won your single number bet in roulette you would receive 35-to-1, which is a 35-chip payoff, plus you'd still keep your original one-chip bet, so you end up with 36 chips. Now if the odds are stated as "for" that means you do not receive back your original bet. If the odds in your single number bet were 35-*for*-1 you would still receive a 35-chip payoff but the casino would keep your original one-chip bet so you would only end up with 35 chips. The only place in a casino where the odds are always stated as "for" is in video poker. You might also come across it on a couple of craps bets where the odds are stated as "for-one" rather than "to-one" in order to give the casino a slightly better edge.

Now, getting back to our roulette examples, let's look at all of the outside bets that you can make and keep in mind that the house edge on all of these outside bets is...do you remember the number?...that's right...5.26%.

There are three bets you can make that will pay you even money, or 1-to-1, which means that if you win, you will get back one dollar for every dollar you bet:

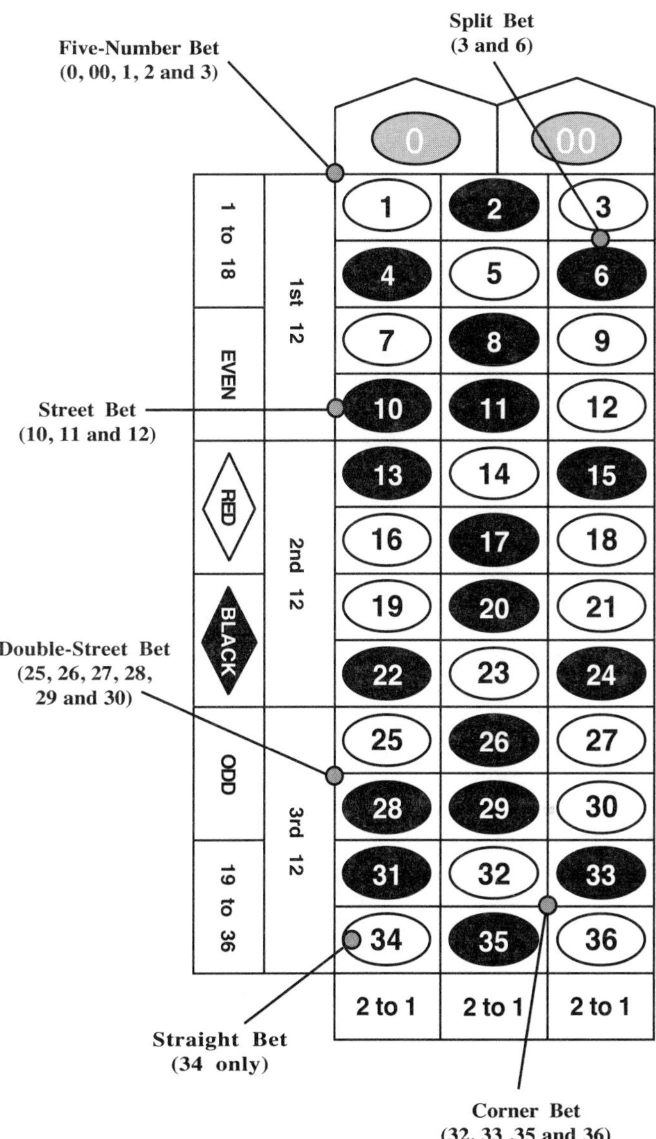

Typical felt layout for placing bets on American double-zero roulette wheel

Red or black - If you put a chip on red then a red number must come up in order for you to win. If the ball lands on a black number, 0 or 00 - you lose. The same thing goes for black - you lose if it comes in red, 0 or 00 and you win if the ball lands on a black number.

Odd or even - If you put a chip on odd then the ball must land on an odd number in order for you to win. If it lands on 0, 00, or an even number - you lose. If you bet on even, you win if an even number shows up and lose if the ball lands on 0, 00 or an odd number.

1 through 18 and 19 through 36 - If you bet on 1 through 18, then you win if a number from 1 through 18 comes in and you lose if the ball lands on 0, 00 or a number higher than 18. Similarly, if you bet on 19 through 36, you win if one of those numbers comes in and you lose on 0, 00 or any number lower than 19.

The only other bets left are the ***dozens*** and columns bets. If you look at the roulette betting layout you can see three areas that each correspond to 12-number sections on the table. The one marked 1st 12 covers the numbers from 1 to 12, the one marked 2nd 12 covers the numbers from 13 to 24 and the other one that's marked 3rd 12 covers the last section of numbers from 25 to 36. If you bet on the 1st 12 you would win if a number from 1 to 12 came in and you would lose if anything else came in, including 0 or 00. The same principle holds true for each of the other dozen bets where you would win if a number in that section came in and you would lose if anything else showed up. All dozens bets pay 2-to-1.

The last bet to look at is the ***column*** bet and that is also a bet that pays 2-to-1. There are three possible column bets you can make and you'll notice that each area corresponds to the numbers in the column directly above it. So, if you put a chip under the first column you will win if any of the numbers in that column come in and you will lose if any other number, including 0 or 00 shows up. Once again, the same rule is in effect for each of the other columns where you would win if the number appears in the column above your bet and you would lose if it doesn't.

All right, now you know all the possible bets and you know how to make them at the table. So, the next question is "How do you win?" and the answer to that is very simple - You have to get lucky! And that's the ONLY way you can win at roulette. As you found out earlier, every bet, except for the 5-number bet, which I'm sure you'll never make, has a house edge of?...that's right...5.26%. So, feel free to put your chips all over the table and then just hope that you're lucky enough to have one of your numbers come up. You see, it just doesn't matter what you do because you'll always have that same house edge of 5.26% working against you on every bet you make.

Now, you may have heard of a system for roulette where you should place your bets only on the numbers that are evenly spaced out around the wheel. For example, if you wanted to play only four numbers, you could bet on 1,2,31 and 32 because when you looked at a roulette wheel, you would notice that if you divided it into four equal parts, you would have a number that appears in each of the four sections. So, is this a good system? Well, actually it's no better and no worse than any other roulette system. The fact is that it's purely a matter of chance where the ball happens to land and it makes no difference whether the numbers you choose are right next to each other or evenly spaced out on the wheel. Each number has an equal chance to occur on every spin of the wheel and the house edge always remains at 5.26%.

You can probably tell that I wouldn't recommend roulette as a good game to play because there are other games that offer much better odds, but if you really insist on playing the game I have three good suggestions for you. #1 - Go to Atlantic City! In Atlantic City if you make an even-money outside bet, like red or black, odd or even, 1 through 18 or 19 through 36 and if 0 or 00 come up, the state gaming regulations allow the casino to take only half of your bet. Because you only lose half of your bet this also lowers the casino edge on these outside bets in half to 2.63%. This rule is only in effect for even-money bets so keep in mind that on all other bets the house edge still remains at that very high 5.26%.

The second suggestion I have for you also involves some travel and here it is: Go to Europe! The game of roulette began in Europe and many casinos over there use a single-zero wheel which makes it a much better game because the house edge on a single-zero roulette wheel is only 2.70%. To make it even better, they have a rule called "en prison" which is similar to the Atlantic City casino rule. If you make an even-money outside bet and the ball lands on 0 you don't lose right away. Instead, your bet is "imprisoned" and you have to let it ride on the next spin. Then, if your bet wins, you can remove it from the table. Because of this rule, the casino edge on this bet is cut in half to 1.35% which makes it one of the best bets in the casino and almost four times better than the same bet when it's made on a standard double-zero roulette wheel in the United States.

Now, if you're not into traveling and you don't think you can make it to Atlantic City or Europe, then you'll just have to settle for suggestion #3 which is: Win quickly! Naturally, this is easier said than done, but in reality, if you want to win at roulette the best suggestion I can give you is that you try to win quickly and then walk away from the table because the longer you continue to bet the longer that big 5.26% house edge will keep eating away at your bankroll. One major principle of gambling is that in order to win you must only play the games that have the lowest casino edge and, unfortunately, roulette is not one of them.

Before closing out this look at roulette, let's take a minute to examine one of the most famous betting systems of all time and the one that many people frequently like to use on roulette. It's called the Martingale system and it is basically a simple system of doubling your bet whenever you lose. The theory behind it is that sooner or later you'll have to win and thus, you will always come out ahead. As an example, let's say you're playing roulette and you bet $1 on red, if you lose you double your next bet to $2 and if you lose that then you double your next bet to $4 and if you lose that you double your next bet to $8 and so forth until you eventually win. Now, when you finally do win you will end up with a profit equal to your original bet, which in this case is $1. If you started the same system with a $5 bet, you would have to bet $10 after your first loss, $20 after your second loss and so forth, but whenever you won you would end up with a $5 profit.

In theory, this sounds like a good idea but in reality it's a terrible system because eventually you will be forced to risk a great amount of money for a very small profit. Let's face it, even if you only wanted to make a $1 profit on each spin of the wheel, sooner or later you will hit a major losing streak where you will have to bet an awful lot of money just to make that $1 profit. For example, if you go eight spins without a winner, you would have to bet $256 on the next spin and if that lost then you'd have to bet $512. Would you really want to risk that kind of money just to make $1? I don't think so. You may think that the odds are highly unlikely that you would lose that many bets in a row, but eventually it will happen and when it does you will suffer some astronomical losses. One other problem with this system is that eventually you won't be able to double your bet because you will have reached the casino maximum, which in most casinos is $500 on roulette. Just keep in mind that the Martingale system works best when it's played for fun on paper and not for real money in a casino. If it was truly a winning system it would have bankrupted the world's casinos years ago.

Baccarat

by Steve Bourie

When you think of Baccarat you probably think of a game that's played by the casino's wealthiest players who sit at a private table and can afford to bet tens of thousands of dollars on the flip of a card and you know what? You're right! The game of Baccarat has always had a reputation as being for the richest gamblers and that usually scared off the average player, but nowadays more and more people are discovering that Baccarat is really a good game for the small stakes player because 1. It has a relatively small advantage for the casino and 2. It's very simple to play.

The mini-Baccarat table is the kind of Baccarat table you're most likely to find in the standard American casino and the game is played pretty much the same as regular Baccarat except that in the mini version all of the hands are dealt out by the dealer and the players never touch the cards. Other than that, the rules are virtually the same. Oh yes, one other difference you'll find is that the betting minimums will always be lower on mini-Baccarat and it's usually pretty easy to find a table with a $10 minimum.

Now, as noted before, the game of Baccarat is very simple to play and that's because the only decision you have to make is what bet you want to make from the three that are available: player, banker or tie. After the players make their bets the game begins and two 2-card hands are dealt from a shoe that contains 8 decks of cards. One hand is dealt for the banker and another hand is dealt for the player. The values of the two cards in each hand are added together and the object of the game is to have a total as close to 9 as possible. After the values of the first two cards in each hand are totaled, a third card can be drawn by either the player, the banker or both. But, the decision as to whether or not a third card should be drawn is not decided by the dealer or the players - it is only decided by the rules of the game.

All of the 10's and all of the face cards are counted as zeros, while all of the other cards from ace though 9 are counted at their face value. So, a hand of Jack, 6 has a total of 6; 10,4 has a total of 4; king, 7 has a total of 7; and ace, queen which would be a great hand in blackjack, only has a total of 1. The other thing about adding the cards together is that no total can be higher than 9. So, if a total is 10 or higher you have to subtract 10 to determine its value. For example, 8,8 totals 16 but you subtract 10 and your total is 6; 9,5 has a total of 4; 8,3 has a total of 1; and 5,5 has a total of 0.

Once again, the object of the game of Baccarat is to have a total as close to 9 as possible, so after the first two cards are dealt if either the player or banker hand has a total of 9 then that's called a "natural" and that hand is the winner. If neither hand has a total of 9 then the next best possible hand is a total of 8 (which is also called a "natural") and that hand would be the winner. If both the player and the banker end up with the same total then it's a tie and neither hand wins.

Now, if neither hand has an 8 or a 9 then the rules of the game have to be consulted to decide whether or not a third card is drawn. Once that's done, the values of the cards are added together again and whichever hand is closest to a total of 9 is the winner. If both hands end up with the same total then it's a tie and neither hand wins.

If you want to bet on the player hand just put your money in the area marked "player" and if you win you'll be paid off at even-money, or $1 for every $1 you bet. The casino advantage on the player bet is 1.36%. If you want to bet on the banker hand you would place your bet in the area marked "banker" and if you win, you'll also be paid off at even-money, but you'll have to pay a 5% commission on the amount you win. So, if you won $10 on your bet, you would owe a 50¢ commission to the house. The 5% commission is only required if you win and not if you lose. The dealer will keep track of the amount you owe by putting an equal amount in a small area on the table that corresponds to your seat number at the table. So, if you're sitting at seat #3 and won $10 on the bank hand the dealer would pay you $10 and then put 50¢ in the #3 box. This lets him know how much you owe the casino in commissions and when you get up to leave the table you'll have to pay the dealer whatever amount is in that box. After adjusting for that 5% commission the casino advantage on the banker bet is 1.17%

Finally, if you want to bet on a tie you would place your bet in the area marked "tie" and if you win you'll be paid off at 8-to-1, or $8 for every $1 you bet. The big payoff sounds nice but actually this is a terrible bet because the casino advantage is a very high 14.1% and this bet should never be made.

As you've seen, the casino advantage in Baccarat is very low (except for the tie bet) and the rules are set in advance so no decisions are made by either the players or the dealer about how to play the cards. This means that, unlike blackjack where you have to decide whether or not you want another card, you have no decisions to make and no skill is involved. This also means that Baccarat is purely a guessing game, so even if you've never played the game before you can sit at a table and play just as well as anyone who's played the game for 20 years! This is the only game in the casino where this can happen and that's why I tell people that Baccarat is an especially good game for the beginning player because you need no special knowledge to take advantage of those low casino edge bets.

The only part of Baccarat that gets a little confusing is trying to understand the rules concerning the draw of a third card, but remember, the rules are always the same at every table and they'll usually have a printed copy of the rules at

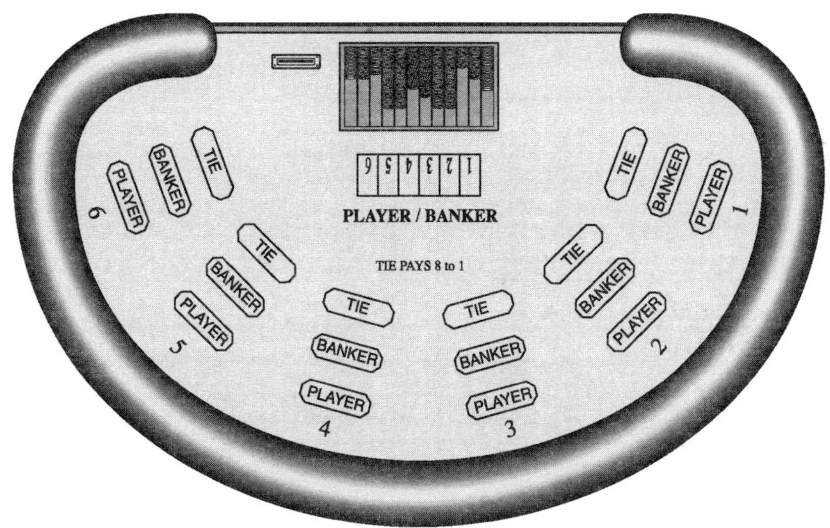

A Sample Mini-Baccarat Table Layout

the table and will give you a copy if you ask for it. After playing the game for awhile you'll start to remember the rules on your own, but until then here's a rundown on how it works:

As noted before, if the first two cards in either hand total 8 or 9, then the game is over and the highest total wins. If the totals are both 8 or both 9 then it's a tie and neither hand wins. For any other total the rules have to be consulted and it's always the player hand that goes first. If the player hand has a total of 6 or 7, it must stand. The only other totals it can possibly have are 0,1,2,3,4 or 5 and for all of those totals it must draw a card.

PLAYER HAND RULES

8,9	STANDS (Natural)
6,7	STANDS
0,1,2,3,4,5	DRAWS

There, that wasn't too hard to understand was it? If the player hand has a total of 6 or 7 it stands and for anything else it has to draw a card. Well, that was the easy part because now it gets a little complicated.

After the player hand is finished the banker hand must take its turn and if its first 2 cards total 0,1 or 2 it must draw a card. If its two cards total 7 it must stand and if the total is 6 it will stand, but only if the player hand did not take a card.

BANK HAND RULES

8,9	STANDS (Natural)
0,1,2	DRAWS
6	STANDS (If player took no card)
7	STANDS

The only other possible totals the bank can have are 3,4,5 or 6 and the decision as to whether or not a 3rd card is drawn depends on the 3rd card that was drawn by the player hand.

When the banker hand has a total of 3 it must stand if the player's 3rd card was an 8 and it must draw if the player's 3rd card was any other card.

IF BANK HAS 3 and

Player's third card is 8 - BANK STANDS
Player's third card is 1,2,3,4,5,6,7,9,10 - BANK DRAWS

When the banker hand has a total of 4 it must stand if the player's 3rd card was a 1,8,9, or 10 and it must draw if the player's 3rd card was any other card.

IF BANK HAS 4 and

Player's third card is 1,8,9,10 - BANK STANDS
Player's third card is 2,3,4,5,6,7 - BANK DRAWS

When the banker hand has a total of 5 it must draw if the player's 3rd card was a 4,5,6 or 7 and it must stand if the player's 3rd card was any other card.

IF BANK HAS 5 and

Player's third card is 1,2,3,8,9,10 - BANK STANDS
Player's third card is 4,5,6,7 - BANK DRAWS

When the banker hand has a total of 6 it must draw if the player's 3rd card was a 6 or 7 and it must stand if the player's 3rd card was any other card.

IF BANK HAS 6 and

Player's third card is 1,2,3,4,5,8,9,10 - BANK STANDS
Player's third card is 6 or 7 - BANK DRAWS

There you have it - those are the rules of Baccarat concerning the draw of a third card. As you saw they were a little complicated, but remember that you don't have to memorize the rules yourself because the dealer will know them and play each hand by those rules, but you can always ask for a copy of the rules at the table to follow along.

Now let's try some sample hands: The player hand has queen,9 for a total of 9 and the banker hand has 4,4 for a total of 8. Which hand wins? Both hands are naturals, but the player hand total of 9 is higher than the banker hand total of 8, so the player hand is the winner.

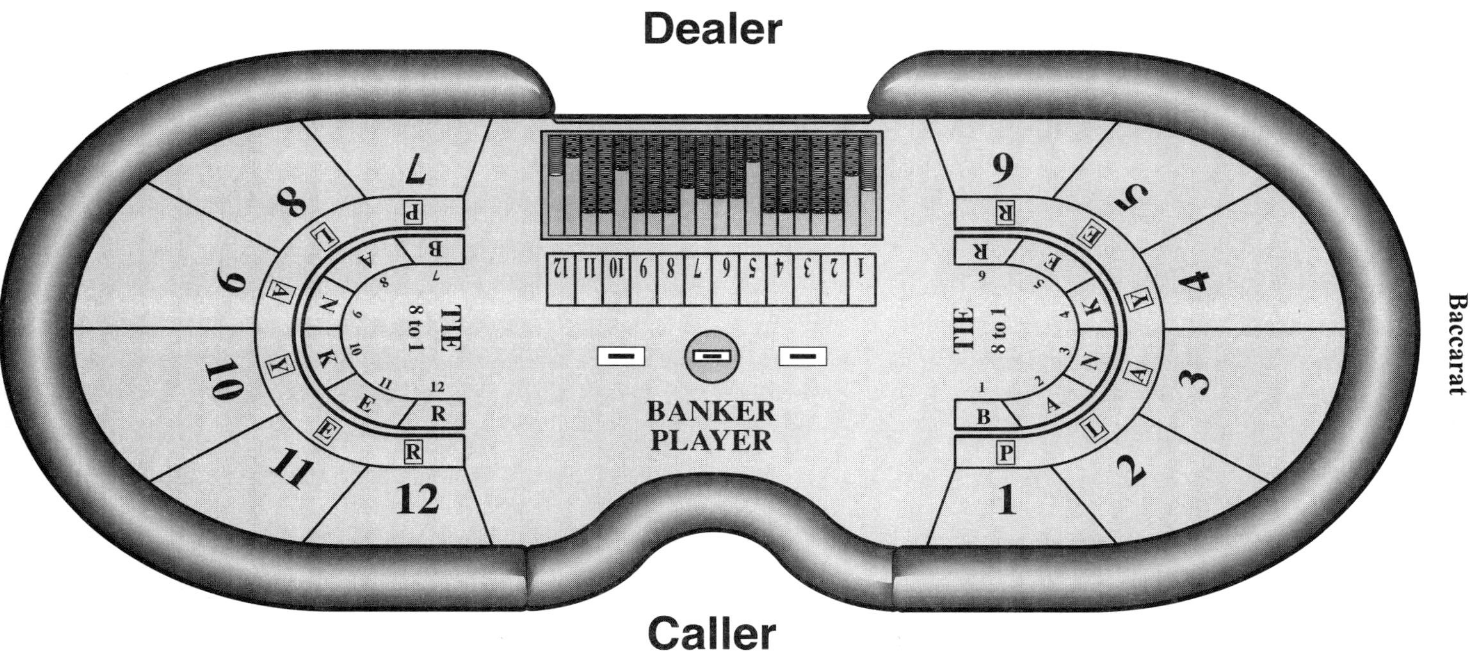

A 12-Seat Baccarat Table Layout

If the player hand has 4,2 for a total of 6 and the banker hand has ace, jack which totals 1, what happens? The player hand must stand on its 6 and the banker hand must always draw when it has a total of 0,1 or 2. Let's say the bank draws a 7 and wins 8 to 6.

What happens when the player hand has king, 5 and the bank hand has 2,4? The player hand must draw and let's say it gets a 7 for a total of 2. The banker hand has a total of 6 and if it could stand on that total it would win because its 6 is higher than the 2 held by the player. Of course, if you were betting on banker that's exactly what you would want to happen but, unfortunately for you, the rules require the bank hand to draw another card whenever its first two cards total 6 and the third card drawn by the player is a 7. So now, instead of having a winning hand you have to hope that the card you draw isn't a 4, giving you a total of 0 or a 5, giving you a total of 1. If either of those cards show up then your winning hand becomes a loser.You also wouldn't want to draw a 6 because that would give you a total of 2 which would give you a tie. In this case let's say that the bank hand goes on to draw an 8 which gives it a total of 3 and it wins 4 to 2.

Baccarat Rules Summary

Player Hand

Total of First Two Cards	
0-1-2-3-4-5	Draws
6-7	Stands
8-9	Natural (Banker cannot draw)

Banker Hand

Total of First Two Cards	DRAWS When Player's Third Card is	STANDS When Player's Third Card is
0-1-2	Always Draws	
3	1-2-3-4-5-6-7-9-0	8
4	2-3-4-5-6-7	1-8-9-0
5	4-5-6-7	1-2-3-8-9-0
6	6-7	1-2-3-4-5-8-9-0
7		Stands
8-9		Stands (Natural)

If the Player's hand does not draw a third card,

then the Banker's hand stands on a total of 6 or more.

If the player hand has 3, ace for a total of 4 and the banker hand has 8,7 for a total of 5, what happens? The player hand must draw and say it gets a 9 for a total of 3. Once again, the banker hand would like to stand on its total because it would win, but the rules have to be consulted first and in this case when the banker's first 2 cards total 5 and the player's third card drawn is a 9 the banker hand must stand, so the banker hand wins 5 to 3.

Finally, let's say the player hand has 4,3 for a total of 7 and the banker hand has 6,10 for a total of 6. The player hand must always stand on totals of 6 or 7 and the banker hand must also stand on its total of 6 because the player hand didn't take a third card. The player hand wins this one 7 to 6.

All right, now that you know how to play Baccarat we come to the important question which is - how do you win? Well, as I said before, if you bet on player you'll only be giving the casino a 1.36% edge and if you bet on banker you'll be giving the casino an even more modest edge of just 1.17%. While both of these are pretty low edges to give the casino you're still stuck with the fact that the casino will always have an edge over you and in the long run the game of Baccarat is unbeatable. So, if that's the case then how do you win? Well, the answer to that is very simple - You have to get lucky! And that's the ONLY way you can win at Baccarat. Of course, this is easier said than done, but fortunately, in the game of Baccarat, you have the option of making two bets that require no skill and both offer the casino a very low edge especially when you compare them to roulette where the house has a 5.26% advantage on a double-zero wheel and slot machines where the edge is about 5% to 15%. I always stress the point that when you gamble in a casino you have to play the games that have the lowest casino edge in order to have the best chance of winning and with that in mind you can see that Baccarat is not that bad a game to play for the recreational gambler.

Now let's take a quick look at one of the most common systems for betting on Baccarat. One thing that many Baccarat players seem to have in common is a belief in streaks and the casinos accommodate these players by providing scorecards at the table that can be used to track the results of each hand. Many players like to bet on whatever won the last hand in the belief that it will continue to come in and they hope for a long streak.

The thinking for these players is that since Baccarat is purely a guessing game it's just like guessing the outcome of a coin toss and chances are that a coin won't alternately come up heads, tails, heads, tails, heads, tails but rather that there will be streaks where the same result will come in for awhile. So, is this a good system? Well, actually, it's no better and no worse than any other system because no matter what you do you'll still have the same casino edge going against you on every bet you make: 1.36% on the player and 1.17% on the banker. The one good thing about a system like this though is that you don't have to sit there and guess what you want to play each time. Instead, you go into the game knowing how you're going to play and you don't have to blame yourself if your guess is wrong, instead you get to blame it on your system!

Craps

by Steve Bourie

At first glance the game of craps looks a little intimidating because of all the various bets you can make but actually the game itself is very simple, so first let me explain the game without any reference to the betting.

Everyone at the craps table gets a turn to roll the dice, but you don't have to roll if you don't want to. The dice are passed around the table clockwise and if it's your turn to roll you simply take two dice and roll them to the opposite end of the table. This is your first roll of the dice which is also called the "come-out" roll. If you roll a 7 or 11 that's called a "natural" and you win, plus you get to roll again. If you roll a 2,3 or 12 those are all called "craps" and you lose, but you still get to roll again. The only other possible numbers you can roll are 4,5,6,8,9 or 10 and if one of those numbers shows up, then that number becomes your "point" and the object of the game is to roll that number again before you roll a 7.

If a 7 shows up before your "point" number does then you lose and the dice move on to the next shooter. If your "point" number shows up before a 7 does, then you have made a "pass." You then win your bet and you get to roll again. That's all there is to the game of craps.

Now that you know how to play the game, let's find out about the different kinds of bets you can make. Two of the best bets you'll find on the craps table are in the areas marked "pass" and "don't pass". When you bet on the "pass" line you're betting that the shooter will win. To make a pass line bet you put your bet right in front of you on the pass line. Pass line bets are paid even-money and the house edge on a pass line bet is 1.41% You can also bet on the "don't pass" line in which case you're betting that the shooter will lose. To make a don't pass bet you put your bet in front of you in the don't pass area. Don't pass bets are also paid even-money and the house edge on them is 1.40%.

In reality, the odds are always 1.41% against the shooter and in favor of the "don't pass" bettor by that same amount. Of course, if you're a "don't pass" bettor the casinos don't want to give you a bet where you have an edge so they have a rule in effect on "don't pass" bets where on the come out roll if the shooter throws a 12, you don't win. You don't lose either, the bet is just considered a "push," or tie, and nothing happens. In some casinos they may make 2 instead of 12 the number that's a push. Just look on the don't pass line and you'll you see the word "bar" and then the number that the casino considers a push. In our illustration it says bar 12, so in this casino your bet on the don't pass line will be a push if the come-out roll is a 12. This rule is what gives the casino its advantage on don't pass bets and it doesn't matter whether the casino bars the 2 or 12 the result is the same 1.40% advantage for the house.

All right, let's say you put $10 on the pass line and you roll the dice. If you roll 7 or 11 you win $10 and if you roll 2,3 or 12 you lose $10. So, what happens if you roll any of the other numbers? Well, as I said before, that number becomes your point and you have to roll that number again before you roll a 7 in order to win your pass line bet.

Once your point is established the dealer at each end of the table will move a marker into the box that corresponds to your point number to let everyone at the table know what your point is. The marker that's used has two different sides. One side is black with the word "off" and the other side is white with the word "on." Before any point is established the marker is kept in the Don't Come box with the black side facing up until you roll a point number and then the dealer turns it over to the white side and moves it inside the box that contains your point number.

For example let's say your come-out roll is a 4. The dealer simply turns the marker over to the white side that says "on" and places it in the 4 box. This lets everyone know that 4 is your point and that you will continue to roll the dice, no matter how long it takes, until you roll a 4, which will make you a winner, or a 7, which will make you a loser.

Now, keep in mind that once your point is established you can't remove your pass line bet until you either win, by throwing your point, or lose, by rolling a 7. The reason for this is that on the come out roll the pass line bettor has the advantage because there are 8 ways to win (by rolling a 7 or 11) and only 4 ways to lose (by rolling a 2, 3 or 12). If a point number is rolled, no matter what number it is, there are then more ways to lose than to win and that's why the bet can't be removed. If you were allowed to remove your bet everyone would just wait for the come-out roll and if they didn't win they would take their bet back which would give them a big advantage over the house and, as you know, casinos don't like that, so that's why you can't remove your bet.

As previously noted, the pass line is one of the best bets you'll find, but there is a way to make it even better because once your point number is established the casino will allow you to make another bet that will be paid off at the true odds. This is a very good bet to make because the casino has no advantage on this bet.

In this instance, since your point was 4, the true odds are 2-to-1 and that's what your bet will be paid off at: $2 for every $1 you bet. This is called an "odds bet," "taking the free odds" or "betting behind the line" and to make this bet you simply put your chips directly behind your pass line bet. There is a limit to how much you're allowed to bet and for many years most casinos allowed a maximum of 2 times the amount of your pass line bet. Nowadays, however, many casinos offer 5 times odds and some casinos are even allowing up to 100 times odds. In the U.S. the Horseshoe casinos offer 100X odds at all of their locations.

Because the casino has no advantage on these bets you are effectively lowering the house edge on your total pass line bet by taking advantage of these free odds bets. For example, the normal house edge on a pass line bet is 1.41% but if you also make a single odds bet along with your pass line bet you will lower the house edge on your total pass line bets to .85%. If the casino offers double odds then the edge on your bets is lowered to .61%. With triple odds the edge is lowered to .47% and if you were to play in a casino that allowed 10 times odds the edge would be lowered to only .18% which means that, statistically speaking, over time, that casino would only make 18¢ out of every $100 you bet on that table. As you can see, the more the casino allows you to bet behind the line, the more it lowers their edge, so it's always a good idea to take advantage of this bet. By the way, free odds bets, unlike regular pass line bets, can be removed or reduced, at any time.

All right, let's make our free odds bet on our point number of 4 by putting $20 behind the line. Then we continue to roll until we either roll a 4 or a 7. If a 4 came up we would get even money on the pass line bet, plus 2-to-1 on the free odds bet, for a total win of $50. But, if we rolled a 7, we would lose both the pass line bet and the free odds bet for a total loss of $30.

In this example we used 4 as our point number, but there are 5 other numbers that could appear and here are the true odds for all of the possible point numbers: the 4 and 10 are 2-to-1; the 5 and 9 are 3-to-2; and the 6 and 8 are 6-to-5. You'll notice that the numbers appear in pairs and that's because each paired combination has the same probability of occurring.

7 = 6 ways	1+6,6+1,2+5,5+2,3+4,4+3
6 = 5 ways	1+5,5+1,2+4,4+2,3+3
8 = 5 ways	2+6,6+2,3+5,5+3,4+4

As you can see there are 6 ways to make a 7 and only 5 ways to make a 6 or 8. Therefore, the true odds are 6-to-5.

7 = 6 ways	1+6,6+1,2+5,5+2,3+4,4+3
4 = 3 ways	1+3,3+1,2+2
10 = 3 ways	4+6,6+4,5+5

There are 6 ways to make a 7 and only 3 ways to make a 4 or 10, so the true odds are 6-to-3, which is the same as 2-to-1;

7 = 6 ways	1+6,6+1,2+5,5+2,3+4,4+3
5 = 4 ways	1+4,4+1,2+3,3+2
9 = 4 ways	3+6,6+3,4+5,5+4

and finally, there are 6 ways to make a 7, but just 4 ways to make a 5 or 9, so the true odds here are 6-to-4 which is the same as 3-to-2.

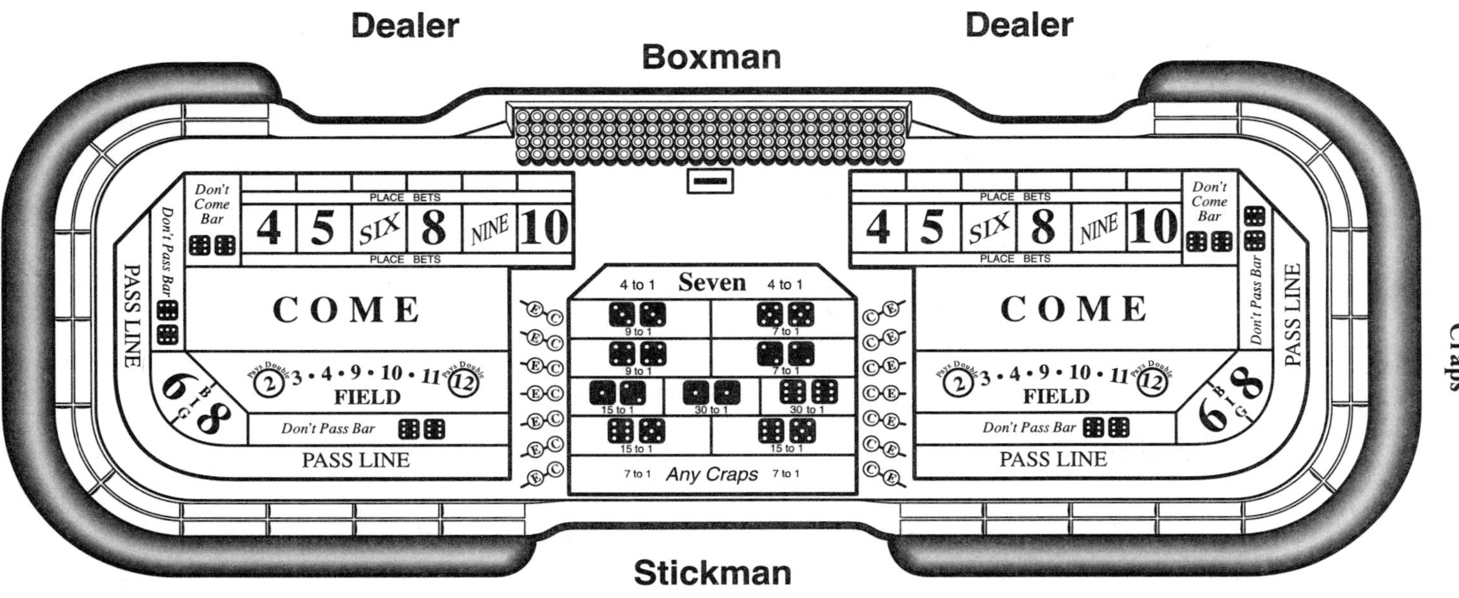

Typical craps table layout

It's important that you remember these numbers, because 1.You want to make sure that you're paid the right amount when you do win and 2. You want to make sure that when you make your odds bets you make them in amounts that are paid off evenly.

As an example, if your point is 5 and you have $5 on the pass line, you wouldn't want to bet $5 behind the line because at 3-to-2 odds the casino would have to pay you $7.50 and they don't deal in change. When making the odds bet on the 5 or 9 you should always bet in even amounts and in the situation just mentioned most casinos would allow you to add an extra $1 so you would have $6 out and they could pay you $9, if you won. The only other situation where this occurs is on the 6 and 8 where the payoff is 6-to-5. So, in that instance you want to make your bets in multiples of $5. Also, if your pass line bet is $15, most casinos will allow you to bet $25 behind the line because, if you win, it's quicker for them to pay you $30, rather than dealing in $1 chips to give you $18 for $15. When situations like this exist, it's good to take advantage of them and bet the full amount you're allowed because that helps to lower the casino edge even more.

We've spent all this time talking about pass line betting, so what about don't pass betting? Well, everything applied to pass line betting works pretty much just the opposite for don't pass betting. If you put $10 on don't pass you would win on the come out roll if the shooter rolled a 2 or 3, you would tie if the shooter rolled a 12, and you would lose if the shooter rolled a 7 or 11. If any other number comes up then that becomes the shooter's point number and if he rolls a 7 before he rolls that same point number, you will win. If he rolls his point number before he rolls a 7, you will lose.

Don't pass bettors are also allowed to make free odds bets to back up their original bets, however, because the odds are in their favor they must lay odds rather than take odds. This means that if the point is 4 or 10, the don't pass bettor must lay 2-to-1, or bet $10 to win $5; on 5 or 9 he must lay 3-to-2, or bet $6 to win $4; and on 6 or 8 he must lay 6-to-5, or bet $6 to win $5. By taking advantage of these free odds bets the casino advantage is slightly lowered on the total don't pass bets to .68% with single odds; .46% with double odds; .34% with triple odds and .12% with 10 times odds. If you want to you can remove, or reduce the amount of your free odds, bet at any time. To make a free odds bet on don't pass you should place your odds bet right next to your original bet and then put a chip on top to connect the two bets. Keep in mind that when you make a free odds bet on don't pass the casino will allow you to make your bet based on the payoff, rather than the original amount of your don't pass bet. In other words, if the casino offered double odds, the point was 4 and you had $10 on don't pass, you would be allowed to bet $40 because you would only win $20 which was double the amount of your original $10 bet. Since you have to put out more money than you'll be getting back, laying odds is not very popular at the craps table and you'll find that the vast majority of craps players would rather bet with the shooter and take the odds. Statistically speaking, it makes no difference whether you are laying or taking the odds because they both have a zero advantage for the house.

One last point about don't pass betting is that once the point is established, the casino will allow you to remove your don't pass bet if you want to - but don't do it! As noted before, on the come out roll the pass line bettor has the advantage because there are 8 rolls that can win and only 4 that can lose, but once the point is established, there are more ways the shooter can lose than win, so at that point the don't pass bettor has the advantage and it would be foolish to remove your bet.

Now, let's take a look at the area marked come and don't come. Since you already know how to bet pass and don't pass, you should easily understand come and don't come because they're the exact same bets as pass and don't pass, except for the fact that you bet them after the point has already been established.

Let's say that the shooter's point is 6 and you make a come bet by putting a $5 chip anywhere in the come box. Well, that's just like making a pass line bet, except that the shooter's next roll becomes the come-out roll for your bet. If the shooter rolls a 7 or 11, you win. If a 2,3, or 12 is rolled you lose, and if anything else comes up then that becomes your point and the shooter must roll that number again before rolling a 7 in order for you to win. In this example if the shooter rolled a 4 the dealer would move your $5 come bet up into the center of the 4 box and it would stay there until either a 4 was rolled, which would make you a winner, or a 7 was rolled which would make you a loser. The house edge on a come bet is the same 1.41% as on a pass line bet. You are allowed free odds on your come bet and you make that bet by giving your chips to the dealer and telling him you want to take the odds. The dealer will then place those chips slightly off center on top of your come bet to show that it's a free odds bet. By the way, if you win, the dealer will put your winnings back in the come bet area so be sure to pick them up off the table or else it will be considered a new come bet.

One other point to note here is that when you make a come bet your bet is always working on every roll, even a come-out roll. However, when you take the odds on your come bets they are never working on the come-out roll. That may sound a little confusing, but here's what it means. In our example the shooter's initial point was 6 and then we made a $5 come bet. The shooter then rolled a 4 which became the point for our come bet. The dealer then moved our $5 come bet to the middle of the 4 box at the top of the table. We then gave $10 to the dealer and said we wanted to take the odds on the 4. On the next roll the shooter rolls a 6 which means he made a pass by rolling his original point number. The next roll will then become the shooter's come-out roll and the odds bet on our 4 will not be working. If the shooter rolls a 7 the pass line bettors will win and we will lose our $5 come bet because he rolled a 7 before rolling a 4. The dealer will then return our $10 odds bet because it wasn't working on the come-out roll. Now, if you want to, you can request that your odds bet be working on the come-out roll by telling the dealer. Then he'll put a marker on top of your bet to show that your odds bet is in effect on the come-out roll.

Naturally, don't come betting is the same as don't pass betting, except again for the fact that the bet isn't made until after the point is established. In this case let's say the point is 5 and you make a don't come bet by placing a $5 chip in the don't come box. Well, once again, that's just like making a don't pass bet except that the shooter's next roll becomes the come-out roll for your bet. If the shooter rolls a 2 or 3, you win. If a 7 or 11 is rolled, you lose. If a 12 is rolled it's a standoff and if anything else comes up then that becomes your point and the shooter must seven-out, or roll a 7, before rolling that point number again in order for you to win. In this example if the shooter rolled a 10 the dealer would move your $5 don't come bet into the upper part of the 10 box and it would stay there until either a 7 was rolled, which would make you a winner, or a 10 was rolled which would make you a loser. The house edge on a don't come bet is the same 1.40% as on a don't pass bet and you can make a free odds bet on your don't come bet by giving your chips to the dealer and telling him you want to lay the odds. The dealer will then place those chips next to and on top of your don't come bet to show that it's a free odds bet. The final point to note here is that don't come bets, as well as the free odds bets on them, are always working - even on the come-out roll.

Now let's talk about place betting and that refers to the 6 numbers you see in the area at the top of the table: 4,5,6,8,9 and 10. Anytime during a roll you can make a bet that one of those numbers will appear before a 7 and if it does you will receive a payoff that is slightly less than the true odds. For example: the true odds are 2-to-1 that a 4 or 10 will appear before a 7. However, if you make a place bet on the 4 or 10 you will only be paid off at 9-to-5 and that works out to a casino advantage of 6.67%.

The true odds of a 5 or 9 appearing before a 7 are 3-to-2, but on a place bet you would only receive a payoff of 7-to-5 which works out to a casino edge of 4.0%. Finally, on the 6 and 8 the true odds are 6-to-5 that one of those numbers will appear before a 7, but on a place bet you would only be paid off at 7-to-6 which means the casino would have an edge of 1.52% on this bet.

As you can see, making a place bet on the 6 or 8 gives the casino its lowest edge and this means that a place bet on the 6 or 8 is one of the best bets you will find on the craps table.

When you want to make a place bet you aren't allowed to put the bet down yourself, you have to let the dealer do it for you. To do this you would just drop your chips down onto the table and tell the dealer what bet you wanted to make. For example you could put three $5 chips down and say "Place the 4,5 and 9." The dealer would then put $5 on the edge of the 4 box, $5 on the edge of the 5 box and $5 on the edge of the 9 box. You'll notice that when the dealer puts your bets on the edge of the boxes they will always be placed in an area that corresponds to where you're standing at the table and this helps the dealer to remember who placed that bet.

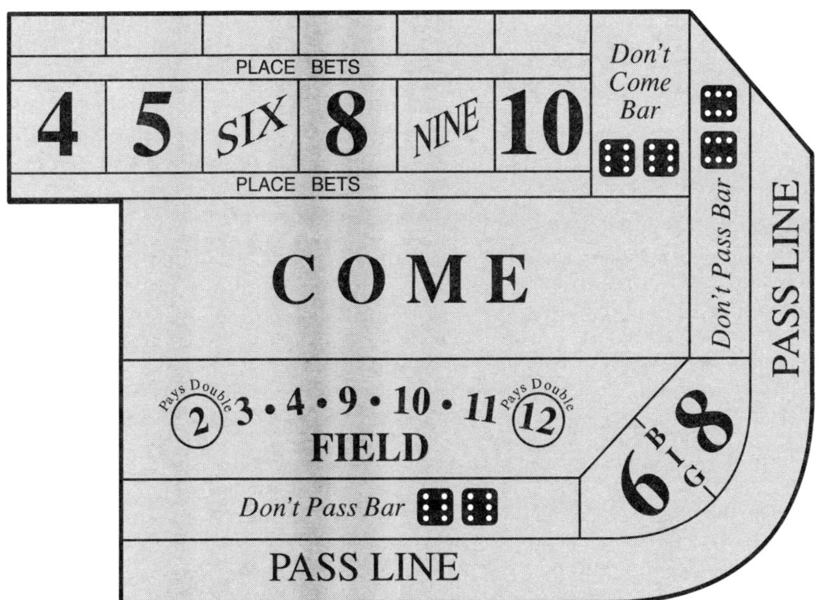

Enlargement of right side of craps layout

When making a place bet you don't have to bet more than one number and you don't have to bet the same amount on each number. You should, however, make sure that you always bet in multiples of $5 whenever you bet on the 4,5,9 or 10 and in multiples of $6 whenever you bet the 6 and 8. This will allow you to always get the full payoff on your bet. If, for example, you bet $3 on the 6 and you won you would only get back even-money, or $3, rather than the $3.50 which your bet should have paid and this results in an even bigger advantage for the casino. Another thing about place bets is that, unlike pass line bets, you can remove your place bets at any time and you do that by telling the dealer you want your bet down and he will take your chips off the table and return them to you. You could also tell the dealer that you didn't want your bet to be working on any particular roll or rolls and you do this by saying for example "off on the 5." The dealer would then put a little button on top of your bet that said "off" and he would remove it when you told him you wanted that number working again.

When we spoke about come bets before I mentioned that come bets are always working on every roll, but that's not the case with place bets because place bets are never working on the come-out roll. If you wanted to, however, you could ask for your place bet to be working on the come out roll by telling the dealer you wanted it working and he would place a button on top of your bet that said "on" to show that your bet was working on the come-out roll.

One last point about place bets is that when you win the dealer will want to know what you want to do for your next bet and you have three choices: if you want to make the same bet just say "same bet" and the dealer will give you your winning chips and leave your original place bet on the table. If you don't want to bet again, just say "take it down" and the dealer will return your place bet along with your winnings. And if you want to double your bet just say "press it" and the dealer will add your winning chips to your other place bet and return any extra chips to you. For example, if you won a $10 place bet on the 5 the dealer would have to give you back $14 in winning chips. If you said "press it" the dealer would add $10 to your place bet and return the remaining $4 in chips to you.

Besides, place betting there is also another way to bet that one of the point numbers will show up before a 7 does and that's called buying a number. A buy bet is basically the same as a place bet except you have to pay a commission of 5% of the amount of your bet and then if you win, the casino will pay you at the true odds. When making a buy bet you should always remember to bet at least $20 because 5% of $20 is $1 and that's the minimum amount the casino will charge you. The reason for the $1 minimum is because that's the smallest denomination chip they have at the craps table and they won't make change for anything under $1. The casino edge on any buy bet for $20 works out to 4.76% so let's take a look at a chart that shows the difference between buying and placing the point numbers.

Point Number	Casino Edge Buy Bet	Casino Edge Place Bet
4 or 10	4.76%	6.67%
5 or 9	4.76%	4.00%
6 or 8	4.76%	1.52%

As you can see the only numbers that you would want to buy rather than place are the 4 and 10 because the 4.76% edge on a buy bet is lower than the 6.67% edge on a place bet. For 5 and 9 the 4.76% edge on a buy bet is slightly worse than the 4.00% edge on a place bet and for the 6 and 8 the 4.76% is a hefty three times higher than the 1.52% edge on the place bet.

To buy the 4 or 10 you would just put your chips down on the layout and tell the dealer what bet you wanted to make. For example, if you put down $21 and said "buy the 10." The dealer will then keep the $1 chip for the house and put your $20 in the same area as the place bets but he'll put a button on top that says "buy" to let him know that you bought the number rather than placed it. Buy bets, just like place bets, can be removed at any time and are always off on the come-out roll. Also, if you do remove your buy bet you will get your 5% commission back.

Besides buy bets where you're betting with the shooter and hoping that a point number will appear before a 7 does, there are also lay bets where you're doing just the opposite - you're betting against the shooter and hoping that a 7 will appear before a point number does.

Lay bets are also paid at the true odds and you have to pay a 5% a commission of the amount you will win rather than the amount you're betting. Once again, when making a lay bet you should always remember to make them based on a minimum payoff of $20 because 5% of $20 is $1 and that's the minimum amount the casino will charge you.

Lay Number	Payoff	Casino Edge
4 or 10	$40 for $20	2.44%
5 or 9	$30 for $20	3.23%
6 or 8	$24 for $20	4.00%

For 4 and 10 you'll have to lay $40 to win $20 and the casino edge is 2.44%; for the 5 and 9 you'll have to lay $30 to win $20 and the casino edge is 3.23%; and for the 6 and 8 you'll have to lay $24 to win $20. The casino edge on that bet is 4.00%.

To make a lay bet you would just put your chips down on the layout and tell the dealer what you wanted to bet. For example, if you put down $41 and said "lay the 10." The dealer would then keep the $1 chip for the house and put your $40 in the same area as the don't come bets but he'll put a button on top that says "buy" to let him know that it's a lay bet. Lay bets, unlike buy bets, are always working on come-out rolls. Lay bets are, however, similar to buy bets in that they can be removed at any time and if you do remove your lay bet you will also receive your 5% commission back.

There are only a few other bets left located on the ends of the table to discuss and two of them are the big 6 and the big 8 which are both very bad bets. To bet the big 6 you place a chip in the big 6 box and then if the shooter rolls a 6 before rolling a 7 you win even money, or $1 for every $1 you bet. To bet the big 8 the same rules would apply: you put your bet in the box and then hope that the shooter rolls an 8 before rolling a 7 so you could win even money on your bet. The big 6 and big 8 can both be bet at any time and both are always working, even on the come-out roll. The casino edge on both the big 6 and the big 8 is 9.1%, which is the biggest edge we've seen so far. But, if you think back about some of the other bets we discussed doesn't this bet sound familiar? It should. This bet is the exact same as a place bet on the 6 or 8, but instead of getting paid off at 7-to-6 we're only getting paid off at even-money! Why would you want to bet the big 6 or big 8 at a house edge of more than 9% instead of making a place bet on the 6 or 8 at a house edge of only 1.5%? The answer is you wouldn't - so don't ever make this bet because it's a sucker bet that's only for people who don't know what they're doing.

The last bet we have to discuss on the player's side of the table is the field bet which is a one-roll bet that will pay even money if a 3,4,9,10 or 11 is rolled and 2-to-1 if a 2 or 12 is rolled. To make a field bet you would just place your chip anywhere in the field box and at first glance it doesn't seem like a bad bet. After all, there are 7 numbers you can win on and only 4 numbers you can lose on! The only problem is that there are 20 ways to roll the 4 losing numbers and only 16 ways to roll the 7 winning numbers and even after factoring in the double payoff for the 2 and 12 the casino winds up with a hefty 5.6% advantage. In some casinos they pay 3-to-1 on the 2 (or the 12) which cuts the casino edge in half to a more manageable 2.8%, but as you've seen there are still much better bets you can make. By the way, if you win on a field bet the dealer will put your winning chips right next to your bet so it's your responsibility to pick them up, or else they'll be considered a new bet!

Now, let's take a look at some of the long-shots, or proposition bets in the center of the table. When you look at these bets one of the first things you'll notice is that, unlike the bets on the other side of the table, the winning payoffs are clearly labeled. The reason they do that is so you can see those big payoffs and want to bet them, but as you'll see, although the payoffs are high, so are the casino advantages.

All of the proposition bets are controlled by the stickman and he is the person who must make those bets for you. So, if you wanted to make a $1 bet on "any craps" you would throw a $1 chip to the center of the table and say "$1 any craps" and the stickman would place that bet in the proper area for you. Then if you won, the stickman would tell the dealer at your end of the table to pay you. You should also be aware that they will only pay you your winnings and keep your original bet in place. If you don't want to make the same bet again, you should tell the stickman that you want your bet down and it will be returned to you.

There are only four proposition bets that are not one-roll bets and they are known as the "hardways." They are the hard 4, hard 6, hard 8 and hard 10. To roll a number the hardway means that the number must be rolled as doubles. For example 3 and 3 is a hard 6, but a roll of 4-2, or 5-1 are both called an easy 6, because they are easier to roll than double 3's.

To win a bet on hard 10 the shooter has to roll two 5's before rolling a 7 or an easy 10 such as 6-4 or 4-6. To win a bet on hard 4 the shooter has to roll two 2's before rolling a 7 or an easy 4 such as 3-1 or 1-3. The true odds of rolling a hard 4 or hard 10 are 8-to-1, but the casino will only pay you 7-to-1 which works out to a casino advantage of 11.1% on both of these bets.

To win a bet on hard 6 the shooter must roll two 3's before rolling a 7 or an easy 6 such as 5-1, 1-5; or 4-2, 2-4. To win a bet on hard 8 the shooter must roll two 4's before rolling a 7 or an easy 8 such as 6-2, 2-6 or 5-3, 3-5. The true odds of rolling a hard 6 or hard 8 are 10-to-1, but the casino will only pay you 9-to-1 which works out to a casino advantage of 9.1% on both of these bets.

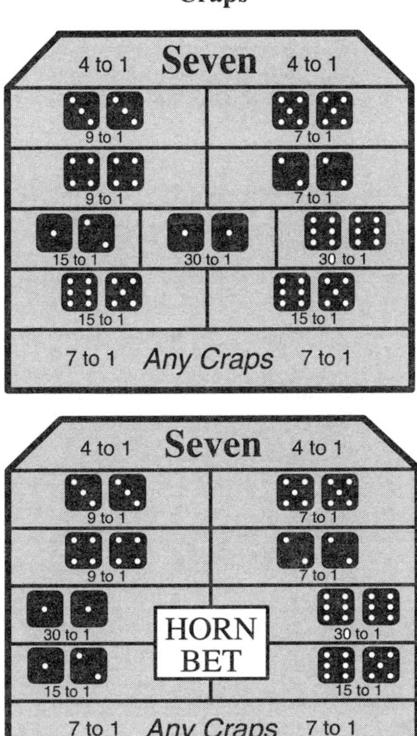

Two different types of proposition bets layouts

As noted before, all of the other proposition bets are one-roll bets which means that the next roll of the dice will decide whether you win or lose. As you'll see, the house edge on all of these bets is very high and they should all be avoided.

For the any craps bet you will win if a 2,3,or 12 is thrown on the next roll and lose if any other number comes up. The true odds are 8-to-1 but the casino will only pay you at 7-to-1 which gives them an edge of 11.1% on this bet and you'll notice that the stickman can put your bet either in the any craps box or, more likely, he'll put it on the circled marked "C" which stands for craps. The reason your bet will be placed in the "C" circle is that it's put in the circle that corresponds to where you're standing at the table and it makes it easier for the stickman to know who that bet belongs to.

For a craps 2 bet you win if the next roll is a 2 and lose if any other number shows up. The true odds are 35-to-1 but the casino will only pay you 30-to-1 which means that the edge on this bet is 13.9% In some casinos the odds for this bet will be shown as 30-for-1 which is actually the same as 29-to-1 and this results in an even bigger edge of 16.7% for the casino.

A craps 12 bet works the same as a craps 2 bet, except that now you will only win if a 12 is thrown. Again, the true odds are 35-to-1 but you will only be paid at 30-to-1 which means the casino edge on this bet is the same 13.9% as in the last craps 2 bet. Also if the bet is shown on the layout as 30-for-1 the casino edge is raised to 16.7%.

For a craps 3 bet you will only win if the next throw is a 3. The true odds are 17-to-1, but the casino will only pay you 15-to-1 which results in a casino advantage of 11.1% Once again, in some casinos the payoff will be shown as 15-for-1 which is the same as 14-to-1 and the house edge in that casino is an even higher 16.7%.

The 11 bet is similar to the craps 3 bet, except that now the only number you can win on is 11. The true odds of rolling an 11 are 17-to-1, but the casino will only pay you 15-to-1 which gives them an 11.1% advantage. Additionally, if the payoff is shown on the layout as 15-for-1 rather than 15-to-1 the casino edge will be even higher at 16.7%. By the way, because 11 sounds so much like 7 you will always hear 11 referred to at the table as "yo" or "yo-leven" to eliminate any confusion as to what number you are referring to. So, if you wanted to bet $5 on 11 you would throw a $5 chip to the stickman and say "$5 yo" and then he will either place it in the 11 box or place it on top of the "E" circle that corresponds to where you're standing at the table.

With a horn bet you are betting on the 2,3,11 and 12 all at once. A horn bet has to be made in multiples of $4 because you're making 4 bets at one time and you'll win if any one of those 4 numbers shows up on the next roll. You'll be paid off at the odds for the number that came in and you'll lose the rest of your chips. For example, if you make an $8 horn bet, this is the same as betting $2 on the 2, $2 on the 3, $2 on the 11 and $2 on the 12. If the number 2 came in you would get paid off at 30-to-1 so you would get back $60 in winnings and the casino would keep the $6 that you lost for the three $2 bets on the 3,11 and 12. The only advantage of a horn bet is that it allows you to make 4 bad bets at once rather than one at a time.

The last proposition bet we have to look at is also the worst bet on the craps table and it's the any 7 bet. With this bet you win if a 7 is rolled and lose if any other number comes up. The true odds are 5-to-1, but the casino will only pay you at 4-to-1 which gives them an edge of 16.7%

So there you have it! We've gone over all the possible bets you can make and now it's time to tell you how to win at the game of craps. Unfortunately, as you've seen, craps is a negative expectation game which means that every bet you make has a built-in advantage for the house. Actually, there is one bet that the casino has no advantage on and do you remember the name of that one? That's right it's the free odds bet and it's great that the casino has no advantage on that bet but the only way you're allowed to make that bet is to first make a negative expectation bet on pass/don't pass or come/don't come, so in essence, there are no bets you can make where you have an advantage over the house and in the long run the game of craps is unbeatable.

So, if that's the case then how do you win? Well, in reality there is only one way to win in craps and that way is to get lucky! Of course, this is easier said than done, but you will find it much easier to come out a winner if you only stick to the bets that offer the casino its lowest edge and those are the only bets you should ever make.

If you want to bet with the shooter I suggest you make a pass line bet, back it up with the free odds and then make a maximum of two come bets that are also both backed up with free odds. For example if double odds are allowed, you could start with a $5 pass line bet and say a 4 is rolled. You would then put $10 behind the line on your 4 and make a $5 come bet. If the shooter then rolled an 8 you would take $10 in odds on your come bet on the 8 and make another $5 come bet. If the shooter then rolled a 5 you would take $10 in odds on your come bet on the 5 and then stop betting. The idea here is that you always want to have a maximum of three numbers working and once you do, you shouldn't make anymore bets until one of your come numbers hits, in which case you would make another come bet, or if your pass line bet wins and then you would follow that up with another pass line bet. The important thing to remember is not to make more than two come bets because you don't want to have too much out on the table if the shooter rolls a 7. By using this betting system you'll only be giving the casino an edge of around .60% on all of your bets and with just a little bit of luck you can easily walk away a winner.

If you wanted to be a little more aggressive with this betting system there are some modifications you could make such as making a maximum of three come bets rather than two, or you could add place bets on the 6 and 8. Remember that a place bet on either the 6 or 8 only gives the casino a 1.52% advantage and that makes them both the next best bets after pass/don't pass and come/don't come. To add the place bets you would start off the same as before, but after you've made your second come bet you would look at the 6 and 8 and if they weren't covered you would then make a $6 place bet on whichever one was open or on both. By adding the place bets on the 6 and 8 you would always have at least three numbers in action and you could have as many as five covered at one time.

One final option with this system is to gradually increase the amount of your pass line and come bets by 50%, or by doubling them, and then backing them up with full odds, but I would only suggest you do this if you've been winning for a while because it could get very expensive if the table was cold and no one was rolling many numbers. Of course, if the table got real cold you could always change your strategy by betting against the shooter and the strategy for that is basically just the opposite of the one I just told you about.

To bet against the shooter you would start with a $5 don't pass bet which you would back up with single free odds and then bet a maximum of two don't come bets that are both backed up with single odds. The reason you don't want to back up your bets with double odds is because when you're betting against the shooter you have to lay the odds which means you're putting up more money than you'll be getting back and, once again, it could get very expensive if a shooter got on a hot roll and made quite a few passes.

For an example of this system let's say you start with a $5 don't pass bet and a 4 is rolled. You would then lay the odds by putting $10 next to your $5 don't pass bet and then make a $5 don't come bet. If the shooter then rolled an 8 you would lay $6 in odds on your don't come bet on the 8 and make another $5 don't come bet. If the shooter then rolled a 5 you would lay $9 in odds on your come bet on the 5 and then stop betting. The idea here is that you always want to have a maximum of three numbers working and once you do that, you shouldn't make anymore bets until, hopefully, the shooter sevens out and all of your bets win. If that does happen, then you would start all over again with a new don't pass bet. Once again, the important thing to remember is not to make more than two don't come bets because you don't want to have too much out on the table if the shooter gets hot and starts to roll a lot of numbers. With this system you'll always have a maximum of three numbers in action and you'll only be giving the casino an edge of about .80% on all of your bets. Some options to bet more aggressively with this system are to increase your free odds bets to double odds rather than single odds and also to make three don't come bets, rather than stopping at two. The choice is up to you but remember that because you must lay the odds and put out more money than you'll be getting back you could lose a substantial amount rather quickly if the roller got hot and made a lot of point numbers.

Now, one last point I want to make about betting craps is that the bankroll you'll need is going to be much bigger than the bankroll you'll need for playing any other casino game. If you're betting with the shooter you'll have one $5 pass line bet with double odds and two come bets with double odds which means that you could have as much as $45 on the table that could be wiped out with the roll of a 7. If you're betting against the shooter you'll have $5 on don't pass with single odds and two don't come bets with single odds which means you could have as much as $44 on the table that could be wiped out if the shooter got on a "hot" roll and made a lot of numbers. As I said before, you need to have an adequate bankroll to be able to ride out the losing streaks that will eventually occur and you need to be able to hold on until things turn around and you start to win.

So how much of a bankroll is enough? Well, I would say about 7 times the maximum amount of money you'll have out on the table is adequate and 10 times would be even better. In both of our examples then you should have a bankroll of at least $300. If you don't have that much money to put out on the table then you might want to consider having less money out on the table by making only one come or don't come bet rather than two or maybe even just limiting your bets to pass and don't pass along with the free odds.

Just remember that it doesn't matter whether you want to bet with the shooter or against the shooter - both of these systems will give you the best chance of winning because they allow the casino only the slightest edge and with a little bit of luck you can easily come out a winner. Good luck!

A Few Last Words

by Steve Bourie

When I sit down to put this book together each year I try to make sure that everything in here will help to make you a better and more knowledgeable gambler when you go to a casino.

I try to include stories that will help you understand how casinos operate, how to choose the best casino games and also how to play those games in the best way possible.

My philosophy with this book is that gambling in a casino is a fun activity and, according to research studies, for about 98% of the people who visit casinos this statement is true. The vast majority of people who gamble in casinos are recreational players who enjoy the fun and excitement of gambling. They know that they won't always win and they also realize that over the long term they will most likely have more losing sessions than winning ones. They also understand that any losses they incur will be the price they pay for their fun and they only gamble with money they can afford to lose. In other words, they realize that casino gambling is a form of entertainment, just like going to a movie or an amusement park, and they are willing to pay a price for that entertainment. Unfortunately, there are also some people who go to casinos and become problem gamblers.

According to Gamblers Anonymous you may be a problem gambler if you answer yes to at least seven of the following 20 questions:

1. Do you lose time from work due to gambling?
2. Does gambling make your home life unhappy?
3. Does gambling affect your reputation?
4. Do you ever feel remorse after gambling?
5. Do you ever gamble to get money with which to pay debts or to otherwise solve financial difficulties?
6. Does gambling cause a decrease in your ambition or efficiency?
7. After losing, do you feel you must return as soon as possible and win back your losses?
8. After a win, do you have a strong urge to return and win more?
9. Do you often gamble until your last dollar is gone?
10. Do you ever borrow to finance your gambling?
11. Do you ever sell anything to finance your gambling?
12. Are you reluctant to use your "gambling money" for other expenses?
13. Does gambling make you careless about the welfare of your family?
14. Do you ever gamble longer than you planned?

15. Do you ever gamble to escape worry or trouble?
16. Do you ever commit, or consider committing, an illegal act to finance your gambling?
17. Does gambling cause you to have difficulty sleeping?
18. Do arguments, disappointments, or frustrations create within you an urge to gamble?
19. Do you have an urge to celebrate good fortune by a few hours of gambling?
20. Do you ever consider self-destruction as a result of your gambling?

If you believe you might have a gambling problem you should be aware that help is available from The National Council on Problem Gambling, Inc. It is the foremost advocacy organization in the country for problem gamblers and is headquartered in Washington, D.C. It was formed in 1972 as a non-profit agency to promote public education and awareness about gambling problems and operates a 24-hour nationwide help line at (800) 522-4700, plus a website at www.ncpgambling.org. Anyone contacting that organization will be provided with the appropriate referral resources for help with their gambling problem.

Another good source for anyone seeking help with a gambling problem is Gambler's Anonymous. They have chapters in many cities throughout the U.S. as well as in most major cities throughout the world. You can see a list of all those cities on their website at www.gamblersanonymous.org or contact them by telephone at (213) 386-8789.

A third program, Gam-Anon, specializes in helping the spouse, family and close friends of compulsive gamblers rather than the gamblers themselves.If you are adversely affected by a loved one who is a compulsive gambler, then Gam-Anon is an organization that may benefit you. They have a website at www.gam-anon.org that lists the cities which host meetings. They can also be contacted by telephone at (718) 352-1671.

I sincerely hope that none of you reading this book will ever have a need to contact any of these worthwhile organizations, but it was an issue that I felt should be addressed.

ALABAMA

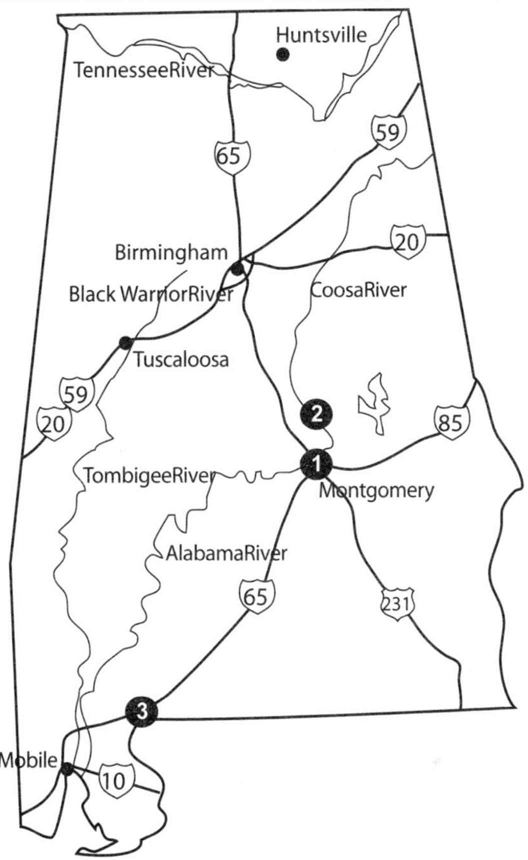

Alabama has three Indian casinos that offer Class II video gaming machines.

Class II video gaming devices look like slot machines, but are actually bingo games and the spinning reels are for "entertainment purposes only." No public information is available concerning the payback percentages on any gaming machines in Alabama.

The minimum gambling age is 21 and all of the casinos are open 24 hours. For Alabama tourism information call (800) 252-2262, or go to: www.alabama.travel.

Wind Creek Casino & Hotel - Montgomery
1801 Eddie Tullis Drive
Montgomery, Alabama 36117
(334) 273-9003
Website: www.windcreekmontgomery.com
Map: **#1**

Toll Free: (888) 772-9946
Rooms: 115 Price Range: $99-$189
Suites: 8 Price Range: $189- $219
Casino Size: 46,000 Square feet
Restaurants: 3
Overnight RV Parking: Free
Senior discount: Various on Mon Noon-4pm if 50+.
Special Features: B.B. King's blues club.

Wind Creek Casino & Hotel - Atmore
303 Poarch Road
Atmore, Alabama 36502
(251) 446-4200
Website: www.windcreekatmore.com
Map: **#3** (55 miles NE. of Mobile)

Room Reservations: (866) 946-3360
Rooms: 236 Price Range: $109-$239
Casino Size: 80,000 Square Feet
Restaurants: 4 (1 open 24 hours) Valet: Free
Buffets: B-$16.95 (Sat/Sun)
L-$11.95/$16.95 (Sat/Sun)
D-$16.95/ $25.95 (Fri/Sat)/$11.95 (Sun)
Overnight RV Parking: Free
Senior Discount: Free breakfast after earning 10 players club points on Mon if 55+

Wind Creek Casino & Hotel - Wetumpka
100 River Oaks Drive
Wetumpka, Alabama 36092-3084
(334) 514-0469
Website: www.windcreekwetumpka.com
Map: **#2** (20 miles N. of Montgomery)

Toll Free: (888) 772-9946
Rooms: 270 Price Range: $109-$158
Suites: 13 Price Range: $179-$289
Casino Size: 39,000 Square Feet
Restaurants: 2
Buffets: B-$9.95 (Thu)/$14.95 (Sat/Sun)
L-$11.95/$16.95 (Sat/Sun)
D-$16.95/$26.95 (Fri-Sun)
Overnight RV Parking: Free
Senior Discount: Free breakfast after earning 10 players club points on Mon if 55+

ARIZONA

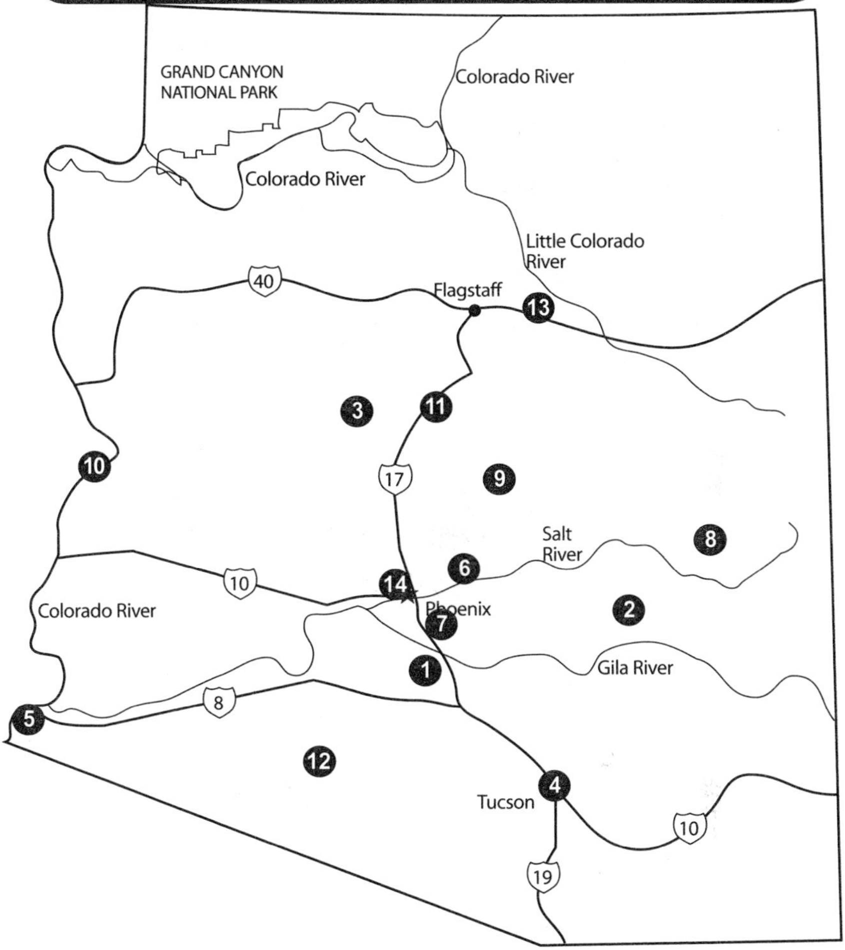

All Arizona casinos are located on Indian reservations and all of them offer slot machines, video poker and video keno. Optional games include: blackjack (BJ), Spanish 21 (S21), let it ride (LIR), casino war (CW), pai gow poker (PGP), three card poker (TCP), Mississippi stud (MS), poker (P), live keno (K), and bingo (BG).

Arizona tribes aren't required to release information on their slot machine percentage paybacks, however, according to the Arizona Department of Gaming, the terms of the compact require each tribes' machines to return the following minimum and maximum paybacks: video poker and video blackjack - 83% to 100%, slot machines - 80% to 100%, keno - 75% to 100%. Each tribe is free to set its machines to pay back anywhere within those limits.

The minimum gambling age is 21 and all casinos are open 24 hours. For more information on visiting Arizona call the state's Office of Tourism at (866) 275-5816 or visit their website at: www.azot.com

Apache Gold Casino Resort
Highway 70 Mile Post 258
San Carlos, Arizona 85501
(928) 475-7800
Map: **#2** (90 miles E. of Phoenix)
Website: www.apache-gold-casino.com

Toll-Free Number: (800) 272-2438
Rooms: 146 Price Range: $69-$119
Suites: 10 Price Range: $139-$161
Restaurants: 2 Liquor: Yes
Buffets: L- $10.99/$14.99 (Fri-Sun)
D- $14.99/$19.99 (Fri)
Casino Size: 10,000 Square Feet
Other Games: BJ (3pm), BG (Wed-Sun),
P (Fri/Sat 3pm)
Overnight RV Parking: Yes
Senior Discount: 15% food and room discount if 55+.
Special Features: Hotel is off-property and is Best Western. 18-hole golf course. Convenience store. 60-space RV Park ($30 per night) w/full hookups and dump station.

Apache Sky Casino
777 Apache Sky Boulevard
Winkelman, Arizona 85192
(800) 272-2438
Website: www.apacheskycasino.com
Map: **#15** (70 miles N. of Tucson)

Restaurants: 1
Casino Hours: 24 Hours Daily
Casino Size: 15,000 Square Feet
Games Offered: Slots, Video Poker, Blackjack
Overnight RV Parking: Yes
Special Features: Affiliated with Apache Gold casino.

Blue Water Casino
11300 Resort Drive
Parker, Arizona 85344
(928) 669-7000
Website: www.bluewaterfun.com
Map: **#10** (160 miles W. of Phoenix)

Toll-Free Number: (888) 243-3360
Rooms: 200 Price Range: $89-$135
Suites: 25 Price Range: $134-$199
Restaurants: 4 Liquor: Yes
Buffet: L-$12.95
D-$12.95/$14.95 (Fri/Sat)
Other Games: BJ, TCP, P, BG
Casino Size: 30,000 Square Feet
Overnight RV Parking: Free (only 1 night)
RV Dump: No
Special Features: 100-slip marina with wakeboard park.

Bucky's Casino & Resort
530 E. Merritt
Prescott, Arizona 86301
(928) 776-5695
Website: www.buckyscasino.com
Map: **#3** (91 miles S.W. of Flagstaff)

Toll-Free Number: (800) 756-8744
Room Reservations: (800) 967-4637
Rooms: 81 Price Range: $129-$189
Suites: 80 Price Range: $159-$229
Restaurants: 3 Liquor: Yes
Other Games: BJ, P
Casino Size: 24,000 Square Feet
Overnight RV Parking: No
Special Features: Located in Prescott Resort Hotel. Free on-site shuttle service.

Casino Arizona 101 & McKellips
524 N. 92nd Street
Scottsdale, Arizona 85256
(480) 850-7777
Website: www.casinoarizona.com
Map: **#6** (15 miles N.E. of Phoenix)

Toll-Free Number: (877) 724-4687
Restaurants: 5 Liquor: Yes
Buffets: B-$19.50(Sun) L-$11.50
D-$16.50 (Sun-Tue)/
$23.50(Wed/Thu)/$21.50(Fri/Sat)
Casino Size: 40,000 Square Feet
Other Games: BJ, LIR, TCP, K, PGP, CW, BG
Overnight RV Parking: Check in with Security
Special Features: 500-seat showroom.

Casino Del Sol
5655 W. Valencia
Tucson, Arizona 85757
(520) 883-1700
Website: www.casinodelsol.com
Map: **#4**

Toll-Free Number: (800) 344-9435
Rooms: 200 Price Range: $116-$209
Suites: 15 Price Range: $299-$339
Restaurants: 5 Liquor: Yes
Buffets: B-$12.00/$28.00 (Sat/Sun)
L-$15.00 (Tue-Fri)
D-$19.00 (Mon-Wed)/$30.00 (Thu)/
$25.00 (Fri-Sat)/$28.00 (Sun)
Casino Size: 22,500 Square Feet
Other Games: BJ, P, BG, TCP, S21, PGP
Overnight RV Parking: Free/RV Dump: No
Special Features: 4,400-seat amphitheater.

Casino of the Sun
7406 S. Camino De Oeste
Tucson, Arizona 85757
(520) 883-1700
Website: www.solcasinos.com
Map: **#4**

Toll-Free Number: (800) 344-9435
Restaurants: 6 Liquor: Yes
Other Games: BJ, UTH, S21, TCP,
PGP, BG, P
Overnight RV Parking: Free/RV Dump: No
Special Features: Smoke shop. Gift shop.

Cliff Castle Casino Hotel
555 Middle Verde Road
Camp Verde, Arizona 86322
(928) 567-7999
Website: www.cliffcastlecasinohotel.com
Map: **#11** (50 miles S. of Flagstaff)

Toll-Free Number: (800) 381-7568
Room Reservation Number: (800) 524-6343
Rooms: 82 Price Range: $69-$89
Suites: 2 Price Range: $79-$109
Restaurants: 7 Liquor: Yes
Buffets: B- $8.00 L- $12.00/$14.00 (Sun)
D- $14.00/$16.99 (Sat)
Casino Size: 14,000 Square Feet
Other Games: BJ, P
Overnight RV Parking: Free/RV Dump: No
Special Features: Casino is in Cliff Castle Lodge. Bowling alley. Kids Quest childcare facility.

Cocopah Resort
15136 S. Avenue B
Somerton, Arizona 85350
(928) 726-8066
Map: **#5** (13 miles S.W. of Yuma)
Website: www.cocopahresort.com

Toll-Free Number: (800) 237-5687
Rooms: 101 Price Range: $77-$107
Suites: 7 Price Range: $127-187
Restaurants: 2 Liquor: Yes
Buffets: B- $8.99 D- $20.99 (Fri/Sat)
Other Games: BJ, BG
Overnight RV Parking: No
Special Features: 18-hole golf course.

Desert Diamond Casino - Sahuarita
1100 West Pima Mine Road
Sahuarita, Arizona 85629
(520) 294-7777
Website: www.desertdiamondcasino.com
Map: **#4**

Toll-Free Number: (866) 332-9467
Restaurants: 3 Liquor: Yes
Buffets: L- $10.99/$16.99 (Sun)
D- $14.99/$21.99 (Fri)
Casino Size: 15,000 Square Feet
Other Games: BJ, S21, K
Overnight RV Parking: Free/RV Dump: No
Special Features: 2,500-seat event center.

Desert Diamond Casino - Tucson
7350 S. Nogales Highway
Tucson, Arizona 85706
(520) 294-7777
Website: www.ddcaz.com
Map: **#4**

Toll-Free Number: (866) 332-9467
Rooms: 140 Rates: $86-$196
Suites: 8 Rates: $266-$350
Restaurants: 3 Liquor: Yes
Buffets: B- $7.99/$14.99 (Sat/Sun)
L- $10.99 (Tue)/$14.99 (Sat/Sun)
D- $14.99 (Wed-Fri/Sun)/$21.99 (Sat)
Casino Size: 15,000 Square Feet
Other Games: BJ, P, TCP, PGP, K, BG, S21
Overnight RV Parking: Free/RV Dump: No
Special Features: Buffet closed Mon-Wed. No bingo Tuesday

Desert Diamond West Valley
91st Ave and Northern Ave
Glendale, Arizona 85305
(520) 294-7777
Website: www.ddcaz.com
Map: **#14** (Suburb of Phoenix)

Restaurants: Food Court Liquor: No
Casino Size: 40,000 Square Feet
Special Features: Free self-serve soft drinks. This casino only offers Class II gaming machines which look like slot machines, but are actually games of bingo and the spinning video reels are for "entertainment purposes only."

Desert Diamond Casino - Why
Highway 86 Mile Post 55
Ajo, Arizona 85321
(866) 332-9467
Website: www.ddcaz.com
Map: **#12** (125 miles S.W. of Phoenix)

Restaurants: 1 Snack Bar
Other Games: Only machines
Overnight RV Parking: No

Fort McDowell Casino
10424 North Fort McDowell Road
Fountain Hills, Arizona 85264
(480) 837-1424
Website: www.fortmcdowellcasino.com
Map: **#6** (25 miles N.E. of Phoenix)

Toll-Free Number: (800) 843-3678
Rooms: 238 Rates: $129-$229
Suites: 8 Rates: $269-$375
Restaurants: 6 Liquor: Yes
Buffets: L- $9.50/$14.50 (Sun)
D-$14.95 (Tue)/$24.95 (Wed)/
$31.95 (Thu)$26.95 (Fri)/
$21.95 (Sat/Sun)
Other Games: BJ, P, K, BG, TCP
Overnight RV Parking: No
Special Features: Free local shuttle. Gift shop.

Harrah's Ak Chin Casino Resort
15406 Maricopa Road
Maricopa, Arizona 85239
(480) 802-5000
Website: www.harrahsakchin.com
Map: **#1** (25 miles S. of Phoenix)

Toll-Free Number: (800) 427-7247
Rooms: 142 Price Range: $80-$215
Suites: 4 Price Range: $160-$280
Restaurants: 4 Liquor: Yes
Buffets: L-$14.99/$21.99 (Sun)
D-$19.99/$29.99 (Fri/Sat)
Casino Size: 43,000 Square Feet
Other Games: BJ, P, K, BG (Wed-Sun), MS,
TCP, LIR, PGP
Overnight RV Parking: Free/RV Dump: No
Senior Discount: Various Mon/Thu if 50+
Special Features: Free local shuttle.

Hon-Dah Resort Casino
777 Highway 260
Pinetop, Arizona 85935
(928) 369-0299
Website: www.hon-dah.com
Map: **#8** (190 miles N.E. of Phoenix)

Toll-Free Number: (800) 929-8744
Rooms: 126 Price Range: $109-$129
Suites: 2 Price Range: $179-$199
Restaurants: 1 Liquor: Yes
Buffets: B- $6.99/$24.99 (Sun)
L- $7.99/$24.99 (Sun)
D- $13.99/$24.99 (Fri)/$17.99 (Sat)
Casino Size: 20,000 Square Feet
Other Games: P
Overnight RV Parking: Must use RV park
Special Features: 258-space RV park ($31.25 per night). Convenience store. Gas station.

Lone Butte Casino
1077 South Kyrene Road
Chandler, Arizona 85226
(520) 796-7777
Website: www.wingilariver.com
Map: **#7** (10 miles S.W. of Phoenix)

Toll-Free Number: (800) 946-4452
Restaurants: 3 Liquor: Yes
Casino Size: 10,000 Square Feet
Other Games: BJ, BG, PGP, TCP
Overnight RV Parking: Free 4 day max/
RV Dump: No

Mazatzal Hotel & Casino
Highway 87 Mile Post 251
Payson, Arizona 85541
(928) 474-6044
Website: www.mazatzal-casino.com
Map: **#9** (90 miles N.E. of Phoenix)

Toll-Free Number: (800) 777-7529
Suites: 40 Prices: $112-$165
Restaurants: 2 Liquor: Yes
Buffets: L- $10.00/$18.00 (Sun)
D- $12.00 (Fri)
Casino Size: 35,000 Square Feet
Other Games: BJ, P, K, BG (Mon-Thu)
Overnight RV Parking: Free/RV Dump: No
Special Features: Offers Stay & Play packages (Sun-Thu) with local motels. Free shuttle. Table games open at 10am

Paradise Casino Arizona
450 Quechan Drive
Yuma, Arizona 85364
(760) 572-7777
Website: www.paradise-casinos.com
Map: **#5** (244 miles W. of Tucson)

Toll-Free Number: (888) 777-4946
Restaurants: 2 Liquor: Yes
Other Games: BG
Overnight RV Parking: Free/RV Dump: No
Special Features: Part of casino is located across the state border in California. Poker offered in CA casino. 10% food discount with players club card.

Spirit Mountain Casino
8555 South Highway 95
Mohave Valley, Arizona 86440
(928) 346-2000
Map: **#12** (15 miles S. of Bullhead City)

Toll-Free Number: (888) 837-4030
RV Reservations: (928) 346-1225
Restaurants: 1 Snack Bar Liquor: Yes
Casino Size: 12,000 Square Feet
Other Games: Only Machines
Overnight RV Parking: Must use RV park.
Special Features: Convenience store. Gas station.

Talking Stick Resort
9700 E. Indian Bend
Scottsdale, Arizona 85256
(480) 850-7777
Website: www.talkingstickresort.com
Map: **#6** (15 miles N.E. of Phoenix)

Toll-Free Number: (866) 877-9897
Rooms: 470 Prices: $139-$189
Suites: 27 Prices: $449-$799
Restaurants: 2 Liquor: Yes
Buffet Prices: B-$11.95/ $33.95 (Sun)
L-$13.95
D-$20.95/ $33.95 (Fri/Sat)
Other Games: BJ, P, TCP, LIR,
CW, K, PGP, BG
Overnight RV Parking: Free 3 day max/RV Dump: No

Twin Arrows Navajo Casino Resort
22181 Resort Blvd
Twin Arrows, Arizona 86004
(928) 856-7200
Website: www.twinarrows.com
Map: **#13** (40 miles E. of Flagstaff)

Toll-Free Number: (855) 946-8946
Rooms: 85 Price Range: $159-$189
Suites: 5 Price Range: $379-$489
Restaurants: 4
Buffets: L-$10.49 D-$14.69/$19.99 (Wed)
Other Games: BJ, TCP, PGP, K, P, BG, S21
Special Features: Located at Twin Arrows exit of Interstate 40. Alcohol is only served in dining areas.

Vee Quiva Hotel & Casino
15091 S. Komatke Lane
Laveen, Arizona 85339
(520) 796-7777
Website: www.wingilariver.com
Map: **#7** (10 miles S.W. of Phoenix)

Toll-Free Number: (800) 946-4452
Rooms: 82 Price Range: $79-$149
Suites: 8 Price Range: $189-$258
Restaurants: 2 Liquor: Yes
Casino Size: 15,000 Square Feet
Other Games: BJ, P, BG, TCP, PGP, MS, S21
Overnight RV Parking: Free 4 day max/
RV Dump: No

Wild Horse Pass Hotel & Casino
5040 Wild Horse Pass Blvd
Chandler, Arizona 85226
(520) 796-7727
Website: www.wingilariver.com
Map: **#7** (25 miles S.E. of Phoenix)

Toll-Free Number: (800) 946-4452
Rooms: 223 Rates: $99-$299
Suites: 19 Rates: $169-$369
Restaurants: 3 Liquor: Yes
Casino Size: 100,000 Square Feet
Other Games: BJ, PGP, LIR, TCP, P
Overnight RV Parking: Free 4 day max/ RV Dump: No
Senior Discount: Various Mon if 55+.
Special Features: 1,400-seat showroom.

Yavapai Casino
1501 E. Highway 69
Prescott, Arizona 86301
(928) 445-5767
Website: www.buckyscasino.com
Map: **#3** (91 miles S.W. of Flagstaff)

Toll-Free Number: (800) 756-8744
Casino Size: 6,000 Square Feet
Restaurants: 1 Snack Bar Liquor: Yes
Overnight RV Parking: No
Special Features: Located across the street from Bucky's Casino. Free local-area shuttle bus.

ARKANSAS

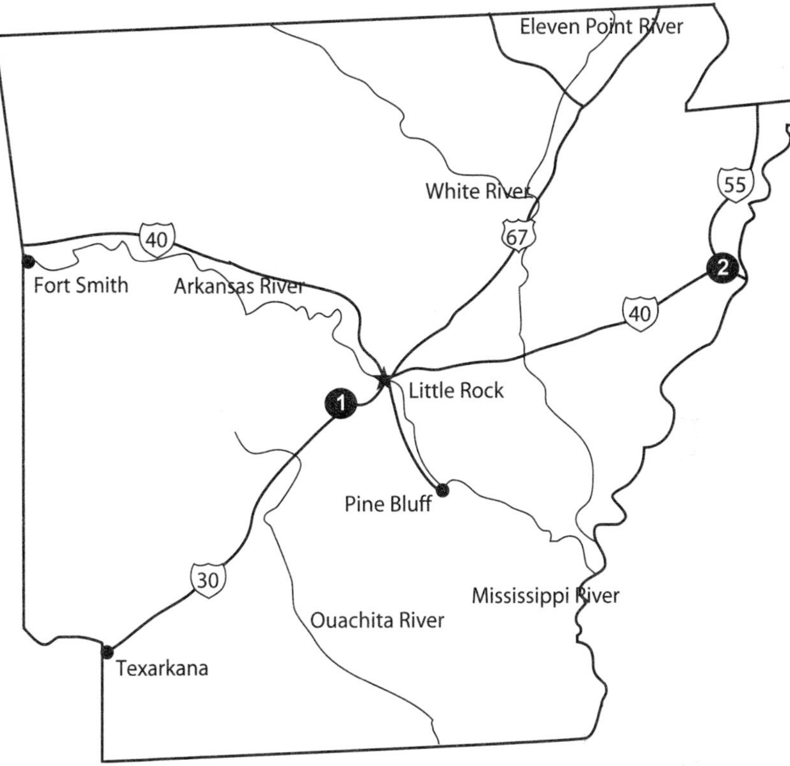

Arkansas has two pari-mutuel facilities featuring "electronic games of skill," which are defined as "games played through any electronic device or machine that affords an opportunity for the exercise of skill or judgment where the outcome is not completely controlled by chance alone."

The games offered are video poker, video blackjack, and "skill" slots where you have two opportunities to spin the reels. The "skill" factor comes into play because after seeing the results of your first spin you then have to decide whether to keep none, one, two, or all three of the symbols on each reel before you spin them again.

Table games offered include: poker (P), let it ride (LIR) and three card poker (TCP).

Gaming regulations require that all of the electronic games of skill must return a minimum of 83%.

For the one year period from July 2016 through June 2017, the average gaming machine's return at Oaklawn was 93.52% and at Southland it was 93.00%

The minimum gambling age is 21 for slots and 18 for pari-mutuel wagering. For more information on visiting Arkansas call the state's tourism office at (800) 628-8725 or visit their website at: www.arkansas.com.

Oaklawn Racing and Gaming
2705 Central Avenue
Hot Springs, Arkansas 71901
(501) 623-4411
Website: www.oaklawn.com
Map: **#1** (55 miles S.W. of Little Rock)

Toll-Free Number: (800) 625-5296
Restaurants: 3
Hours: 10am-3am /6am(Fri/Sat)
Other Games: P, TCP
Admission: Free Parking: Free
Overnight RV Parking: No
Special Features: Live throroughbred racing seasonally. Daily simulcasting of horse racing.

Southland Park Gaming & Racing
1550 North Ingram Boulevard
West Memphis, Arkansas 72301
(870) 735-3670
Website: www.southlandpark.com
Map: **#2** (130 miles E. of Little Rock)

Toll-Free Number: (800) 467-6182
Restaurants: 4
Other Games: P, LIR, TCP
Admission: Free Parking: Free
Preferred Parking: $3/Valet Parking: Free
Buffets: B- $11.99 (Sat)
L- $12.99 (Mon)/$14.99 (Tue-Thu)/ $13.99 (Fri)/$28.99(Sat)/ $16.99(Sun)
D-$16.99 (Mon)/$17.99(Tue-Thu)/ $28.99(Fri/Sat)/ $16.99 (Sun)
Overnight RV Parking: No
Special Features: Live greyhound racing seasonally. Daily simulcasting of greyhound and horse racing. Buffet discount for players club members. Electronic table games.

CALIFORNIA

All California casinos are located on Indian reservations and all are legally allowed to offer electronic gaming machines, blackjack, and other house-banked card games. The games of craps and roulette are not permitted. However, some casinos do offer modified versions of craps and roulette that are played with cards rather than dice or roulette wheels.

Most California card rooms also offer some form of player-banked blackjack, but because they are prohibited by law from playing blackjack, the game is usually played to 22 rather than 21. Additionally, players must pay a commission to the house on every hand they play. The amount will vary depending on the rules of the house but, generally, it's about two to five percent of the total amount bet. There are about 90 card rooms in California and you can see a listing of them on the Internet at: *http://www.cgcc.ca.gov.*

California's tribes aren't required to release information on their slot machine percentage paybacks and the state of California does not require any minimum returns.

Unless otherwise noted, all California casinos are open 24 hours and offer: slots, video poker, and video keno. Optional games offered include: baccarat (B), blackjack (BJ), Spanish 21 (S21), mini-baccarat (MB), poker (P), pai gow poker (PGP), Caribbean stud poker (CSP), let it ride (LIR), three card poker (TCP), four card poker (FCP) bingo (BG), sic bo (SIC) casino war (CW), Mississippi stud (MS) and off track betting (OTB).

The minimum gambling age is 21 at most casinos (at some it's 18) and 18 for bingo or pari-mutuel betting. Look in the "Special Features" listing for each casino to see which allow gambling at 18 years of age.

Although most of the casinos have toll-free numbers be aware that some of those numbers will only work for calls made within California. Also, many of the casinos are in out-of-the-way locations, so it is advisable to call ahead for directions, especially if you will be driving at night.

For more information on visiting California contact the state's department of tourism at (800) 862-2543 or www.visitcalifornia.com.

Agua Caliente Casino
32-250 Bob Hope Drive
Rancho Mirage, California 92270
(760) 321-2000
Website: www.hotwatercasino.com
Map: **#3** (115 miles E. of L. A.)

Toll-Free Number: (888) 999-1995
Gambling Age: 21
Rooms: 340 Price Range: $99-$209
Suites: 22 Price Range $239-$419
Restaurants: 4 Liquor: Yes
Buffets: B- $10.99 (Sat/Sun)
L- $14.99/$24.99 (Sun)
D-$19.99/$24.99 (Fri-Sat)
Other Games: BJ, MB, TCP, S21, LIR, P, PGP
Overnight RV Parking: Only offered at adjacent Flying J truck stop
Special Features: Associated with Spa Casino. Offers card version of craps.

Augustine Casino
84001 Avenue 54
Coachella, California 92236
(760) 391-9500
Website: www.augustinecasino.com
Map: **#8** (125 miles E. of L. A.)

Toll-Free Number: (888) 752-9294
Gambling Age: 21
Restaurants: 2 Liquor: Yes
Buffets: B- $9.95/$12.95 (Sat/Sun)
L- $10.95/$12.95 (Sat/Sun)
D- $13.95/$31.95 (Fri/Sat)
Other Games: BJ, TCP, S21
Overnight RV Parking: No

Barona Valley Ranch Resort and Casino
1932 Wildcat Canyon Road
Lakeside, California 92040
(619) 443-2300
Website: www.barona.com
Map: **#1** (15 miles N.E. of San Diego)

Toll-Free Number: (888) 722-7662
Room Reservations: (877) 287-2624
Gambling Age: 18
Rooms: 397 Price Range: $129-$189
Suites: 9 Price Range: Private Use Only
Restaurants: 8 Liquor: Yes
Buffets: B/L/D-$29.99
Other Games: BJ, B, MB, P, CSP, PGP, MS, TCP, LIR, CW, OTB, FCP, SIC
Overnight RV Parking: Free 3 day Max/ RV Dump: No
Special Features: Offers card versions of roulette and craps. Food court. Wedding chapel. 18-hole golf course. Buffet discounts for players club members.

Bear River Casino Hotel
11 Bear Paws Way
Loleta, California 95551
(707) 733-9644
Website: www.bearrivercasino.com
Map: **#38** (10 miles S. of Eureka)

Toll-Free Number: (800) 761-2327
Gambling Age: 21
Rooms: 105 Prices: $189-$249
Restaurants: 2 Liquor: Yes
Buffet: B- $14.95 (Sun)
Casino Size: 31,000 Square Feet
Other Games: BJ, S21, PGP, TCP
Overnight RV Parking: Yes. Check in with security first
Special Features: Card versions of craps and roulette.

Black Oak Casino
19400 Tuolumne Road North
Tuolumne, California 95379
(209) 928-9300
Website: www.blackoakcasino.com
Map: **#5** (100 miles S.E. of Sacramento)

Toll-Free Number: (877) 747-8777
Gambling Age: 21
Rooms: 148 Price Range: $129-$189
Suites: 16 Price Range: $309-$549
Restaurants: 6 Liquor: Yes
Buffet: B- $13.99 (Sat)/$14.99 (Sun)
L- $9.99/$14.99 (Sun)
D- $22.99 (Fri)/$21.99 (Sat)/ $12.99 (Sun)
Casino Size: 22,000 Square Feet
Other Games: BJ, TCP, LIR, PGP, S21, FCP, MB, P
Overnight RV Parking: No

Blue Lake Casino & Hotel
777 Casino Way
Blue Lake, California 95525
(707) 668-9770
Website: www.bluelakecasino.com
Map: **#34** (10 miles N. of Eureka)

Toll-Free Number: (877) 252-2946
Gambling Age: 21
Rooms: 102 Rates: $140-$165
Suites: 12 Rates: $210-$335
Restaurants: 2 Liquor: Yes
Buffet: B-$15.99 (Sun)
Other Games: BJ, S21, P, TCP, FCP, PGP
Overnight RV Parking: Free/RV Dump: No

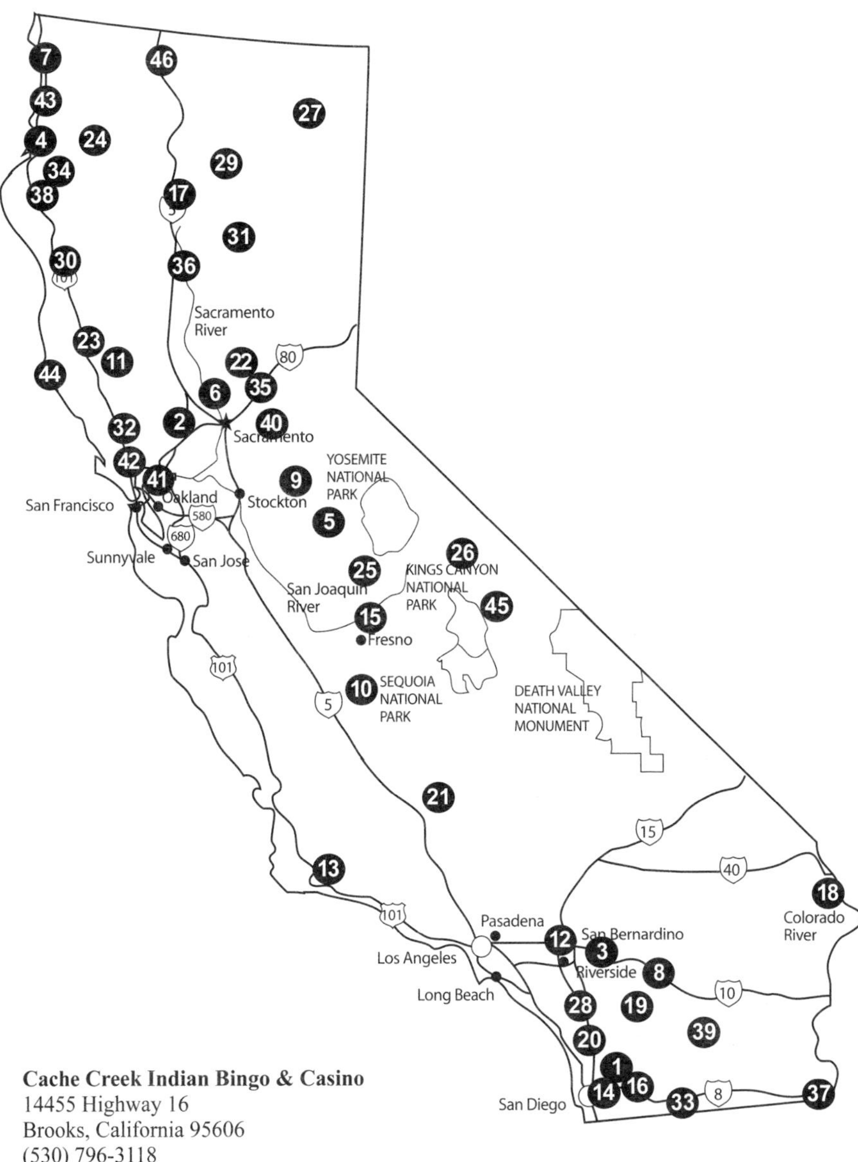

Cache Creek Indian Bingo & Casino
14455 Highway 16
Brooks, California 95606
(530) 796-3118
Website: www.cachecreek.com
Map: **#2** (35 miles N.W. of Sacramento)

Toll-Free Number: (800) 452-8181
Gambling Age: 21
Room Reservations: (888) 772-2243
Rooms: 173 Prices: $159-$309
Suites: 27 Prices: $159-$349
Restaurants: 9 Liquor: Yes
Buffets: L- $14.95 (Fri-Tue)
D- $14.95 (Sun-Tue)/$29.99 (Fri)/ $24.99 (Sat)
Casino Size: 18,000 Square Feet
Other Games: BJ, P, CSP, LIR, PGP, MS, TCP, B, MB, FCP, CW, PG
Overnight RV Parking: Free/RV Dump: No
Special Features: Offers card versions of craps and roulette. Full-service spa. No buffet Wed or Thu. $3 buffet discount for players club members.

Cahuilla Casino
52702 Highway 371
Anza, California 92539
(951) 763-1200
Website: www.cahuillacasino.com
Map: **#19** (30 miles S. of Palm Springs)

Toll-Free Number: (888) 371-2692
Gambling Age: 21
Restaurants: 2 Liquor: Yes
Overnight RV Parking: Free/RV Dump: No

Casino Pauma
777 Pauma Reservation Road
Pauma Valley, California 92061
(760) 742-2177
Website: www.casinopauma.com
Map: **#20** (35 miles N.E. of San Diego)

Toll-Free Number: (877) 687-2862
Gambling Age: 18 Restaurants: 1 Liquor: Yes
Buffet: L-$8.95/$12.95 (Sat/Sun) D-$12.95
Casino Size: 35,000 Square Feet
Other Games: BJ, P, PGP, TCP, MB
Overnight RV Parking: Free/RV Dump: No
Senior Discount: Various Thu if 55+
Special Features: Offers card versions of craps and roulette.

Cherae Heights Casino
27 Scenic Drive
Trinidad, California 95570
(707) 677-3611
Website: www.cheraeheightscasino.com
Map: **#4** (25 miles N. of Eureka)

Toll-Free Number: (800) 684-2464
Gambling Age: 21
Restaurants: 3 Liquor: Yes
Other Games: BJ, S21, PGP, TCP, BG
Overnight RV Parking: Free/RV Dump: No

Chicken Ranch Bingo
16929 Chicken Ranch Road
Jamestown, California 95327
(209) 984-3000
Website: www.chickenranchcasino.com
Map: **#5** (100 miles S.E. of Sacramento)

Toll-Free Number: (800) 752-4646
Gambling Age: 18
Restaurants: 1 Liquor: No
Buffet: B/L- $4.95 (Tue)
Hours: 9am-1am/24 hrs (Wed-Sun)
Casino Size: 30,000 Square Feet
Other Games: Slots only, BG (Thu-Sun)
Overnight RV Parking: No

Chukchansi Gold Resort & Casino
711 Lucky Lane
Coarsegold, California 93614
(559) 692-5200
Website: www.chukchansigold.com
Map: **#25** (35 miles N. of Fresno)

Toll-Free Number: (866) 794-6946
Gambling Age: 21
Rooms: 190 Prices: $136-$279
Suites: 6 Prices: Casino Use Only
Restaurants: 7 Liquor: Yes
Buffets: B- $17.95 (Sun)
L- $14.95/$17.95 (Sun)
D- $19.95/$24.95 (Fri/Sat)
Other Games: BJ, S21, TCP, PGP,
LIR, FCP, MS, MB, B
Overnight RV Parking: Free/RV Dump: No
Senior Discount: Various Tue if 50+

Chumash Casino Resort
3400 East Highway 246
Santa Ynez, California 93460
(805) 686-0855
Website: www.chumashcasino.com
Map: **#13** (40 miles N.W. of Santa Barbara)

Toll-Free Number: (800) 728-9997
Gambling Age: 18
Room Reservations: (800) 248-6274
Rooms: 320 Prices: $155-$335
Suites: 58 Prices: $380-$550
Restaurants: 3 Liquor: Yes
Buffet: D- $24.95
Casino Size: 94,000 Square Feet
Other Games: S21, BJ, P, BG (Sun-Wed), PGP,
TCP, FCP, LIR, MB, MS
Overnight RV Parking: No
Special Features: Spa.

Colusa Casino Resort
3770 Highway 45
Colusa, California 95932
(530) 458-8844
Website: www.colusacasino.com
Map: **#6** (75 miles N. of Sacramento)

Toll-Free Number: (800) 655-8946
Gambling Age: 21
Room Reservations: (877) 869-7829
Rooms: 50 Prices: $99-$139
Suites: 10 Prices: $199-$219
Restaurants: 4 Liquor: Yes
Buffets: B- $10.95/$15.95 (Sat)
L- $10.95/$15.95 (Sat)
D- $14.95/$22.95 (Fri/Sat)
Other Games: BJ, P, TCP, PGP,
BG (Sun-Wed)
Overnight RV Parking: Free/RV Dump: No
Senior Discount: Various Tue/Thu if 50+

Coyote Valley Casino
7751 N. State Street
Redwood Valley, California 95470
(707) 485-0700
Website: www.coyotevalleycasino.com
Map: **#23** (115 miles N. of San Francisco)

Toll-Free Number: (800) 332-9683
Gambling Age: 21
Restaurants: 1 Cafe Liquor: Yes
Other Games: BJ, PGP, P
Overnight RV Parking: Free/RV Dump: No
Senior Discount: Various Mon if 55+

Diamond Mountain Casino and Hotel
900 Skyline Drive
Susanville, California 96130
(530) 252-1100
Website: www.mcah.com
Map: **#31** (160 Miles N.E. of Sacramento)

Toll-Free Number: (877) 319-8514
Gambling Age: 21
Rooms: 63 Prices: $91-$109
Suites: 7 Prices: $154-$189
Restaurants: 2 Liquor: Yes
Casino Size: 26,000 Square Feet
Other Games: BJ, BG (Tue)
Overnight RV Parking: Free/RV Dump: No
Senior Discount: 50% off in Lava Cafe for 55+ from 2-5 pm.

Eagle Mountain Casino
681 South Tule Road
Porterville, California 93257
(559) 788-6220
Website: www.eaglemtncasino.com
Map: **#21** (60 miles S.E. of Fresno)

Toll-Free Number: (800) 903-3353
Gambling Age: 18
Restaurants: 2 Liquor: No
Buffets: L- $7.99 (Wed/Thu)/$9.99 (Fri-Sun)
D- $19.99 (Fri)/$15.99 (Sat)/
$10.99 (Sun)
Casino Size: 9,600 Square Feet
Other Games: BJ, P, S21, PGP
Overnight RV Parking: Free/RV Dump: No
Special Features: Food court with four fast food stations.

Elk Valley Casino
2500 Howland Hill Road
Crescent City, California 95531
(707) 464-1020
Website: www.elkvalleycasino.com
Map: **#7** (84 miles N. of Eureka)

Toll-Free Number: (888) 574-2744
Gambling Age: 21 Restaurants: 1 Liquor: Yes
Casino Size: 23,000 Square Feet
Other Games: BJ, P, BG (Mon/Thu/Fri/Sun)
Overnight RV Parking: No

Fantasy Springs Casino
82-245 Indio Springs Drive
Indio, California 92203
(760) 342-5000
Website: www.fantasyspringsresort.com
Map: **#8** (125 miles E. of Los Angeles)

Toll-Free Number: (800) 827-2946
Gambling Age: 21
Rooms: 250 Prices: $99-$209
Suites: 11 Prices: $350-$599
Restaurants: 6 Liquor: Yes
Buffets: L- $15.99/$24.99 (Sun)
D- $19.99/$24.99 (Sat)
Casino Size: 95,000 Square Feet
Other Games: BJ, S21, MB, LIR, PGP,
TCP, FCP, BG, OTB
Overnight RV Parking: Free/RV Dump: No
Special Features: 24-lane bowling center. 5,000-seat special events center. Card version of craps. Golf course.

Feather Falls Casino
3 Alverda Drive
Oroville, California 95966
(530) 533-3885
Website: www.featherfallscasino.com
Map: **#22** (100 miles N. of Sacramento)

Toll-Free Number: (877) 652-4646
Gambling Age: 21
Rooms: 74 Prices: $79-$89
Suites: 10 Prices: $180-$280
Restaurants: 2 Liquor: Yes
Buffets: B- $8.95/$12.95 (Sat/Sun)
L- $10.95 D- $14.95/$17.95 (Fri/Sat)
Casino Size: 38,000 Square Feet
Other Games: BJ, P
Overnight RV Parking: No
Senior Discount: Various on Mon/Wed if 55+

Garcia River Casino
22215 Windy Hollow Rd
Point Arena, California 95468
(707) 467-5300
Website:www.thegarciarivercasino.com
Map: **#44** (130 miles N. of San Francisco)

Restaurants: 1
Other Games: Gaming Machines Only
Casino Size: 11,000 Square Feet
Hours: 9am - 11pm/1am (Fri/Sat)

Gold Country Casino
4020 Olive Highway
Oroville, California 95966
(530) 538-4560
Website: www.goldcountrycasino.com
Map: **#22** (100 miles N. of Sacramento)

Toll-Free Number: (800) 334-9400
Gambling Age: 21
Rooms: 87 Prices: $99-$169
Restaurants: 3 Liquor: Yes
Buffets: L- $9.99/$11.99 (Sat/Sun)
D- $13.99/$14.99 (Thu)/
$19.99 (Fri/Sat)/$12.99 (Sun)
Other Games: BJ, TCP,
PGP, FCP, BG (Wed-Sun)
Overnight RV Parking: Free/RV Dump: No
Senior discount: 10% off buffet if 55+.
Special Features: 1,200-seat showroom.

Golden Acorn Casino and Travel Center
1800 Golden Acorn Way
Campo, California 91906
(619) 938-6000
Website: www.goldenacorncasino.com
Map: **#33** (40 miles S.E. of San Diego)

Toll-Free Number: (866) 794-6244
Gambling Age: 18
Restaurants: 2 Liquor: Yes
Other Games: BJ
Overnight RV Parking: Free/RV Dump: No
Special Features: 33-acre auto/truck stop and convenience store. Table games open at 2pm/10am Sat/Sun.

Graton Resort & Casino
630 Park Court
Rohnert Park, California 94928
Website: www.gratonresortcasino.com
Map: **#42** (50 miles N. of San Francisco)

Rooms: 200 Prices: $235-$510
Gambling age: 21
Restaurants: 4 Liquor: Yes
Casino Size: 18,000 Square Feet
Other Games: BJ, PGP, TCP, B, FCP, P
Overnight RV Parking: Free/RV Dump: No
Special Features: Casino features a food court with seven fast food restaurants and a Starbucks.

Harrah's Resort Southern California
33750 Valley Center Road
Valley Center, California 92082
(760) 751-3100
Website: harrahssocal.com
Map: **#20** (35 miles N.E. of San Diego)

Toll-Free Number: (877) 777-2457
Gambling Age: 21
Rooms: 552 Prices: $120-$360
Suites: 101 Prices: $150-$609
Restaurants: 7 Liquor: Yes
Buffets: B- $26.99 (Sat/Sun) L-$19.99
D- $27.99/$32.99 (Fri/Sat)
Casino Size: 55,000 Square Feet
Other Games: BJ, PGP, MB, P, MS,
TCP, LIR, FCP
Overnight RV Parking: Free/RV Dump: No
Special Features: Card version of craps and roulette.

Havasu Landing Resort & Casino
5 Main Street
Havasu Lake, California 92363
(760) 858-4593
Website: www.havasulanding.com
Map: **#18** (200 miles E. of L. A.)

Toll Free Number: (800) 307-3610
Gambling Age: 21
Restaurants: 1 Liquor: Yes
Hours: 8:30am-12:30am/2:30am (Fri/Sat)
Other Games: BJ, TCP
Overnight RV Parking: Must use RV park
Casino Size: 6,000 Square Feet
Special Features: Tables open 11:30 am/12:30 pm (Mon-Thu). Marina, RV park ($35-$65 per night). Mobile home rentals.

Hidden Oaks Casino
76700 Covelo Road
Covelo, California 95428
(707) 983-6896
Website: www.hiddenoakscasino.com
Map: **#30** (150 miles N.W. of Sacramento)

Restaurants: 1
Other Games: Gaming machines only
Casino Hours: 12:00pm to 12:00am
Senior Discount: Various Mon if 55+

Hollywood Casino - Jamul
14191 Highway 94
Jamul, California 91935
Map: **#14** (10 miles E. of San Diego)

Gambling Age: 21
Restaurants: 6 Buffets: L- $29.99 (Sun)
Casino Size: 50,000 Square Feet
Other Games: BJ, TCP, FCP, MB, LIR, MS, UTH, PGP

Hopland Sho-Ka-Wah Casino
13101 Nakomis Road
Hopland, California 95449
(707) 744-1395
Website: www.shokawah.com
Map: **#32** (100 miles N. of San Francisco)

Toll Free Number: (888) 746-5292
Gambling Age: 21
Restaurants: 2 Liquor: Yes
Other Games: BJ, BG (Sun-Thu)
Overnight RV Parking: Free/RV Dump: No
Senior Discount: Various Thu if 55+
Special Features: Table games open at 2pm.

Jackson Rancheria Casino & Hotel
12222 New York Ranch Road
Jackson, California 95642
(209) 223-1677
Website: www.jacksoncasino.com
Map: **#9** (60 miles S.E. of Sacramento)

Toll-Free Number: (800) 822-9466
Gambling Age: 21
Rooms: 77 Price Range: $99-$149
Suites: 9 Price Range: $189-$409
Restaurants: 2 Liquor: No
Buffets: L- $10.95 (Mon-Thu)/ $32.95 (Friday-Sunday)
D- $14.95/$16.95 (Thu)/$32.95 (Fri-Sun)
Other Games: BJ, PGP, LIR, TCP, CW, FCP, MB, P
Overnight RV Parking: No
Special Features: Offers card versions of craps and roulette. 805-seat showroom. 100 space RV park ($50-$60 per night)

Konocti Vista Casino Resort & Marina
2755 Mission Rancheria Road
Lakeport, California 95453
(707) 262-1900
Website: www.konocti-vista-casino.com
Map: **#11** (120 miles N. of San Francisco)

Toll-Free Number: (800) 386-1950
Gambling Age: 21 Restaurants: 1 Liquor: Yes
Rooms: 80 Prices: $99-$139
Suites: 5 Prices: $169-$189
Other Games: BJ, PGP
Overnight RV Parking: Must use RV park
RV Dump: Free
Special Features: Marina with 80 slips. 74-space RV park ($38-$41 per night).

Lucky Bear Casino
12510 Highway 96
Hoopa, California 95546
(530) 625-5198
Map: **#24** (30 miles N.E. of Eureka)

Gambling Age: 18 Restaurants: 1 Liquor: No
Hours: 10am-12am/1am (Fri/Sat)
Other Games: BJ, BG
Overnight RV Parking: No
Special Features: Non-smoking casino.

Lucky 7 Casino
350 N. Indian Road
Smith River, California 95567
(707) 487-7777
Website: www.lucky7casino.com
Map: **#7** (100 miles N. of Eureka)

Toll-Free Number: (866) 777-7170
Gambling Age: 21 Restaurants: 1 Liquor: Yes
Casino Size: 24,000 Square Feet
Other Games: BJ, BG (Sun-Tue), P
Senior Discount: Buy $9 lunch special, get $10 Free Play Thu if 55+.
Overnight RV Parking: Free/RV Dump: No

Mono Wind Casino
37302 Rancheria Lane
Auberry, California 93602
(559) 855-4350
Website: www.monowind.com
Map: **#25** (30 miles N.E. of Fresno)

Gambling Age: 21
Restaurants: 1 Liquor: Yes
Casino Size: 10,000 Square Feet
Overnight RV Parking: Free/RV Dump: No

Morongo Casino Resort and Spa
49750 Seminole Drive
Cabazon, California 92230
(951) 849-3080
Website: www.morongocasinoresort.com
Map: **#3** (90 miles E. of L. A.)

Toll-Free Number: (800) 252-4499
Gambling Age: 18
Rooms: 310 Prices: $129-$319
Suites: 32 Prices: $309-$549
Restaurants: 6 Liquor: Yes
Buffets: B- $23.99 (Sat/Sun)
L- $14.95/$20.95 (Wed/Thu)/
$21.95 (Fri/Sat)/$26.95 (Sun)
D- $16.95/$25.95 (Wed/Thu)/
$24.95 (Fri/Sat)/$23.95 (Sun)
Casino Size: 145,000 Square Feet
Other Games: BJ, P, TCP, FCP, MS, LIR,
MB, PGP, BG
Overnight RV Parking: Free/RV Dump: No
Special Features: Card version of craps.

Paiute Palace Casino
2742 N. Sierra Highway
Bishop, California 93514
(760) 873-4150
Website: www.paiutepalace.com
Map: **#26** (130 miles N.E. of Fresno)

Toll-Free Number: (888) 372-4883
Gambling Age: 21
Restaurants: 1 Liquor: Yes
Other Games: BJ, P
Overnight RV Parking: $10/RV Dump: No
Senior Discount: 10% off in restaurant if 50+
Special Features: 24-hour gas station and convenience store.

Pala Casino Spa and Resort
11154 Highway 76
Pala, California 92059
(760) 510-5100
Website: www.palacasino.com
Map: **#20** (35 miles N.E. of San Diego)

Toll-Free Number: (877) 946-7252
Gambling Age: 21
Room Reservations: (877) 725-2766
Rooms: 425 Prices: $139-$299
Suites: 82 Prices: $189-$389
Restaurants: 9 Liquor: Yes
Buffets: B-$30.74 (Sat/Sun)
L-$23.74
D-$30.74/$35.74 (Fri/Sat)
Other Games: BJ, B, MB, TCP, PGP,
MS, LIR, P, BG (Thu)
Overnight RV Parking: Free (park in west lot)
RV Dump: No
Special Features: Offers card versions of craps and roulette. Fitness center and spa. Discount on buffet if players club member. 10-acre, $6.1 million RV Resort with 100 spaces ($50-$80).

Pechanga Resort and Casino
45000 Pechanga Parkway
Temecula, California 92592
(951) 693-1819
Website: www.pechanga.com
Map: **#28** (50 miles N. of San Diego)

Toll-Free Number: (877) 711-2946
Gambling Age: 21
Room Reservations: (888) 732-4264
Rooms: 458 Price Range: $109-$349
Suites: 64 Price Range: $179-$750
Restaurants: 8 Liquor: Yes
Buffets: B- $23.99 (Sat/Sun) L- $20.99
D- $25.99/$30.99 (Fri/Sat)
Other Games: BJ, MB, P, PGP, LIR, TCP, BG
Overnight RV Parking: Must use RV park
RV Dump: $14.00 charge to use
Casino Size: 88,000 Square Feet
Special Features: 168-space RV park ($50-$80 per night). Offers card versions of craps and roulette. Food court with six food outlets.

Pit River Casino
20265 Tamarack Avenue
Burney, California 96013
(530) 335-2334
Website: www.pitrivercasino.com
Map: **#29** (190 miles N. of Sacramento)

Toll-Free Number: (888) 245-2992
Gambling Age: 21
Restaurants: 1 Snack Bar Liquor: No
Casino Hours: 9am-12am/2am (Fri/Sat)
Other Games: BJ, P
Overnight RV Parking: Free/RV Dump: No
Senior Discount: Earn 10 points Mondays, get 50% off food, if 55+
Special Features: Tables open at 4pm/2pm (Sun).

Quechan Casino Resort
525 Algodones Road
Winterhaven, California 92283
(760) 572-3900
Website: www.playqcr.net
Map: **#37** (170 miles E. of San Diego)

Toll-Free Number: (877) 783-2426
Rooms: 158 Price Range: $95-$119
Suites: 8 Price Range: $159-$299
Gambling Age: 21
Restaurants: 2 Liquor: Yes
Other Games: BJ, P, PGP, TCP
Overnight RV Parking: Free/RV Dump: No
Special Features: Part of casino is located across the state border in Arizona. Offers video versions of craps and roulette.

Rain Rock Casino
777 Sharps Road
Yreka, California 96097
Map: **#46** (250 miles N. of Sacramento)

Expected to open early 2018
Casino Size: 36,000 square feet
Special Features: All machines will be Class-II gaming machines based on bingo.

Red Earth Casino
3089 Norm Niver Road
Salton City, California 92274
(760) 395-1700
Website: www.redearthcasino.com
Map: **#39** (114 miles S.E. of Riverside)

Gambling Age: 21
Restaurants: 1 Liquor: Yes
Casino Size: 10,000 Square Feet
Overnight RV Parking: Free/RV Dump: $8

Red Fox Casino
300 Cahto Drive
Laytonville, California 95454
(760) 395-1200
Website: www.redfoxcasino.net
Map: **#30** (150 miles N.W. of Sacramento)

Toll-Free Number: (888) 473-3369
Gambling Age: 18
Restaurants: 1 Snack Bar Liquor: No
Overnight RV Parking: Free/RV Dump: No
Senior Discount: Various Mon if 55+

Red Hawk Casino
5250 Honpie Road
Placerville, California 95667
(530) 677-7000
Website: www.redhawkcasino.com
Map: **#40** (40 miles E of Sacramento)

Toll-Free Number: (888) 573-3495
Gambling Age: 21
Restaurants: 6 Liquor: Yes
Buffets: L- $12.99/$15.99 (Sat)/$19.95 (Sun)
D- $15.99/$31.99 (Fri-Sun)
Other Games: BJ, P, PGP, TCP, LIR,
MB, FCP, B, MS
Special Features: Childcare facility. Shopping arcade. Offers a card version of craps and roulette.

Redwood Hotel Casino
171 Klamath Boulevard
Klamath, California 95548
(707) 482-1777
Website: www.redwoodhotelcasino.com
Map: **#43** (65 miles N of Eureka)

Toll-Free Number: (855) 554-2946
Gambling Age: 21
Hours: 10am-11pm
Rooms: 60 Price Range: $99-$199
Restaurants: 1 Liquor: Yes
Overnight RV Parking: No
Special Features: The only hotel located within the Redwood National & State Parks. Hotel is affiliated with Holiday Inn Express.

River Rock Casino
3250 Hwy 128 East
Geyserville, California 95441
(707) 857-2777
Website: www.riverrockcasino.com
Map: **#32** (75 miles N. of San Fran.)

Gambling Age: 21
Restaurants: 2 Liquor: Yes
Buffets: L- $9.99/$12.99 (Sun)
D- $12.99/$24.99 (Fri)/$19.99 (Sat)
Other Games: BJ, MB, PGP, TCP, S21
Overnight RV Parking: No
Senior discount: 10% off buffet Tue if 55+
Special Features: Buffet closed Tue/Wed

Robinson Rancheria Resort & Casino
1545 East Highway 20
Nice, California 95464
(800) 809-3636
Website: www.rrrc.com
Map: **#11** (115 miles N.W. of Sacramento)

Gambling Age: 21
Rooms: 49 Price Range: $99-$129
Suites: 2 Price Range: $119-$295
Restaurants: 2 Liquor: Yes
Buffets: B - $9.95 (Sun) D- $8.95 (Wed)
Casino Size: 37,500 Square Feet
Other Games: BJ, P, PGP, LIR, TCP,
MB, BG (Wed-Sun)
Overnight RV Parking: Free (one night only)
RV Dump: No
Senior Discount: Various on Wed if 55+.

Rolling Hills Casino
2655 Barham Avenue
Corning, California 96021
(530) 528-3500
Website: www.rollinghillscasino.com
Map: **#36** (115 miles N. of Sacramento)

Toll-Free Number: (888) 331-6400
Gambling Age: 21
Rooms: 90 Price Range: $119-$169
Suites: 21 Price Range: $159-$215
Restaurants: 2 Liquor: Yes
Buffet: B- $10.95 L- $12.95
D- $17.95/$22.95 (Fri)
Casino Size: 60,000 Square Feet
Other Games: BJ, PGP, TCP
Overnight RV Parking: Free in truck lot
Senior Discount: Various Tue/Thu if 50+.
Special Features: 72-space RV park ($35 per night).

Running Creek Casino
635 East Highway 20
Upper Lake, California 95485
(707) 275-9209
Website: www.runningcreekcasino.com
Map: **#11** (120 miles N.W. of Sacramento)

Gambling Age: 21
Restaurants: 2 Liquor: Yes
Buffet: L- $9.99 (Tue-Thu)
D- $9.95 (Tue)/$24.95 (Wed)
Other Games: BJ
Casino Size: 33,000 Square Feet

San Manuel Casino
5797 North Victoria Avenue
Highland, California 92346
(909) 864-5050
Website: www.sanmanuel.com
Map: **#12** (65 miles E. of L. A.)

Toll-Free Number: (800) 359-2464
Gambling Age: 21
Restaurants: 9 Liquor: Yes
Buffet: L- $16.99/$34.99 (Fri)/
$22.99 (Sat/Sun)
D- $21.99/$34.99 (Thu/Fri)/
$29.99 (Sat)/$22.99 (Sun)
Casino Size: 75,000 Square Feet
Other Games: BJ, MB, P, PGP, LIR, TCP, FCP
Overnight RV Parking: Free/RV Dump: No
Special Features: Food Court with four fast food outlets. Buffet discounts for players club members. Offers card versions of craps and roulette.

San Pablo Lytton Casino
13255 San Pablo Avenue
San Pablo, California 94806
(510) 215-7888
Website: www.sanpablolytton.com
Map: **#41** (15 miles N of Oakland)

Gambling Age: 21
Restaurants: 2
Other Games: BJ, TCP, B, PGP
Special Features: All machines are Class-II gaming machines based on bingo. All table game players must place $1 ante for every $100 bet.

Sherwood Valley Casino
100 Kawi Place
Willits, California 95490
(707) 459-7330
Website: www.svrcasino.com
Map: **#11** (130 miles N. of San Francisco)

Gambling Age: 18
Restaurants: 1 Deli Liquor: No
Casino Size: 6,000 Square Feet
Other Games: Slots Only
Overnight RV Parking: Free/RV Dump: No

Soboba Casino
23333 Soboba Road
San Jacinto, California 92583
(951) 665-1000
Website: www.soboba.com
Map: **#3** (90 miles E. of L. A.)

Toll-Free Number: (866) 476-2622
Gambling Age: 21
Restaurants: 1 Liquor: Yes
Casino Size: 52,000 Square Feet
Other Games: BJ, S21, PGP, TCP, FCP
Overnight RV Parking: Free/RV Dump: No
Special Features: Offers card version of roulette.

Spa Resort Casino
140 N. Indian Canyon Drive
Palm Springs, California 92262
(760) 323-5865
Website: www.sparesortcasino.com
Map: **#3** (115 miles E. of L. A.)

Toll-Free Number: (800) 258-2946
Gambling Age: 21
Restaurants: 5 (1 open 24 hours) Liquor: Yes
Buffets: B- $10.99 (Sat/Sun)
L- $9.99 (Mon/Thu/Fri/Sat)/
$24.99 (Sun)
D- $14.99 (Mon/Thurs/Fri/Sat)
Casino Size: 15,000 Square Feet
Other Games: BJ, MB, PGP, TCP
Overnight RV Parking: No
Special Features: Offers card version of roulette.

Spotlight 29 Casino
46200 Harrison Place
Coachella, California 92236
(760) 775-5566
Website: www.spotlight29.com
Map: **#8** (130 miles E. of L. A.)

Toll-Free Number: (866) 377-6829
Gambling Age: 21
Restaurants: 2 Liquor: Yes
Buffets: L-$10.95/$12.95 (Sat/Sun)
D-$15.95/$19.95 (Sat)
Other Games: BJ, S21, UTH, PGP, TCP
Overnight RV Parking: Free/RV Dump: No
Special Features: Three fast-food outlets including McDonald's. 2,200-seat showroom.

Sycuan Resort & Casino
5469 Casino Way
El Cajon, California 92019
(619) 445-6002
Website: www.sycuan.com
Map: **#14** (10 miles E. of San Diego)

Toll-Free Number: (800) 279-2826
Gambling Age: 18
Room Reservations: (800) 457-5568
Restaurants: 5 Liquor: Yes
Buffets: L- $17.95/$26.95 (Sat/Sun) D- $26.95
Casino Size: 73,000 Square Feet
Other Games: BJ, B, S21, P, BG, CW, TCP, CSP, FCP, OTB, PGP, MS
Overnight RV Parking: Free/RV Dump: No
Senior Discount: Various Sun if 55+.
Special Features: Offers card/tile versions of roulette and craps. Three 18-hole golf courses. 500-seat showroom.

Table Mountain Casino & Bingo
8184 Table Mountain Road
Friant, California 93626
(559) 822-2485
Website: www.tmcasino.com
Map: **#15** (15 miles N. of Fresno)

Toll-Free Number: (800) 541-3637
Gambling Age: 18
Restaurants: 3 Liquor: No
Buffet: L- $11.99/$17.99 (Tue)/$12.99 (Fri)
D- $12.99/$21.99 (Tue)/
$13.99 (Fri-Sun)
Other Games: BJ, S21, P, PGP, TCP, BG, CW, FCP
Overnight RV Parking: Free/RV Dump: No
Senior Discount: Buffet discount Mon-Fri if 55+.

Tachi Palace Hotel and Casino
17225 Jersey Avenue
Lemoore, California 93245
(559) 924-7751
Website: www.tachipalace.com
Map: **#10** (50 miles S. of Fresno)

Toll-Free Number: (800) 942-6886
Gambling Age: 18
Room Reservations: (800) 615-8030
Rooms: 215 Price Range: $79-$159
Suites: 40 Price Range: $149-$259
Restaurants: 8 Liquor: Yes
Buffets: B-$15.99 (Sat)/$16.99 (Sun)
L- $11.99
D- $10.99 (Mon)/$22.99 (Thu)/
$19.99 (Fri)/$16.99 (Sat/Sun)
Casino Size: 50,000 Square Feet
Other Games: BJ, P, PGP, TCP, S21, FCP, MB, BG
Overnight RV Parking: Free/RV Dump: No
Senior Discount: $5.99 lunch buffet if 55+.
Special Features: Offers a card-based version of roulette. No buffet Tue/Wed

Thunder Valley Casino
1200 Athens Ave
Lincoln, California 95648
(916) 408-7777
Website: www.thundervalleyresort.com
Map: **#35** (35 miles N.E. of Sacramento)

Toll-Free Number: (877) 468-8777
Gambling Age: 21
Rooms: 297 Price Range: $115-$189
Suites: 40 Price Range: $300-$399
Restaurants: 4 Liquor: Yes
Buffets: B/L-$11.49/$16.95 (Sun)
D-$15.49/$31.99 (Fri)/$29.99 (Sat)
Other Games: BJ, MB, PGP, P, MS, LIR, TCP, FCP
Overnight RV Parking: No
Special Features: Affiliated with Station Casinos of Las Vegas. Five fast-food outlets. Buffet discount with players club card. Card versions of craps and roulette.

Tortoise Rock Casino
Baseline Road
Twentynine Palms, California 92277
(760) 367-9759
Website: www.tortiserockcasino.com
Map: **#8** (125 miles E. of L. A.)

Restaurants: 1
Gambling Age: 18
Casino Size: 30,000 Square Feet
Other Games: P, S21, TCP
Overnight RV Parking: Free/RV Dump: No

Twin Pine Casino & Hotel
22223 Highway 29 at Rancheria Road
Middletown, California 95461
(707) 987-0197
Website: www.twinpine.com
Map: **#32** (100 miles N. of San Francisco)

Toll-Free Number: (800) 564-4872
Rooms: 57 Price Range: $89-$109
Suites: 3 Price Range: $149-$250
Gambling Age: 21
Restaurants: 1 Liquor: No
Other Games: BJ, P, TCP
Overnight RV Parking: No/RV Dump: No
Senior Discount: Various Tue/Thu mornings 8:30 am-11:00 am if 50+.

Valley View Casino Resort
16300 Nyemii Pass Road
Valley Center, California 92082
(760) 291-5500
Website: www.valleyviewcasino.com
Map: **#20** (35 miles N.E. of San Diego)

Toll-Free Number: (866) 843-9946
Gambling Age: 21
Rooms: 100 Price Range: $119-$239
Suites: 8 Price Range: $299-$439
Restaurants: 2 Liquor: Yes
Buffets: L- $9.99/$32.99 (Sat/Sun)
D- $19.99/$32.99 (Fri-Sun)
Other Games: BJ, PGP, TCP
Overnight RV Parking: Free/RV Dump: No
Special Features: Players club members receive $3 off buffets. Offers card-based version of roulette.

Viejas Casino
5000 Willows Road
Alpine, California 91901
(619) 445-5400
Website: www.viejas.com
Map: **#16** (25 miles E. of San Diego)

Toll-Free Number: (800) 847-6537
Rooms: 237 Price Range: $129-$289
Suites: 35 Price Range: $260-$500
Gambling Age: 21
Restaurants: 7 Liquor: Yes
Buffets: L/D- $26.99/$32.99 (Fri-Sun)
Other Games: BJ, B, MB, LIR, TCP
FCP, CW, PGP, BG, OTB
Overnight RV Parking: Free/RV Dump: No
Special Features: 51-store factory outlet shopping center. Buffet discounts for players club members. Card-based versions of craps and roulette.

Win-River Casino
2100 Redding Rancheria Road
Redding, California 96001
(530) 243-3377
Website: www.winrivercasino.com
Map: **#17** (163 miles N. of Sacramento)

Toll-Free Number: (800) 280-8946
Gambling Age: 21
Restaurants: 1 Liquor: Yes
Buffets: B- $24.95 (Sun)
Casino Size: 37,000 Square Feet
Other Games: BJ,TCP, PGP, FCP,
S21, P, BG (Tue-Thu/Sun)
Overnight RV Parking: Free/RV Dump: No
Special Features: Comedy club. Food discounts for players club members. 1,000-seat showroom.

Winnedumah Winn's Casino
135 South Highway 395
Independence, California 93526
(760) 878-2483
Map: **#45** (90 miles E. of Fresno)

Restaurants: 1 Liquor: No
Gambling Age: 18
Other Games: Gaming machines only
Special Features: All machines are Class-II gaming machines based on bingo.

COLORADO

Colorado casinos can be found in the mountain towns of Black Hawk, Central City and Cripple Creek. There are also two Indian casinos (which abide by Colorado's limited gaming rules) in Ignacio and Towaoc.

When casino gambling was initially introduced in 1991 it was limited in that only electronic games (including slots, video poker, video blackjack and video keno) and the table games of poker, blackjack, let it ride and three-card poker were allowed. Plus, a single wager could not exceed $5.

All that changed, however, on July 2, 2009 when the maximum bet was raised to $100, plus the games of craps and roulette were added to the mix. Additionally, the casinos were allowed to stay open for 24 hours, rather than having to be closed between 2 a.m. and 8 a.m.

Here's information, as supplied by Colorado's Division of Gaming, showing the slot machine payback percentages for each city's casinos for the one-year period from July 1, 2016 through June 30, 2017:

	Black Hawk	Central City	Cripple Creek
1¢ Slots	89.70%	90.40%	**91.72%**
5¢ Slots	93.03%	**94.51%**	93.48%
25¢ Slots	92.98%	93.77%	**95.33%**
$1 Slots	93.67%	**95.30%**	95.04%
$5 Slots	94.24%	93.85%	**94.84%**
All	92.45%	92.63%	**93.54%**

These numbers reflect the percentage of money returned on each denomination of machine and encompass all electronic machines including video poker and video keno. The best returns for each category are highlighted in bold print.

The minimum gambling age at all Colorado casinos is 21, including Indian casinos.

For information on visiting Central City, call (303) 582-5251 or visit their website at: www.centralcitycolorado.us.

For information on visiting Black Hawk, call (303) 582-5221, or visit their website at: www.cityofblackhawk.org.

All casinos offer electronic games (slots, video poker, video blackjack and video keno). Some casinos also offer: blackjack (BJ), craps (C), roulette (R), poker (P), let it ride (LIR), Mississippi stud (MS) and three card poker (TCP).

Black Hawk

Map Location: **#1** (35 miles west of Denver. Take U.S. 6 through Golden to Hwy 119. Take Hwy 119 to Black Hawk. Another route is I-70 West to exit 244. Turn right onto Hwy. 6. Take Hwy 6 to 119 and into Black Hawk.)

The casinos in Black Hawk and Central City are located one mile apart. The Black Hawk Shuttle Service provides free transportation throughout Black Hawk and Central City.

Ameristar Black Hawk
111 Richman Street
Black Hawk, Colorado 80422
(720) 946-4000
Website: www.ameristar.com

Toll-Free Number (866) 667-3386
Rooms: 472 Price Range: $149-$289
Suites: 64 Price Range: $379-$539
Restaurants: 5
Buffets: B- $19.99 (Sat/Sun)
L-$13.99/$19.99 (Sat/Sun)
D- $21.95/$33.95 (Sat/Sun)
Casino Size: 46,534 Square feet
Other Games: BJ, P, C, R, MS

Bull Durham Saloon & Casino
110 Main Street
Black Hawk, Colorado 80422
(303) 582-0810
Website: www.bulldurhamcasino.com

Restaurants: 1 (snack bar)
Casino Size: 2,579 Square Feet

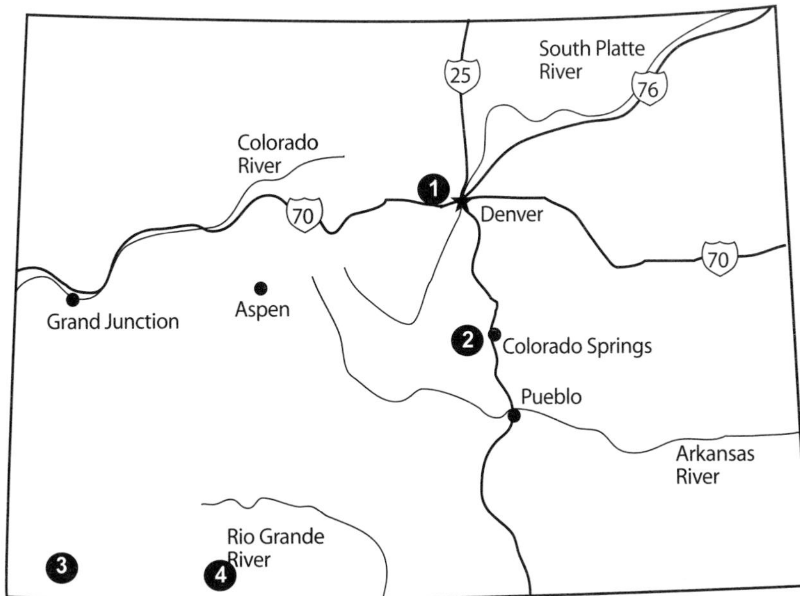

Gilpin Hotel Casino
111 Main Street
Black Hawk, Colorado 80422
(303) 582-1133
Website: www.thegilpincasino.com

Restaurants: 1
Other Games: BJ, C, R
Casino Size: 11,087 Square Feet
Senior Discount: Specials on Tue if 50+.

Golden Gates Casino
261 Main Street
Black Hawk, Colorado 80422
(303) 582-1650
Website: www.thegoldengatescasino.com

Restaurants: 3
Casino Size: 8,004 Square Feet (Golden Gates)
Casino Size: 3,440 Square Feet (Golden Gulch)
Other Games: P, BJ
Special Features: Connected to **Golden Gulch Casino**. Skybridge to **Golden Mardi Gras Casino.**

Golden Mardi Gras Casino
333 Main Street
Black Hawk, Colorado 80422
(303) 582-5600

Restaurants: 1
Casino Size: 17,888 Square Feet
Other Games: BJ, C
Special Features: Skybridge to **Golden Gates Casino.**

Isle of Capri Casino - Black Hawk
401 Main Street
Black Hawk, Colorado 80422
(303) 998-7777
Website: black-hawk.isleofcapricasinos.com

Suites: 130 Price Range: $139-$299
Buffets: B-$8.99 L-$13.99/$23.99 (Sat/Sun)
D- $23.99/$29.99 (Fri-Sun)
Senior Discount: Various Sun if 50+.

Lady Luck Casino
340 Main Street
Black Hawk, Colorado 80422
(303) 582-3000
Website: www.isleofcapricasinos.com

Toll-Free Number (888) 523-9582
Rooms: 140 Price Range: $99-$229
Suites: 24 Price Range: $169-$279
Restaurants: 2 Valet parking: Free
Casino Size: 17,726 Square Feet
Other Games: BJ, P, C, R
Senior Discount: Various Mon/Wed if 40+.
Special Features: Affiliated with Isle of Capri.

The Lodge Casino at Black Hawk
240 Main Street
Black Hawk, Colorado 80422
(303) 582-1771
Website: www.thelodgecasino.com

Rooms: 47 Price Range: $109-$179
Suites: 3 Price Range: Casino Use Only
Restaurants: 3
Buffets: B-$7.99 L-$11.49/$16.99 (Sat/Sun)
D-$17.99/$24.49 (Fri/Sat)
Senior Discount: 50% off breakfast or lunch buffets Mon/Tue if 50+.

Monarch Casino Black Hawk
444 Main Street
Black Hawk, Colorado 80422
(303) 582-1000
Website: www.monarchblackhawk.com

Restaurants: 1
Buffet: B- $7.99/$19.99 (Sat/Sun)
L- $11.99/$19.99 (Sat/Sun)
D- $20.99/$24.99 (Fri-Sun)
Casino Size: 25,860 Square Feet
Other Games: BJ, TCP, R, C
Senior Discount: Various on Mon if 50+.

Red Dolly Casino
530 Gregory Street
Black Hawk, Colorado 80422
Website: www.thereddollycasino.com
(303) 582-1100

Restaurants: 1
Casino Size: 1,992 Square Feet
Casino Hours: 8am-2am

Saratoga Casino
101 Main Street
Black Hawk, Colorado 80422
(303) 582-6162
Website: www.saratogacasinobh.com

Toll-Free Number: (800) 538-5825
Restaurants: 2
Casino Size: 17,129 Square Feet
Other Games: BJ, C, R, TCP, S21
Special Features: 20x odds on craps.

Sasquatch Casino
125 Gregory Street
Black Hawk, Colorado 80422
(303) 582-5582
Website: www.sasquatchcasino.com
Casino Size: 1,827 Square feet
Restaurants: 1 Snack Bar
Casino Hours: 8am-2am/4am (Fri/Sat)

Wild Card Saloon & Casino
112 Main Street
Black Hawk, Colorado 80422
Website: www.thewildcardcasino.net
(303) 582-3412

Restaurants: 1
Casino Size: 2,750 Square Feet
Special Features: Grocery store.

Z Casino
101 Gregory Street
Black Hawk, Colorado 80422
(303) 271-2500
Website: www.zcasinobh.com

Toll-Free Number: (800) 426-2855
Restaurants: 2
Casino Size: 10,471 Square Feet
Other Games: BJ, C

Central City

Map location: **#1** (same as Black Hawk). Central City is located one mile from Black Hawk. Turn left at the third stoplight on Hwy. 119 and proceed up Gregory Street.

Century Casino & Hotel - Central City
102 Main Street
Central City, Colorado 80427
(303) 582-5050
Website: www.cnty.com

Toll-Free Number: (888) 507-5050
Rooms: 22 Price Range $109-$159
Restaurants: 2
Casino Size: 13,899 Square Feet
Other Games: BJ, C, R
Senior Discount: Various Wed/Thu if 50+

Dostal Alley Casino & Microbrewery
1 Dostal Alley
Central City, Colorado 80427
(303) 582-1610
Website: www.dostalalley.net

Restaurants: 1 Snack Bar
Casino Size: 1,041 Square Feet
Casino Hours: 8am-2am
Special Features: Microbrewery.

Famous Bonanza/Easy Street
107 Main Street
Central City, Colorado 80427
(303) 582-5914
Website: www.famousbonanza.com

Toll-Free Number: (866) 339-5825
Restaurants: 1
Casino Size: 5,056 Square Feet (F. Bonanza)
Casino Size: 4,289 Square Feet (Easy Street)
Other Games: BJ, TCP
Casino Hours: 8am-2am/3am (Fri/Sat)

Johnny Z's Casino
132 Lawrence Street
Central City, Colorado 80427
(303) 582-5623
Website: www.johnnyzscasino.com

Restaurants: 1
Casino Size: 35,000 Square Feet
Other Games: BJ, C, TCP
Overnight RV Parking: Free/RV Dump: No
Senior Discount: Various Mon/Tue if 60+

Reserve Casino Hotel
321 Gregory Street
Central City, Colorado 80427
(303) 582-0800
Website: www.reservecasinohotel.com

Toll-Free Number: (800) 924-6646
Room Reservations: (866) 924-6646
Rooms: 118 Price Range $119-$219
Suites: 6 Price Range $199-$349
Senior Discount: Various Mon/Tue if 60+

Cripple Creek

Map Location: **#2** (47 miles west of Colorado Springs. Take exit 141 at Colorado Springs off I-25. Go west on Hwy. 24 to the town of Divide. Turn left onto Hwy. 67 and go 18 miles to Cripple Creek.)

All casinos offer electronic games (slots, video poker, video blackjack and video keno). Some casinos also offer: blackjack (BJ), poker (P), let it ride (LIR) and three card poker (TCP).

Brass Ass Casino
264 E. Bennett Avenue
Cripple Creek, Colorado 80813
(719) 689-2104
Website: www.triplecrowncasinos.com

Restaurants: 1
Casino Size: 7,486 Square Feet
Other Games: BJ, TCP, C, R
Special Features: Connected to **Midnight Rose** and **J.P. McGill's**. Covered parking garage.

Bronco Billy's Casino
233 E. Bennett Avenue
Cripple Creek, Colorado 80813
(719) 689-2142
Website: www.broncobillyscasino.com

Toll Free Number: (877) 989-2142
Restaurants: 4
Other Games: BJ, TCP, C, R
Casino Size: 6,086 Square Feet (Bronco's)
Casino Size: 5,991 Square Feet (Buffalo's)
Senior Discount: Specials Mon/Wed/Fri 8am-6pm if 50+
Special Features: Includes **Buffalo Billy's** Casino.

Century Casino - Cripple Creek
200-220 E. Bennett Avenue
Cripple Creek, Colorado 80813
(719) 689-0333
Website: www.cnty.com

Toll-Free Number: (888) 966-2257
Rooms: 21 Price Range: $109-$119
Suites: 3 Price Range: $119-$219
Restaurants: 1
Casino Size: 5,609 Square Feet
Other Games: BJ, R
Senior Discount: Various Mon/Wed if 50+

Colorado Grande Casino
300 E. Bennett Avenue
Cripple Creek, Colorado 80813
(719) 689-3517
Website: www.coloradogrande.com

Toll Free Number: (877) 244-9469
Rooms: 5 Price Range: $59-$99
Suites: 2 Price Range: $119-$199
Restaurants: 1
Casino Size: 2,569 Square Feet
Senior Discount: Dining discounts if 50+
Special Features: Covered parking garage.

Double Eagle Hotel & Casino
442 E. Bennett Avenue
Cripple Creek, Colorado 80813
(719) 689-5000
Website: www.decasino.com

Toll-Free Reservations: (800) 711-7234
Rooms: 146 Price Range: $89-$139
Suites: 12 Price Range: $159-$500
Restaurants: 3
Casino Size: 14,631 Square Feet (Double Eagle)
Other Games: BJ, R, TCP
Special Features: Players club members get room discount. Covered parking garage. 48-space RV park ($15/$40 with hookups).

Johnny Nolon's Casino
301 E. Bennett Avenue
Cripple Creek, Colorado 80813
(719) 689-2080
Website: www.johnnynolonscasino.com

Restaurants: 1
Casino Size: 3,505 Square Feet

McGill's Hotel & Casino
232 E. Bennett Avenue
Cripple Creek, Colorado 80813
(719) 689-2446
Website: www.triplecrowncasinos.com

Toll-Free Number: (888) 461-7529
Rooms: 36 Price Range: $80-$115
Suites: 5 Price Range: $180-$240
Restaurants: 1
Casino Size: 7,386 Square Feet
Special Features: Connected to **Midnight Rose** and **Brass Ass**. 10% room/food discount for players club members. Covered parking garage.

Midnight Rose Hotel & Casino
256 E. Bennett Avenue
Cripple Creek, Colorado 80813
(719) 689-2865
Website: www.triplecrowncasinos.com

Toll-Free Number: (800) 635-5825
Rooms: 19 Price Range: $90-$120
Restaurants: 2
Casino Size: 9,590 Square Feet
Other Games: P
Special Features: Off-track betting (Thu-Sun). Covered parking garage.

Wildwood Casino At Cripple Creek
119 Carbonate Sreet
Cripple Creek, Colorado 80813
(719) 244-9700
Website: www.wildwoodcasino.net

Toll-Free Number: (877) 945-3963
Valet Parking: Free
Restaurants: 3
Buffet: D-$19.95 (Fri/Sat)
Casino Size: 18,965 Square Feet
Other Games: BJ, P, C, R, LIR
Senior Discount: Various Sun-Thu if 50+
Special Features: Covered parking garage.

Indian Casinos

Sky Ute Casino and Lodge
14826 Highway 172 N.
Ignacio, Colorado 81137
(970) 563-3000
Website: www.skyutecasino.com
Map Location: **#4** (345 miles S.W. of Denver, 20 miles S.E. of Durango)

Toll-Free Number: (888) 842-4180
Room Reservations: (800) 876-7017
Rooms: 36 Price Range: $105-$154
Suites: 3 Price Range: $279-$299
Restaurants: 4 Liquor: Beer/Wine
Senior Discount: Various Wed 9am-9pm, if 50+.
Special Features: 24-space RV park on property ($35 per night). 24-lane bowling alley. Southern Ute Cultural Center and Museum. Free local shuttle.

Ute Mountain Casino & RV Park
3 Weeminuche Drive
Towaoc, Colorado 81334
(970) 565-8800
Website: www.utemountaincasino.com
Map Location: **#3** (425 miles S.W. of Denver, 11 miles S. of Cortez on Hwys. 160/166)

Toll-Free Number: (800) 258-8007
Hotel Reservations: (888) 565-8837
RV Reservations: (800) 889-5072
Rooms: 70 Price Range: $80-$109
Suites: 20 Price Range: $175-$275
Senior Discount: Earn 100 pts. for $10 food voucher Tue, if 50+
Special Features: 84-space RV Park ($35 per night). Ute Tribal Park tours available.

CONNECTICUT

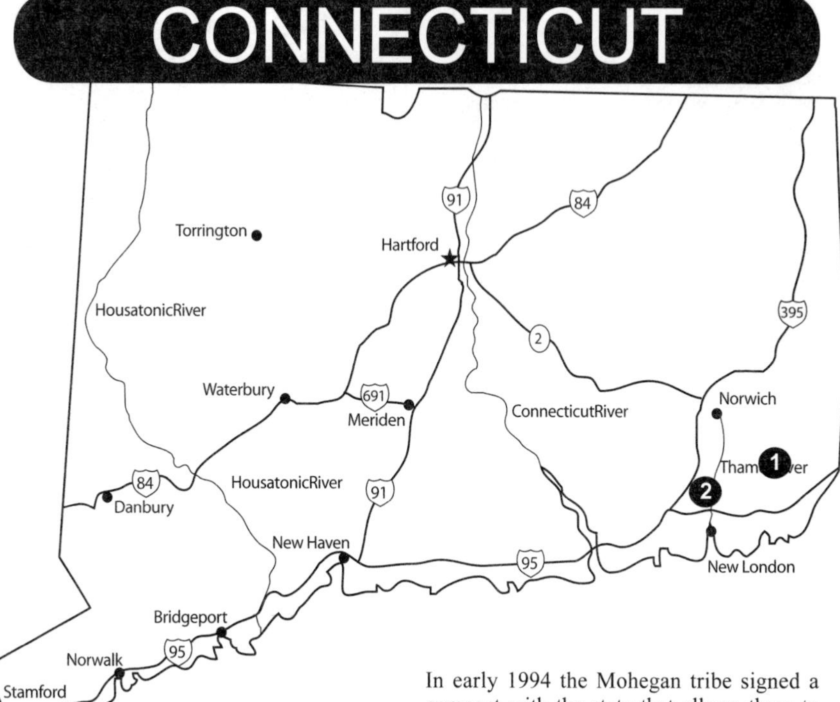

Foxwoods was New England's first casino and it is now the second largest casino in the world.

The Mashantucket Pequot Tribe which operates Foxwoods had to sue the state to allow the casino to open. They argued that since the state legally permitted "Las Vegas Nights," where low-stakes casino games were operated to benefit charities, then the tribe should be entitled to do the same. Eventually, they won their case before the U.S. Supreme Court and began construction of their casino which was financed by a Malaysian conglomerate (after 22 U.S. lenders turned down their loan requests).

When the casino first opened in February 1992, slot machines were not permitted. In January 1993 a deal was made between Governor Weicker and the Pequots which gave the tribe the exclusive right to offer slot machines in return for a yearly payment of 25% of the gross slot revenue. The agreement was subject to cancellation, however, if the state allowed slot machines anywhere else in Connecticut.

In early 1994 the Mohegan tribe signed a compact with the state that allows them to offer casino gambling at their reservation in Uncasville (map location #2). The Pequots gave permission for the Mohegans to have slot machines in their casino. The same 25% of the gross slot revenue payment schedule also applies to the Mohegans. The payment schedules are subject to cancellation, however, if the state legalizes any other form of casino gambling. The Mohegan casino opened in October 1996.

The minimum gambling age at both properties is 18 for bingo and 21 for the casino. Both casinos are open 24 hours. For information on visiting Connecticut call the state's Vacation Center at (800) 282-6863 or visit their website at www.ctbound.org.

The games offered at Foxwoods are: blackjack, craps, roulette, baccarat, mini-baccarat, midi baccarat, big six (money wheel), pai gow poker, pai gow tiles, Caribbean stud poker, let it ride, casino war, Spanish 21, three-card poker, Crazy 4 poker and poker; in addition to bingo, keno and pull tabs. There is also a Race Book offering off-track betting on horses, greyhounds and jai-alai.

Foxwoods Resort Casino, North America's largest casino, has over 300,000 square feet of gaming space. The property features three hotels, over 30 food and beverage outlets, 24 retail shops, an outlet mall with 80 stores, six casinos, Ultimate Race Book, various high limit gaming areas, a 3,600-seat bingo room, a state of the art, smoke-free World Poker Room™ and more than 4,800 electronic gaming machines.

Foxwoods Resort Casino
350 Trolley Line Boulevard
Mashantucket, Connecticut 06338
(860) 312-3000
Website: www.foxwoods.com
Map Location: **#1** (45 miles S.E. of Hartford; 12 miles N. of I-95 at Mystic). From I-95 take exit 92 to Rt. 2-West, casino is 7 miles ahead. From I-395 take exit 79A to Rt. 2A follow to Rt. 2-East, casino is 2 miles ahead.

Hotel Reservations: (800) 369-9663
Rooms: 1,398 Price Range: $119-$699
Suites: 209 Price Range: $229-$1,500
Restaurants: 28 (3 open 24 hours)
Buffets: B- $12.49 L-$19.99 D-$23.99
Casino Size: 323,376 Square Feet
Overnight RV Parking: Free (self-contained only) RV Dump: No
Special Features: Daily resort fee charged in addition to room rate. Three hotels with pool, Grand Pequot Tower hotel spa and beauty salon, golf. Headliner entertainment, The Club and Atrium Lounge. Gift shops. Dream Card Mega Store. Hard Rock Cafe. Dream Card members earn complimentaries at table games, slots, poker and race book. 10% room discount for AAA and AARP members. Two Rees Jones designed golf courses.

In May, 2008 a new casino was added at Foxwoods. Originally called the MGM Grand at Foxwoods, in 2013 it was renamed the Fox Tower. It is connected to the Foxwoods Casino Resort by a covered, moving, walkway.

The property has its own casino offering electronic gaming machines, plus the following games: blackjack, craps, roulette, Spanish 21, and three-card Poker.

The following information is from Connecticut's Division of Special Revenue regarding Foxwoods' slot payback percentages:

Denomination	Payback %
1¢	89.88
2¢	91.57
5¢	90.58
25¢	91.95
50¢	90.16
$1.00	93.45
$5.00	94.08
$10.00	95.11
$25.00	96.16
$100.00	96.76
Average	**92.25**

These figures reflect the total percentages returned by each denomination of slot machine from July 1, 2016 through June 30, 2017.

The games offered at Mohegan Sun are: blackjack, craps, roulette, poker, baccarat, mini-baccarat, pai gow, wheel of fortune, pai gow poker, Caribbean stud poker, let it ride, Spanish 21, Mississippi stud, sic bo, three card poker, four card poker, Texas hold 'em bonus and keno. There is also a race book offering off-track betting on horses, greyhounds and jai-alai.

Mohegan Sun Casino
1 Mohegan Sun Boulevard
Uncasville, Connecticut 06382
(860) 862-8000
Website: www.mohegansun.com
Map Location: **#2** (Take I-95 Exit 76/I-395 North. Take Exit 79A (Route 2A) East. Less than 1 mile to Mohegan Sun Boulevard)

Toll-Free Number: (888) 226-7711
Room Reservations: (888) 777-7922
Sky Tower Rooms: 1,020 Prices: $169-$449
Sky Tower Suites: 180 Prices: $209-$3,500
Earth Tower Rooms: 361 Prices: $179-$699
Earth Tower Suites: 39 Prices: $309-$2,500
Restaurants: 29 (3 open 24 hours)
Buffets (Seasons): B-$12.50 L-$21.00
D-$25.00
Casino Size: 295,000 Square Feet
Overnight RV Parking: Free/RV Dump: No
Special Features: Daily resort fee charged in addition to room rate. Food court with specialty food outlets. Childcare center. On-site gas station. 37-store shopping arcade.

Here's information from Connecticut's Division of Special Revenue regarding Mohegan Sun's slot payback percentages:

Denomination	Payback %
1/4¢	86.03
1/2¢	85.92
1¢	88.95
2¢	88.87
5¢	88.09
25¢	91.42
50¢	91.98
$1.00	93.22
$5.00	93.98
$10.00	96.64
$25.00	95.14
$100.00	93.58
Average	**91.79**

These figures reflect the total percentages returned by each denomination of slot machine from July 1, 2016 through June 30, 2017.

DELAWARE

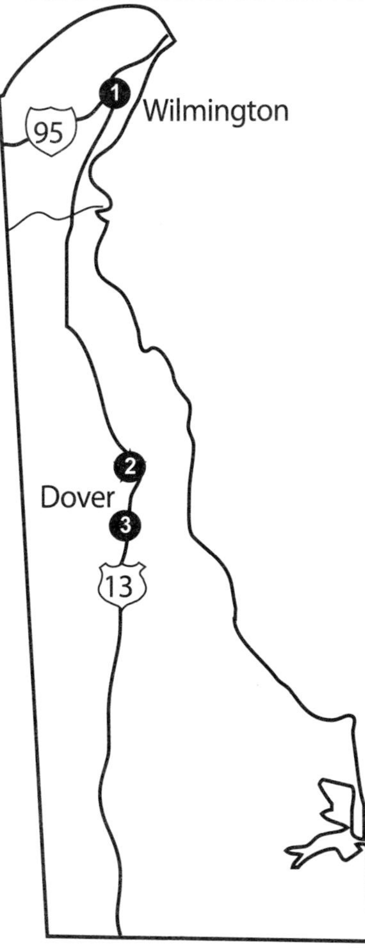

Delaware's three pari-mutuel facilities all feature slot machines. Technically, the machines are video lottery terminals (VLT's) because they are operated in conjunction with the Delaware Lottery. Unlike VLT's in other states, however, Delaware's machines pay out in cash. The VLT's also play other games including: video poker, video keno and video blackjack.

By law, all video lottery games must return between 87% and 95% of all wagers on an annual basis. Games can return above 95% but only with the Lottery Director's approval.

According to figures from the Delaware Lottery for the eleven-month period from June 26, 2016 through May 28, 2017 the average VLT return at Dover Downs was 92.56%, at Delaware Park it was 92.30%, and at Harrington Raceway it was 91.86%.

In mid-2009 the state legalized sports betting for Delaware's three casinos. You can bet on professional and college sporting events, but not on single games-only on multiple games as seen on parlay cards.

In January 2010 the Delaware legislature approved the addition of table games for the state's casinos. All Delaware casinos offer: blackjack, roulette, craps, slots and video poker. Some casinos also offer: mini-baccarat (MB), poker (P), pai gow poker (PGP), Caribbean stud poker (CSP), let it ride (LIR), big 6 (B6), bingo (BG), keno (K), three card poker (TCP), Mississippi stud (MS), casino war (CW), four card poker (FCP) and Spanish 21 (S21).

All casinos are open 24 hours, but they are also closed on Easter and Christmas.

If you want to order a drink while playing, be aware that Delaware gaming regulations do not allow casinos to provide free alcoholic beverages. The minimum gambling age is 21 for slots and 18 for horse racing.

For more information on visiting Delaware call the state's tourism office at (800) 441-8846 or visit their website at: www.visitdelaware.com.

Delaware Park Racetrack & Slots
777 Delaware Park Boulevard
Wilmington, Delaware 19804
(302) 994-2521
Website: www.delawarepark.com
Map: **#1**

Toll-Free Number: (800) 417-5687
Restaurants: 8
Buffets: Brunch: $29.95 (Sun)
Other Games: P, K, TCP, FCP, PGP, MS, S21
Overnight RV Parking: Free/RV Dump: No
Special Features: Live thoroughbred racing seasonally. Daily simulcasting of horse racing.

Dover Downs Hotel Casino
1131 N. DuPont Highway
Dover, Delaware 19901
(302) 674-4600
Website: www.doverdowns.com
Map: **#2**

Toll-Free Number: (800) 711-5882
Rooms: 206 Price Range: $99-$279
Suites: 26 Price Range: $195-$805
Restaurants: 8
Buffets: B-$11.50/$16.50 (Sat/Sun)
L-$15.50 D-$18.50/$24.95 (Fri/Sat)
Casino Size: 91,000 Square Feet
Other Games: S21, TCP, PGP, B, LIR, MS
Overnight RV Parking: Free/RV Dump: Free (Not free during NASCAR events)
Special Features: Casino is non-smoking. Live harness racing seasonally. Daily simulcasting of horse racing. Motorsports speedway with NASCAR racing.

Harrington Raceway & Casino
Delaware State Fairgrounds
U.S. 13 South
Harrington, Delaware 19952
(302) 398-4920
Website: www.harringtonraceway.com
Map: **#3** (20 miles S. of Dover)

Toll-Free Number: (888) 887-5687
Restaurants: 6
Buffets: L- $13.95
D- $17.95/$24.95 (Wed/Fri)/ $21.95 (Sat)
Other Games: MB, P, PGP, TCP, B6, MS, FCP, UTH, S21
Overnight RV Parking: Free/RV Dump: No
Special Features: Live harness racing April-June and August-October. Daily simulcasting of horse racing. Table games open 9am-2am/24-hours (Fri/Sat).

FLORIDA

Florida has three forms of casino gambling: casino boats, Indian casinos and gaming machines at pari-mutuels in two south Florida counties.

The casino boats offer gamblers the opportunity to board ships that cruise offshore where casino gambling is legal. From the west coast the boats travel nine miles out into the Gulf of Mexico. From the East coast they travel three miles out into the Atlantic Ocean.

Unless otherwise noted, all Florida casino boats offer: blackjack, craps, roulette, slots and video poker. Some casinos also offer: mini-baccarat (MB), poker (P), pai gow poker (PGP), three-card poker (TCP), Caribbean stud poker (CSP), let it ride (LIR), bingo (BG) and sports book (SB).

Due to security restrictions, you must present a photo ID at all casino boats or you will not be allowed to board.

For Florida visitor information call (888) 735-2872 or visit their website at: www.visitflorida.com.

Cape Canaveral

Map: **#9** (60 miles S.E. of Orlando)

Victory Casino Cruises - Cape Canaveral
180 Christopher Columbus Drive
Cape Canaveral, Florida 32920
(321) 799-0021
Website: www.victorycasinocruises.com

Toll-Free Number: (855) 468-4286
Gambling Age: 18 Price: $13
Food Service: A la Carte
Schedule: 11am-4pm (Mon-Sat)
12pm-6pm (Sun)
7pm-12am (Sun-Thu)
7pm-12:30am (Fri/Sat)
Buffet Price: $15/$20 (Fri-Sun)
Port Charges: Included Parking: Free
Other Games: MB, TCP, SB, LIR, BG
Special Features: 1,200-passenger *Victory I* departs from Port Canaveral. 6-hour cruise on Sundays.

Jacksonville

Map: **#8**

Victory Casino Cruises - Jacksonville
4378 Ocean Street
Jacksonville, Florida 32233
(855) 468-4286
Website: www.victoryjax.com

THIS SHIP STOPPED SAILING IN 2017. HOWEVER, IT MAY RE-OPEN IN THE FUTURE. CALL FIRST BEFORE TRAVELING TO THIS CASINO!

Toll-Free Number: (855) 468-4286
Gambling Age: 18
Special Features: 1,200-passenger *Victory II* departs from historic Mayport. 6-hour cruise on Sundays.

Port Richey

Map: **#6** (37 miles N.W. of Tampa)

Tropical Breeze Casino
7917 Bayview Street
Port Richey, Florida 34668
(727) 848-3423
Website: www.portricheycasino.com

Toll-Free Number: (844) 386-2789
Gambling Age: 18
Food Service: A la Carte
Shuttle Schedule:
Departs: 11am/3:30pm/7pm (Wed-Mon)
Returns: 5:30pm/9pm/12:00am
Price: $8
Port Charges: Included Parking: Free
Other Games: LIR, TCP
Special Features: 465-passenger Royal Casino 1 stays offshore and a water taxi shuttles passengers back and forth according to above schedule. Shuttle departs from dock on Pithlachascotee River off of US 19 in Port Richey.

Indian Casinos

Florida has eight Indian gaming locations. The Seminole Tribe has seven and the eighth is on the Miccosukee Tribe's reservation.

The Seminoles signed a compact with the state that allows them to offer traditional Class III gaming machines. As part of their compact, five Seminole casinos are also allowed to offer blackjack (BJ), poker (P), baccarat (B), mini-baccarat (MB), Mississippi stud (MS), three card poker (TCP), let it ride (LIR) and pai gow poker (PGP).

The Miccosukee Tribe has not signed a compact and they only offer Class II gaming machines at their casino.

Class II video gaming devices look like slot machines, but are actually bingo games and the spinning reels are for "entertainment purposes only." No public information is available concerning the payback percentages on any gaming machines in Florida's Indian casinos.

All of the casinos are open 24 hours (except Big Cypress) and the minimum gambling age is 18 at all Indian casinos for bingo or poker and 21 for electronic gaming machines and table games.

Miccosukee Resort & Gaming
500 S.W. 177 Avenue
Miami, Florida 33194
(305) 222-4600
Website: www.miccosukee.com
Map: **#1**

Toll-Free Number: (800) 741-4600
Room Reservations: (877) 242-6464
Rooms: 256 Price Range: $99-$149
Suites: 46 Price Range: $129-$209
Restaurants: 6 Liquor: Yes
Other Games: BG, P
Buffets: B-$9.95 L-$11.95
D-$12.95/$30.93 (Fri)
Overnight RV Parking: Free/RV Dump: No

Seminole Casino Big Cypress
30000 Gator Tail Trail
Clewiston, Florida 33440
(954) 214-8817
Website: www.seminolebigcypresscasino.com
Map: **#7** (60 miles N.W. of Fort Lauderdale)

Hours: 10am-6pm/11pm (Fri/Sat)
Restaurants: Snack Bar

Seminole Brighton Casino
17735 Reservation Road
Okeechobee, Florida 34974
(863) 467-9998
Website: www.seminolebrightoncasino.com
Map: **#10** (75 miles N.W. of West Palm Beach)

Toll-Free Number: (866) 222-7466
Restaurants: 1 Liquor: Yes
Casino Size: 24,400 Square Feet
Other Games: P, BG (Wed-Sun)
Overnight RV Parking: No

Seminole Casino Coconut Creek
5550 NW 40th Street
Coconut Creek, Florida 33073
(954) 977-6700
Website: www.seminolecoconutcreekcasino.com
Map: **#2**

Toll-Free Number: (866) 222-7466
Restaurants: 6 Liquor: Yes
Buffet: B-$10/$28 (Sat/Sun)
L-$19 D- $27/$33 (Fri/Sat)
Casino Size: 30,000 Square Feet
Other Games: BJ, MB, TCP, PGP, MS,
P, LIR, CW, S21
Overnight RV Parking: Call ahead.
Special Features: Non-smoking casino on second floor.

Seminole Casino Immokalee
506 South 1st Street
Immokalee, Florida 33934
(941) 658-1313
Website: www.seminoleimmokaleecasino.com
Map: **#4** (35 miles N.E. of Naples)

Toll-Free Number: (800) 218-0007
Rooms: 80 Price Range: $159-$259
Suites: 19 Price Range: $469-$659
Restaurants: 3 Liquor: Yes
Casino Size: 22,000 Square Feet
Other Games: BJ, MB, TCP, PGP,
LIR, P, S21, MS, UTH
Overnight RV Parking: Yes

The Seminole Hard Rock Hotel & Casino in Hollywood features a 130,000-square-foot casino, including a poker room, plus a 500-room hotel with a European-style spa. There is also an adjacent complex featuring a 5,500-seat Hard Rock Live entertainment venue.

Seminole Classic Casino
4150 N. State Road 7
Hollywood, Florida 33021
(954) 961-3220
Website: www.seminoleclassiccasino.com
Map: **#2** (1 miles S. of Fort Lauderdale)

Toll-Free Number: (800) 323-5452
Restaurants: 3 Liquor: Yes
Casino Size: 73,500 Square Feet
Other Games: BJ, MB, TCP, PGP, MS, BG, S21, CW
Overnight RV Parking: Free/RV Dump: No
Special Features: Located one block south of Hard Rock Hotel & Casino Hollywood. Food court with three fast food outlets.

Seminole Hard Rock Hotel & Casino - Hollywood
1 Seminole Way
Hollywood, Florida 33314
(954) 327-7625
www.seminolehardrockhollywood.com
Map: **#2** (1 mile S. of Fort Lauderdale)

Toll-Free Number: (866) 502-7529
Room Reservations: (800) 937-0010
Rooms: 437 Price Range: $179-$399
Suites: 63 Price Range: $309-$479
Restaurants: 3 Liquor: Yes
Buffets: Brunch-$64.95 (Sun)
Casino Size: 130,000 Square Feet
Other Games: BJ, P, CW, S21, MB, TCP, PGP, LIR, MS
Overnight RV Parking: No
Special Features: Food court with five fast-food outlets.. Lagoon-style pool. Health spa.

Seminole Hard Rock Hotel & Casino - Tampa
5223 Orient Road
Tampa, Florida 33610
(813) 627-7625
www.seminolehardrocktampa.com
Map: **#3**

Toll-Free Number: (800) 282-7016
Room Reservations: (800) 937-0010
Rooms: 204 Price Range: $279-$429
Suites: 46 Price Range: $359-$599
Restaurants: 5 Liquor: Yes
Buffets: B-$29.00 (Sun)
L-$20.00/$29.00 (Sun) D- $27.00
Casino Size: 90,000 Square Feet
Other Games: BJ, P, CW, S21, PG, MS
MB, TCP, PGP, LIR, Pai Gow Tiles, UTH
Overnight RV Parking: Call ahead.
Special Features: Food court with four fast food outlets. $5 buffet discount for players club members. Health club.

Pari-Mutuels

Broward County (home county of Fort Lauderdale) and Miami-Dade County both have four pari-mutuel facilities that each offer electronic gaming machines, but no table games.

Florida gaming regulations require a minimum payback of 85% on all gaming machines. From July 1, 2016 through June 30, 2017 the gaming machines at Magic City returned 93.55%, Casino Miami returned 93.48%, Hialeah Park returned 93.47%, Gulfstream Park returned 92.68%, Dania Casino returned 92.64%, Mardi Gras returned 91.67%, Calder returned 91.00%, and The Isle returned 90.91% .

South Florida's pari-mutuel facilities (as well as most pari-mutuels throughout the state), also offer poker. Admission to all casinos is free and they are allowed to be open a maximum of 18 hours per day during the week and 24 hours on the weekends and some holidays.

If you want to order a drink while playing, be aware that Florida gaming regulations do not allow pari-mutuel casinos to provide free alcoholic beverages.

The minimum gambling age is 18 for pari-mutuel betting or poker and 21 for gaming machines.

Calder Casino & Race Course
21001 N. W. 27th Avenue
Miami Gardens, Florida 33056
(305) 625-1311
Website: www.caldercasino.com
Map: **#1**

Toll Free: (800) 333-3227
Hours: 9am-3am/24 hours (Fri/Sat)
Restaurants: 2
Buffets: D-$18.99

Casino Miami
3500 N.W. 37th Avenue
Miami Florida 33142
(305) 633-6400
Website: www.playcasinomiami.com
Map: **#1**

Restaurants: 1 Snack Bar
Hours: 10am-4am/24 hours (Fri/Sat)
Special Features: Live jai-alai seasonally. Daily simulcasting of jai-alai and harness racing.

The Casino @ Dania Beach
301 E. Dania Beach Boulevard
Dania Beach, Florida 33004
(954) 920-1511
Website: www.casinodaniabeach.com
Map: **#2**

Toll-Free Number: (844) 794-6244
Restaurants: 1
Other Games: P
Overnight RV Parking: No
Special Features: Live jai-alai seasonally. Daily simulcasting of thoroughbred/harness racing and jai-alai.

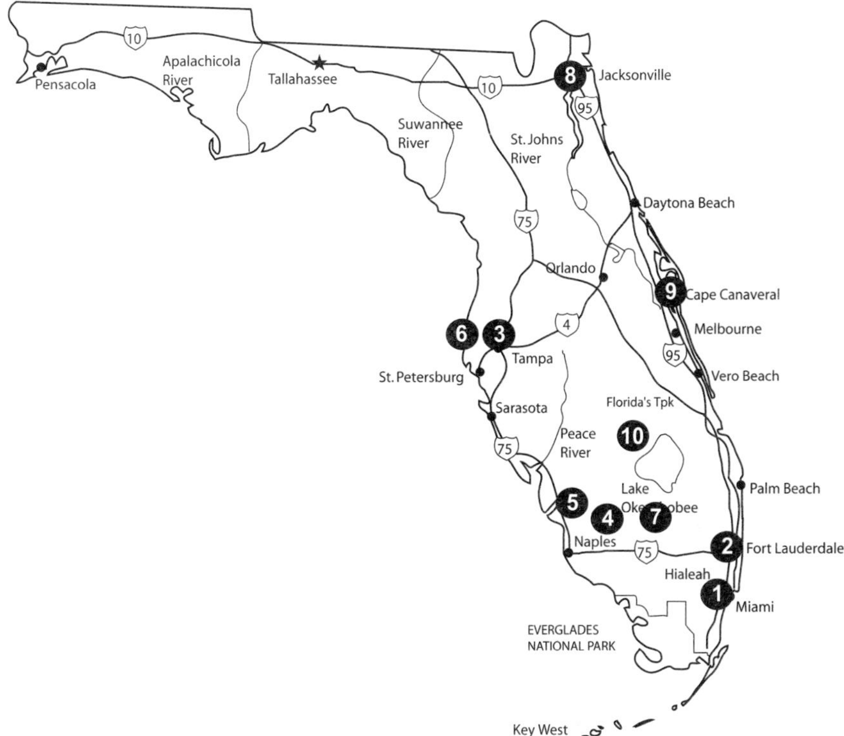

Gulfstream Park Racing & Casino
901 S. Federal Highway
Hallandale Beach, Florida 33009
(954) 454-7000
Website: www.gulfstreampark.com/casino
Map: #**2**

Hours: 9am-3am/ 24 Hours (Fri/Sat)
Restaurants: 3
Overnight RV Parking: No
Special Features: Live thoroughbred racing seasonally. Daily simulcasting of thoroughbred racing. Outdoor shopping area with over 20 shops and restaurants.

Hialeah Park Casino
2200 East 4th Avenue
Hialeah, Florida 33013
(305) 885-8000
Website: www.hialeahparkcasino.com
Map: #1

Restaurants: 4
Casino Hours: 9am-3am/24 hours (Fri/Sat)
Special Features: Live quarter-horse racing seasonally.

Isle Casino Racing Pompano Park
777 Isle of Capri Circle
Pompano Beach, Florida 33069
(954) 972-2000
Website: www.theislepompanopark.com
Map: **#2**

Toll-Free Number: (800) 843-4753
Hours: 9am-3am/24 hours (Fri/Sat)
Restaurants: 4
Buffet: B- $20.99 (Sun) L- $15.99
D- $26.99/ $31.99 (Fri/Sat)
Overnight RV Parking: No
Special Features: Live evening harness racing seasonally. Daily simulcasting of thoroughbred/harness racing and jai-alai.

Magic City Casino
450 NW 37th Avenue
Miami, Florida 33126
305-649-3000
Website: www.magiccitycasino.com
Map: **#1**

Toll-free Number: (888) 566-2442
Hours: 10am-4am/5am (Fri/Sat)
Restaurants: 1
Buffet: L-$12.95 (Sun) D- $15.95 (Fri/Sat)
Special Features: Live dog racing seasonally. Daily simulcasting of dog and harness racing. Buffet discount with players club card.

Mardi Gras Casino
831 N. Federal Highway
Hallandale Beach, Florida 33009
(954) 924-3200
Website: www.mgfla.com
Map: **#2**

Toll-Free Number: (877) 557-5687
Hours: 9am-3am/24 Hours (Fri/Sat)
Restaurants: 4
Overnight RV Parking: No
Special Features: Live dog racing seasonally. Daily simulcasting of dog, thoroughbred and harness races. Poker room is open 24 hours.

GEORGIA

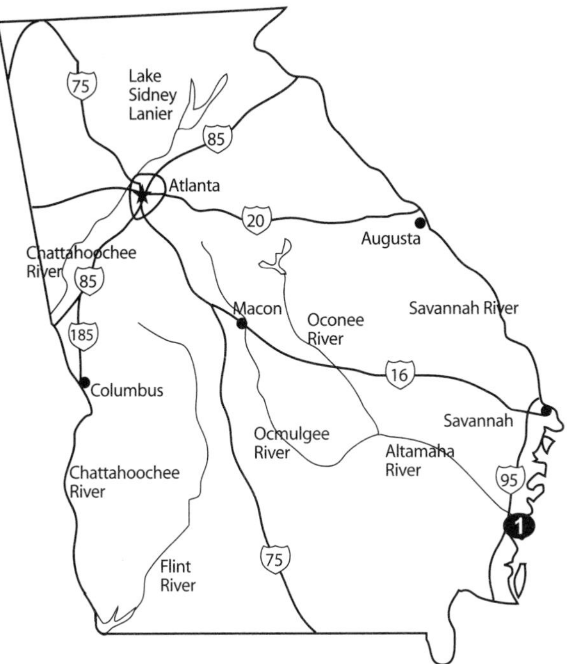

There is one casino boat in Georgia which sails three miles out into international waters where casino gambling is permitted.

The boat offers blackjack, craps, roulette, poker, slots and video poker. Due to security restrictions, you must present a photo ID or you will not be allowed to board.

For information on visiting Georgia call the state's tourism department at (800) 847-4842 or visit their website at www.georgia.org.

Emerald Princess Casino
1 Emerald Princess Drive
Brunswick, Georgia 31523
(912) 265-3558
Website: www.emeraldprincesscasino.com
Map Location: **#1** (75 miles S. of Savannah)

Reservation Number: (800) 842-0115
Gambling Age: 18 Parking: Free
Schedule
11:00am - 4:00pm (Fri/Sat)
1:00pm - 6:00pm (Sun)
7:00pm - 12:00am (Tue-Thu)
7:00pm - 1:00am (Fri/Sat)
Price: $10 Port Charges: Included
Special Features: 400-passenger *Emerald Princess II* sails from Gisco Point, at the southern end of the Sidney Lanier Bridge. Reservations are required for all cruises. Packages with hotel accommodations are available. No one under 18 permitted to board.

IDAHO

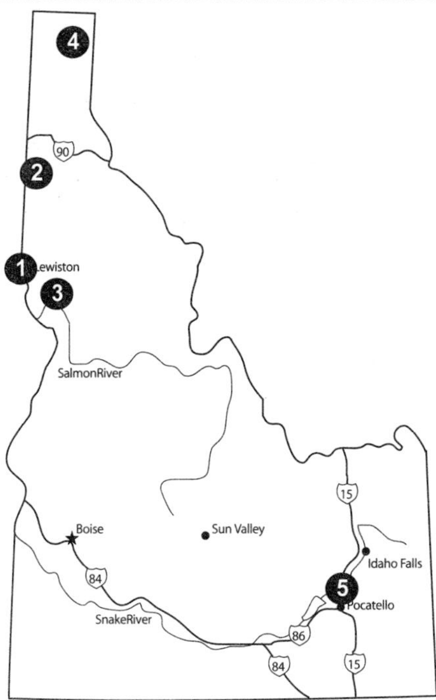

Idaho has seven Indian casinos that offer electronic pull-tab machines and other video games. The machines don't pay out in cash. Instead they print out a receipt which must be cashed by a floor attendant or taken to the cashier's cage. Some casinos also offer bingo (BG), off-track betting (OTB) and poker (P).

The terms of the compact between the tribes and the state do not require any minimum payback percentage that the gaming machines must return to the public.

The minimum gambling age at all casinos is 18 and they are all open 24 hours. For Idaho tourism information call (800) 635-7820 or visit their website: www.visitid.org.

Bannock Peak Casino
1707 W. Country Road
Pocatello, Idaho 83204
(208) 235-1308
Website: www.shobangaming.com
Map: **#5** (5 miles N. of Pocatello)

Restaurants: 1 Snack Bar Liquor: No
Hours: 10am-12am/1am (Fri/Sat)
Casino Size: 5,000 Square Feet
Other Games: Only gaming machines
Overnight RV Parking: Free/RV Dump: No

Clearwater River Casino and Lodge
17500 Nez Perce Road
Lewiston, Idaho 83501
(208) 746-0723
Website: www.crcasino.com
Map: **#1** (250 miles N. of Boise)

Toll-Free Number: (877) 678-7423
Rooms: 47 Price Range: $89-$129
Suites: 3 Price Range $189-$199
Restaurants: 1 Liquor: No
Casino Size: 30,000 Square Feet
Hours: 7am-12am
Other Games: BG (Select Days)
Overnight RV Parking: Free/RV Dump: No
SSpecial Features: 23-space RV park ($25 per night).

Coeur D'Alene Casino Resort Hotel
37914 South Nukwalow
Worley, Idaho 83876
(800) 523-2464
Website: www.cdacasino.com
Map: **#2** (350 miles N. of Boise)

Rooms: 202 Price Range: $79-$200
Suites: 8 Price Range $160-$450
Restaurants: 7 Liquor: Yes Valet Parking: Free
Buffet: B- $11.99 (Fri-Mon)
D- $11.99 (Fri/Sun)/$20.99(Sat)
Casino Size: 30,000 Square Feet
Other Games: K, BG (Fri-Sun), OTB
Overnight RV Parking: $20/RV Dump: No
Special Features: 18-hole golf course. Spa.

Fort Hall Casino
Simplot Road
Fort Hall, Idaho 83203
(208) 237-8778
Website: www.shobangaming.com
Map: **#5** (14 miles N. of Pocatello)

Toll-Free Number: (800) 497-4231
Rooms: 145 Price Range: $149-$229
Suites: 11 Price Range $275-$325
Restaurants: 2 Liquor: No
Casino Size: 15,000 Square Feet
Other Games: BG (Wed-Sun)
Overnight RV Parking: Must use RV Park
Special Features: 27-space RV park ($27 per night).

It'Se-Ye-Ye Casino
419 Third Street
Kamiah, Idaho 83536
(208) 935-7860
Website: www.crcasino.com
Map: **#3** (225 miles N. of Boise)

Restaurants: 1 Liquor: No
Hours: 7am-12am
Casino Size: 2,300 Square Feet
Overnight RV Parking: Free/RV Dump: No

Kootenai River Inn Casino and Spa
7169 Plaza Street
Bonners Ferry, Idaho 83805
(208) 267 8511
Website: www.kootenairiverinn.com
Map: **#4** (450 miles N. of Boise)

Toll-Free Number: (800) 346-5668
Rooms: 47 Price Range: $129-$169
Suites: 4 Price Range $299-$399
Restaurants: 1 Liquor: Yes
Casino Size: 30,000 Square Feet
Other Games: BG (1st and 3rd Wed)
Overnight RV Parking: Free/RV Dump: No
Special Features: Hotel is Best Western. Spa.

Sage Hill Travel Center & Casino
2 North Eagle Road
Blackfoot, Idaho 83221
Map: **#5** (14 miles N. of Pocatello)
Website: www.shobangaming.com
(208) 237-4998

Restaurants: 1
Casino Hours: 6:30am-2am/5am (Fri/Sat)
Casino Size: 13,200 Square Feet
Other Games: Only gaming machines
Special Features: Convenience store and gas station.

ILLINOIS

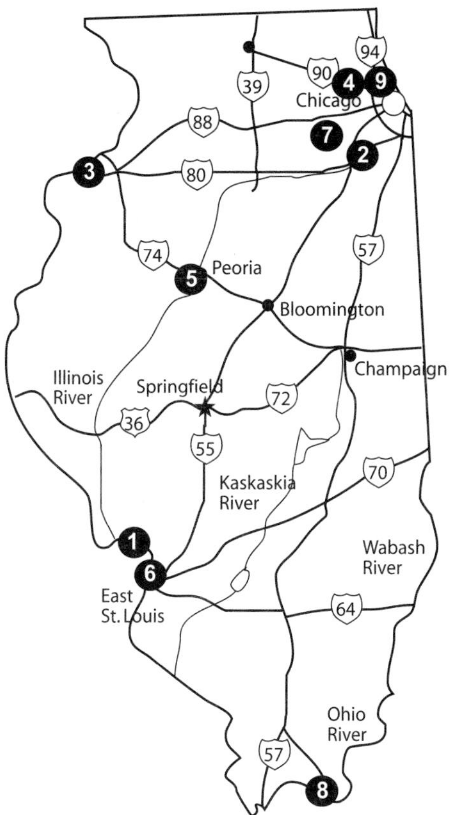

Illinois was the second state to legalize riverboat casinos. Riverboat casinos began operating there in September 1991 with the launching of the first boat: the Alton Belle.

All Illinois riverboats remain dockside and do not cruise. Unlike Mississippi, however, the casinos are not open 24 hours and state law limits the number of gaming licenses to 10.

Here's information from the Illinois Gaming Board showing each casino's average slot payback percentage for the one-year period from July 1, 2016 through June 30, 2017:

CASINO	PAYBACK %
Casino Queen	92.45
Harrah's Joliet	92.05
Hollywood - Joliet	91.31
Argosy Alton	91.10
Par-A-Dice	91.02
Grand Victoria	90.98
Hollywood - Aurora	90.71
Jumer's	90.24
Rivers Casino	90.07
Harrah's Metropolis	89.18

These figures reflect the total percentages returned by each casino for all of their electronic machines.

All casinos are non-smoking and, unless otherwise noted, all casinos offer: slots, video poker, blackjack, craps, roulette and three card poker. Some casinos also offer: let it ride (LIR), baccarat (B), mini-baccarat (MB), poker (P), Ultimate Texas hold em (UTH), Caribbean stud poker (CSP), Mississippi stud (MS), pai gow poker (PGP) and four card poker (FCP).

If you want to order a drink while playing, be aware that Illinois gaming regulations do not allow casinos to provide free alcoholic beverages. The minimum gambling age is 21.

For more information on visiting Illinois contact the state's Bureau of Tourism at (800) 226-6632 or www.enjoyillinois.com

Argosy Casino Alton
1 Piasa Street
Alton, Illinois 62002
(618) 474-7500
Website: www.argosyalton.com
Map: **#1** (260 miles S.W. of Chicago, 25 miles N. of St. Louis, MO)

Toll-Free Number: (800) 711-4263
Restaurants: 3
Buffets: L-$16.99 D-$19.99/$31.99 (Fri/Sat)
Casino Hours: 8am-6am Daily
Casino Size: 23,000 Square Feet
Other Games: UTH
Overnight RV Parking: Yes
Special Features: Casino features a 1,200-passenger modern yacht and a barge docked on the Mississippi River. Table games open at 10am daily. Buffet discount for players club members.

Casino Queen
200 S. Front Street
E. St. Louis, Illinois 62201
(618) 874-5000
Website: www.casinoqueen.com
Map: **#6** (290 miles S.W. of Chicago)

Toll-Free Number: (800) 777-0777
Rooms: 150 Price Range: $89-$169
Suites: 7 Price Range: $149-$699
Restaurants: 4
Buffets: B-$12.95(Sat)/$15.95 (Sun)
L-$11.95/$12.95 (Sat)/$15.95 (Sun)
D-$15.95/$19.95 (Sat)
Casino Hours: 8am-4am/6am (Thu-Sat)
Casino Size: 40,000 Square Feet
Other Games: UTH
Senior Discount: Various Tue 8am-7pm if 50+
Overnight RV Parking: Must use RV park
Special Features: Land-based casino. 140-space RV park ($59+ per night). Sports Bar. MetroLink light-rail station at doorstep.

Grand Victoria Casino
250 S. Grove Avenue
Elgin, Illinois 60120
(847) 468-7000
Website: www.grandvictoriacasino.com
Map: **#4** (41 miles N.W. of Chicago)

Toll Free Number: (888) 508-1900
Restaurants: 4
Buffets: L-$12.99/$15.99 (Sun)
D-$19.99/$34.99(Fri)/
$29.99(Sat/Sun)
Casino Hours: 8:30am-6:30am Daily
Casino Size: 29,850 Square Feet
Other Games: MB, P
Overnight RV Parking: Yes
Special Features: 1,200-passenger paddle wheeler-replica docked on the Fox River. Buffet discount for player's club members. 100x odds on craps.

The Best Places To Play In The Chicago Area

by John Grochowski

Almost from the beginning, legal casino gambling in the Chicago area has been a diverse experience with several markets in one.

Casinos in Illinois were on riverboats restricted to 1,200 gaming positions when they opened their doors starting in 1991, while neighboring Wisconsin had full-scale land-based tribal casinos. When Indiana came on board a few years later, the games were on boats, but the vessels were larger and without the restrictions in gaming positions. And there's competition with Illinois bars, restaurants, truck stops and service organizations, which may have up to five slot machines.

Riverboats no longer sail, even though the Illinois and Indiana casinos nearest Chicago remain on the water, housed in barges or dockside boats. That leaves the following options for Chicago-area players:

Illinois Casinos: Within the Chicago metropolitan area there are five casinos in suburbs and small cities that ring Chicago. Players can choose among Harrah's and Hollywood in Joliet, Hollywood in Aurora, Grand Victoria in Elgin and Rivers in Des Plaines.

Rivers is the closest to Chicago, with Des Plaines neighboring O'Hare Airport about 16 miles from the north Loop. The others are in an arc about 40 to 50 miles from the Loop, with Elgin slightly northwest, Joliet to the southwest and Aurora in between.

The limit on gaming positions remains in force after all these years, Illinois casinos must close for four hours out of each 24, and there is a ban on smoking in public venues in the state. Typically, Illinois casinos use about 1,100 of those positions on slot machines and other electronic gaming devices such as video poker and video keno. Rivers has a larger than usual corps of table players, so its slot total is closer to 1,000

Only the two Joliet casinos have hotels, though all have multiple restaurants, including buffet and steakhouse options. None have showrooms, and in Illinois, when a casino sponsors headliner entertainment, it usually is in cooperation with a partner in the host city.

Indiana Casinos: Actually closer to Chicago than all the Illinois casinos except Rivers, there are four Indiana casinos within the metro area. The largest, Horseshoe in Hammond, is only 16 miles from the South Loop. The others – Ameristar in East Chicago and Majestic Star I and II in Gary, are only a few miles farther east.

All may remain open 24/7, smoking is not banned and there is no limit on the number of games. The casinos there are much larger --- the largest facility, Horseshoe Hammond's barge, has more than 2,800 electronic games and 160-plus table games. One consequence is that there is a much larger selection of new table games in Indiana. If you want to try Blackjack Switch, High Card Flush, Pai-Gow tiles or even a Big Six wheel, you're more likely to find it in Indiana.

Ameristar and Majestic Star have hotels, while Horseshoe prefers to work with Chicago hotel partners. Horseshoe does have a state-of-the-art event center for headliner entertainment, conventions, conferences and more. That's where Horseshoe holds its annual World Series of Poker satellite event.

Outlying Casinos: A little outside the Chicago area, but within easy drives of about an hour and a half, are Blue Chip Casino in Michigan City, Ind., Four Winds Casino in New Buffalo, Mich., Potawatomi Bingo Casino in Milwaukee. Increase the range to a three-hour drive, and that brings in a couple of Illinois casinos, Par-A-Dice casino in Peoria and Jumer's Casino Rock Island.

Blue Chip operates under the same conditions as other Indiana properties and Par-A-Dice and Jumer's operate under Illinois regulations. Potawatomi in Wisconsin and Four Winds in Michigan are full-service, land-based showpieces for those with time to travel a little farther afield.

Illinois bars, restaurants, truck stops and service organizations: Unless prohibited by local ordinance, facilities that receive an Illinois Gaming Board license may operate up to five video gaming machines. Some communities, including the City of Chicago, have opted out, but even so, there are nearly 30,000 machines in operation at such facilities across the state. That's more slots than there are in Illinois' 10 casinos combined.

Each site is limited to five gaming terminals, and the terminals include both slot and video poker games. They are games with random number generators, and work just like casino slots, except there are some restrictions. Credit denominations must range between 5 cents and 25 cents, the maximum wager is $2, and the maximum payout for a single play is $500. A quarter video poker game can't pay the $1,000 jackpot players are used to on quarter machines.

Back in the casinos, let's look at some of the best of gaming in the Chicago area.

Video Poker: Chicago area players have little these days that resembles its video poker hey-day of the mid-2000s. Then, Chicagoans were used to a high volume of 99-percenters-plus payback games – not to mention the 100-percent plus 10-7-5 Double Bonus Poker games with progressive jackpots Empress offered until 2003. They often were often shocked to find pay tables that didn't match up when they visited the Las Vegas Strip. Alas, the video poker oasis has dried up, though there remain some good plays.

Majestic Star in Gary stands as an oasis of high-paying video poker for players with moderate budgets. High payers once were confined to Majestic Star II, but now there's a collection of 99-percenters on Majestic Star I, too. They're not on every machine, so you have to check before you play, but there are 25-cent-50-cent-$1 single-hand machines with a 99.8-percent version of Triple Bonus Poker Plus; Not So Ugly Deuces Wild (99.7); 9-6 Jacks or Better (99.5); 8-5 ACES Bonus Poker (99.4) and more. The one downside is that it takes $100 in play to earn one rewards point on these machines, as opposed to $10 per point on other machines, but the upgrade in payback at the machines is well worth it.

Horseshoe Hammond has a collection of good games for bigger players. You can find NSU Deuces on Triple Play/FivePlay/Ten Play machines at $2, $5 and $10 level. For single-hand players, there's 9-7 Triple Double Bonus Poker (99.58 percent) on $1-$2-$5 and $5-$10-$25 machines, and 9-6 Bonus Poker Deluxe (99.6) on the $5-$10-$25 machines.

Elsewhere, there are opportunities for dollar players, including 9-6 Double Double Bonus Poker (98.98 percent) at. Hollywood Joliet, Harrah's Joliet and Ameristar East Chicago. All have $1 progressives, with the two Joliet casinos both offering three-way progressives --- progressive jackpots on royal flushes, four Aces with a low card kicker, and four Aces without the kicker.

Craps: The addition of Rivers gave the Chicago area a second casino catering to big craps players. Rivers offers 100x odds --- the same as Horseshoe in Hammond. Horseshoe had dramatically changed the face of Chicago area craps after Jack Binion bought the former Empress in 1999. Bringing in 100x odds and $10,000 maximums was a radical change for Chicago, which had been a double-odds kind of town through the mid-1990s.

Now 20x odds have become common among competitors, while Rivers makes it a 100x odds duo.

Blackjack: Most games in the Chicago area use either six or eight decks. Table minimums are high, especially in Illinois where anything under $15 a hand is rare treat for a midweek morning. Even Majestic Star, long the last bastion of $5 tables, has gone to $10 minimums except for the sporadic opening of a $5 Blackjack Switch game.

If you want to play $5 blackjack and don't want to make the longer drive to Jumer's, Par-A-Dice or Blue Chip, your sole option is Harrah's Joliet, which pays only 6-5 on blackjacks at $5 tables. That adds 1.4 percent to the house edge for a total of 1.92 percent against basic strategy players.

Smart players will avoid games like that but in Indiana, you can still play for $5 and get 3-2 payoffs on blackjack. At Majestic Star, $5 tables with continuous shufflers are six decks, dealer hits soft 17, double after split permitted, house edge vs. a basic strategy player 0.63 percent. At $25 tables without the continuous shufflers, dealers stand on all 17s and late surrender is available, reducing the house edge to 0.33 percent. There are a few double-deck games, but with tougher rules, including double down only on two-card 10s and no resplitting of pairs.

Until recent years, the only casinos in the area that had dealers hit soft 17 were Hollywood Aurora and Grand Victoria. Now the most common games on both sides of the state border are six decks with the dealer hitting soft 17, but blackjacks pay 3-2 and you can double down after any first two cards, including after splitting pairs. The house edge is 0.63 percent, and $25 players can get it down to 0.34 percent at the two Joliet casinos where, at that level, dealers stand on soft 17 and players may resplit Aces. Majestic Star drops that a fraction more to 0.33 percent by offering late surrender at its $25 tables.

Other Table Games: You'll find the lowest minimum bets in Indiana. At Majestic Star, $5 tables remain part of the mix. For the high rollers, Horseshoe and Indiana and Rivers in Illinois both have what you're looking for, including max bets of $100,000 a hand at baccarat.

With bigger table pits, Indiana casinos offer much more variety than the Illinois competition. In addition to blackjack and craps, Illinois operations tend to stick with roulette and Caribbean Stud, with a little mini-baccarat, Let It Ride or Three Card Poker in the mix at some casinos. In Indiana, most operators have all those games, and also pick and choose from among Mississippi Stude, pai-gow poker, Spanish 21, Four Card Poker, High Card Flush, Ultimate Texas Hold'Em --- if there's a promising new game, someone in Indiana is likely to try it.

Slot Machines: Along with the rest of the country, Chicago has seen a great expansion in video bonusing slot games, with the hottest trend being toward lower and lower coin denominations. All Chicago area casinos now have penny slots. Horseshoe had been reluctant to join the penny trend, but the nationwide growth and popularity of the games have even casinos that cater to big players clamoring for copper.

Traditional three-reel games remain a big part of the mix at dollars and above, with Majestic Star having the largest selection of quarter three-reelers.

One thing you'll not find in Illinois or Indiana is million-dollar jackpots. Wide-area progressives such as Megabucks that link several different properties to the same jackpot are illegal in Illinois and Indiana. If you're a jackpot chaser, you'll need to go to Potawatomi in Milwaukee or Four Winds in New Buffalo, which both are on the national Native American link.

Slot payouts tend to be higher in Illinois than in Indiana, from quarters on up, but the Indiana casinos pay as much or more than the Illinois operations in nickels and below. Illinois averages tend to hover around 95 percent on dollars, 93 percent on quarters and 88 percent on nickels, 85 percent on pennies while Indiana returns, are around 94 percent on dollars, 92 percent on quarters and 89 percent on nickels and 86 percent on pennies --- with variations from casino to casino, of course.

Harrah's Joliet
151 N. Joliet Street
Joliet, Illinois 60432
(815) 740-7800
Website: www.harrahsjoliet.com
Map: **#2** (43 miles S.W. of Chicago)

Toll-Free Number: (800) 427-7247
Rooms: 200 Price Range: $89-$249
Suites: 4 Price Range: Casino Use Only
Restaurants: 3
Buffets: L-$17.49/$20.99 (Sat)/$26.99 (Sun)
D-$21.99/$36.99 (Fri)/
$26.99 (Sat/Sun)
Casino Hours: 8am-6am Daily
Casino Size: 39,000 Square Feet
Other Games: MB, UTH, P, MS
Overnight RV Parking: No
Special Features: Casino is on a barge docked on the Des Plaines River. Buffet is closed Tue/Wed.

Harrah's Metropolis
100 E. Front Street
Metropolis, Illinois 62960
(618) 524-2628
Website: www.harrahsmetropolis.com
Map: **#8** (Across from Paducah, KY.)

Toll-Free Number: (800) 929-5905
Rooms: 252 Price Range: $55-$159
Suites: 6 Price Range: Casino Use Only
Restaurants: 3
Buffets: B-$16.99 (Sat/Sun)
D-$16.99 (Thu/Sun)/$21.99 (Fri/Sat)
Hours: 9am-5am/7am (Fri/Sat)
Other Games: LIR, MB, MS
Casino Size: 24,269 Square Feet
Overnight RV Parking: Free/RV Dump: No
Special Features: 1,300-passenger sidewheeler-replica docked on the Ohio River. Buffet closed Mon-Wed.

Hollywood Casino - Aurora
1 W. New York Street Bridge
Aurora, Illinois 60506
(630) 801-7000
Website: www.hollywoodcasinoaurora.com
Map: **#7** (41 miles W. of Chicago)

Toll Free Number: (800) 888-7777
Restaurants: 3
Buffets: L-$13.99/$19.99 (Sun)
D-$17.99/$29.99 (Fri)/$20.99 (Sat)
Casino Hours: 8:30am-4:30am/6:30 (Fri/Sat)
Casino Size: 41,384 Square Feet
Other Games: MB, P, MS
Overnight RV Parking: No
Senior Discount: 50% off buffet Wed if 55+
Special Features: Casino is on a barge docked on the Fox River. Buffet discount for players club members. Buffet closed Mon-Tue.

Hollywood Casino - Joliet
151 N. Joliet Street
Joliet, Illinois 60436
(815) 744-9400
Website: www.hollywoodcasinojoliet.com
Map: **#2** (43 miles S.W. of Chicago)

Toll-Free Number: (888) 436-7737
Rooms: 85 Price Range: $99-$149
Suites: 17 Price Range: $129-$179
Casino Hours: 7:30am-5:30am Daily
Restaurants: 4
Buffets: L-$13.99 (Wed-Sat)/$16.99 (Sun)
D-$17.99/$29.99 (Fri)/$22.99 (Sat)
Casino Size: 50,000 square feet
Other Games: MB, P, MS
Overnight RV Parking: Must use RV park
Special Features: 2,500-passenger barge docked on the Des Plaines River. Buffet closed Mon-Tue. 80-space RV park ($36-$42 per night).

Jumer's Casino & Hotel Rock Island
777 Jumer Drive
Rock Island, Illinois 61201
(309) 756-4600
Website: www.jumerscasinohotel.com
Map: **#3** (170 miles W. of Chicago)

Toll-Free Number: (800) 477-7747
Rooms: 205 Price Range: $109-$209
Suites: 7 Price Range: $159-$599
Restaurants: 4
Buffets: B-$8.99 L- $14.99/$19.99 (Sun)
D- $14.99/$19.99 (Fri/Sat)
Casino Hours: 7am-5am Daily
Casino Size: 42,300 Square Feet
Other games: MS, P
Overnight RV Parking: Free/Dump: No

Par-A-Dice Hotel Casino
21 Blackjack Boulevard
East Peoria, Illinois 61611
(309) 698-7711
Website: www.paradicecasino.com
Map: **#5** (170 miles S.W. of Chicago)

Toll-Free Number: (800) 727-2342
Room Reservations: (800) 547-0711
Rooms: 195 Price Range: $99-$139
Suites 13 Price Range: $175-$500
Restaurants: 4
Buffets: B- $7.95 L-$10.99/$14.99 (Sat/Sun)
D-$13.99/$18.99 (Fri/Sat)/
$16.99 (Sun)
Casino Hours: 8am-4am/6am (Fri/Sat)
Casino Size: 26,116 Square Feet
Other Games: MB, LIR, CSP, P, MS, B6
Overnight RV Parking: Free/RV Dump: No
Special Features: 1,600-passenger modern boat docked on the Illinois River. Buffet closed Mon/Tue.

Rivers Casino
3000 S River Road
Des Plaines, Illinois 60018
(847) 795-0777
Website: www.playrivers.com
Map: **#9** (20 miles N.W. of Chicago)

Toll Free Number: (888) 307-0777
Restaurants: 5
Buffets: L-$19.95/$25.95 (Sun)
D-$29.95/$39.95 (Tue)
Casino Hours: 9am-7am Daily
Casino Size: 43,687 Square Feet
Other Games: B, MB, CSP, THB, MS, S21, PGP
Overnight RV Parking: No
Special features: Closest casino to O'Hare airport. Free lounge entertainment nightly.

INDIANA

In June 1993 Indiana became the sixth state to legalize riverboat gambling. All of the state's riverboat casinos offer dockside gambling and, unless otherwise noted, are open 24 hours. The minimum gambling age is 21.

Following is information from the Indiana Gaming Commission regarding average slot payout percentages for the one-year period from July 1, 2016 through June 30, 2017:

CASINO	PAYBACK %
Rising Star	91.61
French Lick	91.61
Indiana Grand	91.55
Hoosier Park	91.48
Blue Chip	91.41
Belterra	90.93
Majestic Star	90.39
Ameristar	90.30
Hollywood	90.10
Horseshoe SI	90.02
Tropicana	89.98
Majestic Star II	89.91
Horseshoe Hammond	89.83

These figures reflect the average percentage returned by each casino for all of their electronic machines including slot machines, video poker, video keno, etc.

Unless otherwise noted, all casinos offer: blackjack, craps, roulette, slots, video poker, video keno and Caribbean stud poker. Optional games include: baccarat (B), mini-baccarat (MB), poker (P), pai gow poker (PGP), three card poker (TCP), Mississippi stud (MS), pai gow (PG), four card poker (FCP), Spanish 21 (S21), big 6 wheel (B6) and let it ride (LIR).

If you want to order a drink while playing, be aware that Indiana gaming regulations do not allow casinos to provide free alcoholic beverages.

NOTE: If you happen to win a jackpot of $1,200 or more in Indiana, the casino will withhold 3.4% of your winnings for the Indiana Department of Revenue. You may, however, be able to get *some* of that money refunded by filing a state income tax return. The $1,200 threshold also applies to any cash prizes won in casino drawings or tournaments.

For more information on visiting Indiana call (800) 289-6646 or visit their website at www.enjoyindiana.com.

Ameristar East Chicago
777 Ameristar Boulevard
East Chicago, Indiana 46312
(219) 378-3000
Website: www.ameristarcasinos.com
Map: **#9** (12 miles E. of Chicago)

Toll-Free Number: (877) 496-1777
Hotel Reservations: (866) 711-7799
Rooms: 286 Prices: $109-$259
Suites: 7 Prices: Casino Use Only
Restaurants: 5
Buffets: B- $17.99 (Sat/Sun)
L- $15.99/$17.99 (Sat/Sun)
D- $19.99/$31.99 (Fri/Sat)
Casino Size: 53,000 Square Feet
Other Games: B, MB, PGP, P, TCP, LIR, MS
Overnight RV Parking: No
Special Features: 3,750-passenger modern yacht docked on Lake Michigan.

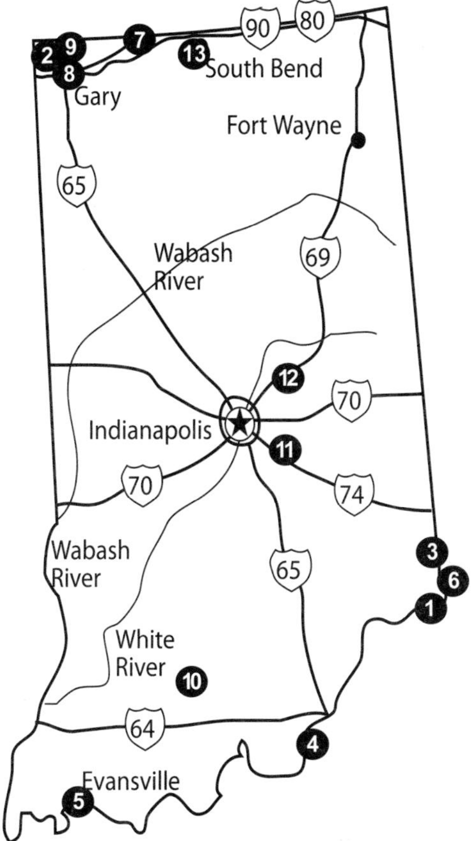

Belterra Casino Resort and Spa
777 Belterra Drive
Florence, Indiana 47020
(812) 427-7777
Website: www.belterracasino.com
Map: **#1** (35 miles S.W. of Cincinnati, Ohio)

Toll-Free Number: (888) 235-8377
Rooms: 600 Price Range: $119-$249
Suites: 8 Price Range: $249-$499
Restaurants: 6
Buffets: B-$14.95 L-$16.95/$20.95 (Sat/Sun)
D-$20.95/$35.95(Fri/Sat)
Casino Size: 38,000 Square Feet
Other Games: P, PGP, TCP, FCP, LIR,
MB, MS, UTH
Overnight RV Parking: Free (must park in back rows of parking lot)/RV Dump: No
Special Features: 2,600-passenger sidewheeler docked on the Ohio River. Health club and spa. 18-hole golf course. 1,500-seat showroom.

Blue Chip Casino & Hotel
777 Blue Chip Drive
Michigan City, Indiana 46360
(219) 879-7711
Website: www.bluechip-casino.com
Map: **#7** (40 miles E. of Chicago)

Toll-Free Number: (888) 879-7711
Rooms: 180 Price Range: $109-$279
Suites: Casino Use Only
Restaurants: 5
Buffets: B-$11.99/$18.99 (Sat/Sun)
L- $15.99/$11.99 (Wed/Fri)
D- $19.99/$24.99 (Thu/Sun)/
$26.99 (Fri)/$31.99 (Sat)
Casino Size: 25,000 Square Feet
Other Games: MB, P, TCP, MS, UTH
Overnight RV Parking: Free/RV Dump: No
Senior Discount: Various Mon if 50+.
Special Features: 2,000-passenger modern yacht docked in a man-made canal.

French Lick Springs Resort & Casino
8670 West State Road 56
French Lick, Indiana 47432
(812) 936-9300
Website: www.frenchlick.com
Map: **#10** (108 miles S. of Indianapolis)

Toll-Free Number: (888) 936-9360
Rooms: 442 Price Range: $189-$339
Restaurants: 11
Buffets: B-$17.99/$21.99 (Sun)
Casino Size: 84,000 Square Feet
Other Games: MB, TCP, FCP, MS
Overnight RV Parking: No/RV Dump: No
Special Features: Two 18-hole golf courses. Full-service spa. 12-space RV park ($60 per night). Six-lane bowling alley. Located on a 3,500-passenger barge in a man-made moat. 10% off buffet for players club members.

Hollywood Casino & Hotel - Lawrenceburg
777 Hollywood Boulevard
Lawrenceburg, Indiana 47025
(812) 539-8000
Website: www.hollywoodindiana.com
Map: **#3** (95 miles S.E. of Indianapolis)

Toll-Free Number: (888) 274-6797
Rooms: 440 Price Range: $89-$259
Restaurants: 4
Buffets: B-$14.99/$21.99 (Sun)
L-$16.99/ $21.99(Sun)
D-$36.99 (Fri)/$26.99 (Sat)/
$24.99 (Sun)
Casino Size: 80,000 Square Feet
Other Games: B6, MB, LIR, P, TCP, PGP,
FCP, B, MS
Overnight RV Parking: Free (only in lot across the street from the casino)/RV Dump: No
Special Features: 4,000-passenger modern yacht docked on the Ohio River. No dinner buffet Mon-Thu.

Horseshoe Casino Hammond
777 Casino Center Drive
Hammond, Indiana 46320
(219) 473-7000
Website: www.chicagohorseshoe.com
Map: **#2** (10 miles E. of Chicago)

Toll-Free Number: (866) 711-7463
Restaurants: 4
Buffets: L/D-$21.99 (Sat/Sun)
Casino Size: 43,000 Square Feet
Other Games: MB, TCP, LIR, P,
B6, PG, B, MS
Overnight RV Parking: Free/RV Dump: No
Special Features: 4,000-passenger barge docked on Lake Michigan. 100x odds on craps

Horseshoe Casino Hotel Southern Indiana
11999 Casino Center Drive SE
Elizabeth, Indiana 47117
(812) 969-6000
Website: www.horseshoe-indiana.com
Map: **#4** (20 miles S. of New Albany)

Toll-Free Number: (866) 676-7463
Reservation Number: (877) 237-6626
Rooms: 503 Prices: Price Range: $89-$229
Restaurants: 4
Buffets: B-$23.99 (Sat/Sun)
L-$20.99 D-$20.99/$34.99 (Fri)/
$29.99 (Sat)
Casino Size: 93,000 Square Feet
Other Games: S21, B, MB, CSP, MS,
P, PGP, LIR, TCP
Senior Discount: Various discounts Wed if 50+
Special Features: 5,000-passenger sidewheeler docked on the Ohio River. Buffet closed Mon/Tue. 18-hole golf course.

The 5,000-passenger *Horseshoe Southern Indiana* is the world's largest riverboat casino.

Majestic Star Casinos & Hotel
1 Buffington Harbor Drive
Gary, Indiana 46406
(219) 977-7777
Website: www.majesticstarcasino.com
Map: **#8** (15 miles E. of Chicago)

Toll-Free Number: (888) 225-8259
Rooms: 300 Price Range: $79-$139
Restaurants: 4
Buffets: B-$10.99 (Sat/Sun)
L-$13.99/$16.99 (Sun)
D-$17.99/$34.95 (Fri/Sat)
Casino Size: 43,000 Square Feet
Other Games: S21, B, MB, MS, CSP, PGP, TCP, LIR, P, B6
Overnight RV Parking: Free/RV Dump: No
Special Features: Two boats: 1,300-passenger and 2,300-passenger modern yachts docked on Lake Michigan.

Rising Star Casino Resort
777 Rising Star Drive
Rising Sun, Indiana 47040
(812) 438-1234
Website: www.risingstarcasino.com
Map: **#6** (40 miles S.W. of Cincinnati)

Toll-Free Number: (800) 472-6311
Rooms: 294 Price Range: $79-$169
Restaurants: 5
Buffets: B-$13.99 L-$14.99/$21.99 (Sat/Sun)
D-$21.99/$25.99 (Tue/Thu)/
$30.99 (Fri/Sat)
Casino Size: 40,000 Square Feet
Other Games: TCP, B6, S21, MS, CSP, LIR, FCP
Overnight RV Parking: Free/RV Dump: No
Senior Discount: Various discounts Mon/Tue if 50+
Special Features: 3,000-passenger paddle wheeler docked on Ohio River. 56-space RV park ($40-$70 per night). Hotel is Hyatt. 18-hole golf course. 1,100-seat showroom. 25x odds on craps.

Tropicana Evansville
421 N.W. Riverside Drive
Evansville, Indiana 47708
(812) 433-4000
Website: www.tropevansville.com
Map: **#5** (168 miles S.W. of Indianapolis)

Toll-Free Number: (800) 342-5386
Rooms: 240 Price Range: $99-$149
Suites: 10 Price Range: $239-$339
Restaurants: 5
Buffets: B-$10.95 L- $13.95/$16.95 (Sun)
D- $17.95/$19.95 (Fri/Sat)
Casino Size: 47,863 Square Feet
Other Games: MB, P, TCP, MS
Overnight RV Parking: No
Senior Discount: Join Club 55, if 55+
Special Features: 2,700-passenger old fashioned paddlewheeler docked on the Ohio River.

Indiana Grand Casino
4300 N. Michigan Road
Shelbyville, Indiana 46176
(317) 421-0000
Website: www.indianagrand.com
Map: **#11** (32 miles S.E. of Indianapolis)

Toll-Free Number: (877) 386-4463
Restaurants: 4
Buffets: L- $13.95/$19.95 (Sun)
D- $18.95/$28.95 (Fri)/
$24.95 (Thu)/$21.95 (Sat)
Casino Size: 70,000 Square Feet
Other Games: P
Special Features: Live thoroughbred and harness racing seasonally. Year-round simulcasting of thoroughbred and harness racing.

Pari-Mutuels

In April 2007, the Indiana state legislature authorized the state's two horse tracks to have up to 2,000 electronic gaming machines.

Both casinos are open 24 hours and the minimum gambling age is 21. The minimum age for pari-mutuel betting is 18.

Hoosier Park
4500 Dan Patch Circle
Anderson, Indiana 46013
(765) 642-7223
Website: www.hoosierpark.com
Map: **#12** (45 miles N.E. of Indianapolis)

Toll-Free Number: (800) 526-7223
Restaurants: 7
Buffets: B-$9.95/$22.95 (Sun)
L-$9.95/$15.95 (Sat)/$22.95 (Sun)
D-$15.95/$26.95 (Fri/Sat)
Other Games: Only Gaming Machines
Casino Size: 92,000 Square Feet
Special Features: Live thoroughbred and harness racing seasonally. Year-round simulcasting of thoroughbred and harness racing.

Indian Casino

Indiana has one Indian casino that is expected to open in early 2018.

Four Winds South Bend
Prairie Avenue and U.S. 31/20 Bypass
South Bend, Indiana
Website: www.fourwindscasino.com
Map: **#13**

EXPECTED TO OPEN EARLY 2018
Toll-Free Number: (866) 494-6371
Restaurants: 4 Liquor: Yes
Buffet: Not Set at Press Time
Casino Size: 55,000 Square Feet
Other Games: Only Gaming Machines
Special Features: This casino will offer Class II gambling which consist of electronic gaming machines which look like slot machines, but are actually games of bingo and the spinning video reels are for "entertainment purposes only."

IOWA

Iowa was the first state to legalize riverboat gambling. The boats began operating on April Fools Day in 1991 and passengers were originally limited to $5 per bet with a maximum loss of $200 per person, per cruise.

In early 1994 the Iowa legislature voted to eliminate the gambling restrictions. Additionally, gaming machines were legalized at three of the state's four pari-mutuel facilities. In mid-2004 a provision was added to allow table games at those three tracks. That same year the state also legalized casinos on moored barges that float in man-made basins of water and no longer required the casinos to be on boats. Iowa also has three Indian casinos.

Here's information, as supplied by the Iowa Racing and Gaming Commission, showing the electronic gaming machine payback percentages for all non-Indian locations for the one-year period from July 1, 2016 through June 30, 2017:

LOCATION	PAYBACK %
Prairie Meadows	91.89
Wild Rose - Emmetsburg	91.32
Catfish Bend	90.97
Riverside	90.79
Wild Rose - Jefferson	90.73
Wild Rose - Clinton	90.71
Diamond Jo Dubuque	90.52
Q Casino	90.52
Grand Falls	90.48
Diamond Jo Worth	90.47
Ameristar	90.35
Rhythm City	90.22
Isle of Capri - Bettendorf	90.13
Hard Rock Casino	90.13
Harrah's	89.63
Casino Queen- Marquette	89.60
Isle of Capri - Waterloo	89.56
Horsehoe Council Bluffs	89.43
Lakeside	89.05

These figures reflect the total percentages returned by each riverboat casino or pari-mutuel facility for all of its electronic machines including: slots, video poker, video keno, etc.

Admission to all Iowa casinos is free and, unless otherwise noted, all casinos are open 24 hours.

All Iowa casinos offer: blackjack, roulette, craps, pai gow poker, Mississippi stud, ultimate Texas hold em, slots and video poker. Some casinos also offer: mini-baccarat (MB), poker (P), pai gow poker (PGP), Caribbean stud poker (CSP), let it ride (LIR), big 6 (B6), bingo (BG), keno (K), Mississippi stud (MS), three card poker (TCP), four card poker (FCP), Spanish 21 (S21) and off-track betting (OTB). The minimum gambling age is 21.

NOTE: If you happen to win a jackpot of $1,200 or more in Iowa, the casino will withhold 5% of your winnings for the Iowa Department of Revenue. If you want to try and get that money refunded, you will be required to file a state income tax return and, depending on the details of your return, you *may* get some of the money returned to you. The $1,200 threshold would also apply to any cash prizes won in casino drawings or tournaments.

For more information on visiting Iowa call the state's tourism department at (800) 345-4692 or visit their website at www.traveliowa.com.

Ameristar Casino Hotel Council Bluffs
2200 River Road
Council Bluffs, Iowa 51501
(712) 328-8888
Website: www.ameristarcasinos.com
Map: **#8** (102 miles S. of Sioux City)

Toll-Free Number: (877) 462-7827
Rooms: 152 Price Range: $129-$259
Suites: 8 Price Range: $240-$349
Restaurants: 5
Buffets: B-$16.99 (Sat/Sun)
L-$12.99/$16.99 (Sat/Sun)
D-$17.99/$29.99 (Fri/Sat)
Casino Size: 38,500 Square Feet
Other Games: S21, TCP, PGP
Overnight RV Parking: No
Special Features: 2,700-passenger sidewheeler replica on the Missouri River.

Casino Queen Marquette
100 Anti Monopoly Street
Marquette, Iowa 52158
(563) 873-3531
Website: www.casinoqueen.com/marquette
Map: **#10** (60 miles N. of Dubuque)

Toll-Free Number: (800) 496-8238
Restaurants: 2
Buffets: B- $14.99 (Sat/Sun)
L- $10.99/$14.99 (Sat/Sun)
D- $14.99/$19.99 (Fri/Sat)
Hours: 9am-2am/24 Hours (Fri/Sat)
Other Games: MS, UTH
Casino Size: 17,925 Square Feet
Overnight RV Parking: Free/RV Dump: No
Senior Discount: Various Wed/Thu if 50+
Special Features: 1,200-passenger paddle wheeler on the Mississippi River.

Catfish Bend Casino - Burlington
3001 Winegard Drive
Burlington, Iowa 52601
(319) 753-2946
Website: www.catfishbendcasino.com
Map: **#9** (180 miles S.E. of Des Moines)

Toll Free Number: (800) 372-2946
Rooms: 20 Price Range: $109-$159
Suites: 20 Price Range: $169-$269
Restaurants: 4
Hours: 8am-3am/24 hours (Fri/Sat)
Casino Size: 23,000 Square Feet
Other Games: S21, P, TCP, FCP,
MB, PGP, UTH
Overnight RV Parking: Free/RV Dump: No
Special features: Land-based casino.

Diamond Jo Casino Dubuque
301 Bell Street
Dubuque, Iowa 52001
(563) 690-4800
Website: www.diamondjodubuque.com
Map: **#7**

Toll-Free Number: (800) 582-5956
Restaurants: 3
Buffets: L-$9.99/$12.99 (Sun)
D-$14.99/$19.99 (Fri/Sat)
Casino Size: 36,683 Square Feet
Other Games: PGP, MS
Overnight RV Parking: Free RV Dump: No
Special features: Land-based casino.

Diamond Jo Casino Worth
777 Diamond Jo Lane
Northwood, Iowa 50459
(641) 323-7777
Website: www.diamondjoworth.com
Map: **#13** (140 miles N. of Des Moines)

Toll-Free Number: (877) 323-5566
Restaurants: 2
Buffets: L-$9.99/$12.99 (Sat/Sun)
D-$14.99/$18.99 (Fri)/$19.99 (Sat)
Casino Size: 36,363 Square Feet
Other Games: TCP, P, MS, UTH
Overnight RV Parking: Free/RV Dump: No
Special features: Land-based casino. Burger King and Subway.

Grand Falls Casino Resort
1415 Grand Falls Boulevard
Larchwood, Iowa 51241
(712) 777-7777
Website: www.grandfallscasinoresort.com
Map: **#4** (17 Miles SE of Sioux Falls, SD)

Toll-Free number: (877)511-4386
Rooms: 88 Price Range: $119-$229
Suites: 10 Price Range: $149-$469
Restaurants: 3
Buffets: B-$8.99 L-$10.99/$17.99 (Sun)
D-$17.99/$18.99 (Wed)/
$20.99 (Fri)/$19.99 (Sat)
Casino Size: 37,810
Other Games: P, PGP, MS, UTH
Overnight RV Parking: No
Special features: Land-based casino. 1,200-seat event center. 14-space RV park ($20-$40 per night).

Hard Rock Hotel & Casino Sioux City
111 3rd Street
Sioux City, Iowa 51101
(712) 226-7600
Website: www.hardrockcasinosiouxcity.com
Map: **#3**

Toll Free Number: (844) 222-7625
Rooms: 50 Price Range: $149-$179
Suites: 4 Price Range: $209-$279
Restaurants: 4
Buffets: B-$12.99 (Sat/Sun)
L-$9.99/$12.99 (Sat/Sun)
D-$14.99/$16.99 (Fri)/$17.99 (Sat)
Casino Size: 20,000 Square Feet
Overnight RV Parking: Yes
Other Games: TCP, PGP, MS, UTH
Special Features: Land-based casino.

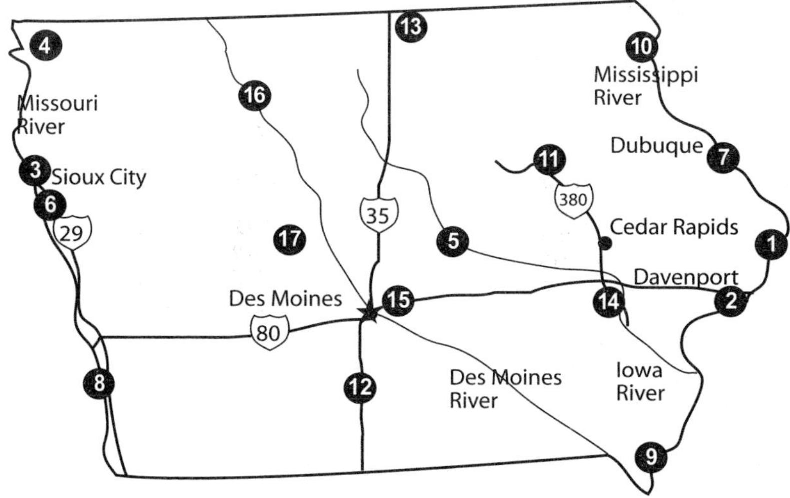

Harrah's Council Bluffs
One Harrah's Boulevard
Council Bluffs, Iowa 51501
(712) 329-6000
Website: www.harrahscouncilbluffs.com
Map: **#8** (102 miles S. of Sioux City)

Toll Free Number: (800) 472-7247
Rooms: 240 Price Range: $99-$295
Suites: 11 Price Range: $250-$325
Restaurants: 3
Buffets: B-$17.99 (Sat-Sun)
L-$14.99
D-$18.99/$22.99 (Fri/Sat)/
$20.99 (Sun)
Casino Size: 33,406 Square Feet
Other Games: TCP, PGP, MS
Overnight RV Parking: Free/RV Dump: No
Special Features: Land-based casino. Buffet discount for players club members.

Isle Casino Hotel - Bettendorf
1777 Isle Parkway
Bettendorf, Iowa 52722
(610) 241-1616
Website: www.isleofcapricasino.com
Map: **#2**

Toll-Free Number: (800) 843-4753
Rooms: 220 Price Range: $119-$260
Suites: 36 Price Range $189-$525
Restaurants: 4
Buffets: B- $9.99/$11.99 (Sat/Sun)
L- $12.99/$13.99 (Sat/Sun)
D- $16.99/$19.99 (Fri-Sun)
Other Games: TCP, PGP, MS
Casino Size: 28,976 Square Feet
Senior Discount: Various on Mon/Wed if 50+
Special Features: 53-slip marina. 50x odds on craps.

Isle Casino Hotel - Waterloo
777 Isle of Capri Boulevard
Waterloo, Iowa 50701
(610) 241-1621
Website: www.theislewaterloo.com
Map: **#11** (90 miles W. of Dubuque)

Toll-Free Number: (800) 843-4753
Rooms: 170 Price Range: $99-$200
Suites: 27 Price Range: $159-$280
Restaurants: 3
Buffets: B-$10.99 (Sat/Sun)
L-$12.99/$15.99 (Sun)
D-$17.99/$19.99 (Fri/Sat)
Other Games: P, MB
Casino Size: 43,142 Square Feet
Overnight RV Parking: Free/RV Dump: No
Special features: Land-based casino.

Lakeside Hotel Casino
777 Casino Drive
Osceola, Iowa 50213
(641) 342-9511
Website: www.lakesidehotelcasino.com
Map: **#12** (50 miles S. of Des Moines)

Toll-Free Number: (877) 477-5253
Suites: 63 Price: $99-$169
Restaurants: 2
Buffets: B- $6.99 (Sun/Mon)
D- $14.99/$18.99 (Thu/Sat)/
$21.99 (Fri)/$16.99 (Sun)
Casino Size: 36,200 Square Feet
Other Games: TCP, PGP
Overnight RV Parking: Free with players club card/
RV Dump: No
Senior Discount: Various on Mon if 50+.
Special Features: Casino is on a barge. 47-space RV park ($20 per night). Fishing/boating dock.

Rhythm City Casino
7077 Elmore Avenue
Davenport, Iowa 52807
(563) 328-8000
Website: www.rhythmcitycasino.com
Map: **#2** (80 miles S.E. of Cedar Rapids)

Toll-Free Number: (844) 852-4386
Restaurants: 3
Buffets: B-$8.99 L-$12.99/$17.99 (Sun)
D-$17.99/$19.99 (Fri/Sat)
Casino Size: 29,692 Square Feet
Other Games: TCP, PGP, P, MS, UTH
Overnight RV Parking: No
Senior Discount: Various Tue 7am-6pm if 50+
Special Features: Land-based casino.

Riverside Casino & Golf Resort
3184 Highway 22
Riverside, Iowa 52327
(319) 648-1234
Website: www.riversidecasinoandresort.com
Map: **#14** (81 miles W. of Davenport)

Toll-Free Number: (877) 677-3456
Rooms: 180 Price Range: $99-$139
Suite: 20 Price Range: $179-$219
Restaurants: 3
Buffets: B-$9.99/$10.99 (Sun)
L-$12.99/$17.99 (Sun)
D-$17.99/$19.99 (Wed/Fri/Sat)
Casino Size: 56,400 Square Feet
Overnight RV Parking: Free/RV Dump: No
Other Games: P, TCP, PGP
Special features: Land-based casino. 18-hole golf course. 1,200-seat showroom.

Wild Rose Casino - Clinton
777 Wild Rose Drive
Clinton, Iowa 52732
(563) 243-9000
Website: www.wildroseresorts.com
Map: **#1** (90 miles E. of Cedar Rapids)

Toll-Free Number: (800) 457-9975
Rooms: 60 Price Range: $79-$119
Suites: 6 Price Range: $149-$199
Restaurants: 2
Buffets: L-$8.99 (Mon/Tue) D-$9.99
Hours: 8am-2am/24 hours (Fri/Sat)
Casino Size: 19,681 Square Feet
Additional Games: PGP, UTH, LIR,
OTB (Fri-Sun)
Overnight RV Parking: Free/RV Dump: No
Special Features: Land-based casino.

Wild Rose Casino - Emmetsberg
777 Main Street
Emmetsburg, Iowa 50536
(712) 852-3400
Website: www.wildroseresorts.com
Map: **#16** (120 miles N.E. of Sioux City)

Toll-Free Number: (877) 720-7673
Rooms: 62 Price Range: $69-$119
Suites: 8 Price Range: $179-$209
Restaurants: 2
Buffets: L- $8.95 (Tues)/$12.95 (Sat/Sun)
D- $12.95 (Sat/Sun)
Other Games: PGP, MS
Hours: 8am-2am/24 Hours (Fri/Sat)
Casino Size: 16,357 Square Feet
Overnight RV Parking: Must use RV park
Senior Discount: Various Tue if 50+
Special features: Land-based casino. 68-space RV park ($15 per night).

Wild Rose Casino - Jefferson
777 Wild Rose Drive
Jefferson, Iowa 50129
(515 386-7777
Website: www.wildroseresorts.com
Map: **#17** (70 miles N.W. of Des Moines)

Rooms: 73 Price Range: $119-$179
Restaurants: 1
Casino Hours: 8am-2am/24 Hours (Fri/Sat)
Other Games: PGP, MS, UTH
Overnight RV Parking: Free/RV Dump: No

Indian Casinos

Blackbird Bend Casino
17214 210th Street
Onawa, Iowa 51040
(712) 423-9646
Website: www.blackbirdbendcasinos.com
Map: **#4** (40 miles S. of Sioux City)

Toll-Free Number: (844) 622-2121
Restaurants: 1
Buffets: B-$5.99/$9.99 (Sun)
L-$8.99/$9.99 (Tue/Sun)
D- $11.99 (Tue)/$10.99/$19.99 (Fri)/
$15.99 (Sat)
Hours: 8am-2am/24 hours (Fri/Sat)
Casino Size: 6,800 Square Feet
Overnight RV Parking: No
Senior Discount: Various Tue if 50+

Meskwaki Bingo Casino Hotel
1504 305th Street
Tama, Iowa 52339
(641) 484-2108
Website: www.meskwaki.com
Map: **#5** (40 miles W. of Cedar Rapids)

Toll-Free Number: (800) 728-4263
Rooms: 390 Price Range: $79-$129
Suites: 14 Price Range: $149-$309
Restaurants: 4 Liquor: Yes
Buffets: B-$8.95/$12.99 (Sun)
L-$9.95/$12.99 (Sun)
D- $12.99/$14.99 (Mon/Wed/Thu)/
$19.99 (Fri)/$16.99 (Sat)
Other Games: MB, P, PGP, MS, UTH
K, BG, Off-Track Betting
Overnight RV Parking: Must Use RV Park
Senior Discount: Various every day if 55+
Special Features: 50-space RV park ($19 per night). Spa.

WinnaVegas Casino
1500 330th Street
Sloan, Iowa 51055
(712) 428-9466
Website: www.winnavegas.biz
Map: **#6** (20 miles S. of Sioux City)

Toll-Free Number: (800) 468-9466
Rooms: 52 Price Range: $85-$122
Suites: 10 Price Range: $190-$220
Restaurants: 2 Liquor: Yes
Buffets: B- $12.49 (Sat/Sun) L-$8.99
D-$12.49/$15.99 (Thu/Sat)/
$18.99 (Fri)
Other Games: P, BG, PGP, MS
Overnight RV Parking: Free/RV Dump: No
Special Features: 20-space RV park ($15/night).

Pari-Mutuels

Horseshoe Casino - Council Bluffs
2701 23rd Avenue
Council Bluffs, Iowa 51501
(712) 323-2500
Website: horseshoecouncilbluffs.com
Map: **#8** (102 miles S. of Sioux City)

Toll-Free Number: (877) 771-7463
Rooms: 158 Price Range: $149-$300
Restaurants: 3
Buffets: L-$15.99/$18.99 (Sat)/$20.99 (Sun)
D- $19.99/$25.99 (Fri/Sat
Casino Size: 78,810 Square Feet
Other Games: P, MB, S21, TCP, FCP
Overnight RV Parking: Free/RV Dump: No
Special Features: Hotel is Hilton Garden Inn. Buffet closed Mon/Tue. Free shuttle service from local hotels. Affiliated with Harrah's. 100x odds on craps.

Prairie Meadows Racetrack & Casino
1 Prairie Meadows Drive
Altoona, Iowa 50009
(515) 967-1000
Website: www.prairiemeadows.com
Map: **#15** (5 miles E. of Des Moines)

Toll-Free Number: (800) 325-9015
Rooms: 148 Price Range: $139-$219
Suites: 20 Price Range: $179-$349
Restaurants: 3
Buffets: B- $8.95/$9.95 (Tue)/$12.95 (Sat/Sun)
L- $9.95/$12.95 (Sat/Sun)
D- $14.95/$17.95 (Wed/Sun)/
$16.95 (Thu)/$18.95 (Fri/Sat)
Casino Size: 85,680 Square Feet
Other Games: MB, P, TCP, PGP, MS, UTH
Overnight RV Parking: Yes
Special Features: Live thoroughbred and quarter-horse racing seasonally. Daily simulcasting of dog and horse racing.

Q Casino
1855 Greyhound Park Road
Dubuque, Iowa 52001
(563) 582-3647
Website: www.qcasinoandhotel.com
Map: **#7**

Toll-Free Number: (800) 373-3647
Rooms: 112 Price Range: $89-$189
Suites: 4 Price Range: $129-$349
Restaurants: 4
Buffets: L- $9.95/$10.95 (Sun)
D- $14.95/$16.95 (Fri/Sat)
Hours: 8am-3am/24 Hours (Fri/Sat)
Casino Size: 47,067 Square Feet
Other Games: P, PGP, MS, UTH
Overnight RV Parking: Free/RV Dump: No
Senior Discount: Various specials Mon if 55+.
Senior Discount: Various specials Wed if 50+.
Special Features: Live greyhound racing seasonally. Greyhound, harness and thoroughbred simulcasting all year. Hotel is Hilton Garden Inn.

KANSAS

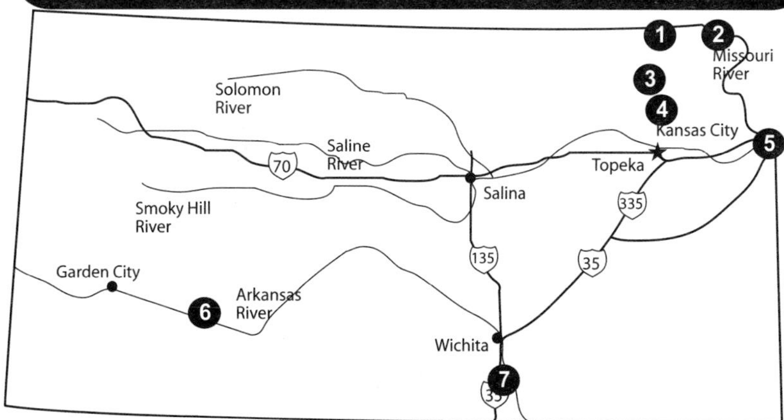

Kansas has four casinos that are state owned and operated. Additionally, there are five Indian casinos in Kansas.

Kansas does not release information about the payback percentages on electronic gaming machines at their casinos. However, gaming regulations require that all machines return no less than 87%.

Unless otherwise noted, all state-run casinos, as well as Indian casinos, are open 24 hours and offer the following games: slot machines, video poker, video keno, blackjack, craps and roulette. Other games include: poker (P), pai gow poker (PGP), mini-baccarat (MB), let it ride (LIR), Mississippi stud (MS), three card poker (TCP) , Ultimate Texas Hold'em (UTH) and bingo (BG). The minimum gambling age is 21 at all casinos.

For information on visiting Kansas call the state's tourism department at (785) 296-2009 or visit their website at www.travelks.com

Boot Hill Casino & Resort
4000 W Comanche Street
Dodge City, Kansas 67801
(620) 682-7777
Website: www.boothillcasino.com
Map: **#6** (155 miles W of Wichita)

Toll-Free Number: (877) 906-0777
Restaurants: 2
Buffets: Brunch - $15.99 (Sun)
Other Games: MB, P, TCP, MS, UTH
Overnight RV Parking: Free/RV Dump: No

Hollywood Casino at Kansas Speedway
777 Hollywood Casino Boulevard
Kansas City, Kansas 66111
(913) 288-9300
Website: www.hollywoodcasinokansas.com
Map: **#5**

Restaurants: 4
Buffets: L - $13.99 D- $16.99/$24.99 (Thu)/ $34.99 (Fri)/$22.99 (Sat)
Casino Size: 80,000 Square Feet
Other Games: MB, P, PGP, TCP, MS, UTH
Overnight RV Parking: Free/RV Dump: No

Kansas Crossing Casino + Hotel
1275 S. Highway 69
Pittsburg, Kansas 66762
(620) 240-4400
Website:www.kansascrossingcasino.com
Map: **#8** (160 miles E of Wichita)

Rooms: 123 Price Range: $99-$149
Restaurants: 1
Casino Size: 18,600 Square Feet
Other Games: TCP, UTH, MS
Senior Discount: Various Wed if 49+
Special Features: Hotel is Hampton Inn.

Kansas Star Casino
777 Kansas Star Drive
Mulvane, Kansas 67110
(316) 719-5000
Website: www.kansasstarcasino.com
Map: **#7** (20 miles S of Wichita)

Restaurants: 5
Buffets: L- $12.99 (Wed-Sat)/$14.99 (Sun)
D- $14.99/$17.99 (Fri/Sat)
Casino Size: 21,000 Square Feet
Other Games: P, TCP, LIR, MS, PGP, MB
Special Features: Buffet closed Mon/Tue.

Indian Casinos

Indian casinos do not release information on their slot machine payback percentages. However, according to tribal-state compacts, "the minimum payback percentage for electronic gaming devices is 80%."

Casino White Cloud
777 Jackpot Drive
White Cloud, Kansas 66094
(785) 595-3430
Website: www.casinowhitecloud.org
Map: **#2** (70 miles N.E. of Topeka)

Toll-Free Number: (877) 652-6115
Restaurants: 1 Liquor: Yes
Buffets: L-$10.00 D-$11.00/$13.00 (Sat)
Casino Size: 21,000 Square Feet
Casino Hours: 9am-1am/3am (Fri/Sat)
Other Games: Machines only, BG (Tue-Sun)
Overnight RV Parking: Free/RV Dump: No
Special Features: Electronic blackjack and roulette.

Golden Eagle Casino
1121 Goldfinch Road
Horton, Kansas 66439
(785) 486-6601
Map: **#3** (45 miles N. of Topeka)
Website: www.goldeneaglecasino.com

Toll-Free Number: (888) 464-5825
Restaurants: 2 Liquor: No
Buffets: B- $7.95 (Sun)
L- $8.95/$10.95 (Sun)
D- $6.95 (Wed-Sun)/$12.95 (Thu)/
$14.95 (Fri)/$18.95 (Sat)
Other Games: BG (Wed-Sun), No Roulette
Overnight RV Parking: Free/RV Dump: No
Special Features: RV hookups available ($10 per night).

Prairie Band Casino & Resort
12305 150th Road
Mayetta, Kansas 66509
(785) 966-7777
Website: www.pbpgaming.com
Map: **#4** (17 miles N. of Topeka)

Toll-Free Number: (888) 727-4946
Rooms: 297 Price Range: $89-$169
Suites: 8 Price Range: Casino Use Only
Restaurants: 3 Liquor: Yes
Buffets: B- $4.99/$17.99 (Sun)
L-$9.99/$17.99 (Sun)
D-$17.99/$27.99 (Fri/Sun)/
$21.99 (Sat)
Casino Size: 33,000 Square Feet
Other Games: BG (Wed-Sun), MB, P, LIR,
TCP, MS, UTH, No Craps
Overnight RV Parking: Must use RV park.
Special Features: 67-space RV park ($30 per night).

Sac & Fox Casino
1322 U.S. Highway 75
Powhattan, Kansas 66527
(785) 467-8000
Map: **#1** (60 miles N. of Topeka)
Website: www.sacandfoxcasino.com

Toll-Free Number: (800) 990-2946
Restaurant: 2 Liquor: Yes
Buffets: L- $12.99 (Sun)
D-$22.99 (Fri)/$17.99 (Sat)/
$12.99 (Sun)
Casino Size: 40,000 Square Feet
Other Games: TCP
Overnight RV Parking: Free/RV Dump: No
Senior Discount: Various Wed, if 50+
Special Features: 24-hour truck stop. Golf driving range. 12-space RV park ($10 per night).

7th Street Casino
777 North 7th Street Trafficway
Kansas City, Kansas 66101
(913) 371-3500
Website: www.7th-streetcasino.com
Map: **#5**

Restaurant: 1 Liquor: Yes
Casino Size: 20,000 Square Feet
Other Games: Only Gaming Machines
Overnight RV Parking: No/RV Dump: No

LOUISIANA

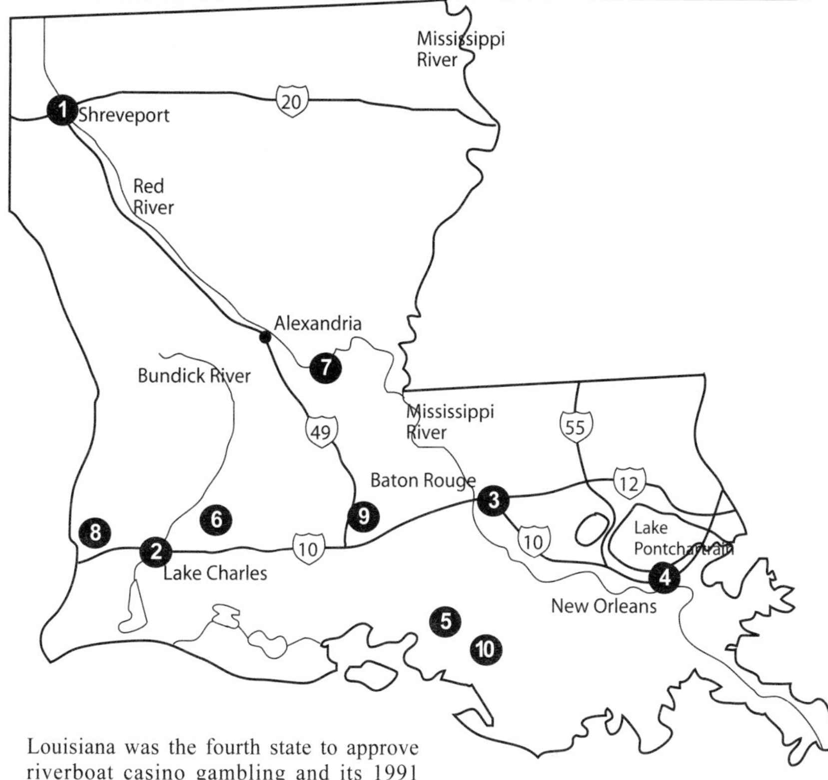

Louisiana was the fourth state to approve riverboat casino gambling and its 1991 gambling law allows a maximum of 15 boats statewide. In 1992 a provision was added for one land-based casino in New Orleans.

The state also has three land-based Indian casinos and four slot machine-only (no video poker or video keno) casinos located at pari-mutuel facilities. Additionally, video poker is permitted at Louisiana truck stops, OTB's and bars/taverns in 31 of the state's 64 parishes (counties). All riverboat casinos in Louisiana are required to remain dockside and all are open 24 hours.

Gaming regulations require that gaming machines in casinos be programmed to pay back no less than 80% and no more than 99.9%. For video gaming machines at locations other than casinos the law requires a minimum return of 80% and a maximum return of 94%.

Louisiana gaming statistics are not broken down by individual properties. Rather, they are classified by region: Baton Rouge (BR), Lake Charles (LC), New Orleans (NO) and Shreveport/Bossier City (SB).

The Baton Rouge casinos consist of the Belle of Baton Rouge, Hollywood Casino, L'Auberge and Evangeline Downs. The Lake Charles casinos include: Isle of Capri, L'Auberge Resort and Delta Downs. New Orleans area casinos are: Amelia Belle, Boomtown, Harrah's (landbased), Treasure Chest and Fairgrounds Raceway. The Shreveport/Bossier city casinos include: Boomtown, Diamond Jack's, Sam's Town, Eldorado, Horseshoe and Harrah's Louisiana Downs.

Here's information, as supplied by the Louisiana State Police-Riverboat Gaming Section, showing the average electronic machine payback percentages for each area's casinos for the 12-month period from June, 2016 through May, 2017:

	BR	LC	NO	SB
1¢	88.56%	88.28%	**88.81%**	88.67%
5¢	91.66%	93.27%	**93.92%**	92.54%
25¢	**92.65%**	92.53%	92.61%	90.97%
$1	**93.76%**	92.08%	92.50%	92.27%
$5	**94.08%**	93.43%	93.17%	92.33%
All	**91.12%**	90.68%	90.35%	90.32%

These numbers reflect the percentage of money returned on each denomination of machine and encompass all electronic machines including video poker and video keno. The best returns for each category are highlighted in bold print.

NOTE: If you happen to win a jackpot of $1,200 or more in Louisiana, the casino will withhold 6% of your winnings for the Louisiana Department of Revenue. If you want to try and get that money refunded, you will be required to file a state income tax return and, depending on the details of your return, you *may* get some of the money returned to you. The $1,200 threshold would also apply to any cash prizes won in casino drawings or tournaments.

All casinos offer: blackjack, craps, roulette, slots, video poker, three card poker and Mississippi stud. Optional games include: Spanish 21 (S21), baccarat (B), mini-baccarat (MB), poker (P), Caribbean stud poker (CSP), pai gow poker (PGP), let it ride (LIR), casino war (CW), four card poker (FCP), big 6 wheel (B6), keno (K), Texas hold 'em Bonus (THB), ultimate Texas hold em (UTH) and bingo (BG). The minimum gambling age is 21 for casino gaming and 18 for pari-mutuel betting.

For more information on visiting Louisiana call the state's tourism department at (800) 633-6970 or visit www.louisianatravel.com

Amelia Belle Casino
500 Lake Palourde Road
Amelia, Louisiana 70340
(985) 631-1777
Website: www.ameliabellecasino.com
Map: **#10** (75 miles S. of Baton Rouge)

Restaurants: 2
Buffets: L- $5.99/$18.75 (Fri)/$9.75 (Sati)
D-$5.99/$18.75 (Fri)/$12.75 (Sat)
Casino Size: 27,928 Square Feet
Other Games: TCP, MS, UTH
Overnight RV Parking: Free (Must park in employee lot)
Special Features: 1,200-passenger paddle wheeler on Bayou Boeuf.

Belle of Baton Rouge
103 France Street
Baton Rouge, Louisiana 70802
(225) 242-2600
Website: www.belleofbatonrouge.com
Map: **#3**

Toll-Free Number: (800) 676-4847
Rooms: 100 Price Range: $79-$109
Suites: 88 Price Range: $200-$550
Restaurants: 4
Buffets: B/L- $12.99 (Sun)
D- $13.99 (Fri/Sat)
Casino Size: 28,500 Square Feet
Other Games: MB, PGP
Overnight RV Parking: Yes/RV dump: No
Special Features: 1,500-passenger paddle wheeler on the Mississippi River.

Boomtown Casino & Hotel Bossier City
300 Riverside Drive
Bossier City, Louisiana 71111
(318) 746-0711
Website: www.boomtownbossier.com
Map: **#1** (across the Red River From Shreveport)

Toll-Free Number: (866) 462-8696
Rooms: 100 Price Range: $90-$185
Suites: 88 Price Range: $119-$219
Restaurants: 4
Buffets: B- $8.95 L- $12.95/$14.95 (Sat-Sun)
D- $18.95/$22.95 (Fri-Sat)/
$20.95 (Sun)
Casino Size: 25,635 Square Feet
Other Games: TCP, UTH
Overnight RV Parking: No
Special Features: 1,925-passenger paddle wheeler on the Red River.

Boomtown Casino New Orleans
4132 Peters Road
Harvey, Louisiana 70058
(504) 366-7711
Website: www.boomtownneworleans.com
Map: **#4** (a suburb of New Orleans)

Toll-Free Number: (800) 366-7711
Restaurants: 5
Buffets: L- $15.95/$19.95 (Sat-Sun)
D- $19.95 (Mon/Wed)/
$24.95 (Tue/Thu)/$29.95 (Fri)/
$27.95 (Sat)/$21.95 (Sun)
Casino Size: 29,027 Square Feet
Other Games: P, MB, PGP, TCP
Overnight RV Parking: Free/RV Dump: No
Senior Discount: Discounted lunch buffet
on Mon if 55+
Special Features: 1,600-passenger paddle wheeler on the Harvey Canal. Family arcade.

Diamond Jacks Casino - Bossier City
711 DiamondJacks Boulevard
Bossier City, Louisiana 71111
(318) 678-7777
Website: www.diamondjacks.com
Map: **#1** (across the Red River from Shreveport)

Toll-Free Number: (866) 552-9629
Suites: 570 Price Range: $59-$169
Restaurants: 3
Buffets: B/L- $9.99 (Sun)
D- $19.99/$26.99 (Fri/Sat)
Casino Size: 29,921 Square Feet
Other Games: S21, FCP, LIR, MS, UTH
Overnight RV Parking: Must use RV park
Special Features: 1,650-passenger paddle wheeler on the Red River. 32-space RV park ($22.50/$25 Fri-Sat). Supervised childcare center. 1,200-seat showroom. Buffet discount for players club members.

Eldorado Casino Shreveport
451 Clyde Fant Parkway
Shreveport, Louisiana 71101
(877) 602-0711
Website: www.eldoradoshreveport.com
Map: **#1**

Suites: 403 Price Range: $69-$229
Restaurants: 5
Buffet: L- $13.50/$17.99 (Sat)/$18.99 (Sun)
D- $22.50 (Mon)/$19.99 (Tue/Sun)/
$18.99 (Wed)/$21.50 (Thu)/
$23.99 (Fri)/$20.99 (Sat)
Casino Size: 28,226 Square Feet
Other Games: MB, P, CSP, LIR, PGP, CW, MS
Overnight RV Parking: Free (Weekdays only)
Special Features: 1,500-passenger paddle wheeler on the Red River.

Golden Nugget Casino - Lake Charles
2550 Golden Nugget Blvd
Lake Charles, Louisiana 70601
(337) 508-7777
Website: www.goldennuggetlc.com

Toll-Free Number: (844) 468-4438
Rooms: 736 Price Range: $169-$429
Suites: 20 Price Range: $699-$1,299
Restaurants: 11
Buffets: B- $13.99/$33.99 (Sun)/$35.99 (Sat)
L-$16.99/$22.99 (Sat/Sun)
D- $33.99 (Mon-Thu/Sun)/
$35.99 (Fri/Sat)
Other Games: B, LIR, P, TCP, PGP, MS, UTH
Senior Discount: Various Wed if 50+
Special Features: 18 hole championship course.

Harrah's New Orleans
228 Poydras Street
New Orleans, Louisiana 70130
(504) 533-6000
Website: www.caesars.com
Map: **#4**

Toll-Free Number: (800) 427-7247
Rooms: 390 Price Range: $170-$259
Suites: 60 Price Range: $359-$699
Restaurants: 10
Buffet: B/L- $15.99/$34.99 (Sat/Sun)
D-$22.99(Mon)/$31.99 (Tue-Thu)/
$34.99 (Fri/Sat)/$29.99 (Sun)
Casino Size: 125,119 Square Feet
Other Games: MB, P, PGP, CSP, LIR,
B, FCP, B6, UTH, P
Overnight RV Parking: No
Special Features: Landbased, non-smoking casino. Five themed gaming areas. Fast food court. Daily live jazz music. Self-parking costs $5 to $30 depending on length of stay. Players club members playing for minimum of 30 rated minutes and earning 15 tier credits, can get validated for up to 24 hours of free parking. Buffet discount for players club members.

Hollywood Casino - Baton Rouge
1717 River Road North
Baton Rouge, Louisiana 70802
(225) 709-7777
Website: www.hollywoodbr.com
Map: **#3**

Toll-Free Number: (800) 447-6843
Restaurants: 3
Buffets: L- $14.95/$17.95 (Sat/Sun)
D- $29.95 (Thu/Fri)
Casino Size: 27,900 Square Feet
Overnight RV Parking: Free/RV Dump: No
Special Features: 1,500-passenger paddle wheeler on the Mississippi River.

Horseshoe Casino Hotel - Bossier City
711 Horseshoe Boulevard
Bossier City, Louisiana 71111
(318) 742-0711
Website: www.horseshoebossiercity.com
Map: **#1** (across the Red River from Shreveport)

Toll-Free Number: (800) 895-0711
Rooms: 606 Price Range: $89-$329
Restaurants: 5
Buffets: B- $16.99 (Sat/Sun)
L- $16.99/$24.99 (Fri)
D- $21.99/$26.99 (Fri)
Casino Size: 28,095 Square Feet
Other Games: MB, P, LIR, TCP, FCP, MS
Overnight RV Parking: Free/RV Dump: No
Special Features: 2,930-passenger paddle wheeler on the Red River. 100x odds on craps.

Isle of Capri Casino - Lake Charles
100 Westlake Avenue
Westlake, Louisiana 70669
(337) 430-0711
Website: www.isleofcapricasinos.com
Map: **#2** (220 miles W. of New Orleans)

Toll-Free Number: (800) 843-4753
Inn Rooms: 241 Price Range: $89-$199
Tower Rooms: 252 Price Range: $139-$249
Restaurants: 4
Buffets: B- $10.99
L- $13.99/$19.99 (Sat)/$17.99 (Sun)
D- $16.99/$22.99 (Fri)/
$19.99 (Sat)/$17.99 (Sun)
Casino Size: 51,569 Square Feet
Other Games: MB, P, TCP, LIR, MS
Overnight RV Parking: Must use RV park
Senior Discount: Various Mon if 50+
Special Features: Two 1,200-passenger paddle wheelers on Lake Charles. 8-space RV park ($20 per night).

L'Auberge Casino Hotel Baton Rouge
777 L'Auberge Avenue
Baton Rouge, Louisiana 70820
(337) 395-7777
Website: www.lbatonrouge.com
Map: **#3**

Toll-Free Number: (866) 261-7777
Rooms: 636 Price Range: $159-$369
Suites: 99 Price Range: $499-$849
Restaurants: 5
Buffet: B- $12.99 L- $15.99/$22.99 (Sat/Sun)
D- $34.99/$36.99 (Fri/Sat)
Casino Size: 29,876 Square Feet
Other Games: MB, B, PGP, P,
TCP, FCP, MS, THB
Overnight RV Parking: No
Senior Discount: Various Tue if 50+
Special Features: 1,600-seat event center

L'Auberge Casino Resort Lake Charles
3202 Nelson Road
Lake Charles, Louisiana 70601
(337) 475-2900
Website: www.llakecharles.com
Map: **#2** (220 miles W. of New Orleans)

Toll-Free Number: (866) 580-7444
Rooms: 636 Price Range: $189-$289
Suites: 99 Price Range: $599-$849
Restaurants: 8 Valet Parking: Free
Buffet: B- $12.99 (Sat/Sun)
L- $14.99/$21.99 (Sat/Sun)
D- $29.99
Casino Size: 27,000 Square Feet
Other Games: MB, B, PGP, LIR, P,
TCP, FCP, THB
Overnight RV Parking: No
Special Features: 18-hole golf course. Spa. Pool with lazy river ride. 1,500-seat event center.

Margaritaville Resort Casino - Bossier City
777 Margaritaville Way
Bossier City, Louisiana 71111
(318) 698-7177
Website: www.margaritavillebossiercity.com
Map: **#1** (across the Red River from Shreveport)

Toll-Free Number: (855) 346-2489
Rooms: 354 Price Range: $79-$269
Suites: 36 Price Range: $319-$589
Restaurants: 4
Buffets: B- $9.99 L- $15.99/$26.99 (Sun)
D- $26.99
Casino Size: 26,624
Other Games: MB, B, TCP, LIR, MS, UTH
Overnight RV Parking: Yes/RV Dump: No

Sam's Town Hotel & Casino Shreveport
315 Clyde Fant Parkway
Shreveport, Louisiana 71101
(318) 424-7777
Website: www.samstownshreveport.com
Map: **#1**

Toll-Free Number: (877) 429-0711
Rooms: 514 Price Range: $75-$179
Restaurants: 4
Buffet: B/L-$14.99 (Sat/Sun)
D-$16.99/$22.99 (Fri/Sat)
Casino Size: 29,194 Square Feet
Other Games: MB, LIR, TCP
Overnight RV Parking: No
Special Features: 1,650-passenger paddle wheeler on the Red River.

Treasure Chest Casino
5050 Williams Boulevard
Kenner, Louisiana 70065
(504) 443-8000
Website: www.treasurechest.com
Map: **#4** (a suburb of New Orleans)

Toll-Free Number: (800) 298-0711
Restaurants: 2
Buffet: L-$11.99/$21.99 (Sat/Sun)
D- $17.99/$19.99 (Mon/Tue/Thu)/
$31.99 (Wed)
Casino Hours: 8am-3am/24 hours (Fri/Sat)
Casino Size: 23,680 Square Feet
Other Games: MB, PGP, TCP, LIR, FCP
Overnight RV Parking: No
Special Features: 1,900-passenger paddle wheeler on Lake Pontchartrain. Hilton Garden Inn located next to casino (504-712-0504).

Indian Casinos

Coushatta Casino Resort
777 Coushatta Drive
Kinder, Louisiana 70648
(800) 584-7263
Website: www.coushattacasinoresort.com
Map: **#6** (35 miles N.E. of Lake Charles)

Room Reservations: (888) 774-7263
Hotel Rooms: 118 Price Range: $149-$229
Suites: 90 Price Range: Casino Use Only
Inn Rooms: 195 Price Range: $109-$159
Lodge Rooms: 92 Price Range: $89-$109
Restaurants: 6 Liquor: Yes
Buffets: B- $12 L- $16/$20 (Sat/Sun)
D- $20/$25 (Thu)/$29 (Fri/Sat)/$23 (Sun)
Casino Size: 105,000 Square Feet
Other Games: MB, P, PGP, LIR, P, TCP,
FCP, MS, BG (Wed-Sun), OTB
Overnight RV Parking: No
Special Features: Land-based casino. 100-space RV park ($25-$65). Video arcade. 18-hole golf course.

Cypress Bayou Casino
832 Martin Luther King Road
Charenton, Louisiana 70523
(337) 923-7284
Website: www.cypressbayou.com
Map: **#5** (75 miles S. of Baton Rouge)

Toll-Free Number: (800) 284-4386
Rooms: 96 Price Range: $89-$139
Suites: 6 Price Range: $149-$299
Restaurants: 5 Liquor: Yes
Casino Size: 27,900 Square Feet
Other Games: MB, P, PGP, TCP,
FCP, MS, BG, OTB
Overnight RV Parking: Free/RV Dump: No
Special Features: Land-based casino. Cigar bar. 30-space RV park ($15-$22 per night; $55 on holidays).

Jena Choctaw Pines Casino
149 Chahta Trails
Dry Prong, Louisiana 71423
(318) 648-7773
Website: www.jenachoctawpinescasino.com
Map: **#5** (75 miles S. of Baton Rouge)

Toll-Free Number: (855) 638-5825
Restaurants: 2 Liquor: Yes
Buffets: L- $9.95/$14.95 (Sun)
D- $14.95/$18.95 (Wed)/
$21.95 (Fri/Sat)
Other Games: P, No Table Games
Overnight RV Parking: Yes
Senior Discount: Various Tue/Wed if 55+

Paragon Casino Resort
711 Paragon Place
Marksville, Louisiana 71351
(318) 253-1946
Website: www.paragoncasinoresort.com
Map: **#7** (30 miles S.E. of Alexandria)

Toll-Free Number: (800) 946-1946
Rooms: 335 Price Range: $118-$159
Suites: 57 Price Range: $155-$355
Restaurants: 6 Liquor: Yes
Buffets: B-$9.99 L-$12.99/$13.99 (Sat/Sun)
D- $18.99/$23.99 (Fri/Sat)
Casino Size: 103,520 Square Feet
Other Games: MB, TCP, PGP, MS, P
Overnight RV Parking: Must use RV park
Special Features: Land-based casino. 185-space RV Park ($25/$35 Fri-Sat). 18-hole golf course.

Pari-Mutuels

Delta Downs Racetrack & Casino
2717 Delta Downs Drive
Vinton, Louisiana 70668
(800) 589-7441
Website: www.deltadowns.com
Map: **#8** (20 miles W. of Lake Charles)

Toll-Free Number: (800) 589-7441
Rooms: 203 Price Range: $109-$299
Suites: 33 Price Range: Casino use only
Restaurants: 3
Buffets: L- $13.99/$17.99 (Sat/Sun)
D- $17.99/$31.99 (Fri/Sat)
Casino Size: 14,901 Square Feet
Other Games: Only slots, no video poker
Overnight RV Parking: Free/RV Dump: No
Special Features: Live thoroughbred and quarter-horse racing seasonally. Daily simulcasting of horse racing. Food court with four fast food outlets.

Evangeline Downs Racetrack & Casino
2235 Creswell Lane Extension
Opelousas, Louisiana 70570
(866) 472-2466
Website: www.evangelinedowns.com
Map: **#9** (30 miles W. of Baton Rouge)

Toll-Free Number: (866) 472-2466
Rooms: 117 Price Range: $109-$159
Restaurants: 3
Buffets: L-$11.99
D-$16.99/$19.99 (Fri)/$18.99 (Sat)
Casino Size: 14,619 Square Feet
Other Games: Only slots, no video poker
Overnight RV Parking: Free/RV Dump: No
Senior Discount: Various Tue if 50 or older
Special Features: Live thoroughbred and quarter-horse racing seasonally. Daily simulcasting of horse racing.

Fair Grounds Racecourse & Slots
1751 Gentilly Boulevard
New Orleans, Louisiana 70119
(504) 944-5515
Website: www.fairgroundsracecourse.com
Map: **#4**

Restaurants: 2
Other Size: 15,000 Square Feet
Other Games: Only slots, no video poker
Casino Hours: 9am-12am/10am-12am (Sun)
Overnight RV Parking: No
Special Features: Live thoroughbred racing seasonally. Daily simulcasting of horse racing.

Harrah's Louisiana Downs
8000 E. Texas Street
Bossier City, Louisiana 71111
(318) 742-5555
Website: www.harrahslouisianadows.com
Map: **#1**

Toll-Free Number: (800) 427-7247
Restaurants: 3
Casino Size: 12,855 Square Feet
Other Games: Only slots, no video poker
Overnight RV Parking: Free/RV Dump: No
Special Features: Live thoroughbred and quarter-horse racing seasonally. Daily simulcasting of horse racing.

MAINE

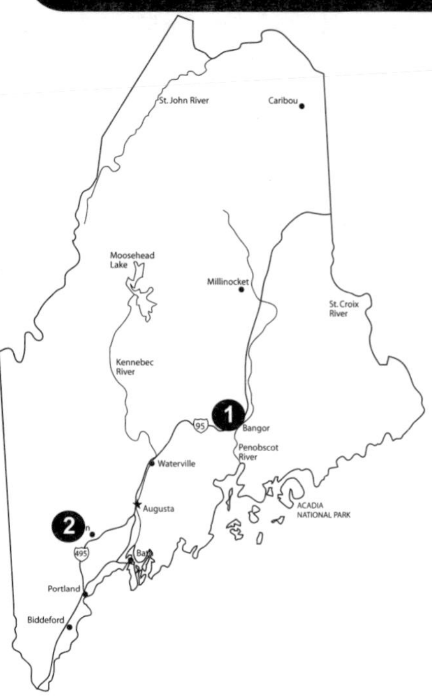

Maine has two racetrack casinos (racinos) that offer electronic gaming machines, as well as live table games.

State gaming regulations require a minimum return of 89% on all machines and during the one-year period from July 1, 2016 through June 30, 2017, the average return on gaming machines at Hollywood Casino was 90.04% and at Oxford Casino it was 91.48%.

Unless otherwise noted, all casinos offer: slots, video poker, video keno, craps, blackjack, roulette, and three card poker. Optional games include: let it ride (LIR), mini baccarat (MB), Big 6 wheel (B6), spanish 21 (S21), ultimate Texas Hold 'em (UTH), Mississippi stud (MS) and Poker (P).

The minimum gambling age is 21 for slots and 18 for pari-mutuel wagering.

For more information on visiting Maine call their Office of Tourism at (888) 624-6345 or visit their website at www.visitmaine.com.

Hollywood Slots Hotel & Raceway
500 Main Street
Bangor, Maine 04401
(207) 262-6146
Website: www.hollywoodcasinobangor.com
Map: **#1**

Toll-Free Number: (877) 779-7771
Rooms: 148 Price Range: $149-$219
Suites: 4 Price Range: $349-$449
Restaurants: 2
Buffets: B/L-$15.99 (Sun)
D-$23.99 (Fri/Sat)
Hours: 8am-3am
Other Games: P
Senior Discount: Various on Sun/Mon if 50+
Special Features: Live harness racing seasonally. Daily simulcasting of horse and harness racing.

Oxford Casino
777 Casino Way
Oxford, Maine 04270
(207) 539-6700
Website: www.oxfordcasino.com
Map: **#2** (55 miles S.W. of Agusta)

Restaurants: 1
Other Games: MB, B6, S21, MS, UTH
Senior Discount: Various on Wed if 50+
Overnight RV Parking: Free (limit 24 hours)/
RV Dump: No

MARYLAND

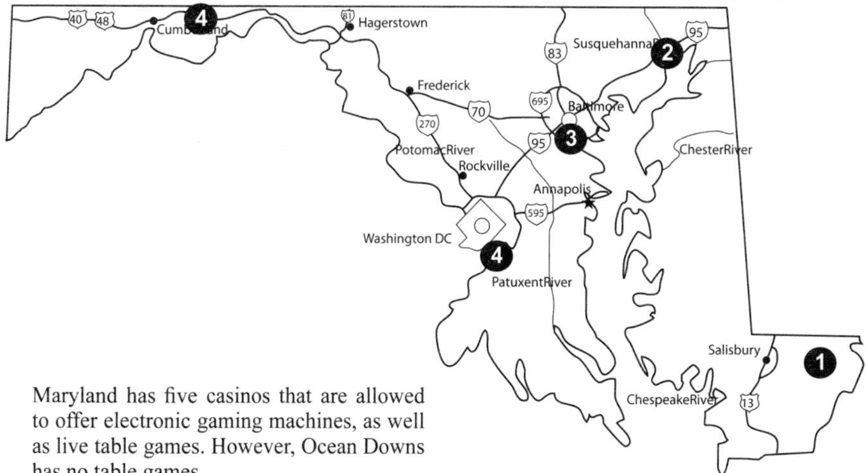

Maryland has five casinos that are allowed to offer electronic gaming machines, as well as live table games. However, Ocean Downs has no table games.

No public information is available about the actual payback percentages on gaming machines in Maryland. However, gaming regulations require a minimum payback of 87% on any one machine and all machines within a casino must have an average payback of 90% to 95%.

All casinos are open 24 hours and, unless otherwise noted, offer: slots, video poker, video keno, craps, blackjack, roulette and three card poker. Optional games include: let it ride (LIR), pai gow poker (PGP), baccarat (B), Ultimate Texas Hold'em (UTH), Mississippi Stud (MS), Poker (P), four card poker (FCP) , big six (B6) and Texas Hold'em Bonus (THB).

If you want to order a drink while playing, be aware that Illinois gaming regulations do not allow casinos to provide free alcoholic beverages. The minimum gambling age is 21 for casinos and 18 for pari-mutuel wagering.

For Maryland tourism information, call (800) 543-1036, or visit their website at www.visitmaryland.com

Casino at Ocean Downs
10218 Racetrack Road
Berlin, Maryland 21811
(410) 641-0600
Website: www.oceandowns.com
Map: **#1** (110 miles SE of Annapolis)

Restaurants: 2
Overnight RV Parking: No
Other Games: Only Gaming Machines.
Special Features: Live harness racing seasonally. Daily simulcasting of thoroughbred and harness racing.

Hollywood Casino - Perryville
1201 Chesapeake Overlook Parkway
Perryville, Maryland 21903
(410) 378-8500
Website: hollywoodcasinoperryville.com
Map: **#2** (30 miles NE of Baltimore)

Restaurants: 2
Other Games: P, TCP, FCP, UTH
Casino Size: 35,000 Square Feet
Overnight RV Parking: No

Horseshoe Casino Baltimore
1525 Russell Street
Baltimore, Maryland 21230
(443) 931-4200
Website: www.caesars.com
Map: **#3** (10 miles SW of Baltimore)

Toll-Free Number: (844) 777-7463
Restaurants: 7
Games offered: B, PGP, TCP, FCP, MS, P, LIR, OTB, UTH
Senior Discount: Various Wed if 55+
Casino Size: 122,000 square feet
Special Features: 100x odds on craps.

Maryland Live! Casino
7002 Arundel Mills Circle #7777
Handover, Maryland 21076
(443) 842-7000
Website: www.marylandlivecasino.com
Map: **#3** (10 miles SW of Baltimore)

Toll-free Number: (855) 563-5483
Restaurants: 8
Buffets: L-$14.99/$19.99 (Sun)
D-$19.99(Thu)/$39.99 (Fri/Sat)
Casino Size: 160,000 Square Feet
Other Games: B, TCP, FCP, PGP, B6, MS, UTH
Senior Discount: Various Mon-Thu if 55+
Special Features: Ram's Head Center Stage entertainment venue. Buffet closed Mon-Wed.

MGM National Harbor
101 MGM National Avenue
Oxon Hill, Maryland 20745
(301) 749-7500
Website: www.mgmnationalharbor.com
Map: **#4** (10 miles S of Washington, D.C.)

Toll-Free Number: (844) 646-6847
Rooms: 308 Price Range: $259-$559
Restaurants: 7
Casino Size: 125,000 Square Feet
Other Games: S21, MB, TCP, FCP, PGP, P, UTH
Senior Discount: Various Wed if 55+
Special Features: 3,000-seat theater. Luxury retail shops. Spa & fitness center.

Rocky Gap Casino Resort
16701 Lakeview Road
Flintstone, Maryland 21530
(301) 784-8400
Website: www.rockygapcasino.com
Map: **#4** (125 miles NW of Baltimore)

Toll-Free Number: (800) 724-0828
Rooms: 195 Price Range: $149-$219
Suites: 5 Price Range: $219-$265
Self-Parking: Free Valet: Free
Buffets: D-$18.50/$20.50 (Fri/Sat)
Restaurants: 4
Other Games: P, B6, MS
Overnight RV Parking: No
Special Features: No buffet Mon/Tue

MASSACHUSETTS

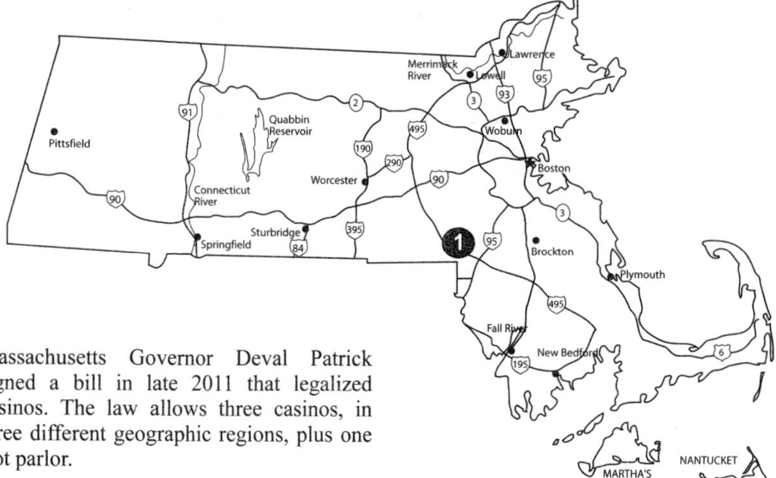

Massachusetts Governor Deval Patrick signed a bill in late 2011 that legalized casinos. The law allows three casinos, in three different geographic regions, plus one slot parlor.

The slot parlor, Plainridge Park Casino, a harness racing track located about 140 miles southwest of Boston, opened June 24, 2015.

The first resort-casino license in Region B (Western Massachusetts) was awarded to MGM Resorts and their $1.3 billion casino, MGM Springfield, is expected to open in late 2018. The second license for Region A (Eastern Massachusetts) was awarded to Wynn Resorts and their $2 billion, Wynn Everett, is expected to open in mid-2019. The final license for Region C (Southeastern Massachusetts) had not yet been awarded as of late 2017.

Additionally, the Mashpee Wampanoag Tribe is planning to build a destination resort casino near Taunton. That facility, First Light Casino, was expected to open by late 2018. However, the project has been hampered by lawsuits which might stop it from being completed.

Massachusetts gaming regulations require a minimum payback of 80% on all gaming machines. From July 1, 2016 through June 30, 2017, the gaming machines at Plainridge Park returned 92.23%

NOTE: If you happen to win a jackpot of $600 or more in Massachusetts, the casino will withhold 5% and send it to the Massachusetts Department of Revenue. You may, however, be able to get some of that money refunded by filing a state income tax return. The $600 threshold also applies to any cash prizes won in casino drawings or tournaments, as well as the fair market value of non-cash prizes such as cars, houses, and trips.

For information on visiting Massachusetts call (800) 447-6277 or visit their web site at www.massvacation.com

Plainridge Park Casino
301 Washington Street
Plainville, Massachusetts 02762
(508) 643-2500
Website: www.plainridgeparkcasino.com
Map: **#1** (140 miles SW of Boston)

Toll-Free Number: (844) 327-4347
Restaurants: 3
Games Offered: Only Gaming Machines
Special Features: Live harness racing seasonally. Daily simulcasting of horse racing. Food court with four fast food outlets.

MICHIGAN

One of Michigan's most popular casinos is actually in Canada. It's Caesars Windsor in Ontario which is just across the river from downtown Detroit.

All winnings are paid in Canadian currency and the minimum gambling age is 19. The casino is open 24 hours and offers the following games: blackjack, Spanish 21, craps, roulette, poker, baccarat, mini-baccarat, big six wheel, pai-gow poker, Caribbean stud poker, three-card poker and let it ride.

Caesars Windsor
377 Riverside Drive East
Windsor, Ontario N9A 7H7
(519) 258-7878
Website: www.caesarswindsor.com
Map: **#12**

PRICES ARE IN CANADIAN DOLLARS
Toll-Free Number: (800) 991-7777
Room Reservations: (800) 991-8888
Rooms: 349 Price Range: $169-$259
Suites: 40 Price Range: $239-$760
Restaurants: 5
Buffets: L-$20.99/$25.24 (Sun)
D-$27.24/$30.24 (Fri/Sat)
Casino Size: 100,000 Square Feet
Overnight RV Parking: Check with security/
RV Dump: No
Special Features: Entire casino is non-smoking. Buffet discount with players club card.

The only casinos in Michigan not on Indian reservations are located in downtown Detroit. All three are open 24 hours and offer the following games: blackjack, craps, roulette, baccarat, mini-baccarat, Caribbean stud poker, three-card poker, pai gow poker, let it ride, big 6 wheel, Spanish 21, Mississippi stud and casino war. No public information is available about the payback percentages on Detroit's gaming machines.

The minimum gambling age at all Detroit casinos is 21 and all three casinos offer free valet parking.

Greektown Casino
555 E. Lafayette Avenue
Detroit, Michigan 48226
(313) 223-2999
Website: www.greektowncasino.com
Map: **#12**

Toll free Number: (888) 771-4386
Rooms: 400 Price Range: $179-$249
Suites: 20 Price Range: $359-$499
Restaurants: 4
Casino Size: 75,000 Square Feet
Other Games: Poker, no Spanish 21
Special Features: Starbucks coffeehouse.

MGM Grand Detroit Casino
1777 Third Avenue
Detroit, Michigan 48226
(313) 393-7777
Website: www.mgmgranddetroit.com
Map: **#12**

Toll-Free Number: (877) 888-2121
Rooms: 335 Price Range: $189-$379
Suites: 65 Price Range: $389-$699
Restaurants: 6
Casino Size: 75,000 Square Feet
Other Games: Poker, Four Card Poker
Overnight RV Parking: No

MotorCity Casino and Hotel
2901 Grand River Avenue
Detroit, Michigan 48201
(313) 237-7711
Website: www.motorcitycasino.com
Map: **#12**

Toll-Free Number: (866) 752-9622
Rooms: 359 Price Range: $179-$259
Suites: 41 Price Range: $439-$799
Restaurants: 4
Buffets: B-$14.00 (Sat/Sun) L-$23.00
D-$28.00/$49.00 (Mon)
Casino Size: 75,000 Square Feet
Other Games: Poker, Ultimate Texas Hold'em
Overnight RV Parking: Free/RV Dump: No

Indian Casinos

Indian casinos in Michigan are not required to release information on their slot machine payback percentages. However, according to officials at the Michigan Gaming Control Board, which is responsible for overseeing the tribal-state compacts, "the machines must meet the minimum standards for machines in Nevada or New Jersey." In Nevada the minimum return is 75% and in New Jersey it's 83%. Therefore, Michigan's Indian casinos must return at least 75% in order to comply with the law.

Unless otherwise noted, all Indian casinos in Michigan are open 24 hours and offer the following games: blackjack, craps, roulette, slots and video poker. Other games offered include: Spanish 21 (S21), craps (C), roulette (R), baccarat (B), mini-baccarat (MB), poker (P), Caribbean stud poker (CSP), let it ride (LIR), three-card poker (TCP), four-card poker (FCP), Ultimate Texas Hold'em (UTH), Mississippi stud (MS), keno (K) and bingo (BG).

The minimum gambling age is 19 at all five Kewadin casinos, plus the Odawa casino resort in Petoskey. It is 21 at all other Indian casinos except for the following seven where it's 18: Leelanau Sands, Turtle Creek, Island Resort, Ojibwa, Ojibwa II, Lac Vieux and Soaring Eagle.

For more information on visiting Michigan call the state's department of tourism at (800) 543-2937 or go to www.michigan.org.

Bay Mills Resort & Casino
11386 Lakeshore Drive
Brimley, Michigan 49715
(906) 248-3715
Website: www.baymillscasinos.com
Map: **#3** (12 miles S.W. of Sault Ste. Marie)

Toll-Free Number: (888) 422-9645
Rooms: 142 Price Range: $79-$169
Suites: 4 Price Range: $150-$220
Restaurants: 4 Liquor: Yes
Buffets: D-$17.99 (Tue)/$29.99 (Fri)/
$21.99 (Sat)
Casino Size: 15,000 Square Feet
Other Games: P, LIR, TCP, UTH
Overnight RV Parking: Must use RV park
Special Features: 76-space RV park ($29/$39 with hookups). 18-hole golf course.

FireKeepers Casino
11177 East Michigan Ave
Battle Creek, Michigan 49014
(269) 962-0000
Website: www.firekeeperscasino.com
Map: **#18**

Toll-Free Number: (877) 352-8777
Restaurants: 5 Liquor: Yes
Buffets: L-$16.95/$21.95 (Sat)
D-$20.95/$29.95 (Fri-Sun)
Casino Size: 107,000 Square Feet
Other Games: MB, TCP, LIR, K, B6,
PGP, P, BG, MS, UTH
Overnight RV Parking: Free/RV Dump: No
Senior Discount: Various Tue if 50+
Special Features: Sports bar. Dance club. Food court. Buffet discount with players club card.

Four Winds Dowagiac
58700 M-51 South
Dowagiac, Michigan 49047
(866) 494-6371
Website: www.fourwindscasino.com
Map: **#21** (110 miles E. of Chicago)

Toll-Free Number: (866) 494-6371
Restaurants: 1 Liquor: Yes
Other Games: No craps, MS
Overnight RV Parking: Free/RV Dump: No
Senior Discount: Various Wed if 55+
Special Features: Table Games open at 10am.

Four Winds Hartford
68600 Red Arrow Highway
Hartford, Michigan 49057
(866) 494-6371
Website: www.fourwindscasino.com
Map: **#21** (110 miles E. of Chicago)

Toll-Free Number: (866) 494-6371
Restaurants: 1 Liquor: Yes Valet Parking: Free
Casino Size: 52,000 Square Feet
Other Games: TCP, MS
Overnight RV Parking: Free/RV Dump: No
Senior Discount: Various Wed if 55+

Four Winds New Buffalo
11111 Wilson Road
New Buffalo, Michigan 49117
(866) 494-6371
Website: www.fourwindscasino.com
Map: **#19** (60 miles E. of Chicago)

Toll-Free Number: (866) 494-6371
Rooms: 415 Price Range: $179-$349
Suites: 36 Price Range: $199-$549
Restaurants: 5 Liquor: Yes
Buffets: L- $18/$36 (Sat)/$24 (Sun)
D-$24/$30 (Fri)/$36 (Sat)
Casino Size: 135,000 Square Feet
Other Games: MB, TCP, PGP, MS, K
Overnight RV Parking: Free/RV Dump: No
Senior Discount: Various Wed if 55+

Gun Lake Casino
1123 129th Ave
Wayland, Michigan 49348
(269) 792-7777
Website: www.gunlakecasino.com
Map: **#20** (23 miles S of Grand Rapids)

Toll-free Number: (866) 398-7111
Restaurants: 2 Liquor: Yes
Buffets: L-$14/$22 (Sat)/$28 (Sun)
D-$22/$28 (Thu/Sat/Sun)/$30 (Fri)
Casino Size: 30,000 Square Feet
Other Games: TCP, MS
Overnight RV Parking: Free/RV Dump: No
Special Features: Food court with four fast food outlets.

Island Resort & Casino
W399 US Highway 2 and US Highway 41
Harris, Michigan 49845
(906) 466-2941
Website: www.islandresortandcasino.com
Map: **#1** (13 miles W. of Escanaba on Hwy. 41)

Toll-Free Number: (800) 682-6040
Rooms: 102 Price Range: $79-$122
Suites: 11 Price Range: $129-$379
Restaurants: 5 Liquor: Yes
Casino Size: 135,000 Square Feet
Other Games: S21, P, TCP, LIR, UTH, BG
Overnight RV Parking: Must use RV park
Senior Discount: Various Wed if 55+
Special Features: 42-space RV park ($20 per night). RV Park open seasonally May 1- Nov 30. Spa.

Kewadin Casino - Christmas
N7761 Candy Cane Lane
Munising, Michigan 49862
(906) 387-5475
Website: www.kewadin.com/christmas
Map: **#9** (40 miles E. of Marquette)

Toll-Free Number: (800) 539-2346
Restaurants: 1 Liquor: Yes
Hours: 9am-1am Daily
Casino Size: 3,060 Square Feet
Other Games: LIR, UTH, No craps/roulette
Overnight RV Parking: Free/RV Dump: No
Senior Discount: Various Wed if 50+
Special Features: Free local-area shuttle service.

Kewadin Casino - Hessel
3 Mile Road
Hessel, Michigan 49745
(906) 484-2903
Website: www.kewadin.com /hessel
Map: **#10** (20 miles N.E. of St. Ignace)

Toll-Free Number: (800) 539-2346
Restaurants: 1 Deli Liquor: Yes
Hours: 9am-10pm/11pm (Fri/Sat)
Casino Size: 6,500 Square Feet
Other Games: Only gaming machines
Overnight RV Parking: Must use RV Park
Senior Discount: Various Wed if 50+
Special Features: 40-space RV park open May-October ($10/$15 with hook-ups per night).

Kewadin Casino - Manistique
5630 West U.S. Highway 2
Manistique, Michigan 49854
(906) 341-5510
Website: www.kewadin.com/manistique
Map: **#11** (95 miles S.E. of Marquette)

Toll-Free Number: (800) 539-2346
Restaurants: 1 Liquor: Yes
Hours: 9am-2am Daily
Casino Size: 25,000 Square Feet
Other Games: Only Gaming Machines
Overnight RV Parking: Free/RV Dump: No
Senior Discount: Various Wed if 50+
Special Features: Free shuttle service from local motels.

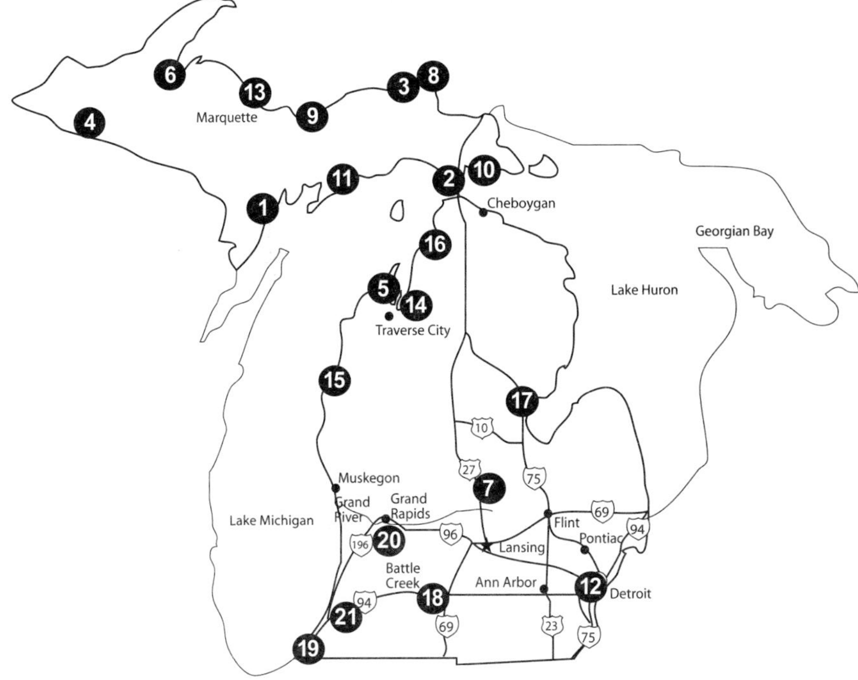

Kewadin Casino Hotel - Sault Ste. Marie
2186 Shunk Road
Sault Ste. Marie, Michigan 49783
(906) 632-0530
Website: www.kewadin.com/sault
Map: **#8**

Toll-Free Number: (800) 539-2346
Rooms: 300 Price Range: $85-$105
Suites: 20 Price Range: $115-$130
Restaurants: 3 Liquor: Yes
Buffets: D-$10.95/$19.95 (Fri)/$22.95 (Sat)
Casino Size: 85,123 Square Feet
Other Games: P, LIR, TCP, BG, K, UTH
Overnight RV Parking: Must use RV park
Senior Discount: Various Wed if 50+
Special Features: Free shuttle service to local motels and airport. Table games open at noon. 64-space RV park ($20 per night) open May-Oct.

Kewadin Casino - St. Ignace
3015 Mackinac Trail
St. Ignace, Michigan 49781
(906) 643-7071
Website: www.kewadin.com/st-ignace
Map: **#2** (50 miles S. of Sault Ste. Marie)

Toll-Free Number: (800) 539-2346
Rooms: 81 Prices: $105-$129
Suites: 11 Prices: $135-$169
Restaurants: 2 Liquor: Yes
Buffets: D-$10.95/$18.99 (Fri)/$22.99 (Sat)
Casino Size: 56,168 Square Feet
Other Games: P, LIR, TCP, UTH
Overnight RV Parking: Must use RV Park.
Senior Discount: Various Wed if 50+.
Special Features: Local motels/hotels offer packages with free shuttle service. Sports bar. 21-space RV park ($15 per night).

Kings Club Casino
12140 W. Lakeshore Drive
Brimley, Michigan 49715
(906) 248-3700
Website: www.4baymills.com
Map: **#3** (12 miles S.W. of Sault Ste. Marie)

Toll-Free Number: (888) 422-9645
Restaurants: 1 Liquor: Yes
Casino Size: 6,500 Square Feet
Hours: 10am-12am/2am (Fri/Sat)
Other Games: Only gaming Machines
Overnight RV Parking: Must use RV park
Special Features: Two miles from, and affiliated with, Bay Mills Resort & Casino. 75-space RV park ($27/$39 w/hookup) at Bay Mills.

Lac Vieux Desert Casino
N 5384 US 45 North
Watersmeet, Michigan 49969
(906) 358-4226
Website: www.lvdcasino.com
Map: **#4** (49 miles S.E. of Ironwood)

Toll-Free Number: (800) 583-3599
Room Reservations: (800) 895-2505
Rooms: 107 Price Range: $75-$110
Suites: 25 Price Range: $110-$135
Restaurants: 1 Liquor: Yes
Buffets: D- $14.95 (Wed/Thu)/$23.95 (Fri)/
$21.95 (Sat)
Casino Size: 25,000 Square Feet
Other Games: P
Overnight RV Parking: Must use RV park
Senior Discount: 10% off in restaurant if 55+
Special Features: 9-hole golf course. 14-space RV park ($15 per night).

Leelanau Sands Casino & Lodge
2521 N.W. Bayshore Drive
Peshawbestown, Michigan 49682
(231) 534-8100
Website: www.leelanausandscasino.com
Map: **#5** (4 miles N. of Sutton's Bay)

Toll-Free Number: (800) 922-2946
Room Reservations: (800) 930-3008
Rooms: 51 Price Range: $120-$160
Suites: 2 Price Range: $160-$180
Restaurants: 2 Liquor: Yes
Casino Size: 29,000 Square Feet
Hours: 8am-2am Daily
Other Games: TCP, BG (Sun/Wed-Fri)
Overnight RV Parking: Free/RV Dump: No
Senior Discount: Various on Tue if 65+.
Special Features: RV hook-ups available for $7 per night.

Little River Casino Resort
2700 Orchard Drive
Manistee, Michigan 49660
(231) 723-1535
Website: www.lrcr.com
Map: **#15** (60 miles S.W of Traverse City)

Toll-Free Number: (888) 568-2244
Rooms: 271 Price Range: $119-$160
Suites: 20 Price Range: $189-$260
Restaurants: 4 Liquor: Yes
Buffets: B-$9.99 L-$11.99
D-$13.99/$29.99 (Fri/Sat)
Casino Size: 75,000 Square Feet
Other Games: LIR, TCP, MS, UTH
Overnight RV Parking: Free/RV Dump: Free
Senior Discount: Various Wed if 55+
Special Features: 95-space RV park open April-October ($25-$45 per night). Spa.

Odawa Casino Resort
1760 Lears Road
Petoskey, Michigan 49770
(231) 439-6100
Website: www.odawacasino.com
Map: **#16** (50 miles S.W of Cheboygan)

Toll-Free Number: (877) 442-6464
Rooms: 127 Price Range: $119-$169
Suites: 10 Price Range- $159-$249
Restaurants: 3 Liquor: Yes
Buffets: B- $7.95/$16.95 (Sun)
L- $11.95/$16.95 (Sun) D- $19.95
Casino Size: 33,000 Square Feet

Other Games: LIR, TCP, P
Overnight RV Parking: Free/RV Dump: No
Senior Discount: Various Wed/Sun 8am-8pm if 50+
Special Features: Hotel is 1/4-mile from casino. Free shuttle service to/from local hotels.

Odawa Casino Mackinaw
1080 S Nicolet Street
Mackinaw City, Michigan 49701
(877) 442-6464
Website: www.odawacasino.com
Map: **#2** (60 miles S. of Sault Ste. Marie)

Toll-Free Number: (877) 442-6464
Restaurants: 1 Snack Bar Liquor: No
Other Games: Class II gaming machines based on bingo

Ojibwa Casino - Marquette
105 Acre Trail
Marquette, Michigan 49855
(906) 249-4200
Website: www.ojibwacasino.com
Map: **#13**

Toll-Free Number: (888) 560-9905
Restaurants: 1 Snack Bar Liquor: Yes
Other Games: LIR
Overnight RV Parking: Free/RV Dump: Yes
Senior Discount: Various Mon if 55+
Special features: 7-space RV Park (Free). Table games open 2pm-2am/12pm-2am (Thu-Sun).

Ojibwa Casino Resort - Baraga
16449 Michigan Avenue
Baraga, Michigan 49908
(906) 353-6333
Website: www.ojibwacasino.com
Map: **#6** (30 miles S. of Houghton)

Toll-Free Number: (800) 323-8045
Rooms: 38 Price Range: $69-$89
Restaurants: 2 Liquor: Yes
Casino Size: 17,000 Square Feet
Other Games: LIR, BG
Overnight RV Parking: Must use RV park
Senior Discount: Various Mon if 55+
Special Features: 12-space RV Park ($20 per night). 8-lane bowling alley. Table games open noon daily.

Saganing Eagles Landing Casino
2690 Worth Road
Standish, Michigan 48658
(888) 732-4537
Website: www.saganing-eagleslanding.com
Map: #**#17**

Toll-Free Number: (888) 732-4537
Restaurants: 1 Liquor: Yes
Casino Size: 32,000 Square Feet
Other Games: Only Gaming Machines
Overnight RV Parking: Must use RV park
Special Features: Electronic versions of blackjack and roulette. 50-space RV park ($20 per night).

Soaring Eagle Casino & Resort
6800 Soaring Eagle Boulevard
Mount Pleasant, Michigan 48858
(888) 732-4537
Website: www.soaringeaglecasino.com
Map: **#7** (65 miles N. of Lansing)

Toll-Free Number: (888) 732-4537
Room Reservations: (877) 232-4532
Rooms: 491 Price Range: $159-$385
Suites: 21 Price Range: $199-$449
Restaurants: 6 Liquor: Yes
Buffets: L-$17.75 D-$19.75
Casino Size: 150,000 Square Feet
Other Games: P, TCP, BG (Wed-Sun)
Overnight RV Parking: Free/RV Dump: No
Senior Discount: Various Thu if 55+
Special Features: Casino is in two separate buildings. Gift shop. Art gallery. Off property RV park with free shuttle ($47-$65 per night)..

Turtle Creek Casino
7741 M-72 East
Williamsburg, Michigan 49690
(231) 534-8888
Website: www.turtlecreekcasino.com
Map: **#14** (8 miles E. of Traverse City)

Toll-Free Number: (800) 922-2946
Rooms: 127 Price Range: $159-$270
Suites: 10 Price Range: $350-$400
Restaurants: 3 Liquor: Yes
Buffets: B-$11.95/$13.95 (Sat/Sun)
D- $25.95/$31.95 (Fri)
Casino Size: 72,000 Square Feet
Other Games: P, TCP, UTH
Overnight RV Parking: Free/RV Dump: No
Senior Discount: Various Thu if 50+

MINNESOTA

All Minnesota casinos are located on Indian reservations and under a compact reached with the state the only table games permitted are card games such as blackjack and poker. Additionally, the only kind of slot machines allowed are the electronic video variety. Therefore, you will not find any mechanical slots that have traditional reels - only video screens.

According to the terms of the compact between the state and the tribes, however, the minimum and maximum payouts are regulated as follows: video poker and video blackjack - 83% to 98%, slot machines - 80% to 95%, keno - 75% to 95%. Each tribe is free to set its machines to pay back anywhere within those limits and the tribes do not not release any information regarding their slot machine percentage paybacks.

The hours of operation are listed for those casinos that are not open on a 24-hour basis and the minimum gambling age is 18 at all casinos.

Unless otherwise noted, all casinos offer: video slots, video poker, video keno and blackjack. Optional games include: poker (P), Caribbean stud poker (CSP), pai gow poker (PGP), three-card poker (TCP), ultimate Texas hold'em (UTH), Mississippi stud (MS), let it ride (LIR) and bingo (BG).

For more information on visiting Minnesota call the state's office of tourism at (800) 657-3700 or go to www.exploreminnesota.com.

Black Bear Casino Resort
1785 Highway 210
Carlton, Minnesota 55718
(218) 878-2327
Website: www.blackbearcasinoresort.com
Map: **#1** (130 miles N. of Twin Cities)

Toll-Free Number: (888) 771-0777
Rooms: 158 Price Range: $89-$125
Suites: 60 Price Range: $99-$159
Restaurants: 4 Liquor: Yes
Buffets:B- $9.99 L- $10.99/$11.99 (Sat/Sun)
D-$11.99/$17.99 (Thu)/
$14.99 (Fri)/$12.99 (Sat)
Casino Size: 65,000 Square Feet
Other Games: P, MS, UTH, BG
Overnight RV Parking: Free/RV Dump: No
Special Features: 18-hole golf course.

Fond-du-Luth Casino
129 E. Superior Street
Duluth, Minnesota 55802
(218) 720-5100
Website: www.fondduluthcasino.com
Map: **#3** (150 miles N.E. of Twin Cities)

Toll-Free Number: (800) 873-0280
Restaurants: 1 Liquor: Yes
Casino Size: 20,000 Square Feet
Other Games: Only blackjack and slots
Overnight RV Parking: No
Senior Discount: Various Tue if 55+
Special Features: One hour free parking in lot adjacent to casino (must be validated in casino). Free shuttle to/from Black Bear Casino.

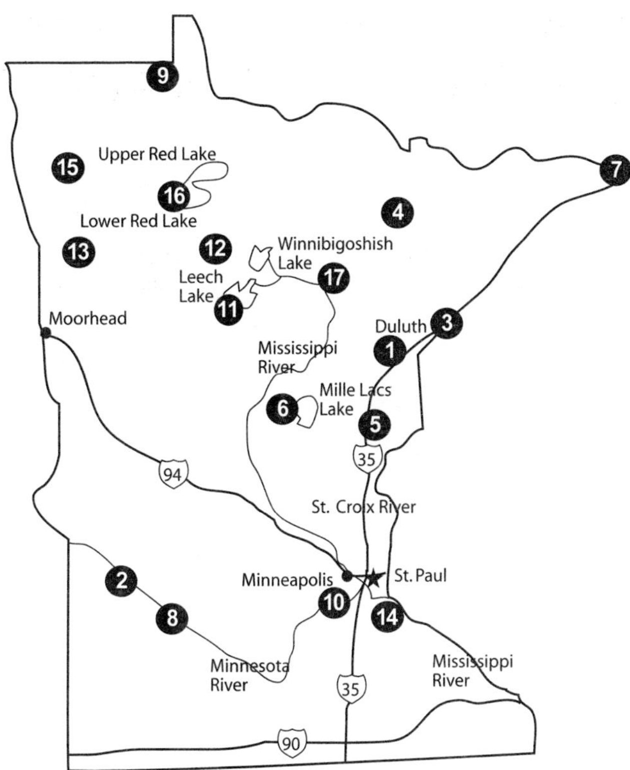

Fortune Bay Resort Casino
1430 Bois Forte Road
Tower, Minnesota 55790
(218) 753-6400
Website: www.fortunebay.com
Map: **#4** (150 miles N.E. of Twin Cities. 24 miles N.E. of Virginia, MN on the S. shore of Lake Vermilion)

Toll-Free Number: (800) 992-7529
Rooms: 83 Price Range: $110-$155
Suites: 33 Price Range: $1349-$350
Restaurants: 4 Liquor: Yes
Buffets: B- $9.95/$13.95 (Sat/Sun)
L- $11.95/$13.95 (Sat/Sun)
D- $16.95/$22.95 (Fri/Sat)/
$21.95 (Mon)
Casino Size: 17,000 Square Feet
Other Games: UTH, P
Overnight RV Parking: Must use RV park
Senior Discount: Various Wed if 50+.
Special Features: Located on S.E. shore of Lake Vermilion. 84-slip marina. 36-space RV Park ($20-$35 per night). Snowmobile and hiking trails. 18-hole golf course.

Grand Casino Hinckley
777 Lady Luck Drive
Hinckley, Minnesota 55037
(320) 384-7777
Website: www.grandcasinomn.com
Map: **#5** (75 miles N. of Twin Cities. One mile E. of I-35's Hinckley exit on Hwy. 48)

Toll-Free Number: (800) 472-6321
Rooms: 485 Price Range: $99-$159 (Hotel)
Price Range: $89-$119 (Inn)
Price Range: $99-$179 (Chalet)
Suites: 52 Price Range: $129-$269
Restaurants: 4 Liquor: Yes
Buffets: B-$11.99 (Sat/Sun)
Casino Size: 54,800 Square Feet
Other Games: P, BG
Overnight RV Parking: Must use RV park
Special Features: 271-space RV park ($29 per night/$38 Fri/Sat). 18-hole golf course. Free pet kennel.

Grand Casino Mille Lacs
777 Grand Avenue
Onamia, Minnesota 56359
(320) 532-7777
Website: www.grandcasinomn.com
Map: **#6** (90 miles N. of Twin Cities. On Highway 169 on the W. shore of Lake Mille Lacs)

Toll-Free Number: (800) 626-5825
Rooms: 284 Price Range: $89-$229
Suites: 14 Price Range: $119-$389
Restaurants: 3 Liquor: No
Buffets: B- $9.99/$11.99 (Sat/Sun)
L- $9.99/$11.99 (Sat/Sun)
D- $13.99/$15.99(Thu)/$26.99 (Fri)/ $16.99 (Sat/Sun)
Casino Size: 42,000 Square Feet
Other Games: P, BG
Overnight RV Parking: Free/RV Dump: No
Special Features: Resort has two hotels (one is off-property). Free pet kennel.

Grand Portage Lodge & Casino
70 Casino Drive
Grand Portage, Minnesota 55605
(218) 475-2401
Website: www.grandportage.com
Map: **#7** (N.E. tip of Minnesota. 300 miles N. of Twin Cities. On Highway 61, five miles from the Canadian border)

Reservation Number: (800) 543-1384
Rooms: 90 Price Range: $79-$135
Suites: 10 Price Range: $135-$205
Restaurants: 1 Liquor: Yes
Casino Size: 15,268 Square Feet
Other Games: BG (Tue/Fri), No Blackjack
Overnight RV Parking: Must use RV park
Special Features: On shore of Lake Superior. Hiking, skiing and snowmobile trails. Gift shop. Marina. 29-space RV park open May-Oct ($35/$40 per night). Free shuttle service to/from Thunder Bay, Ontario.

Jackpot Junction Casino Hotel
39375 County Highway 24
Morton, Minnesota 56270
(507) 697-8000
Website: www.jackpotjunction.com
Map: **#8** (110 miles S.W. of Twin Cities)

Toll-Free Number: (800) 946-2274
Rooms: 253 Price Range: $75-$115
Suites: 23 Price Range: $135-$175
Restaurants: 3 Liquor: Yes
Buffets: B- $9.99 (Sat)/ $15.50 (Sun)
L- $10.99/$15.50 (Sun)
D- $13.50/$22.95 (Fri)/$16.50 (Sat)
Other Games: TCP, UTH, BG (Thu-Mon)
Senior Discount: Various Wed if 50+
Special Features: 70-space RV park ($30-$40 per night). 18-hole golf course.

Little Six Casino
2450 Sioux Trail N.W.
Prior Lake, Minnesota 55372
(952) 403-5525
Website: www.littlesixcasino.com
Map: **#10** (25 miles S.W. of Twin Cities. On County Road 83)

Toll-Free: (800) 262-7799 (Mystic Lake)
Restaurants: 1 Liquor: Yes
Senior Discounts: Various Wed if 55+.
Special Features: 1/4-mile north of Mystic Lake Casino. Free shuttle from Mall of America.

Mystic Lake Casino Hotel
2400 Mystic Lake Boulevard
Prior Lake, Minnesota 55372
(952) 445-9000
Website: www.mysticlake.com
Map: **#10** (25 miles S.W. of Twin Cities. On County Road 83, 3 miles S. of Hwy 169)

Toll-Free Number: (800) 262-7799
Rooms: 510 Price Range: $129-$259
Suites: 76 Price Range: $179-$489
Restaurants: 7 Liquor: Yes
Buffets: L- $13.95/$21.95 (Sat/Sun)
D- $18.95/$19.95 (Fri/Sat)/$37.95 (Sun)
Casino Size: 102,000 Square Feet
Other Games: BG
Overnight RV Parking: Must use RV Park
Senior Discounts: Various Wed if 55+.
Special Features: Free shuttle bus service from Twin Cities area. 122-space RV park ($39/$47 per night spring/summer, $34 fall/winter). Health club. Childcare facility. Spa.

Northern Lights Casino & Hotel
6800 Y Frontage Rd NW
Walker, Minnesota 56484
(218) 547-2744
Website: www.northernlightscasino.com
Map: **#11** (175 miles N. of the Twin Cities. Near the S. shore of Lake Leech four miles S. of Walker, MN at the junction of Highways 371 & 200)

Toll-Free Number: (800) 252-7529
Rooms: 105 Price Range: $100-$120
Suites: 4 Price Range: $120-$190
Restaurants: 2 Liquor: Yes
Buffets: B-$9.95
L-$8.50/$9.95 (Sat/Sun)
D-$11.95/$25.50 (Thurs)/
$16.95 (Fri/Sat)/$13.95 (Sun)
Casino Size: 40,000 Square Feet
Other Games: P
Overnight RV Parking: Free/RV Dump: No
Special Features: 90-foot dome simulates star constellations.

Palace Casino & Hotel
16599 69th Avenue N.W.
Cass Lake, Minnesota 56633
(218) 335-7000
Website: www.palacecasinohotel.com
Map: **#12** (220 miles N.W. of Twin Cities)

Toll-Free Number: (877) 972-5223
Rooms: 64 Price Range: $65-$75
Suites: 16 Price Range $78-$88
Restaurants: 2 Liquor: No
Buffet: L- $8.99 D- $17.99(Fri)/$14.99 (Sat)
Casino Size: 30,000 Square Feet
Other Games: UTH, BG (Thu-Sun)
Overnight RV Parking: Free/RV Dump: Free
Special Features: 15-space RV park offers free parking and hookup.

Prairie's Edge Casino Resort
5616 Prairie's Edge Lane
Granite Falls, Minnesota 56241
(320) 564-2121
Website: www.prairiesedgecasino.com
Map: **#2** (110 miles W. of Twin Cities. Five miles S.E. of Granite Falls on Highway 67 E.)

Toll-Free Number: (866) 293-2121
Rooms: 79 Price Range: $59-$89
Suites: 10 Price Range: $129-$159
Restaurants: 2 Liquor: Yes
Buffets: B/L-$13.95 (Sun)
D-$12.95/$15.95 (Wed)
Casino Size: 36,000 Square Feet
Overnight RV Parking: Must use RV Park
Special Features: 55-space RV park ($25 per night/$30 with hookups). Convenience store. No buffet Mon/Tue.

Seven Clans Casino Red Lake
10200 Route 89
Red Lake, Minnesota 56671
(218) 679-2500
Website: www.sevenclanscasino.com
Map: **#16** (200 miles N.W. of Duluth)

Toll-Free Number: (888) 679-2501
Rooms: 40 Prices: $75-$95
Suites: 16 Price Range $79-$165
Restaurants: 1 Liquor: No
Casino Size: 40,000 Square Feet
Other Games: BG (Sun, No blackjack
Overnight RV Parking: Free/RV Dump: No
Senior Discount: Various Mon if 50+

Seven Clans Casino Thief River Falls
20595 Center Street East
Thief River Falls, Minnesota 56701
(218) 681-4062
Website: www.sevenclanscasino.com
Map: **#15** (275 miles N.W. of Minneapolis)

Toll-Free Number: (800) 881-0712
Suites: 151 Price Range: $75-$210
Restaurants: 2 Liquor: No
Casino Size: 16,000 Square Feet
Overnight RV Parking: Free/RV Dump: No
Senior Discount: Various Mon if 50+ .
Special features: Indoor water park. Malt shop.

Seven Clans Casino Warroad
34966 605th Avenue
Warroad, Minnesota 56763
(218) 386-3381
Website: www.sevenclanscasino.com
Map: **#9** (400 miles N.W. of Twin Cities)

Toll-Free Number: (800) 815-8293
Rooms: 34 Price Range: $85-$119
Suites: 7 Price Range: $159-$179
Restaurants: 2 Liquor: No
Casino Size: 13,608 Square Feet
Other Games: P
Overnight RV Parking: Free/RV Dump: No
Senior Discount: Various Mon if 50+
Special Features: Hotel is Super 8 located one mile from casino with free shuttle service provided.

Shooting Star Casino Bagley
13325 340th Street
Bagley, Minnesota 56676
(218) 935-2701
Website: www.starcasino.com
Map: **#13** (250 miles N.W. of Twin Cities)

Toll-Free Number: (800) 453-7827
Hours: 10am-2am/24 Hours (Fri/Sat)
Restaurants: 1 Liquor: Yes
Games Offered: Video Slots, Video Poker

Shooting Star Casino Hotel
777 Casino Road
Mahnomen, Minnesota 56557
(218) 935-2701
Website: www.starcasino.com
Map: **#13** (235 miles N.W. of Twin Cities)

Room Reservations: (800) 453-7827
Rooms: 360 Price Range: $69-$99
Suites: 30 Price Range: $110-$120
Restaurants: 4 Liquor: Yes
Buffets: B-$7.99 L-$10.50
D-$12.50/$14.99(Thu)/$19.99 (Fri/Sat)
Other Games: P, BG
Overnight RV Parking: Must use RV park
Special Features: 47-space RV park ($30 per night).

Treasure Island Resort & Casino
5734 Sturgeon Lake Road
Red Wing, Minnesota 55089
(651) 388-6300
Website: www.treasureislandcasino.com
Map: **#14** (40 miles S.E. of Twin Cities. Halfway between Hastings and Red Wing, off Highway 61 on County Road 18)

Toll-Free Number: (800) 222-7077
Rooms: 250 Price Range: $109-$159
Suites: 28 Price Range: $179-$249
Restaurants: 3 Liquor: Yes
Buffets: B- $17.50 (Sat/Sun)
L- $13.50/$17.50 (Sat/Sun)
D- $17.50/$28.95 (Thu)/
$19.50 (Fri/Sat)
Casino Size: 110,000 Square Feet
Other Games: B, P, PGP, TCP, UTH, BG
Overnight RV Parking: Must use RV Park
Senior Discount: Various Wed if 50+.
Special Features: 95-space RV park open April-October ($28-$60 per night). 137-slip marina. Dinner and sightseeing cruises.

White Oak Casino
45830 US Hwy 2
Deer River, Minnesota 56636
(218) 246-9600
Website: www.whiteoakcasino.com
Map: **#17** (5 miles N.W. of Grand Rapids)

Toll-Free Number: (800) 653-2412
Restaurants: 1 Snack Bar Liquor: Yes
Casino Size: 11,000 Square Feet
Overnight RV Parking: Free/RV Dump: No
Senior Discount: Various Tue if 50+

Pari-Mutuels

Minnesota has two racetracks that offer the card games of blackjack, poker, pai gow poker, let it ride, Mississippi stud, and four card poker.

The completely nonsmoking card rooms are open 24 hours and admission is free. Players must pay a commission to the card room on each hand played for all games except regular poker, where a rake is taken from each pot. The minimum gambling age is 18.

Canterbury Park
1100 Canterbury Road
Shakopee, Minnesota 55379
(952) 445-7223
Website: www.canterburypark.com
Map: **#10** (22 miles S.W. of Twin Cities)

Horse Track Toll-Free: (800) 340-6361
Card Room Toll-Free: (866) 667-6537
Restaurants: 2
Casino Size: 18,000 Square Feet
Overnight RV Parking: Free/RV Dump: No
Special Features: Live horse racing seasonally. Daily simulcasting of horse racing. Free shuttle service to/from Mall of America.

Running Aces
15201 Running Aces Boulevard
Columbus, Minnesota 55025
(651) 925-4600
Website: www.runaces.com
Map: **#10** (25 miles S.W. of Twin Cities. On County Road 83)

Toll-Free: (877) 786-2237
Restaurants: 1
Other Games: No Let it Ride
Special Features: Live Horse racing seasonally. Daily simulcasting of horse racing.

MISSISSIPPI

Mississippi was the third state to legalize riverboat gambling when it was approved by that state's legislature in 1990. The law restricts casinos to coast waters (including the Bay of St. Louis and the Back Bay of Biloxi) along the Mississippi River and in navigable waters of counties that border the river.

Mississippi law also requires that riverboats be permanently moored at the dock and they are not permitted to cruise. This allows the riverboats to offer 24-hour dockside gambling. The Isle of Capri in Biloxi was the first casino to open on August 1, 1992 followed one month later by The President.

Since the law does not require that the floating vessel actually resemble a boat, almost all of the casinos are built on barges. This gives them the appearance of a land-based building, rather than a riverboat.

Due to the destruction caused by Hurricane Katrina in August 2005, the Mississippi legislature allowed the state's gulf coast casinos to be rebuilt on land within 800-feet of the shoreline and some casinos have been rebuilt in that manner.

The Mississippi Gaming Commission does not break down its slot statistics by individual properties. Rather, they are classified by region. The **Coastal** region includes Biloxi, Gulfport and Bay Saint Louis. The **North** region includes Tunica, Greenville and Lula. The **Central** region includes Vicksburg and Natchez.

With that in mind here's information, as supplied by the Mississippi Gaming Commission, showing the machine payback percentages for each area's casinos for the one-year period from July 1, 2016 through June 30, 2017:

	Coastal	North	Central
1¢ Slots	**91.95%**	91.67%	91.70%
5¢ Slots	94.89%	94.36%	**95.22%**
25¢ Slots	**94.44%**	92.78%	94.04%
$1 Slots	94.05%	**96.27%**	94.31%
$5 Slots	94.47%	**97.93%**	95.09%
All	**92.41%**	92.16%	92.12%

These numbers reflect the percentage of money returned on each denomination of machine and encompass all electronic machines including video poker and video keno. The best returns for each category are highlighted in bold print and you can see that all of the gaming areas offer rather similar returns on their machines.

Unless otherwise noted, all casinos are open 24 hours and offer: slots, video poker, blackjack, craps, roulette and three card poker. Other game listings include: Spanish 21 (S21), baccarat (B), mini-baccarat (MB), poker (P), pai gow poker (PGP), let it ride (LIR), Caribbean stud poker (CSP) Mississippi stud (MS), ultimate Texas hold'em (UTH), big six wheel (B6), four card poker (FCP), casino war (CW) and keno (K). The minimum gambling age is 21.

NOTE: If you happen to win a jackpot of $1,200 or more in Mississippi, the casino will deduct 3% of your winnings and pay it to the Mississippi Tax Commission as a gambling tax. The tax is nonrefundable and the $1,200 threshold would also apply to any cash prizes won in casino drawings or tournaments.

For more information on visiting Mississippi call the state's tourism department at (866) 733-6477 or go to: www.visitmississippi.org

For Biloxi tourism information call (800) 237-9493 or go to: www.gulfcoast.org. For Tunica tourism information call (888) 488-6422 or go to: www.tunicatravel.com.

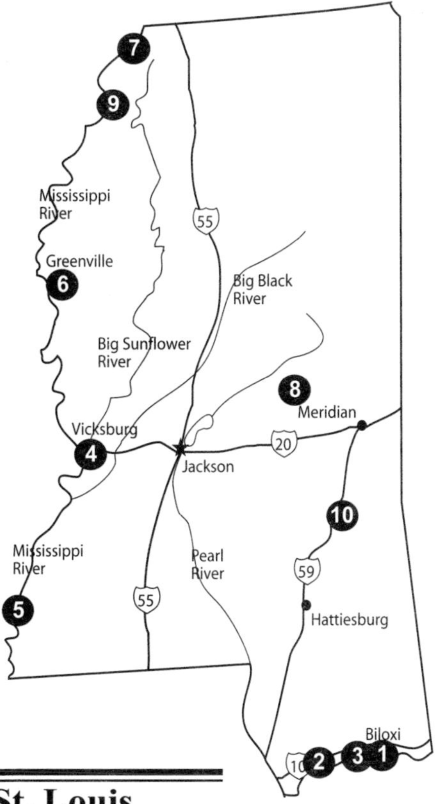

Bay St. Louis

Map: **#2** (on St. Louis Bay, 60 miles E. of New Orleans)

Hollywood Casino Gulf Coast
711 Hollywood Boulevard
Bay St. Louis, Mississippi 39520
(866) 758-2591
Website: www.hollywoodgulfcoast.com

Toll-Free Number: (866) 758-2591
Rooms: 498 Price Range: $69-$179
Suites: 78 Price Range: Casino Use Only
Restaurants: 3
Buffets: B- $9.99 (Sat/Sun)
L-$12.99/$27.99 (Sat/Sun)
D-$20.99/$24.99 (Thu)/$27.99 (Fri-Sun)
Casino Size: 56,300 Square Feet
Other games: MB, PGP, P, MS
Overnight RV Parking: Must use RV park
Special Features: 100-space RV Park ($35/$45 per night). 18-hole golf course. Lazy river pool.

Silver Slipper Casino Hotel
5000 South Beach Boulevard
Bay St. Louis, Mississippi 39520
(228) 469-2777
Website: www.silverslipper-ms.com

Toll-Free Number: (866) 775-4773
Rooms: 110 Price Range: $149-$199
Suites: 19 Price Range: $220-$450
Restaurants: 4
Buffets: L- $12.95/$29.95 (Sun) D- $29.95
Casino Size: 36,826 Square Feet
Other Games: K, MS
Overnight RV Parking: Must use RV park.
Special Features: Land-based casino. 35-space RV park ($25-$35 per night).

Biloxi

Map: **#1** (On the Gulf of Mexico, 90 miles E. of New Orleans)

Beau Rivage Resort & Casino
875 Beach Boulevard
Biloxi, Mississippi 39530
(228) 386-7111
Website: www.beaurivage.com

Toll-Free Number: (888) 750-7111
Rooms: 1,645 Price Range: $89-$300
Suites: 95 Price Range: $139-$450
Restaurants: 8
Buffets: B- $12.99/$15.99 (Sat)/$23.99 (Sun)
L- $15.99/$23.99 (Sun)
D- $22.99/$26.99 (Fri)/ $29.99 (Sat)
Casino Size: 79,808 Square Feet
Other Games: MB, PGP, P, CSP,
LIR, MS, UTH
Overnight RV Parking: No
Special Features: Casino is on a barge. Spa. Beauty salon. 13-store shopping arcade.

Boomtown Casino - Biloxi
676 Bayview Avenue
Biloxi, Mississippi 39530
(228) 435-7000
Website: www.boomtownbiloxi.com

Toll-Free Number: (800) 627-0777
Restaurants: 4
Buffets: L-$13.99/$29.99 (Sat)/$24.99 (Sun)
D- $19.99/$24.99 (Thu/Sun)/$29.99 (Fri/Sat)
Casino Size: 37,891 Square Feet
Other Games: MS, PGP
Overnight RV Parking: Free/RV Dump: No
Special Features: Casino is on a barge. 50-space RV park ($29 to $45 per night).

Golden Nugget - Biloxi
151 Beach Boulevard
Biloxi, Mississippi 39530
(228) 435-5400
Website: www.goldennugget.com

Toll-Free Number: (800) 777-7568
Rooms: 541 Price Range: $89-$259
Suites: 200 Price Range: $129-$429
Restaurants: 5
Buffets: B- $11.99 L- $14.99/$19.99 (Sat/Sun)
D- $19.99 /$29.99 (Thu/$33.99 (Fri-Sun)
Casino Size: 54,728 Square Feet
Other Games: MB, MS, P, PGP, UTH
Overnight RV Parking: Free/RV Dump: No
Senior Discount: Various Wed if 50+
Special Features: Land-based casino. Spa. Beauty salon. Golf packages offered.

Hard Rock Hotel & Casino - Biloxi
777 Beach Boulevard
Biloxi, Mississippi 39530
(228) 374-7625
Website: www.hardrockbiloxi.com

Toll-Free Number: (877) 877-6256
Rooms: 306 Prices: $99-$450
Suites: 64 Prices: $249-$629
Restaurants: 6
Buffets: B-$18.99 (Sat/Sun)
L- $14.99/$18.99 (Sat/Sun)
D-$21.99/$25.99 (Fri/Sat)
Casino Size: 53,800 Square Feet
Other Games: MB, PGP, MS
Overnight RV Parking: No
Special Features: Casino is on a barge. Spa. Nightclub. Collection of rock and roll memorabilia on display.

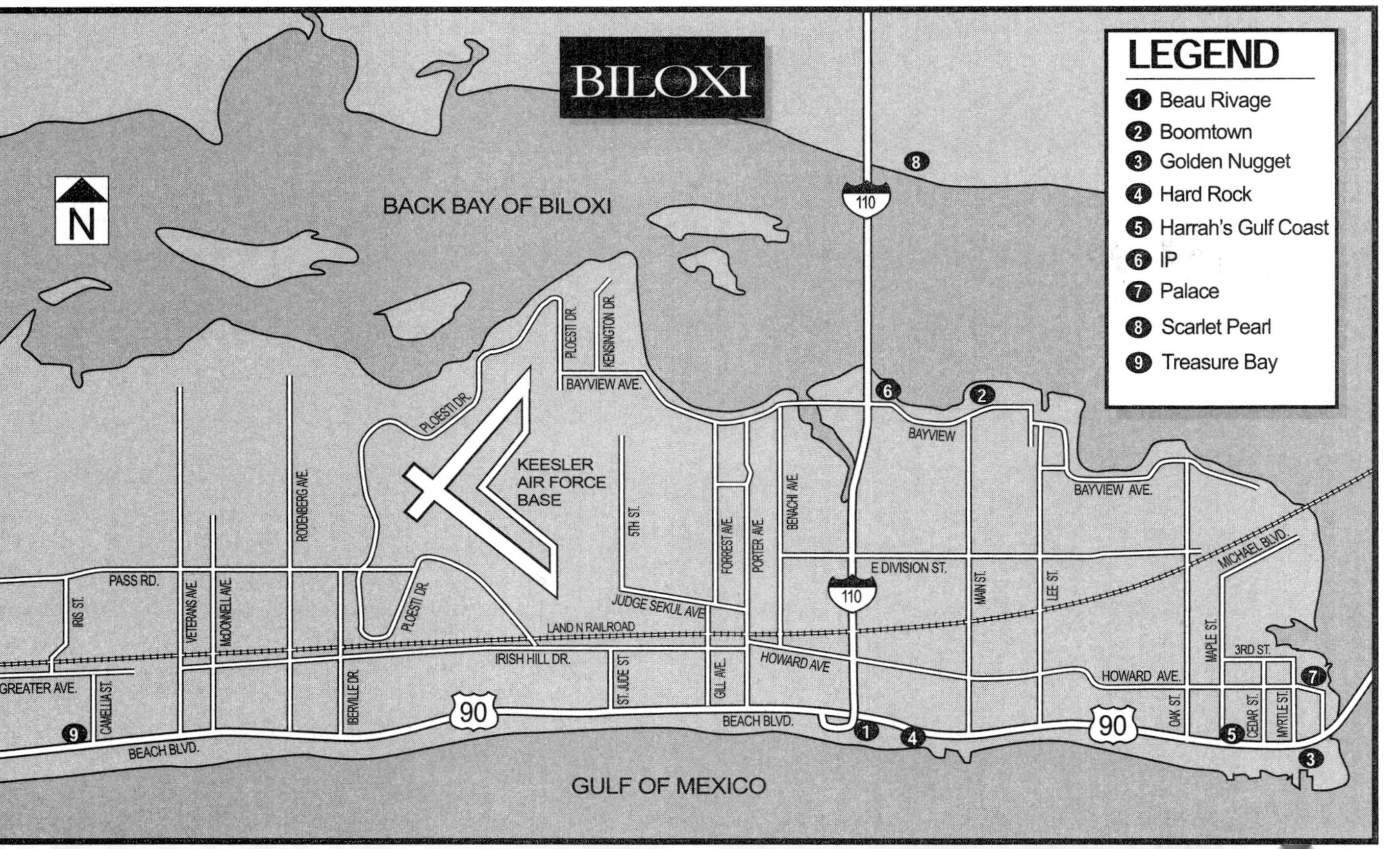
BILOXI
LEGEND
1 Beau Rivage
2 Boomtown
3 Golden Nugget
4 Hard Rock
5 Harrah's Gulf Coast
6 IP
7 Palace
8 Scarlet Pearl
9 Treasure Bay
N
BACK BAY OF BILOXI
GULF OF MEXICO
KEESLER AIR FORCE BASE
110
90
BAYVIEW AVE.
BAYVIEW
PLOESTI DR.
KENSINGTON DR.
5TH ST.
FORREST AVE.
PORTER AVE.
BENACHI AVE.
E DIVISION ST.
MAIN ST.
LEE ST.
MICHAEL BLVD.
MAPLE ST.
3RD ST.
HOWARD AVE.
OAK ST.
CEDAR ST.
MYRTLE ST.
JUDGE SEKUL AVE
LAND N RAILROAD
IRISH HILL DR.
ST. JUDE ST
GILL AVE.
BEACH BLVD.
PASS RD.
IRIS ST.
VETERANS AVE.
McDONNELL AVE.
RODENBERG AVE.
IBERVILLE DR.
GREATER AVE.
CAMELLIA ST.

Harrah's Gulf Coast
265 Beach Boulevard
Biloxi, Mississippi 39530
(228) 436-2946
Website: www.harrahsgulfcoast.com

Toll-Free Number: (800) 946-2946
Rooms: 500 Price Range: $89-$249
Suites: 40 Price Range: $239-$509
Restaurants: 4 (1 open 24 hours)
Buffets: L- $13.99 (Sat/Sun)
D- $17.99/$31.99 (Fri/Sat)
Casino Size: 31,419 Square Feet
Other Games: MB, B, PGP, LIR, MS
Overnight RV Parking: Free/RV Dump: No
Special Features: Land-based casino. Spa. Starbucks coffeehouse.

IP Casino Resort Spa
850 Bayview Avenue
Biloxi, Mississippi 39530
(228) 436-3000
Website: www.ipbiloxi.com

Toll-Free Number: (888) 946-2847
Rooms: 1,088 Price Range: $69-$199
Suites: 14 Price Range: $189-$599
Restaurants: 5
Buffets: B- $11.99 (Sun-Fri)
L- $13.99/$18.99 (Sat)
D- $21.99/$29.99 (Fri/Sat)/$24.99 (Sun)
Casino Size: 81,733 Square Feet
Other Games: MB, PGP, LIR, P, FCP
Overnight RV Parking: Free (Check in with security first)/RV Dump: No
Senior Discount: Various Mon/Wed if 50+
Special Features: Casino is on a barge.

Palace Casino Resort
158 Howard Avenue
Biloxi, Mississippi 39530
(228) 432-8888
Website: www.palacecasinoresort.com

Toll-Free Number: (800) 925-2239
Rooms: 234 Price Range: $79-$249
Suites: 14 Price Range: $159-$525
Restaurants: 3
Buffets: B-$11.99 (Sat/Sun) L-$12.99
D-$20.99/$26.99 (Fri/Sat)
Casino Size: 38,000 Square Feet
Other Games: PGP, MS
Overnight RV Parking: No
Senior Discount: Various Tue if 50+
Special Features: Land-based casino. Marina. 100% smoke-free casino.

Scarlet Pearl Casino Resort
9380 Central Avenue
D'Iberville, Mississippi 39540
(228) 392-1889
Website: www.scarletpearlcasino.com

Toll-Free Number: (888) 266-5772
Rooms: 234 Price Range: $79-$349
Suites: 66 Price Range: $139-$499
Restaurants: 4
Buffets: L- $15.99 /$19.99 (Sat/Sun)
D- $19.99/$29.99 (Fri/Sat)
Casino Size: 60,445 Square Feet
Other Games: MB, PGP, MS, UTH, P
Senior Discount: Various Mon/Wed if 50+
Special features: Land-based casino. Two 18-hole mini golf courses.

Treasure Bay Casino and Hotel
1980 Beach Boulevard
Biloxi, Mississippi 39531
(228) 385-6000
Website: www.treasurebay.com

Toll-Free Number: (800) 747-2839
Rooms: 234 Price Range: $89-$179
Suites: 14 Price Range: $229-$259
Restaurants: 5
Buffets: B- $9.49 L- $12.49 D- $25.99
Casino Size: 28,140 Square Feet
Other Games: PGP, CSP, LIR, MS
Overnight RV Parking: No
Senior Discount: Various Tue/Thu if 50+
Special Features: Land-based casino.

The Best Places To Play On The Gulf Coast
(Biloxi and Gulfport Only)

Roulette- The house edge on a single-zero wheel cuts the house edge from 5.26% down to a more reasonable 2.70%. Unfortunately, there are no casinos on the Gulf Coast that offer single-zero roulette.

Craps- IP is the most liberal of all gulf coast casinos by offering 20X odds on their craps games. All other casinos offer 10X odds.

Blackjack- Gulf Coast casinos offer some decent blackjack games with liberal rules, but all of the casinos hit soft 17, except for Treasure Bay and $100 tables at Beau Rivage. Hitting soft 17 results in an extra mathematical advantage of .20% for the house. All of the recommendations in this section apply to players using perfect basic strategy for each particular game.

Several Gulf Coast casinos offer a single-deck game, but all should be avoided because they all pay 6-to-5 rather than the standard 3-to-2 for winning blackjacks. The casino edge in all of these games is more than 1.50%.

Treasure Bay and Beau Rivage offer the best double-deck game, with the following rules: stand on soft 17, double down on any first two cards, re-split any pair (including aces) and doubling allowed after splitting. This works out to a casino edge of just .14%. The minimum bet is $10 at Treasure Bay and $100 at Beau Rivage. The Golden Nugget, Boomtown, Harrah's and the Palace all have the same game, except they hit soft 17. which brings the casino edge up to .35%.

Hard Rock, Scarlet Pearl, IP and Island View have the same rules as above, but they do not allow re-splitting of aces and that game has a casino edge of .40%.

For six-deck shoe games the best place to play is Beau Rivage, which stands on soft 17, allows doubling down on any first two cards, doubling after splitting, re-splitting of aces and late surrender which gives it a house edge of .26% (this game has a $100 minimum, they also have this same game for lower stakes but the dealer hits on soft 17 and has a house edge of .46%. Harrah's also offers this game.) Treasure Bay has a game where they stand on soft 17, allow doubling down on any first two cards, doubling after splitting and re-splitting of aces. The casino advantage in this game is .34%.

Boomtown, Golden Nugget, Hard Rock, IP, the Palace and Scarlet Pearl all offer an identical game, except they hit soft 17 and that brings the casino edge up to .56%.

Video Poker- Some of the best video poker games on the Gulf Coast for lower limit players are 9/7 Double Bonus (99.11%), 9/6 Double Double Bonus (98.98%), 9/6 Jacks or Better (99.54%), 8/5 Bonus Poker (99.17%) and a version of Deuces Wild called Illinois Deuces (98.91%).

Beau Rivage has Illinois Deuces for $1.

Boomtown offers three games, all in $1 denominations: Illinois Deuces, 8/5 Bonus Poker and 9/6 Double Double Bonus.

The Golden Nugget offers a $1 version of Illinois Deuces, plus $1 9/6 Double Double Bonus.

Harrah's has 9/6 Double Double Bonus for 50-cents, plus Illinois Deuces for quarters and $25.

The IP offers 9/6 Jacks for quarters, 50 cents and $1. There is also $2 9/6 Double Double Bonus. Illinois Deuces is also offered in denominations from 25-cents through $25.

The Palace has 8/5 Bonus for quarters in 10-play.

Treasure Bay has 50-cent and $1 Bonus Poker, 9/6 Double Double Bonus for 50-cents and $1, 9/7 Double Bonus for 50-cents and $1. They also offer Illinois Deuces for 50-cents and $1.

Greenville

Map: **#6** (On the Mississippi River, 121 miles N.W. of Jackson)

Harlow's Casino Resort
4280 Harlows Boulevard
Greenville, Mississippi 38701
(228) 436-4753
Website: www.harlowscasino.com

Toll-Free Number: (866) 524-5825
Rooms: 105 Price Range: $99-$159
Suites: 45 Price Range: $149-$219
Restaurants: 3
Buffets: L- $16.99 (Sun)
D- $16.99/$18.99 (Thu)/$25.99 (Fri/Sat)
Casino Size: 33,000 Square Feet
Other Games: CS, LIR, PGP, MS
Overnight RV Parking: Free/RV Dump: No
Senior Discount: Various Wed if 50+
Special Features: Land-based casino.

Trop Casino Greenville
199 N. Lakefront Road
Greenville, Mississippi 38701
(662) 334-7711
Website: www.tropgreenville.com

Toll-Free Number: (800) 878-1777
Hotel Reservations: (800) 228-2800
Suites: 38 Price Range: $59-$199
Restaurants: 1
Casino Size: 22,822 Square Feet
Other Games: MS
Overnight RV Parking: Free/RV Dump: No
Senior Discount: Various Tue if 50+
Special Features: Casino is on an actual paddlewheel boat.

Gulfport

Map: **#3** (On the Gulf of Mexico, 80 miles E. of New Orleans)

Island View Casino Resort
3300 W. Beach Boulevard
Gulfport, Mississippi 39501
(228) 314-2100
Website: www.islandviewcasino.com

Toll-Free Number: (877) 774-8439
Rooms: 600 Price Range: $89-$199
Restaurants: 5
Buffets: B-$10.99 L-$12.99/$16.99(Sun)
D-$24.99
Casino Size: 82,935 Square Feet
Other Games: PGP, MS
Overnight RV Parking: Free/RV Dump: No
Special Features: Land-based casino.

Lula

Map **#9** (On the Mississippi River, 70 miles S. of Memphis, TN)

Isle of Capri Casino & Hotel - Lula
777 Isle of Capri Parkway
Lula, Mississippi 38644
(610) 241-1627
Website: www.isleofcapricasino.com

Toll-Free Number: (800) 789-5825
Rooms: 485 Price Range: $69-$149
Suites: 40 Price Range: Casino Use Only
Restaurants: 3
Buffets: L-$13.99/$14.99 (Sat)
D-$13.99/$22.99 (Fri)/$23.99 (Sat)
Casino Size: 56,985 Square Feet
Other Games: MS
Overnight RV Parking: Must use RV park.
Senior Discount: Various Wed if 50+
Special Features: 28-space RV Park ($16 per night. First night free if staying two or more).

Natchez

Map: **#5** (on the Mississippi River, 102 miles S.W. of Jackson)

Magnolia Bluffs Casino Hotel
7 Roth Hill Road
Natchez, Mississippi 39120
(601) 235-0045
Website: www.magnoliabluffscasino.com

Toll-Free Number: (888) 505-5777
Rooms: 138 Price Range: $99-$119
Restaurants: 3
Buffets: L- $9/$16.75 (Fri/Sat)
D- $13/$16.75 (Fri/Sat)
Casino Size: 16,032 Square Feet
Other Games: P

Tunica

Map: **#7** (on the Mississippi River, 28 miles S. of Memphis, TN)

Bally's Tunica
1450 Bally Boulevard
Robinsonville, Mississippi 38664
(866) 422-5597
Website: www.ballystunica.com

Toll-Free Number: (866) 422-5597
Restaurants: 3
Buffets: L- $12.99/$17.99 (Sun)
D- $17.99/$26.99 (Fri/Sat)
Casino Size: 46,535 Square Feet
Other Games: MS
Overnight RV Parking: Free/RV Dump: No

Fitz Casino/Hotel
711 Lucky Lane
Robinsonville, Mississippi 38664
(662) 363-5825
Website: www.fitzgeraldstunica.com

Toll-Free Number: (800) 766-5825
Room Reservations: (888) 766-5825
Rooms: 507 Price Range: $49-$119
Suites: 70 Price Range: $79-$159
Restaurants: 2
Buffets: B- $9.99 L- $10.99/$16.99 (Fri/Sat)
D- $17.75/$27.99 (Fri/Sat)
Casino Size: 38,457 Square Feet
Other Games: MS
Overnight RV Parking: Free/RV Dump: No

Gold Strike Casino Resort
1010 Casino Center Drive
Robinsonville, Mississippi 38664
(662) 357-1111
Website: www.goldstrike.com

Room Reservations: (888) 245-7829
Rooms: 1,130 Price Range: $59-$159
Suites: 70 Price Range: $179-$239
Restaurants: 4
Buffets: B-$12.99/$22.99 (Sat/Sun) L-$14.99
D-$22.99/$29.99 (Fri/Sat)
Casino Size: 58,205 Square Feet
Other Games: B, MB, CSP, LIR, FCP, MS
Overnight RV Parking: Free/RV Dump: No
Special Features: Affiliated with MGM Resorts.

Hollywood Casino Tunica
1150 Casino Strip Resort Boulevard
Robinsonville, Mississippi 38664
(662) 357-7700
Website: www.hollywoodtunica.com

Toll-Free Number: (800) 871-0711
Rooms: 437 Price Range: $39-$119
Suites: 57 Price Range: $89-$199
Restaurants: 3
Buffets: B-$9.99 L-$10.99
$17.99/$26.99 (Fri/Sat)
Casino Size: 55,000 Square Feet
Other Games: P, MS
Overnight RV Parking: Must use RV park
Senior Discount: Various Tue if 50+
Special Features: Casino features a collection of Hollywood memorabilia. 123-space RV park ($23 per night).

Horseshoe Casino & Hotel
1021 Casino Center Drive
Robinsonville, Mississippi 38664
(662) 357-5500
Website: www.horseshoetunica.com

Toll-Free Number: (800) 303-7463
Rooms: 200 Price Range: $65-$370
Suites: 311 Price Range: $129-$479
Restaurants: 5
Buffets: B-$23.99 (Sat/Sun)
L-$9.99 D-$14.99/$27.99 (Fri/Sat)
Casino Size: 63,000 Square Feet
Other Games: B, MB, P, LIR, MS, PGP
Overnight RV Parking: Free/RV Dump: No
Special Features: Affiliated with Caesars Entertainment. Bluesville Nightclub. 100x odds on craps. Starbucks coffeehouse.

Resorts Casino Tunica
1100 Casino Strip Resort Boulevard
Robinsonville, Mississippi 38664
(866) 706-7070
Website: www.resortstunica.com

Reservation Number: (866) 676-7070
Rooms: 182 Price Range: $40-$99
Suites: 19 Price Range: $90-$120
Restaurants: 3
Buffets: B- $7.99 L- $10.99
D- $17.99/$19.99 (Thurs)/
$24.99 (Fri/Sat)
Casino Size: 42,902 Square Feet
Overnight RV Parking: Free/RV Dump: Free
Special Features: 18-hole River Bend Links golf course is adjacent to property.

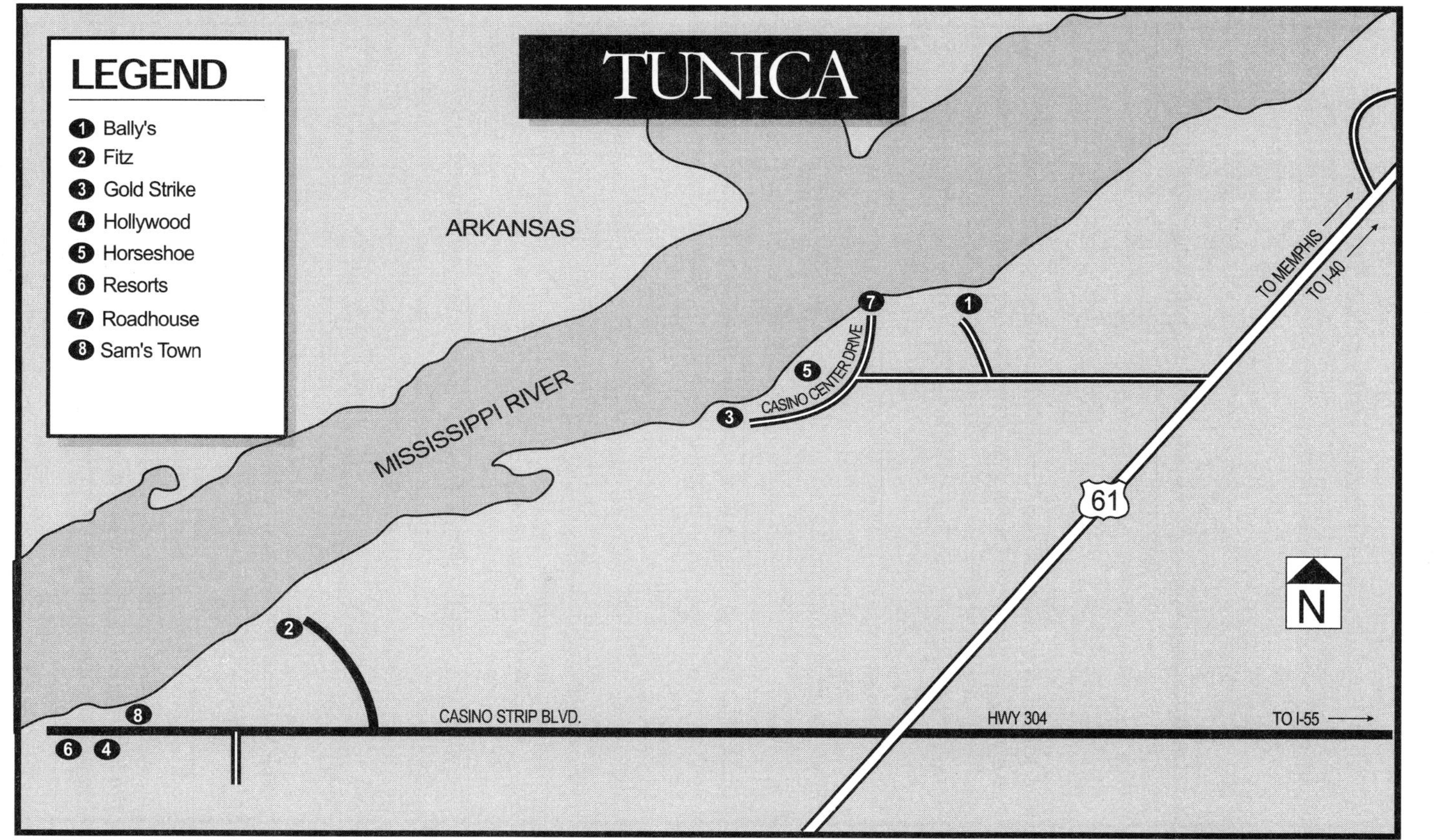
TUNICA
LEGEND
1 Bally's
2 Fitz
3 Gold Strike
4 Hollywood
5 Horseshoe
6 Resorts
7 Roadhouse
8 Sam's Town
ARKANSAS
MISSISSIPPI RIVER
CASINO CENTER DRIVE
TO MEMPHIS
TO I-40
61
N
CASINO STRIP BLVD.
HWY 304
TO I-55

The Best Places To Play in Tunica

Roulette - The house edge on a single-zero wheel cuts the house edge from 5.26% down to a more reasonable 2.70%. Unfortunately, there are no casinos in Tunica that offer single-zero roulette

Craps - All casinos offer 20X odds, except for the Horseshoe which offers 100X odds. Three casinos pay triple (rather than double) on 12 in the field, which cuts the house edge on this bet in half from 5.6 percent to 2.8 percent. The casinos offering this slightly better field bet are: Hollywood, Horseshoe and Gold Strike.

Blackjack - The blackjack games in Tunica are most similar to those offered in downtown Las Vegas. Most casinos offer both single and double-deck games, as well as six-deck shoe games. That's good. The bad part, however, is that dealers hit soft 17 at all casinos, except for Resorts. This results in an extra advantage for the house of .20%. All of the following recommendations apply to players using perfect basic strategy for each particular game.

Only three casinos offer single-deck games and all should be avoided as the casino advantages in these games are .65% and higher.

Bally's, Fitz, Gold Strike and Hollywood all offer the same double-deck games which have the following rules: double down on any first two cards, re-split any pair (including aces), and double down after split. This works out to a casino edge of .35%.

Horseshoe, Resorts, Roadhouse and Sam's Town all offer the same double-deck game as mentioned above, but they don't allow aces to be re-split and that brings the casino edge up slightly to .40%

The six-deck games found at Bally's, Fitz, Gold Strike, Hollywood, Horseshoe and Resorts all have rules identical to the first two-deck games mentioned above and that results in a casino advantage of .56%. Sam's Town has a game similar, but with a slightly higher casino edge of .63% because they won't allow you to re-split aces.

Incidentally, Roadhouse, has the worst six-deck game because they all pay only 6-to-5 for blackjack and that raises the housed edge to almost 2%.

Video Poker - Some of the best video poker games in Tunica for lower limit players are 9/7 Double Bonus (99.11%), 9/6 Double Double Bonus (98.98%), 9/6 Jacks or Better (99.54%), 8/5 Bonus Poker (99.17%) and a version of Deuces Wild called Illinois Deuces (98.91%).

Bally's has both Illinois Deuces and 9/6 Double Double Bonus for $1.

Fitz has 8/5 Bonus for quarters through $5, 9/6 Double Double Bonus for dollars through $5 and Illinois Deuces for quarters on 10-play.

Gold Strike and Horseshoe both have $1 9/7 Double Bonus and $1 9/6 Double Double Bonus. Horseshoe also offers both of those games in $5 denominations.

Roadhouse has 9/6 Jacks in a 100-coin penny game with a progressive and also the same game with an Illinois Deuces pay table. They also offer 9/7 Double Bonus, as well as 9/6 Double Bonus for both $1 and $5.

Sam's Town offers 9/6 Jacks for quarters and $1.

Sam's Town Tunica
1477 Casino Strip Resorts Boulevard
Robinsonville, Mississippi 38664
(662) 363-0711
Website: www.samstowntunica.com

Toll-Free Number: (800) 456-0711
Rooms: 850 Price Range: $39-$119
Suites: 44 Price Range: $69-$169
Restaurants: 3
Buffets: B- $9.99/$14.99 (Sat/Sun)
L- $10.99/$14.99 (Sat/Sun)
D- $17.99/$19.99 (Fri)/$25.99 (Sat)
Casino Size: 48,000 Square Feet
Other Games: LIR, K
Overnight RV Parking: Free/RV Dump: No
Senior Discount: Various Fri if 50+
Special Features: 62-space RV park ($19.99 per night).

Tunica Roadhouse Casino and Hotel
1107 Casino Center Drive
Robinsonville, Mississippi 38664
(662) 363-4900
Website: www.tunica-roadhouse.com

Toll-Free Number: (800) 391-3777
Suites: 140 Price Range: $75-$295
Restaurants: 3
Casino Size: 31,000 Square Feet
Overnight RV Parking: Free/RV Dump: No
Special Features: Affiliated with Caesars Entertainment. All suite hotel with jacuzzi in every room.

Vicksburg

Map: **#4** (on the Mississippi River, 44 miles W. of Jackson)

Vicksburg is one of the most historic cities in the South and is most famous for its National Military Park where 17,000 Union soldiers are buried. The Park is America's best-preserved Civil War battlefield and you can take a 16-mile drive through the 1,858-acre Park on a self-guided tour. In the Park you can also see the U.S.S. Cairo, the only salvaged Union Ironclad. Admission to the Park is $15 per car and allows unlimited returns for seven days.

There are about 10 historic homes in Vicksburg that are open to the public for narrated tours. Admission prices are about $10. Some of the homes also function as Bed and Breakfasts and rooms can be rented for overnight stays.

For more information on visiting Vicksburg call the city's Convention and Visitors Bureau at (800) 221-3536, or visit their website at: www.visitvicksburg.com/

Ameristar Casino Hotel - Vicksburg
4116 Washington Street
Vicksburg, Mississippi 39180
(601) 638-1000
Website: www.ameristarcasino.com

Reservation Number: (800) 700-7770
Rooms: 146 Price Range: $89-$199
Suites: 4 Price Range: $129-$219
Restaurants: 4
Buffets: L- $11.95/$24.95 (Sun)
D-$19.95/$24.95(Wed/Thu/Sun)/
$29.95 (Fri/Sat)
Casino Size: 72,210 Square Feet
Other Games: P, MB, PGP
Overnight RV Parking: Must use RV park.
Special features: 67 space RV park ($30-$35 per night).

Lady Luck Casino Vicksburg
1380 Warrenton Road
Vicksburg, Mississippi 39180
(610) 241-1623
Website: www.isleofcapricasinos.com

Toll-Free Number: (800) 503-3777
Rooms: 82 Price Range: $89-$120
Suites: 7 Price Range: $149-$219
Restaurants: 2
Buffets: L- $11.99/$16.99 (Sun)
DF- $27.95 (Fri/Sat/$16.99 (Sun)/
Casino Size: 25,000 Square Feet
Other Games: No Live Roulette
Overnight RV Parking: Yes
Senior Special: Various Tue if 50+
Special Features: Affiliated with Isle of Capri Casinos

Riverwalk Casino & Hotel
1046 Warrington Road
Vicksburg, Mississippi 39180
(601) 634-0100
Website: www.riverwalkvicksburg.com

Toll-Free Number: (866) 615-9125
Rooms: 80 Price Range: $99-$149
Suites: 4 Price Range: $149-$189
Restaurants: 2
Buffets: L- $19.99 (Sun)
D- $10/$25.99 (Fri)/$32.99 (Sat)
Casino Size: 25,000 square feet
Other Games: MS

WaterView Casino And Hotel
3990 Washington Street
Vicksburg, Mississippi 39180
(601) 636-5700
Website: www.waterviewcasino.com

Toll-Free Number: (877) 711-0677
Rooms: 60 Price Range: $79-$119
Suites: 62 Price Range: $99-$219
Restaurants: 3
Buffets: L- $14.99 (Sat/Sun)
D- $23.99 (Fri/Sat)
Casino Size: 28,000 Square Feet
Other Games: MB, MS
Overnight RV Parking: No

Indian Casinos

Bok Homa Casino
1 Choctaw Road
Heidelberg, Mississippi 39439
Website: www.bokhomacasino.com

Toll-Free Number: (866) 447-3275
Restaurants: 1
Casino Size: 27,000 Square Feet
Other Games: MS
Overnight RV Parking: Free/RV Dump: No
Special Features: Table games open 10am-4am/24 hours (Fri/Sat).

Pearl River Resort
Highway 16 West
Choctaw, Mississippi 39350
(601) 650-1234
Website: www.pearlriverresort.com
Map: **#8** (81 miles N.E. of Jackson)

Toll-Free Number: (800) 557-0711
Room Reservations (866) 447-3275
Silver Star Rooms: 420 Prices: $79-$129
Silver Star Suites: 75 Prices: $179-$579
Golden Moon Rooms: 427 Prices: $69-$119
Golden Moon Suites: 145 Prices: $159-$479
Restaurants: 6 Liquor: Yes
Buffet: B- $21.99 (Sat/Sun)
L-$12.99/$21.99 (Sat/Sun)
D-$13.99/$19.99 (Fri)/$26.99 (Sat)
Silver Star Casino Size: 90,000 Square Feet
Other Games: MB, P
Overnight RV Parking: Free/RV Dump: No
Special Features: Two hotels are across the street from each other. Golden Moon has slots-only casino. 18-hole golf course. 15-acre water park. Health spa. Beauty salon. Shopping arcade with nine stores.

MISSOURI

In November, 1992 Missouri voters approved a state-wide referendum to allow riverboat gambling. That made Missouri the fifth state to approve this form of gambling.

Since Missouri riverboats are not required to cruise, almost all casinos are built on a barge which gives them the appearance of a land-based building, rather than a riverboat.

Unlike dockside gaming in Mississippi, most Missouri casinos are not open 24 hours and the hours of operation are listed for each casino.

Here's information from the Missouri Gaming Commission regarding the payback percentages for each casino's electronic machines for the 12-month period from July 1, 2016 through June 30, 2017:

CASINO	PAYBACK %
River City	90.9
Ameristar-K.C.	90.8
Ameristar-St. Charles	91.0
Hollywood	90.7
Mark Twain	89.4
Isle of Capri - Boonville	90.2
Harrah's N.K.C.	90.3
Argosy	90.4
Lumiere Place	90.2
Isle - Cape Girardeau	89.8
St. Jo Frontier	89.5
Lady Luck	89.3
Isle of Capri K.C.	88.9

These figures reflect the total percentages returned by each casino for all of their electronic machines including slot machines, video poker, video keno, etc.

Unless otherwise noted, all casinos offer: slots, video poker, craps, blackjack, roulette, and three card poker. Optional games include: baccarat (B), mini-baccarat (MB), Caribbean stud poker (CSP), poker (P), pai gow poker (PGP), let it ride (LIR), Spanish 21 (S21), Mississippi stud (MS), ultimate Texas hold 'em (UTH) and four card poker (FCP).

If you want to order a drink while playing, be aware that Missouri gaming regulations do not allow casinos to provide free alcoholic beverages. The minimum gambling age is 21.

NOTE: If you happen to win a jackpot of $1,200 or more in Missouri, the casino will withhold 4% of your winnings for the Missouri Department of Revenue. If you want to try and get that money refunded, you will be required to file a state income tax return and, depending on the details of your return, you may get some of the money returned to you. The $1,200 threshold would also apply to any cash prizes won in casino drawings or tournaments.

For more information on visiting Missouri call the state's Travel Center at (800) 877-1234 or go to: www.visitmo.com.

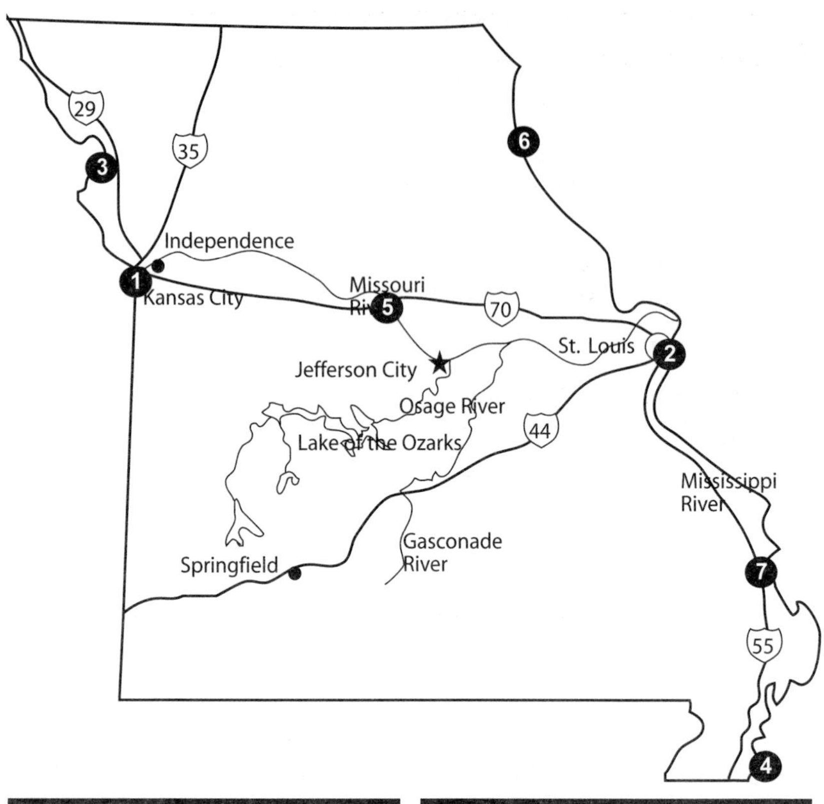

Boonville

Map: **#5** (100 miles E. of Kansas City)

Isle of Capri Casino - Boonville
100 Isle of Capri Boulevard
Boonville, Missouri 65233
(610) 241-1625
Website: www.isleofcapricasino.com

Toll-Free Number: (800) 843-4753
Rooms: 114 Price Range: $109-$179
Suites: 27 Price Range: $159-$229
Restaurants: 3
Buffets: B- $9.99 L- $11.99/$15.99 (Sun)
D- $16.99/$19.99 (Fri/Sat)
Hours: 8am-4:30am/24 Hours (Fri/Sat)
Casino Size: 28,000 Square Feet
Other Games: LIR, No three card poker
Overnight RV Parking: Free (in West lot)
/RV Dump: No
Special Features: 600-passenger barge on the Missouri River.

Cape Girardeau

Map: **#7** (115 miles S. of St. Louis)

Isle of Capri Casino - Cape Girardeau
777 N. Main Street
Cape Girardeau, Missouri 63701
(800) 843-4753
Website: www.isleofcapricasino.com

Toll-Free Number (800) 843-4753
Restaurants: 4
Buffets: L- $11.99/$13.99 (Sun)
D- $15.99/$19.99 (Fri/Sat)
Hours: 8am-4am/24 Hours (Fri/Sat)
Casino Size: 38,304 Square Feet
Other Games: MB, P, PGP, MS
Overnight RV Parking: Free (in West lot)
/RV Dump: No
Senior Discount: Various on Mon if 50+
Special Features: 600-passenger barge on the Mississippi River. 750-seat event center.

The Best Places To Play Blackjack in Kansas City

All Kansas City-area casinos "hit" soft 17. This is slightly more advantageous for the casino than "standing" on soft 17 and it adds an extra .20% to the casino's mathematical edge in all blackjack games.

All four Kansas City casinos offer the same two-deck game and the rules are: dealer hits soft 17 (ace and six), double down on any two cards, split and re-split any pair (except aces), and double allowed after splitting. The casino advantage in this game is .40% against a perfect basic strategy player.

Ameristar and the Isle offer a six-deck blackjack game with the following rules: dealer hits soft 17 (ace and six), double down on any two cards, split and re-split any pair (including aces), and double allowed after splitting. The casino's mathematical edge against a perfect basic strategy player in this game is .56%.

Argosy and Harrah's have a similar game, except they don't allow you to re-split aces and that brings the casino edge up slightly to .63%.

Caruthersville

Map: **#4** (200 miles S. of St. Louis)

Lady Luck Caruthersville
777 East Third Street
Caruthersville, Missouri 63830
(573) 333-6000
Website: www.ladyluckcaruthersville.com

Toll-Free Number: (800) 679-4945
Restaurants: 2
Hours: 9am-3am/24 hours (Fri/Sat)
Casino Size: 21,400 Square Feet
Other Games: MS
Overnight RV Parking: Free/RV Dump: Free
Special Features: 875-passenger sternwheeler on the Mississippi River. 27-space RV park ($40 per night).

Kansas City

Map: **#1**

Ameristar Casino Hotel Kansas City
3200 North Ameristar Drive
Kansas City, Missouri 64161
(816) 414-7000
Website: www.ameristar.com

Toll-Free Number: (800) 499-4961
Rooms: 142 Price Range: $129-$269
Suites: 42 Price Range: $169-$299
Restaurants: 7
Buffets: B- $19.99 (Sun)
L- $15.99/$19.99 (Sun)
D- $19.99/$34.99 (Fri)/$22.99 (Sat)
Casino Size: 140,000 Square Feet
Other Games: MB, P, LIR, PGP
Overnight RV Parking: Free/RV Dump: No
Senior Discount: Various Tue if 50+
Special Features: 4,000-passenger barge adjacent to the Missouri River. Sports Pub. 18-screen movie theater complex. Burger King. 1,384-seat event center.

Argosy Casino Hotel & Spa
777 N.W. Argosy Parkway
Riverside, Missouri 64150
(816) 746-3100
Website: www.argosykansascity.com

Toll-Free Number: (800) 270-7711
Rooms: 250 Price Range: $159-$239
Suites: 8 Price Range: $650
Restaurants: 7
Buffets: B-$12.99/$14.99(Sat)/$16.99 (Sun)
L-$14.99/$16.99 (Sun)
D-$19.99/$27.99 (Fri)/$38.99 (Sat)/ $17.99 (Sun)
Casino Size: 62,000 Square Feet
Other Games: MB, PGP, MS
Overnight RV Parking: No
Senior Discount: Various Tue if 50+
Special Features: 4,675-passenger single-deck Mediterranean-themed barge adjacent to the Missouri River.

Harrah's North Kansas City
One Riverboat Drive
N. Kansas City, Missouri 64116
(816) 472-7777
Website: www.caesars.com

Toll-Free Number: (800) 427-7247
Rooms: 350 Price Range: $109-$249
Suites: 42 Price Range: $139-$299
Restaurants: 4
Buffets: B- $12.99/$17.99 (Sun)
L- $14.99/$17.99 (Sun)
D- $19.99/$26.99 (Fri)/$32.99 (Sat)/ $21.99 (Sun)
Casino Size: 63,300 Square Feet
Other Games: MB, P, PGP
Overnight RV Parking: Free/RV Dump: No
Special Features: 1,700-passenger two-deck barge adjacent to the Missouri River.

Isle of Capri Casino - Kansas City
1800 E. Front Street
Kansas City, Missouri 64120
(816) 855-7777
Website: www.isleofcapricasinos.com

Toll-Free Number: (800) 843-4753
Restaurants: 3
Buffets: B- $16.99 (Sat/Sun)
L- $13.99/$16.99 (Sat/Sun)
D- $20.99/$30.99 (Fri/Sat)
Casino Size: 30,000 Square Feet
Other Games: MB, PGP, MS, UTH, No Three Card Poker
Overnight RV Parking: Free/RV Dump: No
Senior Discount: Various Thu/Sun if 50+
Special Features: 2,000-passenger two-deck Caribbean-themed barge docked in a man-made lake fed by the Missouri River. Closed 5am-6am Wednesdays.

La Grange

Map: **#6** (150 miles N.W. of St. Louis)

Mark Twain Casino
104 Pierce Street
La Grange, Missouri 63448
(573) 655-4770
Website: www.marktwaincasinolagrange.com

Toll-Free Number: (866) 454-5825
Restaurants: 2
Hours: 8am-2am/4am (Fri/Sat)
Casino Size: 18,000 Square Feet
Other Games: UTH
Overnight RV Parking: Must use RV park
Special Features: 600-passenger barge on the Mississippi River. 8-space RV park ($25 per night). Gift shop.

The Best Places To Play Blackjack in St. Louis

Almost all Missouri casinos "hit" soft 17. This is slightly more advantageous for the casino than "standing" on soft 17 and it adds an extra .20% to the casino's mathematical edge. The exception is one table at Lumiere Place where the dealer stands on soft 17.

Hollywood casino offers the best two-deck game. It has a .35% casino advantage against a basic strategy player and the rules are: dealer hits soft 17 (ace and six), double down on any two cards, split and re-split any pair (including aces), and double allowed after splitting. Ameristar and River City offer the same game except you cannot re-split aces. The casino advantage in this game is .40%.

All four St. Louis casinos: Ameristar, Hollywood, Lumiere Place and River City offer a six-deck blackjack game with the following rules: double down on any two cards, split and re-split any pair (including aces), and double allowed after splitting. The casino's mathematical edge against a perfect basic strategy player in these games is .56%.

The above game is also offered at the Casino Queen in nearby E. St. Louis, Illinois but the house stands on soft 17 in that game and it lowers the casino advantage to only .35%. Lumiere Place also has one table with this game. The minimum bet is $25 at Casino Queen and $100 at Lumiere Place.

St. Joseph

Map: **#3** (55 miles N. of Kansas City)

St. Jo Frontier Casino
777 Winners Circle
St. Joseph, Missouri 64505
(816) 279-5514
Website: www.stjofrontiercasino.com

Toll-Free Number: (800) 888-2946
Restaurants: 2
Buffets: L- $14.99 (Sat/Sun)
D- $15.99/$17.99 (Wed/Thu)/$23.99 (Fri/Sat)
Hours: 8am -2am/5am (Fri/Sat)
Casino Size: 18,000 Square Feet
Other Games: MS
Overnight RV Parking: Free/RV Dump: No
Senior Discount: Various Wed if 60+.
Special Features: Casino is on a barge in a moat adjacent to the Missouri River. Buffet closed Sun/Mon.

St. Louis

Map: **#2**

In addition to the four St. Louis-area casinos listed below, the Casino Queen in E. St. Louis, Illinois is also a nearby casino. It is located on the other side of the Mississippi river from downtown St. Louis.

Ameristar Casino St. Charles
1 Ameristar Boulevard
St. Charles, Missouri 63301
(636) 949-7777
Website: www.ameristarcasinos.com

Toll-Free Number: (800) 325-7777
Rooms: 400 Price Range: $159-$279
Restaurants: 8
Buffets: L-$14.95/$21.95 (Sat/Sun)
D- $19.95/$22.95 (Thu/Sun)/
$25.95 (Fri/Sat)
Casino Size: 130,000 Square Feet
Other Games: P, LIR, FCP, MB, MS, PGP, UTH
Overnight RV Parking: No
Senior Discount: Various Wed if 50+
Special Features: 2,000-passenger barge on the Missouri River. Casino closed Wednesdays from 5am to 6am.

Hollywood Casino St. Louis
777 Casino Center Drive
Maryland Heights, Missouri 63043
(314) 770-8100
Website: www.hollywoodcasinostlouis.com

Toll-Free Number: (866) 785-4263
Rooms: 455 Price Range: $129-$259
Suites: 47 Price Range: $179-$359
Restaurants: 6
Buffets: B- $19.99 (Sat/Sun)
L- $13.99/$19.99 (Sat/Sun)
D- $19.99/$17.99 (Tue/Wed)/
$34.99 (Fri)/$25.99 (Sat)
Casino Size: 120,000 Square Feet Total
Other Games: MB, P, PGP, MS,
FCP, CSP, UTH
Overnight RV Parking: Free/RV Dump: No
Senior Discount: Various Mon if 50+.
Special Features: Two 3,200-passenger barges on the Missouri River.

Lumière Place Casino Resort
999 North Second Street
St. Louis, Missouri 63102
(314) 881-7777
Website: www.lumiereplace.com

Toll-Free Number: (877) 450-7711
Suites: 300 Price Range: $149-$309
Restaurants: 4
Buffets: B/L- $14.95 D- $22.95
Casino Size: 75,000 Square Feet
Other Games: MB, P, LIR, FCP, PGP, UTH
Special Features: 2,500-passenger barge floating in a man-made canal 700 feet from the Mississippi River. Property also features 200-room Four Seasons Hotel. Casino closed 6am-8am Wed.

River City Casino & Hotel
777 River City Casino Boulevard
St. Louis, Missouri 63125
(314)388-7777
Website: www.rivercity.com

Toll-Free Number: (888) 578-7289
Rooms: 186 Price Range: $139-$229
Suites: 7 Price Range: $169-$299
Restaurants: 4
Buffets: B- $19.95 (Sun)
L- $13.50/$19.95 (Sat/Sun)
D- $19.95/$34.95 (Wed/Sat)
Casino Size: 90,000 Square Feet
Other Games: P, FCP, MB, MS, PGP, UTH
Overnight RV Parking: No
Senior Discount: Various Tue if 50+

MONTANA

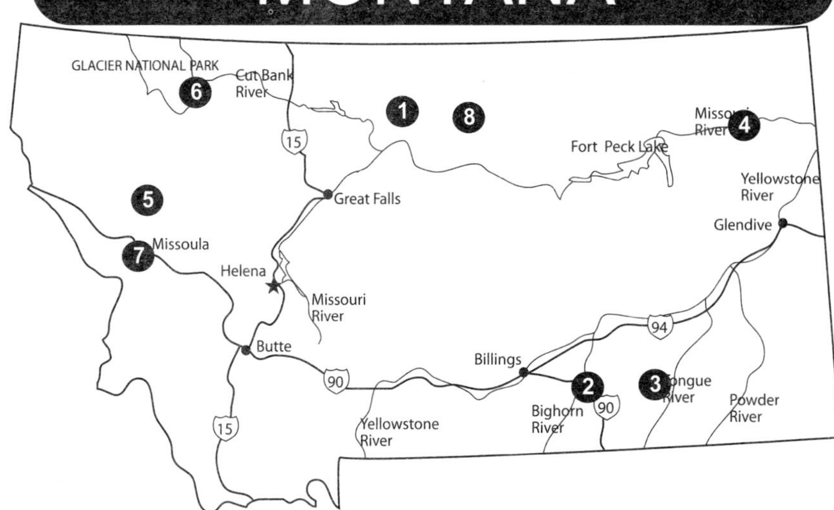

Montana law permits bars and taverns to have up to 20 video gaming devices that play video poker, video keno, or video bingo. These machines are operated in partnership with the state and are not permitted to pay out in cash; instead, they print out a receipt which must be taken to a cashier.

The maximum bet on these machines is $2 and the maximum payout is limited to $800. Montana gaming regulations require these machines to return a minimum of 80%.

All of Montana's Indian casinos offer Class II video gaming devices that look like slot machines, but are actually bingo games and the spinning reels are for "entertainment purposes only."

The maximum bet on the machines in Indian casinos is $5 and the maximum payout is capped at $1,500. According to Montana's Gambling Control Division, there are no minimum payback percentages required for gaming machines on Indian reservations. The minimum gambling age is 18.

For Montana tourism information call (800) 847-4868 or go to: www.visitmt.com

Apsaalooke Nights Casino
71 Heritage Road
Crow Agency, Montana 59022
(406) 638-4440
Map: **#2** (65 miles S.E. of Billings)

Casino Size: 4,000-square feet
Hours: 10am-2am Daily

Charging Horse Casino
1/2 US-212
Lame Deer, Montana 59043
(406) 477-6677
Map: **#3** (90 miles S.E. of Billings on Hwy. 212)

Restaurants: 1 Liquor: No
Hours: 8am-2am Daily
Other Games: Bingo (Wed-Sat)
Overnight RV Parking: Free/RV Dump: No

Fort Belknap Casino
104 Assiniboine Avenue
Harlem, Montana 59526
(406) 353-2235
Website: www.fortbelknapcasino.com
Map: **#8** (155 miles N.E of Great Falls)

Hours: 10am - 2am Daily

Glacier Peaks Casino
416 W Central Avenue
Browning, Montana 59417
(406) 338-2400
Website: www.glacierpeakscasino.com
Map: **#6** (140 miles N.W of Great Falls)

Toll-Free: (877) 238-9946
Rooms: 86 Price Range: $195-$209
Suites: 14 Price Range: $220-$235
Restaurants: 1 Liquor: No
Hours: 8am-2am Daily
Senior Discount: $10 Free play on Wed if 55+
Overnight RV Parking: Free, check in with security first/RV Dump: Free

Gray Wolf Peak Casino
20750 US Highway 93 North
Missoula, Montana 59808
(406) 726-3778
Website: www.graywolfpeakcasino.net
Map: **#7**

Restaurants: 1
Overnight RV Parking: Free/RV Dump: Free

KwaTaqNuk Casino Resort
49708 Highway 93 East
Polson, Montana 59860
(406) 883-3636
Website: www.kwataqnuk.com
Map: **#5** (65 miles N. Of Missoula)

Room Reservations: (800) 882-6363
Rooms: 102 Price Range: $159-$195
Suites: 10 Price Range: $269-$300
Restaurants: 1 Liquor: Yes
Hours: 8am-3am Daily
Overnight RV Parking: Free/RV Dump: Free
Special Features: Two casinos, one is non-smoking.

Northern Winz Hotel & Casino
11275 US Highway 87
Box Elder, Montana 59521
(406) 395-5420
Map: **#1** (90 miles N.E. of Great Falls)

Rooms: 10 Price Range: $59-$89
Hours: 8am-2am/24 hours (Fri/Sat)
Restaurants: 2 Liquor: No
Overnight RV Parking: No
Casino Size: 10,000 Square Feet
Other Games: P (Wed-Sat starting at 6pm)

Northern Winz II
426 Laredo Road
Box Elder, Montana 59521
(406) 395-4863
Map: **#1** (90 miles N.E. of Great Falls)

Restaurants: 1 Liquor: No
Overnight RV Parking: No/RV Dump: No

Silver Wolf Casino
300 Highway 25 East
Wolf Point, Montana 59201
(406) 653-3476
Map: **#4** (180 miles N.E of Billings)

Restaurants: 1 Snack Bar Liquor: No
Hours: 10am-12am/2am (Fri/Sat)
Other Games: Bingo (Thu-Sun)
Overnight RV Parking: Free/RV Dump: No

NEVADA

All Nevada casinos are open 24 hours and, unless otherwise noted, offer: slots, video poker, craps, blackjack, and roulette. The minimum gambling age is 21.

For Nevada tourism information call (800) 237-0774 or go to: www.travelnevada.com.

Other games in the casino listings include: sports book (SB), race book (RB), Spanish 21 (S21), baccarat (B), mini-baccarat (MB), pai gow (PG), poker (P), pai gow poker (PGP), Caribbean stud poker (CSP), crazy 4 poker (C4P), let it ride (LIR), three-card poker (TCP), Mississippi stud (MS), ultimate Texas hold'em (UTH), Texas hold'em bonus (THB), four card poker (FCP), sic bo (SIC), keno (K), big 6 wheel (B6) and bingo (BG).

Amargosa Valley

Map Location: **#8** (91 miles N.W. of Las Vegas on Hwy. 95)

Longstreet Inn Casino & RV Resort
4400 South Highway 373
Amargosa Valley, Nevada 89049
(775) 372-1777
Website: www.longstreetcasino.com

Rooms: 59 Price Range: $99-$119
Casino Size: 2,500 Square Feet
Overnight RV Parking: Must use RV Park
Special Features: 51-space RV Park ($25 per night). 24-hour convenience store.

Battle Mountain

Map Location: **#9** (215 mile N.E. of Reno on I-80)

Owl Club Casino & Restaurant
72 E. Front Street
Battle Mountain, Nevada 89820
(775) 635-2444

Restaurants: 1
Casino Size: 840 Square Feet
Other Games: No table games
Overnight RV Parking: No

Beatty

Map Location: **#10** (120 miles N.W. of Las Vegas on Hwy. 95)

Stagecoach Hotel & Casino
900 East Highway 95
Beatty, Nevada 89003
(775) 553-2419

Reservation Number: (800) 424-4946
Rooms: 80 Price Range: $68-$78
Restaurants: 2
Casino Size: 8,820 Square Feet
Other Games: SB, RB, P (Wed-Sat), B6, no roulette
Overnight RV Parking: Free/RV Dump: No
Special Features: Denny's restaurant. Seven miles from Rhyolite ghost town.

Boulder City

Map Location: **#11** (22 miles S.E. of Las Vegas on Hwy. 93)

Hoover Dam Lodge Hotel & Casino
18000 US Highway 93
Boulder City, Nevada 89005
(702) 293-5000
Website: www.hooverdamlodge.com

Reservation Number: (800) 245-6380
Rooms: 360 Price Range: $80-$125
Suites: 18 Price Range: $109-$160
Restaurants: 3
Casino Size: 17,276 Square Feet
Other Games: SB, RB, No table games
Overnight RV Parking: No

Carson City

Map Location: **#7** (32 miles S. of Reno on Hwy. 395)

Carson Nugget Casino Hotel
507 N. Carson Street
Carson City, Nevada 89701
(775) 882-1626
Website: www.ccnugget.com

Reservation Number: (800) 338-7760
Rooms: 81 Price Range: $69-$89
Restaurants: 3
Casino Size: 28,930 Square Feet
Other Games: SB, RB, P, TCP, K, No roulette
Overnight RV Parking: Free/RV Dump: No
Special Features: Rare gold display. Rooms are at Carson Tahoe Hotel, one block from casino and free shuttle service is provided.

Casino Fandango
3800 S. Carson Street
Carson City, Nevada 89701
(775) 885-7000
Website: www.casinofandango.com

Restaurants: 5
Casino Size: 40,891 Square Feet
Buffets: L-$11.99 (Wed-Fri)/$15.99 (Sat/Sun)
D-$11.99 (Wed/Thu/Sun)/$19.99 (Fri/Sat)
Other Games: SB, RB, P, PGP, TCP, K
Overnight RV Parking: Free/RV Dump: No
Special Features: Buffet closed Mon/Tue.

Gold Dust West - Carson City
2171 East William Street
Carson City, Nevada 89701
(775) 885-9000
Website: www.gdwcasino.com

Toll-Free Number: (877) 519-5567
Rooms: 120 Price Range: $109-$125
Suites: 22 Price Range: $129-$155
Restaurants: 2
Casino Size: 12,000 Square Feet
Other Games: SB, RB, TCP, No roulette
Overnight RV Parking: Must use RV park
Special Features: 48-space RV park ($34-$39). 32-lane bowling center.

Max Casino Carson City
900 S. Carson Street
Carson City, Nevada 89701
(775) 883-0900
Website: www.maxcasinocc.com

Rooms: 92 Price Range: $99-$139
Suites: 3 Price Range: $119-$159
Restaurants: 1
Casino Size: 12,750 Square Feet
Other Games: SB, RB, K, No roulette or craps
Overnight RV Parking: No
Senior Discount: Various Wed if 50+
Special Features: Hotel is Wyndham Garden.

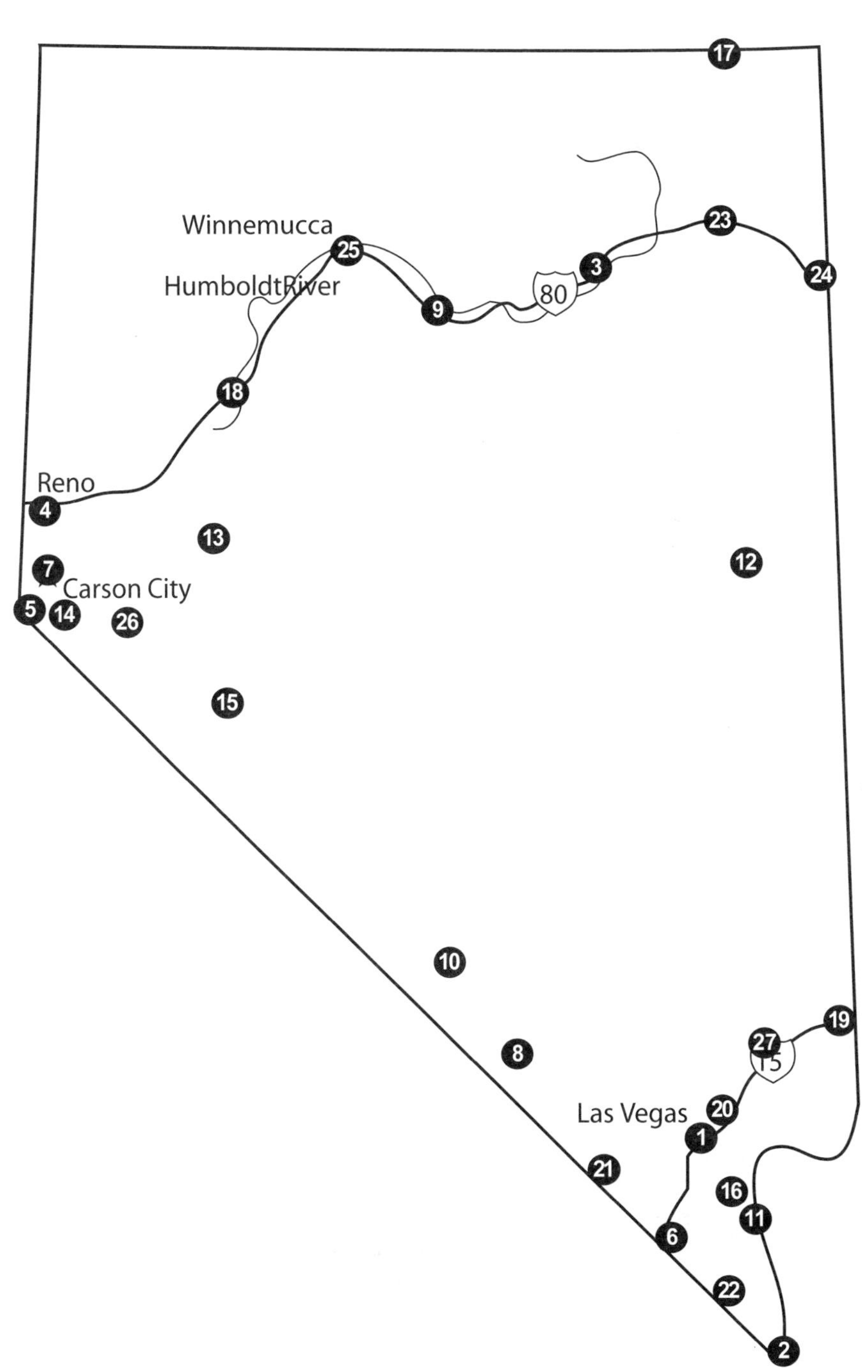
17
Winnemucca
23
25
3
24
HumboldtRiver
80
9
18
Reno
4
13
12
7
Carson City
5
14
26
15
10
19
27
15
8
Las Vegas
20
1
21
16
11
6
22
2

Elko

Map Location: **#3** (289 miles N.E. of Reno on I-80)

Commercial Casino
345 4th Street
Elko, Nevada 89801
(775) 738-3181
Website: www.northernstarcasinos.com

Toll-Free Number: (800) 648-2345
Restaurants: 2
Casino Size: 6,744 Square Feet
Other Games: No table games
Overnight RV Parking: Yes/RV Dump: No
Special Features: Oldest continually operating casino in Nevada. 10-foot-tall stuffed polar bear in casino. Large gunfighter art collection.

Gold Dust West - Elko
1660 Mountain City Highway
Elko, Nevada 89801
(775) 777-7500
Website: www.gdwcasino.com

Restaurants: 2
Casino Size: 12,544
Other Games: SB, RB, TCP, No roulette
Senior Discount: Various Tue if 50+

Red Lion Hotel & Casino
2065 Idaho Street
Elko, Nevada 89801
(775) 738-2111
Website: www.redlionhotelelko.com

Reservation Number: (800) 545-0044
Rooms: 220 Price Range: $89-$139
Suites: 2 Price Range: $259
Restaurants: 3
Casino Size: 16,850 Square Feet
Other Games: SB, RB, P, TCP
Overnight RV Parking: No
Special Features: Starbucks coffeehouse.

Stockmen's Hotel & Casino
340 Commercial Street
Elko, Nevada 89801
(775) 738-5141
Website: www.northernstarcasinos.com

Reservation Number: (800) 648-2345
Rooms: 141 Price Range: $76-$95
Suites: 8 Price Range: $96-$149
Restaurants: 1
Casino Size: 8,441 Square Feet
Other Games: SB, RB, TCP
Overnight RV Parking: Free/RV Dump: No
Special Features: Hotel is Ramada.

Ely

Map Location: **#12** (317 miles E. of Reno on Hwy. 50)

Hotel Nevada & Gambling Hall
501 Aultman Street
Ely, Nevada 89301
(775) 289-6665
Website: www.hotelnevada.com

Reservation Number: (888) 406-3055
Rooms: 51 Price Range: $64-$99
Suites: 12 Price Range: $74-$250
Restaurants: 1
Casino Size: 3,730 Square Feet
Other Games: SB, RB, P, TCP,
No craps or roulette
Special Features: 24-hour Denny's. Display of mining, ranching and railroad artifacts.

Fallon

Map Location: **#13** (61 miles E. of Reno on Hwy. 50)

Bonanza Inn & Casino
855 W. Williams Avenue
Fallon, Nevada 89406
(775) 423-6031

Rooms: 74 Price Range: $59-$89
Restaurants: 1
Casino Size: 5,830 Square Feet
Other Games: SB, RB, K, No table games
Overnight RV Parking: Must use RV park.
Special Features: 20-space RV park ($15 per night). Hotel is Super 8.

Stockman's Casino
1560 W. Williams Avenue
Fallon, Nevada 89406
(775) 423-2117
Website: www.stockmanscasino.com

Toll-Free Number: (855) 423-2117
Restaurants: 2
Casino Size: 8,614 Square Feet
Other Games: SB, RB, No roulette or craps
Senior Discount: Various Tue if 55+
Overnight RV Parking: Free in back
Special Features: Hotel is Holiday Inn Express adjacent to casino.

Gardnerville

Map Location: **#14** (45 miles S. of Reno on Hwy. 395)

Topaz Lodge & Casino
1979 Highway 395 South
Gardnerville, Nevada 89410
(775) 266-3338
Website: www.topazlodge.com

RV/Room Reservations: (800) 962-0732
Rooms: 59 Price Range: $79-$119
Restaurants: 2
Casino Size: 12,800 Square Feet
Other Games: SB, BG, K, TCP, No roulette or craps
Overnight RV Parking: Must use RV park
Special Features: Hotel is Super 8. 60-space RV park ($22 per night).

Hawthorne

Map Location: **#15** (138 miles S.E. of Reno on Hwy. 95)

El Capitan Resort Casino
540 F Street
Hawthorne, Nevada 89415
(775) 945-3321
Website: www.northernstarcasinos.com

Toll Free: (800) 922-2311
Rooms: 103 Price Range: $58-$79
Restaurants: 1
Casino Size: 12,860 Square Feet
Other Games: SB, RB, No table games
Overnight RV Parking: Free/RV Dump: Free
Special Features: Hotel is Travelodge.

Henderson

Map Location: **#16** (15 miles S.E. of Las Vegas on Hwy. 93)

Club Fortune Casino
725 S Racetrack Drive
Henderson, Nevada 89015
(702) 566-5555
Website: www.clubfortunecasino.com

Restaurants: 1
Casino Size: 11,953
Other Games: P
Special Features: $1.99 breakfast special 6am-11am/$2.99 (Sat/Sun). $1 craps. $3 blackjack.

Eldorado Casino
140 Water Street
Henderson, Nevada 89015
(702) 564-1811
Website: www.eldoradocasino.com

Restaurants: 1
Casino Size: 17,756 Square Feet
Other Games: SB, K, BG, No table games
Overnight RV Parking: No
Senior Discount: Various Tue if 50+
Special Features: Affiliated with Boyd Gaming.

Fiesta Henderson Casino Hotel
777 West Lake Mead Parkway
Henderson, Nevada 89015
(702) 558-7000
Website: www.fiestahendersonlasvegas.com

Toll-Free Number: (866) 469-7666
Rooms: 224 Price Range: $39-$149
Suites: 8 Price Range: $135-$259
Restaurants: 4
Buffets: B-$14.99 (Sat/Sun)
L-$9.99/$14.99 (Sat/Sun)
D-$13.99
Casino Size: 73,450 Square Feet
Other Games: SB, RB, PGP, K, BG
Overnight RV Parking: No
Senior Discount: Various Wed if 50+
Special Features: Affiliated with Station Casinos. Buffet discount with players club card.

Green Valley Ranch Resort Spa Casino
2300 Paseo Verde Parkway
Henderson, Nevada 89052
(702) 617-7777
Website: www.greenvalleyranchresort.com

Room Reservations: (866) 782-9487
Rooms: 200 Price Range: $80-$300
Suites: 45 Price Range: $195-$3,500
Restaurants: 8
Buffets: B-$10.99/$20.99 (Sat/Sun)
L-$12.99/$20.99 (Sat/Sun)
D-$19.99/$34.99 (Fri)/$23.99 (Sat)
Casino Size: 144,568 Square Feet
Other Games: SB, RB, B, MB, MS, BG,
P, CSP, PGP, TCP, UTH
Overnight RV Parking: No
Senior Discount: Various Wed if 50+
Special Features: Affiliated with Station Casinos. Spa and fitness center.

Jokers Wild
920 N. Boulder Highway
Henderson, Nevada 89011
(702) 564-8100
Website: www.jokerswildcasino.com

Restaurants: 2
Casino Size: 23,698 Square Feet
Other Games: SB, K
Overnight RV Parking: No
Senior Discount: Various Tue if 50+
Special Features: Affiliated with Boyd Gaming. $1 craps and $3 blackjack.

M Resort • Spa • Casino
12300 Las Vegas Blvd South
Henderson, Nevada 89044
(702) 797-1000
Website: www.themresort.com

Toll-Free Number: (877) 673-7678
Rooms: 355 Price Range: $125-$265
Suites: 35 Price Range: $149-$599
Restaurants: 6
Buffet: L- $16.99/$24.99 (Fri)/$34.99 (Sat/Sun)
D- $24.99/$39.99 (Fri-Sun)
Casino Size: 93,061 Square Feet
Other Games: RB, SB, PGP, MS,
MB, LIR, TCP
Senior Discount: Various Tue if 50+

Railroad Pass Hotel & Casino
2800 S. Boulder Highway
Henderson, Nevada 89002
(702) 294-5000
Website: www.railroadpass.com

Toll-Free Number: (800) 654-0877
Rooms: 100 Price Range: $57-$99
Suites: 20 Price Range: $119-$139
Restaurants: 3
Buffets: B/L-$9.99/$12.99 (Sat/Sun)
D-$9.99/$12.99 (Thu/Sun)/$24.99 (Fri)/
$15.99 (Sat)
Casino Size: 12,803 Square Feet
Other Games: SB, RB, TCP
Overnight RV Parking: No

Skyline Hotel & Casino
1741 N. Boulder Highway
Henderson, Nevada 89011
(702) 565-9116
Website:www.skylinerestaurantandcasino.com

Rooms: 50 Price Range: $119-$169
Restaurants: 1
Casino Size: 4,000 Square Feet
Other Games: SB, RB, P (Fri-Mon),
No craps or roulette
Overnight RV Parking: No
Special Features: $8.95 prime rib special.

Sunset Station Hotel and Casino
1301 W. Sunset Road
Henderson, Nevada 89014
(702) 547-7777
Website: www.sunsetstation.com

Toll-Free Number: (888) 786-7389
Rooms: 448 Price Range: $59-$169
Suites: 18 Price Range: $99-$369
Restaurants: 7
Buffets: B-$9.99/$15.99 (Sun)
L-$11.99/$15.99 (Sun) D-$15.99
Casino Size: 93,703 Square Feet
Other Games: SB, RB, MB, PGP,
LIR, TCP, UTH, K, BG
Overnight RV Parking: No
Senior Discount: Various Wed if 50+
Special Features: Affiliated with Station Casinos. 13-screen movie theater. Childcare center. Food Court with five fast food stations. Buffet discount for players club members.

Jackpot

Map Location: **#17** (Just S. of the Idaho border on Hwy. 93)

Barton's Club 93
1002 Highway 93
Jackpot, Nevada 89825
(775) 755-2341
Website: www.bartonsclub93.com

Toll-Free Number: (800) 258-2937
Rooms: 98 Price Range: $45-$85
Suites: 4 Price Range: $85-$125
Restaurants: 1
Buffets: B- $12.93 (Sat/Sun)
D-$19.93 (Fri/Sat)
Casino Size: 12,550 Square Feet
Other Games: LIR
Overnight RV Parking: Free

Cactus Pete's Resort Casino
1385 Highway 93
Jackpot, Nevada 89825
(775) 755-2321
Website: www.cactuspetes.com

Rooms: 272 Price Range: $89-$159
Suites: 28 Price Range: $149-$219
Restaurants: 3
Buffets: D- $17.95/$27.95 (Fri/Sat)
Casino Size: 24,727 Square Feet
Other Games: SB, RB, P, TCP, LIR, UTH
Overnight RV Parking: Must use RV park
Senior Discount: Various Tue if 50+
Special Features: Casino is affiliated with Pinnacle Entertainment. 91-space RV park ($18-$24 per night). 18-hole golf course.

Horseshu Hotel & Casino
1220 Highway 93
Jackpot, Nevada 89825
(702) 755-7777
Website: www.cactuspetes.com

Rooms: 110 Price Range: $59-$89
Suites: 10 Price Range: $79-$119
Restaurants: 1
Casino Size: 3,377 Square Feet
Other Games: No table games
Overnight RV Parking: No
Special Features: Casino is affiliated with Pinnacle Entertainment.

Jean

Map Location: **#6** (22 miles S.W. of Las Vegas on I-15; 12 miles from the California border)

Terrible's Road House - Jean
1 Main Street
Jean, Nevada 89019
(702) 477-5000
Website: www.stopatjean.com

Reservation Number: (800) 634-1359
Rooms: 800 Price Range: $39-$69
Suites: 13 Price Range: $59-$119
Restaurants: 2
Casino Size: 37,006 Square Feet
Other Games: No craps
Overnight RV Parking: No
Special Features: Table games open 11am-3am. 24-hour Denny's restaurant.

Lake Tahoe

Map Location: **#5** (directly on the Nevada/ California border; 98 miles northeast of Sacramento and 58 miles southwest of Reno).

The area is best known for its many recreational activities with skiing in the winter and water sports in the summer. Lake Tahoe Airport is located at the south end of the basin. The next closest airport is in Reno with regularly scheduled shuttle service by bus.

Incline Village and Crystal Bay are on the north shore of Lake Tahoe, while Stateline is located on the south shore. For South Lake Tahoe information call the Lake Tahoe Visitors Authority at (800) 288-2463 and for North Lake Tahoe information call the Incline Village/Crystal Bay Convention & Visitors Authority at (800) 468-2463.

Here's information, as supplied by Nevada's State Gaming Control Board, showing the slot machine payback percentages for all of the south shore casinos for the fiscal year beginning July 1, 2016 and ending June 30, 2017:

Denomination	Payback %
1¢ Slots	89.04
5¢ Slots	N/A
25¢ Slots	91.41
$1 Slots	93.11
All Slots	93.47

And here's that same information for the north shore casinos:

Denomination	Payback %
1¢ Slots	92.49
5¢ Slots	N/A
25¢ Slots	89.33
$1 Slots	92.79
All Slots	94.32

These numbers reflect the percentage of money returned to the players on each denomination of machine. All electronic machines including slots, video poker and video keno are included in these numbers.

Optional games in the casino listings include: sports book (SB), race book (RB), Spanish 21 (S21), baccarat (B), mini-baccarat (MB), poker (P), pai gow poker (PGP), Caribbean stud poker (CSP), let it ride (LIR), three-card poker (TCP), four card poker (FCP), ultimate Texas hold 'em (UTH), Mississippi stud (MS), keno (K) and bingo (BG).

Cal-Neva Resort Spa & Casino
2 Stateline Road
Crystal Bay, Nevada 89402
(775) 832-4000
Website: www.calnevaresort.com

THIS CASINO WAS CLOSED AT PRESSTIME, BUT IS EXPECTED TO REOPEN AT A LATER DATE.

Reservation Number: (800) 225-6382
Rooms: 199 Price Range: $108-$179
Suites: 18 Price Range: $243-$269
Restaurants: 3
Casino Size: 500 Square Feet
Other Games: Machines only
Overnight RV Parking: No
Special Features: Straddles California/Nevada state line on north shore of Lake Tahoe. European Spa. Three wedding chapels. Florist. Photo studio. Bridal boutique. Gift shop. Airport shuttle. Internet cafe.

Crystal Bay Club Casino
14 State Route 28
Crystal Bay, Nevada 89402
(775) 833-6333
Website: www.crystalbaycasino.com

Restaurants 2
Casino Size: 14,020 Square Feet
Other Games: RB, SB
Overnight RV Parking: No

Grand Lodge Casino at Hyatt Regency
111 Country Club Drive
Incline Village, Nevada 89451
(775) 832-1234
Website: www.grandlodgecasino.com

Toll-Free Number: (800) 327-3910
Rooms: 412 Price Range: $170-$390
Suites: 48 Price Range: $240-$790
Restaurants: 6
Buffets: B-$25.99 (Sat/Sun)
D-$34.99 (Fri/Sat)
Casino Size: 18,900 Square Feet
Other Games: SB, RB, TCP, UTH
Overnight RV Parking: No
Senior Discount: Food/room discounts if 62+
Special Features: On north shore of Lake Tahoe. Two Robert Trent Jones golf courses.

Hard Rock Hotel & Casino Lake Tahoe
50 Highway 50
Stateline, Nevada 89449
(844) 588-7625
Website: www.hardrockcasinolaketahoe.com

Toll-Free Number: (844) 588-7625
Rooms: 521 Price Range: $99-$279
Suites: 18 Price Range: $219-$399
Restaurants: 5
Casino Size: 25,000 Square Feet
Other Games: RB, SB, B, UTH, TCP, PGP
Senior Discount: Join 50+ Rockers Club for various discounts
Special Features: Display of rock and roll memorabilia.

Harrah's Lake Tahoe
15 Highway 50
Stateline, Nevada 89449
(775) 588-6611
Website: www.harrahslaketahoe.com

Reservation Number: (800) 427-7247
Rooms: 463 Price Range: $109-$359
Suites: 62 Price Range: $299-$800
Restaurants: 7
Buffets: Brunch-$24.99 (Sat/Sun)
D-$24.99/$34.99 (Fri)/$37.99 (Sat)
Casino Size: 89,244 Sq Ft (including Harvey's)
Other Games: SB, B, MB, P, PGP, LIR
Overnight RV Parking: No
Senior Discount: Various Mon if 55+
Special Features: Affiliated with Caesars Entertainment. On south shore of Lake Tahoe. Health club. Pet kennel.

Harveys Resort Hotel/Casino - Lake Tahoe
18 Highway 50
Stateline, Nevada 89449
(775) 588-2411
Website: www.harveys.com

Toll-Free Number: (800) 553-1022
Rooms: 704 Price Range: $69-$329
Suites: 36 Price Range: $249-$679
Restaurants: 5
Casino Size: 89,244 Sq Ft (including Harrah's)
Other Games: SB, RB, B, MB, P, PGP, LIR
Overnight RV Parking: No
Senior Discount: Various Mon if 55+
Special Features: Affiliated with Caesars Entertainment. On south shore of Lake Tahoe. 2,000-seat amphitheater. Lake cruises.

Lakeside Inn and Casino
168 Highway 50
Stateline, Nevada 89449
(775) 588-7777
Website: www.lakesideinn.com

Toll-Free Number: (800) 523-1291
Rooms: 124 Price Range: $94-$164
Suites: 8 Price Range: $124-$304
Restaurants: 2
Casino Size: 17,852 Square Feet
Other Games: SB, RB, P
Overnight RV Parking: No
Special Features: On south shore of Lake Tahoe. $5.99 breakfast 11pm-3pm.

Montbleu Resort Casino & Spa
55 Highway 50
Stateline, Nevada 89449
(775) 588-3515
Website: www.montbleuresort.com

Toll-Free Number: (888) 829-7630
Rooms: 403 Price Range: $89-$229
Suites: 37 Price Range: $190-$699
Restaurants: 4
Buffets: B/L- $22.99 (Sun)
D- $22.99 (Fri/Sat)
Casino Size: 45,000 Square Feet
Other Games: SB, RB, TCP, PGP
Overnight RV Parking: No
Senior Discount: Various on Thu if 50+
Special Features: On south shore of Lake Tahoe. Affiliated with Tropicana Resorts. Health spa.

Tahoe Biltmore Lodge & Casino
5 Highway 28
Crystal Bay, Nevada 89402
(775) 831-0660
Website: www.tahoebiltmore.com

Reservation Number: (800) 245-8667
Rooms: 106 Price Range: $69-$129
Suites: 7 Price Range: $139-$189
Restaurants: 2
Buffets: B- $9.95 (Sun)
Casino Size: 10,398 Square Feet
Other Games: SB, RB
Overnight RV Parking: Free/RV Dump: No
Senior Discount: Various Tue if 50+
Special Features: On north shore of Lake Tahoe.

See page 269 for a story on "The Best Places to Gamble in Reno/Tahoe"

Las Vegas

Map Location: **#1**

Las Vegas is truly the casino capital of the world! While many years ago the city may have had a reputation as an "adult playground" run by "shady characters," today's Las Vegas features many world-class facilities run by some of America's most familiar corporate names.

Las Vegas has more motel/hotel rooms - 150,000 - than any other city in the U.S. and it attracts more than 41 million visitors each year. The abundance of casinos in Las Vegas forces them to compete for customers in a variety of ways and thus, there are always great bargains to be had, but only if you know where to look.

H. Scot Krause is a 23-year Las Vegas veteran. He is a freelance writer, gaming industry analyst and researcher who writes the weekly Vegas Values column that appears on the American Casino Guide web site. Here are Scot's picks for the best deals available for a Las Vegas visitor.

Best Appetizer Bargain:
Shrimp Cocktail:
Fremont Casino (Lanai Express): $.99
Skyline Casino (Main Bar) (Henderson): $1.49

With the closing of Du-Par's inside the Golden Gate in 2017, the honor of best shrimp cocktails now moves to Henderson. The Skyline Casino in Henderson offers theirs for a mere $1.49. For a best price bargain downtown, it's the Fremont's 99-cent shrimp cocktail at the Lanai Express counter.

Best Steak Deal:
*Ellis Island, $7.99**
Hard Rock Casino, $7.77

You may find other steak deals in Las Vegas, but the steak special at Ellis Island Casino & Brewery still remains the leader in steak bargains. It's not on the menu but available for the asking 24 hours a day, 7 days a week. For $12.99 (you can get it to down to $7.99*) you get a generous cut of tenderloin cooked to your liking, bread, salad, vegetable of the day, choice of potato and a beer (or root beer) from the microbrewery. *With your Passport Player's Card you can get it down to $7.99 with a $3 discount voucher printed from a kiosk, plus if you play $5 through any machine you can get an additional $1 off and then print out a coupon from a Passport Central kiosk for a voucher. This is not a menu item! Ask your server for the special and they will be happy to take care of you! Second choice would be Mr. Lucky's at the Hard Rock Casino Hotel. The "off-menu," Gambler's Special is an 8-ounce steak that comes with three grilled skewered shrimp, garlic mashed potatoes and salad, all for $7.77 available 24/7.

Best Place to Play Slots:
Rampart Casino
Downtown
South Point (See "Best Video Poker" for slot info.)

This year I am going with Rampart Casino in Summerlin inside the J.W. Marriott. Subjective, of course, but the Rampart recently shared and boasted the payback percentages on all of their slot machines. Numbers are among the best paybacks in Las Vegas, if not the best. Few seem to have challenged them or the numbers, but luck can happen anywhere. Your mileage may vary, but if you're a slot player, I'd try Rampart. Downtown Las Vegas is also a hotbed of activity for slot players and generally the downtown casinos yield a higher payback percentage overall than the Strip. The nice thing about downtown is that you can pop in and out of all of the casinos with ease until you find your lucky casino or machine! You'll even find a few old coin-dropper slots still left downtown for that "old-time" Vegas feel. Others with a good track record for slot payouts include The Palms and South Point.

Best Video Poker:
South Point

South Point's gaming amenities include more than 2,563 of the most popular slot and video poker machines featuring ticket-in, ticket-out technology. They (arguably) offer the most video poker machines with paybacks over 99% of any casino in the city. Combine that with slot club benefits and year-round good promotions and you've got a winning play! Generally, if a casino offers good video poker it follows that the slots may be set to higher payouts too. They want your business, so both tend to be better.

Best Bargain Show:
Mac King, Harrah's

The plaid-suited magician is hilarious and talented and cheap enough to take the whole family. Normally priced around $25-30, tickets can usually be found for far less using coupons, including FREE tickets (usually with the price of a drink.) Check this year's American Casino Guide book for that very coupon! Great afternoon bargain show! See him again for the first time!

Best Free Attractions:
Bellagio Fountains and Conservatoryy
Hard Rock Hotel & Casino (Memorabilia)
Silverton Casino (Aquarium and Bass Pro Shops)

Everyone has their favorite free attraction but the water show at Bellagio is by far a fan favorite for tourists as well as locals. It's quite a dazzling display. Some call it "romantic." While you're there, don't miss the Conservatory inside the hotel. Beautiful displays of flowers, gardens and scenery are changed four times a year depicting the seasons. Often breathtaking and definitely aromatic! My personal favorite? I really enjoy the artifacts, photographs and showcases of various rock and rollers from years past and present at the Hard Rock Hotel & Casino. Check the side halls and alcoves for displays you might ordinarily miss. Display cases are changed throughout the year. I also find the free Aquarium attraction at the Silverton Casino to be fun. It's up-close, relaxing and intriguing. Walking the Bass Pro Shops next to the Aquarium brings the outdoors indoors with displays and attractions you can view for free.

Best Buffet(s)

Generally, the "best buffets" are not exactly "bargains." Usually considered to be among the best (but also pricey) by popular opinion are the buffets at Caesars Palace ($50-$60), Wynn, Bellagio, Cosmopolitan and Planet Hollywood. For a locals casino, Red Rock Resort keeps the prices down and gets high praises. And although they all seem to be constantly changing prices and food selections, for good value, variety, consistency and quality, for my money (or comps) I would give Seasons Buffet (great made-to-order pastas!) at Silverton and Studio B Buffet at M Resort a try. A downtown favorite among tourists and as well as locals is Main Street Station. Perhaps, surprisingly, we find the little Festival Buffet at Fiesta Rancho a top notch favorite for the Mongolian Grill cooking station. The selection of vegetables is great, always cut fresh and sized well. I'm adding Rampart's Buffet to my faves this year too. It's a smaller buffet but many themed nights including Seafood Night and Thursday's New York Deli nights are always excellent and the dessert station is always top notch! Watch for a new buffet opening at the Palms called "Haute Plates." The Stratosphere has also revamped and renamed its buffet, now called "Crafted." (About $21 for dinner.)

Unlike New Jersey, the Nevada Gaming Control Board does not break down its slot statistics by individual properties. Rather, they are classified by area.

The annual gaming revenue report breaks the Las Vegas market down into two major tourist areas: the Strip and downtown. There is also a very large locals market in Las Vegas and those casinos are shown in the gaming revenue report as the Boulder Strip and North Las Vegas areas.

When choosing where to do your slot gambling, you may want to keep in mind the following slot payback percentages for Nevada's fiscal year beginning July 1, 2016 and ending June 30, 2017:

1¢ Slot Machines
The Strip - 88.49%
Downtown - 88.93%
Boulder Strip - 90.57%
N. Las Vegas - 90.82%

5¢ Slot Machines
The Strip - 91.88%
Downtown - 93.39%
Boulder Strip - 96.01%
N. Las Vegas - 95.47%

25¢ Slot Machines
The Strip - 89.97%
Downtown - 94.41%
Boulder Strip - 96.56%
N. Las Vegas - 96.45%

$1 Slot Machines
The Strip - 92.63%
Downtown - 94.76%
Boulder Strip - 95.90%
N. Las Vegas - 95.79%

$1 Megabucks Machines
The Strip - 86.81%
Downtown - 86.95%
Boulder Strip - 87.22%
N. Las Vegas - 87.83%

All Slot Machines
The Strip - 92.00%
Downtown - 92.78%
Boulder Strip - 94.37%
N. Las Vegas - 93.56%

These numbers reflect the percentage of money returned to the players on each denomination of machine. All electronic machines including slots, video poker and video keno are included in these numbers and the highest-paying returns are shown in bold print.

As you can see, the machines in downtown Las Vegas pay out more than those located on the Las Vegas Strip.

Returns even better than the downtown casinos can be found at some of the other locals casinos along Boulder Highway such as Sam's Town and also in the North Las Vegas area. Not only are those numbers among the best returns in the Las Vegas area, they are among the best payback percentages for anywhere in the United States.

This information is pretty well known by the locals and that's why most of them do their slot gambling away from the Strip unless they are drawn by a special players club benefit or promotion.

If you are driving an RV to Las Vegas and want to stay overnight for free in a casino parking lot the only casino that will allow you to do that is Bally's.

Other games in the casino listings include: sports book (SB), race book (RB), Spanish 21 (S21), baccarat (B), mini-baccarat (MB), pai gow (PG), poker (P), pai gow poker (PGP), Caribbean stud poker (CSP), let it ride (LIR), three-card poker (TCP), Mississippi stud (MS), ultimate Texas hold em (UTH), four card poker (FCP), big 6 wheel (B6), sic bo (SIC), keno (K) and bingo (BG).

The Alamo Casino
8050 Dean Martin Drive
Las Vegas, Nevada 89139
(702) 361-1176
Website: www.thealamo.com

Other Games: No craps/roulette
Casino Size: 3,000 Square Feet
Special Features: Truck stop. Burger King restaurant.

Aria Resort & Casino
3730 Las Vegas Boulevard South
Las Vegas, Nevada 89109
(702) 590-7757
Website: www.aria.com

Reservation Number: (866) 359-7757
Rooms: Price Range: $169-$493
Suites: Price Range: $212-$799
Restaurants: 16
Buffet B- $24.99/$32.99 (Sat/Sun)
L-$28.99/$32.99 (Sat/Sun)
D- $37.99/$42.99 (Fri/Sat)
Self-Parking: $7 (1-2 Hrs)/$12 (2 to 4 Hrs)
$15 (4-24 Hrs)
Valet Parking: $20 (0-4 Hrs)/$25 (4-24 Hrs)
Casino Size: 150,000 Square Feet
Other Games: SB, RB, B, MB, P, PG, PGP, LIR, TCP, B6, CW, UTH, FCP
Special Features: Affiliated with MGM Resorts. Located within 76-acre City Center project. Adjacent to 500,000-square-foot Crystals shopping/entertainment complex. 80,000-square-foot spa.

Arizona Charlie's - Boulder
4575 Boulder Highway
Las Vegas, Nevada 89121
(702) 951-9000
Website: www.arizonacharliesboulder.com

Reservation Number: (888) 236-9066
RV Reservations: (800) 970-7280
Rooms: Price Range: $29-$130
Suites: Price Range: $34-$134
Restaurants: 4
Buffets: B-$7.32 (Sun) L-$9.99/$11.99
D-$11.99/$12.99 (Wed)/$18.65 (Fri/Sat)
Casino Size: 47,541 Square Feet
Other Games: SB, RB, PGP, BG, TCP
Special Features: 239-space RV park ($32 per night). Buffet discount with players club card.

Arizona Charlie's - Decatur
740 S. Decatur Boulevard
Las Vegas, Nevada 89107
(702) 258-5200
Website: www.arizonacharliesdecatur.com

Reservation Number: (800) 342-2695
Rooms: Price Range: $45-$130
Suites: Price Range: $54-$139
Restaurants: 5
Buffets: B- $7.99 (Fri/Sat)/$13.32 (Sun)
L- $10.65/$13.32 (Sun)
D- $12.65/$18.65 (Fri/Sat)
Casino Size: 55,227 Square Feet
Other Games: SB, RB, P, PGP, K, BG
Special Features: Buffet discount with players club card.

Bally's Las Vegas
3645 Las Vegas Boulevard S.
Las Vegas, Nevada 89109
(702) 739-4111
Website: www.ballyslv.com

Self-Parking: $7 (1-2 Hrs)/$12 (2 to 4 Hrs)
$15 (4-24 Hrs)
Valet Parking: $20 (0-4 Hrs)/$25 (4-24 Hrs)
Toll-Free Number: (800) 722-5597
Reservation Number: (888) 215-1078
Rooms: Price Range: $52-$193
Suites: Price Range: $1,119-$1,821
Restaurants: 9 hours)
Buffets: Brunch - $95 (Sat/Sun)
Self-Parking: $7 (1-4 Hrs)/$10 (4 to 24 Hrs)
Valet Parking: $13 (0-4 Hrs)/$18 (4-24 Hrs)
Casino Size: 66,187 Square Feet
Other Games: SB, RB, B, MB, P, CW, PG, UTH, PGP, CSP, LIR, TCP, K, BG, MS
Overnight RV Parking: Free/RV Dump: No
Senior Discount: Various if 55+
Special Features: Affiliated with Caesars Entertainment. 20 retail stores.

Bellagio
3600 Las Vegas Boulevard S.
Las Vegas, Nevada 89109
(702) 693-7111
Website: www.bellagioresort.com

Reservation Number: (888) 987-6667
Rooms: 2,688 Price Range: $169-$398
Suites: 308 Price Range: $402-$695
Restaurants: 16
Buffets: B- $23.99/$48.99 (Sat/Sun)
L- $28.99/$48.99 (Sat/Sun)
D- $38.99/$43.99 (Fri/Sat)
Self-Parking: $7 (1-2 Hrs)/$12 (2 to 4 Hrs)
$15 (4-24 Hrs)
Valet Parking: $20 (0-4 Hrs)/$25 (4-24 Hrs)
Casino Size: 156,000 Square Feet
Other Games: SB, RB, B, MB, P, PG,
PGP, CSP, LIR, TCP
Special Features: Affiliated with MGM Resorts. Lake with nightly light and water show. Shopping mall. Two wedding chapels. Beauty salon and spa. Cirque du Soleil's *O* stage show.

Binion's Gambling Hall
128 E. Fremont Street
Las Vegas, Nevada 89101
(702) 382-1600
Website: www.binions.com

Toll-Free Number: (800) 937-6537
Restaurants: 4
Casino Size: 77,800 Square Feet
Other Games: SB, RB, P, PGP, LIR,
TCP, B6
Special Features: Steak House on 24th floor offers panoramic views of Las Vegas. Free souvenior photo taken in front of $1,000,000 cash.

Boulder Station Hotel & Casino
4111 Boulder Highway
Las Vegas, Nevada 89121
(702) 432-7777
Website: www.boulderstation.com

Toll-Free Number: (800) 981-5577
Reservation Number: (800) 683-7777
Rooms: 300 Price Range: $34-$161
Restaurants: 5
Buffets: B-$8.99/$15.99 (Sun)
L-$11.99/$15.99 (Sat/Sun)
D-$15.99/$17.99 (Fri/Sat)
Casino Size: 89,443 Square Feet
Other Games: SB, RB, MB, P, PGP,
TCP, K, BG, B
Senior Discount: Various Wed if 50+
Special Features: 11-screen movie complex. Kids Quest childcare center. Buffet discount for players club members.

Caesars Palace
3570 Las Vegas Boulevard S.
Las Vegas, Nevada 89109
(702) 731-7110
Website: www.caesarspalace.com

Toll-Free Number: (800) 634-6001
Reservation Number: (800) 634-6661
Rooms: 3,349 Price Range: $109-$500
Suites: 399 Price Range: $378-$1,340
Nobu Rooms Price Range: $159-$379
Nobu Suites Price Range: $609-$1,560
Restaurants: 14
Self-Parking: $10 (1-4 Hrs)/$12 (4 to 24 Hrs)
Valet Parking: $15 (0-4 Hrs)/$20 (4-24 Hrs)
Buffets: B- $39.99/$49.99 (Sat/Sun)
L- $39.99/$49.99 (Sat/Sun)
D- $54.99/$57.99 (Fri-Sun
Casino Size: 139,229 Square Feet
Other Games: SB, RB, B, MB, PG, P, MS,
UTH, PGP, LIR, TCP, K
Special Features: Affiliated with Caesars Entertainment. Health spa. Beauty salon. Shopping mall with 125 stores and interactive attractions. *Celine Dion* stage show.

California Hotel & Casino
12 Ogden Avenue
Las Vegas, Nevada 89101
(702) 385-1222
Website: www.thecal.com

Reservation Number: (800) 634-6505
Rooms: 781 Price Range: $55-$175
Suites: 74 Price Range: Casino Use Only
Restaurants: 4
Casino Size: 35,848 Square Feet
Other Games: SB, PGP, LIR, TCP, K
Senior Discount: Various Wed if 50+
Special Features: Affiliated with Boyd Gaming. Offers charter packages from Hawaii.

Casino Royale Hotel & Casino
3411 Las Vegas Boulevard S.
Las Vegas, Nevada 89109
(702) 737-3500
Website: www.casinoroyalehotel.com

Toll-Free Number: (800) 854-7666
Rooms: 151 Price Range: $109-$229
Suites: 3 Price Range: $209-$409
Restaurants: 3
Casino Size: 22,000 Square Feet
Other Games: TCP
Special Features: Outback steakhouse, Denny's and Subway. Refrigerator in every room. White Castle restaurant.

Circus Circus Hotel & Casino
2880 Las Vegas Boulevard S.
Las Vegas, Nevada 89109
(702) 734-0410
Website: www.circuscircus.com

Room Reservations: (877) 224-7287
RV Reservations: (800) 562-7270
Rooms: 3,770 Price Range: $25-$175
Suites: 122 Price Range: $89-$269
Restaurants: 8
Buffets: B/L- $18.99 D-$20.99
Self-Parking: Free
Valet Parking: $10 (0-4 Hrs), $15 (4-24 Hrs)
Casino Size: 123,928 Square Feet
Other Games: SB, RB, P, PGP, MS,
LIR, TCP, B6
Special Features: Affiliated with MGM Resorts. Free circus acts 11am-midnight. Wedding chapel. Midway and arcade games. Indoor Adventuredome theme park.

The Cosmopolitan of Las Vegas
3708 Las Vegas Boulevard South
Las Vegas, Nevada 89109
(702) 698-7000
Website: www.cosmopolitanlasvegas.com

Toll-free Number: (877) 551-7778
Rooms: 2,600 Price Range: $119-$679
Suites: 395 Price Range: $289-$1,299
Restaurants: 16
Buffet: B/L- $28/$36 (Fri-Sun)
D- $42/$49 (Fri-Sun)
Self-Parking: $7 (1-4 Hrs)/$10 (4 to 24 Hrs)
Valet Parking: $13 (0-4 Hrs)/$18 (4-24 Hrs)
Casino Size: 63,628 Square Feet
Other games: RB, SB, LIR, B, MB,
PGP, TCP, CW

The Cromwell Las Vegas
3595 Las Vegas Boulevard S.
Las Vegas, Nevada 89109
(855) 895-3002
Website: www.thecromwell.com

Reservation Number: (844) 426-2766
Rooms: 624 Price Range: $139-$289
Suites: 14 Price Range: $339-$1,250
Restaurants: 2
Self-Parking: $7 (1-4 Hrs)/$10 (4 to 24 Hrs)
Valet Parking: $13 (0-4 Hrs)/$18 (4-24 Hrs)
Casino Size: 33,673 Square Feet
Other Games: P, PGP, MB, UTH,
MS, LIR, TCP
Special Features: Affiliated with Caesars Entertainment. Drai's Beach Club & Nightclub (rooftop); and Drai's After Hours (basement).

The D Las Vegas
301 Fremont Street
Las Vegas, Nevada 89101
(702) 388-2400
Website: www.thed.com

Reservation Number: (800) 274-5825
Rooms: 624 Price Range: $29-$199
Suites: 14 Price Range: $129-$549
Restaurants: 3
Casino Size: 33,673 Square Feet
Other Games: SB, RB, LIR, PGP, TCP, K
Special Features: Fast food court with McDonald's and Krispy Kreme. *Defending the Caveman* stage show.

Downtown Grand Casino
206 North 3rd Street
Las Vegas, Nevada 89101
(855) 384-7263
Website: www.downtowngrand.com

Rooms: 626 Price Range: $39-$289
Suites: 8 Price Range: Casino Use Only
Restaurants: 4
Casino Size: 35,000 Square Feet
Other Games: SB, RB, B, PGP, TCP, B6
Special Features: eSports arena.

Eastside Cannery
5255 Boulder Highway
Las Vegas, Nevada 89122
(702) 856-5300
Website: www.eastsidecannery.com

Reservation Number: (866) 999-4899
Rooms: 190 Price Range: $69-$119
Rooms: 20 Price Range: $109-$189
Restaurants: 3
Buffets: L- $8.99/$9.99 (Thu/Fri)/ $12.99 (Sat/Sun)
D- $11.99/$14.99 (Thu-Sun)
Casino Size: 62,479 Square Feet
Other Games: SB, RB, P, PGP, BG
Senior Discount: Food discounts if 55+
Special Features: Affiliated with Boyd Gaming. Buffet discount with players club card.

El Cortez Hotel & Casino
600 E. Fremont Street
Las Vegas, Nevada 89101
(702) 385-5200
Website: www.elcortezhotelcasino.com

Reservation Number: (800) 634-6703
Rooms: 299 Price Range: $23-$119
Suites: 10 Price Range: $60-$159
Restaurants: 2
Casino Size: 45,300 Square Feet
Other Games: SB ,RB, MB, K
Special Features: Video arcade. Gift shop and ice cream parlor. Barber shop. Beauty salon.

Ellis Island Casino & Brewery
4178 Koval Lane
Las Vegas, Nevada 89109
(702) 733-8901
Website: www.ellisislandcasino.com

Restaurants: 3 (open 24 hours)
Rooms: 289 Price Range: $23-$126
Suites: 12 Price Range $105-$189
Casino Size: 12,316 Square Feet
Other Games: SB, RB
Special Features: Rooms are at Super 8 Motel next door. $7.99 steak dinner (not on menu, must ask for it). On-site microbrewery.

Encore Las Vegas
3131 Las Vegas Boulevard S.
Las Vegas, Nevada 89109
(702) 770-7800
Website: www.encorelasvegas.com

Reservations Number: (888) 320-7125
Suites: 1,800 Price Range: $157-$1,149
Tower Suites: 234 Price Range $255-$8,300
Restaurants: 9
Self-Parking: $7 (1-2 Hrs)/$12 (2 to 4 Hrs) $15 (4-24 Hrs)
Valet Parking: $15 (0-4 Hrs)/$20 (4-24 Hrs)
Casino Size: 186,187 Sq. Ft. (Includes Wynn)
Other Games: SB, RB, B, MB, P, PG, CW, PGP, CSP, LIR, TCP, B6
Special Features: Beach club with three pools. Two nightclubs.

The Best Places To Play In Las Vegas

Roulette- There are 14 casinos in Las Vegas that offer single-zero roulette: Aria, Bellagio, Caesars Palace, Cosmopolitan, Cromwell, Encore, Mandalay Bay, MGM Grand, Mirage, Palazzo, Paris, Venetian and Wynn. This game has a 2.70% edge as compared to the usual 5.26% edge on a double-zero roulette wheel. Be aware that all of these casinos offer single-zero wheels at just some of their roulette games and not all of them. The minimum bet starts at $25 and can go as high as $100.

Craps- 100X odds is the highest offered in Las Vegas and there is only one casino offering that game: The Cromwell. The next best game offers 20x odds and it can be found at Sam's Town, as well as at Main Street Station.

Blackjack- All recommendations in this section apply to basic strategy players. For single-deck games you should always look for casinos that pay the standard 3-to-2 for blackjacks. Many casinos only pay 6-to-5 for blackjack and this increases the casino edge to around 1.5% and they should be avoided. Many casinos also offer a blackjack game called Super Fun 21. This is another game that should be avoided as the casino advantage is around 1%.

The best single-deck game can be found at the El Cortez which offers the following rules: dealer hits soft 17, double down on any first two cards, split any pair, re-split any pair (except aces), and no doubling after splitting. The casino edge in this game is .18% and the minimum bet is $5.

There are three casinos: Four Queens, Hooters and Silverton, that offer a similar single-deck game, but they only allow you to double down on two card totals of 10 or more, and this raises the casino edge to 0.44%

There are six casinos with two-deck games offering the following rules: dealer stands on soft 17, double down on any first two cards, re-split any pair (except aces) and doubling allowed after splitting. The casinos that offer it are: Aria, Bellagio, MGM Grand, Mandalay Bay, Mirage and Treasure Island. The casino edge in these games is .19% with minimum bets of $50 to $100.

The best double-deck game, however, is offered at M Resort. This game has the same rules as the above games except it allows the re-splitting of aces and that brings the casino edge down to .14% The minimum bet at this game is $25.

The remaining best two-deckers in Las Vegas can be found at some casinos that have the same rules as above, with two exceptions: the dealer hits soft 17 and aces can be re-split. The casino advantage is .35% and the game can be found at Aliante, Arizona Charlie's Boulder, Silverton, Tropicana and Westgate. The minimum bet at these casinos is $5 to $25.

For six-deck shoe games the best casinos have these rules: dealer stands on soft 17, double after split allowed, late surrender offered and re-splitting of aces allowed. The casino edge in this game works out to .26% and you can find it at many major casinos: Aria, Bellagio, Caesars Palace, Cosmopolitan, Hard Rock, M Resort, Mandalay Bay, MGM Grand, Mirage, Palazzo, Rio, SLS, Treasure Island, Tropicana, Wynn and the Venetian. The minimum bet at these casinos is usually at least $50, with some at $100.

Almost all of these casinos also offer this same game with identical rules except that they will hit soft 17. The minimums in this game are lower, usually $25, but the casino's mathematical edge is raised to .46%.

Cosmopolitan, Mandalay Bay and SLS offer the best eight deck games. They have the same rules as the .26% six-deck game and the casino advantage is .49% with minimum bets of $10 to $25.

It should also be noted that there are many casino offering six and eight-deck shoe games that only pay 6-to-5 for blackjack, rather than 3-to-2. These games should definitely be avoided as they triple the casino advantage to as high as 2%.

Video Poker- Smart video poker players know that some of the best machines to look for are: 9/6 Jacks or Better (99.54% return), 8/5 Bonus Poker (99.17% return), 10/7 Double Bonus (100.17% return), full-pay Deuces Wild (100.76% return), 10/6 Double Double Bonus (100.07% return) and Not So Ugly Deuces (99.73% return). These games rarely exist at Las Vegas Strip casinos, but they are usually widely available at "locals" casinos along Boulder Highway, or in Henderson or North Las Vegas.

Following is a list of casinos offering some of these better paying video poker games. The abbreviations used for each listing are JB (9/6 jacks or better - 99.54%), BP (8/5 bonus poker - 99.17%), DB (10/7 Double Bonus - 100.17%), DDB (10/6 double double bonus - 100.07%), FPDW (full-pay deuces wild - 100.76%) and NSUD (not so ugly deuces - 99.73%).

Strip-area Casinos
Circus Circus: BP - quarter and $1 (some with progressives)
Cosmopolitan: BP - quarter to $100; JB - fifty cents to $25
Cromwell: JB - quarter; NSUD - quarter; BP - quarter
Ellis Island: JB - nickel to $5; NSUD - nickel to $5;
Gold Coast: JB - quarter to $5; NSUD - quarter to $1; BP - quarter to $10
Hard Rock: BP - $1 to $10
Luxor: BP - $1 to $10
MGM Grand: JB - $1 to $25; BP - $1 to $100
Orleans: BP - quarter to $2; NSUD - quarter
Palace Station: JB- quarter to $1; DB - nickel to $1; DDB - nickel to $1; FPDW - nickel; NSUD - quarter to $1
Palms: JB - quarter to $2; BP - quarter to $25; DDB - quarter and fifty cents; NSUD - fifty-cents and $1
Rio*:* BP - $1 to $100
Silver Sevens: BP - quarter to $1
SLS: BP - $1 to $25
Treasure Island: JB - fifty-cents to $2; BP - fifty-cents to $2
Tropicana: BP - nickel to $25
Tuscany: BP - quarter to $1
Westgate: JB - nickel to $1; NSUD - quarter; BP - quarter to $2
Wynn: JB - $1 to $100; BP - $1 to $100; NSUD - $1 to $100

Downtown Casinos
California: JB - quarter to $1; BP - nickel to $5; DB - quarter to $1; NSUD - nickel to fifty-cents
The D: BP - quarter to $2
El Cortez: JB - $1; DB - quarter and fifty-cents; BP - quarter to $5
Four Queens: JB - quarter to $1; DB - quarter and $1
Fremont: JB - quarter to $1; NSUD - quarter to $1; BP - quarter to $5
Main Street Station: JB - quarter to $1; NSUD - quarter; DB - quarter to $1
Plaza: JB - quarter to $2; BP - quarter to $5; DB - quarter to $2

Locals Casinos- If you are looking for the best video poker in Las Vegas then you may want to make a side trip to some of the casinos along Boulder Highway, as well as in Henderson or North Las Vegas. Most of these casinos offer all of the games listed above in a variety of denominations. The casino company that operates the most locals properties is Station Casinos which owns: Sunset Station, Boulder Station, Texas Station, Santa Fe Station, Palace Station, Green Valley Ranch, Red Rock, Fiesta Henderson and Fiesta Rancho. The other major player is Boyd Gaming, which operates Sam's Town, Gold Coast, Orleans, Suncoast, California, Fremont and Main Street Station. All of these locals casinos will offer good video poker games, coupled with a good players club that will allow you to redeem your points at any of their company-owned casinos.

Excalibur Hotel/Casino
3850 Las Vegas Boulevard S.
Las Vegas, Nevada 89109
(702) 597-7777
Website: www.excalibur.com

Reservation Number: (800) 937-7777
Rooms: 4,008 Price Range: $31-$299
Suites: 46 Price Range: $130-$449
Restaurants: 7
Buffets: B- $18.99/$22.99 (Sat/Sun)
L- $19.99/$22.99 (Sat/Sun)
D- $24.99/$27.99 (Fri/Sat)
Self-Parking: $5 (1-2 Hrs)/$8 (2 to 4 Hrs)
$10 (4-24 Hrs)
Valet Parking: $10 (0-4 Hrs)/$15 (4-24 Hrs)
Casino Size: 98,628 Square Feet
Other Games: SB, RB, P, PGP, LIR,
CW, TCP, B6, K, FCP
Special Features: Affiliated with MGM Resorts. Canterbury wedding chapel. Strolling Renaissance entertainers. Video arcade and midway games. Nightly *Tournament of Kings* dinner show. *Australian Bee Gees* show. *Thunder from Down Under* show. Food Court with fast food outlets.

Flamingo Las Vegas
3555 Las Vegas Boulevard S.
Las Vegas, Nevada 89109
(702) 733-3111
Website: www.flamingolasvegas.com

Reservation Number: (800) 732-2111
Rooms: 3,545 Price Range: $39-$329
Suites: 215 Price Range: $99-$1,129
Restaurants: 6
Buffets: B/L- $21.99/$24.99 (Sat/Sun)
D- $29.99
Self-Parking: $7 (1-4 Hrs)/$10 (4 to 24 Hrs)
Valet Parking: $13 (0-4 Hrs)/$18 (4-24 Hrs)
Casino Size: 72,279 Square Feet
Other Games: SB, RB, MB, P, PGP, MS
LIR, TCP, UTH, K
Special Features: Affiliated with Caesars Entertainment. Health Spa. Shopping arcade. Jimmy Buffet's Margaritaville restaurant. *Legends in Concert* stage show.

Four Queens Hotel/Casino
202 Fremont Street
Las Vegas, Nevada 89101
(702) 385-4011
Website: www.fourqueens.com

Reservation Number: (800) 634-6045
Rooms: 690 Price Range: $39-$169
Suites: 48 Price Range: $110-$259
Restaurants: 3
Casino Size: 27,269 Square Feet
Other Games: SB, RB, UTH, LIR, TCP, K, MS
Special Features: No resort fee charged.

Fremont Hotel & Casino
200 E. Fremont Street
Las Vegas, Nevada 89101
(702) 385-3232
Website: www.fremontcasino.com

Toll-Free Number: (800) 634-6460
Reservation Number: (800) 634-6182
Rooms: 428 Price Range: $45-$149
Suites: 24 Price Range: Casino Use Only
Restaurants: 4
Buffets: B- $9.49/$14.99 (Sat/Sun)
L- $10.49/$14.99 (Sat/Sun)
D- $16.49/$25.99 (Tues/Fri)
Casino Size: 30,244 Square Feet
Other Games: SB, RB, PGP, LIR, TCP, K
Special Features: Affiliated with Boyd Gaming. 99¢ shrimp cocktail at Lanai Express. Only Tony Roma's restaurant in Nevada. Buffet discount with players club card.

Gold Coast Hotel & Casino
4000 W. Flamingo Road
Las Vegas, Nevada 89103
(702) 367-7111
Website: www.goldcoastcasino.com

Toll-Free Number: (888) 402-6278
Rooms: 750 Price Range: $45-$225
Suites: 27 Price Range: $165-$450
Restaurants: 6
Buffets: B-$9.99/$16.99 (Sun)
L-$11.99/$16.99 (Sun)
D- $16.99/$25.99 (Fri)
Casino Size: 88,915 Square Feet
Other Games: SB, RB, MB, PGP, TCP,
K, BG, LIR
Senior Discount: Various Wed if 50+
Special Features: Affiliated with Boyd Gaming. 70-lane bowling center. Showroom.

Golden Gate Hotel & Casino
One Fremont Street
Las Vegas, Nevada 89101
(702) 385-1906
Website: www.goldengatecasino.com

Reservation Number: (800) 426-1906
Rooms: 106 Price Range: $21-$159
Restaurants: None
Casino Size: 12,243 Square Feet
Other Games: SB, RB, TCP, LIR
Special Features: Oldest hotel in Vegas (opened 1906).

The Golden Nugget
129 E. Fremont Street
Las Vegas, Nevada 89101
(702) 385-7111
Website: www.goldennugget.com

Toll-Free Number: (800) 634-3403
Reservation Number: (800) 634-3454
Rooms: 1,805 Price Range: $59-$199
Suites: 102 Price Range: $149-$750
Restaurants: 9
Buffets: B- $14.99/$21.99 (Sat/Sun)
L- $15.99/$21.99 (Sat/Sun)
D-$22.99$24.99 (Thu/Sat)/
$27.99 (Fri)/$25.99 (Sun)
Casino Size: 47,796 Square Feet
Other Games: SB, RB, MB, P, PGP,
LIR, TCP, B6, K
Special Features: World's largest gold nugget (61 pounds) on display. Health spa. Swimming pool with shark tank.

Hard Rock Hotel & Casino
4455 Paradise Road
Las Vegas, Nevada 89109
(702) 693-5000
Website: www.hardrockhotel.com

Toll-Free Number: (800) 473-7625
Rooms: 1,130 Price Range: $49-$389
Suites: 387 Price Range: $99-$429
Restaurants: 8
Casino Size: 59,125 Square Feet
Other Games: SB, RB, B, MB, PGP, P,
UTH, LIR, TCP, B6
Special Features: Rock and Roll memorabilia display. Beach Club with cabanas and sandy beaches. Lagoon with underwater music.

Harrah's Las Vegas
3475 Las Vegas Boulevard S.
Las Vegas, Nevada 89109
(702) 369-5000
Website: www.caesars.com

Toll-Free Number: (800) 392-9002
Reservation Number: (800) 427-7247
Rooms: 2,672 Price Range: $49-$299
Suites: 94 Price Range: $110-$475
Restaurants: 4
Buffets: B-$19.99/$26.99 (Sat/Sun)
L- $23.99/$26.99 (Sat/Sun)
D- $29.99/$32.99 (Fri/Sat)
Self-Parking: $7 (1-4 Hrs)/$10 (4 to 24 Hrs)
Valet Parking: $13 (0-4 Hrs)/$18 (4-24 Hrs)
Casino Size: 90,637 Square Feet
Other Games: SB, RB, MB, P, PG, PGP, B,
UTH, LIR, TCP, CW, K, MS
Special Features: Affiliated with Caesars Entertainment. Mardi Gras-themed casino. Improv Comedy Club. *Mac King* stage show. Fulton Street Food Hall with nine different food stations.

Hooters Casino Hotel
115 East Tropicana Avenue
Las Vegas, Nevada 89109
(702) 739-9000
Website: www.hooterscasinohotel.com

Toll-Free Number: (866) 584-6687
Rooms: 694 Price Range: $39-$195
Suites: 17 Price Range: $205-$500
Restaurants: 4
Casino Size: 25,000 Square Feet
Other Games: SB, RB, LIR, P, PGP, TCP

The Best Vegas Values

By H. Scot Krause

Welcome to "Vegas Values!" It's an exclusive weekly column found only at: americancasinoguide.com, the companion website to this book. The column is updated weekly with some of the best casino promotions found throughout Las Vegas. Below are examples from the "Vegas Values" column. Remember, promotions are subject to change and may be cancelled at anytime. Call ahead to verify before making a special trip.

Arizona Charlie's Boulder and Decatur: You'll need your ace/PLAY card for the café's excellent $5.55 breakfast special of steak or ham, eggs, hash browns & toast. You must present your players card to your server.

Boyd Casinos (Gold Coast, Orleans, Sam's Town or Suncoast): Boyd Casinos (Gold Coast, Orleans, Sam's Town, Suncoast and Fremont): Young at Heart Senior Wednesdays is open to anyone 50 and over. There are $2,500 cash drawings at 4:30 p.m. at each location. Earn 10 points to get a "Buy One, Get One Free Breakfast, Lunch or Dinner Buffet." Earn 50 points and get a free breakfast or lunch buffet. Earn 100 points and get a free dinner buffet or get a $15 Dining Credit after earning 300 points valid after 7:00 p.m. for 24 hours. There is also a "Mystery Multiplier" from 7 a.m.-7 p.m. with a chance to earn up to 50X points for the day. (Promotions are subject to change.)

Cromwell: Offering 100x odds on craps.

El Cortez: Have an IRS tax refund check you're ready to cash? Get a 5% free slot bonus for it. Cash your IRS check (or any government issued check) at the El Cortez main cage and you'll receive an extra 5% (up to $50) in FREE slot play money. The offer generally runs year round. Also, Earn 1,941 points in a day and receive your choice of a FREE pack of cigarettes, a $10 dining voucher at Siegel's 1941, two slices of pizza and a soft drink or draft beer at Pizza Lotto, a $6 Subway voucher or $10 in free slot play. Limit of one redemption per day.

Ellis Island Casino & Brewery: Known for their off-the-menu-great steak special. You get a generous cut of tenderloin cooked to your liking, bread, salad, vegetable of the day, choice of potato and a beer (or root beer) from the microbrewery. The regular price is $12.99, but Passport Players Card members can get it down to $7.99 by jumping through a few hoops. Everyone can swipe their players card to get $3 off for $9.99. Whereas you used to be able to get an additional $2 off by playing $1 in a machine, that requirement has been raised to $5. This steak special is not on the menu. Ask your server for it!

Four Queens: Four Queens: New members signing up for the Royal Players Club receive a FREE t-shirt or canvas tote bag after earning 40 points within the first 24 hours of enrolling (gifts may vary.)

Hard Rock: New sign-ups receive a $5 free bet. Then, play one hour on any table game and receive a $25 dining credit. Or, get $5 in free slot play then, play $20 on your first trip and receive $10 in free slot play.

Jerry's Nugget: Players who join the Jerry's Nugget MoreClub earn free introductory gifts all on their first day's play. Based on slot points earned from 4 am to 11:59 pm on the day they sign up, new members receive the following: 50 base points - $5 comp, 100 base points – Jerry's Nugget t-shirt, 250 base points - $20 comp, and 500 base points - $40 Jerry's Nugget Gift Card. New members earning 1,000 base points or more get to spin for cash and win up to $200. Multiple prizes will be awarded based on the points earned categories. No points will be deducted.

Lucky Club: Seniors 65 and up get 33% off at the restaurant.

M Resort: Comp Buffet Promotion: Must earn points the same day the comp buffet is used - prior to 8 pm to qualify. Offer does not include a line pass. Limit one meal per Marquee Rewards member. Offer not valid during holiday periods. Management reserves all rights to alter or cancel any promotion at any time. Lunch (Monday – Friday): 300 points on Reel Slots, 850 points on Video Poker. Dinner (Monday – Thursday): 450 points on Reel Slots, 1,300 points on Video Poker. Seafood Dinner Buffet (Friday – Sunday): 700 points on Reel Slots, 2,000 points on Video Poker.

Main Street Station: "Score with Four" promotion. Hit any four-of-a-kind, straight flush or royal flush and receive a scratch card for additional cash. Most cards are of the $2 to $5 variety, but they do offer cards valued at $20, $50 and $100, as well as the extremely rare $5,000 cards.

Silverton: All new Silverton Rewards Club members will receive a free gift when signing up for the Rewards Club and will begin participating in the new sign-up program. All new Silverton Rewards Club members will receive up to $200 in free slot play based on the points earned on their first visit. See Silverton Rewards Club for complete rules and details.

Tuscany Casino: Offering new members signing up for the slot club a randomly selected amount of free play, from $5 up to $500, plus a good little Fun Book with some nice coupons in it including matchplays, food discounts, free gifts and comp deals.

Wynn Las Vegas: Offering new members signing up for a Wynn Las Vegas Get $10 in free slot play when you sign up. After earning first 300 points, spin a wheel for a prize ranging from $10 to $10,000 in free slot play, buffets, show tickets and more. Red Card is the same for Encore. Enroll at one or the other, not both.

The LINQ Hotel & Casino
3535 Las Vegas Boulevard S.
Las Vegas, Nevada 89109
(702) 731-3311
Website: www.thelinq.com

Toll-Free Number: (800) 351-7400
Reservation Number: (800) 634-6441
Rooms: 1,088 Price Range: $49-$325
Suites: 225 Price Range: $115-$685
Restaurants: 5
Self-Parking: $7 (1-4 Hrs)/$10 (4 to 24 Hrs)
Valet Parking: $13 (0-4 Hrs)/$18 (4-24 Hrs)
Casino Size: 28,361 Square Feet
Other Games: SB, RB, PGP, LIR, TCP, B6, P
Special Features: Affiliated with Caesars Entertainment. Auto museum (admission charge). Brooklyn Bowl concert venue. Wedding chapel. *Divas* stage show. *Matt Franco Magic Reinvented Nightly* show. 50-story *High Roller* observation wheel with cabins.

Longhorn Casino
5288 Boulder Highway
Las Vegas, Nevada 89122
(702) 435-9170

Website: www.longhorncasinolv.com
Rooms: 150 Price Range: $29-69
Restaurants: 1
Casino Size: 4,825 Square Feet
Other Games: SB, RB, No craps or roulette
Special Features: $4.99 ham steak & eggs, $10.99 Monster Burger, and other restaurant specials.

Free Things To See In Las Vegas!

Conservatory at Bellagio

Looking for some greenery during your Las Vegas stay? The Bellagio Conservatory has got you covered and is completely free! Every season, the Bellagio's 140 expert horticulturists create a breathtaking new scene made up of intricate floral arrangements, gazebos, bridges, and ponds for guests to explore. The themes begin with the Chinese New Year in January and changes for summer, fall, and winter. The conservatory is located inside the Bellagio and is open 24 hours, with live music offered from 5-6pm daily in the south garden.

Lucky Dragon Hotel & Casino
300 Sahara Avenue
Las Vegas, Nevada 89102
Website: www.luckydragonlv.com

Rooms: 2,672 Price Range: $60-$249
Suites: 94 Price Range: $169-$398
Restaurants: 5
Casino Size: 27,500 Square Feet
Special Features: Asian-themed resort. Tea Garden featuring extensive list of tea curated by Las Vegas' only tea sommelier.

Luxor Las Vegas
3900 Las Vegas Boulevard S.
Las Vegas, Nevada 89119
(702) 262-4000
Website: www.luxor.com

Reservation Number (800) 288-1000
Pyramid Rooms: 1,948 Price Range: $37-$299
Pyramid Suites 237 Price Range: $79-$339
Tower Rooms: 2,256 Price Range: $49-$299
Tower Suites 236 Price Range: $89-$469
Restaurants: 6
Buffets: B-$18.99/$22.99 (Sat/Sun)
L-$19.99/$22.99 (Sat/Sun)
D-$24.99/$27.99 (Fri/Sat)
Self-Parking: $5 (1-2 Hrs)/$8 (2 to 4 Hrs)
$10 (4-24 Hrs)
Valet Parking: $10 (0-4 Hrs)/$15 (4-24 Hrs)
Casino Size: 120,000 Square Feet
Other Games: SB, RB, MB, P, PGP,
LIR, TCP, UTH
Special Features: Affiliated with MGM Resorts. 30-story pyramid-shaped hotel with Egyptian theme. *Carrot Top* comedy show. Cirque Du soleil *Criss Angel Mindfreak* Stage show. IMAX theater. *Blue Man Group* stage show.

Main Street Station Hotel & Casino
200 N. Main Street
Las Vegas, Nevada 89101
(702) 387-1896
Website: www.mainstreetcasino.com

Toll-Free Number: (800) 713-8933
Reservation Number: (800) 465-0711
Rooms: 406 Price Range: $45-$150
Suites: 14 Price Range: Casino Use Only
Restaurants: 2
Buffets: B- $8.99/$12.99 (Sat/Sun)
L- $9.99/$12.99 (Sat/Sun)
D- $12.99/$15.99 (Tue/Sat)/$29.99 (Fri)
Casino Size: 26,918 Square Feet
Other Games: PGP, LIR, TCP
Senior Discount: Various Wed if 50+
Special Features: Affiliated with Boyd Gaming. 200-space RV park ($15/$19 per night). Buffet discount for players club members.

Mandalay Bay
3950 Las Vegas Boulevard S.
Las Vegas, Nevada 89119
(702) 632-7777
Web Site: www.mandalaybay.com

Reservation Number: (877) 632-7700
Rooms: 3,220 Price Range: $79-$249
Suites: 424 Price Range: $109-$599
Restaurants: 15
Buffets: B- $18.99/$25.99 (Fri-Sun)
L- $21.99/$25.99 (Fri-Sun) D- $32.99
Self-Parking: $7 (1-2 Hrs)/$10 (2 to 4 Hrs)
$12 (4-24 Hrs)
Valet Parking: $15 (0-4 Hrs)/$20 (4-24 Hrs)
Casino Size: 160,344 Square Feet
Other Games: SB, RB, B, MB, P, PG, PGP, LIR, TCP, B6
Special Features: Affiliated with MGM Resorts. 424-room Four Seasons Hotel on 35th-39th floors. *House of Blues* restaurant. Sand and surf beach with lazy river ride. Shark Reef exhibit (admission charge). Spa. Michael Jackson *ONE* Cirque Du Soleil show

MGM Grand Hotel Casino
3799 Las Vegas Boulevard S.
Las Vegas, Nevada 89109
(702) 891-1111
Website: www.mgmgrand.com

Toll-Free Number: (800) 929-1111
Rooms: 5,005 Price Range: $65-$415
Suites: 752 Price Range: $124-$665
Skylofts: 51 Price Range: $900-$10,000
Restaurants: 15
Buffets: B-$18.99/$29.99 (Sat/Sun)
L-$21.99/$29.99 (Sat/Sun)
D-$29.99/$42.99 (Fri)/$39.99 (Sat)
Self-Parking: $7 (1-2 Hrs)/$10 (2 to 4 Hrs)
$12 (4-24 Hrs)
Valet Parking: $15 (0-4 Hrs)/$20 (4-24 Hrs)
Casino Size: 156,023 Square Feet
Other Games: SB, RB, B, MB, PG, PGP, P, LIR, TCP, C4P, B6, CW
Special Features: Affiliated with MGM Resorts. Largest hotel in America. Topgolf driving range. Cirque du Soleil *Ka* stage show.

The Mirage
3400 Las Vegas Boulevard S.
Las Vegas, Nevada 89109
(702) 791-7111
Website: www.themirage.com

Reservation Number: (800) 374-9000
Rooms: 3,044 Price Range: $79-$349
Suites: 281 Price Range: $169-$1,200
Restaurants: 14
Buffets: B- $18.99/$28.99 (Sat/Sun)
L- $23.99 D- $30.99/$32.99 (Fri/Sat)
Self-Parking: $7 (1-2 Hrs)/$10 (2 to 4 Hrs)
$12 (4-24 Hrs)
Valet Parking: $15 (0-4 Hrs)/$20 (4-24 Hrs)
Casino Size: 97,550 Square Feet
Other Games: SB, RB, B, MB, PG, P, PGP, LIR, TCP, B6
Special Features: Affiliated with MGM Resorts. Siegfried & Roy's Secret Garden and Dolphin Habitat (admission charge). Aquarium display at check-in desk. Simulated volcano with periodic "eruptions." *Terry Fator* and Cirque du Soleil's *Love* stage shows.

Monte Carlo Resort & Casino
3770 Las Vegas Boulevard S.
Las Vegas, Nevada 89109
(702) 730-7777
Website: www.montecarlo.com

Reservation Number: (888) 529-4828
Rooms: 3,002 Price Range: $49-$279
Suites: 259 Price Range: $149-$465
Restaurants: 12
Buffets: B-$18.99/$21.99 (Fri-Sun)
L-$19.99 D-$24.99/$27.99 (Fri-Sun)
Self-Parking: $7 (1-2 Hrs)/$10 (2 to 4 Hrs)
$12 (4-24 Hrs)
Valet Parking: $15 (0-4 Hrs)/$20 (4-24 Hrs)
Casino Size: 101,983 Square Feet
Other Games: SB, RB, MB, B, P, PGP, FCP, LIR, TCP
Special Features: Affiliated with MGM Resorts. Pool with lazy river ride. Health spa.

Free Things To See In Las Vegas!

Fremont Street Experience

This $70 million computer-generated sound and light show takes place 90 feet in the sky over a pedestrian mall stretching four city blocks in downtown Las Vegas and in mid-2004 the entire system was upgraded with new LED modules to provide even crisper and clearer images. It's like watching the world's largest plasma TV with larger-than-life animations, integrated live video feeds, and synchronized music.

There are five differently themed shows nightly. Starting times vary, beginning at dusk, but then begin on the start of each hour through midnight.

New York-New York Hotel & Casino
3790 Las Vegas Boulevard S.
Las Vegas, Nevada 89109
(702) 740-6969
Website: www.nynyhotelcasino.com

Toll-Free Number: (800) 689-1797
Reservation Number: (866) 815-4365
Rooms: 2,024 Price Range: $49-$299
Suites: 12 Price Range: $125-$469
Restaurants: 8
Self-Parking: $7 (1-2 Hrs)/$10 (2 to 4 Hrs) $12 (4-24 Hrs)
Valet Parking: $15 (0-4 Hrs)/$20 (4-24 Hrs)
Casino Size: 90,000 Square Feet
Other Games: SB, RB, MB, PGP, LIR, TCP, B6
Special Features: Affiliated with MGM Resorts. Replica Statue of Liberty and Empire State Building. Roller coaster located on property. Cirque du Soleil's *Zumanity* stage show.

The Orleans Hotel & Casino
4500 West Tropicana Avenue
Las Vegas, Nevada 89103
(702) 365-7111
Website: www.orleanscasino.com

Reservation Number: (800) 675-3267
Rooms: 1,828 Price Range: $45-$149
Suites: 58 Price Range: $199-$499
Restaurants: 10
Buffets: B/L $12.99/$21.99 (Sun)
D- $19.99/ $27.99 (Fri)
Casino Size: 137,000 Square Feet
Other Games: SB, RB, MB, P, PGP, LIR, TCP, K
Special Features: Affiliated with Boyd Gaming. 70-lane bowling center. 18-screen movie theater. Childcare center. 9,000-seat arena. Free shuttle to Gold Coast and Cromwell.

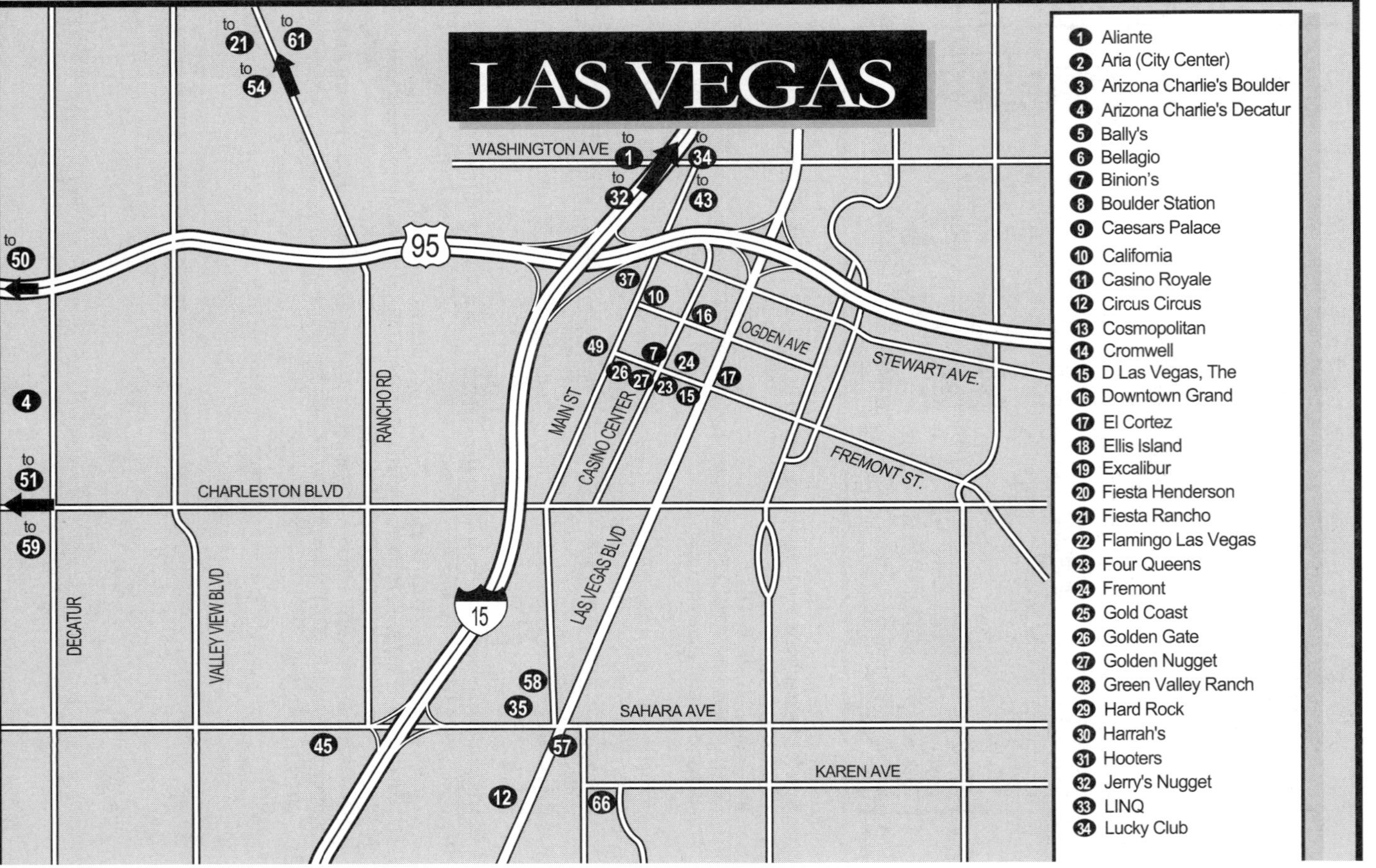

LAS VEGAS
1 Aliante
2 Aria (City Center)
3 Arizona Charlie's Boulder
4 Arizona Charlie's Decatur
5 Bally's
6 Bellagio
7 Binion's
8 Boulder Station
9 Caesars Palace
10 California
11 Casino Royale
12 Circus Circus
13 Cosmopolitan
14 Cromwell
15 D Las Vegas, The
16 Downtown Grand
17 El Cortez
18 Ellis Island
19 Excalibur
20 Fiesta Henderson
21 Fiesta Rancho
22 Flamingo Las Vegas
23 Four Queens
24 Fremont
25 Gold Coast
26 Golden Gate
27 Golden Nugget
28 Green Valley Ranch
29 Hard Rock
30 Harrah's
31 Hooters
32 Jerry's Nugget
33 LINQ
34 Lucky Club
WASHINGTON AVE
95
15
OGDEN AVE
STEWART AVE.
FREMONT ST.
MAIN ST
CASINO CENTER
LAS VEGAS BLVD
RANCHO RD
CHARLESTON BLVD
SAHARA AVE
KAREN AVE
VALLEY VIEW BLVD
DECATUR
to 21
to 61
to 54
to 50
to 51
to 59
to 1
to 34
to 32
to 43

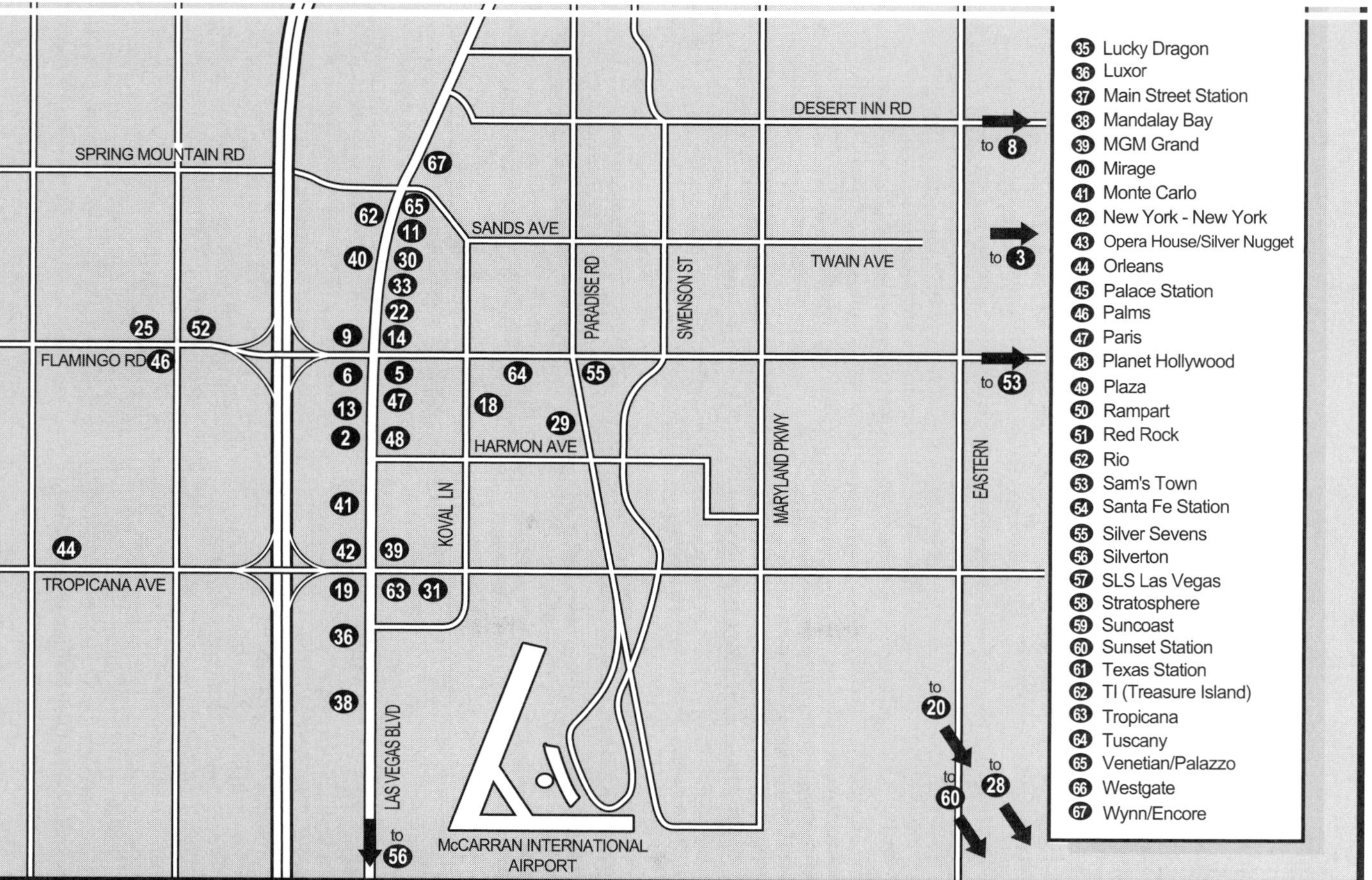

DESERT INN RD
SPRING MOUNTAIN RD
SANDS AVE
TWAIN AVE
PARADISE RD
SWENSON ST
FLAMINGO RD
HARMON AVE
MARYLAND PKWY
EASTERN
KOVAL LN
TROPICANA AVE
LAS VEGAS BLVD
McCARRAN INTERNATIONAL AIRPORT
to 8
to 3
to 53
to 20
to 60
to 28
to 56
35 Lucky Dragon
36 Luxor
37 Main Street Station
38 Mandalay Bay
39 MGM Grand
40 Mirage
41 Monte Carlo
42 New York - New York
43 Opera House/Silver Nugget
44 Orleans
45 Palace Station
46 Palms
47 Paris
48 Planet Hollywood
49 Plaza
50 Rampart
51 Red Rock
52 Rio
53 Sam's Town
54 Santa Fe Station
55 Silver Sevens
56 Silverton
57 SLS Las Vegas
58 Stratosphere
59 Suncoast
60 Sunset Station
61 Texas Station
62 TI (Treasure Island)
63 Tropicana
64 Tuscany
65 Venetian/Palazzo
66 Westgate
67 Wynn/Encore

Palace Station Hotel & Casino
2411 West Sahara Avenue
Las Vegas, Nevada 89102
(702) 367-2411
Website: www.palacestation.com

Reservation Number: (800) 544-2411
Rooms: 949 Price Range: $39-$189
Suites: 82 Price Range: $80-$485
Restaurants: 5
Buffets: B-$8.49/$15.99 (Sun)
L-$10.99 D-$14.99
Casino Size: 84,000 Square Feet
Other Games: SB, RB, B, MB, PG, P, PGP, TCP, K, BG
Senior Discount: Various Wed if 50+
Special Features: Affiliated with Station Casinos. Buffet discount with players club card.

The Palazzo
3355 Las Vegas Boulevard S.
Las Vegas, Nevada 89109
(702) 607-7777
Website: www.palazzo.com

Reservation Number: (888) 283-6423
Suites: 4,046 Price Range: $149-$5,000
Restaurants: 37 (1 open 24 hours)
Casino Size: 138,684 Square Feet
Other Games: SB, RB, B, MB, P, PG, CW, PGP, CSP, LIR, TCP, B6, S21
Special Features: Attached to The Venetian. 90 retail stores. Madame Tussaud's Wax Museum. Canyon Ranch Spa.

The Palms
4321 Flamingo Road
Las Vegas, Nevada 89103
(702) 942-7777
Website: www.palms.com

Toll Free Number: (866) 942-7777
Reservation Number: (866) 942-7770
Rooms: 447 Price Range: $49-$229
Suites: 60 Price Range: $179-$419
Specialty Suites: 9 Prices: $2,500-$40,000
Restaurants: 7
Casino Size: 87,178 Square Feet
Other Games: SB, RB, MB, PGP, UTH, TCP
Special Features: Affiliated with Station Casinos. 14-screen movie theater.

Paris Casino Resort
3655 Las Vegas Boulevard S.
Las Vegas, Nevada 89109
(702) 946-7000
Website: www.parislasvegas.com

Toll-Free Number: (877) 796-2096
Rooms: 2,916 Price Range: $115-$279
Suites: 300 Price Range: $245-$1,345
Restaurants: 14
Buffets: B- $21.99/$23.99 (Sat/Sun)
L- $24.99/$30.99 (Sat/Sun)
D- $30.99/$33.99 (Fri/Sat)
Self-Parking: $7 (1-4 Hrs)/$10 (4 to 24 Hrs)
Valet Parking: $13 (0-4 Hrs)/$18 (4-24 Hrs)
Casino Size: 95,263 Square Feet
Other Games: SB, RB, B, MB, TCP, CW, PG, PGP, LIR, B6, UTH,
Special Features: Affiliated with Caesars Entertainment. Replicas of Paris landmarks. 50-story Eiffel Tower with restaurant/ observation deck. *Anthony Cools* stage show.

Planet Hollywood Resort & Casino
3667 Las Vegas Boulevard S.
Las Vegas, Nevada 89109
(702) 785-5555
Website: www.planethollywoodresort.com

Toll-Free Number: (866) 919-7472
Rooms: 1,878 Price Range: $79-$259
Ultra-Hip Rooms: 466 Price Range: $369-$529
Restaurants: 9
Buffet: B-$21.99/$30.99 (Sat/Sun)
L-$24.99/$30.99 (Sat/Sun)
D-$30.99/$33.99 (Sat/Sun)
Self-Parking: Free
Valet Parking: $13 (0-4 Hrs)/$18 (4-24 Hrs)
Casino Size: 64,470 Square Feet
Other Games: SB, RB, B, MB, P, PGP, UTH, K, BG, CW, MS, LIR, TCP, B6
Special Features: Affiliated with Caesars Entertainment. 130-store retail mall. 7,000-seat Theater of the Performing Arts. Health spa and salon. Britney Spears *Piece of Me* stageshow. *Crazy Girls* stage show. V-theater located in the Miracle Mile Shops offers a variety of stage shows.

Free Things To See In Las Vegas!

Welcome to Las Vegas Sign

Located on the Las Vegas Strip just south of Mandalay Bay is the historic "Welcome to Fabulous Las Vegas" sign. The sign, which was built in 1959 and has since become a well-known Vegas landmark, reads "Welcome to Fabulous Las Vegas, Nevada" on the front and "Drive Carefully" and "Come Back Soon" on the back.

The sign has its own 12-car parking lot and photos can be taken near the sign with ease. The parking lot also has room for two buses and there is access for individuals with disabilities. Parking is free and the sign can be accessed 24 hours a day.

In order to access the "Welcome to Las Vegas" sign parking lot, you must be heading south on Las Vegas Boulevard going away from Mandalay Bay and toward the Las Vegas Outlet Center.

Plaza Hotel & Casino
1 Main Street
Las Vegas, Nevada 89101
(702) 386-2110
Website: www.plazahotelcasino.com

Reservation Number: (800) 634-6575
Rooms: 1,037 Price Range:$29-$152
Suites: 60 Price Range: $106-$329
Restaurants: 3
Casino Size: 51,436 Square Feet
Other Games: SB, RB, PGP, MB, P, LIR, TCP, BG, K
Special Features: Oscar's Steakhouse offers full view of Fremont Street Experience. Food court with four fast food outlets.

Rampart Casino
221 N. Rampart Boulevard
Las Vegas, Nevada 89145
(702) 507-5900
Website: www.rampartcasino.com

Reservation Number: (877) 869-8777
Rooms: 440 Price Range: $123-$229
Suites: 70 Price Range: $209-$399
Restaurants: 6
Buffets: L- $10.99/$16.99 (Sat/Sun)
D- $15.99/$21.99 (Wed)/
$18.99 (Thu)/$16.99 (Sat)
Casino Size: 47,330 Square Feet
Other Games: SB, RB, PGP, TCP, FCP, BG, UTH
Special Features: Hotel is JW Marriott. Golf course. Spa.

Red Rock Resort Spa Casino
11011 W. Charleston Boulevard
Las Vegas, Nevada 89135
(702) 797-7777
Website: www.redrocklasvegas.com

Rooms: 366 Price Range: $80-$269
Suites: 48 Price Range: $280-$1,460
Restaurants: 10
Buffets: B-$10.99/$19.99 (Sun)
L-$14.99/$19.99 (Sun)
D-$20.99/$23.99 (Fri/Sat)
Casino Size: 119,309 Square Feet
Other Games: SB, RB, B, MB, P, PGP, MS, TCP, LIR, K, BG
Special Features: Affiliated with Station Casinos. 16-screen Regal movie complex. 72-lane bowling alley. Childcare center. Full-service spa.

Rio Suites Hotel & Casino
3700 W. Flamingo Road
Las Vegas, Nevada 89103
(702) 252-7777
Website: www.playrio.com

Toll-Free Number: (800) 752-9746
Reservation Number: (866) 746-7671
Suites: 2,563 Price Range: $35-$289
Restaurants: 9
Buffets: B/L- $32.99 (Sat/Sun)
D-$32.99/$34.99 (Fri-Sun)
Seafood Buffet: $20 Upgrade Fee
Casino Size: 117,330 Square Feet
Other Games: SB, RB, MB, P, PG, UTH
MS, PGP, LIR, TCP, C4P, FCP
Special Features: Affiliated with Caesars Entertainment. 20-store shopping mall. Three wedding chapels. *Penn and Teller* stage show.

Sam's Town Hotel & Gambling Hall
5111 Boulder Highway
Las Vegas, Nevada 89122
(702) 456-7777
Website: www.samstownlv.com

Toll-Free Number: (800) 897-8696
Reservation Number: (800) 634-6371
Rooms: 620 Price Range: $38-$160
Suites: 30 Price Range: $89-$209
Restaurants: 6
Buffets: B-$8.99/$14.99 (Sat/Sun)
L-$11.99/$14.99 (Sat/Sun)
D-$12.99/$28.99 (Fri)
Casino Size: 120,681 Square Feet
Other Games: SB, RB, P, LIR,
TCP, K, BG, PGP
Senior Discount: Various Wed if 50+
Special Features: Affiliated with Boyd Gaming. 500-space RV park ($22-$38 per night). Indoor promenade with free laser-light show. 24-hour 56-lane bowling center. 18-theater cinema complex. Childcare center. Buffet discount for players club members.

Santa Fe Station Hotel & Casino
4949 North Rancho Drive
Las Vegas, Nevada 89130
(702) 658-4900
Website: santafestation.sclv.com

Toll Free Number: (866) 767-7770
Rooms: 200 Price Range: $49-$159
Restaurants: 5
Buffets: B-$10.99/$16.99 (Sun)
L-$10.99/$16.99 (Sun)
D-$16.99/$21.99 (Fri/Sat)
Casino Size: 156,401 Square Feet
Other Games: SB, RB, MB, P, PGP,
TCP, UTH, K, BG
Senior Discount: Various Wed if 50+
Special Features: Affiliated with Station Casinos. 60-lane bowling center. 16-screen cinema. Childcare center.

Silver Sevens Hotel and Casino
4100 Paradise Road
Las Vegas, Nevada 89169
(702) 733-7000
Website: www.silversevenscasino.com

Reservation Number: (800) 640-9777
Rooms: 370 Price Range: $49-$129
Restaurants: 2
Buffets: B/L- $12.99 (Sat/Sun)
D- $12.99/$21.99 (Fri/Sat)
Casino Size: 27,225 Square Feet
Other Games: SB, RB, PGP
Senior Discount: Various Wed if 50+
Special features: Buffet discount for players club members.

Silverton Casino Hotel Lodge
3333 Blue Diamond Road
Las Vegas, Nevada 89139
(702) 263-7777
Website: www.silvertoncasino.com

Toll-Free Number: (800) 588-7711
Room Reservations: (866) 722-4608
Rooms: 292 Price Range: $49-$249
Suites: 8 Price Range: $139-$319
Restaurants: 8
Buffets: L- $10.99/$19.99 (Sat/Sun)
D- $16.99/$32.99 (Thu)$22.99 (Fri)/$21.99 (Sat)
Casino Size: 71,829 Square Feet
Other Games: SB, RB, PGP, TCP, UTH
Special Features: Starbucks coffeehouse. Johnny Rockets.

Free Things To See In Las Vegas!

The Fountains at Bellagio

More than one thousand fountains dance in front of the Bellagio hotel, creating a union of water, music and light. The display spans more than 1,000 feet, with water soaring as high as 240 feet. The fountains are choreographed to music ranging from classical and operatic pieces to songs from Broadway shows.

Showtimes are every 30 minutes from 3 p.m (noon on Sat/Sun) until 8 p.m. After 8 p.m. the shows start every 15 minutes until midnight. A list of all musical selections is available on the Bellagio website at: www.bellagio.com.

Slots-A-Fun Casino
2890 Las Vegas Boulevard S.
Las Vegas, Nevada 89109
(702) 734-0410

Restaurants: 1 Subway and Pizza Shop
Casino Size: 16,733 Square Feet
Other Games: No table games
Special Features: Affiliated with Circus Circus Casino.

SLS Hotel & Casino
2535 Las Vegas Boulevard S.
Las Vegas, Nevada 89109
(702) 761-7000
Website: www.slslasvegas.com

Reservation Number: (888) 627-8173
Rooms: 1,350 Price Range: $79-$199
Suites: 250 Price Range: $179-$529
Restaurants: 7
Casino Size: 60,000 Square Feet
Other games: SB, RB, B, MB, PGP, B6, CW, UTH, TCP
Special Features: Hotel is affiliated with Starwood.

South Point Hotel and Casino
9777 Las Vegas Boulevard S.
Las Vegas, Nevada 89183
(702) 796-7111
Website: www.southpointcasino.com

Toll-Free Number: (866) 796-7111
Rooms: 1,325 Price Range: $59-$199
Suites: 25 Price Range: $146-$999
Restaurants: 11
Buffets: B-$9.95/$19.95 (Sat/Sun)
L-$13.95 /$19.95 (Sat/Sun)
D-$19.95/$29.95 (Fri/Sat)
Casino Size: 137,232 Square Feet
Other Games: SB, RB, MB, P, MS, PGP, TCP, UTH, BG
Special Features: 16-screen movie complex. Equestrian center with 4,400-seat arena and 1,200 stalls. 64-lane bowling center. Childcare facility. Health spa.

Stratosphere Hotel & Casino
2000 Las Vegas Boulevard S.
Las Vegas, Nevada 89104
(702) 380-7777
Website: www.stratospherehotel.com

Reservation Number: (800) 998-6937
Rooms: 2,444 Price Range: $76-$129
Suites: 250 Price Range: $159-$229
Restaurants: 7
Buffets: B/L- $16.99/$22.99 (Sat/Sun)
D- $22.99/$23.99 (Thu/Fri/Sun)/$30.99 (Sat)
Casino Size: 80,000 Square Feet
Other Games: SB, RB, P, B6,
PGP, LIR, TCP, CSP
Senior Discount: Tower discount if 55+
Special Features: 109 story Indoor/Outdoor Observation Deck (admission charge). Revolving restaurant at top of tower. Shopping arcade with 30 retail stores.

Suncoast Hotel and Casino
9090 Alta Drive
Las Vegas, Nevada 89145
(702) 636-7111
Website: www.suncoastcasino.com

Reservation Number: (866) 636-7111
Rooms: 432 Price Range: $60-$195
Suites: 40 Price Range: $149-$294
Restaurants: 7
Buffets: B/L-$11.99/$17.99 (Sun)
D-$16.99/$26.99 (Fri)/$21.99 (Sat)
Casino Size: 95,898 Square Feet
Other Games: SB, RB, MB, P, PGP,
TCP, UTH, BG
Senior Discount: Various Wed if 50+
Special Features: Affiliated with Boyd Gaming. 64-lane bowling center. 16-screen movie theater. Childcare center. Seattle's Best coffee shop. Free shuttle to airport.

Treasure Island (TI)
3300 Las Vegas Boulevard S.
Las Vegas, Nevada 89109
(702) 894-7111
Website: www.treasureisland.com

Reservation Number: (800) 944-7444
Rooms: 2,665 Price Range: $88-$179
Suites: 220 Price Range: $129-$259
Restaurants: 9
Buffets: B- $20.9/$27.95 (Sat/Sun)
L- $24.95/$27.95 (Sat/Sun)
D- $30.95/$32.95 (Fri/sat)
Casino Size: 50,335 Square Feet
Other Games: SB, RB, B, MB, P, PG,
PGP, LIR, TCP, B6, K
Special Features: Health spa/salon. Two wedding chapels. Starbucks. Krispy Kreme. Cirque du Soleil's *Mystere* stage show. Marvel comics *Avengers S.T.A.T.I.O.N.* attraction

Tropicana Resort & Casino
3801 Las Vegas Boulevard S.
Las Vegas, Nevada 89109
(702) 739-2222
Website: www.troplv.com

Reservation Number: (888) 381-8767
Rooms: 1,877 Price Range: $74-$139
Suites: 115 Price Range: $275-$1,599
Restaurants: 5
Casino Size: 44,570 Square Feet
Other Games: SB, RB, MB, PGP, B6,
LIR, TCP, MS, UTH
Senior Discount: Various if 65+
Special Features: Wedding chapel. Comedy club.

Tuscany Suites & Casino
255 East Flamingo Road
Las Vegas, Nevada 89169
(702) 893-8933
Website: www.tuscanylv.com

Reservation Number: (877) 887-2261
Suites: 760 Price Range: $55-$2279
Restaurants: 4
Casino Size: 22,450 Square Feet
Other Games: SB
Senior Discount: Various Thu if 50+
Special Features: All suite hotel. Wedding chapel.

Free Things To See In Las Vegas!

Volcano at The Mirage

Another fun Vegas attraction that won't cost you anything is the iconic volcano at the Mirage. The volcano first opened in 1989, but received a $25 million update in 2008. The volcano's choreographed, fire eruptions occur nightly and feature an original soundtrack put together by Grateful Dead drummer Mickey Hart and Indian composer Zakir Hussain. This, combined with sounds from actual volcanic eruptions create a truly thrilling experience. The volcano is located outside the Mirage (you can't miss it!) and eruptions occur at 8 p.m. and 9 p.m. Sunday-Thursday and 8 p.m., 9 p.m. and 10 p.m. Friday and Saturday.

The Venetian Resort Hotel Casino
3355 Las Vegas Boulevard S.
Las Vegas, Nevada 89109
(702) 414-1000
Website: www.venetian.com

Reservation Number: (866) 659-9643
Suites: 4,046 Price Range: $225-$5,000
Restaurants: 42
Casino Size: 138,684 Square Feet
Other Games: SB, RB, S21, B, MB, P, PG, PGP, CSP, C4P, LIR, UTH, TCP, CW, B6
Special Features: Attached to The Palazzo. Recreates city of Venice with canals, gondoliers and replica Campanile Tower, St. Mark's Square, Doge's Palace and Rialto Bridge. 90 retail stores. Madame Tussaud's Wax Museum. Canyon Ranch Spa. *Human Nature* stage show.

Westgate Las Vegas Resort & Casino
3000 Paradise Road
Las Vegas, Nevada 89109
(702) 732-5111
Website: www.westgatedestinations.com

Reservation Number: (888) 796-3564
Rooms: 2,956 Price Range: $65-$135
Suites: 305 Price Range: $189-$1,650
Restaurants: 9
Buffets: B- $16.99/$23.99 (Sat/Sun) L- $19.99/$23.99 (Sat/Sun) D- $24.99
Casino Size: 74,725 Square Feet
Other Games: SB, RB, B, MB, PGP, B6, P, UTH
Special Features: World's largest race and sports book. Health club. Benihana restaurant.

Wild Wild West Casino
3330 West Tropicana Avenue
Las Vegas, Nevada 89103
(702) 740-0000
Website: wildfire.sclv.com

Reservation Number: (702) 739-5003
Rooms: 262 Price Range: $49-$139
Restaurants: 1
Casino Size: 11,250 Square Feet
Other Games: SB, No craps
Special Features: Affiliated with Station Casinos. 24-hour Denny's restaurant. Hotel is Days Inn. 15-acre truck plaza.

Wynn Las Vegas
3131 Las Vegas Boulevard S.
Las Vegas, Nevada 89109
(702) 770-7000
Website: www.wynnlasvegas.com

Toll-Free Number: (888) 320-7123
Rooms: 2,359 Prices: $150-$639
Suites: 351 Prices: $199-$5,600
Restaurants: 18
Buffets: B- $24.99/$35.99 (Sat/Sun)
L- $26.99/$35.99 (Sat/Sun)
D- $42.99/$49.99 (Fri/Sat)
Self-Parking: $7 (1-2 Hrs)/$12 (2-4 Hrs)/
$15 (4-24 Hrs)
Valet Parking: $15 (0-4 Hrs)/$20 (4-24 Hrs)
Casino Size: 186,187 Square Feet
Other Games: SB, RB, B, MB, P, PG,
PGP, LIR, TCP, CW, MS, UTH,B6
Special Features: 150-foot man-made mountain with five-story waterfall. 18-hole golf course.*Le Reve* stage show. Spa and salon.

Laughlin

Map location: **#2** (on the Colorado River, 100 miles south of Las Vegas and directly across the river from Bullhead City, Arizona)

Laughlin is named after Don Laughlin, who owns the Riverside Hotel & Casino and originally settled there in 1966. The area offers many water sport activities on the Colorado River as well as at nearby Lake Mojave.

For Laughlin tourism information call: (800) 452-8445. You can also visit their Website at: www.visitlaughlin.com.

Here's information, as supplied by Nevada's State Gaming Control Board, showing the slot machine payback percentages for all of Laughlin's casinos for the fiscal year beginning July 1, 2016 and ending June 30, 2017:

Denomination	Payback %
1¢ Slots	89.13
5¢ Slots	92.35
25¢ Slots	93.96
$1 Slots	94.83
$1 Megabucks	86.86
$5 Slots	94.01
All Slots	92.31

These numbers reflect the percentage of money returned to the players on each denomination of machine. All electronic machines including slots, video poker and video keno are included in these numbers.

Optional games in the casino listings include: sports book (SB), race book (RB), Spanish 21 (S21), baccarat (B), mini-baccarat (MB), poker (P), pai gow poker (PGP), Caribbean stud poker (CSP), let it ride (LIR), three-card poker (TCP), four card poker (FCP), ultimate Texas hold'em (UTH), Texas hold'em bonus (THB), keno (K), sic bo (SIC), Mississippis stud (MS), big 6 wheel (B6) and bingo (BG).

Aquarius Casino Resort
1900 S. Casino Drive
Laughlin, Nevada 89029
(702) 298-5111
Website: www.aquariuscasinoresort.com

Reservation Number: (800) 662-5825
Rooms: 1,900 Price Range: $49-$189
Suites: 90 Price Range: $119-$299
Restaurants: 6
Buffets: B/L- $13.19/$21.59 (Sun)
D-$16.79/$23.89 (Fri)/$20.39 (Sat)
Casino Size: 57,070 Square Feet
Other Games: SB, RB, LIR, TCP, PGP, UTH
Overnight RV Parking: No
Special Features: Outback Steakhouse. 3,300-seat amphitheater.

Colorado Belle Hotel Casino & Microbrewery
2100 S. Casino Drive
Laughlin, Nevada 89029
(702) 298-4000
Website: www.coloradobelle.com

Reservation Number: (866) 352-3553
Rooms: 1,124 Price Range: $45-$89
Suites: 49 Price Range: $105-$175
Restaurants: 3
Buffets: B- $10.99/$14.99 (Sun)/$19.99 (Sun)
D-$13.99/$24.99 (Sat)/$15.99 (Sun)
Casino Size: 44,953 Square Feet
Other Games: SB, RB, P, TCP, LIR, K
Overnight RV Parking: No
Special Features: Microbrewery. Spa.

Don Laughlin's
Riverside Resort Hotel & Casino
1650 S. Casino Drive
Laughlin, Nevada 89029
(702) 298-2535
Website: www.riversideresort.com

Reservation Number: (800) 227-3849
Rooms: 1,405 Price Range: $49-$119
Executive Rooms: 93 Price Range: $109-$299
Restaurants: 7
Buffets: B-$8.99 L-$9.99/$15.99 (Sun)
D-$15.99/$19.99 (Fri/Sat)
Casino Size: 89,106 Square Feet
Other Games: SB, RB, P, LIR, PGP
TCP, K, BG, UTH
Overnight RV Parking: Must use RV park
Special Features: 740-space RV park ($22-$28) per night). Six-screen cinema. Free classic car exhibit. 34-lane bowling center. Childcare center.

Edgewater Hotel Casino
2020 S. Casino Drive
Laughlin, Nevada 89029
(702) 298-2453
Website: www.edgewater-casino.com

Reservation Number: (866) 352-3553
Rooms: 1,420 Price Range: $29-$129
Suites: 23 Price Range: $95-$195
Restaurants: 5
Buffets: B- $9.99/$14.99 (Sun)
L- $10.99/$14.99 (Sun)
D- $15.99/$22.99 (Fri)/$20.99 (Sat)
Casino Size: 45,927 Square Feet
Other Games: SB, RB, P, PGP, TCP, LIR
Overnight RV Parking: No

Golden Nugget Laughlin
2300 S. Casino Drive
Laughlin, Nevada 89029
(702) 298-7111
Website: www.goldennugget.com

Reservation Number: (800) 237-1739
Rooms: 300 Price Range: $45-$129
Suites: 4 Price Range: $150-$495
Restaurants: 3
Casino Size: 32,600 Square Feet
Other Games: SB, RB, PGP, TCP, K, LIR
Overnight RV Parking: Free/RV Dump: No

Harrah's Laughlin Casino & Hotel
2900 S. Casino Drive
Laughlin, Nevada 89029
(702) 298-4600
Website: www.harrahslaughlin.com

Reservation Number: (800) 427-7247
Rooms: 1,451 Price Range: $29-$250
Suites: 115 Price Range: $179-$299
Restaurants: 5
Buffets: B-$13.99/$17.99 (Sun)
L-$15.99/$17.99 (Sun)
D-$18.99/$20.99 (Thu/Sun)/$28.99 (Fri)/ $23.99 (Sat)
Casino Size: 56,357 Square Feet
Other Games: SB, RB, P, PGP,
TCP, LIR, K
Overnight RV Parking: No
Special Features: Affiliated with Caesars Entertainment. Salon and day spa. Beach and pools. 3,000-seat amphitheater. Cinnabon. Starbucks. Buffet discount for players club members.

Laughlin River Lodge
2700 S. Casino Drive
Laughlin, Nevada 89029
(702) 298-2242
Website: www.laughlinriverlodge.com

Toll-Free Number: (800) 835-7904
Rooms: 995 Price Range: $75-$159
Suites: 8 Price Range: $119-$295
Restaurants: 2
Buffets: B-$9.95 (Sat/Sun)
D-$11.95 (Fri/Sat)
Casino Size: 29,488 Square Feet
Other Games: BG, No table games
Overnight RV Parking: Free/RV Dump: No
Special Features: Health spa.

Pioneer Hotel & Gambling Hall
2200 S. Casino Drive
Laughlin, Nevada 89029
(702) 298-2442
Website: www.pioneerlaughlin.com

Reservation Number: (800) 634-3469
Rooms: 416 Price Range: $32-$110
Suites: 20 Price Range: $95-$149
Restaurants: 2
Casino Size: 16,300 Square Feet
Other Games: SB, RB, TCP
Overnight RV Parking: Free/RV Dump: No
Special Features: Western-themed casino.

Tropicana Laughlin
2121 S. Casino Drive
Laughlin, Nevada 89029
(702) 298-4200
Website: www.troplaughlin.com

Toll-Free Number: (800) 343-4533
Rooms: 1,501 Price Range: $45-$139
Suites: 55 Price Range: $79-$179
Restaurants: 5
Buffets: B- $11.49/$17.99 (Sat/Sun)
D- $13.99/$22.99 (Fri/Sat)
Casino Size: 52,840 Square Feet
Other Games: SB, RB, PGP, BG,
TCP, LIR, MS
Overnight RV Parking: Free/RV Dump: No
Senior Discount: Join Club 50 for discounts
Special Features: Train-shaped swimming pool.

Lovelock

Map Location: **#18** (92 miles N.E. of Reno on I-80)

C Punch Inn & Casino
1440 Cornell Avenue
Lovelock, Nevada 89419
(775) 273-2971
Website: www.cpunchinnandcasino.com

Rooms: 74 Price Range: $79-$99
Spa Rooms: 2 Price Range: $99-$119
Restaurants: 1
Casino Size: 7,000 Square Feet
Other Games: SB, No table games
Overnight RV Parking: Free/RV Dump: No
Special Features: Fully operational cattle ranch and alfalfa farm.

Mesquite

Map Location: **#19** (77 miles N.E. of Las Vegas on I-15 at the Arizona border)

Here's information, as supplied by Nevada's State Gaming Control Board, showing the slot machine payback percentages for all of the Mesquite area casinos for the fiscal year beginning July 1, 2016 and ending June 30, 2017:

Denomination	Payback %
1¢ Slots	90.39
5¢ Slots	96.01
25¢ Slots	95.30
$1 Slots	96.02
$1 Megabucks	86.30
All Slots	94.14

These numbers reflect the percentage of money returned on each denomination of machine and encompass all electronic machines including slots, video poker and video keno.

CasaBlanca Hotel-Casino-Golf-Spa
950 W. Mesquite Boulevard
Mesquite, Nevada 89027
(702) 346-7529
Website: www.casablancaresort.com

Toll-Free Number: (877) 438-2929
Reservation Number: (800) 459-7529
Rooms: 500 Price Range: $39-$79
Suites: 18 Price Range: $69-$199
Restaurants: 3
Buffets: B/L-$8.99 (Sat/Sun)
D-$16.99 (Fri)/$17.99 (Sat)
Casino Size: 27,000 Square Feet
Other Games: SB, RB, PGP, TCP
Overnight RV Parking: Must use RV park
Special Features: 45-space RV park ($25-$35 per night). 18-hole golf course. Health spa.

Eureka Casino & Hotel
275 Mesa Boulevard
Mesquite, Nevada 89027
(702) 346-4600
Website: www.eurekamesquite.com

Reservation Number: (800) 346-4611
Rooms: 192 Price Range: $69-$129
Suites: 18 Price Range: $149-$279
Restaurants: 4
Buffets: B-$16.99 (Sun)
D-$21.99 (Fri)/$16.99 (Sat)
Casino Size: 40,285 Square Feet
Other Games: SB, RB, P, PGP, TCP, LIR, BG
Overnight RV Parking: No
Senior Discount: Various Tue if 55+
Special Features: Spa. Buffet discount with players club card.

Virgin River Hotel/Casino/Bingo
100 E. Pioneer Boulevard
Mesquite, Nevada 89027
(702) 346-7777
Website: www.virginriver.com

Toll-Free Number: (877) 438-2929
Rooms: 720 Price Range: $27-$59
Suites: 2 Price Range: $250
Restaurants: 2
Buffets: B-$6.99 L-$8.99/$10.99 (Sun)
D-$12.99 /$14.99 (Tue/Sat)/
$16.99 (Fri)
Casino Size: 37,000 Square Feet
Other Games: SB, RB, PGP, TCP,
UTH, K, BG
Overnight RV Parking: Free/RV Dump: No
Special Features: 24-lane bowling center.

Minden

Map Location: **#14** (42 miles S. of Reno on Hwy. 395)

Carson Valley Inn
1627 Highway 395 N.
Minden, Nevada 89423
(775) 782-9711
Website: www.cvinn.com

Reservation Number: (800) 321-6983
Hotel Rooms: 146 Price Range: $85-$115
Hotel Suites: 7 Price Range: $129-$189
Lodge Rooms: 75 Price Range: $85-$99
Lodge Suites: 5 Price Range: $99-$119
Restaurants: 3
Casino Size: 22,800 Square Feet
Other Games: SB, RB, P,
TCP, no roulette
Overnight RV Parking: Free/Dump: $5
Special Features: 59-space RV park ($29-$49 per night). 24-hour convenience store. Wedding chapel.

N. Las Vegas

Map Location: **#20** (5 miles N.E. of the Las Vegas Strip on Las Vegas Blvd. N.)

Aliante Casino Hotel & Spa
7300 Aliante Parkway
North Las Vegas, Nevada 89084
(702) 692-7777
Website: www.aliantegaming.com

Toll-Free Number: (877) 477-7627
Rooms: 202 Price Range: $89-$139
Restaurants: 5
Buffets: B-$8.99/$14.99 (Sat/Sun) L- $11.99
D- $15.99/$26.99 (Fri)/$21.99 (Sat)
Casino Size: 125,000 Square Feet
Other Games: SB, RB, TCP, PGP, BG
Overnight RV Parking: No
Special Features: Affiliated with Boyd Gaming. 16-screen Regal Theater.

Bighorn Casino
3016 E. Lake Mead Boulevard
N. Las Vegas, Nevada 89030
(702) 642-1940

Restaurants: 1
Casino Size: 3,740 Square Feet
Other Games: SB, No craps or roulette
Overnight RV Parking: No

Cannery Hotel & Casino
2121 E Craig Road
N. Las Vegas, Nevada 89030
(702) 507-5700
Website: www.cannerycasino.com

Toll-Free Number: (866) 999-4899
Rooms: 201 Price Range: $79-$149
Restaurants: 6
Buffets: B- $8.99 (Sat/Sun)
L- $10.99/$12.99 (Sat/Sun)
D- $15.99/$16.99 (Thu/Fri/Sat)
Casino Size: 79,485 Square Feet
Other Games: RB, SB, P, PGP, BG
Overnight RV Parking: No
Special Features: Affiliated with Boyd Gaming. Property is themed to resemble a 1940's canning factory. Buffet discount for players club members

Fiesta Rancho Casino Hotel
2400 N. Rancho Drive
N. Las Vegas, Nevada 89130
(702) 631-7000
Website: www.fiestarancholasvegas.com

Reservation Number: (800) 731-7333
Rooms: 100 Price Range: $45-$129
Restaurants: 3
Buffets: B- $13.99 (Sat/Sun)
L- $9.99 D- $13.99
Casino Size: 59,951 Square Feet
Other Games: SB, RB, B, MB, PGP, K, BG
Overnight RV Parking: Yes/Dump: No
Senior Discount: Various Wed if 50+
Special Features: Affiliated with Station Casinos. Ice skating arena. Coffee bar. Smoke shop. Buffet discount for players club members.

Jerry's Nugget
1821 Las Vegas Boulevard North
N. Las Vegas, Nevada 89030
(702) 399-3000
Website: www.jerrysnugget.com

Restaurants: 1
Casino Size: 32,511 Square Feet
Other Games: SB, RB, K, BG
Overnight RV Parking: No
Senior Discount: Various Tue if 50+
Special Features: Bakery.

Lucky Club Casino
3227 Civic Center Drive
N. Las Vegas, Nevada 89030
(702) 399-3297
Website: www.luckyclublv.com

Toll-Free Number: (877) 333-9291
Room Reservations: (877) 333-9291
Rooms: 92 Price Range: $39-$69
Suites: 3 Price Range: $100-$129
Restaurants: 1
Casino Size: 16,650 Square Feet
Other Games: SB, RB, No roulette
Overnight RV Parking: No
Senior Discount: Various Sun if 50
Special Features: Closest hotel/casino to Las Vegas Motor Speedway. $9.99 steak & lobster dinner.

The Poker Palace
2757 Las Vegas Blvd. North
N. Las Vegas, Nevada 89030
(702) 649-3799
Website: www.pokerpalace.net

Restaurants: 1
Casino Size: 25,900 Square Feet
Other Games: SB, RB, P, BG,
No craps or roulette
Overnight RV Parking: No

Silver Nugget
2140 Las Vegas Boulevard North
N. Las Vegas, Nevada 89030
(702) 399-1111
Website: www.silvernuggetlv.com

Restaurants: 1
Casino Size: 21,000 Square Feet
Other Games: SB, RB, No roulette or craps
Overnight RV Parking: No
Special Features: 24-lane bowling center.

Texas Station Gambling Hall & Hotel
2101 Texas Star Lane
N. Las Vegas, Nevada 89032
(702) 631-1000
Website: www.texasstation.com

Toll-Free Number: (800) 654-8804
Rooms: 200 Price Range: $39-$139
Restaurants: 4
Buffets: B-$9.99/$15.99 (Sun)
L-$11.99/$15.99 (Sun)
D-$15.99/$16.99 (Thu/Sat)/$18.99 (Fri)
Casino Size: 123,045 Square Feet
Other Games: SB, RB, PGP, K, BG
Overnight RV Parking: No
Senior Discount: Various Wed if 50+
Special Features: Affiliated with Station Casinos. 18-screen movie theater. 60-lane bowling center. Childcare center. Two wedding chapels. 2,000-seat events center. Buffet discount for players club members.

Pahrump

Map Location: **#21** (59 miles W. of Las Vegas on Hwy. 160)

Gold Town Casino
771 S. Frontage Road
Pahrump, Nevada 89048
(775) 751-7777
Website: www.gtowncasino.com

Restaurants: 1
Casino Size: 12,000 Square Feet
Other Games: BG, No table games
Overnight RV Parking: Yes. Free/RV Dump: No
Senior Discount: Various Sun if 55+
Special Features: 24-hour convenience store and gas station. Discount liquor store.

Pahrump Nugget Hotel & Gambling Hall
681 S. Highway 160
Pahrump, Nevada 89048
(775) 751-6500
Website: www.pahrumpnugget.com

Toll Free Number: (866) 751-6500
Rooms: 64 Price Range: $79-$139
Suites: 5 Price Range: $149-$179
Restaurants: 2
Casino Size: 17,400 Square Feet
Other Games: SB, RB, P, UTH,
BG, No roulette
Overnight RV Parking: No
Senior Discount: Various Sun if 55+
Special Features: 24-lane bowling center. Childcare center.

Saddle West Hotel/Casino & RV Park
1220 S. Highway 160
Pahrump, Nevada 89048
(775) 727-1111
Website: www.saddlewest.com

Reservation Number: (800) 433-3987
Rooms: 148 Price Range: $39-$85
Suites: 10 Price Range: $89-$129
Restaurants: 2
Buffets: B/L- $8.95
D- $11.95/$16.95 (Mon/Sat/$18.96 (Fri)
Casino Size: 15,496 Square Feet
Other Games: SB, RB, BG, No table games
Overnight RV Parking: Must use RV park
Special Features: 80-space RV park ($25 per night).

Primm

Map Location: **#6** (25 miles S.W. of Las Vegas on I-15; 9 miles from the California border)

Buffalo Bill's Resort & Casino
31700 Las Vegas Boulevard S.
Primm, Nevada 89019
(702) 382-1212
Website: www.primmvalleyresorts.com

Toll-Free Number: (800) 386-7867
Reservation Number: (888) 774-6668
Rooms: 1,242 Price Range: $29-$95
Suites: 15 Price Range: $89-$125
Restaurants: 4
Casino Size: 61,372 Square Feet
Other Games: SB, RB, P, PGP
Overnight RV Parking: Free/RV Dump: No
Special Features: Amusement park with roller coaster, flume ride and water slides. Movie theater. 6,500-seat arena. Free monorail to Primm Valley and Whiskey Pete's.

Primm Valley Resort & Casino
31900 Las Vegas Boulevard S.
Primm, Nevada 89019
(702) 382-1212
Website: www.primmvalleyresorts.com

Toll-Free Number: (800) 386-7867
Reservation Number: (888) 774-6668
Rooms: 661 Price Range: $35-$105
Suites: 31 Price Range: $113-$178
Restaurants: 4
Buffets: B-$12.49 L-$14.49 D-$17.99
Casino Size: 35,279 Square Feet
Other Games: SB, RB, PGP
Overnight RV Parking: Free/RV Dump: No
Special Features: Free monorail to Whiskey Pete's and Buffalo Bill's. Bonnie & Clyde's "death" car on display. Buffet closed Mon-Thu.

Whiskey Pete's Hotel & Casino
100 Primm Boulevard West
Primm, Nevada 89019
(702) 382-1212
Website: www.primmvalleyresorts.com

Toll-Free Number: (800) 386-7867
Reservation Number: (888) 774-6668
Rooms: 777 Price Range: $39-$109
Suites: 4 Price Range: $139-$219
Restaurants: 2
Casino Size: 36,400 Square Feet
Other Games: SB, RB, P
Overnight RV Parking: Free/RV Dump: No
Special Features: Free monorail to Primm Valley and Buffalo Bill's. Starbucks coffeehouse.

The arch in downtown Reno that welcomes visitors to "The Biggest Little City in the World" is the city's most famous landmark.

Reno

Map Location: **#4** (near the California border, 58 miles N.E. of Lake Tahoe and 32 miles N. of Carson City).

Reno may be best known for its neon arch on Virginia Street which welcomes visitors to "The Biggest Little City in the World." The current arch is actually the fourth one since the original arch was built in 1927. The area also houses the nation's largest car collection at the National Automobile Museum.

For Reno information call the Reno/Sparks Convention & Visitors Authority at (800) 367-7366 or go to: www.visitrenotahoe.com.

Overnight parking of an RV in a casino parking lot is prohibited in Reno.

Here's information, as supplied by Nevada's State Gaming Control Board, showing the slot machine payback percentages for all of the Reno area casinos for the fiscal year beginning July 1, 2016 and ending June 30, 2017:

Denomination	Payback %
1¢ Slots	92.78
5¢ Slots	95.97
25¢ Slots	92.69
$1 Slots	95.70
$1 Megabucks	86.43
$5 Slots	94.90
All Slots	94.68

These numbers reflect the percentage of money returned on each denomination of machine and encompass all electronic machines including slots, video poker and video keno.

Optional games in the casino listings include: sports book (SB), race book (RB), Spanish 21 (S21), baccarat (B), mini-baccarat (MB), pai gow (PG), poker (P), pai gow poker (PGP), Caribbean stud poker (CSP), let it ride (LIR), three-card poker (TCP), four card poker (FCP), ultimate Texas hold'em (UTH), Texas hold'em bonus (THB), big 6 wheel (B6), keno (K) and bingo (BG).

Atlantis Casino Resort
3800 S. Virginia Street
Reno, Nevada 89502
(775) 825-4700
Website: www.atlantiscasino.com

Reservation Number: (800) 723-6500
Rooms: 975 Price Range: $69-$229
Suites: 120 Price Range: $99-$379
Restaurants: 8
Buffets: B-$15.99/$18.99 (Sat)/$29.99 (Sun)
L-$17.99/$18.99 (Sat) /$29.99 (Sun)
D-$24.99/$36.99 (Fri/Sat)
Casino Size: 64,814 Square Feet
Other Games: SB, RB, B, MB, P, PGP, TCP, UTH, K
Senior Discount: Various Mon if 55+
Special Features: Health spa and salon.

Bonanza Casino
4720 N. Virginia Street
Reno, Nevada 89506
(775) 323-2724
Website: www.bonanzacasino.com

Restaurants: 2
Casino Size: 12,484 Square Feet
Other Games: SB, RB, no roulette

Circus Circus Hotel Casino/Reno
500 N. Sierra Street
Reno, Nevada 89503
(775) 329-0711
Website: www.circusreno.com

Reservation Number: (800) 648-5010
Rooms: 1,464 Price Range: $49-$129
Suites: 108 Price Range: $79-$219
Restaurants: 4
Casino Size: 66,679 Square Feet
Other Games: SB, RB, PGP, MS, TCP, THB
Special Features: Affiliated with Eldorado Resorts. Free circus acts. Carnival games. 24-hour gift shop/liquor store. Food court with four fast food outlets.

Club Cal-Neva
38 E. Second Street
Reno, Nevada 89501
(775) 323-1046
Website: www.clubcalneva.com

Toll-Free Number (877) 777-7303
Restaurants: 3
Casino Size: 40,140 Square Feet
Other Games: SB, RB, P, PGP, K

Diamond's Casino
1010 E. 6th Street
Reno, Nevada 89512
(775) 786-5151
Website: www.diamondscasinoreno.com

Ramada Reservations: (888) 288-4982
Rooms: 280 Price Range: $50-$109
Suites: 6 Price Range: $100-$150
Restaurants: 2
Casino Size: 8,000 Square Feet
Other Games: SB, RB, no roulette or craps

Eldorado Hotel Casino
345 N. Virginia Street
Reno, Nevada 89501
(775) 786-5700
Website: www.eldoradoreno.com

Toll-Free Number: (800) 879-8879
Rooms: 817 Price Range: $69-$129
Suites: 127 Price Range: $119-$329
Restaurants: 7
Buffets: B- $11.99/$18.99 (Sat/Sun)
L- $13.99/$18.99 (Sat/Sun)
D- $19.88/$28.99 (Fri-Sun)
Casino Size: 76,500 Square Feet
Other Games: SB, RB, MB, PG, PGP, P, K
Senior Discount: Food discounts if 55+
Special Features: In-house coffee roasting. Pasta shop. Microbrewery. Bakery. Butcher shop. Gelato factory.

The Best Places To Play in Reno/Tahoe

Roulette- The house edge on a single-zero wheel cuts the house edge from 5.26% down to a more reasonable 2.70%. Unfortunately, there are no casinos in Reno/Tahoe that offer single-zero roulette.

Craps- Almost all Reno/Tahoe area casinos offer double odds, or 3x/4x/5x on their crap games. The casino offering the highest odds is The Lakeside Inn in Lake Tahoe which offers 10X odds.

Blackjack- There's good news and bad news for blackjack players in Northern Nevada. The good news is that there is an abundance of single-deck and double-deck games available. The bad news is that all casinos in the Reno/Tahoe area hit soft 17. This results in a slightly higher advantage (.20%) for the casinos. Additionally, some casinos may also restrict your double-downs to two-card totals of 10 or 11 only. The following recommendations apply to basic strategy players.

For single-deck games you should always look for casinos that pay the standard 3-to-2 for blackjacks. Several casinos only pay 6-to-5 for blackjack and this increases the casino edge tremendously. The casino advantage in these games is around 1.5% and they should be avoided.

The best single-deck games can be found at Boomtown and Western Village where they allow you to double down on any first two cards, split any pair and resplit any pair (except aces). The casino edge in this game is .18%. (NOTE: There are numerous casinos that offer a game similar to this one except they will only allow you to double down on totals of 10 or more. This raises the casino edge in this game to .44%).

There are six Reno-area casinos that tie for best place to play double-deck blackjack: Atlantis, Cal-Neva, Eldorado, Grand Sierra, Nugget and Silver Legacy. Their two-deck games have the following rules: double down on any first two cards, split any pair, and resplit any pair (except aces). This works out to a casino edge of .53%. The Hard Rock in Lake Tahoe also has this game.

The best six-deck game can be found in Reno at the Silver Legacy The game's edge is .32% with these rules: double down on any two or more cards, split any pair, resplit any pair (including aces) and double allowed after split.

Next best is a game found at four Lake Tahoe casinos: Harrah's, Harveys, Hyatt Regency and Lakeside Inn. The casino edge here is .56% with the following rules: double down on any two cards, split any pair, resplit any pair (including aces) and double allowed after split.

If you take away resplitting of aces from the previous game then you have a game with a casino edge of .63% which is offered at most other casinos, including: Atlantis, Circus Circus, Eldorado, Grand Sierra, Nugget, the Peppermill and Sands Regency.

Video Poker- Smart video poker players know that some of the best varieties of machines to look for are: 8/5 Bonus Poker (99.17 % return), 9/6 Jacks or Better (99.54% return), 10/6 Double Double Bonus (100.07% return), 10/7 Double Bonus (100.17% return) and full-pay Deuces Wild (100.76% return).

All of these games are available in Northern Nevada, with the exception of full-pay Deuces Wild, which is hard to find. A slightly lesser-paying version, known as Not So Ugly Deuces (NSUD), which returns 99.73%, however, is widely available.

Following is a list of casinos offering the better paying video poker games. The abbreviations used for each listing are BP (8/5 Bonus Poker), JB (9/6 Jacks or Better), DDB (10/6 Double Double Bonus), DB (10/7 Double Bonus), FPDW (Full-Pay Deuces Wild) and NSUD (Not So Ugly Deuces).

Reno/Sparks Casinos:
Atlantis: JB - nickel to quarter (some with progressives); DB - nickel to $2 (some with progressives); DDB - nickel and quarter; BP - nickel to $10 (some with progressives); FPDW - nickel; NSUD - nickel to $10 (some with progressives)
Circus Circus: BP - $1 to $5
Club Cal Neva: JB - fifty-cent and $1; BP - $1
Eldorado: JB - quarter to $5 (some with progressives); NSUD - quarter to $1; BP - quarter to $1
Harrah's Reno: BP - quarter and $1 (one with progressive)
Nugget: JB - penny to $2; BP - penny to $1; NSUD - penny to $2
Peppermill: JB - penny to $100; NSUD - nickel to $100; BP - nickel to $100
Rail City: JB - quarter and $1
Sands Regency: BP - $1 and $2
Silver Legacy: JB - nickel to $1; NSUD - quarter to $1; BP - quarter to $1 (some with progressives); DB - nickel
Western Village: JB - penny to $1; NSUD - penny to $1

Lake Tahoe Casinos:
Harrah's Lake Tahoe: JB - fifty cent to $100; BP - quarter to $100
Harvey's: JB - $5 to $100; BP - quarter to $100 (one with progressive)
Tahoe Biltmore: JB- quarter to $5; BP- $1; NSUD - $1
MontBleu: JB - quarter to $1; BP - quarter to $1

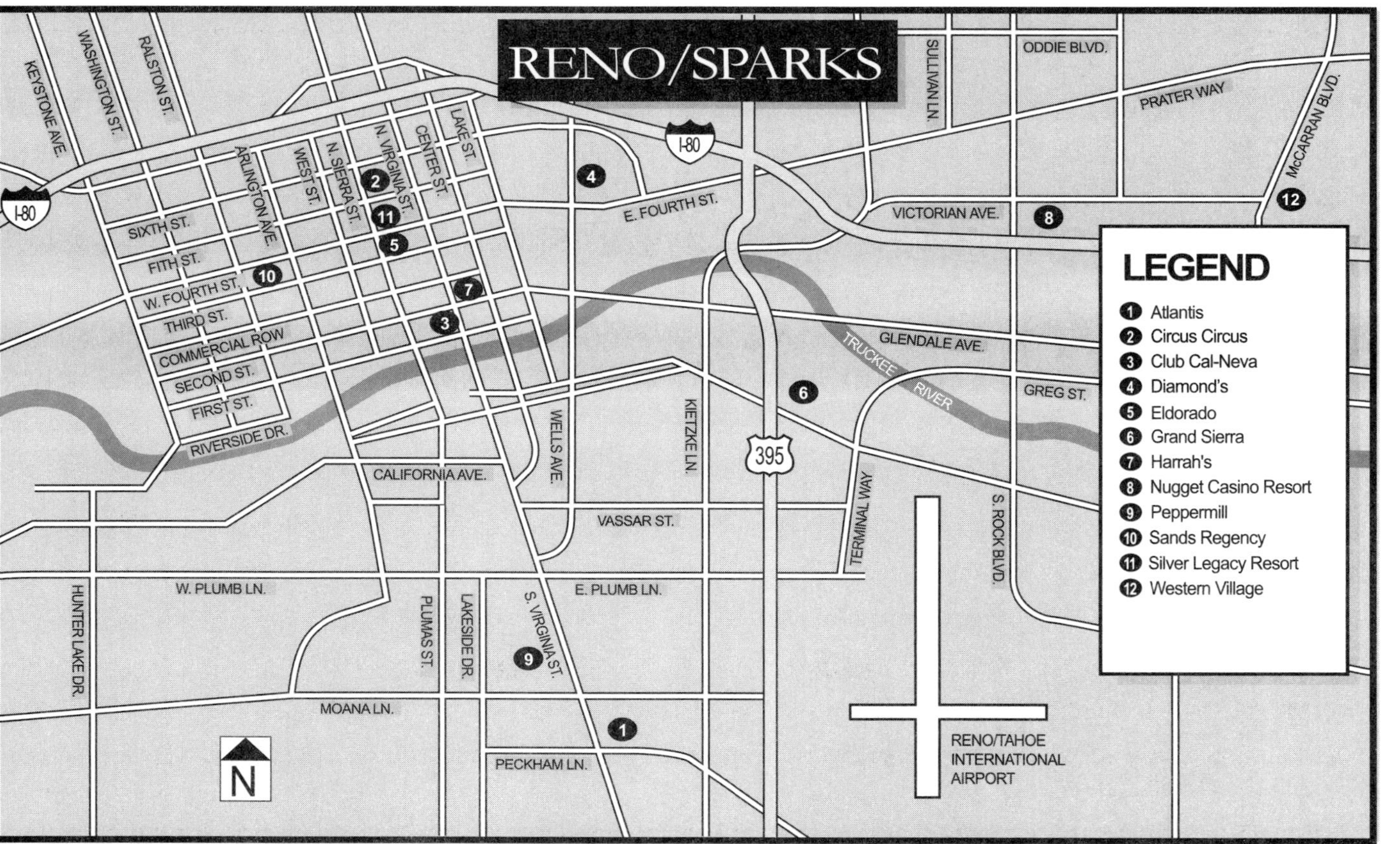
RENO/SPARKS
LEGEND
1 Atlantis
2 Circus Circus
3 Club Cal-Neva
4 Diamond's
5 Eldorado
6 Grand Sierra
7 Harrah's
8 Nugget Casino Resort
9 Peppermill
10 Sands Regency
11 Silver Legacy Resort
12 Western Village
KEYSTONE AVE.
WASHINGTON ST.
RALSTON ST.
I-80
ARLINGTON AVE.
WEST ST.
N. SIERRA ST.
N. VIRGINIA ST.
CENTER ST.
LAKE ST.
SIXTH ST.
FITH ST.
W. FOURTH ST.
THIRD ST.
COMMERCIAL ROW
SECOND ST.
FIRST ST.
RIVERSIDE DR.
E. FOURTH ST.
SULLIVAN LN.
ODDIE BLVD.
PRATER WAY
McCARRAN BLVD.
VICTORIAN AVE.
GLENDALE AVE.
TRUCKEE RIVER
GREG ST.
CALIFORNIA AVE.
WELLS AVE.
KIETZKE LN.
395
TERMINAL WAY
S. ROCK BLVD.
VASSAR ST.
W. PLUMB LN.
E. PLUMB LN.
HUNTER LAKE DR.
PLUMAS ST.
LAKESIDE DR.
S. VIRGINIA ST.
MOANA LN.
PECKHAM LN.
N
RENO/TAHOE
INTERNATIONAL
AIRPORT

Grand Sierra Resort & Casino
2500 E. Second Street
Reno, Nevada 89595
(775) 789-2000
Website: www.grandsierraresort.com

Room Reservations: (800) 501-2651
Rooms: 1,847 Price Range: $59-$199
Suites: 154 Price Range: $299-$599
Restaurants: 7
Buffets: B/L- $16.99/$17.99 (Sat)/
$23.99 (Sun)
D- $20.99/$31.99 (Fri/Sat)/$22.99 (Sun)
Casino Size: 49,140 Square Feet
Other Games: SB, RB, MB, P, PG, PGP,
TCP, K
Senior Discount: Various Wed if 55+
Special Features: 50-lane bowling center. 164-space RV park ($35-$55 summer/$25-$40 winter). Health club. Shopping mall. Family amusement center. Laketop golf driving range. Indoor simulated golf. Two-screen movie theater.

Harrah's Reno
219 N. Center Street
Reno, Nevada 89501
(775) 786-3232
Website: www.harrahsreno.com

Toll-Free Number: (800) 423-1121
Rooms: 886 Price Range: $45-$250
Suites: 60 Price Range: Casino use only
Restaurants: 4
Buffets: B/L-$20.99 (Sat/Sun)
D-$21.99/$29.99 (Fri/Sat)
Casino Size: 40,200 Square Feet
Other Games: SB, RB, MB, FCP,
PGP, LIR, TCP, K
Senior Discount: Buffet discount
Mon-Fri if 55+

Peppermill Hotel Casino Reno
2707 S. Virginia Street
Reno, Nevada 89502
(775) 826-2121
Website: www.peppermillreno.com

Toll-Free Number: (866) 821-9996
Rooms: 1,070 Price Range: $59-$199
Suites: 185 Price Range: $119-$999
Restaurants: 7
Buffets: B-$15.99/$17.99 (Sat)/$23.99 (Sun)
L-$16.99 D-$22.99/$32.99 (Fri/Sat)/
$24.99 (Sun)
Casino Size: 77,058 Square Feet
Other Games: SB, RB, MB, PG, P, PGP,
LIR, TCP, FCP, UTH, K
Senior Discount: Various discounts if 55+
Special Features: Spa.

The Sands Regency Hotel Casino
345 North Arlington Avenue
Reno, Nevada 89501
(775) 348-2200
Website: www.sandsregency.com

Reservation Number: (866) 386-7829
Rooms: 811 Price Range: $39-$79
Suites: 27 Price Range: $99-$249
Restaurants: 6
Buffets: D-$9.99/$13.99 (Fri/Sat)
Casino Size: 25,791 Square Feet
Other Games: SB, RB, P, PGP, TCP, BG

Silver Legacy Resort Casino
407 N. Virginia Street
Reno, Nevada 89501
(775) 325-7401
Website: www.silverlegacy.com

Toll-Free Number: (800) 687-7733
Rooms: 1,720 Price Range: $69-$139
Suites: 150 Price Range: $169-$329
Restaurants: 5
Buffets: B-$11.99/$18.99 (Sat/Sun)
L-$12.99/$18.99 (Sat/Sun)
D-$16.99/$26.99 (Fri/Sat)/
$18.99 (Sun)
Casino Size: 89,200 Square Feet
Other Games: SB, RB, MB, PG, PGP, P,
LIR, TCP, K
Special Features: Affiliated with Eldorado Resorts. Simulated mining machine above casino floor. Comedy club. Rum bar. No buffet Mon-Wed.

Searchlight

Map Location: **#22** (58 miles S. of Las Vegas on Hwy. 95)

Terrible's Road House - Searchlight
100 N. Highway 95
Searchlight, Nevada 89046
(702) 297-1201

Casino Size: 3,910 Square Feet
Other Games: No Table Games
Overnight RV Parking: Free/RV Dump: No

Sparks

Map Location: **#4** (Sparks is a suburb of Reno and is located one mile east of Reno on I-80)

Here's information, as supplied by Nevada's State Gaming Control Board, showing the slot machine payback percentages for all of the Sparks area casinos for the fiscal year beginning July 1, 2016 and ending June 30, 2017:

Denomination	Payback %
1¢ Slots	93.68
5¢ Slots	96.46
25¢ Slots	96.10
$1 Slots	96.08
$5 Slots	96.64
All Slots	94.73

These numbers reflect the percentage of money returned on each denomination of machine and encompass all electronic machines including slots, video poker and video keno.

Alamo Casino & Travel Center
1950 East Greg Street
Sparks, Nevada 89431
(775) 355-8888
Website: www.thealamo.com

Super 8 Room Reservations: (800) 800-8000
Rooms: 64 Price Range: $79-$129
Suites: 7 Price Range: $104-$159
Restaurants: 1
Casino Size: 7,150 Square Feet
Other Games: SB, P, No roulette
Overnight RV Parking: Free/RV Dump: No
Special Features: Motel is Super 8. Truck stop. Post office and gas station.

Nugget Casino Resort
1100 Nugget Avenue
Sparks, Nevada 89431
(775) 356-3300
Website: www.nuggetcasinoresort.com

Toll-Free Number: (888) 868-4438
Rooms: 1,450 Price Range: $40-$139
Suites: 150 Price Range: $109-$295
Restaurants: 6
Buffets: B- $10.99/ (Sat)/$19.99 (Sun)
L-$11.99/$19.99 (Sun)
D-$16.99/$24.99 (Fri/Sat)
Casino Size: 72,300 Square Feet
Overnight RV Parking: Check with security
RV Dump: No
Other Games: SB, RB, P, PGP,
UTH, TCP, K, BG
Special Features: Wedding chapel. Fitness center.

Rail City Casino
2121 Victorian Avenue
Sparks, Nevada 89431
(775) 359-9440
Website: www.railcity.com

Restaurants: 2
Buffets: B/L- $10.77
D- $11.99/$16.99 (Fri/Sat)
Casino Size: 23,854 Square Feet
Other Games: SB, RB, K, No craps or roulette
Overnight RV Parking: No

Western Village Inn & Casino
815 Nichols Boulevard
Sparks, Nevada 89434
(775) 331-1069
Website: www.westernvillagesparks.com

Reservation Number: (800) 648-1170
Rooms: 147 Price Range: $59-$159
Suites: 4 Price Range: $105-$179
Restaurants: 4
Casino Size: 26,452 Square Feet
Other Games: SB, RB
Overnight RV Parking: No/RV Dump: No

Verdi

Map Location: **#4** (4 miles W. of Reno on I-80 at the California border)

Boomtown Hotel & Casino
2100 Garson Road
Verdi, Nevada 89439
(775) 345-6000
Website: www.boomtownreno.com

Toll-Free Number: (800) 648-3790
Room/RV Reservations: (877) 626-6686
Rooms: 318 Price Range: $69-$145
Suites: 20 Price Range: $129-$219
Restaurants: 4
Buffets: D-$36.99 (Fri-Sun) includes lobster
Casino Size: 38,550 Square Feet
Other Games: SB, RB, P, PGP, TCP, K
Overnight RV Parking: Must use RV park
Special Features: Hotel is Best Western. 203-space RV park ($39-$55 per night). 24-hour mini-mart. Indoor family fun center with rides and arcade games. Buffet discount for players club members.

Gold Ranch Casino & RV Resort
350 Gold Ranch Road
Verdi, Nevada 89439
(775) 345-6789
Website: www.goldranchrvcasino.com

RV Reservations: (877) 927-6789
Restaurants: 1
Casino Size: 8,370 Square Feet
Other Games: SB, No table games
Overnight RV Parking: Must use RV park
Special Features: 105-space RV park ($45-$48 per night). 24-hour mini-mart.

Wells

Map Location: **#23** (338 miles N.E. of Reno on I-80)

Alamo Casino Wells
1440 6th Street
Wells, Nevada 89835
(775) 752-3344
Website: www.thealamo.com

Restaurants: 1
Casino Size: 6,100 Square Feet
Other Games: SB, No table games
Overnight RV Parking: Free/RV Dump: No

West Wendover

Map Location: **#24** (Just W. of the Utah border on I-80)

Here's information, as supplied by Nevada's State Gaming Control Board, showing the slot machine payback percentages for all of the Wendover area casinos for the fiscal year beginning July 1, 2016 and ending June 30, 2017:

Denomination	Payback %
1¢ Slots	93.49
5¢ Slots	94.33
25¢ Slots	93.68
$1 Slots	96.01
$5 Slots	96.68
All Slots	94.45

These numbers reflect the percentage of money returned on each denomination of machine and encompass all electronic machines including slots, video poker and video keno.

Montego Bay Casino Resort
680 Wendover Boulevard
W. Wendover, Nevada 89883
(775) 664-4800
Website: www.wendoverfun.com

Toll-Free Number: (800) 217-0049
Rooms: 437 Price Range: $79-$149
Suites: 75 Price Range: $119-$259
Restaurants: 3
Buffets: B-$17.95 (Sat/Sun)
L-$14.95/ $17.95 (Sat/Sun)
D-$17.95/$29.95 (Fri)/$24.95 (Sat)
Casino Size: 49,400 Square Feet
Other Games: SB, RB, P, PGP, LIR,TCP
Overnight RV Parking: Free/RV Dump: No
Senior Discount: Dining discounts if 55+
Special Features: Affiliated with Peppermill Inn and Rainbow casinos. Connected by sky bridge to Wendover Nugget.

Peppermill Inn & Casino
680 Wendover Boulevard
W. Wendover, Nevada 89883
(775) 664-4800
Website: www.wendoverfun.com

Toll-Free Number: (800) 217-0049
Rooms: 302 Price Range: $69-$129
Suites: 42 Price Range: $99-$189
Restaurants: 2
Casino Size: 30,577 Square Feet
Other Games: SB, RB, PGP, LIR, TCP
Overnight RV Parking: Free/RV Dump: No
Senior Discount: Dining discounts if 55+
Special Features: Affiliated with Montego Bay and Rainbow casinos.

Rainbow Hotel Casino
1045 Wendover Boulevard
W. Wendover, Nevada 89883
(775) 664-4800
Website: www.wendoverfun.com

Toll-Free Number: (800) 217-0049
Rooms: 379 Price Range: $69-$139
Suites: 50 Price Range: $99-$219
Restaurants: 4
Buffets: B-$16.95 (Sat/Sun)
L-$13.95/ $16.95 (Sat/Sun)
D-$16.95/$27.95 (Fri)/$23.95 (Sat)
Casino Size: 57,360 Square Feet
Other Games: SB, RB, PGP, LIR, TCP
Overnight RV Parking: Free/RV Dump: No
Senior Discount: Dining discounts if 55+
Special Features: Affiliated with Peppermill Inn and Montego Bay casinos.

Red Garter Hotel & Casino
1225 Wendover Boulevard
W. Wendover, Nevada 89883
(775) 664-2111
Website: www.redgartercasino.com

Toll-Free Number: (800) 982-2111
Rooms: 46 Price Range: $37-$114
Restaurants: 1
Casino Size: 17,342 Square Feet
Other Games: SB, TCP
Overnight RV Parking: No

Wendover Nugget Hotel & Casino
101 Wendover Boulevard
W. Wendover, Nevada 89883
(775) 664-2221
Website: www.wendovernugget.com

Toll-Free Number: (800) 848-7300
Rooms: 500 Price Range: $35-$119
Suites: 60 Price Range: $60-$189
Restaurants: 2
Buffets: B-$16.95 (Sat/Sun)
L-$12.95/ $16.95 (Sat/Sun)
D-$16.95/$27.95 (Fri)/$23.95 (Sat)
Casino Size: 37,074 Square Feet
Other Games: SB, RB, P, TCP,
LIR, PGP, K,
Overnight RV Parking: Must use RV park
Senior Discount: Room/food discounts if 55+
Special Features: 18-space RV park ($35 per night). Connected by sky bridge to Montego Bay. Starbucks coffeehouse.

Winnemucca

Map Location: **#25** (164 miles N.E. of Reno on I-80)

Model T Hotel/Casino/RV Park
1130 W. Winnemucca Boulevard
Winnemucca, Nevada 89445
(775) 623-2588
Website: www.modelt.com

Reservation Number: (800) 645-5658
Rooms: 75 Price Range: $98-$130
Restaurants: 1
Casino Size: 7,053 Square Feet
Other Games: SB, no table games
Overnight RV Parking: Must use RV park
Special Features: Hotel is Quality Inn. 58-space RV park ($30 per night).

Winnemucca Inn
741 W. Winnemucca Boulevard
Winnemucca, Nevada 89445
(775) 623-2565
Website: www.winnemuccainn.com

Reservation Number: (800) 633-6435
Rooms: 105 Price Range: $91-$109
Restaurants: 1
Casino Size: 3,000 Square Feet
Other Games: SB, RB, No table games
Overnight RV Parking: No

Winners Hotel/Casino
185 W. Winnemucca Boulevard
Winnemucca, Nevada 89445
(775) 623-2511
Website: www.winnerscasino.com

Reservation Number: (800) 648-4770
Rooms: 123 Price Range: $49-$89
Suites: 3 Price Range: $69-$99
Restaurants: 2
Casino Size: 10,340 Square Feet
Other Games: SB, RB, BG (Wed/Fri/Sat), TCP
Overnight RV Parking: Free/ Dump: No

Yerington

Map Location: **#26** (60 miles S.E. of Reno on Hwy. Alt. 95)

Pioneer Crossing Casino
11 N. Main Street
Yerington, Nevada 89447
(775) 463-2481
Website: www.pioneercrossingcasino.com

Restaurants: 1 (open 24 hours)
Buffets: B- $8.95 (Sun) D- $8.95 to $15.95
Casino Size: 4,950 Square Feet
Other Games: P, no craps or roulette
Overnight RV Parking: Free/RV Dump: No
Special Features: Movie theater. 12-lane bowling alley.

Indian Casinos

Avi Resort & Casino
10000 Aha Macav Parkway
Laughlin, Nevada 89029
(702) 535-5555
Website: www.avicasino.com
Map Location: **#2**

Toll-Free Number: (800) 284-2946
Rooms: 426 Price Range: $49-$119
Suites: 29 Price Range: $65-$135
Restaurants: 4
Buffets: B-$9.99/$11.99 (Sat)/$22.99 (Sun)
L-$10.99 (Thu/Fri)/$11.99(Sat)/$22.99 (Sun)
D-$15.99/$21.99 (Fri)/$18.99 (Sat)
Casino Size: 25,000 Square Feet
Other Games: SB, RB, P, TCP, PGP, LIR, UTH, K, BG
Overnight RV Parking: Free/RV Dump: No
Special Features: 260-space RV park ($20-$25 per night). On Colorado River with boat dock, launch and private beach. Fast food court. 8-screen cinema. Smoke shop. Childcare center. Buffet discount for players club members.

Moapa Tribal Casino
Interstate 15, Exit 75
Moapa, Nevada 89025-0340
(702) 864-2601
Website: www.moapapaiutes.com
Map Location: **#27** (65 miles N.E. of Las Vegas)

Other Games: Gaming Machines Only
Overnight RV Parking: No
Special Features: Located in travel plaza with gas station and convenience store.

NEW JERSEY

Map Location: **#1** (on the Atlantic Ocean in southeast New Jersey, 130 miles south of New York City and 60 miles southeast of Philadelphia)

All Atlantic City casinos are located along the boardwalk, except for three: Borgata, Harrah's and Golden Nugget. Those three are located in the marina section.

Following is information from the New Jersey Casino Control Commission regarding average slot payout percentages for the 12-month period from July 1, 2016 through June 30, 2017:

CASINO	PAYBACK %
Harrah's	91.7
Borgata	91.6
Caesars	91.0
Bally's A.C.	90.9
Golden Nugget	90.7
Resorts	90.8
Tropicana	90.5

These figures reflect the total percentages returned by each casino for all of their electronic machines which include slot machines, video poker, etc.

All Atlantic City casinos are open 24 hours and, unless otherwise noted, the games offered at every casino are: slots, video poker, craps, blackjack, Spanish 21, roulette, mini-baccarat, Caribbean stud poker, three card poker, four card poker, let it ride, pai gow tiles and pai gow poker. Additional games offered include: sic bo (SB), keno (K), baccart (B), casino war (CW), poker (P), off-track betting (OTB), Texas hold 'em bonus (THB), Mississippi stud (MS), ultimate Texas hold 'em (UTH) and big six wheel (B6). The minimum gambling age is 21.

For more information on visiting New Jersey you can contact the state's Travel & Tourism Department at (800) 537-7397 or go to: www.visitnj.com.

For information only on Atlantic City call (800) 847-4865 or go to: www.atlanticcitynj.com.

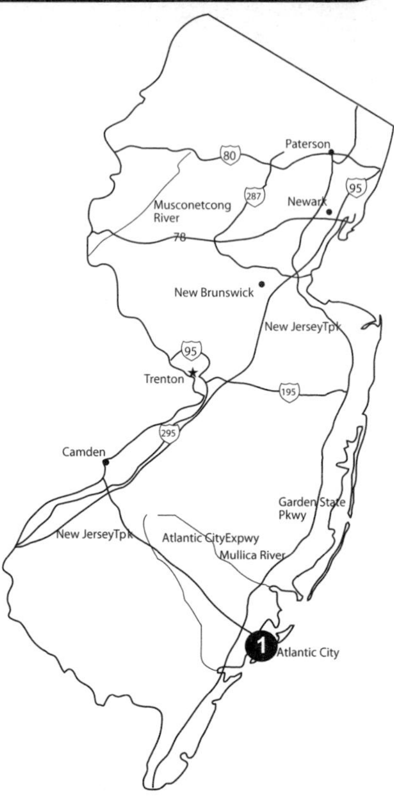

Bally's Atlantic City
1900 Pacific Avenue
Atlantic City, New Jersey 08401
(609) 340-2000
Website: www.ballysac.com

Reservation Number: (800) 225-5977
Rooms: 1,611 Price Range: $109-$389
Suites: 146 Price Range: $219-$599
Restaurants: 10
Casino Size 104,646 Square Feet
Other Games: B6, P, CW
Special Features: Affiliated with Caesars Entertainment. Southern walkway connects to Wild Wild West casino. Parking discount for players club members.

ATLANTIC CITY
BRIGANTINE BLVD.
ATLANTIC AVENUE
PACIFIC AVENUE
NEW JERSEY AVE.
DELAWARE AVE.
MARYLAND AVE.
VIRGINIA AVE.
PENNSLYVANIA AVE.
N CAROLINA AVE.
S CAROLINA AVE.
HURON AVE.
BOARDWALK
ILLINOIS AVE.
INDIANA AVE.
ABSECON BLVD.
OHIO AVE.
MICHIGAN AVE.
ARKANSAS AVE.
MISSOURI AVE.
ATLANTIC CITY EXWY.
MISSISSIPPI AVE.
IOWA AVE.
BRIGHTON AVE.
BOSTON AVE.
PROVIDENCE
ALBANY AVE.
LEGEND
1 Bally's Atlantic City
2 Borgata
3 Caesars
4 Golden Nugget
5 Hard Rock
6 Harrah's
7 Resorts
8 Tropicana
9 Wild Wild West

Borgata Hotel Casino and Spa
One Borgata Way
Atlantic City, New Jersey 08401
(609) 317-1000
Website: www.theborgata.com

Toll-Free Number: (866) 692-6742
Rooms: 2,200 Prices Range: $109-$359
Suites: 600 Price Range: $209-$699
Restaurants: 10
Buffets: B-$16.95/$27.95 (Sun)
L-$19.95/$27.95 (Sun) D-$34.95
Casino Size: 136,667 Square Feet
Other Games: B, B6
Special Features: Affiliated with MGM Resorts. 3,700-seat events center. 1,000-seat music theater. Comedy club. Health spa. Barbershop. Hair and nail salon. Parking discount for players club members.

Caesars Atlantic City
2100 Pacific Avenue
Atlantic City, New Jersey 08401
(609) 348-4411
Website: www.caesarsac.com

Toll-Free Number: (800) 443-0104
Rooms: 979 Price Range: $109-$419
Suites: 198 Price Range: $399-$799
Restaurants: 12
Buffets: Brunch-$29.95 (Sat/Sun)
L-$27.99 D-$34.99/$39.99 (Sat)
Casino Size: 111,812 Square Feet
Other Games: B, SB, B6, THB, MS, UTH
Special Features: Affiliated with Caesars Entertainment. Roman themed hotel and casino. Health spa. Shopping arcade. Parking discount for players club members.

Golden Nugget Atlantic City
Huron Avenue & Brigantine Boulevard
Atlantic City, New Jersey 08401
(609) 441-2000
Website: www.goldennugget.com

Toll-Free Number (800) 777-8477
Reservation Number: (800) 365-8786
Rooms: 568 Price Range: $99-$419
Suites: 160 Price Range: $175-$999
Buffets: B-$15.99 L-$18.99/$23.99 (Sat/Sun)
D-$20.99/$29.99 (Fri)
Casino Size: 70,250 Square Feet
Other Games: B6, P, MS, UTH
Special Features: Adjacent to marina with 640 slips. 3-acre recreation deck with pools, jogging track, tennis courts, miniature golf course and health club. 1,500-seat event center.

Hard Rock Casino Hotel Atlantic City
1000 Boardwalk at Virginia Avenue
Atlantic City, New Jersey 08401
Website: www.hardrockhotels.com

EXPECTED TO OPEN MAY 28, 2018
Rooms: 1,795 Price Range: TBA
Suites: 311 Price Range: TBA
Special Features: Health spa. Hard Rock cafe. 5,000-seat event center. 1,400-seat showroom.

Harrah's Resort Atlantic City
777 Harrah's Boulevard
Atlantic City, New Jersey 08401
(609) 441-5000
Website: www.caesars.com

Reservation Number: (800) 242-7724
Rooms: 2,010 Price Range: $99-$329
Suites: 616 Price Range: $239-$459
Restaurants: 8
Buffets: B- $42.99 (Sun) D- $42.99
Casino Size: 158,966 Square Feet
Other Games: B6, K, P, THB, MS
Special Features: Affiliated with Caesars Entertainment. 65-slip marina. Beauty salon. Miniature golf course (in season). Parking discount for players club members.

The Best Places To Play in Atlantic City

Blackjack: The Golden Nugget offers a single-deck blackjack game that only pays 6-to-5 when you get a blackjack rather than the standard 3-to-2 and this raises the casino advantage in this game to 1.58%. Caesars, Harrah's and the Wild Wild West casino also offer eight-deck games that only pay 6-to-5 for blackjack and the casino advantage in these games is around 2%. All of these are very bad games and all should be avoided.

Other than those 6-to-5 variations, the blackjack games offered at Atlantic City casinos are pretty much all the same: eight-deck shoe games with double down on any first two cards, dealer hits soft 17, pairs can be split up to three times and doubling after splitting is allowed. This works out to a casino edge of .67% against a player using perfect basic strategy and every casino in Atlantic City offers this game. Resorts has some tables where the dealers stand on soft 17 on some of their games. This is the best eight-deck game in the city and the casino advantage advantage is .44%.

If you're willing to make higher minimum bets you can find slightly better games. All casinos offer six-deck games with minimum bets of $25, $50 or $100 per hand where the dealers stand on soft 17 and the casino edge in these games is lowered to .42%. It is offered at every casino in the city, except for Wild Wild West which only offers eight-deck games. Additionally, the Golden Nugget offers the city's best six-deck game because they add late surrender to the above rules, which brings their house advantage down to .34%. The minimum bet on this game is usually $50.

Roulette: When choosing roulette games it's usually best to play in a casino offering a single-zero wheel because the casino advantage is 2.70% versus a double-zero wheel which has a 5.26% advantage. However, that situation is somewhat different in Atlantic City because of certain gaming regulations. On double-zero wheels the casinos can only take one-half of a wager on even money bets (odd/even, red/black, 1-18/19-36) when zero or double-zero is the winning number. This lowers the casino edge on these particular bets to 2.63%, while the edge on all other bets remains at 5.26%. This rule is not in effect on single-zero wheels and virtually all bets on that game have a 2.70% house edge. There are five casinos that have single-zero roulette wheels: Harrah's, Bally's, Borgata, Tropicana and Caesars. You should be aware, however, that almost all of these games are only open on weekends (or by special request) and they require $25-$100 minimum bets.

Craps: All craps tables at Bally's, as well as one table at Golden Nugget, offer 10x odds while all other casinos offer 5x odds.

Video Poker: Full-pay video poker games exist in one form or another at every gaming hall in town, but the casinos have become quite stingy with the comps and other benefits that players can earn on them, especially at the lower levels of play.

Caesars Entertainment (Caesars, Bally's, and Harrah's) is a prime example. While all three properties have full-pay video poker games, quarter players have to play $50 through the machine to earn one Total Rewards Credit, as opposed to $10 per credit on the short-pay games. (One Rewards Credit equals one cent in comps.) Dollar and higher players earn one Reward Credit for every $20 played.

Most video poker games are found in multi-game, multi-denominational machines, where the player can choose whether to play quarters, halves, dollars, or higher. Machines can include a variety of choices and the best games to play are: 9/6 Jacks or Better (99.54%), 8/5 Bonus Poker (99.16%), 9/7 Double Bonus Poker (99.11%), 9/6 Double Double Bonus (98.98%), and 8/6/4 Double Joker Poker.

Borgata has 9/6 Jacks in denominations ranging from 25-cents through $25. Some of these games can be found on Multi-Strike for 25-cents, 50-cents, $1 and $2. There are also 3-play, 5-play and 10-play versions available for $1, $2 and $5. Borgata also has 9/6 Double Double Bonus for quarters through $5, plus 8/5 Bonus games for $1 and $2.

Harrah's has a variety of games that are all available in denominations from $1 through $10. There are three carousels of eight upright machines each with 9/6 Double Double Bonus near the players club booth. Another nearby carousel has 9/6 Jacks or Better, 8/5 Bonus Poker, 9/7 Double Bonus Poker, and a couple varieties of Aces & Faces.

Bally's has 9/6 Jacks or Better for 25-cents through $10. 9/7 Double Bonus for 25-cents to $5, 9/6 Double Double Bonus for 25-cents to $5 (including a couple of Aces & Faces versions of these games).

Golden Nugget has 9/7 Double Bonus and 9/6 Double Double Bonus games for $1, $2 and $5. They also offer $1 Illinois Deuces.

Resorts has 8/5 Bonus Poker in denominations from 25-cents through $1.

The best quarter game in Atlantic City can be found in the Tropicana. A row of five full-pay (99.59%), Five Joker progressive games can be found in an alcove just outside the 10 North lounge. Look for Sigma machines with a purple face glass near the entrance to the women's restroom. The Tropicana also offers 8/5 Bonus for $1.

Caesars offers 9/6 Jacks for quarters (with a progressive) in the video-poker area near the center of the casino, but the jackpot rises slowly. They also have 9/6 Double Double Bonus in denominations ranging from $1 through $100.

Resorts Casino Hotel
1133 Boardwalk
Atlantic City, New Jersey 08401
(609) 344-6000
Website: www.resortsac.com

Toll-Free Number: (800) 334-6378
Rooms: 879 Price Range: $139-$375
Suites: 79 Price Range: $209-$699
Restaurants: 6
Buffets: B/L- $49 (Sun)
Casino Size: 97,707 Square Feet
Other games: B6, THB
Special Features: Indoor/outdoor pools. Margaritaville restaurant. Health spa. 1,350-seat theater. Comedy club. Beachfront bar. Parking discount for players club members.

Tropicana Casino & Resort
2831 Boardwalk
Atlantic City, New Jersey 08401
(609) 340-4000
Website: www.tropicana.net

Toll-Free Number: (800) 843-8767
Rooms: 1,426 Price Range: $99-$349
Suites: 340 Price Range: $149-$479
Restaurants: 10
Buffets: B- $18.95/$24.95 (Sun)
L- $19.95/$24.95 (Sun) D- $29.95
Casino Size: 132,896 Square Feet
Other Games: B6
Special Features: Features "The Quarter," a dining/entertainment complex with 30 stores.

NEW MEXICO

New Mexico's Indian casinos offer an assortment of table games and electronic gaming machines. Additionally, slot machines are allowed at the state's racetracks as well as at about 40 various fraternal and veterans clubs.

New Mexico gaming regulations require that electronic machines at racetracks and fraternal/veterans organizations return a minimum of 80% to a maximum of 96%.

New Mexico's Indian tribes do not make their slot machine payback percentages a matter of public record but the terms of the compact between the state and the tribes require all electronic gaming machines to return a minimum of 80%.

Unless otherwise noted, all New Mexico Indian casinos are open 24 hours and offer: blackjack, craps, roulette, video slots and video poker. Some casinos also offer: Spanish 21 (S21), mini-baccarat (MB), poker (P), pai gow poker (PGP), three card poker (TCP), four card poker (FCP), Caribbean stud poker (CSP), let it ride (LIR), ultimate Texas hold 'em (UTH), Mississippi stud (MS), casino war (CW), big 6 wheel (B6), keno (K), bingo (BG) and off track betting (OTB). The minimum gambling age is 21 for the casinos and 18 for bingo or pari-mutuel betting.

Please note that all New Mexico casinos are prohibited from serving alcohol on the casino floor. If a casino serves alcohol it can only be consumed at the bar and not in the casino itself.

For information on visiting New Mexico call the state's tourism department at (800) 733-6396 or go to: www.newmexico.org.

Apache Nugget Travel Center and Casino
US Highway 550 and NM Highway 537
Dulce, New Mexico 87528
(575) 289-2486
Website: www.apachenugget.com
Map: **#15** (on Jicarilla reservation at intersection of Hwys 550 and 537 near Cuba)

Restaurants: 1 Snack Bar Liquor: No
Other Games: Only gaming machines
Casino Size: 12,000 Square Feet
Hours: 11am-12am/9am-1am (Fri/Sat)
Overnight RV Parking: Free (check in with security first)/RV Dump: No

Buffalo Thunder Resort & Casino
20 Buffalo Thunder Trail
Santa Fe, New Mexico 87506
(505) 455-5555
Website: www.buffalothunderresort.com
Map: **#2**

Room Reservations: (877) 848-6337
Rooms: 350 Price Range: $109-$279
Suites: 45 Price Range: $159-$379
Restaurants: 6 Liquor: Yes
Buffets: D- $15.95/$17.95 (Fri/Sat)
Other Games: P, TCP, OTB
Casino Size: 61,000 Square Feet
Casino Hours: 8am-4am/24 hours (Thu-Sat)
Special Features: Hotel is Hilton. Health Spa. Retail shopping area. Native American art gallery. Buffet closed Mon-Wed.

Camel Rock Casino
17486-A Highway 84/285
Santa Fe, New Mexico 87504
(505) 984-8414
Website: www.camelrockcasino.com
Map: **#2**

Toll-Free Number: (800) 462-2635
Restaurants: 1 Liquor: Yes
Hours: 7am-3am/24 Hours (Thurs-Sat)
Casino Size: 60,000 Square Feet
Other Games: TCP
Overnight RV Parking: Free/RV Dump: No

Casino Apache Travel Center
25845 U.S. Highway 70
Ruidoso, New Mexico 88340
(575) 464-7777
Map: **#4** (90 miles N.E. of Las Cruces)

Restaurants: 1 Liquor: Yes
Other Games: no craps, TCP
Casino Size: 10,000 Square Feet
Senior Discount: Various Mon if 55+
Overnight RV Parking: Free/RV Dump: No
Special Features: Free shuttle service to Inn of the Mountain Gods Casino. Truck stop. Discount smoke shop.

Casino Express
14500 Central Avenue SW
Albuquerque, New Mexico 87120
(505) 552-7777
Map: **#3** (I-40 at exit 140)

Other Games: Only Gaming Machines
Overnight RV Parking: Free/RV Dump: No
Special Features: Adjacent to, and affiliated with, Route 66 Casino.

Cities of Gold Casino Hotel
10-B Cities of Gold Road
Santa Fe, New Mexico 8750
(505) 455-3313
Website: www.citiesofgold.com
Map: **#2** (Intersection of Hwys 84/285/502)

Toll-Free Number: (800) 455-3313
Rooms: 122 Price Range: $65-$139
Suites: 2 Price Range: $149
Restaurants: 2 Liquor: Yes
Buffets: B-$7.99 (Fri-Sun) L-$8.95 D-$10.99/ $7.77 (Fri/Sat)/$11.99 (Sun)
Casino Size: 40,000 Square Feet
Other Games: No Tables Games, BG (Wed-Sun)
Overnight RV Parking: No

Dancing Eagle Casino and RV Park
Interstate 40, Exit 108
Casa Blanca, New Mexico 87007
(505) 552-7777
Website: www.dancingeaglecasino.com
Map: **#1** (40 miles W. of Albuquerque)

Toll-Free Number: (877) 440-9969
Restaurants: 2 Liquor: No
Hours: 8am-4am/24 hours (Fri/Sat)
Casino Size: 21,266 Square Feet
Other Games: No Table Games, BG
Overnight RV Parking: Free/RV Dump: No
Special Features: Located on I-40 at exit 108. Truck stop. 34-space RV park ($10 per night). Grocery store.

Fire Rock Navajo Casino
249 Route 66
Church Rock, New Mexico 87311
(505) 905-7100
Website: www.firerocknavajocasino.com
Map: #**16** (8 miles E of Gallup)

Toll-Free Number: (866) 941-2444
Restaurants: 2 Liquor: No
Hours: 8am-4am/24 Hours (Fri/Sat)
Other Games: BG (Mon-Sat), S21
Casino Size: 64,000 square Feet
Other Games: BG, S21
Senior Discount: Various Tue if 50+

Flowing Water Navajo Casino
2710 East Highway 64
Shiprock, New Mexico 87421
(505) 368-2300
Website: www.flowingwater.com
Map: #**17** (105 miles N of Gallup)

Restaurants: 1
Casino Size: 11,000 square Feet
Other Games: Only Gaming Machines
Senior Discount: Various Tue if 50+

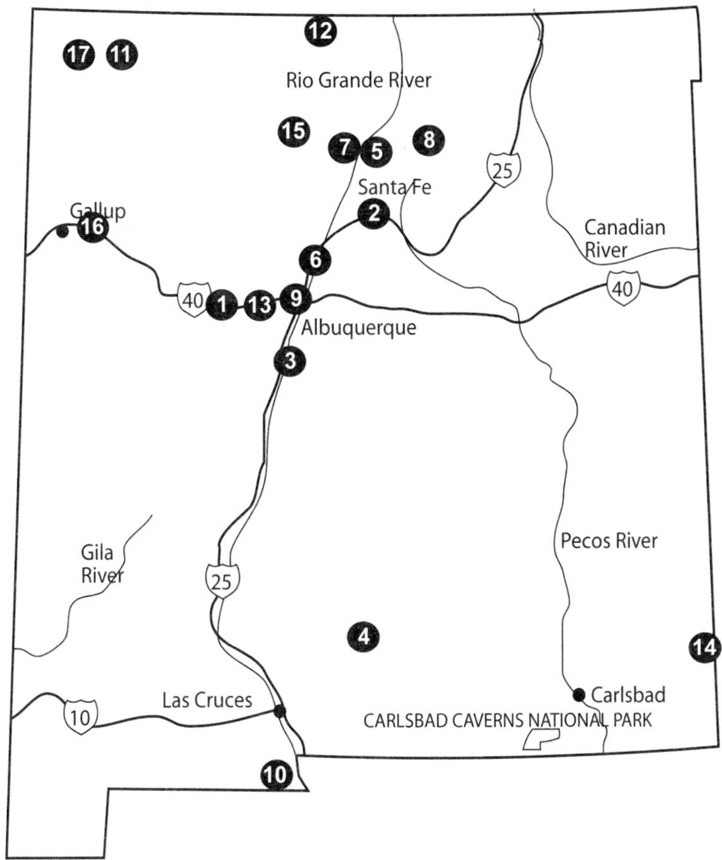

Inn of the Mountain Gods Resort & Casino
287 Carrizo Canyon Road
Mescalero, New Mexico 88340
(575) 464-7059
Website: www.innofthemountaingods.com
Map: **#4** (90 miles N.E. of Las Cruces)

Toll-Free Number: (800) 545-9011
Rooms: 250 Price Range: $129-$249
Suites: 23 Price Range: $269-$399
Restaurants: 5 Liquor: Yes
Buffets: B-$9.99/$13.99 (Sat/Sun)
L-$10.99/$17.99 (Sat/Sun)
D-$11.99/$19.99 (Fri-Sun)
Casino Size: 38,000 Square Feet
Other Games: MB, P, PGP, LIR, UTH, TCP, FCP, MS
Overnight RV Parking: Free/RV Dump: No
Other Games: MB, P, PGP, LIR, UTH, TCP, FCP, MS, BG
Senior Discount: Various Tue if 50+

Isleta Resort Casino
11000 Broadway S.E.
Albuquerque, New Mexico 87105
(505) 724-3800
Website: www.isleta.com
Map: **#3**

Toll-Free Number: (877) 475-3827
Restaurants: 5 Liquor: Yes
Casino Size: 30,000 Square Feet
Other Games: MB, P, BG
Overnight RV Parking: Free/RV Dump: No
Senior Discount: Various Wed if 50+
Special Features: Convenience store. Gas station. Three nine-hole golf courses. Alcohol is only served at sports bar in casino. 50-space RV park ($37 per night).

Nambe Falls Casino
17730 US 84 Fronteg
Santa Fe, New Mexico 87501
(505) 820-5030
Map: **#2**

Casino Size: 7,310 Square Feet
Hours: 8am-4am/2am (Fri/Sat)
Overnight RV Parking: Free/RV Dump: No

Northern Edge Navajo Casino
2752 Indian Service Road 36
Fruitland, New Mexico 87416
(505) 960-7000
Website: www.northernedgenavajocasino.com
Map: **#11** (150 miles N.W of Sante Fe)

Toll-free Number: (877) 241-7777
Rooms: 124 Price Range: $89-$209
Restaurants: 1 Liquor: Yes
Buffets: D-$18.95 (Thu)
Hours: 8am-4am/24 hours (Fri-Sun)
Casino Size: 36,000 square feet
Other Games: TCP, P, S21, MB, PGP
Overnight RV Parking: No
Senior Discount: Various Tue if 50+
Special Features: 24 lane bowling alley. Food court with fast food outlets.

Ohkay Casino Resort
Highway 68
Ohkay Owingeh, New Mexico 87566
(575) 747-1668
Website: www.ohkay.com
Map: **#5** (24 miles N. of Santa Fe)

Toll-Free Number: (800) 752-9286
Rooms: 101 Price Range: $55-$99
Suites: 24 Price Range: $114-$134
Restaurants: 2 Liquor: Yes
Buffets: B- $9.99 L-$12.99 (Sun)
D- $10.99/$23.99 (Fri/Sun)/
$12.99 (Sat)
Casino Size: 30,000 Square Feet
Other Games: Only Gaming Machines
Overnight RV Parking: Free/RV Dump: No
Senior Discount: Various Mon/Wed if 50+
Special Features: Hotel is Best Western. Sporting clays club. Buffet discount for players club members.

Palace West Casino
2S State Road NM-45
Albuquerque, New Mexico 87105
(505) 846-1930
Map: **#3** (at Coors & Isleta Road)

Hours: 8am-4am Daily
Other Games: Only gaming machines
Overnight RV Parking: Free/RV Dump: No
Special Features: Completely nonsmoking.

Route 66 Casino Hotel
14500 Central Avenue SW
Albuquerque, New Mexico 87121
(505) 352-7866
Website: www.rt66casino.com
Map: **#13** (20 miles W. of Albuquerque)

Toll-Free Number: (866) 352-7866
Rooms: 154 Rates: $89-$119
Restaurants: 4 Liquor: Yes
Buffets: L- $11.99/$14.99 (Sun)
D- $11.99 (Mon-Wed)/$13-99 (Thu)/
$26.99 (Fri-Sun)
Other Games: P, PGP, TCP, FCP,
BG, MB, UTH
Overnight RV Parking: Must use RV Park
Special Features: 200-space RV park ($50-$65 per night). Johnny Rockets restaurant. Adjacent to, and affiliated with, Casino Express.

San Felipe Casino Hollywood
25 Hagan Road
Algodones, New Mexico 87001
(505) 867-6700
Website: www.sanfelipecasino.com
Map: **#6** (17 miles N. of Albuquerque)

Toll-Free Number: (877) 529-2946
Restaurants: 2 Liquor: No
Buffets: B- $7.95 L-$9.99 D-$12.99
Other Games: TCP
Senior Discount: Various Mon/Tue if 50+

Sandia Resort & Casino
30 Rainbow Road NE
Albuquerque, New Mexico 87113
(505) 796-7500
Website: www.sandiacasino.com
Map: **#9**

Toll-Free Number: (800) 526-9366
Rooms: 198 Price Range: $195-$226
Suites: 30 Price Range: $269-$399
Restaurants: 4 Liquor: Yes
Buffets: B-$9.95 L-$11.95/$14.95 (Sun)
D-$14.50/$28.95 (Fri/Sat)
Hours: 8am-4am/24 hours (Thu-Sun)
Other Games: P, TCP, PGP, BG, K, MB
Casino Size: 65,000 Square feet
Overnight RV Parking: Free/RV Dump: No
Special Features: 4,200-seat amphitheater. 18-hole golf course. Smoke-free slot room.

Santa Ana Star Casino
54 Jemez Canyon Dam Road
Santa Ana Pueblo, New Mexico 87004
(505) 867-0000
Website: www.santaanastar.com
Map: **#6** (17 miles N. of Albuquerque)

Restaurants: 4 Liquor: Yes
Buffets: L-$9.95 D-$12.95/$25.95 (Fri)
Hours: 8am-4am/24 Hours (Thurs-Sat)
Casino Size: 19,000 Square Feet
Other Games: P, LIR, PGP, TCP, UTH
Overnight RV Parking: Free/RV Dump: No
Senior Discount: Various Mondays if 50+
Special Features: 36-lane bowling alley. 18-hole golf course. Spa. Smoke shop. 3,000-seat event center.

Santa Claran Hotel Casino
460 North Riverside Drive
Espanola, New Mexico 87532
(505) 367-4500
Website: www.santaclaran.com
Map: **#7** (25 miles N of Sante Fe)

Toll-Free Number (866) 244-7625
Rooms: 124 Price Range: $89-$179
Suites: 19 Price Range: $169-$219
Restaurants: 1 Liquor: Yes
Hours: 8am-4am/24 hours (Fri/Sat)
Casino Size: 36,000 square feet
Overnight RV Parking: No
Senior Discount: Various Tue if 50+
Special Features: 24 lane bowling alley.

Sky City Casino Hotel
Interstate 40, Exit 102
Acoma, New Mexico 87034
(505) 552-6123
Website: www.skycity.com
Map: **#1** (50 miles W. of Albuquerque)

Toll-Free Number: (888) 759-2489
Rooms: 132 Price Range: $79-$99
Suites: 15 Price Range: $119-$169
Restaurants: 1 Liquor: Yes
Buffets: B-$7/$9.50 (Sat/Sun)
L- $9/$10 (Sat/Sun)
D- $15.50/$14 (Tue)$14.50 (Wed)/
$22.50 (Fri)/$16 (Sat)
Casino Size: 30,000 Square Feet
Other Games: TCP, BG
Overnight RV Parking: Free/RV Dump: No
Senior Discount: Various Wed if 50+
Special Features: 42-space RV park ($22-$25 per night). No bingo Saturday.

Taos Mountain Casino
700 Veterans Highway
Taos, New Mexico 87571
(575) 737-0777
Website: www.taosmountaincasino.com
Map: **#8** (50 miles N.E. of Santa Fe)

Toll-Free Number: (888) 946-8267
Restaurants: 1 Deli Liquor: No
Hours: 8am-1am/2am (Thu-Sat)
Other Games: no roulette or craps, UTH
Overnight RV Parking: No
Special Features: Entire casino is non-smoking.

Wild Horse Casino & Hotel
13603 US Highway 64
Dulce, New Mexico 87528
(575) 759-3663
Website: www.apachenugget.com
Map: **#12** (95 miles N.W. of Santa Fe)

Room Reservations: (800) 428-2627
Rooms: 43 Price Range: $85-$125
Restaurants: 1 Liquor: Yes
Hours: 11am-1am/
9am-1am (Thu)/2am (Fri/Sat)/12am (Sun)

Pari-Mutuels

The Downs Racetrack and Casino
145 Louisiana Boulevard NE
Albuquerque, New Mexico 87108
(505) 767-7171
Website: www.abqdowns.com
Map: **#9**

Restaurants: 1
Hours: 10am-1am/2am (Thu)4am (Fri/Sat)
Other Games: Only gaming machines
Overnight RV Parking: No
Special Features: Live horse racing seasonally. Daily simulcasting of horse racing.

Ruidoso Downs & Billy The Kid Casino
26225 U.S. Highway 70 East
Ruidoso Downs, New Mexico 88346
(575) 378-4431
Website: www.ruidownsracing.com
Map: **#4** (90 miles N.E. of Las Cruces)

Restaurants: 2
Hours: 10am-11pm/12am (Fri/Sat)
Other Games: Only gaming machines
Overnight RV Parking: No
Senior Discount: Various Wed if 50+
Special Features: Live horse racing seasonally. Daily simulcasting of horse racing.

Sunland Park Racetrack & Casino
1200 Futurity Drive
Sunland Park, New Mexico 88063
(575) 874-5200
Website: www.sunland-park.com
Map: **#10** (5 miles W. of El Paso, TX)

Restaurants: 4
Hours: 10am-1am/2am (Thu)/4am (Fri/Sat)
Other Games: Only gaming machines
Overnight RV Parking: Free/$5 w/hookups
Senior Discount: Various Mon/Wed if 50+
Special Features: Live thoroughbred and quarter-horse racing seasonally. Daily simulcasting of horse racing.

SunRay Park and Casino
#39 Road 5568
Farmington, New Mexico 87401
(505) 566-1200
Website: www.sunraygaming.com
Map: **#11** (150 miles N.W. of Santa Fe)

Restaurants: 1
Hours: 11am-2am/3am (Thu)/4am (Fri)
10am-4am (Sat)/10am-2am (Sun)
Other Games: Only gaming machines
Overnight RV Parking: No
Special Features: Live horse racing seasonally. Daily simulcasting of horse racing.

Zia Park Race Track & Black Gold Casino
3901 W. Millen Drive
Hobbs, New Mexico 88240
(575) 492-7000
Website: www.ziaparkcasino.com
Map: **#14** (70 miles N.E. of Carlsbad)

Toll-Free Number: (888) 942-7275
Restaurants: 3
Hours: 10am-1am/3am (Fri)/9am-3am (Sat)/9am-2am (Sun)
Other Games: Only gaming machines
Special Features: Live horse racing seasonally. Daily simulcasting of horse racing.

NEW YORK

In late 2013 New York passed legislation allowing up to four destination casino resorts in upstate New York. Three have opened and the fourth, Resorts World Catskills, is expected to open by mid-2018.

All casinos offer: blackjack, roulette, craps, slots and video poker. Some casinos also offer: mini-baccarat (MB), poker (P), pai gow poker (PGP), Caribbean stud poker (CSP), let it ride (LIR), big 6 (B6), bingo (BG), keno (K), Mississippi stud (MS), three card poker (TCP), four card poker (FCP) and Spanish 21 (S21).

Here's information, as supplied by the New York Gaming Commission, showing the slot machine payback percentages for all of the casinos for the four-month period from April 1, 2017 through July 31, 2017:

LOCATION	PAYBACK %
Del Lago	91.01
Rivers Casino	90.30
Tioga Downs	91.43

The minimum gambling age is 21. All casinos are open 24 hours, except for Tioga Downs.

Del Lago Resort & Casino
1133 State Route 414
Waterloo, New York 13165
(315) 946-1777
Website: www.dellagoresort.com
Map: **#16** (50 miles S.W. of Syracuse)

Rooms: 165 Rates: $124-$179
Suites: 40 Rates: $240-$590
Restaurants: 5
Buffets: B- $11.95 (Sa)t/$17.95 (Sun)
L- $15.95 D- $21.95
Casino Size: 94,000 Square Feet
Other Games: S21, LIR, TCP, MS, UTH, PGP, MB, CSP, B6
Overnight RV Parking: No
Special Features: Spa.

Resorts World Catskills
Kiamesha Lake, New York 12751
Website: www.rwcatskills.com
Map: **#18** (100 miles N.W. of New York City)

This casino is expected to open in mid-2018.
Suites: 332 Rates: TBA
Casino Size: 100,000 Square Feet
Special Features: Spa. 2,000-seat theater.

Rivers Casino & Resort Schenectady
1 Rush Street
Schenectady, New York 12305
(518) 579-8800
Website: www.riverscasinoandresort.com
Map: **#17**

Rooms: 165 Rates: $116-$279
Restaurants: 6
Casino Size: 50,000 Square Feet
Other Games: B, MB, LIR, TCP, MS, PGP, P
Overnight RV Parking: No
Special Features: Spa.

Tioga Downs
2384 West River Road
Nichols, New York 13812
(888) 946-8464
Website: www.tiogadowns.com
Map: **#14** (30 miles W. of Binghamton)

Toll-Free: (888) 946-8464
Restaurants: 6
Buffets: L- $9.99/$15.99 (Sun)
D- $8.99/$23.99 (Thu)/
$18.99 (Fri/Sat)/$15.99 (Sun)
Casino Size: 19,000 Square Feet
Casino Hours: 9am-3am
Other Games: MB, LIR, TCP, B6, PGP, P, MS
Overnight RV Parking: No
Senior Discount: Various Wed if 50+
Special Features: Live harness seasonally. Daily simulcasting of thoroughbred and harness racing.

Indian Casinos (Class III)

There are six Indian casinos located in upstate New York which offer traditional Class III casino gambling.

All of these casinos are open 24 hours and offer the following games: slot machines, video poker, blackjack, craps, and roulette. Some casinos also offer: Spanish 21 (S21), baccarat (B), mini-baccarat (MB), big six wheel (B6), keno (K), poker (P), pai gow poker (PGP), let it ride (LIR), caribbean stud poker (CSP), three-card poker (TCP), sic bo (SIC), four-card poker (FCP), Mississippi stud (MS), Texas hold'em bonus (THB), ultimate Texas hold'em (UTH) and casino war (CW).

The minimum gambling age is 21 at the three Seneca casinos and 18 at the other casinos. For more information on visiting New York call the state's travel information center at (800) 225-5697 or go to: www.iloveny.com.

Akwesasne Mohawk Casino Resort
873 State Route 37
Hogansburg, New York 13655
(518) 358-2222
Website: www.mohawkcasino.com
Map: **#2** (65 miles W. of Champlain)

Toll-Free Number: (888) 622-1155
Rooms: 145 Price Range: $109-$189
Suites: 5 Price Range: $175-$500
Restaurants: 3 Liquor: Yes
Buffets: B- $13.99 (Sat/Sun)
L- $11.99/$13.99 (Sat/Sun)
D- $18.99/$25.99 (Fri)/$20.99 (Sat)
Casino Size: 40,000 Square Feet
Other Games: S21, LIR, P, TCP, MS,
PGP, FCP, CSP, BG
Overnight RV Parking: Free/RV Dump: No

Seneca Allegany Casino & Hotel
777 Seneca Allegany Boulevard
Salamanca, New York 14779
(716) 945-9300
Website: www.senecaalleganycasino.com
Map: **#12** (65 miles S. of Buffalo)

Toll-Free Number: (877) 873-6322
Rooms: 189 Price Range: $129-$349
Suites: 23 Price Range: $219-$449
Restaurants: 6 Liquor: Yes
Buffets: L -$15 D- $19/$26 (Fri)
Casino Size: 48,000 Square Feet
Other Games: S21, TCP, LIR, FCP,
MS, CSP, THB
Overnight RV Parking: No
Special Features: Buffet discount for players club members.

Seneca Buffalo Creek Casino
1 Fulton Street
Buffalo, New York 14204
(716) 853-7576
www.senecabuffalocreekcasino.com
Map: **#3**

Toll-Free Number: (877) 873-6322
Restaurants: 2 Liquor: Yes
Casino Size: 65,000 Square Feet
Games Offered: S21, LIR, TCP, MS, UTH, CW
Overnight RV Parking: No

Seneca Niagara Casino
310 Fourth Street
Niagara Falls, New York 14303
(716) 299-1100
Website: www.senecaniagaracasino.com
Map: **#4**

Toll-Free Number: (877) 873-6322
Rooms: 574 Price Range: $149-$239
Suites: 30 Price Range: $299-$399
Restaurants: 6 Liquor: Yes
Buffets: B-$14.99 (Sat/Sun) L- $16.99
D-$21.99/$30.99 (Tue)/
$25.99 (Sat/Sun)
Other Games: S21, MB, P, CSP, PGP, MS,
TCP, LIR, FCP, K, B6
Overnight RV Parking: No
Special Features: Buffet discount for players club members.

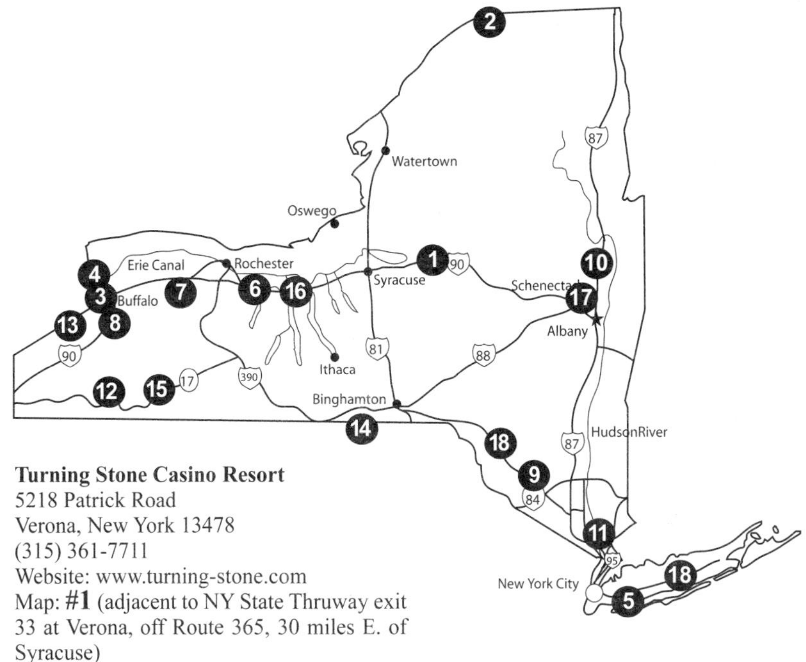

Turning Stone Casino Resort
5218 Patrick Road
Verona, New York 13478
(315) 361-7711
Website: www.turning-stone.com
Map: **#1** (adjacent to NY State Thruway exit 33 at Verona, off Route 365, 30 miles E. of Syracuse)

Toll-Free Number: (800) 771-7711
Rooms: 572 Price Range: $119-$229
Suites: 143 Price Range: $219-$595
Restaurants: 10 Liquor: No
Buffets: B-$21.95 (Sat/Sun)
L-$16.95/ $21.95 (Sat/Sun)
D-$18.95/$20.95 (Tue)/
$25.95 (Fri/Sat)/$23.95 (Sun)
Casino Size: 122,000 Square Feet
Other Games: S21, B, MB, P, LIR, PGP, BG, CSP,TCP, FCP, K, CW, B6, S21, SIC, THB
Overnight RV Parking: No
Senior Discount: Various Wed if 55+
Special Features: Three golf courses. Gift shop. Discount smoke shop. 800-seat showroom. 175-space RV park ($40-$55 per night).

Yellow Brick Road Casino
800 West Genesee St
Chittenango, New York 13037
(315) 366-9400
Website: www.yellowbrickroadcasino.com
Map: **#1** (15 miles E. of Syracuse)

Restaurants: 3 Liquor: Yes
Casino Size: 67,000 Square Feet
Other Games: S21, LIR, TCP, MS, B6

Indian Casinos (Class II)

There are some Indian casinos that offer Class II gambling which consist of electronic gaming machines which look like slot machines, but are actually games of bingo and the spinning video reels are for "entertainment purposes only." No public information is available concerning the payback percentages on the video gaming machines.

All of these casinos have a cashless system whereby you have to go to a cashier cage, or a kiosk, get a "smart" card and deposit money to that card's account. The machines will then deduct losses from, or credit wins to, your account.

Additionally, after playing don't forget to cash out because all remaining credits on cards will be forfeited at the end of the day.

Some of these casinos also offer high-stakes bingo and poker, as shown in the "Other Games" listings.

Lakeside Entertainment
271 Cayuga Street
Union Springs, New York 13160
(315) 889-5416
Website: www.lakesidegaming.com
Map: **#15** (55 miles S. W. of Syracuse)

Restaurants: None Liquor: No
Hours: 10am-11pm/12:30 am (Fri/Sat)
Overnight RV Parking: Free/RV Dump: No

Seneca Gaming - Irving
11099 Route 5
Irving, New York 14081
(716) 549-4389
Website: www.senecagames.com
Map: **#13** (38 miles S.W. of Buffalo)

Toll-Free Number: (800) 421-2464
Restaurants: 1 Liquor: No
Hours: 9:30am-2am/4:30am (Fri/Sat)
Other Games: Bingo
Overnight RV Parking: Free (must check in with security first)/RV Dump: No
Special Features: Discount smoke shop.

Seneca Gaming - Oil Spring
5374 West Shore Road
Cuba, New York 14727
(716) 780-8787
Website: www.senecagames.com
Map: **#15** (80 miles SW of Buffalo)

Hours: 10:30am-11pm daily
Overnight RV Parking: No/RV Dump: No

Seneca Gaming - Salamanca
768 Broad Street
Salamanca, New York 14779
(716) 945-4080
Website: www.senecagames.com
Map: **#12** (65 miles S. of Buffalo)

Toll-Free Number: (877) 860-5130
Restaurants: 1 Snack Bar Liquor: No
Hours: 9:30am-1am/2am (Fri/Sat)
Other Games: Bingo, Poker (Wed-Sun)
Overnight RV Parking: Free (must check in with security first)/RV Dump: No

Pari-Mutuels

New York allows slot machine-type video lottery machines at all New York racetracks, as well as one off-track betting facility. Officially referred to as Video Gaming Machines (VGM's), they are regulated by the New York Lottery.

All VGM's offer standard slot machine-type games, plus keno in denominations from five cents to $10. The machines all accept cash but do not pay out in cash. They print a receipt which must be taken to a cashier.

The VGM's do not operate like regular slot machines or video poker games. Instead, they are similar to scratch-off-type lottery tickets with a pre-determined number of winners. The legislation authorizing the VGM's states, "the specifications for video lottery gaming shall be designed in such a manner as to pay prizes that average no less than ninety percent of sales."

All racetrack casinos also offer electronic versions of roulette, craps and baccarat, except for three racinos in western New York: Hamburg Gaming, Finger Lakes and Batavia Downs.

Here's information, as supplied by the New York Lottery, showing the video gaming machine payback percentages for each of the state's racetracks for the four-month period from April 1, 2017 through July 31, 2017:

LOCATION	PAYBACK %
Resorts World	94.14
Jake's 58	93.27
Empire City	93.10
Monticello	92.21
Saratoga	92.21
Finger Lakes	91.96
Fairgrounds	91.49
Batavia Downs	91.54
Vernon Downs	91.44

All Video Gaming Machine facilities are alowed to be open for 20 hours a day, with varrying hours. Some are open 8am-4am, some are open 9am-5am, etc. and all are non-smoking. Please call to confirm hours if necessary. Admission is free to all facilities and the minimum gambling age is 18 for playing VGM's, as well as for pari-mutuel betting.

Batavia Downs Gaming & Hotel
8315 Park Road
Batavia, New York 14020
(585) 343-3750
Website: www.bataviadownsgaming.com
Map: **#7** (35 miles E. of Buffalo)

Toll-Free: (800) 724-2000
Rooms: 80 Price Range: $98-$152
Suites: 4 Price Range: $199-$239
Restaurants: 4
Overnight RV Parking: No
Senior Discount: Various Mon if 55+
Special Features: Live harness racing seasonally. Daily simulcasting of thoroughbred and harness racing.

Empire City Casino
810 Yonkers Avenue
Yonkers, New York 10704
(914) 968-4200
Website: www.empirecitycasino.com
Map: **#11** (20 miles N. of Manhattan)

Restaurants: 4
Special Features: Live harness racing seasonally. Daily simulcasting of thoroughbred and harness racing.

Finger Lakes Gaming & Racetrack
5857 Route 96
Farmington, New York 14425
(585) 924-3232
Website: www.fingerlakesgaming.com
Map: **#6** (25 miles S. of Rochester)

Restaurants: 5
Buffets: L-$16.95 (Wed-Fri)/$18.95 (Sat/Sun)
D- $20.95 (Wed-Sun)
Casino Size: 28,267 Square Feet
Overnight RV Parking: Call for permission
Senior Discount: Various Wed if 50+
Special Features: Live thoroughbred horse racing seasonally. Daily simulcasting of harness and thoroughbred racing.

Hamburg Gaming at The Fairgrounds
5820 South Park Avenue
Hamburg, New York 14075
(716) 646-6109
Website: www.the-fairgrounds.com
Map: **#8** (15 miles S. of Buffalo)

Toll-Free: (800) 237-1205
Restaurants: 3
Buffets: L- $15.99 D- $ 20.99
Casino Size: 55,000 Square Feet
Overnight RV Parking: Yes
Senior Discount: Various Wed if 55+
Special Features: Live harness racing seasonally. Simulcasting Wed-Sun of thoroughbred and harness racing. Buffet closed Mon/Tue.

Jake's 58 Hotel & Casino
3635 Express Drive North
Islandia, New York 11749
(631) 232-3000
Website: jakes58.com
Map: **#18** (50 miles E. of Manhattan)

Rooms: 200 Price Range:$159 - $179
Suites: 28 Price range: $329 - $399
Restaurants: 1
Casino Hours: 8am - 4am Daily
Casino Size: 100,000 Square Feet
Overnight RV Parking: No
Special Features: Off Track Betting on thoroughbred and harness racing.

Monticello Gaming & Raceway
204 Route 17B
Monticello, New York 12701
(845) 794-4100
Website: monticellocasinoandraceway.com
Map: **#9** (50 miles W. of Newburgh)

Toll-Free: (866) 777-4263
Restaurants: 3
Overnight RV Parking: Free/RV Dump: No
Special Features: Live harness racing seasonally. Daily simulcast of thoroughbred and harness racing.

Resorts World Casino New York City
110-00 Rockaway Boulevard
Jamaica, New York 11420
(718) 215-2828
Website: www.rwnewyork.com
Map: **#5** (15 miles E. of Manhattan)

Toll-Free: (888) 888-8801
Restaurants: 2
Special Features: Live thoroughbred racing seasonally. Daily simulcasting of thoroughbred racing. Food court with five fast food outlets.

Saratoga Casino Hotel
342 Jefferson Street
Saratoga Springs, New York 12866
(518) 584-2110
Website: www.saratogacasino.com
Map: **#10** (25 miles N. of Schenectady)

Toll-Free: (800) 727-2990
Rooms: 104 Price Range: $169-$599
Suites: 13 Price Range: $229-$1,100
Restaurants: 4
Buffets: L- $13.95 D- $15.95
Casino Size: 55,000 Square Feet
Overnight RV Parking: Free
Senior Discount: Various Tue if 55+
Special Features: Live harness racing seasonally. Daily simulcasting of thoroughbred and harness racing. Buffet discount if players club member.

Vernon Downs Casino Hotel
4229 Stuhlman Road
Vernon, New York 13476
(315) 829-2201
Website: www.vernondowns.com
Map: **#1** (30 miles E. of Syracuse)

Toll-Free Number: (877) 888-3766
Suites: 175 Price Range: $129-$199
Restaurants: 5
Buffets: L- $8/$10.99 (Fri/Sat)/$11.99 (Sun)
D- $8/$14.99 (Fri/Sun)/$21.99 (Sat)
Casino Size: 28,000 Square Feet
Overnight RV Parking: Free/RV Dump: No
Senior Discount: Various Tue if 50+
Special Features: Live harness racing seasonally. Daily simulcasting of thoroughbred and harness racing.

Canadian Casinos

If you are traveling to the Buffalo area there are two nearby Canadian casinos just across the border in Niagara Falls, Ontario.

Both casinos are open 24 hours and offer: slots, video poker, blackjack, roulette. Spanish 21, Casino War, Mississippi stud, three card poker and a poker room. Optional games include: baccarat (B), mini-baccarat (MB), big six wheel (B6), keno (K), pai gow poker (PGP), pai gow tiles (Pg), let it ride (LIR), caribbean stud poker (CSP), sic bo (SIC), four-card poker (FCP), Texas hold'em bonus (THB) and ultimate Texas hold'em (UTH).

All winnings are paid in Canadian currency and the minimum gambling age is 19. All prices shown below are in Canadian dollars.

Casino Niagara
5705 Falls Avenue
Niagara Falls, Ontario L2E 6T3
(905) 374-3589
Website: www.casinoniagara.com
Map: **#4**

Toll-Free Number: (888) 946-3255
Restaurants: 2
Buffets: L-$19.95 D-$23.95
Casino Size: 100,000 Square Feet
Other games: Poker, Mississippi stud
Overnight RV Parking: Free/RV Dump: No
Senior Discount: Various Wed if 55+

Fallsview Casino Resort
6380 Fallsview Boulevard
Niagara, Ontario L2G 7X5
(905) 358-3255
Website: www.fallsviewcasinoresort.com
Map: **#4**

Toll-Free Number: (888) 325-5788
Rooms: 340 Price Range: $249-$350
Suites: 28 Price Range: $359-$559
Restaurants: 8
Buffets: B-$13.00/ $25.00 (Sun) L/D-$25.00
Other Games: B, MB, CSP, FCP, LIR, PG,
SIC, THB, UTH
Casino Size: 180,000 Square Feet
Overnight RV Parking: No
Special Features: Additional Hilton and Sheraton hotels connected by walkway. Food court with 10 fast food outlets. Spa/fitness center. 1,500-seat theatre..

NORTH CAROLINA

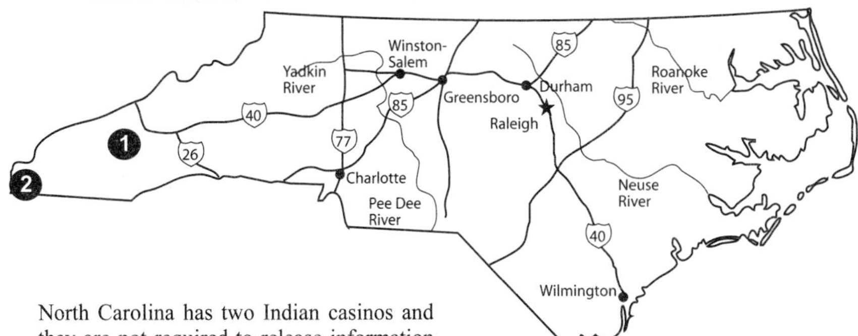

North Carolina has two Indian casinos and they are not required to release information on the payback percentages of their games. However, according to the terms of their compact with the state, the video machines must be games of skill and they are required to return a minimum of 83% to a maximum of 98%.

Some of the slots offered are called "Lock N Roll" and are different than slots you will find in traditional casinos. With these "skill" slots you have two opportunities to spin the reels. The "skill" factor comes into play because after seeing the results of your first spin you then have to decide whether to keep none, one, two, or all three of the symbols on each reel before you spin them again.

The casinos also offer more traditional looking slots, called "Cherokee Raffle Reels." However, once again, they operate differently from regular slot machines because you are actually being entered into a raffle drawing.

Both casinos offer live blackjack, roulette and craps. Optional games include: mini-baccarat (MB), poker (P), let it ride (LIR), Mississippi stud (MS) and three card poker (TCP). Both casinos are open 24 hours and the minimum gambling age is 21.

For more information on visiting North Carolina call the state's division of travel & tourism at (800) 847-4862 or go to: www.visitnc.com.

Harrah's Cherokee Casino
777 Casino Drive
Cherokee, North Carolina 28719
(828) 497-7777
Website: www.harrahscherokee.com
Map: **#1** (55 miles S.W. of Asheville)

Toll-Free Number: (800) 427-7247
Rooms 1,108 Price Range: $149-$499
Suites: 107 Price Range: Casino Use Only
Restaurants: 6 Liquor: Yes
Buffets: L/D- $27.49(Sat)/$33.99 (Sun)
Other Games: MB (Digital), P, LIR, TCP
Overnight RV Parking: No
Special Features: 1,500-seat entertainment pavilion. Buffet closed Tue/Wed.

Harrah's Cherokee Valley River Casino & Hotel
777 Casino Parkway
Murphy, North Carolina 28906
(828) 422-7777
Map: **#2** (55 miles S.W. of Asheville)

Toll-Free Number: (800) 427-7247
Rooms: 300 Price Range: $139-$399
Restaurants: None Liquor: Yes
Casino Size: 50,000 square feet
Other Games: TCP, MS
Special Features: Food court with four fast fast food outlets. Starbucks coffeehouse.

NORTH DAKOTA

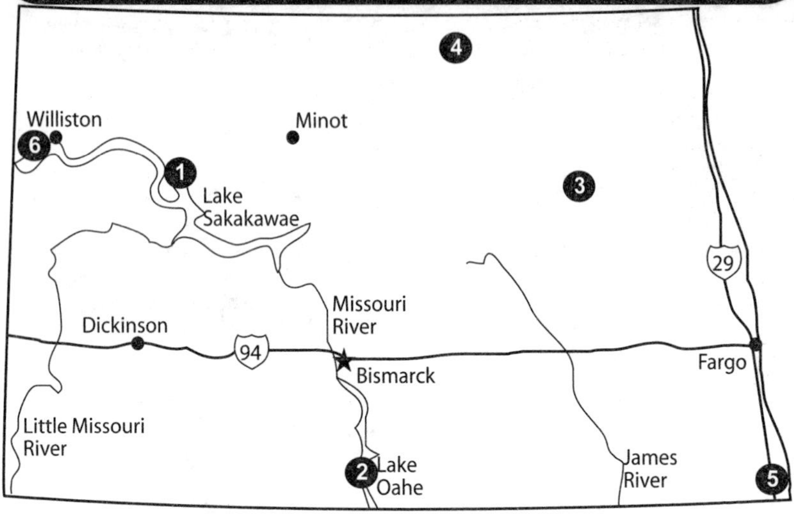

North Dakota has more than 800 sites throughout the state that offer blackjack, with betting limits of $1-$25, for the benefit of charities.

There are also Indian casinos in North Dakota which are limited by law to the following maximum bet limits: blackjack-$100 (two tables in a casino may have limits up to $250), craps-$60, roulette-$50, slots/video poker-$25 and poker-$50 per bet, per round with a maximum of three rounds.

The terms of the state's compact with the tribes require gaming machines to return a minimum of 80% and a maximum of 100%. However, if a machine is affected by skill, such as video poker or video blackjack, the machines must return a minimum of 83%.

All casinos are open 24 hours and offer: blackjack, craps, roulette, slots, video poker and video keno. Optional games include: Spanish 21 (S21), Caribbean stud poker (CSP), let it ride (LIR), ultimate Texas hold em (UTH), poker (P), three-card poker (TCP), keno (K), bingo (BG), big-6 wheel (B6) and off-track betting (OTB). The minimum age requirement is 21 for casino gambling and 18 for bingo.

For information on visiting North Dakota call the state's tourism office at (800) 435-5663 or go to: www.ndtourism.com.

Dakota Magic Casino Resort
16849 102nd Street SE
Hankinson, North Dakota 58041
(701) 634-3000
Website: www.dakotamagic.com
Map: **#5** (50 miles S. of Fargo)

Toll-Free Number: (800) 325-6825
Rooms: 111 Price Range: $79-$129
Suites: 8 Price Range: $150-$240
Restaurants: 4 Liquor: Yes
Buffets: D- $11.95/$17.95(Fri)/$16.95 (Sat)
Casino Size: 24,000 Square Feet
Other Games: P, no roulette
Overnight RV Parking: Free/RV Dump: Fee
Senior Discount: Various on Mon if 55+
Special Features: 27-hole golf course.

Four Bears Casino & Lodge
202 Frontage Road
New Town, North Dakota 58763
(701) 627-4018
Website: www.4bearscasino.com
Map: **#1** (150 miles N.W. of Bismarck)

Toll-Free Number: (800) 294-5454
Rooms: 190 Price: $100
Suites: 30 Price: $149
Restaurants: 3 Liquor: Yes
Buffets: B-$9.95 L-$10.95
D-$19.95/$22.95 (Wed/Thu/Sat)
Other Games: P
Overnight RV Parking: Free/RV Dump: No
Senior Discount: Various Tue if 55+
Special Features: 85-space RV park ($25 per night). Nearby marina. 1,000-seat event center.

Grand Treasure Casino
4418 147th Avenue NW
Trenton, North Dakota 58553
(701) 572-2690
Website: www.grandtreasurecasino.net
Map: **#6** (120 miles N.W of Dickinson)

Casino Size: 5,000 sq ft
Other Games: Machines Only
Senior Discount: Various Mon if 55+

Prairie Knights Casino & Resort
7932 Highway 24
Fort Yates, North Dakota 58528
(701) 854-7777
Website: www.prairieknights.com
Map: **#2** (60 miles S. of Bismarck)

Toll-Free Number: (800) 425-8277
Rooms: 188 Price Range: $100
Suites: 12 Price Range: $150
Restaurants: 2 Liquor: Yes
Buffets: L/D-$10.95
Casino Size: 42,000 Square Feet
Other Games: TCP, UTH, No Roulette
Overnight RV Parking: Must use RV park
Special Features: 16-space RV park ($15 per night) at casino. 32-space RV park ($15 per night) at marina. Free RV dump at marina. Convenience store. Table games open at noon.

Sky Dancer Hotel Casino & Resort
3965 Sky Dancer Way N.E.
Belcourt, North Dakota 58316
(701) 244-2400
Website: www.skydancercasino.com
Map: **#4** (120 miles N.E. of Minot)

Toll-Free Number: (866) 244-9467
Rooms: 70 Price Range: $77-$115
Suites: 27 Price Range: $125-$135
Restaurants: 2 Liquor: Yes
Casino Size: 25,000 Square Feet
Buffets: B- $5.95 L- $7.95
D- $10.95/$21.95 (Fri)/$17.95 (Sat)
Other Games: LIR, OTB (Wed-Sun),
No Craps or Roulette
Overnight RV Parking: Free/RV Dump: Free

Spirit Lake Casino & Resort
7889 ND Highway 57
St. Michael, North Dakota 58370
(701) 766-4747
Website: www.spiritlakecasino.com
Map: **#3** (6 miles S. of Devil's Lake)

Toll-Free Number: (800) 946-8238
Rooms: 108 Price Range: $69-$119
Suites: 16 Price Range: $115-$159
Restaurants: 2 Liquor: No
Buffets: B/L- $9.95 (Sun)
D- $10.95 (Mon/Fri)/$7.95 (Tue)/
$11.95 (Wed/Sat/Sun)/$5.95 (Thu)/
Casino Size: 45,000 Square Feet
Other Games: P, BG (Wed-Sun), No roulette
Overnight RV Parking: Must use RV park
Senior Discount: Various on Monday if 55+
Special Features: 73-space RV park ($25-$35 per night). Smoke shop. 32-slip marina.

OHIO

Ohio has casinos in four cities: Cleveland, Cincinnati, Columbus and Toledo. All of the casinos are non-smoking, open 24 hours and the minimum gambling age is 21.

Unless otherwise noted, all Ohio casinos offer: blackjack, craps, roulette, slots and video poker. Some casinos also offer: mini-baccarat (MB), baccarat (B), poker (P), pai gow poker (PGP), Mississippi stud (MS), sic-bo (SIC), let it ride (LIR), three card poker (TCP), four card poker (FCP), casino war (CW), big six (B6) and bingo (BG).

If you want to order a drink while playing, be aware that Ohio gaming regulations do not allow casinos to provide free alcoholic beverages. Additionally, casinos are not allowed to serve any alcohol between the hours of 2 a.m. and 6 a.m.

NOTE: If you happen to win a jackpot of $1,200 or more in Ohio, the casino will withhold approximately 5% of your winnings for the Ohio Department of Taxation. The $1,200 threshold also applies to any cash prizes won in casino drawings or tournaments.

Additionally, the casino will withhold another approximate 2.5% of your winnings for city taxes in Columbus, Cleveland and Cincinatti. In Toledo, the city tax won't be withheld until you win $2,000, or more. The $1,200 and $2,000 thresholds would also apply to any cash prizes won in casino drawings or tournaments.

Here's information from the Ohio Casino Control Commission regarding the payback percentages for each racino and casino's electronic machines for the six-month period from January 1, 2017 through June 30, 2017:

CASINO	PAYBACK %
JACK Cleveland	92.34
Hollywood Columbus	92.16
JACK Cincinatti	91.58
Belterra	91.08
Miami Valley	91.24
Scito Downs	90.96
Hard Rock	91.06
Hollywood Toledo	91.11
JACK Thistledown	90.87
Dayton Raceway	90.47
Mahoning Valley	90.09

For tourism information, call the Ohio Division of Travel and Tourism at (800) 282-5393, or visit their website at www.discoverohio.com

Hollywood Casino - Columbus
200 Georgesville Road
Columbus, Ohio 43228
(614) 308-3333
Website: www.hollywoodcasinocolumbus.com
Map: #**6**

Toll-Free Number: (855) 617-4206
Restaurants: 4
Buffets: L-$13.99
D-$19.99/$32.99 (Fri)/$27.99(Sat)
Casino Size: 120,000 Square Feet
Other games: TCP, MB, B6, PGP, MS, CW, P
Overnight RV Parking: Free/RV Dump: No
Special Features: Buffet closed Mon/Tue.

Hollywood Casino - Toledo
777 Hollywood Boulevard
Toledo, Ohio 43605
(419) 661-5200
Website: www.hollywoodcasinotoledo.com
Map: #**4**

Toll-Free Number: (877) 777-9579
Buffets: L-$15.99 D-$21.99/$36.99 (Fri) /$32.99 (Sat)
Casino Size: 125,000 square feet
Other games: MB, LIR, P, B6, MS, TCP, UTH

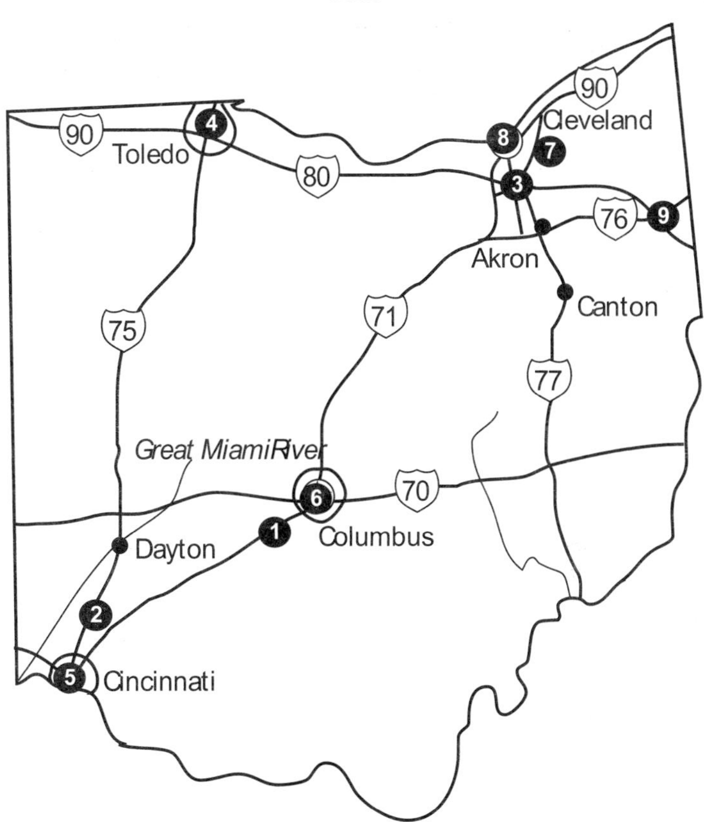

JACK Cincinatti Casino
1000 Broadway Street
Cincinnati, Ohio 45202
(513) 252-0777
Website: www.jackentertainment.com
Map: #**5**

Restaurants: 6
Buffets: L-$17.99/$27.99 (Sat/Sun)
D-$25.99/$24.99 (Thu)/
$29.99 (Fri/Sat)/$35.99 (Sun)
Casino Size: 100,000 Square Feet
Other games: MB, TCP, LIR, MS, B6, P
Senior Discount: Various Wed if 55+
Special features: 100x odds on craps.

JACK Cleveland Casino
100 Public Square
Cleveland, Ohio 44113
(216) 297-4777
Website: www.jackentertainment.com
Map: #**8**

Toll-free Number: (855) 746-3777
Restaurants: 8
Buffet: B-$25.99 (Sat/Sun)
L-$15.99 D-$25.99/$30.99 (Fri/Sat)
Casino Size: 96,000 Square Feet
Games Offered: P, PGP, TCP, FCP,
LIR, MS, UTH
Special features: 100x odds on craps.

Pari-Mutuels

In Ohio, pari-mutuels are allowed to offer video lottery terminals that are regulated by the Ohio Lottery Commission.

All racetrack casinos (racinos) are open 24 hours and the minimum gambling age is 21. The minimum age for pari-mutuel betting is 18.

Belterra Park Gaming & Entertainment Center
6301 Kellogg Road
Cincinnati, Ohio 45230
(513) 232-8000
Website: www.belterrapark.com
Map: **#5**

Restaurants: 4
Buffets: L- $15.95/$22.95 (Sun)
D- $20.95/$31.95 (Fri/Sat)/
$25.95 (Sun)
Senior Discount: Various Tue if 55+
Special Features: Live horse racing seasonally. Daily simulcasting of horse racing.

Hard Rock Rocksino at Northfield Park
10777 Northfield Road
Northfield, Ohio 44067
(330) 908-7625
Website: www.hrrocksinonorthfieldpark.com
Map: #**3** (10 miles SE. of Clevland)

Restaurants: 4
Buffets: L-$15.99/$22.99 (Sun)
D-$22.99/$26.99 (Wed)/$31.99 (Fri/Sat)
Special Features: Live horse racing seasonally. Daily simulcasting of horse racing.

Hollywood Gaming Dayton Raceway
3100 Needmore Road
Dayton, Ohio 45414
(937) 235-7800
Website: www.hollywooddaytonraceway.com
Map: #**1** (10 miles SW. of Columbus)

Toll-Free Number: (844) 225-7057
Restaurants: 1
Special Features: Live harness racing seasonally. Daily simulcasting of horse racing.

Hollywood Gaming Mahoning Valley
655 North Canfield Niles Road
Austintown, Ohio 44515
(877) 788-3777
Website: www.hollywoodmahoningvalley.com
Map: #**9** (45 miles E. of Akron)

Restaurants: 3
Special Features: Live horse racing seasonally. Daily simulcasting of horse racing.

JACK Thistledown Racino
21501 Emery Road
Cleveland, Ohio 44128
(216) 662-8600
Website: www.thistledown.com
Map: #**8**

Restaurants: 4
Senior Discount: Various Tue if 55+
Special Features: Live thoroughbred racing seasonally. Daily simulcasting of harness and horse racing.

Miami Valley Gaming
6000 State Route 63
Lebanon, Ohio 45036
(513) 934-7070
Website: www.miamivalleygaming.com
Map: #**2** (25 miles S. of Dayton)

Toll Free (855) 946-6847
Restaurants: 3
Buffets: L- $13.99/$15.99 (Sun)
D- $18.99/$19.99 (Fri)/$24.99 (Sat)
Special Features: Live Harness racing seasonally. Daily simulcasting of horse racing. Buffet closed Mon/Tue. No lunch buffet Wed.

Scioto Downs Racino
6000 S. High St
Columbus, Ohio 43207
(614) 295-4700
Website: www.sciotodowns.com
Map: #**6**

Restaurants: 3
Buffets: L- $13.99 D- $13.99/
$22.99 (Fri)/$17.99 (Sat)
Senior Discount: Various Wed if 50+
Special Features: Affiliated with Eldorado Resorts. Live harness racing seasonally. Daily simulcasting of harness and horse racing.

OKLAHOMA

All Oklahoma Indian casinos are allowed to offer both Class II and Class III gaming machines.

Most casinos offer only Class II machines which look like slot machines, but are actually games of bingo and the spinning video reels are for "entertainment purposes only." Some casinos also offer traditional Class III slots. In either case, the gaming machines are not allowed to accept or payout in coins. All payouts must be done by a printed receipt or via an electronic debit card. No public information is available concerning the payback percentages on gaming machines in Oklahoma.

Some casinos with card games such as blackjack, let it ride or three-card poker, etc., offer a player-banked version where players must pay a commission to the house on every hand they play. The amount of the commission charged varies, depending on the rules of each casino, but it's usually 50 cents to $1 per hand played. Call the casino to see if they charge a commission.

Traditional roulette and dice games are not permitted in Oklahoma. Instead, the casinos offer card-based versions where the result is determined by playing cards, rather than dice or a roulette wheel.

There are also two horse racing facilities in Oklahoma which feature Class II gaming machines.

All Oklahoma Indian casinos offer gaming machines. Other games include: blackjack (BJ), craps (C), roulette (R), mini-baccarat (MB), poker (P), three-card poker (TCP), pai gow poker (PGP), ultimate Texas hold 'em (UTH), let it ride (LIR), Mississippi stud (MS), bingo (BG) and off-track betting (OTB).

Not all Oklahoma Indian casinos serve alcoholic beverages and the individual listings note which casinos do serve it. Unless otherwise noted, all casinos are open 24 hours. The minimum gambling age is 18 at some casinos and 21 at others.

For more information on visiting Oklahoma call the Oklahoma Tourism Department at (800) 652-6552 or go to: www.travelok.com

Ada Gaming Center - East
1500 North Country Club Road
Ada, Oklahoma 74820
Website: www.adagaming.com
(580) 436-3740
Map: **#2** (85 miles S.E. of Oklahoma City)

Restaurants: 2 (1 snack bar) Liquor: Yes
Casino Size: 9,220 Square Feet
Other Games: BJ, UTH
Overnight RV Parking: No
Special Features: Located in travel plaza with gas station and convenience store.

Ada Gaming Center - West
201 Latta Road
Ada, Oklahoma 74820
(580) 310-0900
Website: www.chickasaw.net
Map: **#2** (85 miles S.E. of Oklahoma City)

Restaurants: 1 Snack Bar Liquor: No
Overnight RV Parking: No
Special Features: Located in travel plaza with gas station and convenience store.

Apache Casino Hotel
2315 East Gore Boulevard
Lawton, Oklahoma 73501
(580) 248-5905
Website: www.apachecasinohotel.com
Map: **#17** (86 miles S.W. of Oklahoma City)

Rooms: 124 Price Range: $109-$187
Suites: 8 Price Range: $239-$329
Restaurants: 2 Liquor: Yes
Buffets: B- $8.99 (Sat/Sun)
Casino Size: 7,700 Square Feet
Other games: BJ, C, UTH
Overnight RV Parking: Free/RV Dump: No
Senior Discount: Various Tue/Thu if 50+

Artesian Hotel Casino Spa
1001 W. 1st Street
Sulphur, Oklahoma 73086
(580) 622-2156
Website: www.artesianhotel.com
Map: **#35** (84 miles S. of Oklahoma City)

Toll-Free Number: (855) 455-5255
Rooms: 81 Price Range: $149-$199
Suites: 4 Price Range: $229-$279
Restaurants: 2 Liquor: Yes
Other Games: BJ, UTH
Overnight RV Parking: Free/RV Dump: No
Senior Discount: Various Wed if 50+
Special Features: Spa.

Black Gold Casino
288 Mulberry Lane (on Route 70)
Wilson, Oklahoma 73463
(580) 668-4415
Website: www.myblackgoldcasino.com
Map: **#39** (112 miles S. of Oklahoma City)

Restaurants: 1 Snack Bar Liquor: No
Casino Size: 3,744 Square Feet
Overnight RV Parking: Free/RV Dump: No
Special Features: Located in travel plaza with gas station and convenience store.

Black Hawk Casino
42008 Westech Road
Shawnee, Oklahoma 74804
(405) 275-4700
Website: www.theblackhawkcasino.com
Map: **#23** (40 Miles E. of Okalhoma City)

Restaurants: 1 Liquor: Yes
Casino Size: 8,600 Sqaure Feet
Other Games: BJ, UTH
Overnight RV Parking: No

Border Casino
22953 Brown Springs Road
Thackerville, Oklahoma 73459
(580) 276-1727
Website: www.mybordercasino.com
Map: **#36** (124 miles S. of Oklahoma City)

Restaurants: 1 Snack Bar Liquor: Yes
Overnight RV Parking: Free/RV Dump: No

Bordertown Casino and Arena
129 W. Oneida Street
Wyandotte, Oklahoma 74370
(918) 666-9401
Map: **#26** (90 miles N.E. of Tulsa)

Restaurants: 1 Liquor: Yes
Special Features: Indoor arena

Buffalo Run Casino
1000 Buffalo Run Boulevard
Miami, Oklahoma 74354
(918) 542-7140
Website: www.buffalorun.com
Map: **#33** (89 miles N.E. of Tulsa)

Rooms: 88 Room Rates: $75-$99
Suites: 12 Room Rates: $85-$115
Restaurants: 3 Liquor: Yes
Other Games: BJ, TCP, UTH
Overnight RV Parking: Free/RV Dump: No
Special Features: 2,000-seat showroom.

Casino Oklahoma
220 E. Cummins Road
Hinton, Oklahoma 73047
(405) 542-4200
Website: www.casinooklahoma.com
Map: **#63** (55 miles W. of Oklahoma City)

Restaurants: 2 Liquor: Yes
Senior Discount: Various Thu at 11am if 55+
Overnight RV Parking: Free/RV Dump: No

Cherokee Casino - Ft. Gibson
107 N. Georgetown Road/US Highway 62
Ft. Gibson, Oklahoma 74434
(918) 684-5507
Website: www.cherokeecasino.com
Map: **#54** (80 miles E. of Tulsa)

Restaurants: 1 Liquor: Yes
Overnight RV Parking: No
Senior Discount: Various Tue if 55+

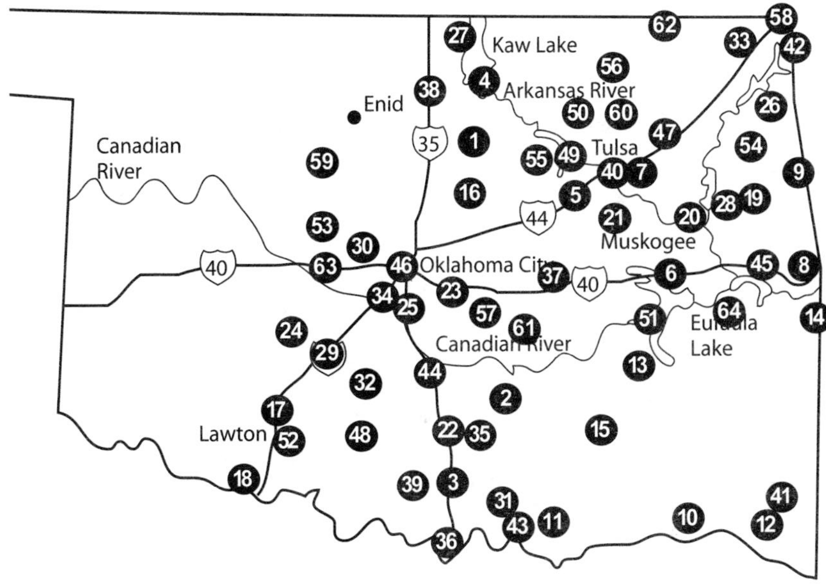

Cherokee Casino - Grove
Highway 59 and East 250 Road
Grove, Oklahoma 74344
(918) 786-1300
Website: www.cherokeecasino.com
Map: **#54** (100 miles N.E. of Tulsa)

Restaurants: 1 Liquor: Yes
Overnight RV Parking: Free/RV Dump: No
Senior Discount: Various Mon/Thu if 50+

Cherokee Casino - Ramona
31501 US 75 Highway
Ramona, Oklahoma 74061
(918) 535-3800
Website: www.cherokeecasino.com
Map: **#60** (30 miles N. of Tulsa)

Restaurants: 1 Liquor: Yes
Senior Discount: Various Tue/Wed if 50+

Cherokee Casino & Hotel - Roland
109 Cherokee Boulevard
Roland, Oklahoma 74954
(800) 256-2338
Website: www.cherokeecasino.com
Map: **#8** (175 miles E. of Oklahoma City)

Rooms: 98 Room Rates: $74-$106
Suites: 12 Room Rates: $119-$179
Restaurants: 2 Liquor: Yes
Buffet: L- $5.99 L- $6.99
D- $8.99/$13.99 (Fri/Sat)
Casino Size: 28,000 Square Feet
Other Games: BJ, R, TCP, UTH
Senior Discount: Various Thu if 50+
Overnight RV Parking: Free/RV Dump: No

Cherokee Casino - Sallisaw
1621 West Ruth Street
Sallisaw, Oklahoma 74955
(918) 774-1600
Website: www.cherokeecasino.com
Map: **#45** (160 miles E. of Oklahoma City)

Toll-Free Number: (800) 256-2338
Restaurants: 1 Liquor: Yes
Casino Size: 22,000 Square Feet
Other Games: OTB
Overnight RV Parking: Free/RV Dump: No

Cherokee Casino - South Coffeyville
1506 North Highway 169
South Coffeyville, Oklahoma 74072
(918) 255-4200
Website: www.cherokeecasino.com
Map: **#62** (70 miles N.E. of Tulsa)

Restaurants: 1 Liquor: Yes
Overnight RV Parking: No

Cherokee Casino - Tahlequah
16489 Highway 62
Tahlequah, Oklahoma 74464
(918) 207-3600
Website: www.cherokeecasino.com
Map: **#19** (83 miles S.E. of Tulsa)

Restaurants: 1 Liquor: No
Overnight RV Parking: Free/RV Dump: No
Senior Special: Various Tue if 50+

Cherokee Casino & Hotel - West Siloam Springs
3426 US Highway 412
West Siloam Springs, Oklahoma 74338
(800) 754-4111
Website: www.cherokeecasino.com
Map: **#9** (85 miles E. of Tulsa)

Toll-Free Number: (800) 754-4111
Rooms: 140 Price Range: $85-$99
Restaurants: 3 Liquor: Yes
Buffets: B-$6.99 (Sat/Sun) L-$8.99
D-$11.99/
Other Games: BJ, R, P, OTB, MS,
UTH, TCP
Overnight RV Parking: Free/RV Dump: No
Senior Discount: Various Tue if 50+

Chisholm Trail Casino
7807 N. Highway 81
Duncan, Oklahoma 73533
(580) 255-1668
Website: www.chisholmtrailcasino.com
Map: **#48** (79 miles S. of Oklahoma City)

Restaurants: 1 Liquor: Yes
Casino Size: 22,000 Square Feet
Other Games: BJ, UTH
Overnight RV Parking: Free/RV Dump: No
Senior Discount: Various Mon if 50+

Choctaw Casino - Broken Bow
1790 South Park Drive
Broken Bow, Oklahoma 74728
(580) 584-5450
Website: www.choctawcasinos.com
Map: **#41** (235 miles S.E. of Oklahoma City)

Restaurants: 1 Liquor: Yes
Overnight RV Parking: Free/ RV Dump: No
Senior Discount: Various Wed if 50+

Choctaw Casino Resort - Durant
4216 South Highway 69/75
Durant, Oklahoma 74701
(580) 920-0160
Website: www.choctawcasinos.com
Map: **#11** (150 miles S.E. of Oklahoma City)

Toll-Free Number: (888) 652-4628
Rooms: 240 Price Range: $109-$279
Suites: 90 Price Range: $239-$550
Restaurants: 8 Liquor: Yes
Buffets: B-$9,99/$19.99 (Sun) L- $16.99
D-$20.99/$26.99 (Fri/Sat)
Casino Size: 36,000 Square Feet
Other Games: BJ, MB, C, R, P, OTB,
TCP, LIR, PGP, UTH
Senior Discount: Various Wed if 50+
Overnight RV Parking: Must use RV Park
Special Features: Spa. 20-lane bowling alley. 4-screen movie theater. 75-space RV park ($45-$55 nightly). 3,000-seat event theater.

Choctaw Casino Resort - Grant
1516 US Highway 271
Grant, Oklahoma 74738
(580) 326-8397
Website: www.choctawcasinos.com
Map: **#10** (200 miles S. of Oklahoma City)

Rooms: 60 Price Range: $119-$169
Restaurants: 2 Liquor: Yes
Buffets: B-$11 (Sat/Sun) L-$13.50
D-$15/$26 (Fri/Sat)
Other Games: BJ, P
Overnight RV Parking: No
Senior Discount: Various Wed if 50+
Special Features: No Dinner Buffet Mon.

Choctaw Casino - Idabel
1425 Southeast Washington Street
Idabel, Oklahoma 74745
(800) 634-2582
Website: www.choctawcasinos.com
Map: **#12** (240 miles S.E. of Oklahoma City)

Restaurants: 1 Liquor: Yes
Casino Size: 11,000 Square Feet
Overnight RV Parking: Must check-in at front desk/RV Dump: No
Senior Discount: Various Wed if 50+

Choctaw Casino - McAlester
1638 South George Nigh Expressway
McAlester, Oklahoma 74501
(918) 423-8161
Website: www.choctawcasinos.com
Map: **#13** (130 miles S.E. of Oklahoma City)

Toll-Free Number: (877) 904-8444
Restaurants: 1 Liquor: Yes
Other Games: BJ
Casino Size: 17,500 Square Feet
Overnight RV Parking: Free/RV Dump: No
Senior Discount: Various Wed if 50+
Special Features: Blackjack games open at 4pm.

Choctaw Casino Hotel - Pocola
3400 Choctaw Road
Pocola, Oklahoma 74902
(918) 436-7761
Website: www.choctawcasinos.com
Map: **#14** (195 miles E. of Oklahoma City)

Toll-Free Number: (800) 590-5825
Rooms: 118 Price Range: $99-$133
Suites: 10 Price Range: $149-$279
Restaurants: 4 Liquor: Yes
Buffet: B/L-$12.99 (Sun) D-$12.99
Other Games: BJ, R, UTH, MS, P TCP
Overnight RV Parking: Free/RV Dump: No
Senior Discount: Various Wed if 50+
Special Features: Buffet closed Mon/Tue.

Choctaw Casino - Stigler
1801 E Main Street
Strigler, Oklahoma 74462
(918) 967-8364
Website: www.choctawcasinos.com
Map: **#64** (150 miles E. of Oklahoma City)

Restaurants: 1 Liquor: No
Hours: 8am-2am/4am (Thu-Sat)
Overnight RV Parking: Free/RV Dump: No

Choctaw Casino - Stringtown
895 North Highway 69
Stringtown, Oklahoma 74569
(580) 346-7862
Website: www.choctawcasinos.com
Map: **#15** (163 miles S.E. of Oklahoma City)

Restaurants: 1 Liquor: Beer Only
Hours: 8am-2am/4am (Thu-Sat)
Senior Discount: Various Wed if 50+
Overnight RV Parking: Free/RV Dump: No

Cimarron Casino
821 W. Freeman Avenue
Perkins, Oklahoma 74059
(405) 547-5352
Website: www.cimarroncasino.com
Map: **#16** (60 miles N. of Oklahoma City)

Restaurants: 2 Liquor: Yes
Other Games: BJ, P
Overnight RV Parking: No
Senior Discount: Various Wed/Fri if 50+

Comanche Nation Casino
402 Southeast Interstate Drive
Lawton, Oklahoma 73501
(580) 250-3030
Website: www.comanchenationcasinos.com
Map: **#17** (86 miles S.W. of Oklahoma City)

Toll-Free Number: (877) 900-7594
Restaurants: 2 Liquor: Yes
Other Games: BJ, TCP, P, UTH
Overnight RV Parking: Free, must get pass from front desk first (with hook ups)/ RV Dump: No
Senior Discount: Various Wed if 55+

Comanche Red River Hotel & Casino
Highway 36 and Highway 70
Devol, Oklahoma 73531
(580) 250-3060
Website: www.comanchenationcasinos.com
Map: **#18** (125 miles S.W. of Oklahoma City)

Toll-Free Number: (877) 849-3992
Rooms: 87 Price Range: $99-$129
Restaurants: 2 Liquor: Yes
Casino Size: 52,500 Square Feet
Other Games: BJ, P, TCP, MS, UTH
Overnight RV Parking: Check-in at front desk (with hook ups)/RV Dump: No
Special Features: Drive-thru smoke shop.

Comanche Spur Casino
9047 US Highway 62
Eldon, Oklahoma 73538
(580) 250-3090
Website: www.comanchenationcasinos.com
Map: **#29** (75 miles S.W. of Oklahoma City)

Restaurants: 1 Snack Bar Liquor: No
Hours: 11am-12am/2am (Fri/Sat)
Overnight RV Parking: No
Senior Discount: Various Wed if 50+
Special features: Smoke shop. Convenience store.

Comanche Star Casino
263171 Highway 53
Walters, Oklahoma 73572
(580) 250-3100
Website: www.comanchenationcasinos.com
Map: **#52** (25 miles S.E. of Lawton)

Restaurants: 1 Liquor: No
Hours: 12pm-11pm/1am (Fri/Sat)
Casino Size: 7,000 Square Feet
Overnight RV Parking: No
Senior Discount: Various Tue if 50+

Creek Nation Casino - Bristow
121 West Lincoln
Bristow, Oklahoma 74010
(918) 367-2260
Website: www.creeknationbristow.com
Map: **#5** (60 miles N.E. of Oklahoma City)

Restaurants: 1 Liquor: No
Hours: 8am-6am
Overnight RV Parking: No

Creek Nation Casino - Checotah
830 North Broadway
Checotah, Oklahoma 74426
(918) 473-5200
Map: **#6** (120 miles E. of Oklahoma City)

Restaurants: 1
Hours: 8am-6am
Casino Size: 8,000 Square Feet
Overnight RV Parking: No
Gambling Age: 18

Creek Nation Casino - Eufaula
806 Forest Avenue
Eufaula, Oklahoma 74432
(918) 689-9191
Map: **#51** (135 miles E. of Oklahoma City)

Restaurants: 1 Snack Bar Liquor: No
Hours: 10am-3am/4am (Thu-Sat)
Overnight RV Parking: No
Gambling Age: 18

Creek Nation Casino - Holdenville
221 East Willow Street
Holdenville, Oklahoma 74848
(405) 379-3321
Map: **#61** (75 miles S.E. of Oklahoma City)

Restaurants: 1 Snack Bar Liquor: No
Hours: 10am-12am/2am (Fri/Sat)
Gambling Age: 18

Creek Nation Casino - Muscogee
3420 West Peak Boulevard
Muskogee, Oklahoma 74403
(918) 683-1825
Website: www.creeknationcasino.net
Map: **#20** (50 miles S.E. of Tulsa)

Restaurants: 1 Liquor: Yes
Other Games: BJ, UTH, TCP
Casino Size: 22,500 Square Feet
Overnight RV Parking: Free/RV Dump: No

Creek Nation Casino - Okemah
1100 S. Woodie Guthrie Street
Okemah, Oklahoma 74859
(918) 623-0051
Map: **#37** (72 miles E. of Oklahoma City)

Restaurants: 1 Snack Bar Liquor: No
Overnight RV Parking: Free/RV Dump: No
Special Features: Gambling age is 18.

Creek Nation Travel Plaza
Highway 75 and 56 Loop
Okmulgee, Oklahoma 74447
(918) 752-0090
Map: **#21** (45 miles S. of Tulsa)

Restaurants: 1 Snack Bar Liquor: No
Overnight RV Parking: Free/RV Dump: No
Special Features: Gas station and convenience store. Burger King.

Davis Trading Post
Interstate 35 and Highway 7
Davis, Oklahoma 73030
(580) 369-5360
Website: www.chickasawtravelstop.com
Map: **#22** (75 miles S. of Oklahoma City)

Restaurants: 1 Liquor: No
Overnight RV Parking: Free/RV Dump: No

Downstream Casino Resort
69300 East Nee Road
Quapaw, Oklahoma 74363
(918) 919-6000
Website: www.downstreamcasino.com
Map: **#58** (On the border of OK, MO, and KS)

Toll-Free Number: (888) 396-7876
Rooms: 200 Price Range: $99-$159
Suites: 22 Price Range: $219-$269
Restaurants: 5 Liquor: Yes
Buffet: B-$9.99/$11.99 (Sun) L-$6.95
D-$16.99/$22.99(Tue)/$18.99 (Thu)/
$20.99 (Fri/Sat)
Casino size: 70,000 Square feet
Other Games: BJ, MB, P, PGP
Special Features: Gambling age is 18. Only casino/hotel in the country located in three states: Oklahoma, Missouri, and Kansas.

Duck Creek Casino
10085 Ferguson Road
Beggs, Oklahoma 74421
(918) 267-3468
Website: www.duckcreekcasino.com
Map: **#21** (35 miles S. of Tulsa)

Restaurants: 1 Liquor: No
Casino Size: 5,000 Square Feet
Overnight RV Parking: No
Senior Discount: Various Tue if 55+

Fire Lake Casino
41207 Hardesty Road
Shawnee, Oklahoma 74801
(405) 878-4862
Website: www.winatfirelake.com
Map: **#23** (38 miles E. of Oklahoma City)

Restaurants: 2 Liquor: Yes
Buffets: B-$6.99 (Sat/Sun) L- $7.99
D- $9.99/$16.99 (Fri)
Other Games: BJ, P, BG, UTH
Overnight RV Parking: Free/RV Dump: No
Senior Discount: Various Sun if 55+

Gold Mountain Casino
1410 Sam Noble Parkway
Ardmore, Oklahoma 73401
(580) 223-3301
Website: www.mygoldmountaincasino.com
Map: **#3** (100 miles S. of Oklahoma City)

Restaurants: 1 Liquor: No
Casino Size: 8,620 Square Feet
Overnight RV Parking: No

Gold River Casino
31064 S. Highway 281
Anadarko, Oklahoma 73005
(405) 247-4700
Website: www.goldriverok.com
Map: **#24** (60 miles S.W. of Oklahoma City)

Restaurants: 1 Liquor: Yes
Casino Size: 12,000 Square Feet
Casino Hours: 9am-4am/24 hrs (Fri/Sat)
Senior Discount: Various Tue if 55+
Overnight RV Parking: Free/RV Dump: No

Golden Pony Casino
109095 Okemah Street
Okemah, Oklahoma 74859
(918) 582-4653
Website: www.goldenponycasino.com
Map: **#37** (72 miles E. of Oklahoma City)

Toll-Free Number: (877) 623-0072
Restaurants: 1 Liquor: No
Overnight RV Parking: Free/RV Dump: No
Senior Discount: Various Mon if 50+

Goldsby Gaming Center
1038 West Sycamore Road
Norman, Oklahoma 73072
(405) 329-5447
Website: www.goldsbycasino.com
Map: **#25** (21 miles S. of Oklahoma City)

Restaurants: 1 Liquor: Yes
Other Games: BG (Wed-Sun)
Casino Size: 23,007 Square Feet
Overnight RV Parking: No

Grand Casino Hotel & Resort
777 Grand Casino Boulevard
Shawnee, Oklahoma 74804
(405) 964-7263
Website: www.grandresortok.com
Map: **#23** (38 miles E. of Oklahoma City)

Rooms: 242 Price Range: $129-$179
Suites: 20 Price Range: $149-$199
Restaurants: 5 Liquor: Yes
Buffets: L- $11.45/$14.45 (Sun)
D- $14.45/$29.95 (Fri/Sat)
Casino Size: 125,000 Square Feet
Other Games: BJ, C, R, P, TCP, UTH, K
Overnight RV Parking: $50 per night
Special Features: 3,000-seat event center.

Grand Lake Casino
24701 S. 655 Road
Grove, Oklahoma 74344
(918) 786-8528
Website: www.grandlakecasino.com
Map: **#26** (80 miles N.E. of Tulsa)

Toll-Free Number: (800) 426-4640
Rooms: 30 Price Range: $69-$79
Restaurants: 2 Liquor: Yes
Casino Size: 45,000 Square Feet
Overnight RV Parking: No

Hard Rock Hotel & Casino Tulsa
770 W Cherokee Street
Catoosa, Oklahoma 74015
(918) 384-7800
Website: www.hardrockcasinotulsa.com
Map: **#7** (a suburb of Tulsa)

Toll-Free Number: (800) 760-6700
Rooms: 130 Price Range: $109-$199
Suites: 20 Price Range: $209-$600
Restaurants: 5 Liquor: Yes
Buffets: B-$8.95 L-$10.95
D-$17.95/$23.99 (Fri/Sat)
Casino Size: 80,000 Square Feet
Other Games: BJ, C, R, P, TCP, UTH
Overnight RV Parking: Free/RV Dump: No

High Winds Casino
61475 E. 100 Road
Miami, Oklahoma 74354
(918) 541-9463
Website: www.highwindscasino.com
Map: **#33** (89 miles N.E. of Tulsa)

Restaurants: 1 Liquor: Yes
Overnight RV Parking: Free/RV Dump: No

Indigo Sky Casino
70220 East US Highway 60
Wyandotte, Oklahoma 74370
(888) 992-7591
Website: www.indigoskycasino.com
Map: **#26** (90 miles N.E. of Tulsa)

Toll-Free: (888) 992-7591
Rooms: 100 Room Rates:$119-$149
Suites: 17 Price Range: $149-$209
Restaurants: 2 Liquor: Yes
Other Games: BJ, P, OTB, BG
Overnight RV Parking: Must use RV park
Special Features: 45-space RV Park ($15/night)

Ioway Casino
338445 East Highway 66
Chandler, Oklahoma 78349
(405) 258-0051
Website: www.iowaycasino.com
Map: **#65** (40 miles N. E. of Okla. City)

Restaurants: 1 Liquor: Yes
Hours: 10am-2am/24 hours (Fri/Sat)

Kickapoo Casino - Harrah
25230 East Highway 62
Harrah, Oklahoma 73045
(405) 964-4444
Website: www.kickapoo-casino.com
Map: **#23** (31 miles E. of Oklahoma City)

Restaurants: 1 Liquor: Yes
Hours: Noon-4am
Other Games: BJ, UTH
Overnight RV Parking: Free/RV Dump: No

Kickapoo Casino - Shawnee
38900 W. MacArthur Drive
Shawnee, Oklahoma 74804
(405) 395-0900
Website: www.kickapoo-casino.com
Map: **#23** (38 miles E. of Oklahoma City)

Restaurants: 1 Snack Bar Liquor: Yes
Overnight RV Parking: Free/RV Dump: No

Kiowa Casino
198131 Highway 36
Devol, Oklahoma 73531
(580) 299-3333
Website: www.kiowacasino.com
Map: **#18** (125 miles SW of Oklahoma City)

Toll-Free Number: (866) 370-4077
Restaurants: 3 Liquor: Beer Only
Buffets: B-$11.50 (Sun)
L-$9.50/$11.50 (Sun)
D-$11.50/$24.99 (Wed)/$12.99 (Thu/Fri)
Other Games: BJ, TCP, UTH
Overnight RV Parking: Free/RV Dump: No
Special Features: No table games Monday.

Lucky Star Casino - Canton
301 NW Lake Road
Canton, Oklahoma 73724
(580) 886-2490
Website: www.luckystarcasino.org
Map: **#59** (60 miles N. W. of Okla. City)

Restaurants: 1 Snack Bar Liquor: Beer
Hours: 10am-11pm/24 hours (Fri/Sat)
Casino Size: 2,200 Square Feet
Overnight RV Parking: Free/RV Dump: No
Special Features: Gambling age is 18.

Lucky Star Casino - Clinton
10347 N2274 Road
Clinton, Oklahoma 73601
(580) 323-6599
Website: www.luckystarcasino.org
Map: **#29** (85 miles W. of Oklahoma City)

Restaurants: 1 Liquor: Beer
Other Games: BJ, TCP, UTH
Overnight RV Parking: Free/RV Dump: No
Special Features: Gambling age is 18.

Lucky Star Casino - Concho
7777 North Highway 81
Concho, Oklahoma 73022
(405) 422-6500
Website: www.luckystarcasino.org
Map: **#30** (35 miles N.W. of Oklahoma City)

Restaurants: 1 Liquor: Yes
Other Games: BJ, P
Casino Size: 40,000 Square Feet
Overnight RV Parking: Free/RV Dump: Free
Special Features: Gambling age is 18. Free RV hookups (must register first).

Lucky Star Casino - Hammon
20413 Highway 33
Hammon, Oklahoma 73650
(580) 473-2010
Website: www.luckystarcasinos.com
Map: **#66** (120 miles W. of Okla. City)

Restaurants: 1 Deli Liquor: Beer Only
Hours: 10am-2am Daily
Overnight RV Parking: Free/RV Dump: No
Special Features: Gambling age is 18.

Lucky Star Casino - Watonga
1407 S. Clarence Nash Boulevard
Watonga, Oklahoma 73772
(580) 623-7333
Website: www.featherwarrior.com
Map: **#53** (70 miles N. W. of Okla. City)

Restaurants: 1 Snack Bar Liquor: Beer
Hours: 10am-2am Daily
Casino Size: 2,200 Square Feet
Overnight RV Parking: Free/RV Dump: No
Special Features: Gambling age is 18.

Lucky Turtle Casino
64499 East Highway 60
Wyandotte, Oklahoma 74370
(918) 678-3767
Map: **#42** (90 miles N.E. of Tulsa)
Website: luckyturtle.wyandottecasinos.com

Restaurants: 1 Liquor: No
Casino Size: 4,000 Square Feet
Overnight RV Parking: No
Senior Discount: Various Wed if 50+
Special Features: Convenience store.

Madill Gaming Center
902 South First Street
Madill, Oklahoma 73446
(580) 795-7301
Website: www.madillgaming.com
Map: **#31** (122 miles S. of Oklahoma City)

Restaurants: 1 Liquor: No
Casino Size: 2,071 Square Feet
Overnight RV Parking: No
Special Features: Smoke shop.

Native Lights Casino
12375 N. Highway 77
Newkirk, Oklahoma 74647
(580) 448-3100
Website: www.nativelightscasino.com
Map: **#27** (106 miles N. of Oklahoma City)

Toll-Free Number: (877) 468-3100
Restaurants: 1 Liquor: Yes
Hours: 10am-12am/3am (Fri/Sat)
Overnight RV Parking: Free/RV Dump: No

Newcastle Gaming Center
2457 Highway 62 Service Road
Newcastle, Oklahoma 73065
(405) 387-6013
Website: www.mynewcastlecasino.com
Map: **#34** (19 miles S. of Oklahoma City)

Restaurants: 2 Liquor: Yes
Casino Size: 44,622 Sqaure Feet
Other Games: BJ, B, R, K, OTB,
TCP, MS, UTH
Overnight RV Parking: Free/RV Dump: No
Senior Discount: Various Sun if 50+

One Fire Casino
1901 North Wood Drive
Okmulgee, Oklahoma 74447
(918) 756-8400
Website: www.onefirecasino.com
Map: **#21** (45 miles S. of Tulsa)

Restaurants: 1 Liquor: Yes
Casino Size: 10,000 Square Feet
Overnight RV Parking: Free/RV Dump: No
Senior Discount: Various Tue if 50+

Osage Casino - Bartlesville
222 Allen Road
Bartlesville, Oklahoma 74003
(918) 699-7740
Website: www.osagecasinos.com
Map: **#56** (50 miles N. of Tulsa)

Toll-Free Number (877) 246-8777
Restaurants: 2 Liquor: No
Buffet: D- $9.99 (Thu/Sun)/$27.99 (Fri)/
$16.99 (Sat)
Other Games: BJ, TCP, UTH
Senior Discount: Various Mon/Tue if 50+

Osage Casino - Hominy
39 Deer Avenue
Hominy, Oklahoma 74035
(918) 699-7740
Website: www.osagecasinos.com
Map: **#49** (44 miles N.W. of Tulsa)

Toll-Free Number (877) 246-8777
Restaurants: 1 Liquor: Yes
Hours: 10am-2am/4am (Thu-Sat)
Senior Discount: Various Mon/Tue if 50+

Osage Casino - Pawhuska
2017 E. 15th Street (at Highway 99)
Pawhuska, Oklahoma 74056
(918) 699-7740
Website: www.osagecasinos.com
Map: **#50** (a suburb of Tulsa)

Toll-Free Number (877) 246-8777
Restaurants: 1 Liquor: No
Hours: 10am-2am/4am (Thu-Sat)
Overnight RV Parking: Free/RV Dump: No
Senior Discount: Various Mon/Tue if 50+

Osage Casino - Ponca City
64464 U.S. Highway 60
Ponca City, Oklahoma 74601
(918) 699-7740
Website: www.osagecasinos.com
Map: **#5** (50 miles N.W. of Tulsa)

Toll-Free Number (877) 246-8777
Suites: 50 Price Range: $119-$259
Restaurants: 1 Liquor: Yes
Other Games: BJ, TCP, UTH
Senior Discount: Various Mon/Tue if 50+
Overnight RV Parking: No

Osage Casino - Sand Springs
301 Blackjack Drive (on Highway 97T)
Sand Springs, Oklahoma 74063
(918) 699-7740
Website: www.osagecasinos.com
Map: **#40** (a suburb of Tulsa)

Toll-Free Number: (877) 246-8777
Restaurants: 1 Liquor: Yes
Buffet: B-$8.95 (Sat/Sun)
Senior Discount: Various Mon/Tue if 50+
Overnight RV Parking: No

Osage Casino - Skiatook
5591 West Rogers Boulevard
Skiatook, Oklahoma 74070
(918) 699-7740
Website: www.osagecasinos.com
Map: **#60** (17 miles N. of Tulsa)

Toll-Free Number: (877) 246-8777
Suites: 50 Price Range: $119-$259
Restaurants:1 Liquor: Yes
Other Games: BJ, TCP, UTH
Senior Discount: Various Mon/Tue if 50+
Overnight RV Parking: No

Osage Casino - Tulsa
951 W. 36th Street North
Tulsa, Oklahoma 74127
(918) 699-7740
Website: www.osagecasinos.com
Map: **#40**

Toll-Free Number: (877) 246-8777
Restaurants: 1 Liquor: Yes
Casino Size: 47,000 Square Feet
Other Games: BJ, TCP, UTH
Senior Discount: Various Mon/Tue if 50+
Overnight RV Parking: Free/RV Dump: No

Outpost Casino
67901 East 100 Road
Wyandotte, Oklahoma 74370
(918) 666-6770
Map: **#42** (90 miles N.E. of Tulsa)

Restaurants: 1 Liquor: Beer Only
Overnight RV Parking: Free/RV Dump: No
Special Features: Gambling age is 18.

Prairie Moon Casino
202 South Eight Tribes Trail
Miami, Oklahoma 74354
(918) 542-8670
Website: www.miaminationcasinos.com
Map: **#33** (89 miles N.E. of Tulsa)

Restaurants: 1 Liquor: No
Overnight RV Parking: No
Special Features: Gambling age is 18.

Prairie Sun Casino
3411 P Street NW
Miami, Oklahoma 74354
(918) 541-2150
Website: www.miaminationcasinos.com
Map: # **33** (89 miles N.E. of Tulsa)

Restaurants: 1 Snack Bar Liquor: Yes
Casino Size: 11,000 Square Feet
Overnight RV Parking: No
Special Features: Gambling age is 18.

Quapaw Casino
58100 E. 64h Road
Miami, Oklahoma 74354
(918) 540-9100
Website: www.quapawcasino.com
Map: **#33** (89 miles N.E. of Tulsa)

Restaurants: 1 Liquor: Yes
Other Games: BJ
Overnight RV Parking: Free up to 3 days/
RV Dump: No
Senior Discount: Various Wed if 50+

River Bend Casino Hotel
100 Jackpot Place
Wyandotte, Oklahoma 74370
(918) 678-4946
Website: www.wyandottecasinos.com
Map: **#26** (90 miles N.E. of Tulsa)

Toll-Free Number: (866) 447-4946
Rooms: 80 Price Range: $89-$119
Suites: 12 Price Range: $119-$149
Restaurants: 3 Liquor: Yes
Other Games: BJ, TCP, UTH
Overnight RV Parking: Free/RV Dump: No
Special Features: Special events center offers bowling, billiards and live events.

River Mist Casino
14313 Old Highway 99
Konowa, Oklahoma 74849
(405) 217-0176
Website: www.snocasinos.com
Map: **#2** (75 miles S.E. of Oklahoma City)

Restaurants: None Liquor: No
Hours: 10am-12am/2am (Fri/Sat)

River Spirit Casino Resort
8330 Riverside Parkway
Tulsa, Oklahoma 74137
(918) 299-8518
Website: www.riverspirittulsa.com
Map: **#40**

Toll-Free Number: (888) 748-3731
Rooms: 463 Price Range: $109-$209
Suites: 20 Price Range: $209-$289
Restaurants: 5 Liquor: Yes
Buffets: B-$21.95 (Sun)
L-$11.95/$21.95(Sun)
D-$15.95/$22.95 (Thu)/
$19.95 (Fri)/$23.95 (Sat)
Casino Size: 81,000 Square Feet
Other Games: BJ, B, P, UTH
Senior Disc: Buffet discount Mon-Sat if 50+
Overnight RV Parking: Free/RV Dump: No
Special Features: Separate non-smoking casino. Free shuttle to/from local hotels.

Riverwind Casino
1544 West State Highway 9
Norman, Oklahoma 73072
(405) 322-6000
Website: www.riverwind.com
Map: **#25** (21 miles S. of Oklahoma City)

Toll-Free Number: (888) 440-1880
Rooms: 100 Price Range: $109-$209
Restaurants: 2 Liquor: Yes
Buffets: B- $10.99 (Wed)/$15.99 (Sun)
L- $13.99/$15.99 (Sun)
D- $19.99/$24.99 (Sat)/$18.99 (Sun)
Casino Size: 60,000 Square Feet
Other Games: BJ, B, R, P, OTB,
TCP, UTH, K
Senior Discount: Various Wed if 50+
Overnight RV Parking: Free/RV Dump: No
Special Features: 1,500-seat showroom. Food court with four fast food outlets.

Sac and Fox Casino - Stroud
356120 E 926 Road
Stroud, Oklahoma 74079
(918) 968-2540
Website: www.snfcasino.com
Map: **#5** (60 miles N.E. of Oklahoma City)

Restaurants: 1 Liquor: Yes
Casino Size: 8,600 Sqaure Feet
Casino Hours: 10am-2am Daily
Overnight RV Parking: No

Salt Creek Casino
1600 Highway 81
Pocasset, Oklahoma 73079
(405) 459-4000
Website: www.saltcreekcasino.com
Map: **#34** (50 miles S.W. of Oklahoma City)

Restaurants: 2 Liquor: Yes
Overnight RV Parking: No
Other Games: BJ, UTH

Seminole Nation Casino
11277 Highway 99
Seminole, Oklahoma 74868
(405) 217-0176
Website: www.snocasinos.com
Map: **#57** (60 miles S.E of Oklahoma City)

Restaurants: 1 Liquor: Yes
Overnight RV Parking: No

Seminole Nation Smoke Shop
36625 Highway 270
Wewoka, Oklahoma 74884
(405) 217-0176
Website: www.snocasinos.com
Map: **#57** (60 miles E. of Oklahoma City)

Restaurants: 1 Snack Bar Liquor: No
Casino Size: 3,424 Square Feet
Overnight RV Parking: No
Hours: 10am-12am/2am (Fri/Sat)
Senior Discount: Various Sun if 55+
Special Features: Convenience store.

Seven Clans Casino - Chilocco
12901 N. Highway 77
Newkirk, Oklahoma 74647
(580) 448-3210
Website: www.sevenclans.com
Map: **#27** (106 miles N. of Oklahoma City)

Restaurants: 1 Deli Liquor: Yes
Overnight RV Parking: No

Seven Clans Casino Hotel - First Council
12875 North Highway 77
Newkirk, Oklahoma 74647
(877) 725-2670
Website: www.myfirstwin.com
Map: **#27** (Just south of the Kansas state line)

Rooms: 66 Price Range: $99-$109
Suites: 20 Price Range: $119-$139
Restaurants: 1 Liquor: Yes
Casino Size: 125,000 Square Feet
Other Games: BJ, BG, TCP, UTH
Overnight RV Parking: Free/RV Dump: No
Special Features: 3,000-seat event center.

Seven Clans Casino - Paradise
7500 Highway 177
Red Rock, Oklahoma 74651
(580) 723-4005
Website: www.firstcouncilcasinohotel.com
Map: **#1** (82 miles N. of Oklahoma City)

Toll-Free Number: (866) 723-4005
Restaurants: 1 Liquor: Yes
Casino Size: 23,000 Square Feet
Other Games: BJ, UTH
Overnight RV Parking: No
Senior Discount: Various Thu if 55+
Special Features: Convenience store and gas station.

Seven Clans Casino - Perry
5111 Kaw Street
Perry, Oklahoma 73077
(580) 336-7260
Website: www.sevenclans.com
Map: **#67** (65 miles N. of Okla. City)

Restaurants: 1 Deli Liquor: Yes
Overnight RV Parking: Free/RV Dump: No
Senior Discount: Various Tue if 55+
Special Features: Drive-through smoke shop.

Seven Clans Casino - Red Rock
8401 Highway 177
Red Rock, Oklahoma 74651
(580) 723-1020
Website: www.sevenclans.com
Map: **#1** (82 miles N. of Oklahoma City)

Restaurants: 1 Deli Liquor: Yes
Overnight RV Parking: No

Southwind Casino - Braman
9695 N. Highway
Braman, Oklahoma 74632
(580) 385-2441
Website: www.southwindcasino.com
Map: **#27** (106 miles N. of Okla. City)

Restaurants: 1 Liquor: Yes
Overnight RV Parking: Free/RV Dump: No

Southwind Casino - Kanza
9601 U.S. 177
Braman, Oklahoma 74632
(580) 385-24444
Website: www.southwindcasino.com
Map: **#27** (106 miles N. of Okla. City)

Casino Hours: 8am-12am/2am (Fri/Sat)
Overnight RV Parking: Free/RV Dump: No
Special Features: Located in a truck stop. Located one block from Braman Casino. o

Southwind Casino - Newkirk
5640 North LaCann Drive
Newkirk, Oklahoma 74647
(580) 362-2578
Website: www.southwindcasino.com
Map: **#27** (106 miles N. of Oklahoma City)

Toll-Free Number: (866) 529-2464
Restaurants: 1 Liquor: Yes
Other Games: BG (Thu-Mon), OTB
Casino Hours: 10am-11pm/2am (Fri/Sat)
Senior Discount: Various Mon/Wed if 55+
Overnight RV Parking: Free/RV Dump: No

The Stables Casino
530 H Street Southeast
Miami, Oklahoma 74354
(918) 542-7884
Website: www.the-stables.com
Map: **#33** (89 miles N.E. of Tulsa)

Toll-Free Number: (877) 774-7884
Restaurants: 1 Liquor: Yes
Overnight RV Parking: No
Senior Discount: Various Wed if 55+

Stone Wolf Casino & Grill
54251 S 349 Road
Pawnee, Oklahoma 74058
(918) 454-7777
Website: www.stonewolfcasino.com
Map: **#55** (57 miles N.W. of Tulsa)

Restaurants: 1 Liquor: No
Hours: 8am-2am/24hrs (Fri-Sun)
Senior Discount: Various Thu if 55+

Sugar Creek Casino
5304 North Broadway
Hinton, Oklahoma 73047
(405) 542-2946
Website: www.sugarcreekcasino.net
Map: **#63** (55 miles W. of Oklahoma City)

Restaurants: 2 Liquor: Yes
Buffets: L- $$9.99 (Sat)
Other Games: BJ, UTH
Overnight RV Parking: No
Senior Discount: Various Mon if 55+

Texoma Gaming Center
1795 Highway 70 East
Kingston, Oklahoma 73439
(580) 564-6000
Website: www.mytexomacasino.com
Map: **#43** (130 miles S. of Oklahoma City)

Restaurants: 1 Liquor: Yes
Casino Size: 8,800 Square Feet
Overnight RV Parking: No
Special Features: Convenience store.

Thunderbird Casino - Norman
15700 East State Highway 9
Norman, Oklahoma 73026
(405) 360-9270
Website: www.playthunderbird.com
Map: **#25** (21 miles S. of Oklahoma City)

Toll-Free Number: (800) 259-5825
Restaurants: 1 Liquor: Yes
Hours: 9am-2am/24 Hours (Fri/Sat)
Other Games: BJ, TCP
Casino Size: 40,000 Square Feet
Overnight RV Parking: Free

Thunderbird Casino - Shawnee
2051 S. Gordon Cooper Drive
Shawnee, Oklahoma 74801
(405) 273-2679
Website: www.playthunderbird.com
Map: **#23** (38 miles E. of Oklahoma City)

Toll-Free Number: (800) 259-5825
Restaurants: 1 Deli Liquor: Yes
Hours: 9am-12am/2am (Fri/Sat)

Tonkawa Gasino
10700 Allen Drive
Tonkawa, Oklahoma 74653
(580) 628-2624
Website: www.tonkawacasino.com
Map: **#38** (91 miles N. of Oklahoma City)

Toll-Free Number: (877) 648-2624
Restaurant: No Liquor: No
Hours: 11am-11pm Daily
Overnight RV Parking: Free/RV Dump: No
Special Features: Convenience store. Gas station.

Tonkawa Hotel & Casino
16601 W. South Avenue
Tonkawa, Oklahoma 74653
(580) 628-2624
Website: www.tonkawacasino.com
Map: **#38** (91 miles N. of Oklahoma City)

Restaurants: 1 Liquor: Yes
Hours: 10am-2am Daily
Overnight RV Parking: Free/RV Dump: No
Special Features: New hotel expected to open by early 2018.

Trading Post Casino
291 Agency Road
Pawnee, Oklahoma 74058
(918) 762-4466
Map: **#55** (57 miles N.W. of Tulsa)

Restaurants: 1 Liquor: No
Casino Size: 3,600 Square Feet
Hours: 7am-2am/11pm (Sun)
Overnight RV Parking: No
Special Features: Convenience store. Gas station.

Treasure Valley Casino
12252 Ruppe Road
Davis, Oklahoma 73030
(580) 369-2895
Website: www.treasurevalleycasino.com
Map: **#22** (75 miles S. of Oklahoma City)

Rooms: 55 Price Range: $104-$119
Suites: 4 Price Range: $159-$209
Restaurants: 2 Liquor: Yes
Casino Size: 19,666 Square Feet
Other Games: BJ, TCP, UTH
Overnight RV Parking: Free/RV Dump: No
Special Features: Gambling age is 18.

Washita Casino
30639 Highway 145
Paoli, Oklahoma 73074
(405) 484-7777
Website: www.washitacasino.com
Map: **#44** (52 miles S. of Oklahoma City)

Restaurants: 1 Liquor: Yes
Casino Size: 6,335 Square Feet
Overnight RV Parking: No
Special Features: Convenience store.

Wilson Travel Plaza
288 Mulberry Lane
Wilson, Oklahoma 73463
(580) 668-9248
Map: **#39** (112 miles S. of Oklahoma City)

Restaurants: 1 Snack Bar Liquor: No
Overnight RV Parking: Free/RV Dump: No
Special Features: Convenience store. Gas station.

WinStar World Casino and Resort
777 Casino Avenue
Thackerville, Oklahoma 73459
(580) 276-4229
Website: www.winstarworldcasino.com
Map: **#36** (124 miles S. of Oklahoma City)

Toll-Free Number: (800) 622-6317
Rooms: 1,159 Price Range: $99-$279
Suites: 240 Price Range:$129-$399
Restaurants: 10 Liquor: Yes
Buffets: L- $18.99/$23.99 (Sun)
D- $23.99/$28.99 (Fri-Sun)
Other Games: BJ, C, R, MB, P, MS, LIR, TCP, UTH, PGP, OTB, K
Casino Size: 169,824 Square Feet
Overnight RV Parking: Free/RV Dump: No
Senior Discount: Free buffet Wed/Thu if 50+
Special Features: 153-space RV ($30/$40 per night)

Pari-Mutuels

Oklahoma has two horse tracks which offer Class II electronic video gaming machines as well as pari-mutuel betting on horse races. Admission is free to the casinos, but there is an admission charge for horse racing. The minimum gambling age is 18.

Cherokee Casino Will Rogers Downs
20900 S. 4200 Road
Claremore, Oklahoma 74019
(918) 283-8800
Website: www.cherokeecasino.com
Map: **#47** (30 miles N.E. of Tulsa)

Restaurants: 1 Liquor: Yes
Hours: 10am-1am/4am (Fri/Sat)
Overnight RV Parking: Must use RV park
Senior Discount: Various Wed if 50+
Special Features: Live horse racing seasonally. Daily simulcasting of horse racing. 400-space RV park ($32 per night/$10 without hookups).

Remington Park Racing • Casino
One Remington Place
Oklahoma City, Oklahoma 73111
(405) 424-1000
Website: www.remingtonpark.com
Map: **#46**

Toll-Free Number: (800) 456-4244
Restaurants: 1
Buffet: D- $24.95 (Thu)
Overnight RV Parking: No
Senior Discount: Various Tue if 55+
Special Features: Live horse racing seasonally. Daily simulcasting of horse racing. Buffet discount for players club members.

OREGON

Oregon law permits bars and taverns to have up to six video lottery terminals that offer various versions of video poker. Racetracks are allowed to have no more than 10 machines. The maximum bet allowed is $2.50 and the maximum single payout on any machine is capped at $600.

These machines are the same as regular video gaming devices but are called lottery terminals because they are regulated by the state's lottery commission which receives a share of each machine's revenue. The machines accept cash but do not pay out in cash; instead, they print out a receipt which must be taken to a cashier.

According to figures from the Oregon Lottery, during its fiscal year from July 1, 2016 through June 30, 2017, the VLT's had an approximate return of 92.22%.

There is also one racetrack, Portland Meadows, which offers instant racing betting machines. While these machines may appear to be regular slot machines, they are actually based on unidentified past horse races and the reels are for entertainment purposes only.

There are nine Indian casinos in operation in Oregon. According to the governor's office which regulates the Tribe's compacts, "there is no minimum payback percentage required on the Tribe's machines. Each Tribe is free to set their own limits on their machines."

All casinos offer blackjack, slots and video poker. Some casinos also offer: craps (C), roulette (R), poker (P), Pai Gow Poker (PGP), Spanish 21 (S21), let it ride (LIR), three card poker (TCP), four card poker (FCP), big 6 wheel (B6), bingo (BG), keno (K) and off track betting (OTB). Unless otherwise noted, all casinos are open 24 hours and the minimum gambling age is 21 (18 for bingo).

For Oregon tourism information call (800) 547-7842 or go to: www.traveloregon.com.

Chinook Winds Casino Resort
1777 N.W. 44th Street
Lincoln City, Oregon 97367
(541) 996-5825
Website: www.chinookwindscasino.com
Map: **#4** (45 miles W. of Salem)

Toll-Free Number: (877) 423-2241
Rooms: 227 Price Range: $79-$119
Suites: 81 Price Range: $185-$249
Restaurants: 5 Liquor: Yes
Buffets: B-$10.95/$19.95 (Sun) L-$11.95
D-$17.95/$21.95 (Fri)/$20.95 (Sat)
Other Games: C, R, P, LIR, TCP,
PGP, UTH, K, BG
Overnight RV Parking: Free/RV Dump: No
Senior Discount: Buffet discount if 55+
Special Features: Childcare center. 18-hole golf course. Must earn 40 points on players card and RV park is free for up to three nights.

Indian Head Casino
3636 Highway 26
Warm Springs, Oregon 97741
(541) 460-7777
Website: www.indianheadgaming.com
Map: **#5** (100 miles E. of Portland)

Restaurants: 2 Liquor: Yes
Casino Size: 25,000 Square Feet
Overnight RV Parking: Free/RV Dump: No
Senior Discount: Various Tue if 50+

Kla-Mo-Ya Casino
34333 Highway 97 North
Chiloquin, Oregon 97624
(541) 783-7529
Website: www.klamoyacasino.com
Map: **#7** (20 miles N. of Klamath Falls)

Toll-Free Number: (888) 552-6692
Restaurants: 1 Liquor: Yes
Overnight RV Parking: Free/RV Dump: No
Senior Discount: Various Mon if 55+

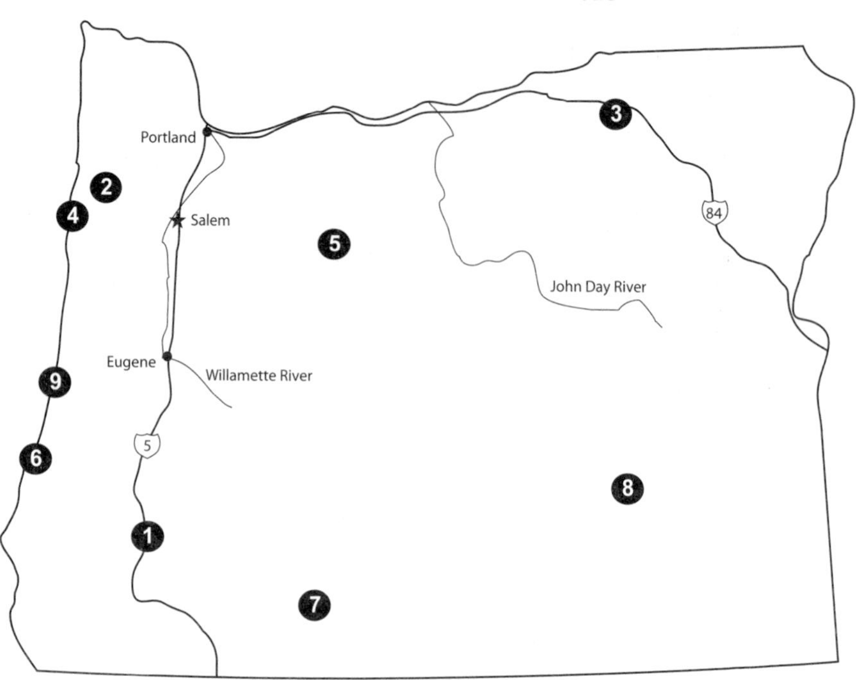

The Mill Casino Hotel
3201 Tremont Street
North Bend, Oregon 97459
(541) 756-8800
Website: www.themillcasino.com
Map: **#6** (75 miles S.W. of Eugene)

Toll-Free Number: (800) 953-4800
Rooms: 109 Price Range: $139-$189
Suites: 3 Price Range: $169-$259
Restaurants: 4 Liquor: Yes
Buffets: D-$9.99 (Mon)/$16.99 (Fri/Sat)
Other Games: C, R, S21, PGP, TCP
Overnight RV Parking: Must use RV park
Senior Discount: Various Mon if 55+
Special Features: 102-space RV park ($35-$70 per night spring/summer; $25-$35 fall/winter). Free local shuttle. Room and food discounts for players club members. Table games open at 3pm.

Seven Feathers Hotel & Casino Resort
146 Chief Miwaleta Lane
Canyonville, Oregon 97417
(541) 839-1111
Website: www.sevenfeathers.com
Map: **#1** (80 miles S. of Eugene)

Toll-Free Number: (800) 548-8461
Rooms: 146 Price Range: $99-$179
Restaurants: 4 Liquor: Yes
Buffets: L- $8.99 (Sat)
D- $12.99/$27.99 (Thu)/
$22.99 (Fri)/$17.99 (Sat)/$15.99 (Sun)
Casino Size: 27,300 Square Feet
Other Games: C, R, B, LIR, PGP,
TCP, FCP, K, BG
Senior Discount: Various Thu if 55+
Overnight RV Parking: Must use RV park
Special Features: 191-space RV park ($39-$55 per night). 18-hole golf course.

Spirit Mountain Casino
27100 SW Salmon River Highway
Grand Ronde, Oregon 97347
(503) 879-2350
Website: www.spiritmountain.com
Map: **#2** (85 miles S.W. of Portland)

Toll-Free Number: (800) 760-7977
Rooms: 94 Price Range: $89-$149
Suites: 6 Price Range: $169-$219
Restaurants: 4 Liquor: Yes
Buffets: B-$9.95 L-$10.95/$16.95 (Sun)
D-$15.95/$24.95 (Fri)/$19.95 (Sat/Sun)
Other Games: C, R, P, PGP, LIR, TCP, K, BG
Overnight RV Parking: Free/RV Dump: Free
Senior Discount: Various on Mon if 55+
Special Features: Childcare center. Players club members receive a room discount.

Three Rivers Casino & Hotel
5647 US Highway 126
Florence, Oregon 97439
(877) 374-8377
Website: www.threeriverscasino.com
Map: **#9** (61 miles W. of Eugene)

Toll-Free Number: (877) 374-8377
Rooms: 90 Price Range: $89-$139
Suites: 4 Price Range: $190- $250
Restaurants: 5 Liquor: Yes
Buffets: B- $13.99 (Sun) L- $9.99
D- $9.99 (Mon)/$12.99 (Tue-Thu)/
$17.99 (Fri)/$25.99(Sat)
Other Games: C, R, P, K, BG, LIR, PGP
Overnight RV Parking: Free/RV Dump: No
Senior Discount: Food discount Mon if 55+

Three Rivers Casino Coos Bay
1297 Ocean Boulevard
Coos Bay, Oregon 97420
(877) 374-8377
Website: www.threeriverscasino.com
Map: **#6** (75 miles S.W. of Eugene)

Toll-Free Number: (877) 374-8377
Restaurants: 1
Special Features: This casino offers Class II gambling which consist of electronic gaming machines which look like slot machines, but are actually games of bingo and the spinning video reels are for "entertainment purposes only."

Wildhorse Resort & Casino
46510 Wildhorse Boulevard
Pendleton, Oregon 97801
(541) 278-2274
Website: www.wildhorseresort.com
Map: **#3** (211 miles E. of Portland)

Toll-Free Number: (800) 654-9453
Rooms: 100 Price Range: $89-$139
Suites: 5 Price Range: $129- $229
Restaurants: 5 Liquor: Yes
Buffets: B/L- $12.95 (Sat)/$18.95 (Sun)
D- $15.95
Casino Size: 80,000 Square Feet
Other Games: C, R, P, TCP, K, BG
Overnight RV Parking: Free/RV Dump: No
Senior Discount: Various Tue if 55+
Special Features: 100-space RV park ($31-$45 per night). Cultural Institute. 18-hole golf course. Health spa. Childcare center.

PENNSYLVANIA

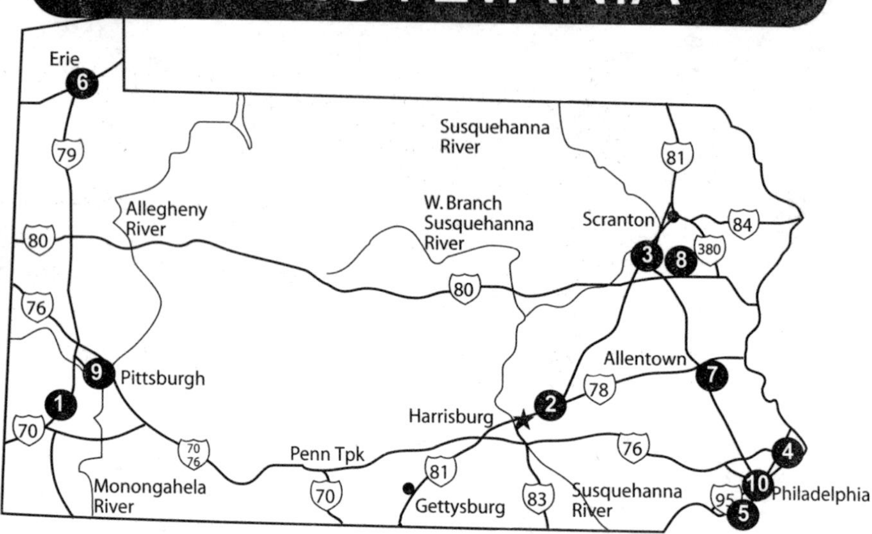

In July 2004 the Pennsylvania legislature authorized the legalization of slot machines at 14 locations throughout the state: seven racinos, five stand-alone casinos, and two hotel resorts. All casinos can have up to 5,000 machines, except the resort licensees, which are allowed up to 600.

The final stand-alone license was awarded to Live! Hotel and Casino which will be building a $425 million project housing a 200,000-square-foot gaming floor, a 220-room hotel and a 1,000-seat music venue.

The resort will be located at 900 Packer Avenue in South Phildelphia and the earliest it is expected to open is late 2018.

Unless otherwise noted, all casinos offer: slots, video poker, craps, blackjack, roulette, three card poker, mini-baccarat and Pai-gow poker. Optional games include: baccarat (B), poker (P), ultimate Texas hold 'em (UTH), Texas hold'em bonus (THB), let it ride (LIR), pai gow (PG), big 6 wheel (B6), Spanish 21 (S21), four card poker (FCP), Sic-Bo (SIC), Mississippi stud (MS) and casino war (CW).

Pennsylvania gaming regulations require that gaming machines return a minimum of 85%. Following is information from the Pennsylvania Gaming Control Board regarding average slot payout percentages for the one-year period from July 1, 2016 through June 30, 2017:

CASINO	PAYBACK %
Parx Casino	90.95
Valley Forge	90.59
Mount Airy	90.36
The Meadows	90.06
Mohegan Sun at PD	90.17
Sands Bethlehem	89.93
Harrah's Philadelphia	90.07
The Rivers	89.72
Presque Isle	89.44
Sugar House	89.68
Lady Luck Nemacolin	89.35
Hollywood Casino at PN	89.22

The minimum gambling age is 18 for pari-mutuel betting and 21 at casinos. All casinos are open 24 hours and admission is free. However, the casinos at the two hotel resorts are not open to the general public. You must be a guest of the resort in order to play at their casinos. However, you can buy a guest pass for temporary admission.

For more information on visiting Pennsylvania call their Office of Tourism at (800) 237-4363 or visit their website at www.visitpa.com.

Lady Luck Nemacolin
4067 National Pike
Farmington, Pennsylvania 15437
(724) 329-7500
Website: www.nemacolin.com/casino
Map: **#11** (60 miles S.E. of Pittsburgh)

Toll-Free Number: (888) 523-9582
Room Reservations: (866) 344-6957
Rooms: 300 Price Range: $259-$579
Suites: 27 Price Range: $349-$2,299
Other Games: MS, B6, FCP, no pai gow poker
Restaurants: 3
Senior Discount: Various Fri if 50+
Special Features: Located at Nemacolin Woodlands Resort. Casino is affiliated with Isle of Capri Casinos. You must be a guest of the resort for admittance to the casino, or buy a $10 gift card to get access for a 24-hour period. You can also buy an annual membership for $45 which allows unlimited admission for two, plus discounts on various amenities.

Mount Airy Resort & Casino
312 Woodland Road
Mount Pocono, Pennsylvania 18344
(570) 243-4800
Website: www.mounttairycasino.com
Map: **#8** (30 miles S.E. of Scranton)

Toll-Free Number: (877) 682-4791
Rooms: 175 Price Range: $189-$389
Suites: 25 Price Range: $269-$439
Restaurants: 5
Buffets: L/D-$19.99
Casino Size: 68,000 Square Feet
Other Games: P, LIR, B, B6, FCP, S21, MS, PG
Special Features: 18-hole golf course. Spa.

Rivers Casino
777 Casino Drive
Pittsburgh, Pennsylvania 15212
(412) 231-7777
Website: www.theriverscasino.com
Map: **#9**

Toll-free Number: (877) 558-0777
Restaurants: 5
Buffets: L- $14.99 D- $19.99
Other Games: B, P, B6, FCP, LIR, MS, UTH
Special Features: Free parking for players club members who play and earn points on card.

Sands Casino Resort Bethlehem
77 Sands Boulevard
Bethlehem, Pennsylvania 18015
Website: www.pasands.com
Map: **#7** (60 miles N of Philadelphia)

Toll-Free number: (877) 726-3777
Rooms: 288 Price Range: $149-$359
Suites: 22 Price Range: $259-$459
Restaurants: 8
Buffets: L- $16.95/$19.45 (Thu/Fri)/
$21.45 (Sat)/$24.95 (Sun)
D-$16.95/$19.45 (Thu)/$30.95 (Fri)/
$44.95 (Sat)/$24.95 (Sun)
Other Games: B, PG, P, B6, LIR,
CSP, CW, SIC
Senior Discount: Various Tue if 55+
Special Features: Spa. Outlet shopping center.

Sugar House Casino
1001 N Delaware Avenue
Philadelphia, Pennsylvania 19125
(267) 232-2000
Website: www.sugarhousecasino.com
Map: **#10**

Toll-Free number: (877) 477-3715
Restaurants: 4
Casino Size: 45,000 Square Feet
Other Games: P, B, PG, S21, MS, UTH

Valley Forge Convention Center Casino
1160 First Avenue
King of Prussia, Pennsylvania 19406
(610) 354-8118
Website: www.vfcasino.com
Map: **#10** (15 miles N.w of Philadelphia)

Room Reservations: Valley Forge Scanticon Hotel (610) 265-1500
Restaurants: 2
Casino Size: 33,000 Square Feet
Other Games: B, PG, B6, S21, UTH
Special Features: One hotel attached to convention center: Radisson Hotel Valley Forge www.radissonvalleyforge.com You must be a guest of the hotel for admittance to the casino, or buy a $10 gift card to get access for a 24-hour period. You can also buy a three-month membership for $20 which allows unlimited admission for two people, plus a 10% discount in the restaurants. Food court with four fast food outlets.

Pari-Mutuels

Harrah's Philadelphia Casino & Racetrack
777 Harrah's Boulevard
Chester, Pennsylvania 19013
(484) 490-1800
Website: www.harrahsphilly.com
Map: **#5** (8 miles S. of Philadelphia airport)

Toll-Free Number: (800) 480-8020
Restaurants: 5
Other Games: S21, B, FCP, LIR, SIC, UTH, P, MS
Special Features: Live harness racing seasonally. Daily simulcast of harness and thoroughbred racing.

Hollywood Casino at Penn National
777 Hollywood Boulevard
Grantville, Pennsylvania 17028
(717) 469-2211
Website: www.hollywoodpnrc.com
Map: #2 (16 miles N.E. of Harrisburg)

Restaurants: 4
Buffets: B-$16.99 (Sun) L-$14.99
D-$14.99/$26.99 (Fri/Sat)/$16.99 (Sun)
Casino Size: 45,000 Square Feet
Other Games: S21, FCP, P, LIR, B6
Special Features: Live thoroughbred horse racing seasonally. Daily simulcast of harness and thoroughbred racing. Buffet closed Monday and Tuesday.

The Meadows Racetrack & Casino
210 Racetrack Road
Washington, Pennsylvania 15301
(724) 225-9300
Website: www.meadowsgaming.com
Map: **#1** (25 miles S.W. of Pittsburgh)

Toll-Free number: (877) 726-3777
Rooms: 140 Price Range: $139-$169
Suites: 15 Price range: $199-$249
Restaurants: 3
Other Games: P, LIR, FCP, B, B6, MS
Special Features: Live harness seasonally. Daily simulcast of harness and thoroughbred racing. Food court with five fast food outlets.

Mohegan Sun at Pocono Downs
1280 Highway 315
Wilkes-Barre, Pennsylvania 18702
(570) 831-2100
Website: www.mohegansunpocono.com
Map: **#3** (20 miles S.W. of Scranton)

Toll-Free number: (888) 946-4672
Rooms: 238 Price Range: $119-$329
Restaurants: 8
Buffets: L- $15.99/$19.99 (Sun)
D-$19.99/$25.99 (Fri/Sat)
Other Games: S21, LIR, P, PG, MS
Special Features: Live harness racing seasonally. Daily simulcast of harness and thoroughbred racing. Buffet closed Mon/Tue.

Parx Casino and Racing
3001 Street Road
Bensalem, Pennsylvania 19020
(215) 639-9000
Website: www.parxcasino.com
Map: **#4** (18 miles N.E. of Philadelphia)

Toll-Free Number: (888) 588-7279
Restaurants: 3
Other Games: P, FCP, B6, B, PG
Special Features: Thoroughbred horse racing seasonally. Daily simulcast of harness and thoroughbred racing.

Presque Isle Downs & Casino
8199 Perry Highway
Erie, Pennsylvania 16509
(814) 860-8999
Website: www.presqueisledowns.com
Map: **#6**

Toll-Free Number: (866) 374-3386
Restaurants: 4
Buffet: L-$19.99 (Sat/Sun)
D-$26.99 (Fri)/$19.99 (Sat)
Other Games: LIR, P, MS
Special Features: Live thoroughbred horse racing seasonally. Daily simulcast of harness and thoroughbred racing. Buffet closed Monday to Thursday.

RHODE ISLAND

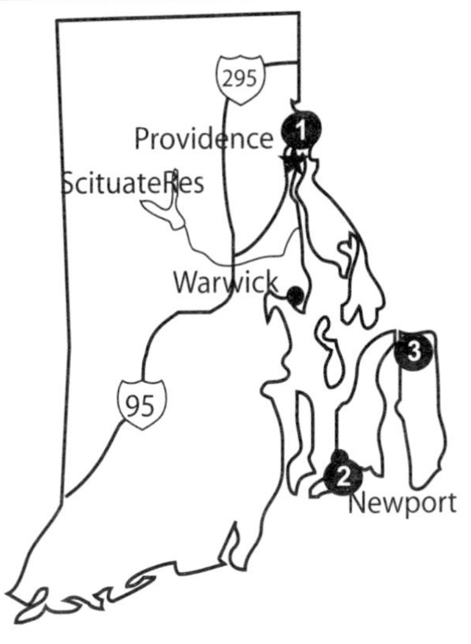

Rhode Island has two pari-mutuel facilities which both feature video lottery terminals (VLT's). These machines are the same as regular video gaming devices but are called lottery terminals because they are regulated by the state's lottery commission which receives a share of each machine's revenue. The machines accept cash but don't pay out in cash; instead, they print out a receipt which must be taken to a cashier.

All VLT's are programmed to play at least six different games: blackjack, keno, slots and three versions of poker (jacks or better, joker poker and deuces wild).

According to figures from the Rhode Island Lottery for the one-year period from July 1, 2016 through June 30, 2017 the average VLT return at Twin River was 90.91% and at Newport Grand it was 91.08%.

Twin River Casino offers live table games, but Newport Grand does not. However, the owners of Newport Grand are building a new casino in Tiverton (Map location **#3**) which will offer slots as well as table games. That casino is expected to open in mid-2018 and it will replace Newport Grand which would then close. For more information on that new casino, go to twinrivertiverton.com/

The minimum gambling age in Rhode Island is 18. For information on visiting Rhode Island call the state's tourism division at (800) 556-2484 or go to: www.visitrhodeisland.com.

Newport Grand Casino
150 Admiral Kalbfus Road
Newport, Rhode Island 02840
(401) 849-5000
Website: www.newportgrand.com
Map: **#2**

Toll-Free Number: (800) 451-2500
Restaurants: 1
Hours: 10am-1am/ 2am (Fri/Sat)
Overnight RV Parking: No
Special Features: Daily simulcasting of horse racing, dog racing and jai-alai. Digital versions of blackjack and roulette.

The games offered at Twin River are blackjack, craps, roulette, Spanish 21, pai gow poker, three card poker, let it ride, poker room and big 6 wheel.

Twin River Casino
100 Twin River Road
Lincoln, Rhode Island 02865
(401) 723-3200
Website: www.twinriver.com
Map: **#1** (10 miles N. of Providence)

Toll-Free Number: (877) 827-4837
Restaurants: 5
Overnight RV Parking: No
Special Features: Daily (except Tuesday) simulcasting of horse and dog racing. Three food courts with 10 fast food outlets.

SOUTH CAROLINA

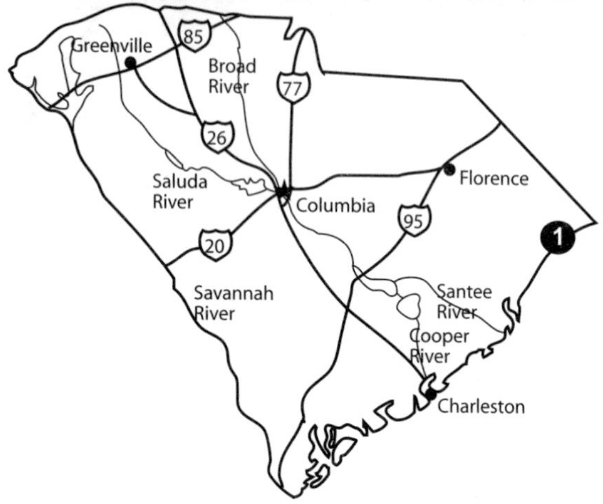

South Carolina has one casino boat which sails three miles out into international waters where casino gambling is permitted.

Big M Casino offers: blackjack, craps, roulette, three card poker, let it ride, slots and video poker. Due to security restrictions, you must present a photo ID or you will not be allowed to board.

For more information on visiting South Carolina go to: www.discoversouthcarolina.com or call their tourism department at (800) 872-3505.

The Big "M" Casino
4491 Waterfront Avenue
Little River, South Carolina 29566
(843) 249-9811
Website: www.bigmcasino.com
Map Location: **#1** (35 miles N. of Myrtle Beach)

Reservation Number: (877) 250-5825
Ship's Registry: U.S. Gambling Age: 21
Buffet: $13 am cruise/ $18 pm cruise
Schedule:
10:00am - 3:30pm (Sat-Mon) **Ship I**
11:00am - 4:30pm (Tue-Sun) **Ship II**
5:30pm - 10:30pm (Mon/Sat) **Ship I**
6:30pm - 11:30pm (Tue-Sun) **Ship II**
Price: $25
Port Charges: None Parking: Free
Special Features: 600-passenger *Big M Casino I* and *Big M Casino II* sail from Little River waterfront. Free shuttle available from Myrtle Beach. Must be 21 or older to board.

SOUTH DAKOTA

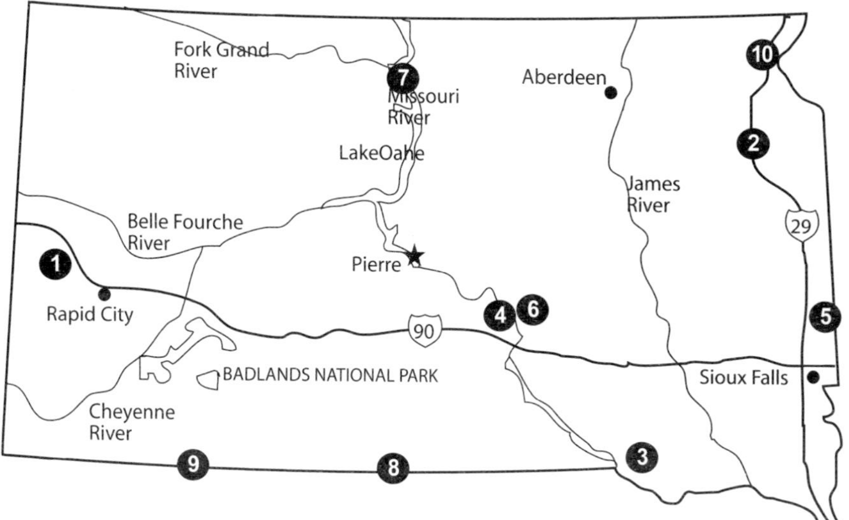

South Dakota's bars and taverns are allowed to have up to 10 video lottery terminals (VLT's) that offer the following games: poker, keno, blackjack and bingo.

These machines are the same as regular video gaming devices but are called lottery terminals because they are regulated by the state's lottery commission which receives a share of each machine's revenue.

The machines accept cash but don't pay out in cash; instead, they print out a receipt which must be taken to a cashier. The maximum bet is $2 and the maximum payout allowed is $1,000.

Slot machines, as well as blackjack, roulette, craps and poker are only permitted at Indian casinos and in Deadwood.

Deadwood was once most famous for being the home of Wild Bill Hickok who was shot to death while playing cards in the No. 10 Saloon. The hand he held was two pairs: black aces and black eights, which is now commonly referred to as a "dead man's hand." Wild Bill is buried in the local cemetery along with another local celebrity: Calamity Jane.

The first casinos in Deadwood opened on November 1, 1989. All of the buildings in the downtown area are required to conform with the city's authentic 1880's architecture. Many of the casinos are located in historic structures but there are also some new structures which were designed to be compatible with the historic theme of the town. The old No. 10 Saloon is still operating and you can actually gamble in the same spot where old Wild Bill bit the dust!

South Dakota law limits each casino licensee to a maximum of 30 slot machines and no one person is allowed to hold more than three licenses. Some operators combine licenses with other operators to form a cooperative which may look like one casino but in reality it's actually several licensees operating under one name.

The state's gaming laws originally limited blackjack, poker, let it ride and three-card poker bets to a maximum of $5, however, in July 2012 the law was changed to allow maximum bets of $1,000.

In addition to the Deadwood casinos, there are also nine Indian casinos in South Dakota. These casinos are also subject to the $1,000 maximum bet restrictions.

Here are statistics from the South Dakota Commission on Gaming for the payback percentages on all of Deadwood's slot machines for the one-year period from July 1, 2016 through June 30, 2017:

Denomination	Payback %
1¢ Slots	90.73
5¢ Slots	93.79
25¢ Slots	90.74
$1 Slots	92.35
$5 Slots	92.21
All	91.04

Unless otherwise noted, all casinos are opened 24 hours.

The Deadwood Trolly runs a scheduled shuttle service to all of the casinos that operates from 7 am to 1am weekdays and 7 am to 3 am on weekends. The cost is $1 per ride.

Unless otherwise noted, all casinos offer slot machines and video poker. Some casinos also offer: blackjack (BJ), craps (C), roulette (R), let it ride (LIR), three-card poker (TCP), ultimate Texas hold 'em (UTH), Mississippi stud (MS) and poker (P). Most of the Indian casinos also offer bingo (BG).

The minimum gambling age is 21 at all Deadwood and Indian casinos (18 for bingo at Indian casinos). South Dakota's casinos have very liberal rules about allowing minors in casinos and virtually all of the casinos will allow children to enter with their parents until about 8 p.m. Additionally, South Dakota is the only jurisdiction that will allow children to stand next to their parents while they are gambling.

For South Dakota tourism information call (800) 732-5682. For information on visiting Deadwood call the city's Chamber of Commerce at (800) 999-1876, or visit their website at www.deadwood.org.

Deadwood

Map: **#1** (in the Black Hills, 41 miles N.W. of Rapid City. Take I-90 W. Get off at the second Sturges exit and take Hwy. 14-A into Deadwood)

Best Western Hickok House
137 Charles Street
Deadwood, South Dakota 57732
(605) 578-1611
Website: www.bestwesternhickokhouse.com

Best Western Reservations: (800) 837-8174
Rooms: 38 Price Range: $98-$299
Restaurants: 1
Special Features: Hot tub and sauna.

Buffalo-Bodega Gaming Complex
658 Main Street
Deadwood, South Dakota 57732
Website: www.buffalobodega.com
(605) 578-1162

Restaurants: 1
Special Features: Oldest bar in Deadwood. Steakhouse restaurant.

Bullock Hotel
633 Main Street
Deadwood, South Dakota 57732
(605) 578-1745
Website: www.historicbullock.com

Reservation Number: (800) 336-1876
Rooms: 26 Price Range: $129-$169
Suites: 2 Price Range: $219-$259
Restaurants: 1
Special Features: Deadwood's oldest hotel.

Nestled in the Black Hills of South Dakota, the entire city of Deadwood has been designated a national historic landmark. Free historic walking tours are offered daily.

Cadillac Jack's Gaming Resort
360 Main Street
Deadwood, South Dakota 57732
(605) 578-1500
Website: www.cadillacjacksgaming.com

Toll Free Number: (866) 333-9195
Rooms: 92 Price Range: $99-$159
Suites: 11 Price Range: $165-$349
Restaurants: 1
Casino Size: 10,000 Square Feet
Other Games: BJ, C, R, P, TCP, MS, UTH
Special Features: Hotel is part of Choice Hotels. Free valet parking.

Celebrity Hotel & Casino
629 Main Street
Deadwood, South Dakota 57732
(605) 578-1909
Website: www.celebritycasinos.com

Toll-Free Number: (888) 399-1886
Rooms: 9 Price Range: $79-$164
Suites: 3 Price Range: $184-$254
Other Games: BJ
Special Features: Free auto and movie memorabilia museum. Blackjack offered 5pm-2am Wed-Sat only.

Deadwood Comfort Inn & Suites
225 Cliff Street
Deadwood, South Dakota 57732
(605) 578-7550
Website: www.deadwoodcomfortinn.com/

Reservation Number: (800) 961-3096
Rooms: 66 Price Range: $129-$159
Suites: 5 Price Range: $149-$199
Restaurants: 1
Special Features: Family amusement arcade and mini-golf. Affiliated with Choice Hotels.

Deadwood Dick's Saloon and Gaming Hall
51 Sherman Street
Deadwood, South Dakota 57732
(605) 578-3224
Website: www.deadwooddicks.com

Toll Free Number: (877) 882-4990
Rooms: 5 Price Range: $89-$179
Suites: 6 Price Range: $119-$269
Restaurants: 1
Special Features: Antique mall with 25 dealers.

Deadwood Gulch Gaming Resort
304 Cliff Street
Deadwood, South Dakota 57732
(605) 578-1294
Website: www.deadwoodgulch.com

Reservation Number: (800) 695-1876
Rooms: 95 Price Range: $99-$199
Suites: 5 Price Range: $225-$299
Restaurants: 2
Casino Size: 7,500 Square Feet
Special Features: Free breakfast for hotel guests.

Deadwood Mountain Grand
1906 Deadwood Mountain Drive
Deadwood, South Dakota 57732
(605) 559-0386
Website: www.deadwoodmountaingrand.com

Toll-free Number: (877) 907-4726
Rooms: 90 Price Range: $129-$219
Suites: 8 Price Range: $209-$389
Restaurants: 2
Casino Size: 7,500 Square Feet
Other Games: BJ, TCP, UTH
Senior Discount: Various Tue if 50+
Special Features: Hotel is Holiday Inn. 2,500-seat entertainment center.

Deadwood Station Bunkhouse and Gambling Hall
68 Main Street
Deadwood, South Dakota 57732
(605) 578-3476
Website: www.deadwoodstation.com

Toll-Free Number: (855) 366-6405
Rooms: 28 Price Range: $99-$129
Restaurants: 1

First Gold Hotel & Gaming
270 Main Street
Deadwood, South Dakota 57732
(605) 578-9777
Website: www.firstgold.com

Reservation Number: (800) 274-1876
Rooms: 190 Price Range: $79-$159
Suites: 5 Price Range: $129-$219
Restaurants: 2
Buffets: B/L- $10.95 D- $17.95/$26.95 (Fri/Sat)
Casino Size: 11,000 Square Feet
Other Games: BJ, TCP, MS
Special Features: RV park located next door. Includes **Blackjack** and **Horseshoe** casinos.

Gold Country Inn Gambling Hall and Cafe
801 Main Street
Deadwood, South Dakota 57732
(605) 578-2393
Website:www.goldcountrydeadwood.com

Reservation Number: (800) 287-1251
Rooms: 53 Price Range: $69-$109
Restaurants: 1

Gold Dust Casino & Hotel
688 Main Street
Deadwood, South Dakota 57732
(605) 578-2100
Website: www.golddustgaming.com

Rooms: 42 Price Range: $129-$259
Restaurants: 1
Casino Size: 30,000 Square Feet
Other Games: BJ, R, TCP, UTH
Special Features: Hotel is at 25 Lee Street, one block from casino. Largest gaming complex in Deadwood with eleven casinos. Free continental breakfast for hotel guests. Includes **French Quarter**, **Legends** and **Silver Dollar** casinos.

Hickok's Hotel and Casino
685 Main Street
Deadwood, South Dakota 57732
(605) 578-2222
Website: www.hickoks.com

Rooms: 18 Price Range: $79-$129
Suites: 4 Price Range: $139-$189
Restaurants: 1 Snack Bar
Special Features: Includes **B.B. Cody's.**

Iron Horse Inn
27 Deadwood Street
Deadwood, South Dakota 57732
(605) 717-7530
Website: www.ironhorseinndeadwood.com

Toll Free Number: (844) 245-6180
Rooms: 19 Price Range: $109-$159
Suites: 4 Price Range: $129-$189
Casino Size: 1,000 Square Feet

The Lodge at Deadwood
100 Pine Crest Lane
Deadwood, South Dakota 57732
(605) 571-2132
Website: www.deadwoodlodge.com

Toll-Free Number: (877) 393-5634
Rooms: 100 Price Range: $119-$169
Suites: 40 Price Range: $179-$299
Restaurants: 2
Casino Size: 11,000 Square Feet
Other Games: BJ, TCP, P, CW, MS, UTH
Special Features: Electronic version of roulette.

Lucky 8 Gaming Hall/Super 8 Motel
196 Cliff Street
Deadwood, South Dakota 57732
(605) 578-2535
Website: www.deadwoodsuper8.com

Reservation Number: (800) 800-8000
Rooms: 47 Price Range: $49-$129
Suites: 4 Price Range: $99-$149
Restaurants: 1 Snack Bar
Special Features: Video arcade. Free continental breakfast for hotel guests.

Main Street Deadwood Gulch Bar
560 Main Street
Deadwood, South Dakota 57732
(605) 578-1207

Martin & Mason Hotel
33 Deadwood Street
Deadwood, South Dakota 57732
(605) 722-3456
Website: www.martinmasonhotel.com

Rooms: 6 Prices: $179-$199
Suites: 2 Prices: $230-$389
Restaurants: 1
Special Features: Includes **Wooden Nickel Casino and Lee Street Station.**

Midnight Star
677 Main Street
Deadwood, South Dakota 57732
(605) 578-1555
Website: www.themidnightstar.com

Toll-Free Number: (800) 999-6482
Restaurants: 1
Other Games: BJ, TCP
Special Features: Sports bar & grill. Display of Kevin Costner movie memorabilia. Blackjack open Wed-Sun.

Mineral Palace Hotel & Gaming
601 Main Street
Deadwood, South Dakota 57732
(605) 578-2036
Website: www.mineralpalace.com

Reservation Number: (800) 847-2522
Rooms: 71 Price Range: $79-$179
Suites: 4 Price Range: $139-$389
Restaurants: 1
Other Games: BJ, R, TCP

Mustang Sally's
634 Main Street
Deadwood, South Dakota 57732
(605) 578-2025

Restaurants: 1

Old Style Saloon #10
657 Main Street
Deadwood, South Dakota 57732
(605) 578-3346
Website: www.saloon10.com

Toll-Free Number: (800) 952-9398
Restaurants: 1
Casino Size: 4,000 Square Feet
Other Games: BJ, P, TCP
Hours: 11am-9pm/10pm (Fri/Sat)
Special Features: Wild Bill's chair and other old west artifacts on display. Includes **The Utter Place** card room.

Oyster Bay/Fairmont Hotel
628 Main Street
Deadwood, South Dakota 57732
(605) 578-2205

Restaurants: 1
Special Features: Historic restoration of 1895 brothel, spa and underground jail cell. Oyster bar.

Silverado - Franklin Historic Hotel & Gaming Complex
709 Main Street
Deadwood, South Dakota 57732
(605) 578-3670
Website: www.silveradofranklin.com

Toll-Free Number: (800) 584-7005
Rooms: 80 Price Range: $39-$129
Suites: 15 Price Range: $59-$209
Restaurants: 2
Buffets: B-$11.95/$16.95 (Sun)
L-$12.95/$16.95 (Sun)
D-$17.95/$27.95 (Fri/Sat)
Casino Size: 20,000 Square Feet
Other Games: BJ, C, R, P, LIR, TCP, CSP, FCP, UTH
Senior Discount: Various Wed if 50+

Tin Lizzie Gaming
555 Main Street
Deadwood, South Dakota 57732
(605) 578-1715
Website: www.tinlizzie.com

Toll-Free Number: (800) 643-4490
Rooms: 59 Price Range: $69-$149
Suites: 5 Price Range: $159-$249
Restaurants: 3
Buffets: B-$10.99 L-$9.99
D-$15.99/$26.99 (Fri/Sat)
Casino Size: 8,300 Square Feet
Other Games: BJ, C, R, LIR, TCP, UTH
Senior Discount: Various if 50+
Special Features: Hotel is Hampton Inn. Includes **Four Aces** casino.

Veterans of Foreign War
10 Pine Street
Deadwood, South Dakota 57732
(605) 722-9914

Hours: 9:30am-12am Daily

Indian Casinos

Dakota Connection
46102 County Highway 10
Sisseton, South Dakota 57262
(605) 698-4273
Website: www.dakotaconnection.com
Map: **#10** (165 miles N. of Sioux Falls)

Toll-Free Number: (800) 542-2876
Restaurants: 1 Liquor: No
Buffets: B- $8.99 (Sat/Sun) L- $10.99 (Sun)
Hours: 8am-2am/24 Hours (Fri/Sat)
Other Games: BG
Overnight RV Parking: Free must register at players club/RV Dump: No
Special Features: Convenience store. Gas station.

Dakota Sioux Casino & Hotel
16415 Sioux Conifer Road
Watertown, South Dakota 57201
(605) 882-2051
Website: www.dakotasioux.com
Map: **#2** (104 miles N. of Sioux Falls)

Toll-Free Number: (800) 658-4717
Rooms: 88 Price Range: $55-$99
Suites: 12 Price Range: $89-$199
Restaurants: 2 Liquor: Yes
Buffets: B/L- $8.95 (Sat/Sun)
D- $12.95 (Sun)/$19.95 (Sat)
Other Games: BJ, P
Overnight RV Parking: Free/RV Dump: Free
Senior Discount: Various Mon if 50+
Special Features: 9-space RV park ($10 per night). Room discount for players club members.

East Wind Casino
US Highway 18
Martin, South Dakota 57551
(605) 685-1140
Website: www.eastwindcasino.com

Restaurants: 1 Deli Liquor: no
Senior Discount: Various Wed if 55+

Fort Randall Casino Hotel
38538 East Highway 46
Pickstown, South Dakota 57367
(605) 487-7871
Website: www.fortrandallcasino.com
Map: **#3** (100 miles S.W. of Sioux Falls)

Room Reservations: (800) 362-6333
Rooms: 57 Price Range: $65-$81
Suites: 2 Price Range: $81-$115
Restaurants: 1 Liquor: Yes
Buffets: D-$17.95 (Sat)
Other Games: BJ, R (Fri/Sat), P (Wed/Fri/Sat), BG (Thu-Sun)
Overnight RV Parking: Free/RV Dump: Free
Senior Discount: Various Wed if 50+
Special Features: Room discount for players club members.

Golden Buffalo Casino
321 Sitting Bull Street
Lower Brule, South Dakota 57548
(605) 473-5577
Website: www.thegoldenbuffalocasino.com
Map: **#4** (45 miles S.E. of Pierre)

Rooms: 38 Price Range: $55-$80
Restaurants: 1 Liquor: Yes
Hours: 8am-12:30am/2am (Fri/Sat)
Casino Size: 9,000 Square Feet
Overnight RV Parking: Free/RV Dump: Free

Grand River Casino and Resort
2 U.S. 12
Mobridge, South Dakota 57601
(605) 845-7104
Website: www.grandrivercasino.com
Map: **#7** (240 miles N.E. of Rapid City)

Toll-Free Number: (800) 475-3321
Rooms: 38 Price Range: $80-$110
Suites: 2 Price Range: $150-$200
Restaurants: 1 Liquor: Yes
Buffets: B- $8.95 (Sat/Sun)
D-$10.50/$17.95 (Sun)
Other Games: BJ, P
Overnight RV Parking: Free/RV Dump: No
Special Features: 10-space RV park ($17 per night). Room discount for players club members.

Lode Star Casino & Hotel
1003 SD Highway 47
Fort Thompson, South Dakota 57339
(605) 245-6000
Website: www.thelodestarcasino.com
Map: **#6** (150 miles N.W. of Sioux Falls)

Rooms: 50 Price Range: $59-$75
Restaurants: 1 Liquor: Yes
Hours: 7am-2am/4am (Thu-Sat)
Other Games: BJ, P (Mon/Thu/Sat)
Overnight RV Parking: Free/RV Dump: No
Senior Discount: Various Mon if 50+
Special Features: Hotel is off-property and free shuttle is provided.

Prairie Wind Casino & Hotel
25 Casino Drive
Oglala, South Dakota 57764
(605) 867-6300
Website: www.prairiewindcasino.com
Map: **#9** (85 miles S.E. of Rapid City)

Toll-Free Number: (800) 705-9463
Rooms: 78 Price Range: $69-$109
Suites: 6 Price Range: $149-$299
Restaurants: 1 Liquor: No
Buffets: B-$9.95 (Sat/Sun)
D-$12.95/$25.95 (Thu)/$21.95 (Fri)
Other Games: BJ, BG, P, TCP
Overnight RV Parking: Free/RV Dump: No
Senior Special: Various Thu if 50+

Rosebud Casino
370421 Highway 83 (on SD/NE stateline)
Mission, South Dakota 57555
(605) 378-3800
Website: www.rosebudcasino.com
Map: **#8** (22 miles S. of Mission)

Toll-Free Number: (800) 786-7673
Rooms: 58 Price Range: $99-$115
Suites: 2 Price Range: $109-$139
Restaurants: 2 Liquor: Yes
Buffets: B/L-$11.99 (Sun)
D- $10.99/$13.99 (Thu-Sun)
Other Games: BJ, BG (Tue-Sat)
Overnight RV Parking: Free/RV Dump: No
Senior Discount: Various Wed if 50+
Special Features: Hotel is Quality Inn. 15-space RV park ($20 per night).

Royal River Casino & Hotel
607 S. Veterans Street
Flandreau, South Dakota 57028
(605) 997-3746
Website: www.royalrivercasino.com
Map: **#5** (35 miles N. of Sioux Falls on I-29)

Toll-Free Number: (877) 912-5825
Rooms: 108 Price Range: $106-$127
Suites: 12 Price Range: $139-$160
Restaurants: 1 Liquor: Yes
Buffets: B-$5.99 (Sat)/$10.99 (Sun)
L-$8.99/$10.99 (Sun)
D-$9.99/$16.99 (Fri)/
$14.99 (Sat)/$7.99 (Sun)
Casino Size: 17,000 Square Feet
Other Games: BJ, R, MS, UTH
Overnight RV Parking: Free/RV Dump: No
Senior Discount: Various Thu if 55+
Special Features: 21-space RV park ($10 per night).

Turtle Creek Crossing Casino
28281 US Highway 18
Mission, South Dakota 57555
(605) 856-2329
Map: **#8** (100 miles S. of Pierre)

Casino Hours: 8am-8pm
Games Offered: Gaming Machines Only

TEXAS

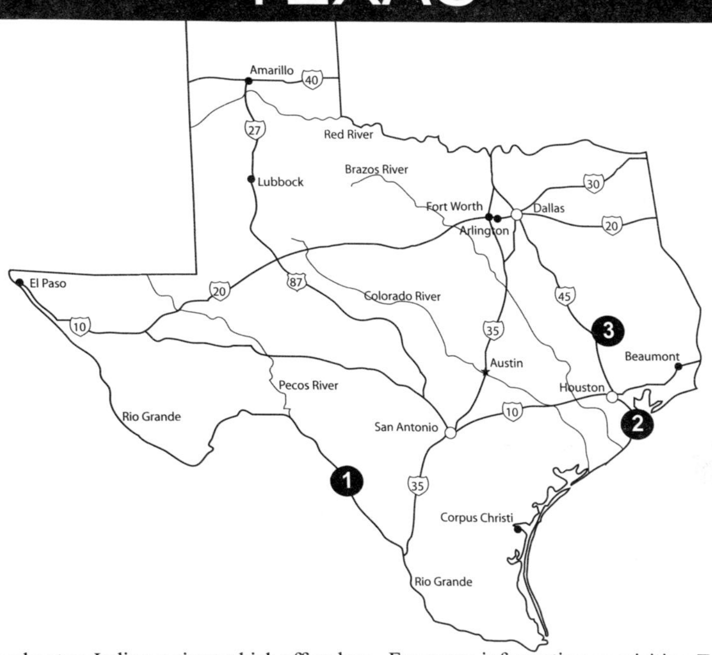

Texas has two Indian casinos which offer class II gaming machines based on bingo. One of them also offers pull tab machines, bingo and poker. The minimum gambling age is 21 and the casinos are open 24 hours daily.

The state is in a legal fight to try and shut down Naskila Gaming but at the time of publication the casino was still open. Be sure to call first if planning a trip.

Class II video gaming devices look like slot machines, but are actually bingo games and the spinning reels are for "entertainment purposes only." No public information is available concerning the payback percentages on any gaming machines in Texas' Indian casino.

Texas also has one casino boat which sails nine miles out into the Gulf of Mexico where casino gambling is permitted. The boat offers: blackjack, craps, roulette, three card poker, a sports book, slots and video poker. You must provide a photo ID or you won't be allowed to board.

For more information on visiting Texas call (800) 888-8839 or go to: www.traveltex.com.

Jacks or Better Casino
715 N. Holiday Drive
Galveston, Texas 77550
(409) 356-9148
Website: www.jacksorbettercasino.com/
Map: **#2** (50 miles S.E. of Houston)

Reservation Number: (877) 844-4725
Gambling Age: 18 Ship's Registry: U.S.
Meal Service: A la Carte
Price: $5 for all cruises
Schedule:
10:30am-4:30pm (Fri/-Sat)
6:30pm - 12:30am (Fri/Sat)
1:00pm - 8:00pm (Sun)
Port Charges: Included Parking: Free
Special Features: 150-passenger ship. Must be 18 or older to board.

Kickapp Lucky Eagle Casino Hotel
794 Lucky Eagle Drive
Eagle Pass, Texas 78852
(830) 758-1936
Website: www.luckyeagletexas.com
Map: **#1** (140 miles S.W. of San Antonio)

Toll-Free Number: (888) 255-8259
Rooms: 240 Price Range: $99-$209
Suites: 9 Price Range: $124-$269
Restaurants: 6 Liquor: Yes
Buffets: L- $9,99 D- $14.99
Casino Size: 16,000 Square Feet
Games Offered: Class II Gaming Machines based on bingo, pull tab machines, bingo hall (Wed-Sun) and poker room.
Overnight RV Parking: Free/RV Dump: Free
Special Features: 20-space RV park ($15 per night).

Naskila Gaming
540 State Park Road 56
Livingston, Texas 77351
(936) 563-2946
Website: www.naskila.com
Map: **#3** (75 miles N.E. of Houston)

Restaurants: 1 Liquor: No
Casino Size: 15,000 square feet
Games Offered: Class II Gaming Machines based on bingo

WASHINGTON

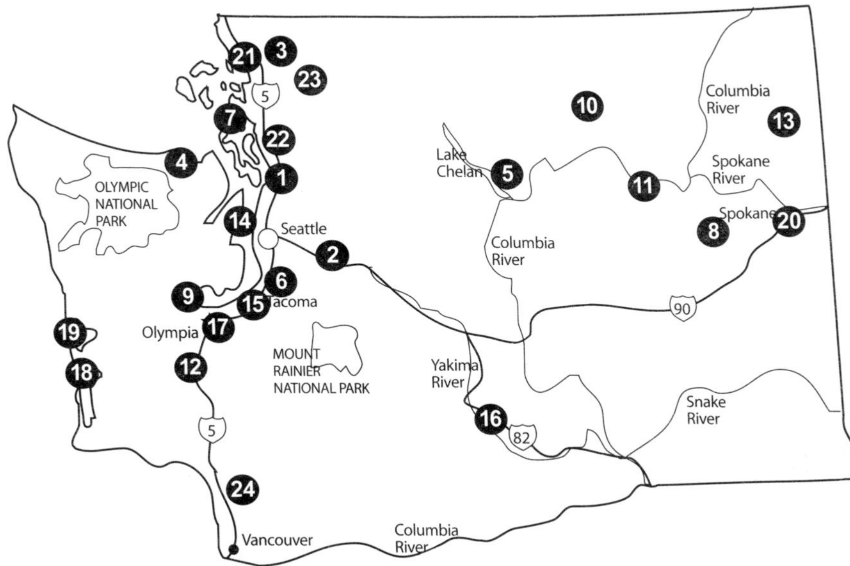

The Indian casinos operating in Washington all have compacts with the state allowing them to offer table games, as well as electronic 'scratch' ticket games which use a finite number of tickets with a predetermined number of winners and losers.

These video gaming machines have a maximum bet of $20.

The Tribes are not required to release information on their slot machine percentage paybacks. However, according to the terms of the compact between the Tribes and the state, the minimum prize payout for electronic 'scratch' ticket games is 75%.

Most Washington casinos are open on a 24-hour basis. The hours of operation are noted in each casino's listing for those not open 24 hours.

All casinos offer blackjack, craps, roulette, slots, video poker and pull tabs. Optional games offered include: baccarat (B), mini-baccarat (MB), poker (P), pai gow poker (PGP), Caribbean stud poker (CSP), three-card poker (TCP), ultimate Texas hold em (UTH), four card poker (FCP), Spanish 21 (S21), big 6 wheel (B6), keno (K), Off-Track Betting (OTB) and bingo (BG).

The minimum gambling age is 21 at most casinos (at some it's 18) and 18 for bingo or pari-mutuel betting. Look in the "Special Features" listing for each casino to see which allow gambling at 18 years of age.

Although most of the casinos have toll-free numbers be aware that some of these numbers will only work for calls made within Washington.

For more information on visiting Washington call their tourism department at (800) 544-1800 or go to: www.experiencewashington.com.

Angel of the Winds Casino
3438 Stoluckquamish Lane
Arlington, Washington 98223
(360) 474-9740
Website: www.angelofthewinds.com
Map: **#22** (50 miles N. of Seattle)

Rooms: 125 Price Range: $114-$189
Suites:6 Price Range: $209-$279
Restaurants: 2 Liquor: Yes
Buffet: B-$9.99/$16.99 (Sat/Sun)
L-$10.99 D-$15.99/$24.99 (Fri-Sun)
Other Games: P, TCP, PGP, UTH, K
Senior Discount: Various Mon if 50+
Overnight RV Parking: Free/RV Dump: No

BJ's Bingo
4411 Pacific Highway East
Fife, Washington 98424
(253) 922-0430
Website: www.bjs-bingo.com
Map: **#15** (a suburb of Tacoma)

Restaurants: 1
Other games: BG, No table games
Overnight RV Parking: Call ahead
Senior Discount: Various Sun/Mon if 55+

Chewelah Casino
2555 Smith Road
Chewelah, Washington 99109
(509) 935-6167
Website: www.chewelahcasino.com
Map: **#13** (50 miles N. of Spokane)

Toll-Free Number: (800) 322-2788
Restaurants: 1 Liquor: Yes
Hours: 8am-2am
Casino Size: 22,000 Square Feet
Other Games: S21
Overnight RV Parking: Free/RV Dump: No
Senior Discount: Various Wed if 55+
Special Features: One block from Double Eagle Casino. 10-space RV park ($15 per night). Gambling age is 18.

Coulee Dam Casino
515 Birch Street
Coulee Dam, Washington 99116
(509) 633-0766
Website: www.colvillecasinos.com
Map: **#11** (85 miles N.W of Spokane)

Toll-Free Number: (800) 556-7492
Restaurants: 1 Liquor: Yes
Other Games: Only Gaming Machines
Overnight RV Parking: Free/RV Dump: No
Special Features: Gambling age is 18.

Elwha River Casino
631 Stratton Road
Port Angeles, Washington 98363
(360) 452-3005
Website: www.elwharivercasino.com
Map: **#4** (70 miles N.W. of Seattle via ferry)

Restaurants: 1 Liquor: No
Other Games: Only Gaming Machines
Hours: 10am-12am/4am (Fri/Sat)

Emerald Queen Hotel & Casino at Fife
5700 Pacific Highway East
Fife, Washington 98424
(253) 594-7777
Website: www.emeraldqueen.com
Map: **#15** (a suburb of Tacoma)

Toll-Free Number: (888) 820-3555
Rooms: 130 Price Range: $99-$129
Suites: 10 Price Range: $179-$229
Restaurants: 3 Liquor: Yes
Buffets: L-$13.95/$19.95 (Sun) D-$19.95
Other Games: Only Gaming Machines
Overnight RV Parking: No
Senior Discount: Buffet discount if 60+
Special Features: Free shuttle to other Emerald Queen casino.

Emerald Queen Casino at I-5
2024 East 29th Street
Tacoma, Washington 98404
(253) 594-7777
Website: www.emeraldqueen.com
Map: **#15**

Toll-Free Number: (888) 831-7655
Restaurants: 2 Liquor: Yes
Buffets: L-$13.95/$24.95 (Sun) D-$24.95
Other Games: S21, MB, PGP, LIR, TCP, B6, UTH
Senior Discount: Buffet discount if 60+
Overnight RV Parking: Free/RV Dump: No
Special Features: Sports bar. Free shuttle to other Emerald Queen casino.

ilani Casino Resort
1 Cowlitz Way
Ridgefield, Washington 98642
(877) 464-5264
Website: www.ilaniresort.com
Map: #**24** (20 miles N. of Vancouver, WA)

Toll-Free Number: (877) 464-5264
Restaurants: 8
Casino Size: 100,000 square feet
Other Games: MB, S21, PGP, TCP, UTH

Little Creek Casino Resort
91 West Highway 108
Shelton, Washington 98584
(360) 427-7711
Website: www.little-creek.com
Map: **#9** (23 miles N. of Olympia off Hwy 101/108 interchange)

Toll-Free Number: (800) 667-7711
Rooms: 92 Price Range: $99-$139
Suites: 6 Price Range: $169-$229
Restaurants: 5 Liquor: Yes
Buffets: B-$8.95/$16.95 (Sun) L-$12.95
D-$16.95/$24.95 (Fri/Sat)
Hours: 8am-5am/24 hours (Thu-Sun)
Casino Size: 30,000 Square Feet
Other Games: P, PGP, K, BG
Overnight RV Parking: Free/RV Dump: No
Senior Discount: Various Mon-Wed if 50+
Special Features: Indoor pool. Gift shop.

Lucky Dog Casino
19330 N. Highway 101
Skokomish, Washington 98584
(360) 877-5656
Website: www.myluckydogcasino.com
Map: **#9** (23 miles N. of Olympia)

Toll-Free Number: (877) 582-5948
Restaurants: 2 Liquor: Yes
Hours: 9am-12am/2am (Fri/Sat)/1am (Sun)
Casino Size: 2,500 Square Feet
Other Games: Only Gaming Machines
Special Features: 20-space RV park ($34-$39 per night).

Lucky Eagle Casino
12888 188th Avenue SW
Rochester, Washington 98579
(360) 273-2000
Website: www.luckyeagle.com
Map: **#12** (26 miles S. of Olympia)

Toll-Free Number: (800) 720-1788
Rooms: 65 Price Range: $99-$135
Suites: 4 Price Range: $138-$265
Restaurants: 5 Liquor: Yes
Buffets: L-$13.95/$15.95 (Sun)
D-$17.95/$25.95 (Fri/Sat)
Casino Size: 75,000 Square Feet
Other Games: S21, PGP, TCP, UTH, K, BG
Overnight RV Parking: Must use RV park
Senior Discount: Various specials Mon if 50+
Special Features: 20-space RV park ($25 per night).

Mill Bay Casino
455 Wapato Lake Road
Manson, Washington 98831
(509) 687-6911
Website: www.colvillecasinos.com
Map: **#5** (200 miles N.E. of Seattle on the N. shore of Lake Chelan)

Toll-Free Number: (800) 648-2946
Restaurants: 2 Liquor: Yes
Other Games: S21, PGP, FCP
Overnight RV Parking: Free/RV Dump: No
Senior Discount: Various Wed if 55+
Special Features: Gambling age is 18.

Muckleshoot Casino
2402 Auburn Way South
Auburn, Washington 98002
(253) 804-4444
Website: www.muckleshootcasino.com
Map: **#6** (20 miles S. of Seattle)

Toll-Free Number (800) 804-4944
Restaurants: 5 Liquor: Yes
Buffets: B-$18.95 (Sat/Sun)
L-$14.95/$18.95 (Sat/Sun)
D-$19.95/$25.95 (Fri/Sat/Sun)
Other Games: S21, MB, P, PGP, TCP, BG, UTH
Overnight RV Parking: Free/RV Dump: No
Special Features: Two casinos in separate buildings, one is non-smoking.

Nooksack Northwood Casino
9750 Northwood Road
Lynden, Washington 98264
(360) 734-5101
Website: www.northwood-casino.com
Map: **#3** (14 miles N. of Bellingham)

THIS CASINO CLOSED JUNE 16, 2017 BUT IS EXPECTED TO RE-OPEN IN THE FUTURE. CALL FIRST BEFORE VISITING THIS CASINO.
Toll-Free Number (877) 777-9847
Restaurants: 2 Liquor: Yes
Buffets: D-$10.95 (Wed)/$4.95 (Thu)/
$19.95 (Fri)/$12.95 (Sat)
Hours: 9am-2am/3am (Fri/Sat)
Casino Size: 20,000 Square Feet
Other Games: Only Gaming Machines
Overnight RV Parking: Free/RV Dump: No
Senior Discount: Various Tue if 40+
Special Features: RV hook-ups available for $30 per night/$7 if players club member.

Northern Quest Resort & Casino
100 N Hayford Road
Airway Heights, Washington 99001
(509) 242-7000
Website: www.northernquest.com
Map: **#20** (10 miles W. of Spokane)

Toll-Free Number (877) 871-6772
Rooms: 200 Prices $129-$219
Suites: 50 Prices: $249-$369
Restaurants: 4 Liquor: Yes
Buffets: B/L-$12.95/$16.95 (Sun)
D-$16.95/$29.95 (Fri)/$21.95 (Sat)
Casino Size: 21,500 Square Feet
Other Games: S21, PGP, TCP, K, OTB, P
Overnight RV Parking: Free/RV Dump: No
Senior Discount: Various Tue if 55+
Special Features: New RV park expected to open in early 2018.

The Point Casino
7989 Salish Lane NE
Kingston, Washington 98346
(360) 297-0070
Website: www.the-point-casino.com
Map: **#14** (18 miles W. of Seattle via Bainbridge Ferry)

Toll-Free Number (866) 547-6468
Rooms: 85 Price Range: $89-$119
Suites: 9 Price Range: $125-$199
Restaurants: 2 Liquor: Yes
Buffets: D- $17.95 (Wed-Fri)/$24.95 (Sat)
Casino Size: 18,500 Square Feet
Other Games: S21, PGP, P
Overnight RV Parking: Free/RV Dump: No
Senior Discount: Various on Sun if 55+
Special Features: Table games open at 4pm/2pm (Fri-Sun). Buffet closed Mon/Tue.

Quil Ceda Creek Nightclub & Casino
6410 33rd Avenue N.E.
Tulalip, Washington 98271
(360) 716-1700
Website: www.quilcedacreekcasino.com
Map: **#1** (30 miles N. of Seattle)

Toll-Free Number: (888) 272-1111
Restaurants: 1 Liquor: Yes
Casino Size: 52,000 Square Feet
Other Games: S21, PGP, TCP, UTH
Overnight RV Parking: Free/RV Dump: No
Special Features: One mile from Tulalip Casino.

Quinault Beach Resort and Casino
78 Route 115
Ocean Shores, Washington 98569
(360) 289-9466
Website: www.quinaultbeachresort.com
Map: **#19** (90 miles W. of Tacoma)

Toll-Free Number: (888) 461-2214
Rooms: 159 Price Range: $129-$209
Suite: 9 Price Range: $289-$449
Restaurants: 4 Liquor: Yes
Buffets: D-$16.95 (Wed)/$29.95 (Fri)
Casino Size: 16,000 Square Feet
Other Games: S21, P, TCP
Overnight RV Parking: Free (must register first at front desk)/RV Dump: No
Senior Discount: Buffet discount if 50+
Special Features: Spa. RV park charges $10 per night Fri/Sat.

Red Wind Casino
12819 Yelm Highway SE
Olympia, Washington 98513
(360) 412-5000
Website: www.redwindcasino.com
Map: **#17**

Toll-Free Number: (866) 946-2444
Restaurants: 4 Liquor: Yes
Buffets: B-$14.95 (Sat)/$19.95 (Sun)
L-$15.95/$19.95 (Sun)
D-$22.95/$29.95 (Fri/Sat)
Hours: 8am-5am/24 hrs (Thu-Sun)
Casino Size: 12,000 Square Feet
Other Games: S21, PGP, TCP, K, UTH
Overnight RV Parking: Free/RV Dump: No
Senior Discount: 25% off food if 55+

7 Cedars Casino
270756 Highway 101
Sequim, Washington 98382
(360) 683-7777
Website: www.7cedarscasino.com
Map: **#4** (70 miles N.W. of Seattle via ferry)

Toll-Free Number: (800) 458-2597
Restaurants: 4 Liquor: Yes
Buffets: L-$13.95 (Fri/Sat)
D-$21.95 (Fri/Sat)
Hours: 9am-3am/4am (Fri/Sat)
Other Games: S21, P, PGP, K, BG, UTH
Overnight RV Parking: Free (Must check-in at cashier cage first)/RV Dump: No
Senior Discount: Various on Mon if 50+

Shoalwater Bay Casino
4112 Highway 105
Tokeland, Washington 98590
(360) 267-2048
Website: www.shoalwaterbaycasino.com
Map: **#18** (75 miles S.W. of Olympia)

Toll-Free Number: (866) 834-7312
Restaurants: 1 Liquor: Yes
Hours: 10am-Midnight/2am (Fri/Sat)
Casino Size: 10,000 Square Feet
Other Games: Only Gaming Machines
Overnight RV Parking: Free (Check with security first)/RV Dump: No

Silver Reef Hotel • Casino • Spa
4876 Haxton Way
Ferndale, Washington 98248
(360) 383-0777
Website: www.silverreefcasino.com
Map: **#21** (7 miles N. of Bellingham)

Toll-Free Number: (866) 383-0777
Rooms: 105 Price Range: $129-$159
Suites: 4 Price Range: $279-$319
Restaurants: 4 Liquor: Yes
Buffets: L-$12.95/$16.95 (Sun)
D-$18.95/$23.95 (Fri)/$19.95(Sat)
Casino Size: 48,000 Square Feet
Other Games: S21, PGP, TCP, FCP, UTH
Senior Discount: Various on Mon if 50+
Overnight RV Parking: Free/RV Dump: No
Special Features: Buffet closed Wednesday.

Skagit Valley Casino Resort
5984 N. Darrk Lane
Bow, Washington 98232
(360) 724-7777
Website: www.theskagit.com
Map: **#7** (75 miles N. of Seattle)

Toll-Free Number: (877) 275-2448
Rooms: 74 Price Range: $99-$139
Suites: 29 Price Range: $179-$219
Restaurants: 3 Liquor: Yes
Buffets: B-$15.99 (Sat/Sun)
L-$9.99/ $15.99 (Sat/Sun)
D-$14.99/$21.50 (Fri)/$24.95 (Sat)
Hours: 9am-3am/5am (Fri/Sat)
Casino Size: 26,075 Square Feet
Other Games: S21, PGP
Overnight RV Parking: No
Senior Discount: Various on Tue if 50+
Special Features: Two 18-hole golf courses. Health spa.

Snoqualmie Casino
37500 SE North Bend Way
Snoqualmie, Washington 98065
(425) 888-1234
Website: www.snocasino.com
Map: **#2** (30 miles E. of Seattle)

Restaurants: 5 Liquor: Yes
Buffets: L-$15.95/$18.95 (Sat/Sun)
D-$28.95/$44.95 (Tue)/$25.95 (Mon)
Other Games: S21, B, PGP, P

Suquamish Clearwater Casino Resort
15347 Suquamish Way NE
Suquamish, Washington 98392
(360) 598-8700
Website: www.clearwatercasino.com
Map: **#14** (15 miles W. of Seattle via Bainbridge Ferry)

Toll-Free Number: (866) 609-8700
Rooms: 70 Price Range: $139-$189
Suites: 15 Price Range: $169-$219
Restaurants: 4 Liquor: Yes
Buffets: L-$13.95
D-$18.95/$28.95 (Fri)/$26.25 (Sat)
Casino Size: 22,000 Square Feet
Other Games: P, PGP, TCP, LIR, K
Overnight RV Parking: Free/RV Dump: No
Senior Discount: Buffet discount if 55+
Special features: Seattle and Edmonds Ferries fee reimbursed with qualified play. 18-hole golf course. Gambling age is 18. Table games open 11am.

Swinomish Casino & Lodge
12885 Casino Drive
Anacortes, Washington 98221
(360) 293-2691
Website: swinomishcasinoandlodge.com
Map: **#7** (70 miles N. of Seattle, between I-5 and Anacortes on Hwy. 20)

Toll-Free Number: (888) 288-8883
Rooms: 98 Price Range: $129-$179
Suites: 4 Price Range: $279-$349
Restaurants: 3 Liquor: Yes
Casino Size: 23,000 Square Feet
Other Games: S21, PGP, TCP, FCP, UTH, K
Overnight RV Parking: Must use RV park
Senior Discount: Various on Tue if 50+
Special Features: 35-space RV park ($27-$35 per night). Gift shop.

Tulalip Casino
10200 Quil Ceda Boulevard
Tulalip, Washington 98271
(360) 716-6000
Website: www.tulalipcasino.com
Map: **#1** (30 miles N. of Seattle)

Toll-Free Number: (888) 272-1111
Rooms: 370 Price Range: $179-$239
Suites: 23 Price Range: $249-$429
Restaurants: 9 Liquor: Yes
Buffets: B-$12.95/$18.95 (Sat/Sun)
L-$14.50/$18.95 (Sat/Sun)
D-$19.95/$21.95 (Fri-Sun)/$27.95 (Tue)
Casino Size: 45,000 Square Feet
Other Games: S21, MB, P, PGP, UTH,
TCP, FCP BG
Overnight RV Parking: Free/RV Dump: No
Special Features: 3,000-seat amphitheatre. One mile from Quil Ceda Creek Casino. Bingo hall is one mile away with free shuttle service.

12 Tribes Casino
28968 US Highway 97
Omak, Washington 98841
(509) 422-4646
Website: www.colvillecasinos.com
Map: **#10** (165 miles N.E. of Seattle)

Toll-Free Number: (800) 559-4643
Rooms: 68 Price Range: $99-$189
Suites: 12 Price Range: $179-$229
Restaurants: 2
Casino Size: 56,000 Square Feet
Senior Discount: Various Tue if 55+
Special Features: 21-space RV park ($30 per night). Spa.

Two Rivers Casino & Resort
6828-B Highway 25 South
Davenport, Washington 99122
(509) 722-4000
Website: www.two-rivers-casino.com
Map: **#8** (60 miles W. of Spokane)

Toll-Free Number: (800) 954-2946
Restaurants: 1 Liquor: No
Hours: 12pm-10pm/Closed Tue/Wed
Casino Size: 10,000 Square Feet
Overnight RV Parking: Must use RV park
Senior Discount: Various on Fri if 55+
Other Games: Only Gaming Machines and Blackjack
Senior Discount: Various Sun if 55+
Special Features: Regular slots. 100-space RV park ($28-$35 per night). 260-slip marina and beach. Gambling age is 18. Open seasonally May-October.

Yakama Legends Casino
580 Fort Road
Toppenish, Washington 98948
(509) 865-8800
Website: www.legendscasino.com
Map: **#16** (20 miles S. of Yakima)

Toll-Free Number: (877) 726-6311
Rooms: 200 Price Range: $109-$159
Restaurants: 2 Liquor: No
Buffets: B-$14.95 (Sun)
L-$12.96/$29.95 (Thu)
D-$12.95/$28.95 (Thu)/$14.95 (Sun)
Casino Size: 45,000 Square Feet
Other Games: S21, P, PGP, K
Overnight RV Parking: Free/RV Dump: No
Senior Discount: Various on Tue if 55+
Special Features: Indoor waterfall. Gambling age is 18.

Card Rooms

Card rooms have been legal in Washington since 1974. Initially limited to just five tables per location, the law was changed in 1996 to allow up to 15 tables. One year later, a provision was added to allow house-banked games. Permissible games include: blackjack, Caribbean stud poker, pai gow poker, let it ride, casino war and numerous other card games. Baccarat, craps, roulette and keno are not allowed.

The maximum bet at each card room is dependent on certain licensing requirements and is capped at either $25 or $100. Additionally, the rooms can be open no more than 20 hours per day. These card rooms are now commonly called "mini-casinos." The minimum gambling age in a card room is 18.

Each city and county has the option to ban the card rooms so they are not found in every major city (Seattle has none). Due to space limitations we don't list all of the Washington card rooms in this book.

For a list of card rooms, we suggest that you contact the Washington State Gambling Commission at (360) 486-3581, or visit their website at: www.wsgc.wa.gov

WEST VIRGINIA

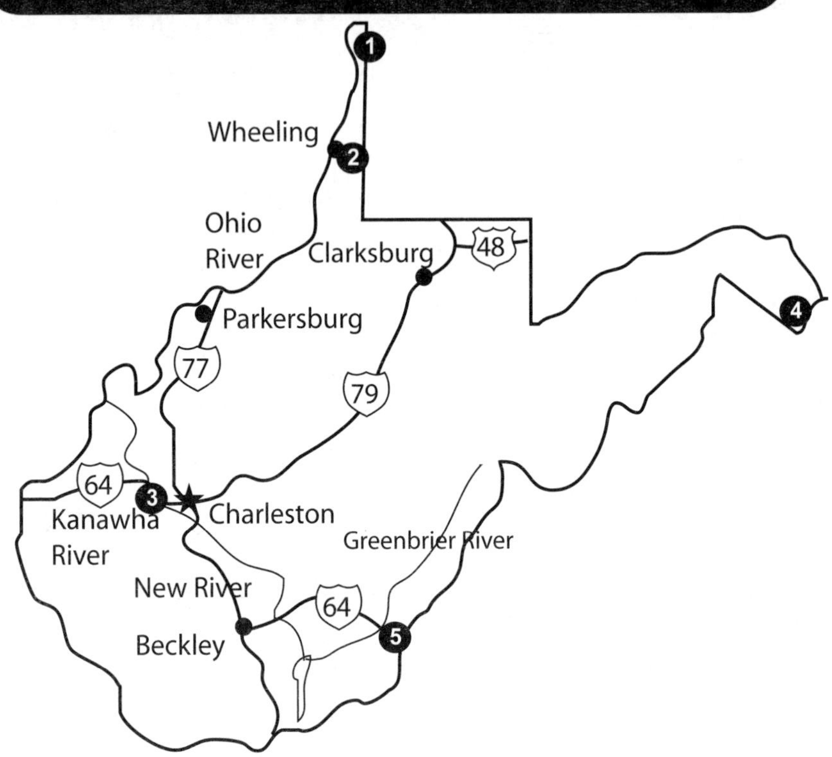

West Virginia has four pari-mutuel facilities and one resort hotel that feature video lottery terminals. The VLT's are the same as regular video gaming devices but are called lottery terminals because they are regulated by the state's lottery commission which receives a share of each machine's revenue.

West Virginia law requires that VLT's return a minimum of 80% to a maximum of 95%. VLT games include: slots, blackjack, keno and numerous versions of poker. The minimum gambling age is 21.

For the one-year period from July 1, 2016 through June 30, 2017 the average return on VLT's was: 88.59% at Mountaineer Park, 90.66% at Mardi Gras, 89.28% at Wheeling Island, 89.92% at Charles Town Races.

West Virginia law also allows bars, as well as restaurants that serve alcohol, to have up to five VLT's. Fraternal organizations are also allowed to have up to 10 VLT's. All of these machines are identical to the machines found at the racetracks, except they only print out tickets and do not pay out in cash.

All West Virgina casinos also offer the following table games: blackjack, craps, roulette and three card pokere. Optional games offered include: poker (P), pai gow poker (PGP), four card poker (FCP), Caribbean stud poker (CSP), mini-baccarat (MB), Spanish 21 (S21), Mississippi stud (MS) and big 6 wheel (B6).

All casinos are open 24 hours, except for the Greenbriar facility. For West Virginia tourism information call (800) 225-5982 or go to: www.callwva.com.

The Casino Club at The Greenbrier
300 W. Main Street
White Sulphur Springs, West Virginia 24986
(304) 536-1110
Website: www.greenbrier.com
Map: **#5** (120 miles S.E. of Charleston)

Toll-free Number: (855) 453-4858
Rooms: 238 Price Range: $209-$499
Restaurants: 6
Casino Hours: 11am-3am/4am (Fri/Sat)
Casino Size: 75,000 square Feet
Other Games: B, MB, P
Special Features: Casino only open to hotel guests, sporting club or golf/tennis club members, or convention/event attendees. Men required to wear jackets after 7 p.m.

Hollywood Casino at Charles Town Races
750 Hollywood Drive
Charles Town, West Virginia 25414
(304) 725-7001
Website: www.ctownraces.com
Map: **#4** (320 miles N.E. of Charleston)

Toll-Free Number: (800) 795-7001
Rooms: 132 Price Range: $119-$189
Suites: 18 Price Range: $219-$329
Restaurants: 5
Buffets: L-$13.99/$15.99 (Sat)/$21.99 (Sun)
D-$17.99/$44.99 (Fri)/$25.99 (Sat)
Other Games: MB, LIR, FCP, B6, PGP, P
Overnight RV Parking: Free/RV Dump: No
Special Features: Live thoroughbred racing seasonally. Daily simulcasting of horse and dog racing. No buffet Mon/Tue.

Mardi Gras Casino & Resort
1 Greyhound Drive
Cross Lanes, West Virginia 25313
(304) 776-1000
Website: www.mardigrascasinowv.com
Map: **#3** (10 miles N.W. of Charleston)

Toll-Free Number: (800) 224-9683
Rooms: 132 Price Range: $129-$169
Suites: 21 Price Range: $189-$219
Restaurants: 3
Buffets: D- $18.99 (Fri/Sat only)
Casino Size: 30,000 Square Feet
Other Games: B6, P, MS
Overnight RV Parking: Free/RV Dump: No
Senior Discount: Various Tue if 50+
Special Features: Live dog racing seasonally. Daily simulcasting of horse and dog racing.

Mountaineer Casino Racetrack & Resort
1420 Mountaineer Circle
New Cumberland, West Virginia 26047
(304) 387-2400
Website: www.moreatmountaineer.com
Map: **#1** (35 miles N. of Wheeling)

Toll-Free Number: (800) 804-0468
Rooms: 238 Price Range: $129-$169
Suites: 20 Price Range: $179-$239
Restaurants: 5
Buffets: L-$12.99 D-$15.99/21.99 (Fri)/$18.99 (Sat)
Other Games: S21, P, FCP, LIR, MS
Overnight RV Parking: Free/RV Dump: No
Special Features: Live thoroughbred racing seasonally. Daily simulcasting of horse/dog racing. 18-hole golf course. Spa and fitness center.

Wheeling Island Hotel Casino Racetrack
1 S. Stone Street
Wheeling, West Virginia 26003
(304) 232-5050
Website: www.wheelingisland.com
Map: **#2**

Toll-Free Number: (877) 946-4373
Rooms: 142 Price Range: $89-$169
Suites: 9 Price Range: $149-$229
Restaurants: 4
Buffets: B-$9.99 (Sat)/$18.99 (Sun)
L-$14.99/$26.99 (Fri)/$19.99 (Sat)/ $18.99 (Sun) D-$17.99/$25.99 (Fri)/$19.99 (Sat)
Casino Size: 50,000 Square Feet
Other Games: P, LIR, UTH
Overnight RV Parking: Free/RV Dump: No
Senior Discount: Various on Wed if 50+
Special Features: Live dog racing seasonally. Daily simulcasting of horse and dog racing.

WISCONSIN

All Wisconsin casinos are located on Indian reservations.

The Tribes are not required to release information on their slot machine percentage paybacks, but according to the terms of the compact between the state and the tribes "for games not affected by player skill, such as slot machines, the machine is required to return a minimum of 80% and a maximum of 100% of the amount wagered."

All casinos offer blackjack, slots and video poker. Some casinos also offer: craps (C), roulette (R), mini baccarat (MB), Mississippi stud (MS), poker (P), Pai Gow Poker (PGP), three card poker (TCP), four card poker (FCP), let it ride (LIR), ultimate Texas hold 'em (UTH), big 6 wheel (B6), bingo (BG), keno (K) and off-track betting (OTB). Unless otherwise noted, all casinos are open 24 hours and the minimum gambling age is 21 (18 for bingo).

For visitor information contact the state's department of tourism at (800) 432-8747 or their website at: www.travelwisconsin.com.

Bad River Lodge Casino
73370 U.S. Highway 2
Odanah, Wisconsin 54861
(715) 682-7121
Website: www.badriver.com
Map: **#1** (halfway between Ironwood, MI and Ashland, WI; 45 miles east of Duluth, MN on US 2)

Toll-Free Number: (800) 777-7449
Rooms: 42 Price Range: $99-$119
Suites: 8 Price Range: $119-$129
Restaurants: 1 Liquor: Yes
Casino Size: 19,200 Square Feet
Hours: 8am-2am Daily
Other Games: TCP, LIR
Overnight RV Parking: Free/RV Dump: Free
Senior Discount: Dining specials if 55+.
Special Features: 20-space RV park ($10/$20 per night). Gas station. Grocery store.

Ho-Chunk Gaming Black River Falls
W9010 Highway 54 East
Black River Falls, Wisconsin 54615
(715) 284-9098
Website: www.ho-chunkgaming.com
Map: **#8** (110 miles M.W. of Madison on Hwy. 54, 4 miles E. of I-94)

Toll-Free Number: (800) 657-4621
Rooms: 60 Price Range: $49-$98
Suites: 6 Price Range: $93-$130
Restaurants: 2 Liquor: Yes
Buffets: L-$8.98/$10 (Fri/Sat)/$11.95 (Sun)
D-$12.50/$14.98 (Tue)/
$19.98 (Fri/Sat)
Open 24 hours daily Memorial to Labor Day
Size: 35,000 Square Feet
Other Games: BG, TCP, No craps or roulette
Overnight RV Parking: Free/RV Dump: No
Senior Discount: Various Mon if 50+
Special Features: Food/hotel discounts for players club members.

Ho-Chunk Gaming Madison
4002 Evan Acres Road
Madison, Wisconsin 53718
(608) 223-9576
Website: www.ho-chunkgaming.com
Map: **#17**

Toll-Free Number: (888) 248-1777
Restaurants: 1 Liquor: Yes
Casino Size: 22,000 Square Feet
Other Games: Only Gaming Machines
Senior Discount: Various Wed if 50+
Special Features: Casino offers only Class II machines which look like slot machines, but are actually games of bingo and the spinning video reels are for "entertainment purposes only." Smoke-free casino.

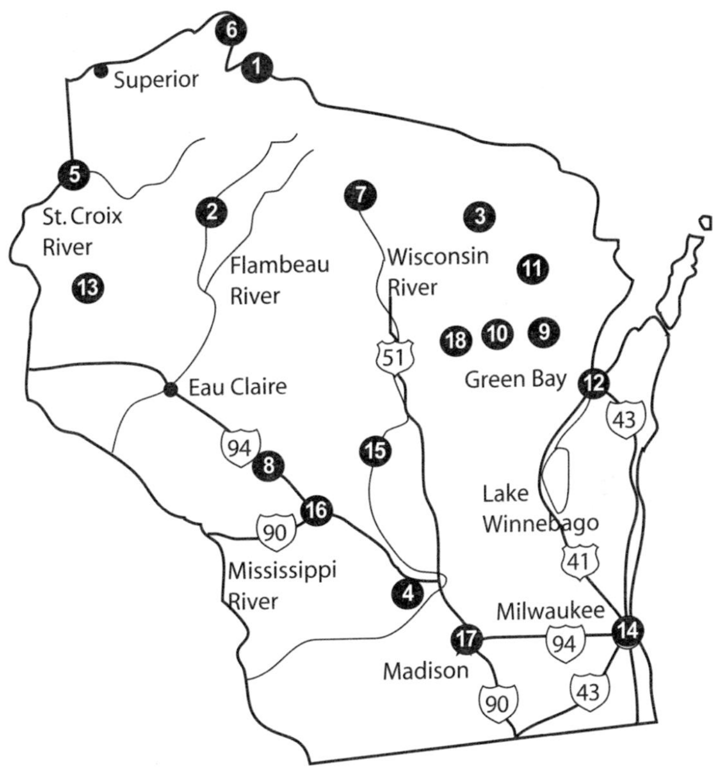

Ho-Chunk Gaming Nekoosa
949 County Road G
Nekoosa, Wisconsin 54457
(715) 886-4560
Website: www.ho-chunkgaming.com
Map: **#15** (50 miles S. of Wausau)

Toll-Free Number: (800) 782-4560
Restaurants: 2 Liquor: Yes
Other Games: R, UTH, TCP, MS
Overnight RV Parking: Free (must check-in first with security)/RV Dump: No
Senior Discount: Specials on Thu if 55+
Special Features: Smoke and gift shop. Convenience store. Electronic table games.

Ho-Chunk Gaming Tomah
27867 Highway 21
Tomah, Wisconsin 54660
(608) 372-3721
Website: www.ho-chunkgaming.com
Map: **#16** (3 miles E. of Tomah on Hwy 21)

Toll-Free Number: (866) 880-9822
Restaurants: 1 Snack Bar Liquor: No
Hours: 8am-Midnight/2am (Fri/Sat)
Casino Size: 2,000 Square Feet
Other Games: Only Gaming Machines
Special Features: Convenience store. Open 24 hours Fri-Sat during the summer.

Ho-Chunk Gaming Wisconsin Dells
S3214 Highway BD
Baraboo, Wisconsin 53913
(608) 356-6210
Website: www.ho-chunkgaming.com
Map: **#4** (40 miles N. of Madison.)

Toll-Free Number: (800) 746-2486
Rooms: 295 Price Range: $119-$159
Suites: 20 Price Range: $279-$299
Restaurants: 4 Liquor: Yes
Buffets: B-$7.99 (Sat/Sun)
L-$9.99/$11.99 (Sat/Sun)
D-$12.99/$35 (Wed)/$17.99 (Fri)/$30 (Sat)
Casino Size: 90,000 Square Feet
Other Games: C, R, P, TCP, B, FCP, UTH
OTB, BG (Tue-Sun)
Overnight RV Parking: Free/RV Dump: No
Senior Discount: Various Tue/Thu if 50+
Special Features: Smoke shop. Free local shuttle. Childcare center. 49-space RV park ($29-$79 per night)

Ho-Chunk Gaming Wittenberg
N7198 US Highway 45
Wittenberg, Wisconsin 54499
(608) 372-3721
Website: www.ho-chunkgaming.com
Map: **#18** (3 miles E. of Tomah on Hwy 21)

Toll-Free Number: (866) 910-0150
Restaurants: 1 Snack Bar Liquor: Yes
Casino Size: 2,000 Square Feet
Other Games: Only Gaming Machines
Overnight RV Parking: Free/RV Dump: No
Special Features: Convenience store.

IMAC Casino/Bingo
2100 Airport Drive
Green Bay, Wisconsin 54313
(800) 238-4263
Website: www.oneidacasino.net
Map: **#12** (across from Austin Straubel Airport, take Interstate 43 to Highway 172)

Other Games: BG, OTB, no blackjack
Hours: 8am-12am/2am (Fri/Sat)
Restaurants: 1 Liquor: Yes
Overnight RV Parking: $15 per night
Special features: Free shuttle service to Oneida's main casino and Mason Street Casino.

Lake of the Torches Resort Casino
510 Old Abe Road
Lac du Flambeau, Wisconsin 54538
(715) 588-7070
Website: www.lakeofthetorches.com
Map: **#7** (160 miles N.W. of Green Bay. Heading N. on Hwy. 51, go left on Hwy. 47, 12 miles to casino)

Toll-Free Number: (800) 258-6724
Rooms: 88 Price Range: $109-$149
Suites: 13 Price Range: $139-$189
Restaurants: 3 Liquor: Yes
Buffets: B-$8.45/$12.95 (Sun)
D-$16.95/$12.95 (Thu)/
$16.95 (Fri)/$24.95 (Sat)
Other Games: C, P, BG (Wed-Sun)
Overnight RV Parking: Free/RV Dump: No
Senior Discount: Various Mon if 55+
Special Features: Players club members get room and other discounts.

LCO Casino, Lodge & Convention Center
13767 W County Road B
Hayward, Wisconsin 54843
(715) 634-5643
Website: www.lcocasino.com
Map: **#2** (55 miles S.E. of Duluth, MN. 3 miles N.E. of Hayward on county trunk B)

Toll-Free Number: (800) 526-2274
Rooms: 53 Price Range: $59-$89
Suites: 22 Price Range: $89-$139
Restaurants: 1 Liquor: Yes
Buffets: B-$9.95 (Sat/Sun)
L-$9.95 D-$13.95/$20.95 (Fri)
Casino Size: 35,000 Square Feet
Other Games: C, R, P
Overnight RV Parking: Free (must register first at customer service)/RV Dump: No
Senior Discount: Various Tue if 55+
Special Features: Adjacent 8-space RV park ($25 per night). Sports lounge. Gift shop.

Legendary Waters Resort & Casino
37600 Onigaming Drive
Red Cliff, Wisconsin 54814
(715) 779-3712
Website: www.legendarywaters.com
Map: **#6** (70 miles E. of Duluth, MN on Hwy. 13)

Toll-Free Number: (800) 226-8478
Rooms: 40 Price Range: $70-$145
Suites: 7 Price Range: $149-$229
Restaurants: 3 Liquor: Yes
Buffets: B-$10 (Sun)
Other Games: P
Overnight RV Parking: Must use RV park
Senior Discount: Various Mon if 50+
Special Features: Campground and 34-space RV park ($40 per night). 45-slip marina.

Menominee Casino Resort
N277 Highway 47/55
Keshena, Wisconsin 54135
(715) 799-3600
Website: www.menomineecasinoresort.com
Map: **#9** (40 miles N.W. of Green Bay on Hwy. 47)

Toll-Free Number: (800) 343-7778
Rooms: 100 Price Range: $109-$125
Suites: 8 Price Range: $159-$179
Restaurants: 4 Liquor: Yes
Buffets: B/L- $14.00 (Sun)
D- $10/$17.00 (Fri)/$20.00 (Sat)
Casino Size: 33,000 Square Feet
Other Games: C, R, P, LIR, MS,
TCP, BG, UTH
Overnight RV Parking: Must use RV park
Senior Discount: Various Mon if 50+
Special Features: 60-space RV park ($20 per night). Gift shop. Smoke shop. No bingo Tues.

Mole Lake Casino & Lodge
3084 Highway 55
Mole Lake, Wisconsin 54520
(715) 478-3200
Website: www.molelake.com
Map: **#3** (100 miles N.W. of Green Bay)

Toll-Free Number: (800) 236-9466
Rooms: 65 Price Range: $71-$93
Suites: 10 Price Range: $81-$136
Restaurants: 2 Liquor: Yes
Hours: 7am-2am/3 am (Fri/Sat)
Other Games: BG (Fri-Tue)
Overnight RV Parking: Free/RV Dump: No
Special Features: Motel is two blocks from casino. No blackjack on Tue/Wed.

North Star Mohican Casino Resort
W12180 County Road A
Bowler, Wisconsin 54416
(715) 787-3110
Website: www.northstarcasinoresort.com
Map: **#10** (50 miles N.W. of Green Bay)

Toll-Free Number: (800) 952-0195
Rooms: 130 Price Range: $89-$119
Restaurants: 3 Liquor: Yes
Casino Size: 66,000 square Feet
Other Games: C, R, LIR, TCP, UTH
BG (Sun-Wed/Fri)
Overnight RV Parking: Free/RV Dump: Fee
Special Features: 57-space RV park ($29-$39 per night). Smoke shop. $10 freeplay with each night's stay at RV park.

Oneida Bingo & Casino
2020 Airport Drive
Green Bay, Wisconsin 54313
(920) 494-4500
Website: www.oneidacasino.net
Map: **#12** (across from Austin Straubel Airport, take Interstate 43 to Highway 172)

Toll-Free Number: (800) 238-4263
Restaurants: 2 Liquor: Yes
Hours: 10am-4am (Tables)/24 Hours (Slots)
Other Games: C, R, P, LIR, MB, UTH,
TCP, FCP, BG
Overnight RV Parking: No/$15 at IMAC
Special Features: Casino is connected to Radisson Inn, call for rates (800) 333-3333. Free local shuttle. Smoke shop. Food court with three fast food outlets.

Oneida Casino - Mason Street
2522 W. Mason Street
Green Bay, Wisconsin 54313
(920) 494-4500
Website: www.oneidacasino.net
Map: **#12**

Toll-Free Number: (800) 238-4263
Restaurant: 2
Casino Size: 38,000 square feet
Other games: Gaming Machines Only
Overnight RV Parking: Free/RV Dump: No

Oneida Casino One-Stop Packerland
3120 S. Packerland Drive
Green Bay, Wisconsin 54303
(920) 496-5601
Website: www.oneidacasino.net
Map: **#12**

Restaurant: 1 Snack Bar Liquor: No
Casino Size: 5,000 Square Feet
Other games: Gaming Machines Only
Overnight RV Parking: No

Oneida Casino Travel Center
5939 Old Highway 29 Drive
Pulaski, Wisconsin 54313
(920) 865-7919
Website: www.oneidacasino.net
Map: **#12**

Restaurant: 1
Casino Size: 5,800 Square Feet
Other games: Gaming Machines Only
Overnight RV Parking: Free/RV Dump: No

Potawatomi Hotel & Casino
1721 W. Canal Street
Milwaukee, Wisconsin 53233
(414) 645-6888
Website: www.paysbig.com
Map: **#14**

Toll-Free Number: (800) 729-7244
Rooms: 381 Price Range: $159-$409
Suites: 17 Price Range: Casino Use Only
Restaurants: 7 Liquor: Yes
Buffets: B-$18.00 (Sun)
L- $15.00
D- $15.00 (Tue/Thu)/
$41.00 (Wed/Fri)/$24.00 (Sat)
Casino Size: 38,400 Square Feet
Other Games: S21, C, R, P, PGP, TCP, MS,
UTH, CW, B, LIR, FCP, BG, OTB
Overnight RV Parking: Free/RV Dump: No
Special Features: Smoke-free casino on 2nd floor. No dinner buffet Sunday or Monday.

Potawatomi Carter Casino Hotel
618 Highway 32
Wabeno, Wisconsin 54566
(715) 473-2021
Website: www.cartercasino.com
Map: **#11** (85 miles N. of Green Bay on Hwy. 32)

Toll-Free Number: (800) 487-9522
Rooms: 70 Price Range: $98-$123
Suites: 29 Price Range: $190-$255
Restaurants: 2 Liquor: Yes
Casino Size: 25,000 Square Feet
Other Games: C, R, LIR, TCP, BG (Wed-Sun)
Overnight RV Parking: Free. Must register at Guest Services
Senior Discount: Specials on Thu if 50+
Special Features: 24-hour gas station and convenience store. Craps/roulette open 6pm Sat/Sun.

St. Croix Casino Danbury
30222 State Road 35 - 77
Danbury, Wisconsin 54830
(715) 656-3444
Website: www.stcroixcasino.com
Map: **#5** (26 miles E. of Hinckley, MN)

Toll-Free Number: (800) 238-8946
Rooms: 47 Price Range: $84-$234
Restaurants: 4 Liquor: Yes
Buffets: B-$4.99 (Fri)/$8.99 (Sat/Sun)
L-$7.99
D- $9.99/$12.99 (Wed)/$10.99 (Fri)
Casino Size: 22,500 Square Feet
Other Games: C, R
Overnight RV Parking: Must use RV park
Special Features: 45-space RV park ($22 per night). Room discount for players club members. Gambling age is 21. Craps and roulette only offered Wes-Sun.

St. Croix Casino - Hertel Express
4384 State Road 70
Webster, Wisconsin 54893
(715) 349-5658
Website: www.stcroixcasino.com
Map: **#5** (26 miles E. of Hinckley, MN)

Restaurants: 1
Other Games: Machines only
Overnight RV Parking: Must use RV park
Special Features: Gambling age is 21. 16-space RV park ($27 per night).

WYOMING

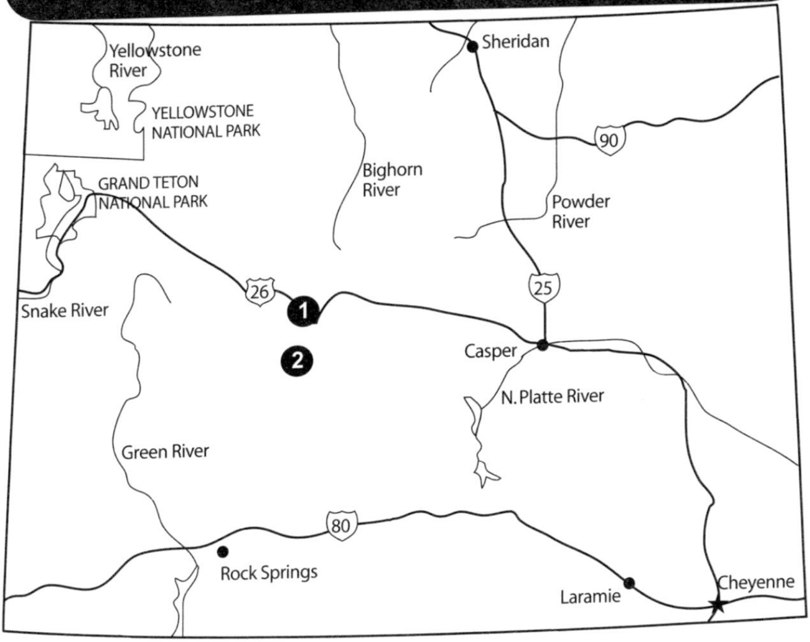

Wyoming's Indian casinos offer Class II bingo-type gaming machines, plus traditional Class III slot machines. Two of the casinos also offers some card-based table games.

The machines don't pay out in cash. Instead they print out a receipt which must be cashed by a floor attendant or taken to the cashier's cage. You can also make bets via a cashless system whereby you get a "smart" card and deposit money to that card's account. The machines will then deducts losses from, or credit wins to, your account.

No public information is available regarding the payback percentages on Wyoming's gaming machines. Unless otherwise noted, the casinos are open 24 hours and the minimum gambling age is 18.

For Wyoming tourism information call (800) 225-5996 or visit their website at: www.wyomingtourism.org

789 Casino
10369 Highway 789
Riverton, Wyoming 82501
(307) 857-9450
Website: www.play789casino.com
Map: **#1** (125 miles W. of Casper)

Restaurants: 1 Liquor: No
Casino Size: 7,000 Square Feet
Other Games: Bingo
Overnight RV Parking: No
Senior Discount: Various Tue if 55+

Little Wind Casino
800 Blue Sky Highway 132
Arapahoe, Wyoming 82520
(307) 438-7000
Website: www.littlewindcasino.com
Map: **#2** (140 miles W. of Casper)

Restaurants: 1 Liquor: No
Casino Size: 1,920 Square Feet
Overnight RV Parking: Free/RV Dump: No
Senior Discount: Various on Tue if 55+
Special Features: Convenience store. Gas station.

Shoshone Rose Casino & Hotel
5690 U.S. Highway 287
Lander, Wyoming 82520
(307) 206-7001
Website: www.thesrcasino.com
Map: **#2** (140 miles W. of Casper)

Rooms: 55 Price Range: $99-$149
Suites: 5 Price Range: $229-249
Restaurants: 1 Liquor: No
Casino Size: 7,000 Square Feet
Other games: Blackjack, Ultimate Texas Hold 'em
Overnight RV Parking: Free/RV Dump: No
Senior Discount: Various Mon if 55+

Wind River Hotel and Casino
10269 Highway 789
Riverton, Wyoming 82501
(307) 885-2600
Website: www.windrivercasino.com
Map: **#1** (125 miles W. of Casper)

Toll-Free Number: (866) 657-1604
Rooms: 80 Price Range: $85-$155
Suites: 10 Price Range: $250-$300
Restaurants: 2 Liquor: No
Other Games: Blackjack, Three Card Poker, Roulette, Poker, Ultimate Texas Hold 'em
Casino Size: 8,000 Square Feet
Senior Discount: Various Tue if 55+
Special Features: Smoke shop. Gas station.

Casino Index

A

Ada Gaming Center - East 301
Ada Gaming Center West 301
Agua Caliente Casino 129
Akwesasne Mohawk Casino Resort 290
Alamo Casino (Las Vegas) 238
Alamo Casino & Travel Center 273
Alamo Casino Wells 275
Aliante Casino & Hotel 263
Amelia Belle Casino 184
Ameristar Black Hawk 142
Ameristar Casino Council Bluffs 175
Ameristar Casino Hotel Kansas City 221
Ameristar Casino Hotel - Vicksburg 218
Ameristar Casino St. Charles 223
Ameristar East Chicago 170
Angel of the Winds Casino 336
Apache Casino Hotel 301
Apache Gold Casino Resort 122
Apache Nugget Travel Center and Casino 283
Apache Sky 122
Apsaalooke Nights Casino 225
Aquarius Casino Resort 260
Argosy Casino Alton 164
Argosy Casino Hotel & Spa 222
Aria Resort & Casino 239
Arizona Charlie's - Boulder 239
Arizona Charlie's - Decatur 239
Artesian Hotel Casino Spa 302
Atlantis Casino Resort 268
Augustine Casino 129
Avi Resort & Casino 277

B

Bad River Lodge Casino 344
Bally's Atlantic City 278
Bally's Las Vegas 239
Bally's Tunica 213
Bannock Peak Casino 161
Barona Valley Ranch Resort and Casino 130
Barton's Club 93 233
Batavia Downs Gaming 293
Bay Mills Resort & Casino 195
Bear River Casino Hotel 130
Beau Rivage Resort & Casino 208
Bellagio 240
Belle of Baton Rouge 184
Belterra Casino Resort and Spa 171
Belterra Park Gaming & Entertainment Center 300
Best Western Hickok House 326
Bighorn Casino 264
Big "M" Casino, The (S.Carolina) 324
Binion's Gambling Hall 240
BJ'S Bingo 336
Black Bear Casino Resort 200
Blackbird Bend Casino 179
Black Gold Casino 302
Black Hawk Casino 302
Black Oak Casino 130
Blue Chip Casino & Hotel 171
Blue Lake Casino & Hotel 130
Blue Water Casino 122
Bok Homa Casino 218
Bonanza Casino 268
Bonanza Inn & Casino 230
Boomtown Casino - Biloxi 208
Boomtown Casino & Hotel Bossier City 185
Boomtown Casino New Orleans 185
Boomtown Hotel & Casino 274
Boot Hill Casino & Resort 181
Border Casino 302
Bordertown Casino and Arena 302
Borgata Hotel Casino And Spa 280
Boulder Station Hotel & Casino 240
Brass Ass Casino 146
Bronco Billy's Casino 146
Bucky's Casino & Resort 122
Buffalo Bill's Resort & Casino 266
Buffalo-Bodega Gaming Complex 326
Buffalo Run Casino 302
Buffalo Thunder Resort & Casino 283
Bull Durham Saloon & Casino 142
Bullock Hotel 326

C

C Punch Inn & Casino 262
Cache Creek Indian Bingo & Casino 131
Cactus Pete's Resort Casino 233
Cadillac Jacks's Gaming Resort 327
Caesars Atlantic City 280
Caesars Palace 240
Caesars Windsor 194
Cahuilla Casino 132
Calder Casino & Race Course 156
California Hotel & Casino 241
Cal-Neva Resort Spa & Casino 234
Camel Rock Casino 283
Cannery Hotel & Casino 264
Canterbury Park 205
Carson Nugget Casino Hotel 228
Carson Valley Inn 263
CasaBlanca Hotel-Casino-Golf-Spa 262
Casino Apache Travel Center 284
Casino Arizona 101 & McKellips 122
Casino at Ocean Downs 191
Casino Club at The Greenbrier 343
Casino @ Dania Beach, The 156
Casino Del Sol 123
Casino Express 284
Casino Fandango 228
Casino Miami 156

Casino Niagara 294
Casino of the Sun 123
Casino Oklahoma 302
Casino Pauma 132
Casino Queen 164
Casino Queen Marquette 176
Casino Royale Hotel & Casino 241
Casino White Cloud 182
Catfish Bend Casino - Burlington 176
Celebrity Hotel & Casino 327
Century Casino - Cripple Creek 146
Century Casino & Hotel - Central City 145
Charging Horse Casino 225
Cherae Heights Casino 132
Cherokee Casino - Ft. Gibson 302
Cherokee Casino - Grove 303
Cherokee Casino & Hotel - Roland 303
Cherokee Casino - Ramona 303
Cherokee Casino - Sallisaw 303
Cherokee Casino - South Coffeyville 304
Cherokee Casino - Tahlequah 304
Cherokee Casino & Hotel - West Siloam Springs 304
Cherokee Casino Will Rogers Downs 316
Chewelah Casino 336
Chicken Ranch Bingo 132
Chinook Winds Casino Resort 317
Chisholm Trail Casino 304
Choctaw Casino - Broken Bow 304
Choctaw Casino - Idabel 305
Choctaw Casino - McAlester 305
Choctaw Casino - Pocola 305
Choctaw Casino Resort - Durant 304
Choctaw Casino Resort - Grant 304
Choctaw Casino - Stigler 305
Choctaw Casino - Stringtown 305
Chukchansi Gold Resort & Casino 132
Chumash Casino Resort 132
Cimarron Casino 305
Circus Circus Hotel & Casino (Las Vegas) 241
Circus Circus Hotel Casino/Reno 268
Cities of Gold Casino Hotel 284
Clearwater River Casino and Lodge 162
Cliff Castle Casino Hotel 123
Club Cal-Neva 268
Club Fortune Casino 231
Cocopah Casino 123
Coeur D'Alene Casino Resort Hotel 162
Colorado Belle Hotel Casino & Microbrewery 260
Colorado Grande Casino 146
Colusa Casino Resort 133
Comanche Nation Casino 305
Comanche Red River Hotel & Casino 306
Comanche Spur Casino 306
Comanche Star Casino 306
Commercial Casino 230
Cosmopolitan of Las Vegas, The 241
Coulee Dam Casino 336
Coushatta Casino Resort 188
Coyote Valley Casino 133
Creek Nation Casino - Bristow 306
Creek Nation Casino - Checotah 306
Creek Nation Casino - Eufaula 306
Creek Nation Casino - Holdenville 306
Creek Nation Casino - Muscogee 306
Creek Nation Casino - Okemah 307
Creek Nation Travel Plaza 307
Cromwell Las Vegas, The 241
Crystal Bay Club Casino 234
Cypress Bayou Casino 188

D

Dakota Connection 330
Dakota Magic Casino Resort 296
Dakota Sioux Casino & Hotel 330
Dancing Eagle Casino and RV Park 284
Davis Trading Post 307
Deadwood Comfort Inn & Suites 327
Deadwood Dick's Saloon and Gaming Hall 327
Deadwood Gulch Gaming Resort 328
Deadwood Mountain Grand 328
Deadwood Station Bunkhouse and Gambling Hall 328
Del Lago Resort 289
Delaware Park Racetrack & Slots 152
Delta Downs Racetrack & Casino 189
Desert Diamond Casino - Sahuarita 123
Desert Diamond Casino - Tucson 123
Desert Diamond Casino - Why 124
Desert Diamond West Valley 124
Diamond Jacks Casino - Bossier City 185
Diamond Jo Casino Dubuque 176
Diamond Jo Casino Worth 176
Diamond Mountain Casino and Hotel 133
Diamond's Casino 268
D Las Vegas 242
Don Laughlin's Riverside Resort Hotel & Casino 261
Dostal Alley Casino & Microbrewery 145
Double Eagle Hotel & Casino 146
Dover Downs Hotel Casino 152
Downs Racetrack and Casino 288
Downstream Casino Resort 307
Downtown Grand Casino 242
Duck Creek Casino 307

E

Eagle Mountain Casino 133
Eastside Cannery 242
East Wind Casino 330
Edgewater Hotel Casino 261
El Capitan Resort Casino 231
El Cortez Hotel & Casino 242
Eldorado Casino 231

Eldorado Casino Shreveport 185
Eldorado Hotel Casino (Reno) 268
Elk Valley Casino 133
Ellis Island Casino & Brewery 242
Elwha River Casino 336
Emerald Princess Casino 159
Emerald Queen Casino - I-5 337
Emerald Queen Hotel & Casino - Fife 336
Empire City Casino 293
Encore Las Vegas 242
Eureka Casino & Hotel 263
Evangeline Downs Racetrack & Casino 189
Excalibur Hotel/Casino 245

F

Fair Grounds Racecourse & Slots 189
Fallsview Casino Resort 294
Famous Bonanza/Easy Street 145
Fantasy Springs Casino 133
Feather Falls Casino 134
Fiesta Henderson Casino Hotel 232
Fiesta Rancho Casino Hotel 264
Finger Lakes Gaming & Racetrack 293
FireKeepers Casino 195
Fire Lake Casino 307
Fire Rock Navajo Casino 284
First Gold Hotel & Gaming 328
Fitz Casino/Hotel 214
Flamingo Las Vegas 245
Flowing Water Navajo Casino 284
Fond-du-Luth Casino 200
Fort Belknap Casino 225
Fort Hall Casino 162
Fort McDowell Casino 124
Fort Randall Casino Hotel 331
Fortune Bay Resort Casino 201
Four Bears Casino & Lodge 297
Four Queens Hotel/Casino 245
Four Winds Dowagiac 195
Four Winds Hartford 195
Four Winds New Buffalo 196
Four Winds South Bend 174
Foxwoods Resort Casino 149
Fremont Hotel & Casino 245
French Lick Springs Resort & Casino 172

G

Garcia River Casino 134
Gilpin Hotel Casino 143
Glacier Peaks Casino 226
Gold Coast Hotel & Casino 245
Gold Country Casino 134
Gold Country Inn Gambling Hall and Cafe 328
Gold Dust Casino & Hotel 328
Gold Dust West - Carson City 228
Gold Dust West - Elko 230
Golden Acorn Casino and Travel Center 134
Golden Buffalo Casino 331
Golden Eagle Casino 182
Golden Gate Hotel & Casino 246
Golden Gates Casino 143
Golden Mardi Gras Casino 143
Golden Nugget Atlantic City 280
Golden Nugget - Biloxi 208
Golden Nugget Casino - Lake Charles 186
Golden Nugget Laughlin 261
Golden Nugget, The (Las Vegas) 246
Golden Pony Casino 308
Gold Mountain Casino 307
Gold Ranch Casino & RV Resort 274
Gold River Casino 307
Goldsby Gaming Center 308
Gold Strike Casino Resort 214
Gold Town Casino 265
Grand Casino Hinckley 201
Grand Casino Hotel & Resort 308
Grand Casino Mille Lacs 202
Grand Falls Casino Resort 176
Grand Lake Casino 308
Grand Lodge Casino at Hyatt Regency 235
Grand Portage Lodge & Casino 202
Grand River Casino and Resort 331
Grand Sierra Resort & Casino 272
Grand Treasure Casino 297
Grand Victoria Casino 164
Graton Resort & Casino 134
Gray Wolf Peak Casino 226
Greektown Casino 194
Green Valley Ranch Resort Spa Casino 232
Gulfstream Park Racing & Casino 157
Gun Lake Casino 196

H

Hamburg Casino at The Fairgrounds 293
Hard Rock Casino Hotel Atlantic City 280
Hard Rock Hotel & Casino - Biloxi 208
Hard Rock Hotel & Casino Lake Tahoe 235
Hard Rock Hotel & Casino (Las Vegas) 246
Hard Rock Hotel & Casino Sioux City 176
Hard Rock Hotel & Casino Tulsa 308
Hard Rock Rocksino at Northfield Park 300
Harlow's Casino Resort 212
Harrah's Ak Chin Casino Resort 124
Harrah's Cherokee Casino 295
Harrah's Cherokee Valley River Casino & Hotel 295
Harrah's Council Bluffs 177
Harrah's Gulf Coast 210
Harrah's Joliet 168
Harrah's Lake Tahoe 235
Harrah's Las Vegas 246
Harrah's Laughlin Casino & Hotel 261
Harrah's Louisiana Downs 189
Harrah's Metropolis 168
Harrah's New Orleans 186

Harrah's North Kansas City 222
Harrah's Philadelphia Casino & Racetrack 322
Harrah's Reno 272
Harrah's Resort Atlantic City 280
Harrah's Resort Southern California 134
Harrington Raceway & Casino 152
Harveys Resort Hotel/Casino - Lake Tahoe 235
Havasu Landing Resort & Casino 135
Hialeah Park Casino 157
Hickok's Hotel and Casino 328
Hidden Oaks Casino 135
High Winds Casino 308
Ho-Chunk Gaming Black River Falls 344
Ho-Chunk Gaming Madison 344
Ho-Chunk Gaming Nekoosa 345
Ho-Chunk Gaming Tomah 345
Ho-Chunk Gaming Wittenberg 346
Ho-Chunk Gaming Wisconsin Dells 346
Hollywood Casino at Charles Town Races 343
Hollywood Casino at Kansas Speedway 181
Hollywood Casino at Penn National 322
Hollywood Casino - Aurora 168
Hollywood Casino - Baton Rouge 186
Hollywood Casino Gulf Coast 207
Hollywood Casino - Columbus 298
Hollywood Casino & Hotel - Lawrenceburg 172
Hollywood Casino - Jamul 135
Hollywood Casino - Joliet 168
Hollywood Casino - Perryville 191
Hollywood Casino St. Louis 224
Hollywood Casino - Toledo 298
Hollywood Casino Tunica 214
Hollywood Gaming Dayton Raceway 300
Hollywood Gaming Mahoning Valley 300
Hollywood Slots Hotel & Raceway 190
Hon-Dah Resort Casino 124
Hoosier Park 174
Hooters Casino Hotel 246
Hoover Dam Lodge Hotel & Casino 228
Hopland Sho-Ka-Wah Casino 135
Horseshoe Casino Baltimore 192
Horseshoe Casino - Council Bluffs 180
Horseshoe Casino Hammond 172
Horseshoe Casino Hotel - Bossier City 186
Horseshoe Casino & Hotel (Mississippi) 214
Horseshoe Casino Hotel Southern Indiana 172
Horseshu Hotel & Casino 233
Hotel Nevada & Gambling Hall 230

I

ilani Casino Resort 337
IMAC Casino/Bingo 346
Indiana Grand Casino 174
Indian Head Casino 317
Indigo Sky Casino 308
Inn of the Mountain Gods Resort & Casino 285
Ioway Casino 309
IP Casino Resort Spa 210
Iron Horse Inn 328
Island Resort & Casino 196
Island View Casino Resort 213
Isle Casino Hotel - Bettendorf 177
Isle Casino Hotel - Waterloo 178
Isle Casino Racing Pompano Park 158
Isle of Capri Casino - Black Hawk 143
Isle of Capri Casino - Boonville 220
Isle of Capri Casino - Cape Girardeau 220
Isle of Capri Casino & Hotel - Lula 213
Isle of Capri Casino - Kansas City 222
Isle of Capri Casino - Lake Charles 186
Isleta Resort Casino 285
It'Se-Ye-Ye Casino 162

J

JACK Cincinatti Casino 299
JACK Cleveland Casino 299
Jackpot Junction Casino Hotel 202
Jacks or Better Casino 333
Jackson Rancheria Casino & Hotel 135
JACK Thistledown Racino 300
Jake's 58 Hotel & Casino 293
Jena Choctaw Pines Casino 188
Jerry's Nugget 264
Johnny Nolon's Casino 146
Johnny Z's 145
Jokers Wild 232
Jumer's Casino & Hotel Rock Island 169

K

Kansas Crossing Casino + Hotel 181
Kansas Star Casino 181
Kewadin Casino - Christmas 196
Kewadin Casino - Hessel 196
Kewadin Casino Hotel - Sault Ste. Marie 197
Kewadin Casino - Manistique 196
Kewadin Casino - St. Ignace 197
Kickapoo Casino - Harrah 309
Kickapoo Casino - Shawnee 309
Kickapp Lucky Eagle Casino Hotel 334
Kings Club Casino 198
Kiowa Casino 309
Kla-Mo-Ya Casino 317
Konocti Vista Casino Resort & Marina 135
Kootenai River Inn Casino and Spa 162
KwaTaqNuk Casino Resort 226

L

Lac Vieux Desert Casino 198
Lady Luck Caruthersville 221
Lady Luck Casino (Colorado) 144
Lady Luck Casino Vicksburg 218
Lady Luck Nemacolin 321
Lake of the Torches Resort Casino 346
Lakeside Hotel Casino 178
Lakeside Entertainment 292

Lakeside Inn & Casino 235
L'Auberge Casino Hotel Baton Rouge 187
L'Auberge Casino Resort Lake Charles 187
Laughlin River Lodge 261
LCO Casino, Lodge & Convention Center 346
Leelanau Sands Casino & Lodge 198
Legendary Waters Resort & Casino 347
LINQ Hotel & Casino, The 248
Little Creek Casino Resort 337
Little River Casino Resort 198
Little Six Casino 202
Little Wind Casino 350
Lode Star Casino & Hotel 331
Lodge at Deadwood, The 329
Lodge Casino at Black Hawk, The 144
Lone Butte Casino 124
Longhorn Casino 248
Longstreet Inn Casino & RV Resort 227
Lucky 7 Casino 136
Lucky 8 Gaming Hall/Super 8 Motel 329
Lucky Bear Casino 135
Lucky Club Casino 264
Lucky Dog Casino 337
Lucky Dragon Hotel Casino 249
Lucky Eagle Casino 337
Lucky Star Casino - Canton 309
Lucky Star Casino - Clinton 309
Lucky Star Casino - Concho 309
Lucky Star Casino - Hammon 309
Lucky Star Casino - Watonga 310
Lucky Turtle Casino 310
Lumière Place Casino Resort 224
Luxor Las Vegas 249

M

Madill Gaming Center 310
Magic City Casino 158
Magnolia Bluffs Casino 213
Main Street Deadwood Gulch Bar 329
Main Street Station Hotel & Casino 249
Majestic Star Casinos & Hotel 173
Mandalay Bay 250
Mardi Gras Casino 158
Mardi Gras Casino & Resort (West Virginia) 343
Margaritaville Resort Casino - Bossier City 187
Mark Twain Casino 222
Martin & Mason Hotel 329
Maryland Live! Casino 192
Max Casino Carson City 228
Mazatzal Hotel & Casino 125
McGill's Hotel & Casino 147
Meadows Racetrack & Casino, The 322
Menominee Casino Resort 347
Meskwaki Bingo Casino Hotel 179
MGM Grand Detroit Casino 194
MGM Grand Hotel Casino 250
MGM National Harbor 192
Miami Valley Gaming 300
Miccosukee Resort & Gaming 154
Midnight Rose Hotel & Casino 147
Midnight Star 329
Mill Bay Casino 337
Mill Casino Hotel, The 318
Mineral Palace Hotel & Gaming 329
Mirage, The 250
Moapa Tribal Casino 277
Model T Hotel/Casino/RV Park 276
Mohegan Sun at Pocono Downs 322
Mohegan Sun Casino 150
Mole Lake Casino & Lodge 347
Monarch Casino Black Hawk 144
Mono Wind Casino 136
Montbleu Resort Casino & Spa 235
Monte Carlo Resort & Casino 250
Montego Bay Casino Resort 275
Monticello Gaming & Raceway 293
Morongo Casino Resort and Spa 136
MotorCity Casino and Hotel 194
Mountaineer Casino Racetrack & Resort 343
Mount Airy Resort & Casino 321
M Resort Spa Casino 232
Muckleshoot Casino 338
Mustang Sally's 329
Mystic Lake Casino Hotel 203

N

Nambe Falls Casino 286
Naskila Gaming 334
Native Lights Casino 310
Newcastle Gaming Center 310
Newport Grand Casino 323
New York-New York Hotel & Casino 251
Nooksack Northwood Casino 338
Northern Edge Navajo Casino 286
Northern Lights Casino & Hotel 203
Northern Quest Resort & Casino 338
Northern Winz Hotel & Casino 226
Northern Winz II 226
North Star Mohican Casino Resort 347
Nugget Casino Resort 274

O

Oaklawn Racing and Gaming 128
Odawa Casino Mackinaw 199
Odawa Casino Resort 198
Ohkay Casino Resort 286
Ojibwa Casino - Marquette 199
Ojibwa Casino Resort - Baraga 199
Old Style Saloon #10 329
One Fire Casino 310
Oneida Bingo & Casino 347
Oneida Casino - Mason Street 347
Oneida Casino One-Stop Packerland 348
Oneida Casino Travel Center 348
Orleans Hotel & Casino, The 251

Osage Casino - Bartlesville 310
Osage Casino - Hominy 310
Osage Casino - Pawhuska 311
Osage Casino - Ponca City 311
Osage Casino - Sand Springs 311
Osage Casino - Skiatook 311
Osage Casino - Tulsa 311
Outpost Casino 311
Owl Club Casino & Restaurant 227
Oxford Casino 190
Oyster Bay/Fairmont Hotel 330

P

Pahrump Nugget Hotel & Gambling Hall 265
Paiute Palace Casino 136
Pala Casino Spa and Resort 136
Palace Casino & Hotel (Minnesota) 203
Palace Casino Resort (Mississippi) 210
Palace Station Hotel & Casino 254
Palace West Casino 286
Palazzo, The 254
Palms, The 254
Par-A-Dice Hotel Casino 169
Paradise Casino Arizona 125
Paragon Casino Resort 188
Paris Casino Resort 254
Parx Casino and Racing 322
Pearl River Resort 218
Pechanga Resort and Casino 137
Peppermill Hotel Casino Reno 272
Peppermill Inn & Casino 275
Pioneer Crossing Casino 276
Pioneer Hotel & Gambling Hall 262
Pit River Casino 137
Plainridge Park Casino 193
Planet Hollywood Resort & Casino 254
Plaza Hotel & Casino 255
Point Casino, The 338
Poker Palace, The 264
Potawatomi Carter Casino Hotel 348
Potawatomi Hotel & Casino 348
Prarie Band Casino 182
Prairie Knights Casino & Resort 297
Prairie Meadows Racetrack & Casino 180
Prairie Moon Casino 311
Prairie's Edge Casino Resort 203
Prairie Sun Casino 311
Prairie Wind Casino & Hotel 331
Presque Isle Downs & Casino 322
Primm Valley Resort & Casino 266

Q

Q Casino 180
Quapaw Casino 312
Quechan Casino Resort 137
Quil Ceda Creek Nightclub & Casino 338
Quinault Beach Resort and Casino 339

R

Rail City Casino 274
Rain Rock Casino 137
Railroad Pass Hotel & Casino 232
Rainbow Hotel Casino 275
Rampart Casino 255
Red Dolly Casino 144
Red Earth Casino 137
Red Fox Casino 137
Red Garter Hotel & Casino 276
Red Hawk Casino 138
Red Lion Hotel & Casino 230
Red Rock Resort Spa Casino 255
Red Wind Casino 339
Redwood Hotel Casino 138
Remington Park Racing & Casino 316
Reserve Casino Hotel 145
Resorts Casino Hotel 282
Resorts Casino Tunica 214
Resorts World Catskills 289
Resorts World Casino New York City 294
Rhythm City Casino 178
Rio Suite Hotel & Casino 256
Rising Star Casino Resort 173
River Bend Casino Hotel 312
River City Casino & Hotel 224
River Mist Casino 312
River Rock Casino 138
Rivers Casino (Illinois) 169
Rivers Casino (Pennsylvania) 321
Rivers Casino & Resort Schenectady 289
Riverside Casino & Golf Resort 178
River Spirit Casino Resort 312
Riverwalk Casino & Hotel 218
Riverwind Casino 312
Robinson Rancheria Resort & Casino 138
Rocky Gap Casino Resort 192
Rolling Hills Casino 138
Rosebud Casino 331
Route 66 Casino 286
Royal River Casino & Hotel 332
Ruidoso Downs & Billy The Kid Casino 288
Running Aces 205
Running Creek Casino 138

S

Sac and Fox Casino - Stroud 312
Sac & Fox Casino (Kansas) 182
Saddle West Hotel/Casino & RV Park 265
Saganing Eagles Landing Casino 199
Sage Hill Travel Center & Casino 162
Salt Creek Casino 312
Sam's Town Hotel & Casino Shreveport 187
Sam's Town Hotel & Gambling Hall 256
Sam's Town Tunica 217
Sandia Resort & Casino 287
Sands Casino Resort Bethlehem 321

Sands Regency Hotel Casino, The 272
San Felipe Casino Hollywood 286
San Manuel Casino 139
San Pablo Lytton Casino 139
Santa Ana Star Casino 287
Santa Claran Hotel Casino 287
Santa Fe Station Hotel & Casino 256
Saratoga Casino 144
Saratoga Casino Hotel 294
Sasquatch Casino 144
Scarlet Pearl Casino Resort 210
Scioto Downs Racino 300
Seminole Brighton Casino 154
Seminole Casino Big Cypress 154
Seminole Casino Coconut Creek 154
Seminole Casino Immokalee 154
Seminole Classic Casino 155
Seminole Hard Rock
Hotel & Casino - Hollywood 155
Seminole Hard Rock
Hotel & Casino - Tampa 156
Seminole Nation Casino 313
Seminole Nation Smoke Shop 313
Seneca Allegany Casino & Hotel 290
Seneca Buffalo Creek Casino 290
Seneca Gaming - Irving 292
Seneca Gaming - Oil Spring 292
Seneca Gaming - Salamanca 292
Seneca Niagara Casino 290
Seven Cedars Casino 339
Seven Clans Casino - Chilocco 313
Seven Clans Casino Hotel - First Council 313
Seven Clans Casino - Paradise 313
Seven Clans Casino - Perry 313
Seven Clans Casino Red Lake 204
Seven Clans Casino - Red Rock 313
Seven Clans Casino Thief River Falls 204
Seven Clans Casino Warroad 204
Seven Feathers Hotel & Casino Resort 318
789 Casino 349
7th Street Casino 182
Sherwood Valley Casino 139
Shoalwater Bay Casino 339
Shooting Star Casino Hotel 204
Shoshone Rose Casino 350
Silverado - Franklin Historic Hotel & Gaming
Complex 330
Silver Legacy Resort Casino 273
Silver Nugget 265
Silver Reef Hotel Casino Spa 339
Silver Sevens Hotel and Casino 256
Silver Slipper Casino 207
Silverton Casino Hotel Lodge 256
Silver Wolf Casino 226
Skagit Valley Casino Resort 339
Sky City Casino Hotel 287
Sky Dancer Hotel Casino & Resort 297
Skyline Hotel & Casino 232
Sky Ute Casino and Lodge 147
Slots-A-Fun Casino 257
SLS Hotel & Casino 257
Snoqualmie Casino 340
Soaring Eagle Casino & Resort 199
Soboba Casino 139
Southland Park Gaming & Racing 128
South Point Hotel and Casino 257
Southwind Casino - Braman 313
Southwind Casino - Kanza 314
Southwind Casino - Newkirk 314
Spa Resort Casino 139
Spirit Lake Casino & Resort 297
Spirit Mountain Casino (Arizona) 125
Spirit Mountain Casino (Oregon) 319
Spotlight 29 Casino 139
Stables Casino, The 314
Stagecoach Hotel & Casino 227
St Croix Casino Danbury 348
St. Croix Casino - Hertel Express 348
St. Jo Frontier Casino 223
Stockman's Casino 231
Stockmen's Hotel & Casino 230
Stone Wolf Casino & Grill 314
Stratosphere Hotel & Casino 258
Sugar Creek Casino 314
Sugar House Casino 321
Suncoast Hotel and Casino 258
Sunland Park Racetrack & Casino 288
SunRay Park and Casino 288
Sunset Station Hotel and Casino 233
Suquamish Clearwater Casino Resort 340
Swinomish Casino & Lodge 340
Sycuan Resort & Casino 140

T

Table Mountain Casino & Bingo 140
Tachi Palace Hotel and Casino 140
Tahoe Biltmore Lodge & Casino 236
Talking Stick Resort 125
Taos Mountain Casino 287
Terrible's Roadhouse - Jean 233
Terrible's Roadhouse - Searchlight 273
Texas Station Gambling Hall & Hotel 265
Texoma Gaming Center 314
Three Rivers Casino Coos Bay 319
Three Rivers Casino & Hotel 319
Thunderbird Casino - Norman 314
Thunderbird Casino - Shawnee 314
Thunder Valley Casino 140
Tin Lizzie Gaming 330
Tioga Downs 289
Tonkawa Gasino 315
Tonkawa Hotel & Casino 315
Topaz Lodge & Casino 231
Tortoise Rock Casino 141
Trading Post Casino 315
Treasure Bay Casino and Hotel 210

Treasure Chest Casino 187
Treasure Island Resort & Casino 204
Treasure Island (TI) 258
Treasure Valley Casino 315
Trop Casino Greenville 212
Tropical Breeze Casino 153
Tropicana Casino & Resort (Atlantic City) 282
Tropicana Evansville 174
Tropicana Laughlin 262
Tropicana Resort & Casino (Las Vegas) 258
Tulalip Casino 340
Tunica Roadhouse Casino and Hotel 217
Turning Stone Casino Resort 291
Turtle Creek Casino 199
Turtle Creek Crossing Casino 332
Turtle Mountain Mini-Casino 297
Tuscany Suites & Casino 258
Twelve Tribes Casino 340
Twin Arrows Navajo Casino Resort 125
Twin Pine Casino & Hotel 141
Twin River Casino 323
Two Rivers Casino & Resort 341

U

Ute Mountain Casino & RV Park 147

V

Valley Forge Convention Center Casino 321
Valley View Casino Resort 141
Vee Quiva Hotel & Casino 125
Venetian Resort Hotel Casino, The 259
Vernon Downs Casino Hotel 294
Veterans of Foreign War 330
Victory Casino Cruises - Cape Canaveral 153
Victory Casino Cruises - Jacksonville 153
Viejas Casino 141
Virgin River Hotel/Casino/Bingo 263

W

Washita Casino 315
WaterView Casino And Hotel 218
Wendover Nugget Hotel & Casino 276
Western Village Inn & Casino 274
Westgate Las Vegas Resort & Casino 259
Wheeling Island Racetrack
& Gaming Center 343
Whiskey Pete's Hotel & Casino 266
White Oak Casino 205
Wild Card Saloon & Casino 144
Wild Horse Casino & Hotel (New Mexico) 287
Wild Horse Pass Hotel & Casino (Arizona) 126
Wildhorse Resort & Casino (Oregon) 319
Wild Rose Casino - Clinton 179
Wild Rose Casino - Emmetsberg 179
Wild Rose Casino - Jefferson 179
Wild Wild West Casino 259
Wildwood Casino At Cripple Creek 147
Wilson Travel Plaza 315
Wind Creek Casino & Hotel - Atmore 120
Wind Creek Casino & Hotel - Montgomery 119
Wind Creek Casino & Hotel - Wetumpka 120
Wind River Hotel and Casino 350
WinnaVegas Casino 180
Winnedumah Winn's Casino 141
Winnemucca Inn 276
Winners Hotel/Casino 276
Win-River Casino 141
WinStar World Casino And Resort 315
Wynn Las Vegas 260

Y

Yakama Legends Casino 341
Yavapai Casino 126
Yellow Brick Road Casino 291

Z

Z Casino 145
Zia Park Race Track & Black Gold Casino 288

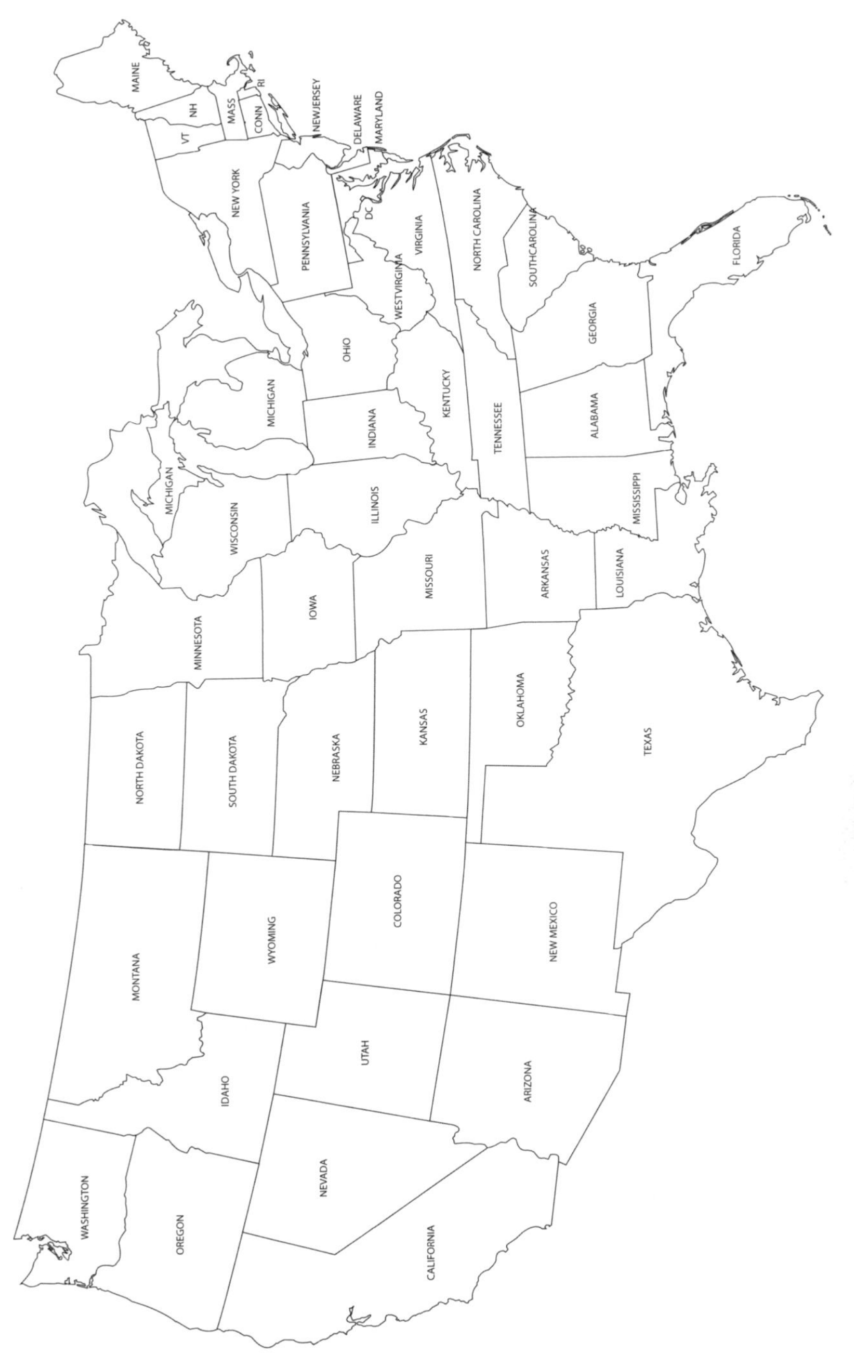
MAINE
NH
VT
MASS
RI
CONN
NEW YORK
NEWJERSEY
DELAWARE
MARYLAND
DC
PENNSYLVANIA
WESTVIRGINIA
VIRGINIA
NORTH CAROLINA
SOUTHCAROLINA
GEORGIA
FLORIDA
OHIO
MICHIGAN
INDIANA
KENTUCKY
TENNESSEE
ALABAMA
MISSISSIPPI
MICHIGAN
WISCONSIN
ILLINOIS
MISSOURI
ARKANSAS
LOUISIANA
IOWA
MINNESOTA
NORTH DAKOTA
SOUTH DAKOTA
NEBRASKA
KANSAS
OKLAHOMA
TEXAS
MONTANA
WYOMING
COLORADO
NEW MEXICO
IDAHO
UTAH
ARIZONA
WASHINGTON
OREGON
NEVADA
CALIFORNIA

Notice

Casino Vacations Press, Inc. and/or its parent or subsidiaries, will not be responsible if a participating merchant refuses to honor a coupon offer in this book. However, we will try to secure compliance. Additionally, Casino Vacations Press, Inc. and/or its parent or subsidiaries, disclaims all alleged liability, for bodily injury or property damage resulting from any accident, event or occurrence on, or resulting from the use of the premises of the participating merchants. Casino Vacations Press, Inc. and/or its parent or subsidiaries, disclaims all warranties, expressed or implied, or otherwise imposed by law, regarding the condition of those premises or the safety of same. Casino Vacations Press, Inc. and/or its parent or subsidiaries, disclaims all alleged vicarious liability for bodily injury or property damage resulting from the acts or ommissions of the participating merchants.

Coupon Directory

Colorado
Double Eagle/Gold Creek 363
Monarch 363

Florida
Mardi Gras 363/365

Illinois, Joliet
Harrah's Joliet 365

Mississippi, Bay St Louis
Silver Slipper 367

Mississippi, Biloxi
Beau Rivage 367

Mississippi, Tunica
Hollywood............367/369

Nevada, Lake Tahoe
Grand Lodge at Hyatt Regency....369
Hard Rock 369

Nevada, Las Vegas
Aliante............371
Arizona Charlie's Boulder 373
Arizona Charlie's Decatur............373
Bally's 373
Bighorn 375
Binion's 377
Bonanno's Pizza (6 locations)......377/379
Boulder Station 379
California 379/381
Cannery 381
Club Fortune 383
D, The............383/385
Downtown Grand............385/387
Ellis Island 387/389
Fat Burger 389
Fiesta Henderson............391
Fiesta Rancho............391
Five Star Helicopter Tours 391
Flamingo (Carlos N Charlies)......393
Flamingo (Legends in Concert) ...393
Flamingo (Margaritaville)............393
Flamingo (Uno Salon)............395
Four Queens 395/397
Fremont, The............397/399
Gambler's General Store............399
Gold Coast 401
Golden Gate 403
Green Valley Ranch 403
Haagen Dazs (4 locations) 405
Harrah's............405
Hooters............407
Jerry's Nugget 409
Johnny Rockets 411
Klondike............411
LA Subs (2 locations)............413
LINQ (Divas) 413
LINQ (ameriCAN)............413/415
LINQ (Chayo) 415
Longhorn............415/417
Lucky Club............417/419
Luxor (Bodies) 419
Luxor (Tacos &Tequila)............421
Luxor (Titanic) 421
Main Street Station 421/423
Mandalay Bay (Guinness Store)..423/425
Mandalay Bay (House of Blues)..425/427
Mandalay Bay (Ri Ra Irish Pub)..427
MGM Grand (CSI Experience)....427
Nathan's (6 locations) 429
New York Pretzel (3 locations) 429
Original Chicken Tender (2 locations) 429/431
Orleans 431/433
Palace Station............433
Pan Asian (4 locations) 433
Paris (Eiffel Tower)............435
Paris (Anthony Cools Show) 435
Planet Hollywood (Buffet)............435
Planet Hollywood (PBR Bar).......437
Planet Hollywood (Theaters) 437
Planet Hollywood (V Card) 439
Plaza............439/443
Rampart............443/445
Red Rock............445
Rio............445/447
Sam's Town............447/449
Santa Fe Station 449
Silver Nugget 451
Silver Sevens............453

Silverton.....................................453/455
SLS...455
South Point..................................457
Stratosphere................................457
Sun Coast 459
Sunset Station..............................459
Tacos & Ritas (2 locations)..........461
Texas Station 461
Tuscany 461/463
Venetian (Grand Canal Shops).....463
Venetian (Madame Tussauds) 465
Venetian (Prime Burger) 465
Venetian (Rockhouse) 465/467
Venetian (San Gennaro Burger)...467
Wild West Horseback..................467
Wildfire 469
William Hill 469

Nevada, Laughlin
Colorado Belle 471
Edgewater 471/473
Harrah's.......................................473
Tropicana 475

Nevada, Pahrump
Pahrump Nugget/Gold Town/
Lakeside Casino 475/77

Nevada, Primm
Primm Valley...............................477

Nevada, Reno Area
Atlantis..479
Harrah's Reno 479

COUPON CHANGES

Coupon offers can change without notice.
To see a list of any coupon changes, go to:
americancasinoguide.com/coupon-changes.html

We will list any coupon changes on that page.

AMERICAN CASINO GUIDE

Play $30 Get $10 FREE!

Play $30 and receive $10 in CasinoPlay. Must be a Premier Club member. Offer expires December 31, 2018. See reverse for full details.

A current American Casino Guide Discount Card must be presented when redeeming this coupon, or offer is void

AMERICAN CASINO GUIDE

2-4-1 Breakfast or Lunch buffet

Present this coupon with your Club Monarch card to the cashier at The Buffet and receive one *free* breakfast or lunch buffet with the purchase of a second buffet at the regular price. ***See back for details.***

A current American Casino Guide Discount Card must be presented when redeeming this coupon, or offer is void

AMERICAN CASINO GUIDE

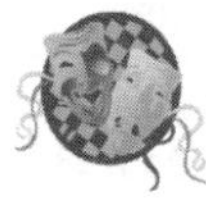

MARDI GRAS CASINO

FREE Dessert with Purchase of an Entrée

Present this coupon at The French Quarter Restaurant located on the 3rd floor to receive one dessert free when an entrée is purchased at regular menu price. See reverse for details.

A current American Casino Guide Discount Card must be presented when redeeming this coupon, or offer is void

americancasinoguide.com

442 E. Bennett Avenue
Cripple Creek, CO 80813
www.decasino.com
(800) 711-7234
(719) 689-5000

Must present coupon. Limit one coupon per customer per day. Not valid for use with any other coupons, ads or promotions. Must be 21 years of age and a Premier Club Member. Membership in Premier Club is free. Management reserves the right to cancel or change this promotion at any time. Valid through December 31, 2018.

Offer void if coupon is copied or sold

americancasinoguide.com

P.O. Box 9 | 488 Main St.
Black Hawk, CO 80422 | 303.582.1000

Expires December 30, 2018. Valid daily. Excludes holidays or special events. No cash value. Gratuity not included. Must be 21. Not valid in combination with any other offer. Non-transferable. Management reserves all rights. Must be a Club Monarch member. ***Not a club member? Join today! It's fun,it's easy, it's free.***

Club Member #________________

Offer Code #ACG2018C1

Offer void if coupon is copied or sold

americancasinoguide.com

831 N. Federal Highway, Hallandale Beach, FL 33009 • (877) 557-5687 • (954) 924-3200

Must be 21 years of age to purchase & consume alcohol. Not valid on any other offer or special. Limit one coupon per person. Cannot be combined with any other offer.

Original coupon must be presented (no photocopies). Tax and gratuity not included. Management reserves the right to cancel or alter this coupon without prior notice. Offer expires 12/30/18.

When gambling is no longer a game…call 1-888-ADMIT-IT.

Offer void if coupon is copied or sold

AMERICAN CASINO GUIDE

MARDI GRAS CASINO

Receive $10 Bonus Play

Present this coupon at the Mardi Gras Casino Players' Club to receive $10 free bonus play. See reverse for details.

A current American Casino Guide Discount Card must be presented when redeeming this coupon, or offer is void

AMERICAN CASINO GUIDE

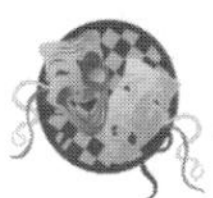

MARDI GRAS CASINO

Buy One Entrée, Get One FREE

Present this coupon at the French Quarter Restaurant and Bar to receive one entrée free when an entrée is purchased at regular menu price. See reverse for details.

A current American Casino Guide Discount Card must be presented when redeeming this coupon, or offer is void

AMERICAN CASINO GUIDE

Buy One Buffet Get One FREE

Present this coupon at Flavors The Buffet, along with your Total Rewards® card, to receive one FREE buffet with the purchase of one buffet. All ages welcome. See reverse for full details.

A current American Casino Guide Discount Card must be presented when redeeming this coupon, or offer is void

MARDI GRAS CASINO

831 N. Federal Highway, Hallandale Beach, FL 33009 • (877) 557-5687 • (954) 924-3200

Must be 21 years of age or older and a Players' Club Member. Membership is free. Cannot be redeemed for cash. No reproduction allowed. Bonus play is not transferable into or out of the State of Florida.

Bonus play will be downloaded onto your Players' Club card. Management reserves the right to modify, amend or cancel this coupon at any time. Offer expires 12/30/18 and is valid once per year. The State of Florida assumes no liability. Limit one coupon per account per year. When gambling is no longer a game... call 1-888-ADMIT-IT.

MARDI GRAS CASINO

831 N. Federal Highway, Hallandale Beach, FL 33009 • (877) 557-5687 • (954) 924-3200

Must be 21 years of age to purchase & consume alcohol. Free entrée must be of equal or lesser value than purchased entrée. Not valid on any other offer or special. Cannot be combined with any other offer.

Limit one coupon per person. Original coupon must be presented (no photocopies). Tax and gratuity not included. Management reserves the right to cancel or alter this coupon without prior notice. Offer expires 12/30/18. When gambling is no longer a game… call 1-888-ADMIT-IT.

151 N. Joliet Street
Joliet, IL 60432
(815) 740-7800
harrahsjoliet.com

Offer valid on cash purchases only. Valid for dine in only. Alcohol and gratuity not included. Some restrictions apply. Not valid at any other outlet. See Total Rewards for complete details. Valid Total Rewards card required. In some cases a valid government issued picture ID may also be required. Subject to rules available at venue. This offer is non-transferable, non-negotiable, subject to availability, cannot be combined with any other discount, promotion or complimentary offer. Alteration, duplication or unauthorized use voids this offer. Some blackout dates may apply. Harrah's reserves the right to change or cancel this program at any time upon IGB approval. Harrah's employees and their immediate families are not eligible. Must be 21 years or older to gamble. Know When Stop Before You Start® If you or someone you know has a gambling problem, crisis counseling and referral services can be accessed by calling 1-800-GAMBLER (1-800-426-2537). ©2017, Caesars License Company, LLC. All rights reserved. Offer expires 12/30/18.

AMERICAN CASINO GUIDE

Buy One Buffet Get One Free!

(or 50% off when dining alone)

Buy one lunch or dinner at Jubilee Buffet and get one free (or 50% off when dining alone). See reverse for details.

A current American Casino Guide Discount Card must be presented when redeeming this coupon, or offer is void

AMERICAN CASINO GUIDE

An MGM Resorts Luxury Destination

10% Off Room Rate

Receive 10 percent off prevailing room rate by calling (888) 567-6667 and mentioning offer code ACG18. See reverse for full details.

A current American Casino Guide Discount Card must be presented when redeeming this coupon, or offer is void

AMERICAN CASINO GUIDE

HOLLYWOOD Casino®

TUNICA, MS

Buy One Epic Buffet and Get One Free!

Enjoy two buffets for the price of one at Hollywood's Epic Buffet! Dine and play among movie memorabilia in an authentic Hollywood atmosphere 7 days a week! See reverse for details.

Exp: 12/31/18

#87005

A current American Casino Guide Discount Card must be presented when redeeming this coupon, or offer is void

americancasinoguide.com

5000 South Beach Blvd.
Bay St. Louis, MS 39520
www.silverslipper-ms.com
1-866-SLIPPER

Present this coupon to Players Services to redeem offer. Must be a Slipper Rewards member to participate. Membership is free; must be 21 years or older. Not valid on holidays or holiday weekends.

Limit one coupon, per person for the duration of the promotion. Not valid with any other offer. Management reserves all rights. Offer expires 12/24/18.

2018ACG

Offer void if coupon is copied or sold

americancasinoguide.com

RESORT & CASINO • BILOXI

An MGM Resorts Luxury Destination

875 Beach Boulevard
Biloxi, MS 39530
(228) 386-7111 • (888) 567-6667
www.beaurivage.com

A credit card guarantee will be required at the time of booking and at check-in for incidentals. Advance reservations required. Reservations canceled with less than 24-hour notice will forfeit first night room and tax deposit. May not be used during holidays. Resort fees may apply and will be collected upon check-in. Offer is non-transferable, subject to availability, and may not be used in conjunction with any other M life® Rewards offer. Gaming restriction patrons prohibited. Must be 21 years of age. ©2017 MGM Resorts International®. Beau Rivage reserves all rights. Gambling Problem? Call 1-888-777-9696.

Offer void if coupon is copied or sold

americancasinoguide.com

Sign up for a Marquee Rewards® card at the Player Services Counter. Marquee Rewards cards are free with valid, state issued ID. Then present this coupon at the Epic Buffet along with your Marquee Rewards card to receive your buy-one-get-one-free Epic Buffet® offer. Must be 21 years of age or older to redeem.

Hollywood Casino Tunica reserves the right to modify or cancel this promotion at anytime without prior notice. Offer not valid on Friday or Saturday. This coupon cannot be combined with any other promotion. Valid only at Hollywood Casino Tunica. Not transferable. One coupon per Player account. Offer void if sold. Offer expires 12/31/18.

TUNICA, MS

1150 Casino Strip Resorts Blvd.
Tunica Resorts, MS 38664
(800) 871-0711
(662) 357-7700
hollywoodcasinotunica.com

Offer void if coupon is copied or sold

AMERICAN CASINO GUIDE

HOLLYWOOD Casino®

TUNICA, MS

Room Rates From $59 (Sun-Thu)

Special packages available! Call 1-800-871-0711 for reservations. See reverse for details.

Exp: 12/31/18

A current American Casino Guide Discount Card must be presented when redeeming this coupon, or offer is void

AMERICAN CASINO GUIDE

Play $20 Get $40 Free Slot Play!

Present this coupon at the Backstage Pass/Bank to receive $40 in Free Slot Play after playing $20 on your Backstage Pass card. See reverse for more details.

Group 5510

A current American Casino Guide Discount Card must be presented when redeeming this coupon, or offer is void

AMERICAN CASINO GUIDE

$10 FREE Slot Play

Present this coupon at the Players Advantage Club® booth, sign up for a card, or present your current card, and receive $10 in FREE slot play. See reverse for more details.

A current American Casino Guide Discount Card must be presented when redeeming this coupon, or offer is void

americancasinoguide.com

Offer valid for American Casino Guide readers. Must be 21 years of age or older. Subject to availability. Valid for one night only, must present coupon.

Offer subject to change or cancellation at any time without prior notice. Valid only at Hollywood Casino Tunica. Not transferable. One coupon per Player account. Offer void if sold. Offer expires 12/31/18.

TUNICA, MS

1150 Casino Strip Resorts Blvd.
Tunica Resorts, MS 38664
(800) 871-0711
(662) 357-7700
hollywoodcasinotunica.com

Offer void if coupon is copied or sold

americancasinoguide.com

Hard Rock Hotel & Casino Lake Tahoe
50 Highway 50, Stateline, NV 89449
(844) 588-7625
www.hardrockcasinolaketahoe.com

Must be Backstage Pass member to redeem, membership is free. Present voucher to Backstage Pass/Bank to enroll. Cannot be redeemed for cash. Non-negotiable. Not valid with any other offer. Must be 21or older, with valid ID, to redeem. No photocopies accepted. Management reserves all rights. Offer expires December 30, 2018.

Offer void if coupon is copied or sold

americancasinoguide.com

111 Country Club Drive
Incline Village, NV 89451
(775) 832-1234
(800) 327-3910

Must be 21 years of age, or older. Valid once per account per calendar year. One offer per account. Management reserves the right to alter or change promotion at any time. Expires 12/31/18.

Offer void if coupon is copied or sold

AMERICAN CASINO GUIDE

TWO FOR ONE BUFFET

Must be an Aliante Players Club member. Must purchase one Medley Buffet at regular price, to receive a second buffet, of equal or lesser value, for free or 50% off a single buffet. Valid once per 12 month period. See reverse for full details.

A current American Casino Guide Discount Card must be presented when redeeming this coupon, or offer is void

AMERICAN CASINO GUIDE

Aliante™

CASINO + HOTEL + SPA

New Members
Earn 100 points, get a Free Gift

Must be a new Aliante Players Club member. Present this original coupon to the Players Club when signing up. 100 points must be earned on day of sign up. You keep the points. See reverse for more details.

A current American Casino Guide Discount Card must be presented when redeeming this coupon, or offer is void

AMERICAN CASINO GUIDE

$10 MATCH PLAY

Must be an Aliante Players Club member. Present this original coupon at the Pit to redeem. No cash value. See reverse for more details.

A current American Casino Guide Discount Card must be presented when redeeming this coupon, or offer is void

Aliante™
CASINO + HOTEL + SPA

7300 Aliante Parkway
North Las Vegas, NV 89084
702-692-7777
aliantegaming.com

Present this coupon to receive a buy one, get one free buffet at Medley Buffet or 50% off a single buffet. Must be an Aliante Players Club member. Membership is free. Gratuity not included. No cash value. Must be 21 years of age or older to redeem. Not valid with any other offer. Not valid on holidays or peak days. Present this coupon to receive a buy one, get one free buffet at Medley Buffet or 50% off a single buffet. Management reserves all rights. Expires 12/30/2018. Settle to 50045

Offer void if coupon is copied or sold

Aliante™
CASINO + HOTEL + SPA

7300 Aliante Parkway
North Las Vegas, NV 89084
702-692-7777
aliantegaming.com

New members only. Must sign up for an Aliante Players Club card. Earn 100 points and present his coupon at the Players Club to receive a free gift. 100 points must be earned on day of sign up. Void if copied or altered. Must be 21 years of age or older. Not valid with any other offer. Management reserves all rights. Expires 12/30/2018.

Offer void if coupon is copied or sold

Aliante™
CASINO + HOTEL + SPA

7300 Aliante Parkway
North Las Vegas, NV 89084
702-692-7777
aliantegaming.com

No cash value. This offer is non-transferable. One coupon per person per day. Coupon is good for one bet, win or lose. Even money table game bets and coupon only pays even money. Must be 21 years of age. Void if copied or altered. Must present players club card and valid photo I.D. to redeem. Valid only on Blackjack: main bets only. Roulette: outside even money bets only. Craps: pass or don't pass, and/or field. Please gamble responsibly. See Players Club for complete details. Management reserves all rights. Expires 12/30/2018.

Offer void if coupon is copied or sold

AMERICAN CASINO GUIDE

2-For-1 Buffet

Present this coupon to the **ace** | PLAY Center at Arizona Charlie's Boulder to receive one FREE buffet when you purchase one buffet at the regular price. See reverse for details.

ace | PLAY card # ______________________

A current American Casino Guide Discount Card must be presented when redeeming this coupon, or offer is void

AMERICAN CASINO GUIDE

2-For-1 Buffet

Present this coupon to the **ace** | PLAY Center at Arizona Charlie's Decatur to receive one FREE buffet when you purchase one buffet at the regular price. See reverse for details.

ace | PLAY card # ______________________

A current American Casino Guide Discount Card must be presented when redeeming this coupon, or offer is void

AMERICAN CASINO GUIDE

20% OFF

Redeem at the Bally's Spa or Salon for 20% off any service. See reverse for details.

A current American Casino Guide Discount Card must be presented when redeeming this coupon, or offer is void

4575 Boulder Highway
Las Vegas, NV 89121
702.951.5800
800.362.4040
ArizonaCharliesBoulder.com

Must be 21 years of age or older. Must present **ace** | PLAY card and surrender the original coupon (no photocopies) to the **ace** | PLAY Center representative for a voucher. Resale prohibited. No cash value. Maximum two people per coupon. Tax and tip are not included. Not valid for takeout. Management reserves the right to change or cancel this promotion at any time without notice. Valid January 2 - December 19, 2018.

740 S. Decatur Boulevard
Las Vegas, NV 89107
702.258.5200
800.342.2695
ArizonaCharliesDecatur.com

Must be 21 years of age or older. Must present **ace** | PLAY card and surrender the original coupon (no photocopies) to the **ace** | PLAY Center representative for a voucher. Resale prohibited. No cash value. Maximum two people per coupon. Tax and tip are not included. Not valid for takeout. Management reserves the right to change or cancel this promotion at any time without notice. Valid January 2 - December 19, 2018.

3645 Las Vegas Blvd. S.
Las Vegas, NV 89109
702-967-4111
BallysLasVegas.com

Limit 1 coupon per guest. No cash value. Not valid on previously purchased services. Cannot be combined with any other offer. Subject to availability. Blackout dates may apply. Management reserves all rights. Offer subject to change or cancellation without notification. Offer expires 12/30/18.

AMERICAN CASINO GUIDE

$5 Blackjack Matchplay

Present this coupon at any blackjack table, along with your Bigshot Players Club card, prior to the start of a hand and we'll match your bet of $5 if you win. See reverse for details.

A current American Casino Guide Discount Card must be presented when redeeming this coupon, or offer is void

AMERICAN CASINO GUIDE

2-for-1 Lunch or Dinner Entrée

Buy one lunch or dinner entrée in our restaurant and get one entrée of equal or lesser value FREE! Present to server before ordering. See reverse for more details.

A current American Casino Guide Discount Card must be presented when redeeming this coupon, or offer is void

AMERICAN CASINO GUIDE

$20 Free Play for $10

Present this coupon at the Bigshot Players Club booth to receive $20 in Free Play for only $10. Valid for new and current members. See reverse for more details.

A current American Casino Guide Discount Card must be presented when redeeming this coupon, or offer is void

3016 E. Lake Mead Blvd.
N. Las Vegas, NV 89030
(702) 642-1940

Limit: one coupon per person, per month. Cannot be redeemed for cash. Must be 21 or older. Cannot be combined with any other offer or promotion. Non-transferable. Offer void if sold.

Must present original coupon (no photocopies). Not responsible for lost or stolen coupon. Management reserves all rights. Offer may be changed or discontinued at anytime at the discretion of management. Offer expires December 30, 2018.

3016 E. Lake Mead Blvd.
N. Las Vegas, NV 89030
(702) 642-1940

Limit one coupon per person. Must be 21 years or older. Purchase one lunch or dinner entrée to receive the second one of equal or lesser value free. Not valid on take out orders. Coupon is void if altered or duplicated. Must present original coupon (no photocopies).

Tax, beverages and gratuity are not included. Not valid with any other offers or discounts. Management reserves the right to cancel or modify offer at any time. Coupon has no cash value. Offer expires December 30, 2018.

3016 E. Lake Mead Blvd.
N. Las Vegas, NV 89030
(702) 642-1940

Must be 21 years of age or older. Cannot be combined with any other offer or promotion. Non-transferable. Offer void if sold. Limit one coupon per account, per calendar year.

Must present original coupon (no photocopies). Not responsible for lost or stolen coupon. Management reserves all rights. Offer may be changed or discontinued at anytime at the discretion of management. Offer expires December 30, 2018.

AMERICAN CASINO GUIDE

Double Points (Up to 500) for members of Club Binion's

Double your Club Binion's points (up to 500) with this coupon! See reverse for more details.

A current American Casino Guide Discount Card must be presented when redeeming this coupon, or offer is void

AMERICAN CASINO GUIDE

2-for-1 Binion's Famous Hamburger at Binion's Café

Buy one of Binion's famous hamburgers at Binion's Café and get one FREE! See reverse for more details.

A current American Casino Guide Discount Card must be presented when redeeming this coupon, or offer is void

AMERICAN CASINO GUIDE

Bonanno's®
NEW YORK PIZZERIA

Buy One Pizza Get One Free

Present this coupon at Bonanno's New York Pizzeria, purchase a whole pizza and get a second whole pizza free! See reverse for details.

A current American Casino Guide Discount Card must be presented when redeeming this coupon, or offer is void

128 East Fremont St.
Las Vegas, NV 89101
800.937.6537 • 702.382.1600
www.binions.com

Strictly limited to one coupon per person per 12 month period. Coupon has no cash value. Must be 21 years or older. Points must be earned on day of redemption. Offer valid for Club Binion's members only. Double points will be added to account within 48 hours. Not valid with any other offers. Management reserves the right to cancel or modify offer at any time without notice. Coupon is void if altered or duplicated. Offer expires December 27, 2018.

americancasinoguide.com

128 East Fremont St.
Las Vegas, NV 89101
800.937.6537 • 702.382.1600
www.binions.com

Strictly limited to one coupon per person per 12 month period. Must be 21 years or older. Must redeem coupon at Club Binion's to receive voucher for Binion's Café. Purchase one hamburger (of equal or greater value) to receive the second one free. Offer valid only at Binion's Café. Coupon is void if altered or duplicated. Tax, alcoholic beverages and gratuity are not included. Not valid with any other offers or discounts. Management reserves the right to cancel or modify offer at any time. Coupon has no cash value. Offer expires December 27, 2018.

Offer void if coupon is copied or sold

americancasinoguide.com

MGM Grand Food Court
Luxor Food Court
Flamingo Food Court
Mandalay Bay Food Court

Must present coupon to cashier prior to ordering. Offer has no cash value. Not valid with any other offer. One coupon per person. Subject to change or cancellation without prior notice. Offer valid through December 31, 2018.

Offer void if coupon is copied or sold

Bonanno's®
NEW YORK PIZZERIA

Buy One Item Get One Free

Present this coupon at Bonanno's New York Pizzeria, purchase any menu item and get a second menu item of equal or lesser value free! See reverse for details.

A current American Casino Guide Discount Card must be presented when redeeming this coupon, or offer is void

AMERICAN CASINO GUIDE

2-For-1 Buffet
(Monday-Thursday)

Buy one Feast Buffet and get the second Feast Buffet FREE. Offer valid Monday-Thursday. See reverse for more details.

A current American Casino Guide Discount Card must be presented when redeeming this coupon, or offer is void

AMERICAN CASINO GUIDE

5X Point Multiplier

Before your play, present this coupon to the B Connected Club for activation. See reverse side for details.

A current American Casino Guide Discount Card must be presented when redeeming this coupon, or offer is void

americancasinoguide.com

MGM Grand Food Court
Luxor Food Court
Flamingo Food Court
Mandalay Bay Food Court

Must present coupon to cashier prior to ordering. Offer has no cash value. Not valid with any other offer. One coupon per person. Subject to change or cancellation without prior notice. Offer valid through December 31, 2018.

Offer void if coupon is copied or sold

americancasinoguide.com

4111 Boulder Hwy
Las Vegas, NV 89121
(702) 432-7777
boulderstation.sclv.com

This voucher entitles bearer to one free breakfast, lunch or dinner in the Feast Buffet when accompanied by a cash paying guest. Tax and gratuity not included. One voucher per person/subscriber. Voucher must be presented to cashier. Vouchers are not transferable and are not redeemable for cash. Must be 21 or older. Not a line pass. Not valid on holidays, Not valid with any other offer. Offer may be changed or discontinued at any time at the discretion of management. Original vouchers only. Offer is void if sold. Offer expires December 20, 2018. Settle to: #88-942

Offer void if coupon is copied or sold

americancasinoguide.com

12 East Ogden Avenue
Las Vegas, NV 89101
(800) 634-6505
thecal.com

Before your play, present this coupon to the B Connected Club for activation. This offer cannot be used in conjunction with any other offer, floor-wide promotion, or event. Point multipliers are not valid on select machines. Max 100,000 bonus promotion points. See B Connected for complete details. Must be 21 or older and have an active B Connected Card. Management reserves all rights. Expires 12/30/18. Offer code: AC185X

Offer void if coupon is copied or sold

AMERICAN CASINO GUIDE

Earn 500 points, Get a Free Buffet
(Keep the points)

Earn 500 base points playing slots then present this original coupon and B Connected Card to the B Connected Club, and receive a voucher that will entitle bearer to one FREE dinner buffet at the Garden Court Buffet located at Main Street Station. Excludes seafood night. See reverse side for details.

A current American Casino Guide Discount Card must be presented when redeeming this coupon, or offer is void

AMERICAN CASINO GUIDE

New Members Play $25 Get $10

Present this coupon when signing up for a new B Connected card to be eligible for Play $25 and Get $10 slot play. See reverse for full details.

A current American Casino Guide Discount Card must be presented when redeeming this coupon, or offer is void

AMERICAN CASINO GUIDE

2-For-1 Buffet

Purchase one buffet at regular price and receive a second buffet of equal or lesser value free. See reverse for more details.

A current American Casino Guide Discount Card must be presented when redeeming this coupon, or offer is void

americancasinoguide.com

12 East Ogden Avenue
Las Vegas, NV 89101
(800) 634-6505
thecal.com

Before your play, present this coupon to the B Connected Club for activation. Earn 500 base points playing slots on same day original coupon is presented to the B Connected Club for redemption. Limit one coupon per B Connected account. Excludes Friday night seafood buffet. This coupon has no cash value, cannot be combined with any other offer or used more than once. Reproduction, sale, barter or transfer are prohibited and render this coupon void. Management reserves the right to change or discontinue this offer without notice. Must be 21 or older and have an active B Connected Card. Not valid on holidays. Expires 12/30/18. Offer code: AC18FB

Offer void if coupon is copied or sold

americancasinoguide.com

California Hotel Casino
12 East Ogden Avenue
Las Vegas, NV 89101
(800) 634-6505
thecal.com

Fremont Hotel & Casino
200 Fremont St
Las Vegas, NV 89101
(800) 634-6460
fremontcasino.com

Main Street Station
200 North Main Street
Las Vegas, NV 89101
(800) 713-8933
mainstreetcasino.com

Present this coupon when signing up for a new B Connected card at your choice of casinos- the California, Fremont, or Main Street Station to be eligible for the Play & Get slot play. One Play & Get offer per new B Connected account. Slot play refers to non-cashable downloadable machine credits and will be uploaded to your B Connected account, pin number is required. Slot play is non-transferable and cannot be used with any other offer. You must be 21 or over to participate. Slot play will expire 24 hrs after coupon redemption. Management reserves the right to modify or cancel this promotion without prior notice. See the B Connected Club for additional details. Expires 12/30/2018. Offer code: AC18NM

Offer void if coupon is copied or sold

americancasinoguide.com

2121 E. Craig Road
N. Las Vegas, NV 89030
(702) 507-5700
(866) 999-4899
www.cannerycasino.com

Must present CAN Club card, valid photo ID and coupon to cashier to redeem. Coupon has no cash value, must be 21 or older to redeem. Limit one coupon redemption per person. Excludes holidays. Cannot be combined with any other offer or discount. Valid at Cannery on Craig Road only. Management reserves all rights. Offer expires 12/30/18.

Settle to comp: 90600

Offer void if coupon is copied or sold

AMERICAN CASINO GUIDE

$50 in FREE Slot Play!

How Fortune8!

Get $50 in free slot play when you've earned 5,000 base points in one 24-hour period from 12:01a.m.–11:59p.m. See reverse for details.

A current American Casino Guide Discount Card must be presented when redeeming this coupon, or offer is void

AMERICAN CASINO GUIDE

the D LAS VEGAS

Get out of Blackjack Hand for Free

(push your bet on 22)

Redeem this coupon at player's club and have your bet pushed when you get a 22. Maximum $25 bet. See reverse side for full details.

A current American Casino Guide Discount Card must be presented when redeeming this coupon, or offer is void

AMERICAN CASINO GUIDE

the D LAS VEGAS

$25 Match Play

Bet $25 on any even-money bet and we'll pay you $50 if you win. Present this coupon at Club D to receive your free $25 match play. See reverse side for full details.

A current American Casino Guide Discount Card must be presented when redeeming this coupon, or offer is void

americancasinoguide.com

725 S Racetrack Road
Henderson, NV 89015
(702) 566-5555
ClubFortunecasino.com

Present this voucher to the Player Rewards Center during normal operation hours 8a.m.-10p.m. Must be or become a Player Rewards Card member to redeem. Cannot be used in conjunction with any other free slot play offer. Limit of one (1) free slot play coupon per person and Player Rewards card. Not valid with any other offer. Management reserves all rights. Group #5991. Expires 11:59p.m. 12/30/18.

Offer void if coupon is copied or sold

americancasinoguide.com

301 E. Fremont Street
Las Vegas, NV 89101
(702) 388-2400
www.TheD.com

Voucher must be redeemed at Club D prior to play. Offer valid for blackjack only (not valid on Super Fun 21). Bonus is not paid on double downs or pair splits. Limit one offer per account per calendar year. Maximum bonus payout not to exceed $25. A minimum buy-in of $100 is required.

Valid government issued ID required to join Club D. Must be 21 or older. Membership is free. Management reserves all rights. No cash value. Offer expires December 29, 2018.

Offer void if coupon is copied or sold

americancasinoguide.com

301 E. Fremont Street
Las Vegas, NV 89101
(702) 388-2400
www.TheD.com

Voucher must be surrendered to Club D to receive free match play offer. Good for one bet only, win or lose, (pushes play again). Limit one offer per account per calendar year.

Valid government issued ID required to join Club D. Must be 21 or older. Membership is free. Management reserves all rights. No cash value. Offer expires December 29, 2018.

Offer void if coupon is copied or sold

Here is your
American Casino Guide
Discount Card.

Cut out this card
and carry it with you!

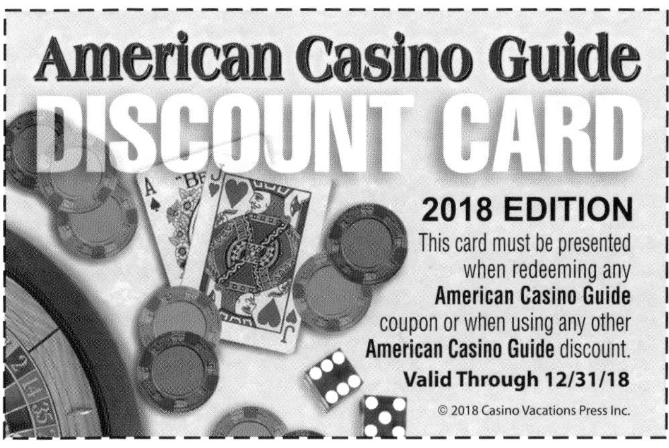

You <u>must</u> present this card to a merchant whenever you redeem an *American Casino Guide* coupon.

Do not lose this card.
No replacements will be given.

This card identifies you as the purchaser of an ***American Casino Guide*** and it entitles you to all of the benefits offered through our coupon program.

Print Name

Valid through December 31, 2018

This card ***must be presented*** when redeeming any *American Casino Guide* coupon or when using any other *American Casino Guide* discount.

AMERICAN CASINO GUIDE

the D LAS VEGAS

Up to $100 Free Play

Earn $5 in free play for every 50 points earned on slots or video poker. Maximum bonus of $100. See reverse side for full details.

A current American Casino Guide Discount Card must be presented when redeeming this coupon, or offer is void

AMERICAN CASINO GUIDE

FREE Deck of Cards

Redeem at Grand Rewards Players Club.
See reverse for details.

A current American Casino Guide Discount Card must be presented when redeeming this coupon, or offer is void

AMERICAN CASINO GUIDE

DOWNTOWN GRAND HOTEL & CASINO

Earn 25 Points and receive $10 in Free Slot Play

Redeem at Grand Rewards Players Club.
See reverse for details.

A current American Casino Guide Discount Card must be presented when redeeming this coupon, or offer is void

301 E. Fremont Street
Las Vegas, NV 89101
(702) 388-2400
www.TheD.com

Voucher must be redeemed at Club D prior to play. Receive $5 free slot play for every 50 points earned up to a $100 maximum bonus. Any bonus must be redeemed within the first 24-hours of play and can be redeemed one time only. Player keeps points earned. Limit one offer per account per calendar year. Cannot be used in conjunction with Club D new member sign-up bonus.

Valid government issued ID required to join Club D. Must be 21 or older. Membership is free. Management reserves all rights. No cash value. Offer expires December 29, 2018.

americancasinoguide.com

206 N. 3rd Street
Las Vegas NV 89101
(855) DT-GRAND
www.downtowngrand.com

Must be a be GRAND REWARDS member and at least 21 or older to redeem. Maximum of one (1) coupon per GRAND REWARDS member. Must present at GRAND REWARDS Players Club for redemption. Deck of Cards are while supplies lasts. Deck of Cards have no cash value and are non-transferable. Downtown Grand Hotel & Casino has the right to modify or cancel the offer at any time. Cannot be combined with any other offers. Management reserves all rights. Coupon expires 12/29/18

Offer void if coupon is copied or sold

americancasinoguide.com

206 N. 3rd Street
Las Vegas NV 89101
(855) DT-GRAND
www.downtowngrand.com

Must be a GRAND REWARDS member and at least 21 or older to redeem. Maximum of one (1) coupon per GRAND REWARDS member. Points must be earned same day. Free Slot Play will be valid for 72 hours from time earned. Offer is non-transferable and has no cash value. Downtown Grand Hotel & Casino has the right to modify or cancel the offer at any time. Cannot be combined with any other offers. Management reserves all rights. Coupon expires 12/29/18

Offer void if coupon is copied or sold

AMERICAN CASINO GUIDE

DOWNTOWN GRAND HOTEL & CASINO

Buy One Get One FREE Cocktail at Freedom Beat

Redeem at Grand Rewards Players Club.
See reverse for details.

A current American Casino Guide Discount Card must be presented when redeeming this coupon, or offer is void

AMERICAN CASINO GUIDE

DOWNTOWN GRAND HOTEL & CASINO

FREE Appetizer with purchase of an Entrée at Triple George Grill

Redeem at Grand Rewards Players Club.
See reverse for details.

A current American Casino Guide Discount Card must be presented when redeeming this coupon, or offer is void

AMERICAN CASINO GUIDE

Play $10 and get up to $100 free play

(with your Passport Players Club Card)

Play $10 on slots or video poker and get up to $100 free play. Upon playing $10 through any Ellis Island slot or video poker machine, you will be enrolled into the Spin and Win promotion. See reverse for details.

Name____________________ PPC________________

A current American Casino Guide Discount Card must be presented when redeeming this coupon, or offer is void

americancasinoguide.com

DOWNTOWN
GRAND
HOTEL & CASINO

206 N. 3rd Street
Las Vegas NV 89101
(855) DT-GRAND
www.downtowngrand.com

Must be a GRAND REWARDS member and at least 21 or older to redeem. Maximum of one (1) coupon per GRAND REWARDS member. Receive one (1) free drink with purchase of a drink of equal or lesser value. Valid at Freedom Beat. Gratuity not included. Downtown Grand Hotel & Casino has the right to modify or cancel the offer at any time. Cannot be combined with any other offers. Offer is non-transferable and has no cash value. Management reserves all rights. Coupon expires 12/29/18

Offer void if coupon is copied or sold

americancasinoguide.com

206 N. 3rd Street
Las Vegas NV 89101
(855) DT-GRAND
www.downtowngrand.com

Must be a GRAND REWARDS member and at least 21 or older to redeem. Valid at Triple George Grill only. Free Appetizer with the purchase of an Entrée. Maximum value $15. Valid for dine-in only. Gratuity not included. Downtown Grand Hotel & Casino has the right to modify or cancel the offer at any time. Cannot be combined with any other offers. Offer is non-transferable and has no cash value. Management reserves all rights. Coupon expires 12/29/18

Offer void if coupon is copied or sold

americancasinoguide.com

4178 Koval Lane
Las Vegas, NV 89169
(702) 733-8901
www.ellisislandscasino.com

Must be playing with Passport Player's Club card, membership is free. Upon playing $10 through any slot or video poker machine, present this coupon at the Passport Players Club, you will be "Enrolled" into the spin and win promotion at the passport Central Kiosk. Participate in the promotional game where you can win $10 - $100 in Slot free play. Free play will automatically post in your account same day. Free play must be played through once to cash out. Limit one voucher per customer. One time only. No cash value. Not valid in conjunction with any other offer. Must be 21 years or older to redeem. Management reserves the right to cancel or change this offer at any time. Offer expires December 30, 2018.

Offer void if coupon is copied or sold

AMERICAN CASINO GUIDE

Play $5 and Receive an Ellis Island T-Shirt

Present this coupon, along with your Passport Players Club Card, to the promotions booth after playing $5 to receive your exclusive limited edition t-shirt. See reverse for more details.

Name____________________________PPC______________________

A current American Casino Guide Discount Card must be presented when redeeming this coupon, or offer is void

AMERICAN CASINO GUIDE

$10 Match Play for Any Even-Money Table Game Bet

Present this coupon, along with your Passport Players Club Card, to the promotions booth to receive your $10 Match Play coupon. See reverse for more details.

Name____________________________PPC______________________

A current American Casino Guide Discount Card must be presented when redeeming this coupon, or offer is void

AMERICAN CASINO GUIDE

2-for-1 Drink

Present this coupon at the Fat Bar Las Vegas to receive two well drinks or two select draft beers for the price of one. See reverse for details.

A current American Casino Guide Discount Card must be presented when redeeming this coupon, or offer is void

americancasinoguide.com

4178 Koval Lane
Las Vegas, NV 89169
(702) 733-8901

www.ellisislandscasino.com

Must be 21 years of age or older. Original coupon must be presented (no photocopies) along with your Passport Players Club Card. Membership in Passport Players Club must be in good standing. Resale prohibited. Limit one offer per calendar year per person. Management reserves the right to cancel or alter this coupon without prior notice. Offer expires 12/30/18.

Offer void if coupon is copied or sold

americancasinoguide.com

4178 Koval Lane
Las Vegas, NV 89169
(702) 733-8901
www.ellisislandscasino.com

Must be 21 years of age or older. Original coupon must be presented (no photocopies) along with your Passport Players Club Card. Membership in Passport Players Club must be in good standing. Resale prohibited. Limit one offer per calendar year per person. Management reserves the right to cancel or alter this coupon without prior notice. Offer expires 12/30/18.

Offer void if coupon is copied or sold

americancasinoguide.com

3763 Las Vegas Blvd S
Las Vegas, NV 89109
(702) 736-4733
FatBurger.com

This coupon is good for two (2) well drinks or two (2) select draft beers for the price of one (1) at Fat Bar located in front of Fatburger on the Las Vegas Strip. Minimum $7 purchase required. Must present coupon when ordering. Limit of one coupon per person. No cash value. Management reserves all rights. Offer not valid 12/31/17. Offer expires 12/30/18.

Offer void if coupon is copied or sold

AMERICAN CASINO GUIDE

Royal Flush Capital of the World.

2-For-1 Buffet
(Monday-Thursday)

Buy one Festival Buffet and get the second Festival Buffet free. Offer valid Monday-Thursday. See reverse for more details.

A current American Casino Guide Discount Card must be presented when redeeming this coupon, or offer is void

AMERICAN CASINO GUIDE

Royal Flush Capital of the World.

2-For-1 Buffet
(Monday-Thursday)

Buy one Festival Buffet and get the second Festival Buffet free. Offer valid Monday-Thursday. See reverse for more details.

A current American Casino Guide Discount Card must be presented when redeeming this coupon, or offer is void

AMERICAN CASINO GUIDE

Grand Canyon Helicopter Tours – Fly Below the Rim!

$75 OFF Grand Canyon West Rim Helicopter Tour

HELICOPTER TOURS

180 Degree Panoramic Views

First Class/VIP Configuration

Mercedes-Benz Hotel Transfers

A current American Casino Guide Discount Card must be presented when redeeming this coupon, or offer is void

Royal Flush Capital of the World.

777 W Lake Mead Pkwy
Henderson, NV 89015
(702) 558-7000
www.fiestahenderson.sclv.com

This voucher entitles bearer to one free lunch or dinner in the Festival Buffet when accompanied by a cash paying guest. Tax and gratuity not included. One voucher per person/subscriber. Voucher must be presented to cashier. Vouchers are not transferable and are not redeemable for cash. Must be 21 or older. Not a line pass. Not valid on holidays, Not valid with any other offer. Offer may be changed or discontinued at any time at the discretion of management. Original vouchers only. Offer is void if sold. Offer expires 12/20/18. Settle to: #88-942

Royal Flush Capital of the World.

2400 N Rancho Dr
N. Las Vegas, NV 89130
(702) 631-7000
www.fiestarancho.sclv.com

This voucher entitles bearer to one free lunch or dinner in the Festival Buffet when accompanied by a cash paying guest. Tax and gratuity not included. One voucher per person/subscriber. Voucher must be presented to cashier. Vouchers are not transferable and are not redeemable for cash. Must be 21 or older. Not a line pass. Not valid on holidays, Not valid with any other offer. Offer may be changed or discontinued at any time at the discretion of management. Original vouchers only. Offer is void if sold. Offer expires 12/20/18. Settle to: #88-942

Ask about our Extended Air Tour or our 30 min, 1 hour and 2 Hour Landing and Adventure Tours.

Grand Canyon West Rim
$75 OFF!

5 STAR Grand Canyon West Rim Helicopter Tours Include:

- ★ ***Luxury Mercedes-Benz Motorcoach Hotel Pickup***
- ★ ***Complimentary Refreshments at Our Air Terminal***
- ★ ***Luxurious State-of-the-Art Jet Helicopters***
- ★ ***All Forward-facing Leather Seats with 180° Panoramic Views***
- ★ ***Narrated Pilot Commentary and In-flight Music***

Secure your seats NOW!
Call 7a-10p, mention "ACG"
5StarHelicopterTours.com

702-565-7827

All Tours Include Luxury Mercedes-Benz Las Vegas Area Hotel Pickup & Drop-off!

Must mention CODE "ACG" at time of booking to receive discount. Must call direct. Not valid with any other offer or discount.
Copyright © 5 STAR Grand Canyon Helicopter Tours, LLC. FAA Certified Air Carrier No. 5S9A1230. Follow us on

Offer expires 12/30/18

AMERICAN CASINO GUIDE

Second Round

of Frozen House Margarita free
Classic, Strawberry or Mango

Order your Frozen House Margarita, and the second round is on us. Gratuity not included. Coupon holds no cash value. Cannot be combined with another offer. Not valid if reproduced. Any attempts to sell or auction shall nullify this offer. Management reserves all rights. Must present offer at the time of order.

A current American Casino Guide Discount Card must be presented when redeeming this coupon, or offer is void

AMERICAN CASINO GUIDE

2-FOR-1 TICKETS

Redeem at the Flamingo Box Office for 2-for-1 Golden Circle or Main Floor tickets to Legends in Concert. See reverse for details.

Offer code: LCACG

A current American Casino Guide Discount Card must be presented when redeeming this coupon, or offer is void

AMERICAN CASINO GUIDE

Buy One Who's To Blame Margarita Get One FREE!

Present this coupon to your server, before ordering, and receive two Who's To Blame Margaritas for the price of one. See reverse for details.

A current American Casino Guide Discount Card must be presented when redeeming this coupon, or offer is void

americancasinoguide.com

3555 Las Vegas Blvd. South Las Vegas, NV, 89109. Caesars Entertainment License Company, LLC, Ph (702) 522 9254. Inside the Flamingo Hotel www.carlosncharlieslv.com

Must be 21 or older to gamble. Know When To Stop Before You Start. ®Gambling Problem? Call 1-800-522-4700. ©2012, Caesars Entertainment License Company, LLC. Expiration date of 12/30/18.

Offer void if coupon is copied or sold

americancasinoguide.com

3555 Las Vegas Blvd. S.
Las Vegas, NV 89109
702-733-3111
Flamingo.com

Present coupon at time of purchase to redeem. Limit three free tickets per coupon. No cash value. Golden Circle tickets are $88.78 inclusive, Main Floor tickets are $79.06. Not valid on previously purchased tickets. Cannot be combined with any other offer. Subject to availability. Blackout dates may apply. Management reserves all rights. Offer subject to change or cancellation without notification. Offer expires 12/30/18.

Offer void if coupon is copied or sold

americancasinoguide.com

Located at The Flamingo
3555 Las Vegas Blvd. S.
Las Vegas, NV 89109
702-733-3302
www.margaritaville.com

Coupon must be presented upon ordering. Must be 21 or older. Gratuity not included. Limit one per person. Coupon has no cash value. May not be combined with any other offer. Management reserves all rights. Expires 12/29/18.

Offer Code: BOGOMACG

Offer void if coupon is copied or sold

AMERICAN CASINO GUIDE

$10 Off Any Service of $50 or More

Redeem at the Uno Salon at the Flamingo Las Vegas for $10 off any service of $50 or more. See reverse for details.

A current American Casino Guide Discount Card must be presented when redeeming this coupon, or offer is void

AMERICAN CASINO GUIDE

Double Points (Up to 500) for members of the Royal Players Club™

Double your Royal Players Club™ points (up to 500) with this coupon! See reverse for more details.

A current American Casino Guide Discount Card must be presented when redeeming this coupon, or offer is void

AMERICAN CASINO GUIDE

2-for-1 Lunch or Dinner Entrée in Magnolia's

Buy one lunch or dinner entrée in Magnolia's and get one entrée FREE! See reverse for more details.

A current American Casino Guide Discount Card must be presented when redeeming this coupon, or offer is void

americancasinoguide.com

3555 Las Vegas Blvd. S.
Las Vegas, NV 89109
702-733-3111
Flamingo.com

Limit 1 coupon per guest. No cash value. Not valid on previously purchased services. Cannot be combined with any other offer. Subject to availability. Blackout dates may apply. Management reserves all rights. Offer subject to change or cancellation without notification. Offer expires 12/30/18.

Offer void if coupon is copied or sold

americancasinoguide.com

202 Fremont Street
Las Vegas, NV 89101
(702) 385-4011
(800) 634-6045
www.fourqueens.com

Strictly limited to one coupon per person per 12 month period. Coupon has no cash value. Must be 21 years or older. Points must be earned on day of redemption. Offer valid for Royal Players Club™ members only. Double points will be added to account within 48 hours. Management reserves the right to cancel or modify offer at any time without notice. Not valid with any other offer. Coupon is void if altered or duplicated. Offer expires December 27, 2018.

Offer void if coupon is copied or sold

americancasinoguide.com

202 Fremont Street
Las Vegas, NV 89101
(702) 385-4011
(800) 634-6045
www.fourqueens.com

Strictly limited to one coupon per person per 12 month period. Must be 21 years or older. Must redeem coupon at the Royal Players Club to receive voucher for Magnolia's. Purchase one lunch or dinner entrée (equal or greater value) to receive the second one free. Offer valid only in Magnolia's. Coupon is void if altered or duplicated. Tax, alcoholic beverages and gratuity are not included. Not valid with any other offers or discounts. Management reserves the right to cancel or modify offer at any time. Coupon has no cash value. Offer expires December 27, 2018.

Offer void if coupon is copied or sold

AMERICAN CASINO GUIDE

Mike Hammer Show

comedy & magic

2-for-1 Show Tickets

Buy one ticket to the Mike Hammer Comedy Magic Show and receive a second one FREE.

See reverse for more details.

A current American Casino Guide Discount Card must be presented when redeeming this coupon, or offer is void

AMERICAN CASINO GUIDE

Spirit of the King

Elvis Tribute Show

2-for-1 Show Tickets

Buy one ticket to the Spirit of the King Elvis Tribute Show and receive a second one FREE.

See reverse for more details.

A current American Casino Guide Discount Card must be presented when redeeming this coupon, or offer is void

AMERICAN CASINO GUIDE

5X Point Multiplier

Before your play, present this coupon to the B Connected Club for activation. See reverse side for details.

A current American Casino Guide Discount Card must be presented when redeeming this coupon, or offer is void

americancasinoguide.com

202 Fremont Street
Las Vegas, NV 89101
(877) 935-2844
mikehammershow.com

Show open to ages 13+. Must be 21 to redeem coupon.Must redeem coupon at the Four Queens Box Office to receive second ticket for free with purchase of one at full price. Coupon is void if altered or duplicated. Tax and box office fees are not included. Not valid with any other offers or discounts. **Show times: 7pm Tuesday-Saturday.** Subject to availability. Management reserves the right to cancel or modify offer at any time. Coupon has no cash value. Offer expires December 29, 2018.

Offer void if coupon is copied or sold

americancasinoguide.com

202 Fremont Street
Las Vegas, NV 89101
(877) 935-2844
mikehammershow.com

Show open to ages 13+. Must be 21 to redeem coupon.Must redeem coupon at the Four Queens Box Office to receive second ticket for free with purchase of one at full price. Coupon is void if altered or duplicated. Tax and box office fees are not included. Not valid with any other offers or discounts. **Show times: 9pm Tuesday-Saturday**. Subject to availability. Management reserves the right to cancel or modify offer at any time. Coupon has no cash value. Offer expires December 29, 2018.

Offer void if coupon is copied or sold

americancasinoguide.com

200 Fremont St
Las Vegas, NV 89101
(800) 634-6460
fremontcasino.com

Before your play, present this coupon to the B Connected Club for activation. This offer cannot be used in conjunction with any other offer, floor-wide promotion, or event. Point multipliers are not valid on select machines. Max 100,000 bonus promotion points. See B Connected for complete details. Must be 21 or older and have an active B Connected Card. Management reserves all rights. Expires 12/30/18. Offer code: AC185X

Offer void if coupon is copied or sold

AMERICAN CASINO GUIDE

Earn 500 points, Get a Free Buffet

(Keep the points)

Earn 500 base points playing slots then present this original coupon and B Connected Card to the B Connected Club, and receive a voucher that will entitle bearer to one FREE dinner buffet at the Paradise Buffet. Excludes seafood nights. See reverse side for details.

A current American Casino Guide Discount Card must be presented when redeeming this coupon, or offer is void

AMERICAN CASINO GUIDE

New Members Play $25 Get $10

Present this coupon when signing up for a new B Connected card to be eligible for Play $25 and Get $10 slot play. See reverse for full details.

A current American Casino Guide Discount Card must be presented when redeeming this coupon, or offer is void

AMERICAN CASINO GUIDE

GAMBLERS GENERAL STORE

THE WORLD'S LARGEST GAMBLING SUPERSTORE! OPEN 7 DAYS A WEEK!

PERSONALIZED POKER CHIPS • CARDS • ROULETTE • BLACKJACK • CRAPS
GAMBLING TABLES • RAFFLE DRUMS • AWARD WHEELS • BOOKS • VIDEOS

10% Off Your Purchase!

Save 10% on your order from the largest Gambling Superstore in the world! We are located in Las Vegas, Nevada and offer genuine casino quality gaming products that can be used in casinos, homes, offices or parties.

A current American Casino Guide Discount Card must be presented when redeeming this coupon, or offer is void

americancasinoguide.com

200 Fremont St
Las Vegas, NV 89101
(800) 634-6460
fremontcasino.com

Before your play, present this coupon to the B Connected Club for activation. Earn 500 base points playing slots on same day original coupon is presented to the B Connected Club for redemption. Limit one coupon per B Connected account. Excludes Tuesday and Friday night seafood buffet. This coupon has no cash value, cannot be combined with any other offer or used more than once. Reproduction, sale, barter or transfer are prohibited and render this coupon void. Management reserves the right to change or discontinue this offer without notice. Must be 21 or older and have an active B Connected Card. Not valid on holidays. Expires 12/30/18. Offer code: AC18FB

Offer void if coupon is copied or sold

americancasinoguide.com

California Hotel Casino
12 East Ogden Avenue
Las Vegas, NV 89101
(800) 634-6505
thecal.com

Fremont Hotel & Casino
200 Fremont St
Las Vegas, NV 89101
(800) 634-6460
fremontcasino.com

Main Street Station
200 North Main Street
Las Vegas, NV 89101
(800) 713-8933
mainstreetcasino.com

Present this coupon when signing up for a new B Connected card at your choice of casinos- the California, Fremont, or Main Street Station to be eligible for the Play & Get slot play. One Play & Get offer per new B Connected account. Slot play refers to non-cashable downloadable machine credits and will be uploaded to your B Connected account, pin number is required. Slot play is non-transferable and cannot be used with any other offer. You must be 21 or over to participate. Slot play will expire 24 hrs after coupon redemption. Management reserves the right to modify or cancel this promotion without prior notice. See the B Connected Club for additional details. Expires 12/30/2018. Offer code: AC18NM

Offer void if coupon is copied or sold

americancasinoguide.com

9:00AM-5:30PM
Monday-Saturday
9:00AM-4:30PM
Sunday

Call: (702) 382-9903 or (800) 522-1777

800 South Main Street Las Vegas, Nevada 89101

Email: store@ggslv.com **Web: gamblersgeneralstore.com**

Limit one coupon per order. Not valid with any other offer. Must present coupon at store, or mention code "ACG" when ordering by telephone or on our website. Valid through 12/31/18.

Offer void if coupon is copied or sold

AMERICAN CASINO GUIDE

GOLD COAST®
HOTEL & CASINO · LAS VEGAS

Earn 200 Points, Get Free Buffet (Keep the points)

Earn 200 points playing slots then present this original coupon and B Connected Card to the B Connected Club, and receive a voucher that will entitle bearer to one FREE breakfast, lunch or regular dinner buffet. See reverse side for details.

A current American Casino Guide Discount Card must be presented when redeeming this coupon, or offer is void

AMERICAN CASINO GUIDE

GOLD COAST®
HOTEL & CASINO · LAS VEGAS

Get $20 off when you spend $40 in Cornerstone

Present this coupon to your server, before ordering, to get $20 off any check total of $40 or more at Cornerstone, the Classic American Steakhouse. See reverse for details.

A current American Casino Guide Discount Card must be presented when redeeming this coupon, or offer is void

AMERICAN CASINO GUIDE

GOLD COAST®
HOTEL & CASINO · LAS VEGAS

$10 Match Play

Present this original coupon and B Connected Card to the B Connected Club for a match play voucher. Voucher and equal wager of real chips or cash should be presented to the dealer. See reverse side for details.

A current American Casino Guide Discount Card must be presented when redeeming this coupon, or offer is void

GOLD COAST
HOTEL & CASINO · LAS VEGAS

Gold Coast Hotel & Casino
4000 W. Flamingo Road
Las Vegas, NV 89103
(702) 367-7111 • (800) 331-5334
www.goldcoastcasino.com

Must be 21 or older and have an active B Connected Card. Not valid on Holidays. Earn 200 points playing slots on same day original coupon is presented to B Connected Club to obtain voucher. Limit one coupon per person. Excludes Friday night dinner buffet. This coupon has no cash value, cannot be combined with any other offer or used more than once. Reproduction, sale, barter or transfer are prohibited and render this coupon void. Management reserves the right to change or discontinue this offer without notice. Expires 12/30/18.

americancasinoguide.com

GOLD COAST
HOTEL & CASINO · LAS VEGAS

Gold Coast Hotel & Casino
4000 W. Flamingo Road
Las Vegas, NV 89103
(702) 367-7111 • (800) 331-5334
www.goldcoastcasino.com

Must present B Connected Card with valid ID to redeem. B Connected membership is free. Dining area only. $20 dining credit applied to minimum check total of $40 or more. Valid through December 30, 2018. Excludes holidays. Limit one offer per check. Cannot be combined with any other offer. Gratuity not included. Must be 21 years or older to redeem.

Offer void if coupon is copied or sold

americancasinoguide.com

GOLD COAST
HOTEL & CASINO · LAS VEGAS

Gold Coast Hotel & Casino
4000 W. Flamingo Road
Las Vegas, NV 89103
(702) 367-7111 • (800) 331-5334
www.goldcoastcasino.com

Must be 21 or older and have an active B Connected Card. Limit one coupon per person and limit one coupon per wager. Coupon good for play on any Gold Coast casino table game but excludes live poker. Good for one decision on even-money bets only. Win or lose, coupon is claimed by the house. If you tie then the coupon may be re-bet. This coupon has no cash value, cannot be combined with any other offer or used more than once. Reproduction, sale, barter or transfer are prohibited and render this coupon void. Management reserves the right to change or discontinue this offer without notice. Expires 12/30/18.

Offer void if coupon is copied or sold

AMERICAN CASINO GUIDE

$25 FREE PLAY for earning 200 points

Earn 200 points while playing with your Club 1906 card and receive $25 FREE slot play. Offer valid for new members only. See reverse side for full details.

A current American Casino Guide Discount Card must be presented when redeeming this coupon, or offer is void

AMERICAN CASINO GUIDE

$25 Match Play

Bet $25 on any even-money bet and we'll pay you $50 if you win. Present this coupon at Club 1906 to receive your free $25 match play. See reverse side for full details.

A current American Casino Guide Discount Card must be presented when redeeming this coupon, or offer is void

AMERICAN CASINO GUIDE

GREEN VALLEY RANCH

2-For-1 Buffet

(Monday-Wednesday)

Buy one Feast Buffet and get the second Feast Buffet free. Offer valid Monday-Wednesday. See reverse for more details.

A current American Casino Guide Discount Card must be presented when redeeming this coupon, or offer is void

americancasinoguide.com

One Fremont Street
Las Vegas, NV 89101
(702) 385-1906
Reservations (800) 426-1906

Offer valid for new members only. Voucher must be surrendered to Club 1906 at time of sign-up and required points must be earned the same day. Limit one offer per account. Cannot be used with any other new member offer.

Valid government issued ID required to join Club 1906. Must be 21 or older. Membership is free. Management reserves all rights. No cash value. Offer expires December 29, 2018.

Offer void if coupon is copied or sold

americancasinoguide.com

One Fremont Street
Las Vegas, NV 89101
(702) 385-1906
Reservations (800) 426-1906

Voucher must be surrendered to Club 1906 to receive free match play offer. Good for one bet only, win or lose, (pushes play again). Limit one offer per account per calendar year.

Valid government issued ID required to join Club 1906. Must be 21 or older. Membership is free. Management reserves all rights. No cash value. Offer expires December 29, 2018.

Offer void if coupon is copied or sold

americancasinoguide.com

GREEN VALLEY RANCH

2300 Paseo Verde Pkwy
Las Vegas, NV 89052
(702) 617-7777
www.greenvalleyranch.sclv.com

This voucher entitles bearer to one free breakfast, lunch or dinner in the Feast Buffet when accompanied by a full price, cash paying guest. Tax and gratuity not included. One voucher per person/subscriber. Voucher must be presented to cashier. Vouchers are not transferable and are not redeemable for cash. Must be 21 or older. Not a line pass. Not valid on holidays, Not valid with any other offer. Offer may be changed or discontinued at any time at the discretion of management. Original vouchers only. Offer is void if sold. Offer expires 12/19/18. Settle to: #88-942

Offer void if coupon is copied or sold

AMERICAN CASINO GUIDE

Buy One Get One Free

Present this coupon at any Haagen Dazs shop listed on the back, purchase your choice of any menu item and receive your choice of a second menu item of equal or lesser value free!

A current American Casino Guide Discount Card must be presented when redeeming this coupon, or offer is void

AMERICAN CASINO GUIDE

10% OFF

Redeem at the Harrah's Las Vegas Spa for 10% off any 50-minute spa treatment. See reverse for details.

A current American Casino Guide Discount Card must be presented when redeeming this coupon, or offer is void

AMERICAN CASINO GUIDE

Two FREE Tickets With Drink Purchase

Receive two free tickets to The Mac King Comedy Magic Show with purchase of one drink per person. See reverse for details.

A current American Casino Guide Discount Card must be presented when redeeming this coupon, or offer is void

MGM Grand Hotel - Food Court
New York New York Hotel
Fashion Show Mall

Must present coupon to cashier prior to ordering. Offer has no cash value. Not valid with any other offer. One coupon per person. Subject to change or cancellation without prior notice. Offer valid through December 31, 2018.

Harrah's

3475 Las Vegas Blvd. S.
Las Vegas, NV 89109
702-369-5000
harrahs.com

Valid at The Spa at Harrah's Las Vegas only. Limit 1 treatment per coupon. No cash value. Not valid on previously purchased services. Cannot be combined with any other offer. Subject to availability. Blackout dates may apply, including December 25 through 31. Management reserves all rights. Offer subject to change or cancellation without notification. Offer expires 12/30/18.

Harrah's

3475 Las Vegas Blvd. S.
Las Vegas, NV 89109
702-369-5000
harrahs.com

Show times Tuesday through Saturday at 1 p.m. and 3 p.m. Seating begins 45 minutes before show time. Seating is limited on a space available basis. Present this ticket at the Harrah's Las Vegas Box Office to redeem your free ticket for two. One drink minimum ($10.95 per person/plus tax & gratuity). Offer expires 12/31/18

Additional Offer: Upgrade to VIP Line Pass & VIP Seating for only $6.00 per person and also receive 2-for-1 buffet. Offer expires 12/31/18.

AMERICAN CASINO GUIDE

HOOTERS
Casino Hotel • Las Vegas

Play $10 Get $10 in Free Play

Play $10 on slots or video poker and get $10 in Free Play. $10 in Free Play will be credited to your Rewards Club+ account once you have played $10 on any Hooters Casino slot or video poker machine. See reverse for full Details.

Name____________________ Club #____________________

A current American Casino Guide Discount Card must be presented when redeeming this coupon, or offer is void

AMERICAN CASINO GUIDE

HOOTERS
Casino Hotel • Las Vegas

$10 Match Play for Any Even-Money Table Game Bet

Make a $10 even-money bet at blackjack, craps or roulette with this coupon and your Rewards Club+ and receive a FREE $10 Match Bet! See reverse for full details.

A current American Casino Guide Discount Card must be presented when redeeming this coupon, or offer is void

AMERICAN CASINO GUIDE

HOOTERS
Casino Hotel • Las Vegas

Buy 10 Wings Get 10 FREE!

Present this coupon to your server in Hooters Restaurant at Hooters Casino Hotel to receive 10 FREE wings when you buy 10 wings at regular price. See Reverse for full details.

Offer Code: 30555

A current American Casino Guide Discount Card must be presented when redeeming this coupon, or offer is void

americancasinoguide.com

HOOTERS
Casino Hotel ◆ Las Vegas

115 East Tropicana Avenue
Las Vegas, Nevada 89109
(702) 739-9000
(800) 726-7366
www.hooterscasinohotel.com

Coupon must be presented to Rewards Club+ prior to play beginning. $10 in play must be recorded on Rewards Club+ card. Membership is free. Once the $10 in play threshold on a slot or video poker machines has been met, $10 in Free Play will be downloaded on to your Rewards Club+ card. Free Play must be played through once to cash out. Free Play cannot be used on any Wide Area Progressive machine. Limit one voucher per customer. Offer can only be used once per calendar year. No cash value. Not valid in conjunction with any other offer. Must be 21 years of age or older to redeem. Management reserves the right to alter, change or cancel without notice. A current American Casino Guide Discount Card must be presented when redeeming this coupon or offer is void. Offer expires December 30, 2018.

Offer void if coupon is copied or sold

americancasinoguide.com

HOOTERS
Casino Hotel ◆ Las Vegas

115 East Tropicana Avenue
Las Vegas, Nevada 89109
(702) 739-9000
(800) 726-7366
www.hooterscasinohotel.com

Must be 21 years of age or older and a Rewards Club+ member. Make a $10 minimum even-money bet at any blackjack, craps or roulette game, along with this original coupon (no photocopies), and receive a $10 Match Bet. Good for one decision on even money bets only. Win or lose, coupon is claimed by the house. If you tie, then coupon may be re-bet. No cash value. Limit one voucher per customer. Offer can only be used once per calendar year. Not valid with any other offer. Management reserves the right to alter, change or cancel without notice. Offer expires December 30, 2018.

Offer void if coupon is copied or sold

americancasinoguide.com

HOOTERS
Casino Hotel ◆ Las Vegas

115 East Tropicana Avenue
Las Vegas, Nevada 89109
(702) 739-9000
(800) 726-7366
www.hooterscasinohotel.com

Present this coupon to your server in Hooters Restaurant at Hooters Casino Hotel, Las Vegas. Gratuity not included. Non-transferable. Dine in only. Must be a Rewards Club+ member. One offer per Rewards Club+ member. One offer per table. Offer good at Hooters Restaurant at Hooters Casino in Las Vegas only. Offer valid 24/7. Management reserves the right to alter, change or cancel without notice. Offer expires December 30, 2018.

Offer void if coupon is copied or sold

JERRY'S NUGGET CASINO

$10 Table Games Match Play

Redeem at The MoreClub and receive a $10 table games match play. See reverse for details.

A current American Casino Guide Discount Card must be presented when redeeming this coupon, or offer is void

JERRY'S NUGGET CASINO

$10 Bingo Bucks added to $10 Required Bingo Buy-In

Redeem at The MoreClub and receive $10 bingo bucks added to your $10 bingo buy-in. See reverse for details.

A current American Casino Guide Discount Card must be presented when redeeming this coupon, or offer is void

JERRY'S NUGGET CASINO

$10 Free Slot Play

Redeem at The MoreClub and receive $10 free slot play. See reverse for details.

A current American Casino Guide Discount Card must be presented when redeeming this coupon, or offer is void

JERRY'S NUGGET CASINO

1821 Las Vegas Boulevard North
N. Las Vegas, NV 89030
(702) 399-3000 • www.jerrysnugget.com

Limit one coupon per customer from January 1, 2018 thru December 31, 2018. Must be a MoreClub member. MoreClub membership is free. Present original coupon to The MoreClub and receive a $10 table games match play. No photocopies will be honored. A $10 minimum bet is required. Match play surrendered after first hand. Good for one hand, one wager. Player rating required at time of play. Cannot be redeemed for cash. Not valid with any other offer. Must be 21 years of age or older to redeem. Management reserves all rights. Offer expires December 31, 2018.

JERRY'S NUGGET CASINO

1821 Las Vegas Boulevard North
N. Las Vegas, NV 89030
(702) 399-3000 • www.jerrysnugget.com

Limit one coupon per customer from January 1, 2018 thru December 31, 2018. Must be a MoreClub member. MoreClub membership is free. Present original coupon to The MoreClub and receive $10 bingo bucks at the Jerry's Nugget Bingo Hall with $10 bingo buy-in. No photocopies will be honored. Valid for one bingo session. Minimum $10 bingo buy-in required. Cannot be redeemed for cash. Not valid with any other offer. Must be 21 years of age or older to redeem. Management reserves all rights. Offer expires December 31, 2018.

JERRY'S NUGGET CASINO

1821 Las Vegas Boulevard North
N. Las Vegas, NV 89030
(702) 399-3000 • www.jerrysnugget.com

Limit one coupon per customer from January 1, 2018 thru December 31, 2018. Must be a MoreClub member. MoreClub membership is free. Present original coupon to The MoreClub to receive $10 free slot play. No photo copies will be honored. Free slot play will be activated when you play at any eligible game. Free slot play valid for 48 hours. Cannot be redeemed for cash. Not valid with any other offer. Must be 21 years of age or older to redeem. Management reserves all rights. Offer expires December 31, 2018.

FREE Burger and Milkshake

Present this coupon at any Johnny Rockets listed on the back, purchase any burger and milkshake and receive a second burger and milkshake FREE! See reverse for details.

A current American Casino Guide Discount Card must be presented when redeeming this coupon, or offer is void

AMERICAN CASINO GUIDE

$10 Free Slot Play

Double Your New Member Sign Up Bonus!

Get $10 in FREE slot play when you sign up as a new member at the Klondike Sunset Casino. See reverse for more details.

A current American Casino Guide Discount Card must be presented when redeeming this coupon, or offer is void

AMERICAN CASINO GUIDE

Free Entrée

Receive One Free Entrée at Sarah's Kitchen

Receive one FREE entrée at Sarah's Kitchen located inside the Klondike Sunset Casino. See reverse for more details.

A current American Casino Guide Discount Card must be presented when redeeming this coupon, or offer is void

Fashion Show Mall • Bally's Hotel & Casino
Venetian Hotel Grand Canal Shops • Luxor Food Court
Meadows Mall Food Court • Excalibur Hotel Casino
Flamingo Hotel Food Court • MGM Grand Food Court
Mandalay Bay Food Court

Must present coupon to cashier prior to ordering. Offer has no cash value. Not valid with any other offer. One coupon per person. Subject to change or cancellation without prior notice. Offer valid through December 31, 2018.

Klondike Sunset Casino
444 W. Sunset Rd.
Henderson, NV 89011
702.826.3866
www.klondikesunset.com

Must be 21 years of age or older and present a valid photo ID. Must sign up as a new Player's Club member to receive the offer. Player's Club membership is free. Valid one time only. No cash value. Management reserves all rights. Expires 12/31/18.

Klondike Sunset Casino
444 W. Sunset Rd.
Henderson, NV 89011
702.826.3866
www.klondikesunset.com

Must be a Player's Card member or sign up as a new member to receive the offer. Player's Club membership is free. Does not include beverage or tip. Limit one coupon per customer. Cannot be combined with any other coupon or offer. Management reserves all rights. Must be 21 or older. Expires 12/31/18.

AMERICAN CASINO GUIDE

Buy One Get One Free

Present this coupon at any L.A. Subs, purchase your choice of any sub sandwich or salad and get a second sub sandwich or salad of equal or lesser value free! See reverse for details.

A current American Casino Guide Discount Card must be presented when redeeming this coupon, or offer is void

AMERICAN CASINO GUIDE

2-FOR-1 TICKETS

Redeem at The LINQ Box Office for 2-for-1 tickets to Frank Marino's Divas. See reverse for details.

Offer code: _DBO

A current American Casino Guide Discount Card must be presented when redeeming this coupon, or offer is void

AMERICAN CASINO GUIDE

ameriCAN

beer & cocktails

2-For-1 Cocktail

Present this coupon at ameriCAN to receive two well cocktails for the price of one before 9 p.m. See reverse for details.

A current American Casino Guide Discount Card must be presented when redeeming this coupon, or offer is void

Luxor Food Court
Flamingo Hotel Food Court

Must present coupon to cashier prior to ordering. Offer has no cash value. Not valid with any other offer. One coupon per person. Subject to change or cancellation without prior notice. Offer valid through December 31, 2018.

3535 Las Vegas Blvd. S
Las Vegas, NV 89109
800-351-7400
TheLinqlv.com

Present coupon at time of purchase to redeem. Limit 4 per coupon. Not valid on drink or dining packages. No cash value. Not valid on previously purchased tickets. Cannot be combined with any other offer. Subject to availability. Blackout dates may apply. Management reserves all rights. Offer subject to change or cancellation without notification. Offer expires 12/30/18.

The Promenade at The Linq
3535 S Las Vegas Blvd
Las Vegas, NV 89109

Valid on any well drink. Free drink of equal or lesser value. Gratuity not included. Limit one per person. Coupon has no cash value. May not be combined with any other offer. Must be 21 years of age or older. Management reserves all rights. Expires 12/29/18.

AMERICAN CASINO GUIDE

ameriCAN
beer & cocktails

2-For-1 Draft Beer

Present this coupon at ameriCAN to receive two draft beers for the price of one before 9 p.m. See reverse for details.

A current American Casino Guide Discount Card must be presented when redeeming this coupon, or offer is void

AMERICAN CASINO GUIDE

Buy One Chayo Margarita Get One FREE!

Present this coupon to your server, before ordering, and receive two Chayo Margaritas for the price of one. See reverse for details.

A current American Casino Guide Discount Card must be presented when redeeming this coupon, or offer is void

AMERICAN CASINO GUIDE

$5 Blackjack Matchplay

Present this coupon at any blackjack table, along with your Bigshot Players Club card, prior to the start of a hand and we'll match your bet of $5 if you win. See reverse for details.

A current American Casino Guide Discount Card must be presented when redeeming this coupon, or offer is void

The Promenade at The Linq
3535 S Las Vegas Blvd
Las Vegas, NV 89109

Valid on any draft beer. Free drink of equal or lesser value. Gratuity not included. Limit one per person. Coupon has no cash value. May not be combined with any other offer. Must be 21 years of age or older. Management reserves all rights. Expires 12/29/18.

CHAYO

MEXICAN KITCHEN + TEQUILA BAR

LAS VEGAS

The LINQ Hotel and Casino
3545 S Las Vegas Blvd #4
Las Vegas, NV 89109
(702) 691-3773

Coupon must be presented upon ordering. Must be 21 or older. Gratuity not included. Limit one per person.

Coupon has no cash value. May not be combined with any other offer. Management reserves all rights. Expires 12/29/18.

5288 Boulder Highway
Las Vegas, Nevada 89122
(702) 435-9170
(800) 825-0880

Limit: one coupon per person, per month. Cannot be redeemed for cash. Must be 21 or older. Cannot be combined with any other offer or promotion. Non-transferable. Offer void if sold.

Must present original coupon (no photocopies). Not responsible for lost or stolen coupon. Management reserves all rights. Offer may be changed or discontinued at anytime at the discretion of management. Offer expires 12/29/18.

AMERICAN CASINO GUIDE

$10 Free Play for $5

Present this coupon to cashier cage at Longhorn Casino to receive $10 in Free Play for $5. See reverse for details.

A current American Casino Guide Discount Card must be presented when redeeming this coupon, or offer is void

AMERICAN CASINO GUIDE

Free Ace For Blackjack!

Present this coupon at any blackjack table, along with your Bigshot Players Club card, prior to the start of a hand and your first card will be an ace. See reverse for details.

A current American Casino Guide Discount Card must be presented when redeeming this coupon, or offer is void

AMERICAN CASINO GUIDE

Free Deck of Cards or Dice

Present this coupon at guest services and receive either a free deck of cards or a pair of dice. See reverse for more details.

A current American Casino Guide Discount Card must be presented when redeeming this coupon, or offer is void

americancasinoguide.com

5288 Boulder Highway
Las Vegas, Nevada 89122
(702) 435-9170
(800) 825-0880

Present this voucher to the cashier and receive $10 in free play for just $5. Limit one coupon per account per calendar year. Must present original coupon (no photocopies).

Must be a Bigshot Players Club member and 21 years of age or older. Not valid in conjunction with any other offer. Management reserves the right to cancel or change this offer at any time. Offer expires 12/29/18.

Offer void if coupon is copied or sold

americancasinoguide.com

5288 Boulder Highway
Las Vegas, Nevada 89122
(702) 435-9170
(800) 825-0880

Maximum bet $5. Must be 21 or older. Cannot be combined with any other offer or promotion. Non-transferable. Offer void if sold. Limit: one coupon per person, per month.

Must present original coupon (no photocopies). Not responsible for lost or stolen coupon. Management reserves all rights. Offer may be changed or discontinued at anytime at the discretion of management. Offer expires 12/29/18.

Offer void if coupon is copied or sold

americancasinoguide.com

(702) 399-3297 • (877) 333-9291
3227 Civic Center Drive
N. Las Vegas, NV 89030

Restrictions apply. See Players' club for complete rules. Limit one coupon per customer. Must be a new member. This offer is non-transferable, non refundable and has no cash value. MUST mention ACG. Must present and surrender this coupon upon use. No exceptions. Not available in conjunction with any other offer, Management reserves all rights. Must be 21 or older. Offer subject to change or cancellation at any time without notice. Offer expires December 30, 2018.

Offer void if coupon is copied or sold

AMERICAN CASINO GUIDE

Buy One Entrée Get One Free

(or 50% one entrée when dining alone)

Purchase one entrée at Lucy's Bar & Grill and get a second entrée for FREE, or get 50% off one entrée when dining alone. See reverse for details.

A current American Casino Guide Discount Card must be presented when redeeming this coupon, or offer is void

AMERICAN CASINO GUIDE

$10 Table Games Match Bet

Place a $10 even-money bet with this voucher at Lucky Club, along with your players' card, and get an extra $10 if you win! See reverse for more details.

A current American Casino Guide Discount Card must be presented when redeeming this coupon, or offer is void

AMERICAN CASINO GUIDE

BODIES

THE EXHIBITION

30% Off Admission

Located inside the Luxor Resort, this exhibition showcases real full-bodies and organs, providing a detailed, three-dimensional vision of the human form rarely seen outside of an anatomy lab, or a morgue. Present this coupon at the box office to receive 30% off each adult admission for up to 4 people.

A current American Casino Guide Discount Card must be presented when redeeming this coupon, or offer is void

(702) 399-3297 • (877) 333-9291
3227 Civic Center Drive
N. Las Vegas, NV 89030

Present this original coupon to your server in Lucy's Bar & Grill, along with your My Points Las Vegas Club card, to receive one FREE entree with the purchase of another entree at the regular price, or 50% off a single entree when dining alone. The FREE entree must be of equal or lesser value. Not valid for to-go orders. Limit: one coupon per customer, per month. No cash value. Must be 21 years of age or older. Tax and gratuity not included. Management reserves all rights. Offer expires 12/30/18.

Offer void if coupon is copied or sold

(702) 399-3297 • (877) 333-9291
3227 Civic Center Drive
N. Las Vegas, NV 89030

Present this coupon to Lucky Club Players' Club for redemption. Valid for new and existing members. Limit one per calendar year. Offer is non-transferrable and has no cash value. Offer cannot be combined with any other offer. Management reserves all rights. Must be 21 years or older with a valid form of ID. Offer expires December 30, 2018.

Offer void if coupon is copied or sold

BODIES

THE EXHIBITION

The Bodies exhibition is open daily at 10 a.m. with last admission at 9 p.m. For more information and pricing, please call (800) 557-7428 or visit www.bodiestickets.com. Located in the Luxor Resort on Las Vegas Boulevard (The Strip). Management reserves all rights. Not valid with any other discount. Expires December 31, 2018. **Offer Code: YD**

Offer void if coupon is copied or sold

AMERICAN CASINO GUIDE

FREE Appetizer With Purchase of Two Entrees

Present this coupon to your server when ordering to get a FREE appetizer with the purchase of 2 entrees at Tacos & Tequila located inside the Luxor Las Vegas. See reverse for more details.

A current American Casino Guide Discount Card must be presented when redeeming this coupon, or offer is void

AMERICAN CASINO GUIDE

TITANIC

THE ARTIFACT EXHIBITION

30% Off Admission

Located inside the Luxor Resort, the epic story of the "ship of dreams" is revived through Titanic: The Artifact Exhibition. Present this coupon at the box office to receive 30% off each adult admission for up to 4 people.

A current American Casino Guide Discount Card must be presented when redeeming this coupon, or offer is void

AMERICAN CASINO GUIDE

5X Point Multiplier

Before your play, present this coupon to the B Connected Club for activation. See reverse side for details.

A current American Casino Guide Discount Card must be presented when redeeming this coupon, or offer is void

americancasinoguide.com

3500 Las Vegas Blvd S.
Las Vegas, NV 89109
(702) 262-4555
Luxor.com

Present this coupon to your server when ordering to get a FREE appetizer with the purchase of 2 entrees. Appetizer Sampler not available with this offer. Limit: one coupon per customer, per calendar month. No cash value. Must be 21 years of age or older. Tax and gratuity not included. Resale prohibited. Management reserves all rights. Offer expires 12/30/18.

Offer void if coupon is copied or sold

americancasinoguide.com

TITANIC
THE ARTIFACT EXHIBITION

The Titanic exhibition is open daily at 10 a.m. with last admission at 9 p.m. For more information and pricing, please call (800) 557-7428 or visit www.titanictix.com. Located in the Luxor Resort on Las Vegas Boulevard (The Strip). Management reserves all rights. Not valid with any other discount. Expires December 31, 2018.

Offer Code: YD

Offer void if coupon is copied or sold

americancasinoguide.com

200 North Main Street
Las Vegas, NV 89101
(800) 713-8933
mainstreetcasino.com

Before your play, present this coupon to the B Connected Club for activation. This offer cannot be used in conjunction with any other offer, floor-wide promotion, or event. Point multipliers are not valid on select machines. Max 100,000 bonus promotion points. See B Connected for complete details. Must be 21 or older and have an active B Connected Card. Management reserves all rights. Expires 12/30/18. Offer code: AC185X

Offer void if coupon is copied or sold

AMERICAN CASINO GUIDE

Earn 500 points, Get a Free Buffet (Keep the points)

Earn 500 base points playing slots then present this original coupon and B Connected Card to the B Connected Club, and receive a voucher that will entitle bearer to one FREE dinner buffet at the Garden Court Buffet. Excludes seafood night. See reverse side for details.

A current American Casino Guide Discount Card must be presented when redeeming this coupon, or offer is void

AMERICAN CASINO GUIDE

New Members Play $25 Get $10

Present this coupon when signing up for a new B Connected card to be eligible for Play $25 and Get $10 slot play. See reverse for full details.

A current American Casino Guide Discount Card must be presented when redeeming this coupon, or offer is void

AMERICAN CASINO GUIDE

$5 Off The Perfect Pint Experience

Receive $5 off the Individual Perfect Pint Experience, offered at $20 per person. See reverse for more details.

A current American Casino Guide Discount Card must be presented when redeeming this coupon, or offer is void

americancasinoguide.com

200 North Main Street
Las Vegas, NV 89101
(800) 713-8933
mainstreetcasino.com

Before your play, present this coupon to the B Connected Club for activation. Earn 500 base points playing slots on same day original coupon is presented to the B Connected Club for redemption. Limit one coupon per B Connected account. Excludes Friday night seafood buffet. This coupon has no cash value, cannot be combined with any other offer or used more than once. Reproduction, sale, barter or transfer are prohibited and render this coupon void. Management reserves the right to change or discontinue this offer without notice. Must be 21 or older and have an active B Connected Card. Not valid on holidays. Expires 12/30/18. Offer code: AC18FB

Offer void if coupon is copied or sold

americancasinoguide.com

California Hotel Casino
12 East Ogden Avenue
Las Vegas, NV 89101
(800) 634-6505
thecal.com

Fremont Hotel & Casino
200 Fremont St
Las Vegas, NV 89101
(800) 634-6460
fremontcasino.com

Main Street Station
200 North Main Street
Las Vegas, NV 89101
(800) 713-8933
mainstreetcasino.com

Present this coupon when signing up for a new B Connected card at your choice of casinos- the California, Fremont, or Main Street Station to be eligible for the Play & Get slot play. One Play & Get offer per new B Connected account. Slot play refers to non-cashable downloadable machine credits and will be uploaded to your B Connected account, pin number is required. Slot play is non-transferable and cannot be used with any other offer. You must be 21 or over to participate. Slot play will expire 24 hrs after coupon redemption. Management reserves the right to modify or cancel this promotion without prior notice. See the B Connected Club for additional details. Expires 12/30/2018. Offer code: AC18NM

Offer void if coupon is copied or sold

americancasinoguide.com

The Shoppes at Mandalay Place
3930 Las Vegas Blvd S. #129
Las Vegas, NV 89119
(702) 632-7773

Receive $5 off the Individual Perfect Pint Experience, offered at $20 per person. Guests who take advantage of this offer receive a 20-ounce official Guinness glass filled with a pint of Guinness, personalized certificate and framed photograph. Must be 21 or older. This offer cannot be combined with other promotions. No cash value. Must present original coupon (no photocopies).Management reserves all rights. Valid through 12/30/18.

Offer void if coupon is copied or sold

AMERICAN CASINO GUIDE

10% Off All GUINNESS® Merchandise After Spending $50

Receive a 10% discount on all GUINNESS® official merchandise inside the Guinness Store Las Vegas after spending $50 on full price items only. See reverse for details.

A current American Casino Guide Discount Card must be presented when redeeming this coupon, or offer is void

AMERICAN CASINO GUIDE

Buy One Drink Get One FREE

Buy one drink at the House of Blues Restaurant & Bar and get a second drink FREE. See reverse for full details.

A current American Casino Guide Discount Card must be presented when redeeming this coupon, or offer is void

AMERICAN CASINO GUIDE

Complimentary Hat at HOB Gear Shop

Receive a complimentary baseball cap at the House of Blues Company Store with the purchase of a t-shirt of $30 or more. See reverse for full details.

A current American Casino Guide Discount Card must be presented when redeeming this coupon, or offer is void

americancasinoguide.com

The Shoppes at Mandalay Place
3930 Las Vegas Blvd S. #129
Las Vegas, NV 89119
(702) 632-7773

Receive a 10% discount on all GUINNESS® official merchandise inside the Guinness Store Las Vegas after spending $50 on full price items only. This offer cannot be combined with other promotions. No cash value. Must present original coupon (no photocopies).Management reserves all rights. Valid through 12/30/18.

Offer void if coupon is copied or sold

americancasinoguide.com

Located at
Mandalay Bay Hotel & Casino
3950 Las Vegas Blvd South
Las Vegas, NV 89119
702-632-7600
www.houseofblues.com/lasvegas

Good for one domestic beer, well drink or house wine, valid at the bar only. Free drink must be of equal or lesser value. Must present this coupon when ordering drink. Limit one coupon per customer. Not valid with any other offers or holidays. Offer is non-transferable and has no cash value. Must be 21+ with valid ID. Management reserves all rights. Expires 12/30/18

Offer void if coupon is copied or sold

americancasinoguide.com

Located at
Mandalay Bay Hotel & Casino
3950 Las Vegas Blvd South
Las Vegas, NV 89119
702-632-7600
www.houseofblues.com/lasvegas

T-shirt purchase of $30 or more required. Free baseball cap is a $20 value. Must present this coupon when purchasing retail item. Limit one coupon per customer. Not valid with any other offers. Not valid on previous purchases. Offer is non-transferable and has no cash value. Management reserves all rights. Expires 12/30/18

Offer void if coupon is copied or sold

AMERICAN CASINO GUIDE

Family & Friends
50% Off Adult Ticket
to Gospel Brunch

Present this coupon when booking your Gospel Brunch ticket to receive the 50% discount. See reverse for details.

A current American Casino Guide Discount Card must be presented when redeeming this coupon, or offer is void

AMERICAN CASINO GUIDE

RíRá
IRISH PUB & RESTAURANT

15% Off
Full Price
Menu Items

Present this coupon to your server, before ordering, to receive 15% off full price food items on the Breakfast, Brunch, Lunch, Dinner and Dessert menus. See reverse for more details.

A current American Casino Guide Discount Card must be presented when redeeming this coupon, or offer is void

AMERICAN CASINO GUIDE

CSI:
THE EXPERIENCE®
BUY 1 GET 1 FREE
CODE: ACG

A current American Casino Guide Discount Card must be presented when redeeming this coupon, or offer is void

americancasinoguide.com

Located at
Mandalay Bay Hotel & Casino
3950 Las Vegas Blvd South
Las Vegas, NV 89119
702-632-7600
www.houseofblues.com/lasvegas

Subject to availability. Must present coupon when booking adult Gospel Brunch ticket to receive discounted offer. Limit one coupon per customer. Not valid with any other offers or on holidays. Offer is non-transferable and has no cash value. Management reserves all rights. Expires 12/30/18.

Offer void if coupon is copied or sold

americancasinoguide.com

The Shoppes at
Mandalay Place
3930 Las Vegas Blvd S.
Las Vegas, NV 89119
(702) 632-7771
rira.com/lasvegas

This offer cannot be combined with other promotions. Limit: one coupon per customer, per calendar month.

No cash value. Must be 21 years of age or older. Tax and gratuity not included. Resale prohibited. Management reserves all rights. Offer expires 12/30/18.

Offer void if coupon is copied or sold

americancasinoguide.com

THE EXPERIENCE®
LOCATED INSIDE MGM GRAND

3799 LAS VEGAS BLVD SOUTH
LAS VEGAS, NV 89109
702-891-5749
CSIEXHIBIT.COM

REDEEM COUPON AT CSI: THE EXPERIENCE UPON TICKET PURCHASE. LIMIT 4 PER COUPON. NO CASH VALUE. NOT VALID ON PREVIOUSLY PURCHASED TICKETS. MAY NOT BE COMBINED WITH OTHER OFFERS OR DISCOUNTS. MANAGEMENT RESERVES ALL RIGHTS. OFFER EXPIRES 12/29/2018

Offer void if coupon is copied or sold

AMERICAN CASINO GUIDE

Buy One Get One Free

Present this coupon at any Nathan's listed on the back, purchase your choice of any menu item and receive your choice of a second menu item of equal or lesser value free!

A current American Casino Guide Discount Card must be presented when redeeming this coupon, or offer is void

AMERICAN CASINO GUIDE

Buy One Get One Free

Present this coupon at any New York Pretzel listed on the back, purchase your choice of any menu item and receive your choice of a second menu item of equal or lesser value free!

A current American Casino Guide Discount Card must be presented when redeeming this coupon, or offer is void

AMERICAN CASINO GUIDE

Free Hand Battered Chicken Tenders & Fresh Cut Fries

Present this coupon at Original Chicken Tender, buy any meal and receive a second meal of equal or lesser value free! See reverse for details.

A current American Casino Guide Discount Card must be presented when redeeming this coupon, or offer is void

americancasinoguide.com

MGM Grand Hotel • Flamingo Food Court
New York New York Hotel and Casino
Luxor Hotel • Monte Carlo Food Court
Fashion Show Mall Food Court • Bally's Hotel
Mandalay Bay Hotel and Casino

Must present coupon to cashier prior to ordering. Offer has no cash value. Not valid with any other offer. One coupon per person. Subject to change or cancellation without prior notice. Offer valid through December 31, 2018.

Offer void if coupon is copied or sold

americancasinoguide.com

Venetian Hotel Grand Canal Shoppes
MGM Grand Hotel - Star Lane Mall
New York New York Hotel - MGM Entrance

Must present coupon to cashier prior to ordering. Offer has no cash value. Not valid with any other offer. One coupon per person. Subject to change or cancellation without prior notice. Offer valid through December 31, 2018.

Offer void if coupon is copied or sold

americancasinoguide.com

Luxor Food Court
MGM Grand Food Court

Must present coupon to cashier prior to ordering. Offer has no cash value. Not valid with any other offer. One coupon per person. Subject to change or cancellation without prior notice. Offer valid through December 31, 2018.

Offer void if coupon is copied or sold

AMERICAN CASINO GUIDE

Buy One Breakfast Item Get One Free

Present this coupon at Original Chicken Tender, purchase any breakfast menu item and receive a second breakfast menu item of equal or lesser value FREE! See reverse for details.

A current American Casino Guide Discount Card must be presented when redeeming this coupon, or offer is void

AMERICAN CASINO GUIDE

The ORLEANS℠

HOTEL & CASINO · LAS VEGAS

$10 Table Games Match Play

Present this original coupon and B Connected Card to the B Connected Club for a match play voucher. Voucher and equal wager of real chips or cash should be presented to the dealer. See reverse side for details.

A current American Casino Guide Discount Card must be presented when redeeming this coupon, or offer is void

AMERICAN CASINO GUIDE

HOTEL & CASINO · LAS VEGAS

Two Showroom Tickets For The Price of One

This coupon entitles the bearer to one free ticket of equal value for purchase of one ticket to any show in The Orleans Showroom. Present coupon at The Orleans Showroom box office. See reverse side for details.

A current American Casino Guide Discount Card must be presented when redeeming this coupon, or offer is void

americancasinoguide.com

Luxor Food Court
MGM Grand Food Court

Must present coupon to cashier prior to ordering. Offer has no cash value. Not valid with any other offer. One coupon per person. Subject to change or cancellation without prior notice. Offer valid through December 31, 2018.

Offer void if coupon is copied or sold

americancasinoguide.com

4500 W. Tropicana Ave.
Las Vegas, NV 89103
(702) 365-7111
(800) ORLEANS
www.orleanscasino.com

Must be 21 or older and have an active B Connected Card. Limit one coupon per person and limit one coupon per wager. Coupon good for play on any Orleans casino table game but excludes live poker. Good for one decision on even-money bets only. Win or lose, coupon is claimed by the house. If you tie then the coupon may be re-bet. This coupon has no cash value, cannot be combined with any other offer or used more than once. Reproduction, sale, barter or transfer are prohibited and render this coupon void. Management reserves the right to change or discontinue this offer without notice. Expires 12/30/18.

Offer void if coupon is copied or sold

americancasinoguide.com

4500 W. Tropicana Ave.
Las Vegas, NV 89103
(702) 365-7111
(800) ORLEANS
www.orleanscasino.com

Bearer must be at least 21 years of age and prepared to present a photo ID. Limit one coupon per person. Coupon has no cash value and cannot be combined with any other offer or used more than once. Reproduction, sale, barter and transfer are prohibited and render this coupon void. Management reserves all rights. Offer expires December 31, 2018.

Offer void if coupon is copied or sold

AMERICAN CASINO GUIDE

The ORLEANS℠

HOTEL & CASINO · LAS VEGAS

Get $15 off when you spend $30 in Bailiwick

Present this coupon to your server, before ordering, to get $15 off any check total of $30 or more at Bailiwick, the Hub of Bites, Sips & Sounds. See reverse for details.

A current American Casino Guide Discount Card must be presented when redeeming this coupon, or offer is void

AMERICAN CASINO GUIDE

2-For-1 Buffet

(Monday-Thursday)

Buy one Feast Buffet and get the second Feast Buffet free. Offer valid Monday-Thursday. See reverse for more details.

A current American Casino Guide Discount Card must be presented when redeeming this coupon, or offer is void

AMERICAN CASINO GUIDE

Buy one Two-Entree Meal Get One 50% Off

Present this coupon at Pan Asian Express, purchase any two entree meal and get a second one 50% off! See reverse for details.

A current American Casino Guide Discount Card must be presented when redeeming this coupon, or offer is void

americancasinoguide.com

4500 W. Tropicana Ave.
Las Vegas, NV 89103
(702) 365-7111
(800) ORLEANS
www.orleanscasino.com

Must present B Connected Card with valid ID to redeem. B Connected membership is free. Dining area only. $15 dining credit applied to minimum check total of $30 or more. Valid through December 30, 2018. Excludes holidays. Limit one offer per check. Cannot be combined with any other offer. Gratuity not included. Must be 21 years or older to redeem.

Offer void if coupon is copied or sold

americancasinoguide.com

2411 W Sahara Ave
Las Vegas, NV 89102
(702) 367-2411
www.palacestation.sclv.com

This voucher entitles bearer to one free breakfast, lunch or dinner in the Feast Buffet when accompanied by a cash paying guest. Tax and gratuity not included. One voucher per person/subscriber. Voucher must be presented to cashier. Vouchers are not transferable and are not redeemable for cash. Must be 21 or older. Not a line pass. Not valid on holidays, Not valid with any other offer. Offer may be changed or discontinued at any time at the discretion of management. Original vouchers only. Offer is void if sold. Offer expires December 20, 2018. Settle to: #88-942

Offer void if coupon is copied or sold

americancasinoguide.com

Bally's Hotel & Casino
MGM Grand Food Court
Flamingo Food Court
Mandalay Bay Food Court

Must present coupon to cashier prior to ordering. Offer has no cash value. Not valid with any other offer. One coupon per person. Subject to change or cancellation without prior notice. Offer valid through December 31, 2018.

Offer void if coupon is copied or sold

AMERICAN CASINO GUIDE

EIFFEL TOWER
EXPERIENCE

2-For-1 Daytime Tickets

Redeem at the Paris Box Office for 2-for-1 admission to the Eiffel Tower Ride. See reverse for details.

Offer code: AMCAS2012

A current American Casino Guide Discount Card must be presented when redeeming this coupon, or offer is void

AMERICAN CASINO GUIDE

Anthony Cools

Free Upgrade to VIP Seating

Get a FREE upgrade to VIP seating with the purchase of a regular price ticket to the Anthony Cools Hypnotism show. Valid for up to two tickets. Coupon must be presented at the box office. See back for full details.

A current American Casino Guide Discount Card must be presented when redeeming this coupon, or offer is void

AMERICAN CASINO GUIDE

spice market buffet

20% OFF

Redeem at the Spice Market Buffet to receive 20% OFF admission. See reverse for details.

Offer code: 20BUF

A current American Casino Guide Discount Card must be presented when redeeming this coupon, or offer is void

3655 Las Vegas Blvd. S
Las Vegas, NV 89109
702-946-7000
ParisLasVegas.com

Present coupon at time of purchase to redeem. Limit 4 per coupon. Offer is only good on daytime tickets. No cash value. Not valid on previously purchased tickets or Express Pass Tickets. Cannot be combined with any other offer. Subject to availability. Service fees apply. Blackout dates may apply. Management reserves all rights. Offer subject to change or cancellation without notification. Offer expires 12/30/18

Paris Las Vegas Casino & Hotel
3655 Las Vegas Boulevard S.
Las Vegas, NV 89109
(702) 946-7000 or visit
www.parislasvegas.com

Subject to availability. Show times subject to change. Offers cannot be combined. Coupon must be presented at time of purchase and is only available through the box office. Management reserves all rights. Not for resale. Valid through 12/30/18. Offer Code: AMCAS2014

3667 Las Vegas Blvd S
Las Vegas, NV 89109
702-785-5555
planethollywoodresort.com

Valid at Planet Hollywood Casino and Hotel only. Must present physical coupon to cashier for redemption. Not valid in conjunction with Buffet of Buffets®. Maximum four (4) discounts per coupon. Gratuity not included. Valid at designated restaurant only. Subject to availability. Not valid for take-out. Blackout dates may apply including holidays. Valid picture ID required. Offer is non-transferable. Cannot be used in conjunction with any other offer or promotion. Must be at least 21 years of age. No exchanges, replacements, substitutions or trade-outs. Any attempt to sell, auction or otherwise transfer shall nullify this offer. Additional restrictions may apply. Management reserves all rights. Trademarks used herein are owned by Caesars License Company, LLC and its affiliated companies. Must be 21 or older to gamble. Know When To Stop Before You Start.® Gambling Problem? Call 1-800-522-4700. ©2015. **Offer expires 12/30/18**

V THEATER SAXE THEATER

2-for-1 Show Tickets

Offer valid for the following shows:

VEGAS! THE SHOW • V - The Ultimate Variety Show • Zombie Burlesque
The Mentalist • Beatleshow Orchestra

Present this coupon when you buy 1 full price General Admission ticket and receive a second ticket of equal or lesser value FREE (or 50% off the price of a retail show ticket). See back for full details.

ACGF4ADG-001

A current American Casino Guide Discount Card must be presented when redeeming this coupon, or offer is void

2-For-1 Cocktail or Draft Beer

Present this coupon at PBR Rock Bar to receive two well cocktails or domestic draft beers for the price of one before 9pm. See reverse for details.

A current American Casino Guide Discount Card must be presented when redeeming this coupon, or offer is void

AMERICAN CASINO GUIDE

Free Appetizer with Purchase of Two Entrées

Present this coupon to your server before ordering to receive one complimentary appetizer with the purchase of two entrées at PBR Rock Bar & Grill.
See reverse for more details.

A current American Casino Guide Discount Card must be presented when redeeming this coupon, or offer is void

americancasinoguide.com

V THEATER **SAXE THEATER**

In the Miracle Mile Shops at Planet Hollywood - 3663 Las Vegas Blvd.
For show information call (866) 932-1818

Valid on General Admission only, upgrades available at the box office. May not be combined with any other offer or applied to prior purchase. Applicable tax & service fees will apply. No cash value. Subject to availability, management reserves all rights. Offer only valid at the V Theater & Saxe Theater Box Office. Offer expires December 31, 2018.

Offer void if coupon is copied or sold

americancasinoguide.com

Miracle Mile Shops at Planet Hollywood
3663 S Las Vegas Blvd #730
Las Vegas, Nevada 89109

Valid on any well drink, or domestic draft beer. Free drink of equal or lesser value. Gratuity not included. Limit one per person. Coupon has no cash value. May not be combined with any other offer. Must be 21 years of age or older. Management reserves all rights. Expires 12/29/18.

Offer void if coupon is copied or sold

americancasinoguide.com

Miracle Mile Shops at Planet Hollywood
3663 S Las Vegas Blvd #730
Las Vegas, Nevada 89109

Blackout dates apply. Gratuity not included. Limit one coupon per table. Coupon has no cash value. May not be combined with any other offer. Must be 21 years of age or older. Management reserves all rights. Expires 12/29/18.

Offer void if coupon is copied or sold

AMERICAN CASINO GUIDE

2-for-1 Vegas Nightclub Pass

Present this coupon to the V Theater or Saxe Theater Box office to get two V Card Vegas Nightclub Passes for the price of one. See reverse for full details.

A current American Casino Guide Discount Card must be presented when redeeming this coupon, or offer is void

AMERICAN CASINO GUIDE

Buy One Milkshake Get One Free

Present this coupon at Brightside Breakfast & Burgers, before ordering, to get one free milkshake, when you buy one at the regular price. See reverse for details

A current American Casino Guide Discount Card must be presented when redeeming this coupon, or offer is void

AMERICAN CASINO GUIDE

50% Off Pizza

Present this coupon at Pop Up Pizza, before ordering, to receive 50% off the price of one menu item. See reverse for details.

A current American Casino Guide Discount Card must be presented when redeeming this coupon, or offer is void

In the Miracle Mile Shops at Planet Hollywood - 3663 Las Vegas Blvd.
For information call (866) 932-1818 or visit vcardlasvegas.com

Please present this coupon to the V Theater or Saxe Theater Box office to receive one V Card Vegas Nightclub Pass with the purchase of another at full price. Not valid with any other offer or applied to prior purchase. Management reserves all rights. Box office hours 9 a.m. - 9 p.m. Offer expires December 30, 2018.

HOTEL • CASINO • BINGO

1 Main Street
Las Vegas, NV 89101
(702) 386-2110
(800) 634-6575
www.PlazaHotelCasino.com

Purchase one milkshake to receive a second one, of equal or lesser value, free. Gratuity not included. Limit one per person. Coupon has no cash value. May not be combined with any other offers or promotions. Management reserves all rights. Offer expires 12/29/18

Settle to #89219

HOTEL • CASINO • BINGO

1 Main Street
Las Vegas, NV 89101
(702) 386-2110
(800) 634-6575
www.PlazaHotelCasino.com

Valid for dine in only. Gratuity not included. May not be combined with any other offer or promotion. Must present coupon before ordering. Coupon has no cash value. Management reserves all rights. Offer expires 12/29/18.

AMERICAN CASINO GUIDE

FREE 777 Slot Tournament Entry

(10 a.m. Session Only)

Present coupon at the Royal Rewards Center for FREE entry into 10 a.m. 777 Slot Tournament. See reverse for details.

A current American Casino Guide Discount Card must be presented when redeeming this coupon, or offer is void

AMERICAN CASINO GUIDE

$10 Match Play

Redeem this coupon at the Royal Rewards Center for validation. See reverse for details.

A current American Casino Guide Discount Card must be presented when redeeming this coupon, or offer is void

AMERICAN CASINO GUIDE

Free Glass of Wine at Oscar's Beef-Booze-Broads

Redeem this coupon at Oscar's for a free glass of wine with a purchase of an entrée. Reservations recommended. See reverse for details.

A current American Casino Guide Discount Card must be presented when redeeming this coupon, or offer is void

americancasinoguide.com

1 Main Street
Las Vegas, NV 89101
(702) 386-2110
(800) 634-6575
www.PlazaHotelCasino.com

Must be a Royal Rewards members. Valid for same day of joining club only for one time redemption. Tournament held every Wednesday, Thursday and Friday. Prizes paid in Free Slot Play to 1st-5th Place. Management reserves all rights. See Royal Rewards Center for additional details. Offer expires 12/29/18.

Offer void if coupon is copied or sold

americancasinoguide.com

1 Main Street
Las Vegas, NV 89101
(702) 386-2110
(800) 634-6575
www.PlazaHotelCasino.com

Valid coupon with Royal Rewards card required for redemption. Coupon must be in its original format and may not be copied in any way. Present validated voucher to any table game prior to the start of the hand. Valid on straight up Blackjack, Craps & Roulette. Valid for even money bets only. Coupons are nontransferable and cannot be combined. Must be 21 years of age or older. No cash value. Win or lose, coupon is claimed by the house. If you tie, coupon may be re-bet. Management reserves all rights. Offer expires 12/29/18

Offer void if coupon is copied or sold

americancasinoguide.com

1 Main Street
Las Vegas, NV 89101
(702) 386-2110
(800) 634-6575
www.PlazaHotelCasino.com

Coupon must be surrendered to server before ordering. Must be 21 or older to redeem. Gratuity not included. Coupon only valid with purchase of an entrée. House wine only. Not applicable to group bookings. May not be combined with any other offer. Coupon has no cash value. Management reserves all rights. Offer expires 12/29/18.

Offer void if coupon is copied or sold

AMERICAN CASINO GUIDE

2-For-1 Drink

Redeem this coupon at any casino bar.
See reverse for details.

A current American Casino Guide Discount Card must be presented when redeeming this coupon, or offer is void

AMERICAN CASINO GUIDE

$10 Match Play for Any Even-Money Table Game Bet

Make a $10 even-money bet on blackjack, craps or roulette with this coupon and your Rampart Rewards card and receive a $10 Match Bet! See reverse for details.

A current American Casino Guide Discount Card must be presented when redeeming this coupon, or offer is void

AMERICAN CASINO GUIDE

2-For-1 Buffet

(or 50% off when dining alone)

Buy one buffet and get a second one FREE (or 50% off when dining alone). When using as 2-for-1 coupon both buffets must be redeemed on same visit. See reverse for more details.

A current American Casino Guide Discount Card must be presented when redeeming this coupon, or offer is void

1 Main Street
Las Vegas, NV 89101
(702) 386-2110
(800) 634-6575
www.PlazaHotelCasino.com

Valid on well drinks, domestic beers, house wines, soda or water. Free drink of equal or lesser value. Gratuity not included. Limit one per person. Must be 21 years of age or older. Coupon has no cash value. May not be combined with any other offers or promotions. Management reserves all rights. Settle to #82200. Offer expires 12/29/18.

221 N. Rampart Boulevard
Las Vegas, NV 89128
(702) 507-5900
(877) 869-8777
www.RampartCasino.com

Must be 21 or older and a Rampart Rewards member. Make a $10 even-money bet at any blackjack, craps or roulette game, with this original coupon (no photocopies), and your Rampart Rewards card to receive a $10 Match Bet. Good for one decision on even money bets only. Win or lose, coupon is claimed by the house. If you tie, then coupon may be re-bet. No cash value. Limit: one coupon per customer, per year. Not valid with any other offer. Management reserves all rights. Valid through 12/30/18.

221 N. Rampart Boulevard
Las Vegas, NV 89128
(702) 507-5900
(877) 869-8777
www.RampartCasino.com

Present this coupon to the cashier at time of purchase. Must be 21 or older to reeem. Tax and gratuity not included. Coupon not redeemable for cash. Must have Rampart Rewards card. Original coupon (no photocopies) must be presented to the cashier. One coupon per customer. Not valid with any other coupon or offer. Management reserves all rights. Valid through 12/30/18.

AMERICAN CASINO GUIDE

30% Off Spa

Redeem at Spa Aquae at the Rampart Casino for 30% off any spa treatment. See reverse for details.

A current American Casino Guide Discount Card must be presented when redeeming this coupon, or offer is void

AMERICAN CASINO GUIDE

red rock

CASINO · RESORT · SPA

2-For-1 Buffet

(Monday-Thursday)

Buy one Feast Buffet and get the second Feast Buffet free. Offer valid Monday-Thursday. See reverse for more details.

A current American Casino Guide Discount Card must be presented when redeeming this coupon, or offer is void

AMERICAN CASINO GUIDE

CARNIVAL WORLD & SEAFOOD BUFFET

$5 Off

Redeem at the Carnival World Buffet® at Rio Las Vegas for $5 off buffet admission. See reverse for details.

Offer code: CB5TZ

A current American Casino Guide Discount Card must be presented when redeeming this coupon, or offer is void

americancasinoguide.com

221 N. Rampart Boulevard
Las Vegas, NV 89128
(702) 507-5900
(877) 869-8777
www.RampartCasino.com

Limit one treatment per coupon. No cash value. Not valid on previously purchased services or on waxing. Cannot be combined with any other offer, package or discount. Subject to availability. Blackout dates may apply. Management reserves all rights. Offer subject to change or cancellation without notification. Valid through 12/30/18.

Offer void if coupon is copied or sold

americancasinoguide.com

11011 W Charleston Blvd
Las Vegas, NV 89135
(702) 797-7777
www.redrock.sclv.com

This voucher entitles bearer to one free breakfast, lunch or dinner in the Feast Buffet when accompanied by a full price, cash paying guest. Tax and gratuity not included. One voucher per person/subscriber. Voucher must be presented to cashier. Vouchers are not transferable and are not redeemable for cash. Must be 21 or older. Not a line pass. Not valid on holidays, Not valid with any other offer. Offer may be changed or discontinued at any time at the discretion of management. Original vouchers only. Offer is void if sold. Offer expires 12/20/18. Settle to: #88-942

Offer void if coupon is copied or sold

americancasinoguide.com

3700 W. Flamingo Rd.
Las Vegas, NV 89103
702-777-7777
RioLasVegas.com

Present coupon at time of purchase to redeem. Limit 4 per coupon. Excludes Buffet of Buffets passes. No cash value. Not valid on previously purchased tickets. Cannot be combined with any other offer. Subject to availability. Blackout dates may apply. Management reserves all rights. Offer subject to change or cancellation without notification. Offer expires 12/30/18

Offer void if coupon is copied or sold

AMERICAN CASINO GUIDE

VOODOO
STEAK

$10 Off Entrée

Redeem at Voodoo Steak at Rio Las Vegas for $10 off your entrée. See reverse for details.

Offer code: ACGR1

A current American Casino Guide Discount Card must be presented when redeeming this coupon, or offer is void

AMERICAN CASINO GUIDE

2-FOR-1 TICKETS

Redeem at the Rio Box Office for 2-for-1 tickets to X Rocks. See reverse for details.

A current American Casino Guide Discount Card must be presented when redeeming this coupon, or offer is void

AMERICAN CASINO GUIDE

SAM'S TOWN®

Earn 200 points, Get a Free Buffet

(Keep the points)

Earn 200 points playing slots then present this original coupon and B Connected Card to the B Connected Club, and receive a voucher that will entitle bearer to one FREE breakfast, lunch or regular dinner buffet. See reverse side for details.

A current American Casino Guide Discount Card must be presented when redeeming this coupon, or offer is void

3700 W. Flamingo Rd.
Las Vegas, NV 89103
702-777-7777
RioLasVegas.com

Minimum purchase of 2 entrees. Tax & gratuity not included. No cash value. Not valid on previously purchased services. Cannot be combined with any other offer. Subject to availability. Blackout dates may apply. Management reserves all rights. Offer subject to change or cancellation without notification. Offer expires 12/30/18

americancasinoguide.com

3700 W. Flamingo Rd.
Las Vegas, NV 89103
702-777-7777
RioLasVegas.com

Present coupon at time of purchase to redeem. Must be 18 or older. Limit 4 per coupon. No cash value. Not valid on previously purchased tickets. Cannot be combined with any other offer. Subject to availability. Blackout dates may apply. Management reserves all rights. Offer subject to change or cancellation without notification. Offer expires 12/30/18

Offer void if coupon is copied or sold

americancasinoguide.com

Sam's Town Hotel & Gambling Hall
5111 Boulder Highway
Las Vegas, NV 89122
(702) 456-7777 • (800) 897-8696
www.samstownlv.com

Must be 21 or older and have an active B Connected Card. Not valid on Holidays. Earn 200 points playing slots on same day original coupon is presented to B Connected Club to obtain voucher. Limit one coupon per person. Excludes specialty night dinners and brunch. This coupon has no cash value, cannot be combined with any other offer or used more than once. Reproduction, sale, barter or transfer are prohibited and render this coupon void. Management reserves the right to change or discontinue this offer without notice. Expires 12/30/18

Offer void if coupon is copied or sold

AMERICAN CASINO GUIDE

SAM'S TOWN®

Two FREE Drinks at any Casino Bar For NEW Members

Present this coupon when signing up for a new B Connected Card to receive two FREE well, call or draft beers at any casino bar. See reverse for more details.

Offer Validation Stamp Here

A current American Casino Guide Discount Card must be presented when redeeming this coupon, or offer is void

AMERICAN CASINO GUIDE

SAM'S TOWN®

One FREE Room Night

Pay for two nights and get a third night FREE! Good Sunday through Thursday. Holidays and convention periods excluded. Blackout dates may apply. Subject to availability. For reservations call 1-800-634-6371 and ask for offer "ACG18"

A current American Casino Guide Discount Card must be presented when redeeming this coupon, or offer is void

AMERICAN CASINO GUIDE

2-For-1 Buffet

(Monday-Thursday)

Buy one Feast Buffet and get the second Feast Buffet free. Offer valid Monday-Thursday. See reverse for more details.

A current American Casino Guide Discount Card must be presented when redeeming this coupon, or offer is void

americancasinoguide.com

SAM'S TOWN®

Sam's Town Hotel & Gambling Hall
5111 Boulder Highway
Las Vegas, NV 89122
(702) 456-7777 • (800) 897-8696
www.samstownlv.com

Present this coupon when signing up for a new B Connected card to receive two free well, call or draft beers at any casino bar. Must be 21 years of age or older. Coupon cannot be used in conjunction with any other offer. Management reserves right to change or cancel offer at any time. Must present B Connected Card with coupon for redemption. Coupon has no cash value. Expires 12/30/18. One per customer.

AM85994

Offer void if coupon is copied or sold

americancasinoguide.com

SAM'S TOWN®

Sam's Town Hotel & Gambling Hall
5111 Boulder Highway
Las Vegas, NV 89122
(702) 456-7777 • (800) 897-8696
www.samstownlv.com

This voucher entitles the bearer to one free room night at Sam's Town Hotel & Casino, with the purchase of two nights at the prevailing rate. Must have advance reservations. Must present voucher upon check-in. Not valid in conjunction with any other offer. Management reserves the right to cancel this promotion at any time. Credit card or cash deposit required. Guest is responsible for all incidental charges. Must be 21 or older. Limit one free room per person. Offer expires 12/28/18

Offer void if coupon is copied or sold

americancasinoguide.com

4949 N Rancho Dr
Las Vegas, NV 89130
(702) 658-4900
www. santafestation.sclv.com

This voucher entitles bearer to one free breakfast, lunch or dinner in the Feast Buffet when accompanied by a cash paying guest. Tax and gratuity not included. One voucher per person/subscriber. Voucher must be presented to cashier. Vouchers are not transferable and are not redeemable for cash. Must be 21 or older. Not a line pass. Not valid on holidays or specialty nights. Not valid with any other offer. Offer may be changed or discontinued at any time at the discretion of management. Original vouchers only. Offer is void if sold. Offer expires December 20, 2018. Settle to: #88-942

Offer void if coupon is copied or sold

AMERICAN CASINO GUIDE

SILVER NUGGET CASINO

Buy One Entrée Get One Free

(or 50% one entrée when dining alone)

Purchase one entrée at the Hometown Kitchen and get a second entrée for FREE, or get 50% off one entrée when dining alone. See reverse for details.

A current American Casino Guide Discount Card must be presented when redeeming this coupon, or offer is void

AMERICAN CASINO GUIDE

SILVER NUGGET CASINO

Free Deck of Cards or Dice

Present this coupon at guest services and receive either a free deck of cards or a pair of dice. See reverse for more details.

A current American Casino Guide Discount Card must be presented when redeeming this coupon, or offer is void

AMERICAN CASINO GUIDE

$10 Table Games Match Bet

Place a $10 even-money bet with this voucher at Silver Nugget, along with your players' card, and get an extra $10 if you win! See reverse for more details.

A current American Casino Guide Discount Card must be presented when redeeming this coupon, or offer is void

CASINO

2140 Las Vegas Blvd. N.
N. Las Vegas, Nevada 89030
(702) 399-1111

Present this original coupon to your server in the Hometown Kitchen, along with your My Points Las Vegas Club card, to receive one FREE entree with the purchase of another entree at the regular price, or 50% off a single entree when dining alone. The FREE entree must be of equal or lesser value. Not valid for to-go orders. Limit: one coupon per customer, per month. No cash value. Must be 21 years of age or older. Tax and gratuity not included. Management reserves all rights. Offer expires 12/30/18.

americancasinoguide.com

CASINO

2140 Las Vegas Blvd. N.
N. Las Vegas, Nevada 89030
(702) 399-1111

Restrictions apply. See Players' club for complete rules. Limit one coupon per customer. Must be a new member. This offer is non-transferable, non refundable and has no cash value. MUST mention ACG. Must present and surrender this coupon upon use. No exceptions. Not available in conjunction with any other offer, Management reserves all rights. Must be 21 or older. Offer subject to change or cancellation at any time without notice. Offer expires 12/30/18.

Offer void if coupon is copied or sold

americancasinoguide.com

CASINO

2140 Las Vegas Blvd. N.
N. Las Vegas, Nevada 89030
(702) 399-1111

Present this coupon to Silver Nugget Players' Club for redemption. Valid for new and existing members. Limit one per calendar year. Offer is non-transferrable and has no cash value. Offer cannot be combined with any other offer. Management reserves all rights. Must be 21 years or older with a valid form of ID. Offer expires December 30, 2018.

Offer void if coupon is copied or sold

AMERICAN CASINO GUIDE

SILVER SEVENS
HOTEL & CASINO

Buy One Dinner Buffet
Get One Free
(or 50% off when dining alone)

Purchase one dinner buffet at the S7 Buffet and get the second one free, or get 50% off one buffet when dining alone. See reverse for details.

A current American Casino Guide Discount Card must be presented when redeeming this coupon, or offer is void

AMERICAN CASINO GUIDE

SILVER SEVENS
HOTEL & CASINO

Buy One Entrée
Get One Free
(or 50% off one entrée when dining alone)

Purchase one entrée at the Sterling Spoon Café and get a second entrée for FREE, or get 50% off one entrée when dining alone. See reverse for details.

A current American Casino Guide Discount Card must be presented when redeeming this coupon, or offer is void

AMERICAN CASINO GUIDE

2-For-1
Seasons Buffet
(or 50% off when dining alone)

Must be a Silverton Rewards Club member. Must purchase one Seasons buffet at regular price, to receive a second buffet, of equal or lesser value, for free. Good for one time use only. See reverse for more details.

A current American Casino Guide Discount Card must be presented when redeeming this coupon, or offer is void

SILVER SEVENS
HOTEL & CASINO
Not your average VEGAS

4100 Paradise Rd
Las Vegas, NV 89169
(702) 733-7000
www.silversevenscasino.com

Present A-Play Club coupon and A-Play® Club Card at the buffet or cafe when paying for meal. Must be 21 years or older. Tax and gratuity not included. Complimentary value up to $19.99. Void if copied. Limit one coupon per day, per party. No cash value. May not be combined with any other coupon offer or discount; full retail pricing applies. Management reserves the right to cancel or discontinue this offer without prior notice. Not valid without A-Play® Club Card. Settle to: 464. Offer Expires 12/28/18.

americancasinoguide.com

SILVER SEVENS
HOTEL & CASINO
Not your average VEGAS

4100 Paradise Rd
Las Vegas, NV 89169
(702) 733-7000
www.silversevenscasino.com

Present A-Play Club coupon and A-Play® Club Card at the buffet or cafe when paying for meal. Must be 21 years or older. Tax and gratuity not included. Receive one FREE entrée of equal or lesser value with the purchase of one entrée at regular price or receive 50% off one entrée. Limit one coupon per day, per party. No cash value. May not be combined with any other coupon offer or discount; full retail pricing applies. Management reserves the right to cancel or discontinue this offer without prior notice. Not valid without A-Play® Club Card. Settle to: 465. Offer Expires 12/28/18.

Offer void if coupon is copied or sold

americancasinoguide.com

SILVERTON
Casino • Hotel • Las Vegas

Silverton Casino Hotel
3333 Blue Diamond Road
Las Vegas, NV 89139
www.silvertoncasino.com
702-263-7777 • 866-946-4373

Receive one FREE lunch, brunch or dinner buffet with the purchase of a second lunch, brunch or dinner buffet at regular price. Must be a Silverton Rewards Club member. Good for one time use only. Present this original coupon to the cashier along with your Silverton Rewards card to the cashier at Seasons Buffet. Coupon has no cash value, cannot be combined with any other offer or promotion and is non-transferable. Not valid on holidays. Management reserves all rights. Must be 21 years or older with a valid form of ID. Offer does not include gratuity. Offer is void if sold. Settle to #D148 Expires 12/30/18.

Offer void if coupon is copied or sold

AMERICAN CASINO GUIDE

Free Starter With Purchase Of An Entree

Present this coupon along with your Silverton Rewards card and valid photo ID at WuHu Noodle to redeem. See reverse for more details.

A current American Casino Guide Discount Card must be presented when redeeming this coupon, or offer is void

AMERICAN CASINO GUIDE

SLS LAS VEGAS®

HOTEL & CASINO

$25 Match Play

Place a $25 even-money bet and get an extra $25 if you win! Visit the Club 52 Desk to receive this offer. See reverse side for more details.

A current American Casino Guide Discount Card must be presented when redeeming this coupon, or offer is void

AMERICAN CASINO GUIDE

SLS LAS VEGAS®

HOTEL & CASINO

Earn 250 slot points, get $10 FREE play

Get $10 FREE play when you earn 250 slot points. Visit the Club 52 Desk to receive this offer. See reverse side for more details.

A current American Casino Guide Discount Card must be presented when redeeming this coupon, or offer is void

Silverton Casino Hotel
3333 Blue Diamond Road
Las Vegas, NV 89139
www.silvertoncasino.com
702-263-7777 • 866-946-4373

Present this coupon along with your Silverton Rewards card and valid photo ID at WuHu Noodle to redeem. Maximum value $10. Offer is valid for one Starter item with purchase of an entrée. Offer cannot be combined with other offers or promotions. Valid for one use through December 28, 2018. Must be 21 years or older. Management reserves all rights. Settle to # D148.

SLS LAS VEGAS®
HOTEL & CASINO

CLUB 52

2535 S Las Vegas Blvd., Las Vegas, NV 89109 • (702) 761-7000 • www.slslasvegas.com

Visit the Club 52 Desk to receive offer. Must be a Club 52 member and 21 years of age to qualify. Guest must swipe at any casino kiosk to print out match play offer after showing coupon to the Club 52 Desk. Guest must place a bet with their own money equal to the Match Play and the casino will pay the equivalent of the voucher and the player's matched chip(s) on a winning bet. Match Play is only valid for a single bet, win or lose, and only on even money bets only. Limit one Match Play per person. Offer valid one time January 1, 2018 – December 31, 2018. Management reserves all rights.

SLS LAS VEGAS®
HOTEL & CASINO

CLUB 52

2535 S Las Vegas Blvd., Las Vegas, NV 89109 • (702) 761-7000 • www.slslasvegas.com

Visit the Club 52 Desk to receive offer. Must be a Club 52 member and 21 years of age to qualify. Slot Points must be earned the same day of promotion enrollment. Guest must swipe at any casino kiosk to accept offer after showing coupon to the Club 52 Desk. Upon earning slot points, guest must swipe at kiosk to receive free play offer. Offer valid one time January 1, 2018 – December 31, 2018. Management reserves all rights.

AMERICAN CASINO GUIDE

Earn 300 points, Get Free Buffet (Keep the points)

Earn 300 points playing slots then present this original coupon and players club card to the players club, and receive a voucher that will entitle bearer to one FREE breakfast, lunch or regular dinner buffet. See reverse side for details.

A current American Casino Guide Discount Card must be presented when redeeming this coupon, or offer is void

AMERICAN CASINO GUIDE

FREE Appetizer With Purchase of Entrée at Don Vito's

Present this coupon to your server when ordering to get a FREE appetizer with the purchase of an entrée at Don Vito's Italian Restaurant located inside the South Point. See reverse for more details.

A current American Casino Guide Discount Card must be presented when redeeming this coupon, or offer is void

AMERICAN CASINO GUIDE

STRATOSPHERE
HOTEL | CASINO | TOWER

Two-For-One Tower Admission Tickets

Get one FREE Tower Admission ticket with the purchase of one Tower Admission ticket at full price.
(See back for full details.)

2000 Las Vegas Blvd. S. • Las Vegas, NV 89104 • 800.99.TOWER • 702.380.7777

A current American Casino Guide Discount Card must be presented when redeeming this coupon, or offer is void

americancasinoguide.com

9777 S Las Vegas Blvd
Las Vegas, NV 89183
(702) 796-7111• (866) 791-7626
www.southpointcasino.com

Must be 21 or older and have an active The Club Card. Not valid on Holidays. Earn 300 points playing slots on same day original coupon is presented to The Club to obtain voucher. Limit one coupon per person. Excludes brunch and seafood buffets. Gratuity not included. This coupon has no cash value, cannot be combined with any other offer or used more than once. Reproduction, sale, barter or transfer are prohibited and render this coupon void. Management reserves the right to change or discontinue this offer without notice. Expires 12/30/18. **Coupon Code 6452**

Offer void if coupon is copied or sold

americancasinoguide.com

9777 S Las Vegas Blvd
Las Vegas, NV 89183
(702) 796-7111• (866) 791-7626
www.southpointcasino.com

Present this coupon to your server when ordering to get a FREE appetizer with the purchase of one entrée. Limit: one coupon per customer, per calendar month. No cash value. Must be 21 years of age or older. Tax and gratuity not included. Resale prohibited. Management reserves all rights. Offer expires 12/30/18. **Coupon Code 6453**

Offer void if coupon is copied or sold

americancasinoguide.com

STRATOSPHERE

HOTEL | **CASINO** | TOWER

OFFER CODE: ACG_TWR

To view special offers, go to StratosphereHotel.com
(Coupon must be presented at the Stratosphere Ticket Center.)

Management reserves all rights. Valid through December 30, 2018. Must be at least 18 years of age unless accompanied by an adult. Subject to availability. Offers cannot be combined. Not for resale. Offer void if coupon is copied or sold.

Blackout dates apply. Not available on New Year's Eve.

Offer void if coupon is copied or sold

AMERICAN CASINO GUIDE

2-For-1
Breakfast or
Lunch Buffet
(or 50% off when dining alone)

Buy one breakfast or lunch buffet and get a second one FREE (or 50% off when dining alone). Offer valid Monday–Saturday. Coupon has no cash value, must be 21 years of age or older. Must be a B Connected member to redeem. See reverse for full details.

A current American Casino Guide Discount Card must be presented when redeeming this coupon, or offer is void

AMERICAN CASINO GUIDE

5X
Points!

Present this coupon to the B Connected Club and receive 5X points for one day's play from 12:01am-11:59pm. See reverse for more details.

A current American Casino Guide Discount Card must be presented when redeeming this coupon, or offer is void

AMERICAN CASINO GUIDE

2-For-1
Buffet
(Monday-Thursday)

Buy one Feast Buffet and get the second Feast Buffet free. Offer valid Monday-Thursday. See reverse for more details.

A current American Casino Guide Discount Card must be presented when redeeming this coupon, or offer is void

americancasinoguide.com

HOTEL & CASINO · LAS VEGAS

(702) 636-7111 • 1-877-677-7111
9090 Alta Dr
www.suncoastcasino.com

Present this coupon to St. Tropez Buffet cashier. Tax and Gratuity is not included Original coupon (no photocopies) must be presented at the time of purchase. This offer is not valid with any other offer or promotion and is not valid on holidays. This offer is void if sold. Management reserves the right to change or cancel this offer at anytime. Offer expires 12/20/18

Offer Code: SBFAO14L6

B Connected Membership # ______________________________

Offer void if coupon is copied or sold

americancasinoguide.com

HOTEL & CASINO · LAS VEGAS

(702) 636-7111 • 1-877-677-7111
9090 Alta Dr
www.suncoastcasino.com

Present this coupon to the B Connected Club with your B Connected Membership card. This offer cannot be used with any other offer or point multiplier offer. Must be 21 years of age. Maximum 100,000 points. Management reserves the right to change or cancel this offer at any time. Limit one coupon per person. Offer Expires 12/20/18

Group Codes: 5XAMER16E 5XAMER16R 5XAMERI6S

Offer void if coupon is copied or sold

americancasinoguide.com

1301 W Sunset Rd
Henderson, NV 89014
(702) 547-7715
www.sunsetstation.sclv.com

This voucher entitles bearer to one free breakfast, lunch or dinner in the Feast Buffet when accompanied by a cash paying guest. Tax and gratuity not included. One voucher per person/subscriber. Voucher must be presented to cashier. Vouchers are not transferable and are not redeemable for cash. Must be 21 or older. Not a line pass. Not valid on holidays, Not valid with any other offer. Offer may be changed or discontinued at any time at the discretion of management. Original vouchers only. Offer is void if sold. Offer expires December 20, 2018. Settle to: #88-942

Offer void if coupon is copied or sold

AMERICAN CASINO GUIDE

TACOS & 'RITAS

50% Off Giant Margarita With Any Purchase

Present this coupon at Tacos & 'Ritas, make any purchase and receive 50% off a giant 44oz frozen margarita in a souvenir glass! See reverse for details.

A current American Casino Guide Discount Card must be presented when redeeming this coupon, or offer is void

AMERICAN CASINO GUIDE

2-For-1 Buffet
(Monday-Thursday)

Buy one Feast Buffet and get the second Feast Buffet Free. Offer valid Monday-Thursday. See reverse for more details.

A current American Casino Guide Discount Card must be presented when redeeming this coupon, or offer is void

AMERICAN CASINO GUIDE

TUSCANY SUITES & CASINO

Earn 300 Points, Get $10 Free Slot Play

Present this coupon to the Tuscany Players Club after earning 300 same-day base points to receive $10 in free slot play. Valid for new or current members. See reverse side for details.

A current American Casino Guide Discount Card must be presented when redeeming this coupon, or offer is void

americancasinoguide.com

TACOS & 'RITAS

Venetian Hotel Casino Floor Food Court
MGM Grand Food Court

Must present coupon to cashier prior to ordering. Offer has no cash value. Not valid with any other offer. One coupon per person. Subject to change or cancellation without prior notice. Offer valid through December 31, 2018.

Offer void if coupon is copied or sold

americancasinoguide.com

Gambling Hall & Hotel

2101 Texas Star Ln
North Las Vegas, NV 89032
(702) 631-1000
www.texasstation.sclv.com

This voucher entitles bearer to one free breakfast, lunch or dinner in the Feast Buffet when accompanied by a cash paying guest. Tax and gratuity not included. One voucher per person/subscriber. Voucher must be presented to cashier. Vouchers are not transferable and are not redeemable for cash. Must be 21 or older. Not a line pass. Not valid on holidays, Not valid with any other offer. Offer may be changed or discontinued at any time at the discretion of management. Original vouchers only. Offer is void if sold. Offer expires December 20, 2018. Settle to: #88-942

Offer void if coupon is copied or sold

americancasinoguide.com

255 E Flamingo Road
Las Vegas, NV 89169
(702) 893-8933 • (877) 887-2261
www.tuscanylv.com

Base points only. No multipliers. Bearer must be at least 21 years of age and prepared to present a photo ID. Limit one coupon per person per 30-day period. Coupon has no cash value and cannot be combined with any other offer or used more than once. Reproduction, sale, barter and transfer are prohibited and render this coupon void. Management reserves all rights. Offer expires 12/31/18.

Offer void if coupon is copied or sold

AMERICAN CASINO GUIDE

2-for-1 Entrée, Burger or Taco at Pub 365

Present this coupon, along with your Tuscany Players Club Card, to your server at Pub 365 to buy one entrée, burger or taco and receive one of equal, or lesser value, for free. See reverse for more details.

A current American Casino Guide Discount Card must be presented when redeeming this coupon, or offer is void

AMERICAN CASINO GUIDE

TUSCANY SUITES & CASINO

10% Off Room Rate!

Save 10% on your room rate when you book directly with Tuscany Suites & Casino. See reverse side for details.

A current American Casino Guide Discount Card must be presented when redeeming this coupon, or offer is void

AMERICAN CASINO GUIDE

GRAND CANAL SHOPPES
THE VENETIAN | THE PALAZZO

FASHION SHOW LAS VEGAS

Free Savings Book

Enjoy thousands in savings throughout the Strip's premier shopping destinations! Present this coupon at the Fashion Show Guest Services or the Apothecary at Grand Canal Shoppes. While supplies last. Expires 12/31/18.

A current American Casino Guide Discount Card must be presented when redeeming this coupon, or offer is void

255 E Flamingo Road
Las Vegas, NV 89169
(702) 893-8933 • (877) 887-2261
www.tuscanylv.com

Buy one entrée, burger or taco and receive one of equal or lesser value for free. Present coupon and Tuscany Players Club card to server for redemption. Valid only at Pub 365. Dine-in only. Does not include tax or gratuity. Limit one per customer. Not valid with any other offer. No cash value. Management reserves all rights. Offer expires 12/31/18.

255 E Flamingo Road
Las Vegas, NV 89169
(702) 893-8933 • (877) 887-2261
www.tuscanylv.com

When making your direct booking at www.tuscanylv.com, the Group Code to enter is "SOCIAL" Offer based on availability. Limit one per person. Offer for recipient only and is non-transferrable. Valid ID required for check-in. A major credit card or $200 cash deposit is required at check-in. Offer cannot be combined with any other offer or discount and is not available for groups or conventions. Management reserves all rights. Offer expires 12/29/18.

GRAND CANAL
SHOPPES

THE VENETIAN | THE PALAZZO

Located inside The Venetian and The Palazzo across from Fashion Show and TI
24-Hour Shopping Line
(702) 414-4500
www.grandcanalshoppes.com

LAS VEGAS

Located on the Strip across from Wynn Las Vegas, The Palazzo and TI
Guest Services (702) 369-8382
www.thefashionshow.com

AMERICAN CASINO GUIDE

Madame Tussauds
LAS VEGAS

2-For-1 General Admission

Receive one FREE ticket with the purchase of a full-price adult general admission ticket at Madame Tussauds Interactive Wax Attraction located in front of the Venetian Resort on Las Vegas Boulevard. See reverse for details.

5106

A current American Casino Guide Discount Card must be presented when redeeming this coupon, or offer is void

AMERICAN CASINO GUIDE

PRIMEBURGER
boutique burgers, crafted fries, spirits & shakes

Free Milkshake With Purchase

Present this coupon at Primeburger in the Venetian Hotel Grand Canal Shoppes, and receive a free non-alcoholic milkshake with the purchase of any menu item.

A current American Casino Guide Discount Card must be presented when redeeming this coupon, or offer is void

AMERICAN CASINO GUIDE

ROCKHOUSE
LAS VEGAS

2-For-1 Cocktail or Draft Beer

Present this coupon at Rockhouse to receive two well cocktails or domestic draft beers for the price of one before 9 p.m. See reverse for details.

A current American Casino Guide Discount Card must be presented when redeeming this coupon, or offer is void

americancasinoguide.com

Madame Tussauds
LAS VEGAS

Who would you like to meet at the world famous Madame Tussauds Las Vegas? Featuring over 100 lifelike wax figures of your favorite celebrities, Madame Tussauds removes the velvet ropes and allows you to get up close to your favorite stars!

Madame Tussauds Las Vegas is open daily at 10 a.m. For more information and pricing, please call (866) 841-3739 or visit madametussauds.com. Located in front of the Venetian Resort on Las Vegas Blvd (The Strip). Not valid with any other discount promotion. Expires December 31, 2018.

Offer void if coupon is copied or sold

americancasinoguide.com

PRIMEBURGER

boutique burgers, crafted fries, spirits & shakes

Venetian Hotel Grand Canal Shoppes

Must present coupon to cashier prior to ordering. Offer has no cash value. Not valid with any other offer. One coupon per person. Subject to change or cancellation without prior notice. Offer valid through December 31, 2018.

Offer void if coupon is copied or sold

americancasinoguide.com

Grand Canal Shoppes at the Venetian
3355 S Las Vegas Blvd, #3200
Las Vegas, Nevada

Valid on any well drink, or domestic draft beer. Free drink of equal or lesser value. Gratuity not included. Limit one per person. Coupon has no cash value. May not be combined with any other offer. Must be 21 years of age or older. Management reserves all rights. Expires 12/29/18.

Offer void if coupon is copied or sold

AMERICAN CASINO GUIDE

ROCKHOUSE

LAS VEGAS

Free Pitcher of Domestic Draft Beer with $25 Purchase

Present this coupon at Rockhouse to receive a free pitcher of domestic draft beer with a purchase of $25 or more. See reverse for details.

A current American Casino Guide Discount Card must be presented when redeeming this coupon, or offer is void

AMERICAN CASINO GUIDE

BURGER San Gennaro

Buy One Get One Free

Present this coupon at the San Gennaro Burger in the Venetian Casino Floor Food Court, purchase your choice of any menu item and receive your choice of a second menu item of equal or lesser value free!

A current American Casino Guide Discount Card must be presented when redeeming this coupon, or offer is void

AMERICAN CASINO GUIDE

$40 Off Sunset Dinner Ride

Present this coupon at time of purchase to receive $40 off the regular price of the sunset dinner ride. See reverse for details.

A current American Casino Guide Discount Card must be presented when redeeming this coupon, or offer is void

ROCKHOUSE
LAS VEGAS

Grand Canal Shoppes at the Venetian
3355 S Las Vegas Blvd, #3200
Las Vegas, Nevada

Valid on any domestic draft only. Limit one coupon per table. Gratuity not included. Coupon has no cash value. Must be 21 years of age or older. Management reserves all rights. Expires 12/29/18.

BURGER
San Gennaro

Venetian Hotel Casino Floor Food Court

Must present coupon to cashier prior to ordering. Offer has no cash value. Not valid with any other offer. One coupon per person. Subject to change or cancellation without prior notice. Offer valid through December 31, 2018.

2470 Chandler Ave Suite 11
Las Vegas, NV 89120
(702) 792-5050
wildwesthorsebackadventures.com

Present this coupon at time of purchase to receive $40 off the regular price of the sunset dinner ride. No cash value. Offer valid for all party members.

This adventure includes roundtrip transportation, a 1.5 hour trail ride in beautiful Glendale, a mouthwatering steak BBQ dinner, spectacular views, and memories that will last a lifetime. Management reserves all rights and may change or cancel this promotion at any time without notice. Offer is valid through December 23, 2018.

AMERICAN CASINO GUIDE

$20 For $10 at Wild Grill

Present this coupon to your server before ordering to receive $20 in food for only $10. See reverse for more details.

A current American Casino Guide Discount Card must be presented when redeeming this coupon, or offer is void

AMERICAN CASINO GUIDE

FREE $25 Mobile Sports Bet For New Members

Present this coupon at any Full Service William Hill Sports Book location in Nevada to receive a $25 Free Mobile Sports Bet with your new Mobile Sports account. See reverse for more details.

A current American Casino Guide Discount Card must be presented when redeeming this coupon, or offer is void

AMERICAN CASINO GUIDE

FREE $2 Virtual Racing Bet For New Members

Present this coupon at participating Full Service William Hill Sports Book locations in Nevada to receive a $2 Free Virtual Racing Bet with your new Mobile Sports account or William Hill Rewards Club account. See reverse for more details.

A current American Casino Guide Discount Card must be presented when redeeming this coupon, or offer is void

1901 N Rancho Dr
Las Vegas, NV 89106
(702) 648-3801
www.wildfire.sclv.com

This voucher entitles bearer to $20 worth of Wild Grill Dining for only $10. **Offer is valid at any Wild Grill including Wildfire Boulder, Wildfire Lanes, Wildfire Rancho, or Wildfire Sunset.** Tax and gratuity not included. One voucher per person/ subscriber. Voucher must be presented to cashier. Vouchers are not transferable and are not redeemable for cash. Must be 21 or older. Not a line pass. Not valid on holidays. Not valid with any other offer. Offer may be changed or discontinued at any time at the discretion of management. Original vouchers only. Offer is void if sold. Offer expires 12/21/18. Settle to: #88-113

For locations visit:
www.williamhill.us

Offer Expires December 31, 2018. Must be 21 years of age or older to participate. $25 minimum deposit required. Offer is non-transferable, may not be used in conjunction with any other offer or promotion and has no cash value. Member must not have previously established any William Hill Mobile Sports account. See official rules for details. Limit one coupon per person. Management reserves all rights.

For participating locations visit:
www.williamhill.us

Must be 21 years of age or older to participate. Visit www.williamhill.us to find participating William Hill Sports Book offering Virtual Racing. Offer is non-transferable, may not be used in conjunction with any other offer or promotion and has no cash value. Member must not have previously established any William Hill Mobile Sports or Rewards Club account. See official rules for details. Limit one coupon per person. Management reserves all rights. Offer expires December 31, 2018.

AMERICAN CASINO GUIDE

COLORADO BELLE
CASINO • RESORT • LAUGHLIN

One FREE Night!

Buy one night at $39 and get your second night FREE!
Advance reservations required. Must present coupon at check-in.
Call (800) 477-4837 Mon-Fri 9am – 4:30pm. Mention Code ACGCB.

A current American Casino Guide Discount Card must be presented when redeeming this coupon, or offer is void

AMERICAN CASINO GUIDE

COLORADO BELLE
CASINO • RESORT • LAUGHLIN

FREE Pints Draft Beer

Buy one regularly priced entree and receive a free Pints draft Beer!
Redeem this coupon at Colorado Belle's Pints Brewery. Must be at least 21. See reverese for details.

Comp# 63150

A current American Casino Guide Discount Card must be presented when redeeming this coupon, or offer is void

AMERICAN CASINO GUIDE

EDGEWATER
CASINO • RESORT • LAUGHLIN

One FREE Night!

Buy one night at $49 and get your second night FREE!
Advance reservations required. Must present coupon at check-in.
Call (800) 677-4837 Mon-Fri 9am – 4:30pm. Mention Code ACGEW.

A current American Casino Guide Discount Card must be presented when redeeming this coupon, or offer is void

americancasinoguide.com

COLORADO BELLE
CASINO • RESORT • LAUGHLIN

2100 S Casino Dr
Laughlin, NV 89029
(702) 298-4000
(800) 477-4837
www.coloradobelle.com

Must be at least 21 with valid photo ID. Subject to availability. Credit Card required to reserve room. Rate based on standard room. Valid Sunday – Wednesday. Excludes holidays and special events. Subject to change/cancellation. Limit one coupon per stay. Non-negotiable. No cash value. May not be redeemed by Edgewater or Colorado Belle employees. Management reserves all rights. Valid through 12/29/2018.

Offer void if coupon is copied or sold

americancasinoguide.com

COLORADO BELLE
CASINO • RESORT • LAUGHLIN

2100 S Casino Dr
Laughlin, NV 89029
(702) 298-4000
(800) 477-4837
www.coloradobelle.com

Gratuity not included. Must be at least 21. Subject to change/cancellation. No cash value, non-refundable, non-negotiable. Only original coupons accepted. May not be redeemed by Edgewater/Colorado Belle employees. May not be combined with any other offer/discount. Valid through 12/29/2018. Comp # 63150

Offer void if coupon is copied or sold

americancasinoguide.com

2020 S Casino Dr
Laughlin, NV 89029
(702) 298-2453
(800) 677-4837
www.edgewater-casino.com

Must be at least 21 with valid photo ID. Subject to availability. Credit Card required to reserve room. Rate based on standard room. Valid Sunday – Wednesday. Excludes holidays and special events. Subject to change/cancellation. Limit one coupon per stay. Non-negotiable. No cash value. May not be redeemed by Edgewater or Colorado Belle employees. Management reserves all rights. Valid through 12/29/2018.

Offer void if coupon is copied or sold

AMERICAN CASINO GUIDE

EDGEWATER
CASINO • RESORT • LAUGHLIN

2-For-1 Buffet
(or 50% off when dining alone)

Buy one buffet at regular price and get a second one free (or 50% off when dining alone). Redeem this Coupon at Edgewater's Grand Buffet. See reverse for details.

Comp # 63025

A current American Casino Guide Discount Card must be presented when redeeming this coupon, or offer is void

AMERICAN CASINO GUIDE

Buy One Buffet - Get One FREE!

Present this coupon and your Total Rewards® card at the Fresh Market Square Buffet at Harrah's Laughlin to buy one buffet (brunch or dinner) and receive one buffet FREE! Valid at Harrah's Laughlin only. Offer code: 176

A current American Casino Guide Discount Card must be presented when redeeming this coupon, or offer is void

AMERICAN CASINO GUIDE

Buy One Entree - Get One FREE!

Present this coupon and your Total Rewards® card at the Beach Cafe at Harrah's Laughlin at time of seating to buy one entree at the Beach Cafe and receive one entree of equal, or lesser value, FREE! Valid at Harrah's Laughlin only. Offer code: 176

A current American Casino Guide Discount Card must be presented when redeeming this coupon, or offer is void

americancasinoguide.com

2020 S Casino Dr
Laughlin, NV 89029
(702) 298-2453
(800) 677-4837
www.edgewater-casino.com

Gratuity not included. Must be at least 21. Subject to change/cancellation. No cash value, non-refundable, non-negotiable. Only original coupons accepted. May not be redeemed by Edgewater/Colorado Belle employees. May not be combined with any other offer/discount. Valid through 12/29/2018. Comp # 63025

Offer void if coupon is copied or sold

americancasinoguide.com

2900 South Casino Drive
Laughlin, Nevada 89029
(702) 298-4600 • (800) HARRAHS
www.harrahs.com

Management reserves the right to modify this offer at any time without prior notice. Original coupon must be presented (no photocopies), along with Total Rewards® card. Not valid on weekends (Friday/Saturday) or holidays. Cannot be used in conjunction with any other offer. Must be 21 or older to redeem. Coupon has no cash value. Limit one coupon per person per visit. Subject to availability. Gratuity not included. Offer valid through 12/15/18. Must be 21 years or older to gamble. Know When To Stop Before You Start.® Gambling Problem? Call 1-800-522-4700. ©2017, Caesars License Company, LLC.

Offer void if coupon is copied or sold

americancasinoguide.com

2900 South Casino Drive
Laughlin, Nevada 89029
(702) 298-4600 • (800) HARRAHS
www.harrahs.com

Management reserves the right to modify this offer at any time without prior notice. Original coupon must be presented (no photocopies), along with Total Rewards® card. Not valid on weekends (Friday/Saturday) or holidays. Cannot be used in conjunction with any other offer. Must be 21 or older to redeem. Limit one coupon per person per visit. Subject to availability. Gratuity not included. Offer valid through 12/15/18. Must be 21 years or older to gamble. Know When To Stop Before You Start.® Gambling Problem? Call 1-800-522-4700. ©2017, Caesars License Company, LLC.

Offer void if coupon is copied or sold

AMERICAN CASINO GUIDE

TROPICANA

LAUGHLIN

A TROPICANA ENTERTAINMENT PROPERTY

2-for-1 Roundhouse Buffet

Enjoy breakfast, brunch or dinner at the Roundhouse Buffet at Tropicana Laughlin. Must be a Trop Advantage Card member. Must purchase one buffet at regular price to receive second buffet for free.

Coupon #121

A current American Casino Guide Discount Card must be presented when redeeming this coupon, or offer is void

AMERICAN CASINO GUIDE

2-for-1 Entrée

Present this coupon to the players club for a 2-for-1 entrée at the Pahrump Nugget Café, Gold Town Café or Lakeside Café. Not valid with any other offers. See reverse for more details.

A current American Casino Guide Discount Card must be presented when redeeming this coupon, or offer is void

AMERICAN CASINO GUIDE

LAKESIDE CASINO & RV PARK PAHRUMP, NV

$10 in FREE Slot Play

New members only, present this coupon at the players club booth at the Pahrump Nugget, Gold Town or Lakeside casino and receive $10 in FREE slot play! See reverse for more details.

A current American Casino Guide Discount Card must be presented when redeeming this coupon, or offer is void

americancasinoguide.com

TROPICANA
LAUGHLIN
A TROPICANA ENTERTAINMENT PROPERTY

Tropicana Laughlin Hotel & Casino
2121 South Casino Drive
Laughlin, NV 89029
www.troplaughlin.com
702-298-4200 * 1-800-343-4533

Receive ONE FREE breakfast, brunch or dinner buffet with purchase of a breakfast, brunch or dinner buffet at regular price. Must be a Trop Advantage Card member. Valid for one time redemption. One coupon per transaction. Coupon is not valid on holidays or blackout dates. Restaurant hours of operation vary. Present original coupon and Trop Advantage Card to cashier. Coupon has no cash value, cannot be combined with any other offer or promotion and excludes gratuity. Management reserves all rights. Must be 21 or older to redeem. Offer valid Jan. 2, 2018 through Dec. 27, 2018.

Offer void if coupon is copied or sold

americancasinoguide.com

PAHRUMP, NV

681 S. Highway 160
Pahrump, NV 89048
(775) 751-6500
(866) 751-6500
www.pahrumpnugget.com

Present this coupon to the players club. Excludes Nye County residents. Must be at least 21 years of age. Must show a valid photo I.D and a players club card.

Limit one coupon per person. Not valid with any other offer. Coupon has no cash value. Management reserves the right to cancel or modify this offer at any time. Max value $10. Resale prohibited. Expires 12/31/18

Offer void if coupon is copied or sold

americancasinoguide.com

PAHRUMP, NV

681 S. Highway 160
Pahrump, NV 89048
(775) 751-6500
(866) 751-6500
www.pahrumpnugget.com

This coupon is valid for new player club members only. Not valid with any other offer or discount. Limit one coupon per person. Excludes Nye County residents. Must be at least 21 years of age. Must show a valid photo I.D. Coupon has no cash value. Management reserves the right to cancel or modify this offer at any time. Offer expires 12/31/18

Offer void if coupon is copied or sold

AMERICAN CASINO GUIDE

One FREE Hotel or RV Night Stay!

Pay for one room night at the full rate and receive the second room night FREE at either the Pahrump Nugget or RV Space at Lakeside. See reverse side for more details.

A current American Casino Guide Discount Card must be presented when redeeming this coupon, or offer is void

AMERICAN CASINO GUIDE

25% Off Hotel Room

Get 25% off your room rate by calling (888) 774-6668 to reserve and mention offer code TPCAS18. Must be 21 or older. Offer valid Sunday-Thursday. Not valid on holidays and subject to availability. Must present coupon at check-in. See reverse for full details.

A current American Casino Guide Discount Card must be presented when redeeming this coupon, or offer is void

AMERICAN CASINO GUIDE

15% Off Entire Bill at Primm & Proper

Receive 15% off your entire bill at Primm & Proper located inside Primm Valley Resort & Casino. Offer is valid 7 days a week. Coupon must be presented at checkout. See reverse for full details.

A current American Casino Guide Discount Card must be presented when redeeming this coupon, or offer is void

CASINO GROUP
PAHRUMP, NV

681 S. Highway 160
Pahrump, NV 89048
(775) 751-6500
(866) 751-6500
www.pahrumpnugget.com

Valid Sunday through Thursday for consecutive night stays in the same room or space. Excludes Nye county residents. Holidays and special events excluded. Subject to availability. Must have advance reservations by calling 866-751-6500 or 888-558-5253 and must advise the Pahrump Nugget Hotel agent or Lakeside RV agent that you are calling for the American Casino Guide offer. Must present and surrender this coupon upon check-in. No exceptions. Management reserves the right to modify or cancel this promotion at any time. Not valid with any other offer. Customer required to place credit card on file at check-in. Customer responsible for all other additional charges. Must be 21 or older. Limit one free room or RV Space per coupon. Expires 12/31/18

31900 Las Vegas Blvd S,
Primm, NV 89019
(702) 386-7867
www.primmvalleyresorts.com

Present coupon at check-in to receive 25% prevailing room rate. Blackout dates may apply. Offer cannot be combined with any other offer or promotional discount. No cash value. Resort fee applies on non-complimentary room nights. Credit card required when making reservation. Must be 21 years of age or older to redeem this offer. Management reserves all rights to modify, change or cancel this offer at any time without prior notice. Offer Expires 12/28/18.

31900 Las Vegas Blvd S,
Primm, NV 89019
(702) 386-7867
www.primmvalleyresorts.com

Present coupon at checkout to receive 15% off your food bill. Offer cannot be combined with any other offer or promotional discount. No cash value. Must be 21 years of age or older to redeem this offer. Management reserves all rights to modify, change or cancel this offer at any time without prior notice. Offer expires 12/28/18.

Settle to 1000